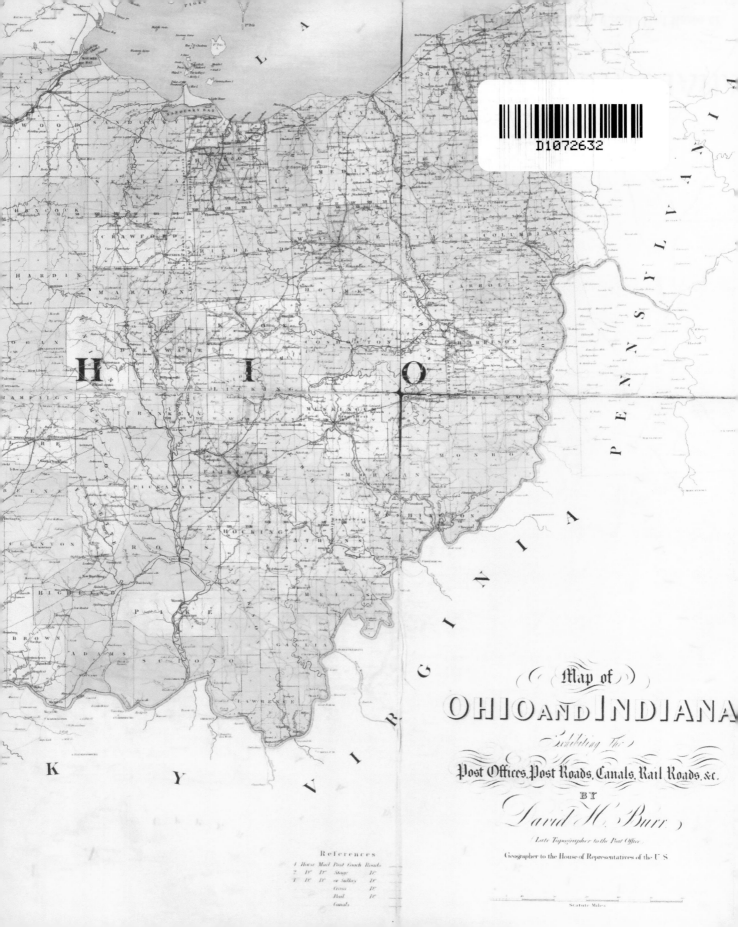

Map of
OHIO AND INDIANA
Exhibiting the
Post Offices, Post Roads, Canals, Rail Roads, &c.
BY
David H. Burr
Late Topographer to the Post Office.
Geographer to the House of Representatives of the U S

References
1 Horse Mail Post Coach Roads
2 D⁰ D⁰ Stage D⁰
T D⁰ D⁰ or Sulkey D⁰
Cross D⁰
Rail D⁰
Canals

Statute Miles

Parallel Lives

Two Hoosier Chemists from Peru

By George Fleck

WILLIAMSBURG, MASSACHUSETTS

The photograph on the cover, taken
about 2000 by Smith College
photographer M. Richard Fish, shows
the author with one of the many
equal-arm two-pan balances used in
laboratory instruction at Smith in the
middle of the twentieth century.

Published by The Impress Group
Williamsburg, Massachusetts

First printing
Library of Congress QD11
Dewey 540.9
ISBN 978-1-5323-2617-2

Printed in the United States

Table of Contents

Preface ix

I. Parallel Paths 3

    Education in Turn-of-the-Century Indiana 7

    Mary Fredericke Mueller and Gustave Adolph Germann 14

    Albert Fredrick Ottomar Germann 18

    Doctoral Study in Europe 34

    Western Reserve University 41

    How did Ida and Albert Meet? 44

    Frank Erhart Emmanuel Germann 46

    Frank Follows Albert to Geneva 51

    Cornell University 54

    How did Martha and Frank Meet? 56

    Sources and References 63

II. Colorado: the School of Mines, and then the University 83

    Colorado School of Mines 87

    The University of Colorado 93

    John Bernard Ekeley 96

    An Office, a Lab, and a Research Group 103

    The Chemistry of Photography 105

    A Sabbatical, The Ku Klux Klan, and Cornell 109

    Fluorescence and Phosphorescence 112

    From Duboscq to Beckman and Cary 124

    An Adventure in Europe 127

    Subterranean Carbon Dioxide 127

    A New Scholarly Journal 131

    Changing of the Guard 139

    Professional Leadership Roles 143

    Retirement 144

    Sources and References 147

III. Western Reserve, then to Stanford, and back to Cleveland 167

    Phosgene 175

    Theories of Solvent Systems 184

    Laboratory Products Company 196

    S.M.A. 208

    Carotene 211

    Germann Assembles a Research Group 214

    The Valparaiso Interlude 219

    Sources and References 220

IV. Valparaiso 239

    A Focused History of Education in Valparaiso 240

    Brown's Revival 246

    The Ku Klux Klan Enters 258

    Fort Wayne Lutherans Seize an Opportunity 265

    Dr. A. F. O. Germann Receives a Call 274

    William Herman Theodore Dau 282

    Biological Evolution in the Curriculum 288

    The Germann Administration 296

    Return to Cleveland 302

    Sources and References 304

V. Nutritional Research Associates 321

    Quintrex 324

    South Whitley 327

    Lee Eve 334

    Robert Hicks 336

    Hubert A. Stump 353

    Peter and Charles Kaadt 356

    Fred Fox, Hugo Fox, and Fred Graham 367

    Prince Immanuel of Jerusalem 375

    Valentine Hennig 379

    Nutritional Research Associates 382

    Sources and References 388

A. Graduate Students of Frank Erhart Emmanuel Germann 409

B. Graduate Students of Albert Fredrick Ottomar Germann 415

Index 420

Preface

WRITING OF THIS BOOK began in 1951, when Harold F. Tschantz and Charles Marshall Bowerman (editors and publishers of the weekly *South Whitley Tribune*), assigned the author to interview Dr. Albert F. O. Germann for a feature article on "The Carrot Factory" in South Whitley, Indiana. The high school student met with the dignified, soft-spoken, and personable scientist. The student was given a tour of the chemical laboratory of Nutritional Research Associates. Dr. Germann answered every question asked, directly and clearly.

More than six decades later, it is clear that many other questions could have been asked in that interview. Answers to unasked questions, in some cases, can still be extracted from extant documents and from personal interviews. The carrot factory newspaper article ["Percolated Carrots Source of Health," *South Whitley Tribune*, vol. 65, no. 51 (Thursday afternoon, June 28, 1951), pp. 1 and 7] was but a preliminary introduction to a much larger story, a lively story that speaks today to a wider audience, within a much broader geographical, cultural, and historical context.

The story, as it unfolds in this book, is told in the twenty-first century with many of the biases of the author: a transplanted Hoosier from a family of educators, a physical chemist, and a long-time college teacher. Many of his interpretations are grounded in the small town of South Whitley (population then about a thousand) as well as in small and intimate academic communities nestled in colleges, universities, and research laboratories. Many of the folk in the story flourished in the first half of the twentieth century; the author's professional career is set in the last half of that century. Although a generation apart, the author and some of characters in the story walked similar paths. In some cases, there were personal interactions.

When brothers Albert Fredrick Ottomar Germann and Frank Erhart Emmanuel Germann were born in the 1880s, few of their Hoosier contemporaries were destined for formal education beyond the local district common schools. Both Germanns *did* continue their schooling, graduating from Peru (Indiana) High School and then from Indiana University, with baccalaureate degrees in chemistry or physics. Inorganic chemistry, organic chemistry, and physics had experienced remarkable advances in the 1800s, especially in Europe. The brothers both entered physical chemistry when this fledgling scientific specialty was poised for a twentieth-century revolution, both in theory and in the laboratory. The research by the Germann brothers, initially in the United States and then in Europe, contributed to this revolution. Their early accomplishments were recognized with earned doctoral degrees, awarded by the University of Geneva in Switzerland.

Chapter 1 describes two careers begun in academic institutions with familiar names—Indiana University, University of Wisconsin, Cornell University, and Western Reserve University. The names are familiar now, today signifying academic strength, excellence, and prestige. But the institutions were young, small, and struggling when Albert and Frank began their parallel careers. Albert and Frank came of age in the years when American education and American physical science were also coming of age.

Readers will not miss the pervasive Lutheran connections. Readers may be prepared for the urgent invitation to Albert from the Lutheran University Association of Fort Wayne, Indiana, to play a pivotal role in the Lutheranization of Valparaiso University. Readers may not be prepared for the role played in the drama by the Ku Klux Klan. The Indiana and Colorado Klan appear in Chapters 1 and 2. The Indiana Klan appears in Chapters 4 and 5.

The Germann brothers were typical neither of their neighbors nor of their generation. But their lives, their aspirations, their careers, and their influences provide many insights into a panorama of changes—and often progress—in education, scientific research, medicine, nutrition, and industry in the twentieth century. South Whitley, the town where Albert Germann and his family finally settled, was typical neither of its neighboring communities nor of small-town Midwestern America. Nevertheless, interactions of diverse (sometimes idiosyncratic, charismatic, enigmatic, or even unscrupulous) individuals in South Whitley provide many insights into that panorama of changes.

The biographies of Albert Fredrick Ottomar Germann and Frank Erhart Emmanuel Germann are the central themes of this book. Because their relationships with other folk can be understood by knowing something about those other folk, many mini-biographies appear throughout the book. Significant characters in the narratives were born in the 1800s, some in frontier communities. Many were born only one or two generations after the first pioneer settlements of Europeans in Ohio, Indiana, Illinois, Iowa, Nebraska, and Missouri.

In examining the South Whitley venue in the concluding chapter, vignettes of Lee LeVere Eve, Robert Emmet Hicks, Hubert A. Stump, Peter and Charles Kaadt, Fred and Hugo Eugene Fox, Frederick Milo Graham, Prince Immanuel of Jerusalem, Valentine Hennig, Vernon Jersey, Robert John Cross, and Otto Ungnade illuminate the locale of Nutritional Research Associates and of Ger Manner. With this cast of characters in South Whitley, the early-twentieth-century narrative in Chapter 5 can be read as prelude to twenty-first century America: pioneering productive science side by side with fraudulent pseudoscience, risk-taking free enterprise sometimes combined with blatant exploitation, communities evolving to maintain coherence in spite of divisive centrifugal forces. Each reader can judge whether the reader's world of today is fundamentally different with respect to the nature, effect, and significance of such contrasts, conflicts, and attempts at resolutions.

Parallel Lives

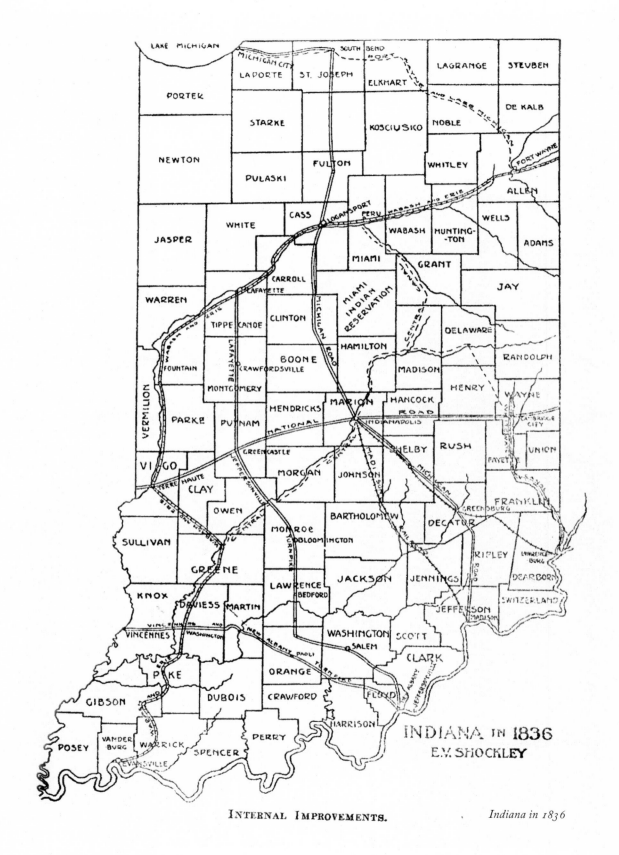

INTERNAL IMPROVEMENTS. *Indiana in 1836*

I.

Parallel Paths

B ROTHERS Albert Fredrick Ottomar Germann (1886–1976) and Frank Erhart Emmanuel Germann (1887–1974) were born and raised in a Lutheran family in Peru, Miami County, Indiana. This book is their story.

Peru was already settled by Europeans, and indeed had become an organized and bustling city, when Albert and Frank were born there. Churches and schools had been established. Peru had become the political, commercial, manufacturing, and transportation center for the surrounding farming communities.

Only sixty years earlier, Miami County had been part of the Miami Nation, a home for Native Americans. Under provisions of the Treaty of Mississinewa, signed in 1826 in Wabash, Indiana, the United States forced the Miami Nation to surrender most of its land to the United States. Representatives of the Miami Nation and representatives of the United States met at the Forks of the Wabash in Huntington, Indiana, between 1833 and 1840, to negotiate three more treaties. Miami County was then carved out of the Miami Indian Reservation.

In 1846, the Miami Nation, by then the last indigenous tribe in Indiana, was compelled by the United States Government to leave the Wabash River Valley for Kansas Territory, and then for Indian Territory in what is now the State of Oklahoma. Some very determined leaders stayed in Indiana, pursuing land claims for a hundred years. Two thousand Native Americans remain in Miami County. Fragile connections between Miamis in Indiana and Miamis in Oklahoma were strengthened in 1972 and 1974 when Indiana Miami Chief William Hale and Oklahoma Miami Chief Forest Olds met with officials of Miami University in Oxford, Ohio. The position of Coordinator of Miami Tribe Relations was created in April 1994 at Miami University. The Myaamia Center at Miami University was established in 2001 to assist language and cultural revitalization efforts by the Miami Tribe of Oklahoma.

European settlers who first came to Miami County in the 1800s found what they considered wilderness frontier. In anticipation of the arrival of Europeans, the Federal Government had surveyed the land. At least on maps, the land was divided into Congressional Townships, and subdivided into Sections. A standard township was a square, six miles long and six miles wide. Except for surveying errors and practical problems arising from rivers, lakes, and swamps, each of the thirty-six sections in a township was a square, one mile long and one mile wide. A standard section contained 640 acres. The surveyed land was ready to be purchased from the Federal Government at the United States General Land Office in Fort Wayne for settlement, development, and exploitation.

Peru Township was organized in 1834. The Town of Peru, on the banks of the Wabash River, was incorporated in 1848. The town became the City of Peru in 1867. Peru built a municipal water system in 1879, initially pumping water from the Wabash River into a reservoir. Those waterworks, distributing river water by gravity to 101 hydrants, were largely justified for fire protection. In 1900, the City let contracts for drilling thirteen deep wells to provide an alternative to river water for domestic uses. Sewers were put in later. Electricity came to Peru in fall 1885. That was five years after Wabash, fifteen miles east of Peru, became the first electrically lighted city in the world. The first improved streets in Peru had a macadam surface, compacted layers of small stones cemented with stone dust and water into a hard pavement. Broadway was paved with bricks in summer 1901, followed by a section of Main Street.

Albert and Frank Germann lived as youngsters and as young men in the City of Peru. Their father was a carpenter in Peru, and their maternal grandfather was a downtown merchant. Albert and Frank walked to school, first to a Lutheran elementary school and then to Peru High School. Both brothers were hard workers. They excelled in their studies. They also had significant role models. Much credit for their strong interest in academics and for their scholastic achievements is surely due their proud parents, Mary Fredericke Mueller (1864–1942) and Gustave Adolph Germann (1860–1940). Mary and Gustave continued throughout the following decades to provide guidance for their sons. Both parents lived to celebrate the successes of their sons.

Albert and Frank had other family and community role models. Their cousin Edwin Jacob Germann had attended Ohio Normal University and Wittenberg College in Ohio, before coming west into Indiana to join the faculty of Rochester Normal College, twenty-five miles north of Peru. Martha Constantia Keyl Theobald, wife of Jacob Theobald (to whom Gustave Adolph Germann was apprenticed when he first came to Peru) was a daughter of the Rev. Ernst Gerhard Wilhelm Keyl. Rev. Keyl was a graduate of Leipzig University and an influential Lutheran leader known and respected throughout the Midwest. Lutherans, insisting on an educated clergy, valued education highly and supported many schools. Love of learning and the value of education were transmitted to Albert and Frank by folks within their family, within their church, and within the wider community.

As the story of the Germann brothers unfolds, many mentors appear. Ross Franklin Lockridge Sr., history teacher and then Principal of Peru High School, was influential in encouraging these two star pupils to apply to Indiana University. At college, Instructor of Chemistry Frank Curry Mathers directed Albert's undergraduate chemistry research project, and sparked Albert's interest in physical chemistry. Associate Professor of Chemistry Oliver Brown gave Albert practical information about the physical chemistry faculty at the University of Wisconsin. Louis Kahlenberg and J. Howard Mathews at the University of Wisconsin gave advice to Albert about doctoral study in Europe. Among Frank's collegiate mentors at Indiana University were Professor of Physics Arthur Lee Foley and Associate Professor of Physics Rolla Roy Ramsey. Frank sought (and obtained) career advice from Indiana University President William Lowe Bryan in a personal meeting in December, 1913.

Albert and Frank each became a distinguished physical chemist. The sub-discipline of physical chemistry was still in its infancy when the brothers began their formal education, and their career paths were not well trodden by predecessors. American original research in the chemical sciences was just beginning to blossom. With sound practical advice from faculty mentors, Albert and Frank each traveled to Europe to complete their formal scientific education under the tutelage of scientists with reputations throughout the Western world. A doctoral or postdoctoral sojourn to European laboratories was a familiar trek for chemists at the University of Wisconsin, where Albert became a graduate student and where Frank took a summer-school course in physical chemistry.

Their doctoral research in Europe, each with the distinguished physical chemist

Philippe-Auguste Guye at the University of Geneva, resulted in an impressive list of publications in prestigious scientific journals. Published experimental research was becoming a significant aspect of the credentials required for academic advancement in the sciences; "publish or perish" had already become a reality at leading American universities when Albert and Frank took their first jobs. Each Germann brother benefited from the professional recognition of being a published author, and each Germann brother survived pitfalls of the publish-or-perish system. Each brother flourished academically and professionally.

Albert and Frank each taught school as they worked their way through college. After college, they taught to finance their education in graduate school and to gain experience at the lectern and in the teaching laboratory. Each then had teaching careers in universities. Throughout this book are biographical vignettes of their teachers, their colleagues, and especially their students, vignettes included to provide glimpses of the education landscape of the times and to indicate how teachers and students mutually influenced individual lives and careers.

The story of each brother, from family beginnings in Miami County to their illustrious research achievements in chemistry, physics, and engineering, is impressive but largely untold to Hoosier audiences. Surprising documented stories abound—heroic rescue of a Hoosier university that in 1907 was said to be second in enrollment in the United States only to Harvard, significant roles in the United States radium industry, recognition for developing practical methods of exploiting underground carbon dioxide, experimental and theoretical exploration of phosgene (the infamous World War I poison gas) as a chemical solvent, founding of companies that had major impacts on human nutrition and on domestic agriculture. Conflicts involving the emerging medical, biomedical, and bionutritional sciences became focused and very public in the small town of South Whitley, Indiana, home of Ger Manner. Each brother was an active participant in the maturing of fledgling academic, scientific, and engineering enterprises that helped shape and reshape the cultural and economic landscape of America.

Education in Turn-of-the-Century Indiana

At the close of the nineteenth century, educational institutions in Indiana were evolving rapidly. Fundamental issues of academic independence, financing, and governance had swirled around Indiana schools, colleges, and universities throughout their early history. Hoosier educational institutions remained entangled with politics, religion, and nativism into the twentieth century. Those educational institutions were boldly entering the twentieth century when Albert and Frank began their schooling at St. John's Christian Day School in the small City of Peru. Each brother then attended the local public high school.

With a Peru High School diploma as his highest academic credential, each brother found a teaching position in a rural school near Peru. In what would now be called work-study programs, each young man worked his way through Indiana University in Bloomington, 130 miles south of Peru. Their courses at Indiana University were sandwiched between teaching assignments in Miami County public schools. Then, atypical of their college classmates, each entered a postgraduate program in physical science after graduating from the University.

The second Indiana state constitution (the Constitution of 1851) mandated "a general and uniform system of Common Schools, wherein tuition shall be without charge, and equally open to all." The State Board of Education adopted (on November 15, 1853) the standard textbooks for the district common schools in Indiana, establishing a uniform statewide public elementary school curriculum. This academic curriculum emphasized reading, spelling, grammar, elocution, literature, and arithmetic. The teacher's only classroom technology needed for implementing this curriculum was chalk and a chalkboard. Students often brought their own slates. Fifty years later, a Hoosier [Charles Allen Prosser (1871–1952)] would lead efforts to add vocational subjects to the curriculum. Instrumental in formulating the 1853 curriculum was Presbyterian minister and first Wabash College faculty member Caleb Mills (1806–1879), often called the father of the Indiana public education system. Caleb Mills was a vigorous exponent of the philosophy of strict separation of public education from dictates of organized religion. He became Indiana Superintendent of Public Instruction in 1854.

The textbooks recommended in 1853:

McGuffey's Newly Revised Eclectic Primer, With Pictorial Illustrations (Cincinnati: Winthrop B. Smith, 1849). *"Intended as an Introduction to McGuffey's Eclectic First Reader."*

William Holmes McGuffey, *The Eclectic First Reader for Young Children, Consisting of Progressive Lessons in Reading and Spelling, Mostly in Easy Words of One and Two Syllables* (Cincinnati: Truman and Smith, 1838).

McGuffey's Newly Revised Eclectic Second Reader, Containing Progressive Lessons in Reading and Spelling (Cincinnati: Winthrop B. Smith, 1848).

McGuffey's Newly Revised Eclectic Third Reader, Containing Selections in Prose and Poetry, With Rules for Reading and Exercises in Articulation, Defining, etc. (Cincinnati: Winthrop B. Smith, 1853).

McGuffey's Newly Revised Eclectic Fourth Reader, Containing Elegant Extracts in Prose and Poetry, With Rules for Reading, and Exercises in Articulation, Defining, etc. (Cincinnati: Winthrop B. Smith, 1853).

McGuffey's Newly Revised Rhetorical Guide, or, Fifth Reader of the Eclectic Series, Containing Elegant Extracts in Prose and Poetry, With Copious Rules and Rhetorical Exercises (Cincinnati: Winthrop B. Smith, 1853).

Noble Butler, *A Practical Grammar of the English Language* (Louisville: John P. Morton and Company, 1846).

McGuffey's Newly Revised Eclectic Spelling Book, Showing the Exact Sound of Each Syllable, According to the Most Approved Principles of English Orthoepy (Cincinnati: Winthrop B. Smith, 1846).

William Greenleaf Webster, *A Speller and Definer* (Louisville: John P. Morton, 1845).

Samuel Augustus Mitchell, *Mitchell's Ancient Geography, Designed for Academies, Schools, and Families* (Philadelphia: S. Augustus Mitchell, 1834).

Joseph Ray, *Ray's Eclectic Arithmetic on the Inductive and Analytic Methods of Instruction: Designed for Common Schools and Academies*, 16th ed. (Cincinnati: Truman and Smith, 1841).

The Cincinnati firm of Truman and Smith (a partnership of William T. Truman and Winthrop B. Smith) published several mathematics textbooks authored by Joseph

Ray (1807–1855), beginning in 1834. In 1833, William Holmes McGuffey (1800–1873) signed a contract with Truman and Smith for a series of graded reading textbooks. Sales of Ray's math books and McGuffey's *Readers* were to exceed two hundred million copies during the last half of the nineteenth century. The Truman and Smith partnership dissolved in 1841. Smith formed the Winthrop B. Smith Publishing Company, with rights to publish the Ray and the McGuffey textbooks. Smith took immediate advantage of the 1853 Indiana textbook recommendations, publishing stereotype editions of McGuffey's *First, Second, Third,* and *Fourth Readers* as "Smith's Indiana Series" (Cincinnati: Winthrop B. Smith Publishing Company, 1853).

Under the 1851 constitution, the township became the rural school unit as well as the rural political unit throughout the state. Indiana was the first state to make the *township* the school unit. For most of Indiana, the rural common schools were one-room, one-teacher schools, managed by elected township trustees. The trustees hired and fired the teachers. The trustees had responsibility for finances.

There was a lot of neighborhood influence in the management of each school. Many of the teachers were from families in the township. Other teachers "boarded around," staying in the more well-to-do homes. In 1853, most of the teachers were self-taught. They had read parts of the *King James Bible* and had memorized selected verses. They were familiar with the prescribed textbooks. Fifty years later, a typical teacher in a common school was a recent graduate of a public high school, or had studied in one of the many short-lived seminaries supported by religious denominations.

For critics from the outside, Indiana rural schools represented a maze of contradictions: a statewide-standardized curriculum implemented by individual elected township trustees who employed teachers with minimal credentials. Only a rare township trustee had run for office on a platform that advocated higher qualifications for teachers in his district common schools. A typical township trustee in an Indiana farming community was elected because voters believed that he could maintain country roads and bridges, and that he could dig the ditches and lay the clay tiles needed to drain wetlands so that land could be cleared and farmed.

Indiana was chosen by outside, well-funded groups as a laboratory for educational "reform," for modernizing rural culture to conform to values of twentieth century upper-class urban society. President Theodore Roosevelt's 1908 Commission on Country Life concluded that fundamental change in every aspect of rural life would be needed if citizens in small towns and rural areas were to catch up with their city cousins. John D. Rockefeller, through his General Education Board (founded in 1901, with a million-dollar starter grant from Rockefeller), in 1923 chose Indiana's Johnson and LaGrange counties "to demonstrate to Hoosiers and other Midwest-erners the necessity and wisdom of fundamental change in rural education." Johnson and LaGrange were "County Unit Demonstration Projects," intended to show that efficiency and centralized control would improve education and encourage scientific farming methods. The undisguised intent of many reformers was to ensure that farm-ers would supply sufficient food for a burgeoning urban population. Reformers argued that redirected rural education was required for survival of the newly indus-trialized cities. Citizens in Johnson and LaGrange counties were not convinced. Most believed that they were being patronized.

In the first years of the twentieth century, seemingly benign slogans such as "con-solidate into county-unit schools" and "save the public schools" were rallying cries for bitter educational battles involving covert regional, political, ethnic, and religious agendas. State Superintendent Caleb Mills preached separation of public education from religion, but his recommended textbooks placed Protestantism in every public classroom of the state. William Holmes McGuffey wrote seven of those textbooks, each designed to instill Presbyterian Calvinist beliefs and behavioral norms in stu-dents. McGuffey's colleague Joseph Ray found many ways to inject morality into the word problems of his state-recommended arithmetic text.

Indiana Quakers objected to some of McGuffey's views. The Indiana Yearly Meeting of Friends commissioned Indiana chemist and physician John Thomas Plummer (1807–1864) to write primers whose contents were appropriate for Quaker children. He wrote *The Little Child's First Reader: Adapted to Either Mode of Teach-ing—By Letters or By Words* (Friends' Educational Series. Philadelphia: T. Ellwood Zell, 1862) and *The Second Reader: A Collection of Reading in Prose and Verse, Adapted for Use in Schools and Families* (published posthumously in the Friends' Educational Series, Cincinnati: R. W. Carroll, 1867).

There was pressure in Lutheran communities across Indiana to perpetuate the German language. Lutheran schools needed German alternatives to the McGuffey *Readers*. Conrad Witter played a central role in making German alternatives available. He established the "Verlag der Conrad Witter'schen Schulbuchhandlung" bookstore and publishing facility at the corner of Walnut and Second streets in St. Louis in 1850. In 1857, he published the fourth edition of the *Evangelische Katechismus* of the Evangelischer Kirchenverein des Westens (Evangelical Church Union of the West, 1840–1866). He was a contributor to (and in 1857 the Midwestern publisher of) an American edition of *F. P. Wilmsen's deutscher Kinderfreund für Schule und Haus.* He published *A New Pocket-Dictionary of the English and German Languages* (1866, 386 pages).

Early in the 1860s, Witter published his own German–English first, second, and third readers. During the next two decades, he published many new editions and revisions, as well as textbooks targeted to German classes in public schools.

The Witter firm faced a formidable competitor in 1886 when Van Antwerp, Bragg and Company in Cincinnati announced a complete line of textbooks for German–American common schools. This line included five volumes of the *Eclectic German Readers* series, and a guide to writing Kurrentschrift, a form of German-language cursive handwriting. Almost all text was printed with German blackletter typefaces. Authors of each book were William H. Weick and Constantin Grebner.

Concordia Publishing House in St. Louis began publication of German *Readers* for Lutheran schools. Concordia may have acquired publication rights from Conrad Witter. Concordia Publishing House, founded in 1869, remains the publishing arm of The Lutheran Church–Missouri Synod. The first *Reader* was for upper classes and appeared in 1887: *Lesebuch für ober-classen Evangelisch–Lutherische Schulen.* In rapid succession came *Erstes Lesebuch für Evangelisch–Lutherische Schulen, Zweites Lesebuch für Evangelisch–Lutherische Schulen, Drittes Lesebuch für Evangelisch–Lutherische Schulen,* and *Lesebuch für mittel-classen Evangelisch–Lutherische Schulen.* In most cases, the corporate author was given as Deutsche Evangelisch–Lutherische Synode von Missouri, Ohio und Andern Staaten (German Evangelical Lutheran Synod of Missouri, Ohio, and Other States). Concordia Publishing House also published a series of arithmetic textbooks, *Practical Arithmetic for the Common Schools of North America*, parts 1, 2, 3, and 4. The author, Herman Duemling (1845–1913), taught science and mathematics at Concordia College in Fort Wayne, Indiana. Duemling reappears in Chapter 4.

There was no pretense of separating schooling and religion in St. Paul's Lutheran School in Fort Wayne. St. Paul's School, established in 1837, claims to be "the first elementary school—public or private—in Indiana." It continues as a member of The Lutheran Schools consortium (preschools, seventeen elementary schools, and one high school) in the greater Fort Wayne region. Albert and Frank Germann attended St. John's Christian Day School, established in 1860 by St. John's Lutheran Church in Peru. They also attended the public Peru High School, and after graduation taught in Miami County public schools. We note in Chapter 4 that Methodists opened the Valparaiso [Indiana] Male and Female College in 1859, Presbyterians opened the Valparaiso Collegiate Institute in 1861, Lutherans opened the Valparaiso German–English Lutheran Parochial School in 1864, and Catholics held classes at their Valparaiso Saint Paul Academy as early as 1867. Each of those four religious schools enrolled elementary school children as well as older students. There appears to have been no religious test for admission; each school needed students if it were to thrive, or at least to survive.

The Ku Klux Klan in the mid-1920s chose Indiana for full-scale assaults on religious schools as part of their "100 percent Americanism" agenda. The Klan focused explicitly on Catholic schools, but astute Lutheran leaders were wary of Klan-proposed state legislation which, had it been enacted and implemented, could have crippled Lutheran schools and could have challenged the credentials of Lutheran-educated teachers. We shall see in Chapter 2 how the Klan sought (but failed) in 1925 to exert control over the administration of the University of Colorado. An attempt in 1923 by the Klan to purchase Valparaiso University is related in Chapter 4. The influence of the Indiana Klan in the 1920s is visible in the South Whitley, Indiana, setting of Ger Manner and Nutritional Research Associates. This Klan influence is documented in Chapter 5.

Collegiate institutions were established early in Indiana history—Vincennes (1801), Indiana University (1820), Hanover (1827), Wabash (1832), Franklin (1834), DePauw (1837), Concordia (1839), Saint Mary's (1841), Notre Dame (1842), Taylor (1846), Earlham (1847), Butler (1850), Evansville (1854), Valparaiso (1859), Manchester (1860), Indiana State (1865), Purdue (1869). Those early years were often precarious.

Some began as academies, seminaries, or post-common-school institutions. Vincennes University was founded as Jefferson Academy. Presbyterian minister John Finley Crowe (1787–1860) in 1827 opened Hanover Academy in a log cabin near his home. Wabash College was originally Wabash Teachers Seminary and Manual Labor College, founded on November 21, 1832, by nine men who met at the home of Presbyterian pastor James Thomson in Crawfordsville. DePauw University opened as Indiana Asbury University, named after Methodist Bishop Francis Asbury (1745–1816). Concordia Theological Seminary was founded in Fort Wayne in 1846 by Wilhelm Sihler (1801–1885) to educate pastors for German Lutheran immigrants to the United States. In July 1841, Anne-Thérèse Guérin (1798–1856) and the Sisters of Providence opened St. Mary's Academy for Young Ladies, which later became Saint Mary-of-the-Woods College. University of Notre Dame du Lac began with two pre-college students in 1842; the Indiana General Assembly chartered the school in 1844. Taylor University in 1846 was Fort Wayne Female College, established by the North Indiana Conference of the Methodist Episcopal Church. It was renamed for missionary bishop William Taylor (1821–1902); it moved to Upland in 1893. Earlham in 1847 was a co-educational Quaker boarding high school; it became Earlham College in 1859. Ovid Butler (1801–1881) on January 15, 1850, founded North Western Christian University, which became Butler University in 1877. The University of Evansville traces its history to 1854, when John Moore in Moores Hill, Indiana, founded Moores Hill Male and Female Collegiate Institute. Manchester University was founded in Roanoke, Indiana, as the Roanoke Classical Seminary for Otterbein College; Otterbein had been founded in Westerville, Ohio, in 1847 by the Church of the United Brethren in Christ. Indiana University opened in 1820 as Indiana State Seminary, but classes for its first dozen students began only in 1825. Indiana State Normal School opened in 1865 in Terre Haute; it became Indiana State University in 1965. Its Eastern Division was established in Muncie in 1918, and by 1965 had become Ball State University. Purdue University had a President but neither faculty nor students until 1874.

Most (except Indiana University, Indiana State Normal School, and Purdue University) had explicit religious roots and church financing. Many faculty members were clerics. Each of those seventeen survived (many of their cohorts did not), albeit with evolution of their missions, often with name and location changes, and sometimes with traumatic transitions. In this chapter, the focus is on Indiana University in Bloomington. You will notice, when reading Chapter 4, that Valparaiso University is an example of dramatic evolution of mission, with major name changes and with traumatic transitions. Only the physical location of its campus provided nominal institutional continuity. Indeed, an argument has been made for a founding-date of 1925 (instead of 1859) for Valparaiso.

Throughout this book, note is made of the propensity of some educational institutions to award diplomas and degrees with apparent lack of constraint and with scant attention to principle. The examples cited are unique neither to Indiana, nor to the nineteenth and twentieth centuries.

Mary Fredericke Mueller and Gustave Adolph Germann

Gustave Adolph Germann (July 4, 1860–December 31, 1940) was born close to Indiana, just east of the Ohio–Indiana state line, in Harrison Township, Van Wert County, Ohio. Harrison Township is adjacent to Allen County, Indiana. Fort Wayne, the county seat of Allen County, plays pivotal roles throughout Germann family stories.

Fort Wayne, the "Summit City," lies at the confluence of the St. Joseph and St. Mary's rivers, the place where those two western-flowing rivers merge to form the eastern-flowing Maumee River. The Maumee River, known by Native Americans as Miami of the Lake, flows into Lake Erie. Kekionga, on the present site of Fort Wayne, was the capital of the Miami Nation. Because the site lies on a portage between Lake Erie and the Wabash River, French traders built a fort there in 1697. Fort Wayne partisans call the portage the "eastern continental divide." The Miami Nation regained control of Kekionga in 1763, and defeated United States military forces in the army's two attempts to secure the area. General Anthony Wayne then led the Legion of the United States on an expedition that resulted in the destruction of Kekionga. On October 22, 1794, the Legion captured the Wabash–Erie portage. A new fort was built, christened Fort Wayne.

Gustave Germann was a son of Maria Elisabetha Hofmann (February 24, 1823–August 4, 1878) and Georg Peter Germann (August 16, 1815–August 12, 1901), Prussian Lutherans who immigrated about 1840 from Hessen-Homberg. Gustave and one of his four brothers (Gustave also had five sisters) drove by horse and wagon from Van Wert County to Miami County in March 1877.

The cross-country drive by horse and wagon was an adventure. The present system of state roads and national highways in northeastern Indiana had scarcely been imagined in 1877. Federal survey teams had established the north–south section lines on the ground in each Congressional Township in 1822 and 1823, beginning implementation of Thomas Jefferson's plan to divide the public domain lands into uniform rectangles. Surveyors then set the perpendicular east–west section lines. Country roads eventually formed a grid, with many of those roads along section lines. That checkerboard pattern is obvious today when farmland is viewed from an airplane flying over northwestern Ohio and northern Indiana. In 1877, most roads between Van Wert County and Miami County were the responsibility of the adjacent landowners. Many roads were impassable several months each year, and some existed just in surveyor's notebooks. Only the important roads had any semblance of an all-weather surface. Most of the now familiar oblique highways were constructed in the twentieth century as direct routes to connect established towns and cities.

Gustave Germann served a three-year carpentry apprenticeship in Peru with Jacob C. Theobald. Jacob was a Lutheran immigrant from Bavaria who had come to Peru in 1861. Jacob became active in local politics, and was elected to the Peru City Council. By 1895, he was President of the Standard Cabinet Manufacturing Company in Peru at 151–159 East Canal Street, next to the Wabash River and next to remnants of the Wabash and Erie Canal.

Planning the Wabash and Erie Canal, financing the canal, and building the canal had profound effects on Indiana. The 1826 Treaty of Mississinewa granted easements for the canal over lands still owned and occupied by the Miami Nation. Construction work on the canal began at its Fort Wayne crest in February 1832. When completed in 1843, the Wabash and Erie Canal extended 468 miles from Toledo, Ohio, up and over the Fort Wayne portage (a wooden aqueduct over the St. Mary's River near Main Street), then toward the southeast corner of Whitley County, to Huntington, through Peru, and on to Evansville, Indiana. The canal joined the Ohio River at Evansville. The canal was a segment of a navigable inland water route from the Port of New York City to the Port of New Orleans. A restored Wabash and Erie Canal Toll House can still be seen in downtown Peru.

The fully functioning canal had a short life. The last canal boat docked in Huntington in 1874. The canal's mercantile consequences for Fort Wayne, Huntington, and Peru were substantial and generally positive. Financial consequences for the state were disastrous. Before the many engineering problems of the canal could be discovered and remedied, direct competition by railroads rendered canals in Indiana economically untenable. The new railroads ruined the canal, but benefited the cities of Fort Wayne, Huntington, Peru, and (as we shall see in Chapter 5) the small town of South Whitley.

Jacob Theobald married Mary Shireman of Germany in March 1865. Mary died in 1873. Jacob then married Martha Constantia Keyl in 1874. Martha was the second daughter of Sophie Amilie Vogel and Ernst Gerhard Wilhelm Keyl (1804–1872). Rev. E. G. W. Keyl was President from 1855 to 1868 of the Eastern District of the German Evangelical Lutheran Synod of Missouri, Ohio, and Other States. He was an influential leader in the movement to join with other Lutheran denominations to form the Evangelical Lutheran Synodical Conference of North America, forerunner of the present Lutheran Church–Missouri Synod.

Gustave Adolph Germann established himself first as a carpenter, then as a builder, and eventually as a successful building contractor in Peru. On Thursday, September 11, 1884, he married Mary Fredericke Mueller (1864–1942), daughter of Elizabeth Akerly and Jacob F. Mueller. Jacob Mueller was a Peru merchant, already well accepted in the business community. In spite of strong pressures within the Lutheran churches of the area to perpetuate the German language, the Mueller family became Millers, and St. Johannes Evangelical Lutheran Church in Peru became St. John's Evangelical Lutheran Church. In the 1895 Peru city street directory, the residence of G. A. and Mary F. Germann appears as 310 West Main Street. This address listing remained unchanged until 1906, when it became 123 West 3rd Street. The listing was still 123 West 3rd Street until at least 1939.

Lutherans had key roles in many of the stories told in this book. Three sons of Maria Elisabetha Hofmann and Georg Peter Germann became Lutheran ministers.

One son was a pastor near Decatur, Illinois, serving a Lutheran church that no longer exists as a separate congregation. Another son, the Rev. Carl (Charles) Adam Germann (November 22, 1851–March 17, 1932), was born in Van Wert County. He attended a Lutheran elementary school and a local public high school in Van Wert County. Then he became a student at the Lutheran Concordia Seminary in St. Louis, attending from 1869 to 1873. Charles was ordained at St. Johannes Evangelical Lutheran Church in Peru on Sunday, August 24, 1873. He served as pastor of the Peru church from 1873 to 1883, and then accepted a call from Trinity Lutheran Church, Utica, New York. Trinity had been founded in Utica in 1881 as the German Evangelical Lutheran Trinity Congregation, with C. J. Oelschlaeger of Ohio as pastor. In 1883, Trinity became one of the first Lutheran churches in central New York to join the Missouri Synod. Charles Germann served as pastor of Trinity until 1920, and then as pastor emeritus until his death.

Charles Germann married Agnes Magdalena Keyl in 1873. One son, Alfred W. Germann, became a church organist. Another son, Gary E. Germann, became a Lutheran minister. Agnes Magdalena Keyl was the fifth daughter of Sophie Amilie Vogel and E. G. W. Keyl.

Another son of Maria and Georg, the Rev. Peter Friedrich Germann, was born in Van Wert County on August 22, 1849. He married Caroline Emilie Keyl (1851–1924) in 1874 in Fort Smith, Arkansas. Caroline Emilie was the third daughter of Sophie Amilie Vogel and E. G. W. Keyl. Caroline's twin brother, Hermann Wilhelm Keyl, was married and working as an upholsterer in Peru in 1882. Peter Friedrich Germann died in Peru on March 31, 1935.

Jacob Germann was yet another son of Maria and Georg. Jacob was born August 13, 1835. He married Emelia (Emma) Maria Sigrest on November 24, 1862, in Ohio. They had five children. Emma died in Harrison Township, Van Wert County, in 1876. At least three of their children [Bertha, Regina M. (Maria?), and Edwin Jacob] came to Indiana. A son Julius was living in the village of Wren, Van Wert County, Ohio, in 1918. Jacob died March 27, 1918, in Fort Wayne, at the home of his daughter Regina. He had moved to Fort Wayne in 1905, becoming a member of Emmaus Evangelical Lutheran Church.

Regina married Theodore F. Brase (July 2, 1861–May 31, 1939), a Fort Wayne native. As a young boy, T. F. Brase assisted his father, who owned and operated boats that hauled grain from Toledo through Fort Wayne to Cincinnati on the Wabash and Erie Canal. The canal had opened for boats from Fort Wayne to Huntington in July 1835, and was in full operation through Peru to Evansville by summer 1843. Most of the Indiana segments of the canal had been supplanted by railroads by the time Theodore was born. The last docking in Huntington was in 1874. From 1896 to his retirement in 1932, Theodore Brase was a sales representative for Mayflower Mills, manufacturer of flour and feeds in Fort Wayne. He was a member of Emmaus Evangelical Lutheran Church.

Edwin Jacob Germann (1869–1942) enrolled at Wittenberg College (Springfield, Ohio) during the academic year 1887–1888. Ministers of the English Evangelical Lutheran Synod of Ohio founded Wittenberg (since 1957, Wittenberg University) in 1845. Edwin reported his home as Van Wert in 1892–1893 when he was a junior (studying piano) in the Music Department of Ohio Normal University (now Ohio Northern University) in Ada, Ohio. He was one of the initial faculty of Rochester Normal College in Rochester, Indiana, twenty-five miles north of Peru. Physician Winfield Scott Shafer (1852–1916) founded the College in 1895. Edwin was Professor of Music. An accomplished cornetist, Edwin organized (and directed) the Rochester Normal College brass band (1895–1904). When Rochester Normal

College closed in 1912, Edwin and his wife Edith Poor moved to Fort Wayne, where they established the Sherwood School of Piano and Voice. They were members of Emmaus Evangelical Lutheran Church. After Edith's death in 1934, Edwin lived with his sister, Regina Germann Brase, in Fort Wayne.

Bertha Germann did not marry.

Albert Fredrick Ottomar Germann

Albert Fredrick Ottomar Germann was born in Peru on Thursday, February 18, 1886, son of Mary Fredericke Mueller and Gustave Adolph Germann. Albert attended St. John's Christian Day School in Peru. The school, established in 1860 by St. Johannes Evangelical Lutheran Church, has continued virtually uninterrupted. In 2013, it was a thriving preschool and kindergarten, supported by the St. John's congregation but open to all.

Albert attended Peru High School from 1900 to 1904. It was an exciting time in the educational life of the city. Philanthropist Andrew Carnegie (1835–1919) gave funds to Peru in 1901 to construct a public library building. Before then, the library books of Peru were shelved in Peru High School. The site chosen for the Carnegie Library was 102 East Main Street (the northeast corner of Main and Huntington streets) in the center of the city. City officials placed the cornerstone on Thursday, February 6, 1902, and the impressive building opened in 1903. The library continues in the same building.

Albert was the Freshman Class representative on the staff of the first yearbook published by the school. Referring to the calendar year 1901, the yearbook was titled *Naughty-One*. The second volume of the Peru High School annual was titled *Narcissus*. The youth Narcissus in Greek mythology was the son of the river god Cephissus and the nymph Leiriope. Narcissus was in love with his own reflection, and the yearbook editors announced that their book was a one-time, golden opportunity for socially acceptable narcissism. The yearbook has retained the title *Narcissus* to this day.

The photograph of Albert in the 1904 *Narcissus* has the caption: "Albert has the honor of having more credits than any one in school. In fact, he could have graduated last year if there had not been a regulation against finishing in 3½ years. He is one of the charter members of the debating class, in which profession he has undying and everlasting fame." Albert did not gain everlasting fame as debater or orator, but he was to spend many years as an effective and convincing teacher, lecturer, and discussion leader in classrooms.

Financial support for the *Narcissus* came in part from book sales and in large part from advertisements. Advertisements placed by local merchants were numerous but small. The largest advertisement in the 1902 *Narcissus* was full-page, from Indiana University in Bloomington. The ad boasted that the University had grown from 28 graduates in 1881 to 164 graduates in 1901. This boast was intended to be an inducement for Peru students to apply to Indiana University. Albert did apply. His application was accepted. He enrolled. He would earn two degrees in chemistry from Indiana University.

Albert Germann graduated from Peru High School in 1904. That high school diploma was credential enough for Albert to teach public school in Miami County. The Pipe Creek Township Trustee hired Albert to teach at Bunker Hill High School in southern Miami County. Albert Germann "served as township principal and high school teacher at Reserve in Butler Township, in 1905. In the alternate periods between school work he attended Indiana University at Bloomington until he succeeded in being graduated 'with high distinction,' from the state university in 1909, with the degree A.B." In 1962, Bunker Hill High School disappeared when Maconaquah School Corporation was formed, consolidating Clay High School and Bunker Hill High School. The now-extinct community of Reserve was near the unincorporated village of Peoria on the Mississinewa River.

Some twenty-first century educational critics deplore what they view as excessive specialization in the education of those students who concentrate on science, technology, engineering, and mathematics. Albert Germann, alternating between teaching a wide range of academic subjects in Miami County schools and mastering college-level courses at Indiana University, had no opportunity to ignore the connections between the sciences and the humanities. He spent the five years between high school graduation and university graduation pursuing a liberal arts education while gaining the specialized knowledge and skills needed for graduate study in chemistry. He was also "keeping school" and "teaching school," managing classrooms and learning teaching methods "on the job."

We shall observe throughout this book the gradual but relentless consolidation of one-teacher schools during the first quarter of the twentieth century. There were

ten one-teacher schools in Butler Township in 1905. Most were heated in the winter
with wood—seasoned local hardwood, burned in a potbellied stove located in the
center of the classroom. If the teacher were fortunate, enough firewood was supplied
(already dried, split, and stacked) by the township trustee or by neighboring families.
Water came from an outdoor hand pump installed over a dug well, or from an iron-
bound oaken bucket lowered and raised with a windlass above the well. The well
might be ten to twenty feet deep, depending on the ground water level and the skill
of the well diggers. There would be one or two outhouses (privies), ideally located far
enough away from the well to minimize groundwater contamination. It would be
another thirty years until there were sanitary standards for outdoor toilets, longer
before the standards were implemented and enforced, and even longer before rural
school buildings were connected to functional sewerage systems.

The Germann brothers were not unique in working their way through college by
teaching in rural schools. It was commonplace in Indiana in 1905 for a man to teach
in the public schools for a few years before moving on to another profession or to a
career in higher education. Unmarried women (and widows) with the same credentials typically continued their careers in the classroom. Two decades later, it was still
unusual for a married woman to be hired to teach in an Indiana public school, and
even later before it was common for a woman to be hired to teach in the same school
building where her husband taught.

The Indiana University Registrar confirms that Albert entered Indiana University in Bloomington, Indiana, on Friday, June 24, 1904, and that he received the
degree of Bachelor of Arts in Chemistry on Wednesday, June 23, 1909. He joined
Epsilon Chapter (the Indiana University chapter) of the national chemistry fraternity Alpha Chi Sigma. He also attended meetings of the Concordia Club, a campus
Lutheran organization.

Chemistry lecture and recitation rooms, laboratories, and faculty offices were in
a newly reconstructed Wylie Hall. Wylie Hall had been built in 1884, the first building on the "new campus" in Dunn's Woods at the east edge of Bloomington. The red
brick building was originally two stories with a tower and spire, housing the Department of Chemistry and the University Library. Thomas Charlton Van Nüys (1844–
1898), Head of the Chemistry Department in 1884, was intimately involved with
design of the laboratories. Van Nüys had spent the year 1876 working in new laboratories at the Kaiser-Wilhelm-Universität in Strasbourg, and had closely observed

what German architects then considered state of the art in laboratory design.

Enrollments increased. Ten years after Wylie Hall opened, students reported that "both the large qualitative and quantitative laboratories and the small room for the study of toxicology are crowded with students. Bacteriology will be added to the curriculum upon the return of Professor Lyons from Germany, and even next year it may be necessary to devote the whole of Wylie Hall to Chemistry."

A fire on Wednesday, February 7, 1900, possibly caused by an explosion in a chemistry laboratory, destroyed the upper part of the building. Wylie Hall was rebuilt as a three-story building without a tower. In the intervening years between 1884 and 1900, new ideas had arisen about design of laboratory facilities for research and teaching. Many of the architectural innovations that were incorporated in the rebuilding plans came directly from European experiences of faculty members Robert Lyons and Louis Davis. They had recently visited chemistry laboratories in Heidelberg, Wiesbaden, Munich, Copenhagen, Berlin, and Marburg. Wylie Hall was rebuilt to be a twentieth-century chemistry teaching and research facility.

When did Albert's interest in chemistry begin? We know that he discovered a congenial, supportive, and stimulating environment within the Indiana University Department of Chemistry. When Albert Germann matriculated as an undergraduate in 1904, the small chemistry faculty was composed of Robert Edward Lyons (abt 1867–1946), Professor and Head of the Department; Louis Sherman Davis (born 1867), Associate Professor; Oliver W. Brown (1873–1967), Assistant Professor; Dean of Women Mary Bidwell Breed (1870–1949), Assistant Professor; and Frank Curry Mathers (1881–1973), Instructor. Not all of these faculty members were in residence in Bloomington at the same time, and those in residence were not all teaching undergraduate chemistry courses. Robert Lyons and Louis Davis were also members of the faculty of the new Indiana University School of Medicine. The School of Medicine had been organized in 1903.

Albert Germann thrived in the atmosphere created by these four men and one woman—educators, scholars, and influential members of the University community. It was a department with a tradition of undergraduate research. It was a department in touch with exciting chemistry developments in Europe and in the United States. It was a department that enabled Albert Germann to prepare himself for entrance into a competitive academic world.

Robert Lyons received the A.B. degree from Indiana University in 1889. He began experimental research as an undergraduate with Thomas Charlton Van Nüys, Head of the Chemistry Department. Lyons investigated procedures for the quantitative chemical analysis of urine, and continued that research as a graduate assistant. Lyons received the A.M. degree in Chemistry from Indiana University in 1890. Professor Van Nüys had studied chemistry in Germany three times, and he encouraged Lyons to do likewise. Lyons travelled to Germany for doctoral study with physical chemist Friedrich Krafft (1852–1923), receiving the Ph.D. from the University of Heidelberg (Ruprecht-Karls-Universität Heidelberg) in 1895. He also studied chemistry and visited laboratories in Wiesbaden, Munich, Copenhagen, and Berlin. When Lyons returned to Bloomington, the President made him Head of the Department of Chemistry, replacing T. C. Van Nüys who became Professor Emeritus in 1895 at age 51. Van Nüys retired because of failing health.

Louis Sherman Davis received the A.B. degree in 1891 and the A.M. degree in 1892, both from Indiana University. He became an Instructor of Chemistry at Indiana University in 1892, and was promoted to Associate Professor in 1895. He was granted a leave of absence to study at Philipps-Universität Marburg, a public university in the German principality of Hesse. Philipps-Universität was founded in 1527, and is the oldest university in the world founded as a Protestant institution. Chemistry was just emerging from its alchemical antecedents when, in 1609, Philipps-Universität established the world's first professorship in chemistry. Louis Sherman Davis received his chemistry doctorate from Philipps-Universität in 1896 and returned to Bloomington. Dr. Davis resigned from the Indiana University faculty on January 30, 1905. Davis was immediately replaced by Frederick Lafayette Shinn (A.B. 1901, A.M. 1902, both degrees from Indiana University). Shin had been a graduate student at Yale and was completing graduate study at the University of Wisconsin. He was awarded the Ph.D. in physical chemistry by the University of Wisconsin in 1906 with the dissertation "On the Optical Rotary Power of Salts in Dilute Solutions."

Oliver W. Brown attended high school in Kokomo, Indiana, received the B.S. degree from Earlham College in 1895, the A.M. degree from Indiana University in 1896, and an honorary D.Sc. degree from Huntington College (Huntington, Indiana) in 1941. He was a graduate student of physical chemist Wilder Dwight Bancroft at Cornell University, and he taught at Colorado School of Mines before joining the Indiana University faculty in 1899. He retired from Indiana University in 1943.

Oliver Brown was an electrochemist, with a special interest in batteries.

Indiana University Vice-President William Lowe Bryan recruited Mary Bidwell Breed for a newly created position: Dean of Women. Bryan had spent two years in his search for the University's first Dean of Women. The Dean was to be a senior member of the University's academic administration. Dr. Bryan, himself Professor of Psychology, felt it essential that the Dean be a member of the faculty and bring strong academic credentials to the office. Dr. Breed certainly had impressive credentials. She had four academic degrees, including a doctorate based on chemical research conducted at the University of Heidelberg. She had taught college science courses. She had published the results of her experimental chemical research in the *American Chemical Journal*, had presented her research at the Franklin Institute, and had published her doctoral research as a monograph. She had more than a decade of experience at two women's colleges.

Mary Bidwell Breed (1870–1949), Ada Louise Comstock (1876–1973), and Marion Talbot (1858–1948)—the first Deans of Women at the universities of Indiana, Wisconsin, Minnesota, and Chicago—were trailblazers in women's collegiate education. Each was an influential educational administrator during decades when women began to get access to opportunities that had generally been open only to men. Albert Germann did not know that Dr. Breed and her compatriots were blazing a trail for him. The trail for him was to lead to his appointment in 1913 as Instructor in Chemistry for the women in The College for Women of Western Reserve University in Cleveland, Ohio. Western Reserve had established The College for Women in 1888.

Born September 15, 1870, in Pittsburgh, Mary Breed attended Pennsylvania Female College, Pittsburgh (East End), Pennsylvania, for four years. She graduated with the degree *Artium Baccalaurea* (A.B.) in 1889. In 1890, she enrolled in Bryn Mawr College, a woman's college founded five years earlier by Quakers in Bryn Mawr, Pennsylvania, eleven miles from Philadelphia. Bryn Mawr in 1892 was the first in the nation to grant students the right to make all the rules governing their conduct, and the obligation to enforce those rules. Mary Breed in 1892–1893 was a member of the Executive Committee of the Self-Government Association, and also President of the Undergraduate Association. At Bryn Mawr, she majored in chemistry, and conducted experimental chemical research under the direction of Prof. Edward Harrison Keiser. On Tuesday, February 21, 1893, in her junior year, she and

Prof. Keiser attended a meeting of the Chemical Section of the Franklin Institute in Philadelphia. She read a research paper, "On Phenolphthalein and Methylorange as Indicators," which she had submitted in January. At least three members of the audience contributed to a discussion following the paper. In her senior year, she conducted experimental research involving the quantitative analysis of palladium diammonium chloride. Her objective was determination of the atomic weight of palladium. Bryn Mawr awarded her the A.B. degree in 1894.

She entered the graduate program at Bryn Mawr, continuing research with Prof. Edward Harrison Keiser. These experiments involved chemical reactions of magnesium with a series of alcohols. She was Assistant in the Chemical Laboratory and a Graduate Scholar. Mary Bidwell Breed received the A.M. degree in Chemistry from Bryn Mawr College in 1895.

Bryn Mawr awarded Mary Breed a European Fellowship for the year 1894–1895. She spent her wanderjahr visiting laboratories in Paris, in Italy, and especially in Heidelberg. The Ruprecht-Karls-Universität Heidelberg, founded in 1386, would become a coeducational institution in 1899, but not in time for Mary Breed to enroll. Instead, she became a private student of Viktor Meyer (1848–1897), Professor of Chemistry at Heidelberg. Robert Lyons, her future colleague at Indiana University, was also at Heidelberg, completing his doctorate with physical chemist Friedrich Krafft. When she returned to the United States, Bryn Mawr named her a "Graduate Fellow by Courtesy" while she wrote her doctoral thesis, *The Polybasic Acids of Mesitylene.* The 31-page thesis was published in the inaugural volume of *Bryn Mawr College Monographs,* Monograph Series, vol. 1, no. 1 (June 1901). She was a member of the Graduate Club Executive Committee in 1899–1900. Bryn Mawr awarded her the degree of Doctor of Philosophy in Chemistry in 1901.

While finishing her doctorate, she served on the faculty of the Pennsylvania College for Women in 1897–1898 and 1898–1899. This was a return to her alma mater, Pennsylvania Female College. In 1890, its name had changed to Pennsylvania College for Women. In 1955, it became Chatham College. Since 2007, it has been Chatham University. She taught "Botany," "General Biology," "Physics," "General Chemistry," and "Theories of Modern Science." She was the only faculty member in science.

Indiana University appointed Mary Breed to the positions of Assistant Professor of Chemistry and Dean of Women at the same time. In a November 1, 1901, President's Report announcing the appointment of Breed, Vice-President William Lowe

Bryan noted that she would serve as the Dean of Women and "will teach a part of the time and devote the remainder of the time to the interests of the young women students." She did teach a section in "General Chemistry" (Chemistry 2) and "Selected Chapters in Theoretical Chemistry: Atomic Theory, the Periodic Law, and Theory of Solutions" (Chemistry 23) in 1901–1902. She taught no further courses, and probably was not an active participant in the affairs of the Chemistry Department after her first year. Her name remained on the masthead of the Chemistry Department offerings in the *Indiana University Catalogue* until 1906. She served as an alumna member of the Bryn Mawr Academic Committee in 1903–1904 and 1904–1905.

Breed was the first Dean of Women at Indiana University, serving from 1901 to 1906. She was one of only three deans. Another of those three was also Vice-President of the University. She was the first female dean at the University. Her reputation spread beyond the boundaries of the state. In 1906, she was vigorously recruited by the University of Missouri to become Advisor of Women and Head of Read Hall, the women's dormitory. She went to Missouri, and was an effective administrator there from 1906 to 1912. During the academic year 1912–1913, she was Associate Head and Teacher of English at St. Timothy's School in Catonsville, Maryland. This was the transitional year when the headship and ownership of the preparatory school passed from its founders to Jane Rives Heath and Louisa McEndree Fowler. From 1913 to 1929, Mary Breed was Dean (and later a transformational Director) of the Margaret Morrison Carnegie College of Carnegie Institute of Technology in Pittsburgh. She died on her 79th birthday, September 15, 1949.

Perhaps the chemist who provided the most encouragement to Albert was Frank Curry Mathers. Frank Mathers was born in a one-room log cabin four miles south of Bloomington. He graduated from Bloomington High School in 1899. Mathers received the A.B. degree in Chemistry from Indiana University in 1903, and the A.M. in 1905. He was probably a graduate teaching assistant in 1904–1905, and he may have taught in the general chemistry laboratory when Albert took that course. Frank Mathers was granted a leave of absence from 1905 to 1907 to work toward his 1907 Ph.D. at Cornell University, Ithaca, New York. His Ph.D. research, directed by Professor Louis Munroe Dennis (1863–1936), was a study of the atomic weight of indium.

Among the advanced courses taught by Frank Mathers at Indiana University when Albert was a student in the Department were "Electro-Chemistry," "Assaying," "Physical Chemistry," and "Seminary in Electro-Chemistry and Applied Physical

Chemistry." He filed for a United States Patent for "Process for Electrolytic Deposition of Metals" on April 21, 1909, obtaining Patent 931944A on August 24, 1909. Mathers offered Albert Germann the opportunity to begin experimental electrochemical research as an undergraduate, probably while Albert was enrolled in the "Seminary in Electro-Chemistry and Applied Physical Chemistry."

The textbook used in the beginning chemistry courses (Chemistry 1 and 2) was written by Ira Remsen (1846–1927). A copy of Remsen's 1901 *A College Text-Book of Chemistry* is still in the Indiana University Library. In the Preface, Remsen wrote: "Especial attention has been given to the parts dealing with matters pertaining to physical chemistry ... In the opinion of the author the time has not yet come for the abandonment of the study of elements and their compounds in what some are pleased to call the old fashioned way. Indeed it seems essential that such study must always form the basis of the higher or spiritual study of chemistry." Remsen founded *The American Chemical Journal* in 1879, and was President of The John Hopkins University from 1901 to 1913. He was elected to the National Academy of Sciences of the United States of America in 1882. Two of his students wrote in his National Academy of Sciences Biographical Memoir: "Ira Remsen was for many years the outstanding figure in American chemistry. When the history of the development of the science in this country is written, the fact will be evident that through his influence the serious study of chemistry and the output of new knowledge very rapidly increased. Much had been accomplished by a few gifted men in America before Remsen's day, but he opened up a life work in chemistry as a career to many, and developed a spirit of research that spread over the country." Remsen was the author of several widely adopted chemistry textbooks, each published by a leading American textbook publishing house: Henry Holt and Company, Edwin Ginn and Company, or D. C. Heath and Company.

There were other men of previous generations who were touted as role models for aspiring chemists at Indiana University. Two such men were Harvey Washington Wiley and Richard Dale Owen.

Harvey Washington Wiley (1844–1930) was born in a log farmhouse near the village of Kent, Republican Township, Jefferson County, Indiana. He attended nearby Hanover College on the banks of the Ohio River, just outside the City of Madison (the county seat of Jefferson County). Wiley graduated with an A.B. degree in 1867 and an A.M. in 1870. He entered Indiana Medical College, where he received the

M.D. degree in 1871. Wiley taught Greek and Latin at North Western Christian University (renamed Butler University in 1875) for two years, and then taught Indiana's first laboratory course in chemistry (at Indiana Medical College), beginning in 1873. Wylie Hall chemistry laboratories in Bloomington were not completed until 1884. He studied for only a few months at Harvard College, before receiving a Harvard B.S. degree in 1873. He then joined the faculty of the newly opened Purdue University in 1874. He was also appointed Indiana State Chemist. "Wiley was offered the position of Chief Chemist in the U. S. Department of Agriculture by George Loring, the Commissioner of Agriculture, in 1882. Loring was seeking to replace Peter Collier, his current Chief Chemist, with someone who could employ a more objective approach to the study of sorghum, the potential of which as a sugar source, was far from proven. Wiley accepted the offer after being passed over for the presidency of Purdue, allegedly because he was 'too young and too jovial,' unorthodox in his religious beliefs, and also a bachelor." Wiley gained national recognition by providing the crucial leadership for Congressional passage of the landmark Federal Pure Food and Drug Act of 1906.

Richard Dale Owen (1810–1890) became Chair of Natural Philosophy at Indiana University in 1864, after serving in the Mexican–American War (April 1846–February 1848) and the United States Civil War. Of an even earlier generation, his background was very different from that of Frank Mathers or Harvey Wiley. Born in Scotland, he was the youngest son of Robert Owen, founder of the utopian community of New Harmony on the Wabash River in southwestern Indiana. Young Richard learned his first chemistry and physics in Switzerland, and continued studies in both chemistry and physics at Anderson's Institution in Glasgow. He taught at Western Military Institute, Georgetown, Kentucky, and received the M.D. degree from the Medical College of Nashville. He became the Indiana State Geologist (and by virtue of his position as State Geologist, an ex officio member of the Indiana University faculty) in 1860. In 1867, Richard Owen was named Professor of Natural Science and Chemistry at Indiana University. While remaining on the Indiana University faculty, he became the first president of Purdue University, serving for two years (1872–1874) when the institution had no buildings, no faculty, and no students.

The professional careers of Owen and Wiley, and the early careers of Mathers and Germann, illustrate the evolution in Midwestern United States during a century from natural philosophy (embracing chemistry, physics, mineralogy, geology, medicine, agriculture, and more) to chemistry as a separate scientific discipline, and then to electrochemistry as a narrow specialty in physical chemistry for laboratory research and scholarly publication.

As early as 1865, technological innovations began to make chemistry laboratories major consumers of plumbed-in, running water. This was a time when domestic running water was a rarity in the Midwest, and when scant attention was being paid to the chemical and bacteriological purity of drinking water. Lack of water was a serious concern in Bloomington. Existing waterworks were utterly inadequate. The campus was located on high ground. There was little usable groundwater, and there were no major rivers or lakes in the vicinity. University President William Lowe Bryan in 1909 appointed a faculty committee, including chemist Robert Edward Lyons, physicist Arthur Lee Foley, geologists Edgar Roscoe Cumings and Joshua William Beede, and mathematician Ulysses S. Hanna, to propose a solution. Dr. Hanna had been City Engineer of Bloomington since 1904. Their recommendation, accepted by the Board of Trustees, was to build a reservoir, three miles northeast of Bloomington, to supply water by gravity only to the campus. Arthur Foley was architect and engineer for the reservoir dam. Construction began in 1910.

In the meantime, while Albert Germann was learning experimental techniques in the Wylie Hall chemistry laboratories, campus officials were imposing water restrictions for many uses. But in Wylie Hall, cooling water was flowing freely through distillation condensers. Flowing water was being used to wash chemical glassware, and to rinse off and dilute toxic, corrosive, or reactive chemicals. Water aspirators were used for vacuum filtrations. Hirsch and Büchner filter funnels, requiring water aspirators, were being used routinely for chemical preparations. Gooch crucibles, also requiring water aspirators, were in use for gravimetric quantitative analysis. It has been estimated that, "even in modest use, [lab water aspirators discharge] 50,000 gallons of water per aspirator over the course of a year." Water from the reservoir would come none too soon.

Upon receiving his baccalaureate diploma in 1909, Albert immediately began graduate studies in chemistry at Indiana University.

Although the Indiana Constitution of 1816 promised a public university, Indiana University in Bloomington actually began in 1820 as Indiana State Seminary. There were no classes until 1825, when Presbyterian minister Baynard Rush Hall (1793–1863) became the first (and for two years the only) teacher. There were twelve students in 1825, and the curriculum consisted largely of Greek and Latin. The faculty doubled when Presbyterian John Hopkins Harney (1806–1868) was hired in 1827 to teach mathematics and perhaps also "the natural sciences."

The school's nominal status rose to Indiana College in 1828, and then to Indiana University in 1838. For the rest of the nineteenth century, it was a *university* in name only. The first M.S. degree in Chemistry went to Samuel Brown Wylie (1854–1890) in 1882. Although an occasional master's degree was awarded during the next two decades, it was not until 1904 that the Graduate School was established. In each of the years 1908, 1909, and 1910, Indiana University awarded just two master's degrees in chemistry, and in 1910 (as we shall see), one of the candidates was in residence at the University of Wisconsin. Leo Lehr Carrick, a 1911 graduate of Valparaiso University, would earn the first Indiana University Ph.D. in Chemistry in 1921. Valparaiso University in 1911 was the largest educational establishment in Indiana, perhaps second in enrollment in the United States only to Harvard University. We shall return to Valparaiso in Chapter 4.

Albert Germann was in Bloomington just until the end of summer 1909. The Indiana University *Bulletin* (published in May 1909) listed him as a Teaching Fellow within the Department of Chemistry for the coming year, but (as we shall soon see) he did not assist in any chemistry courses at Indiana University during fall or spring semesters of the academic year 1909–1910. His electrochemical experimental research on a mercurous perchlorate voltmeter, under the direction of Frank Mathers, was completed during the summer. Germann had begun that research while an undergraduate.

In addition to being in partial fulfillment of the requirements for the degree of Master of Arts in Chemistry, his thesis (reporting on research with Frank Mathers) was also the basis for two research publications: Frank C. Mathers and Albert F. O. Germann, "Studies on Perchloric Acid: Mercurous Perchlorate Voltameter," *Indiana University Studies*, vol. 1, no. 5 (1910), pp. 41–49; and Frank C. Mathers and Albert F. O. Germann, "Mercurous Perchlorate Electrolytic Meter," *Transactions of the American Electrochemical Society*, vol. 19, pp. 69–80 (1911). These publications were the first in what was to become an impressive list of contributions to the scientific literature by Albert Germann.

How did the international scientific community become aware of Albert Germann's first scholarly publications? Not every college, university, or research library had files of *Indiana University Studies* or of *Transactions of the American Electrochemical Society*, and scientists with modest incomes had to be very selective when choosing their own personal paid subscriptions. Chemists could keep abreast of current research by consulting one of the three international chemical abstracting periodicals—*Chemisches Zentralblatt, Chemical Abstracts,* or the Abstracts Section of the *Journal of the Chemical Society* [London]. Publication of *Chemical Abstracts* began in January 1907, under the auspices of the American Chemical Society. Chemical Abstracts Service has continued its monitoring, abstracting, and indexing of the world's chemistry-related literature into the twenty-first century.

In 1910 or 1911, a person who had become aware of a research paper not available locally might mail a reprint-request penny postcard to the author. Journals at that time routinely printed separate copies of articles, often with covers, so that authors could respond easily to such reprint requests. An author could submit an order for a supply of these offprints or reprints when returning corrected proofs to the publisher. This practice continued beyond the 1960s, but became less needed with universal availability of photocopiers, widespread access to interlibrary loan services, somewhat limited internet access to publications, and pressure from some institutions for "internet open access" to scholarly publications.

Albert Germann remained a candidate for the Master of Arts in Chemistry throughout the 1909–1910 academic year. Indiana University conferred the A.M. degree on Wednesday, June 22, 1910.

Notwithstanding his enrollment in the Indiana University chemistry graduate program, Albert Germann was attracted to the physical chemistry program at the University of Wisconsin in Madison. The field of physical chemistry was new, and very much in the limelight. Its birth as an academic discipline is often dated with the first issue of the journal *Zeitschrift für physikalische Chemie, Stöichiometrie und Verwandtschaftslehre* in February 1887. The first English-language journal of physical chemistry, *The Journal of Physical Chemistry,* was founded in the United States in 1896. The field gained scientific prominence when physical chemists Jacobus van 't Hoff (1852–1911), Svante Arrhenius (1859–1927), and Wilhelm Ostwald (1853–1932) received the first, third, and ninth Nobel chemistry prizes in 1901, 1903, and 1909.

Mary Bidwell Breed, when she was a chemistry graduate student in 1895, wrote that this field "is usually spoken of as 'the new science of physical chemistry,' though the giving of such a name to it is somewhat misleading. It is not physical chemistry any more than it is chemical physics. It is really the science of phenomena which we cannot explain either by chemistry or by physics alone, but which we are endeavoring to explain by combining the resources of the two."

Professional networking, then and now, plays a central role in career opportunities and choices. Indiana University Associate Professor Oliver Brown had spent summers 1902 and 1903, and then the academic year 1903–1904, doing electrochemical research at the University of Wisconsin. He was a reliable source of practical information for Albert Germann about physical chemistry at Wisconsin. So was Frederick Shinn, who joined the Indiana chemistry faculty in 1905 while completing doctoral study at the University of Wisconsin with Professor Louis Albrecht Kahlenberg (1870–1941), Chair of the Wisconsin Chemistry Department. Kahlenberg was a physical chemist who had studied with Theodore William Richards (1868–1928). Richards in 1914 would be the first American to be awarded the Nobel Prize in Chemistry. In 1908, Kahlenberg hired physical chemist Joseph Howard Mathews (1880–1970) as Instructor in Chemistry at Wisconsin. Mathews, who was to be a mentor of Albert Germann, had also studied with T. W. Richards. Only a few years earlier, as an undergraduate at Wisconsin, Mathews had studied with Kahlenberg.

Albert Germann moved to Madison and became an Assistant in Chemistry at the University of Wisconsin for the academic year 1909–1910. He arrived in Madison at the beginning of a major development in the hands-on, laboratory-oriented collegiate chemistry curriculum. Germann began research in the Laboratory of Physical Chemistry, under the direction of J. Howard Mathews. Germann constructed much of his own apparatus. He submitted a University of Wisconsin master's thesis entitled "The Use of a Dewar Flask in Measurements of Heats of Neutralization." In his research experiments, Albert measured the heat evolved when an acid is mixed with a base. He mixed the reactants in a double-wall Dewar glass vacuum flask to minimize heat flow between the reacting solution and the external environment. Professor Kahlenberg, as chair of the chemistry department, approved the thesis on August 5, 1910. Germann was awarded the M.Sc. degree in Chemistry by the University of Wisconsin in 1910.

We shall note in subsequent chapters that contemporary requirements for the master's degree varied widely from institution to institution, and in some cases the requirement was at best minimal. Noteworthy is that both Indiana University and the University of Wisconsin had a thesis requirement for the master's degree in chemistry. In practice, the thesis requirement in both cases for Albert Germann was substantive; each of his master's theses was of sufficient quality to be published in a prestigious scholarly journal.

Germann's University of Wisconsin master's thesis was typewritten, accompanied with a skillfully drawn diagram of the apparatus and with three graphs competently hand drawn on cross-section paper. Within two months, Mathews and Germann had made some editorial changes, added two references to the research literature, revised a few calculations, perfected the drawing and graphs for reproduction, and submitted the thesis to the *Journal of Physical Chemistry,* where the text was set in type and published in January 1911.

Mathews concluded the *Journal of Physical Chemistry* paper with a sentence (added to the original thesis) that evaluates the pedagogical importance of the apparatus that Germann had designed, constructed, and tested: "The working parts are simple, and if necessary can be made by a student of ordinary skill, thus making it both a convenient and reliable method for laboratory use in classes of physical and thermochemistry." Mathews was already developing a laboratory course in physical chemistry that was to become standard in chemistry curricula throughout the United States. Germann was a teaching assistant in this course, using the textbook *Laboratory Exercises in Physical Chemistry* by Frederick Hutton Getman (1877–1941), published in 1904 by John Wiley & Sons, New York.

Mathews began to try new laboratory exercises whose directions he had mimeographed to supplement the Getman lab manual. Germann's M.Sc. thesis provided instructions for one of these new student experiments. Mathews later collaborated with Wisconsin colleagues Farrington Daniels (1889–1972) and John Warren Williams (1898–1988) to publish *Experimental Physical Chemistry* (New York: McGraw-Hill Book Company, 1929; 475 pages). That book, in seven editions and with added authors from the Wisconsin chemistry faculty, was the market leader among physical chemistry laboratory textbooks until the 1970s.

Major American suppliers of laboratory equipment and supplies responded by featuring specialized apparatus for the new laboratory exercises. Such apparatus appeared in the catalogs of Eimer and Amend of Pittsburgh; Will Corporation of Rochester, New York; Arthur H. Thomas Company and Scientific Materials Company (after 1925, Fisher Scientific) of Philadelphia; and Central Scientific Company

(CENCO), E. H. Sargent & Company, and W. M. Welch Mfg. Co. of Chicago.

Albert Germann's thesis was prepared in a form that would serve as a model for the written laboratory reports required in Wisconsin-type physical chemistry laboratory courses throughout the country and throughout the century. His thesis was the basis for Experiment 21 ("Heat of Neutralization," pp. 76–80) in the first edition of *Experimental Physical Chemistry*.

As an Assistant in Chemistry in 1909–1910, Albert taught students in the physical chemistry laboratory on the third floor of a new chemistry building that had been built in 1905. The entrance on University Avenue was impressive, with six Ionian columns within a Bedford oolitic limestone frame. The interior was of wood timber construction, faced with sand-lime brick. That building, with two major additions, would serve the Chemistry Department for more than half a century. It was also home of the School of Pharmacy. The chemistry library and the pharmacy library were both in the building.

Unlike the situation in Bloomington, there were no conservation restrictions on water use. The university campus was sited on the shores of the 9,740-acre Lake Mendota, fed by the Yahara River. Lake Mendota was an irresistible source of an apparently unlimited supply of water. The new chemistry building had potable water, hot and cold untreated lake water, distilled water, and steam supplied to laboratories via separate piping systems. Potable water came from the City of Madison waterworks. Lake water, used for all campus purposes except cooking and drinking, came from a pumping station whose origins dated from 1876 when the first Science Hall was being built. "Distilled water" was condensed steam, distributed to labs through galvanized iron piping, largely used for rinsing laboratory glassware. For chemically pure water, there was a tin-lined still that delivered water to a glass carboy. Filled carboys were moved to laboratories with a hand truck. Pure water was a precious commodity. The still filled a five-gallon carboy in an hour, using forty gallons of cooling water flowing through its condenser. For ultrapure water, water from the still was probably redistilled from an alkaline permanganate solution by an individual researcher.

Doctoral Study in Europe

In the nineteenth century, American academic chemists often went to Europe to complete a doctorate or for postdoctoral research. We have noted that Thomas Charlton Van Nüys, Robert Edward Lyons, Louis Sherman Davis, and Mary Bidwell Breed, members of the Indiana University Chemistry Department, travelled to Germany and Denmark for their research and for visits to chemical laboratories. Louis Kahlenberg had been a graduate student in Leipzig. He was a valuable source of advice to Albert about doctoral study in Europe.

J. Howard Mathews also had practical advice, but from a different perspective. After receiving his master's degree from Wisconsin in 1905, he went to Harvard to study with Theodore William Richards. "During Mathews' first year, Richards informed him that next year he would be an exchange professor at the University of Berlin; Mathews could work with assistant professor Gregory Baxter and finish in 1907. Mathews hid his disappointment.... Mathews told Richards he preferred to find a teaching position for a year so that he could complete his work with him. Mathews was successful in finding a temporary instructorship in physical and industrial chemistry at Case Institute of Applied Science in Cleveland." Mathews returned to Harvard in 1907, and completed his doctorate in 1908 with T. W. Richards.

Richards had a great deal of experience in European universities. After receiving a Harvard doctorate under Josiah Parsons Cooke (1827–1894) in 1886, he received a John Parker Fellowship. Harvard's Parker Fellowship for European study, created in 1873 by the bequest of Mrs. Anna Parker, provided one of the first American travel stipends for scholars. Richards spent a semester in Göttingen, where he worked on a problem in analytical chemistry with P. E. Jannach and on vapor density determinations with Viktor Meyer (1848–1897). The second semester was spent visiting active research labs in other universities in Germany, France, Switzerland, and England. On his return to America, he became a member of the Harvard faculty. After Cooke's death in 1894, Richards took over the instruction in physical chemistry. To strengthen his qualifications for the subject, he spent a semester with Friedrich Wilhelm Ostwald (1853–1932; Nobel laureate 1909) in Leipzig and a semester with Walther Hermann Nernst (1864-1941; Nobel laureate 1920) in Göttingen.

Albert Germann decided to follow the examples of such American chemists as Louis Kahlenberg and T. W. Richards. Germann left Madison and traveled to Europe at the end of summer 1910. He entered a doctoral program at the University of Geneva (Université de Genève) in Geneva, Switzerland. He was a graduate student there from the winter semester 1910–1911 through the winter semester 1911–1912.

From an American perspective, the Université de Genève is an ancient institution. It traces its history back to the 1559 founding of a Collège (a grammar school) and an Académie (an advanced school) in Geneva by Reformation theologian John Calvin (1509–1564). The Académie de Genève became a theological and humanistic seminary. During the Scientific Revolution of the eighteenth century, the Académie was also home to scholars in law, philosophy, and the sciences. When a medical school was established in 1873, the Académie became the secular Université de Genève.

Philippe-Auguste Guye (1862–1922) directed Germann's research in the physical chemistry laboratory (Laboratoire de Chemie physique de l' Université de Genève). Guye had earned his Ph.D. at the University of Geneva, with research under the direction of Carl Gräbe. Guye was Professor of Physical Chemistry at the University. In 1892, he had been elected to the "Chaire extraordinaire de chimie théorique et technique." In 1903, Professor Guye founded the first Swiss journal of chemistry, the *Journal de Chimie Physique*. Italian photochemist Giacomo Luigi Ciamician (1857–1922), "the founder of green chemistry," would later nominate Guye five times (1917, 1918, 1919, 1920, and 1921) for the Nobel Prize in Chemistry. Guye would be awarded the Davy Medal of the Royal Society of London in 1921 "for his researches in physical chemistry."

The academic lineage of Philippe-Auguste Guye can be traced back to Antoine-Laurent Lavoisier (1743–1794), Claude Louis Berthollet (1748–1822), and Antoine François, comte de Fourcroy (1755–1809), collaborators and key contributors to the eighteenth-century transformation of practical and descriptive alchemy into systematic and quantitative chemistry. Guye's mentor Carl Gräbe (1841–1927) earned his Ph.D. in chemistry in 1862 from the University of Heidelberg, with research under the direction of Robert Wilhelm Eberhard Bunsen (1811–1899). Bunsen received the Ph.D. from the University of Göttingen in 1831, with chemical research in the laboratory of Friedrich Stromeyer (1776–1835). Stromeyer's doctorate was an M.D. from the University of Göttingen in 1800; Stromeyer studied chemistry under Louis Nicolas Vauquelin (1763–1829), who in turn learned his experimental chemistry as an assistant to Antoine François, comte de Fourcroy, from 1783 to 1791.

Albert Germann could later claim to be an academic descendant of chemists Lavoisier, Berthollet, and Fourcroy. As we shall see, so could Frank Germann.

Albert Germann joined a research group that included "MM. Arni et Bell, des Drs G. Baume, A. F. O. Germann et de Mlle [A.] Gillay." This group, under the direction of Ettore Cardoso in the Laboratoire de Chemie physique de l' Université de Genève, was determining the critical temperatures of the gases C_2H_4, N_2O, H_2S, CO_2, C_2N_2, NH_3, and HCl. The critical temperature of a substance is the highest temperature at which vapor of the substance can be liquefied by increasing the pressure. Above that temperature, distinct liquid and gas phases cannot coexist, regardless of pressure. Albert Germann determined the critical temperature of HCl to be 51.40 °C. He and Georges Baume were also co-authors of an experimental research paper on thermodynamic properties of mixtures.

Germann's primary research concentration at the University of Geneva involved extremely precise measurements of the density of pure oxygen. He was aware of the earlier work of Edward Williams Morley (1838–1923), Hurlbut Professor of Natural History and Chemistry at Western Reserve College in Ohio. Morley gained fame among physicists for the Michelson–Morley experiments, investigations that cast doubt on the existence of luminiferous æther. Morley has been credited with introduction of the laboratory method of chemistry instruction at Western Reserve in September 1869, perhaps the first such course in any college west of the Appalachians.

For Germann, however, Morley's reputation was as the chemist who had made the most precise and most reliable measurements of the atomic weight of oxygen. Morley published his definitive work in 1895. At that time, the atomic weight of each element was usually determined by reference to hydrogen equal to 1.000…, but experimentally the atomic weights of most elements required a precise value for oxygen. Morley had determined the densities of both oxygen and hydrogen, thus the ratio of their atomic weights. In practice, Morley had measured the atomic weight of oxygen.

Morley reported his results for oxygen in terms of the *normal liter:* the mass of a liter of oxygen gas at the freezing temperature of water and at a pressure of 760 mm of mercury. Guye and Germann adopted the same definition.

Beyond merely replicating Morley's work, Germann looked for possible sources of uncertainty in Morley's experiments. He designed and executed experiments to reduce such experimental error. To reduce the possibility of contamination of oxygen samples, Germann used his glass-blowing expertise to construct apparatus that min-imized physical contact of oxygen with any material other than glass. In particular, no rubber tubing was in contact with an oxygen sample. For each measurement, Ger-mann introduced the oxygen into a sealed glass globe. He attached the globe to other parts of the apparatus with a ground-glass joint, and closed the globe with a ground-glass stopcock. The joint and the stopcock required a lubricant; Germann chose the particular lubricant with a view to minimizing chemical reaction with oxygen. He periodically removed and replaced the lubricant. Because of the possibility that size of the globe could affect the results, Germann used four globes of different capaci-ties: 252.004 mL, 410.27 mL, 455.72 mL, and 872.33 mL. To provide confidence in the precision of pressure measurements, he made simultaneous determinations with four independent mercury manometers of different diameters. He adjusted the pres-sure to 760 mm of mercury when the globe was immersed in an ice-water slurry and thus (by definition of the Celsius temperature scale) at zero °C.

Because oxygen gas has a density comparable to the density of laboratory air, each weighing necessarily included compensation for the buoyancy exerted by the laboratory atmosphere. That "buoyancy correction" was often comparable in magni-tude to the weight of the gas sample itself. To verify that the buoyancy correction took proper account of the weight of the glass bulb, Germann blew two of the inter-mediate-volume glass globes with walls of significantly different thickness; the 410.27 mL globe weighed 67 g, whereas the 455.72 mL globe, volume 1.11 times greater, weighed 118 g, mass 1.76 times greater.

Albert Germann compared his experimental value (normal liter of oxygen = 1.42905 g) with Morley's average of his forty-one observations (normal liter of oxygen = 1.42900 g). This excellent agreement was confirmation of the nineteenth-century results of Edward Williams Morley. Germann also saw this agreement as validation of his own twentieth-century experiments and his own experimental techniques.

Today, nuclear masses are determined by comparison with the isotope carbon twelve, ^{12}C. When Morley was active in the laboratory, no chemist suspected that there were isotopes of hydrogen, oxygen, and carbon. It was the English radio-chemist Frederick Soddy (1877–1956, Nobel laureate 1921) who suggested the existence of isotopes of the heavy elements to explain his experiments (1904 to 1914) and experiments of his older colleague Ernest Rutherford (1871–1937, Nobel laureate 1908) involving the radioactive decay of uranium to radium. Joseph

John Thomson (1856–1940, Nobel laureate 1906) in 1912 was the first to find evidence of isotopes of a non-radioactive element. It was not until 1929 that William Francis Giauque (1895–1982) and Herrick Lee Johnston (1898–1965) reported the oxygen isotopes ^{17}O and ^{18}O.

Albert Germann received a Ph.D. or Sc.D. degree (precisely: doctorat ès sciences physiques et chimiques) from the University of Geneva on January 15, 1914. His sixty-three-page doctoral thesis, published as a printed book, was entitled "Révision de la densité de l'oxygène, contribution à la determination de la densité l'air à Genève." Philippe-Auguste Guye's *Journal de Chimie physique* published a shorter version.

As a student at Indiana University, Albert joined the national chemistry fraternity Alpha Chi Sigma. The *General Directory of Alpha Chi Sigma Fraternity* (January 1, 1911) indicates that, in 1911, he was living in Geneva, Switzerland, and his home address was 123 West 3rd Street, Peru, Indiana. That was the Germann family home address from 1906 until at least 1939.

Albert did not spend the year 1912–1913 in Geneva. He was in Germany, at the University of Berlin (Königlichen Friedrich-Wilhelms-Universität zu Berlin). The official record lists him as a student of chemistry at the University of Berlin for the 1912 summer semester. Jacobus van 't Hoff had been professor of physical chemistry there from 1895 until his death in 1911. When Albert arrived, physical chemist Walther Hermann Nernst (1864–1941; Nobel laureate 1920) was a professor at the University of Berlin. Also at Berlin was Max Karl Ernst Ludwig Planck (1858–1947; Nobel laureate 1918), a founder of quantum theory. Together, Nernst and Planck are often credited with formulating the Third Law of Thermodynamics. It was an exciting place to be immersed in cutting-edge physical chemical research.

The laboratory apparatus available in Bloomington and in Madison when Albert Germann was initiated into experimental chemistry was mostly imported from England, France, and Germany. Carl Friedrich Zeiss (1816–1888) and Ernst Abbe (1840–1905) in Jena had international reputations for constructing and marketing fine optical instruments. Friedrich Otto Schott (1851–1935) opened a glassmaking laboratory (Jenaer Glaswerk) in Jena in 1882. He had financial support from Zeiss, Abbe, and the Prussian government. For Zeiss and Abbe, Schott created apochromatic lenses that bring three different wavelengths of light into focus in the same plane. By 1893, Schott had invented borosilicate glass for thermometers and laboratory glassware. By 1870, both Paul Bunge (1839–1888) in Hamburg and Florenz Sartorius (1846–1925) in

Göttingen were producing precision analytical balances. Philippe-Auguste Guye used a modified Sartorius balance for the gas density measurements in his laboratory. Albert took the opportunity when in Germany to locate sources of specialized laboratory equipment. Importation into the United States halted during the Great War, but the Zeiss, Abbe, Schott, and Sartorius firms survived the war and prospered afterwards. Their names still signify high precision and high quality. Zeiss still signifies high sales; with corporate headquarters in Germany, Carl Zeiss ranked number ten internationally among instrumentation firms in 2012 sales.

With a career in research chemistry contemplated, it was to Albert's professional advantage while in Europe to learn first-hand about sources of specialty "fine chemicals"—reagent-grade, high-purity chemical compounds, often produced and sold in small quantities. Many of the names of suppliers are still familiar to chemists, although the business enterprises have undergone many mergers and acquisitions, as well as financial and geo-political ups-and-downs. As we shall see in Chapters 3 and 5, Albert Germann would become one of these chemical entrepreneurs within a couple of decades. Here we shall indicate the origins of some of best-known chemical companies—Merck & Company, BASF, Bayer, Ciba-Geigy, du Pont, Baker and Adamson, and Mallinckrodt. Then, as now, ownership and operations often crossed national boundaries.

Friedrich Jacob Merck (1621–1678) purchased an apothecary shop in Darmstadt, Germany, in 1668. In 1827, Heinrich Emmanuel Merck (1794–1855) transformed the Merck family pharmacy into a drug manufacturing enterprise. The German firm, E. Merck AG, opened a United States sales office in 1887. Merck & Company began production in Rahway, New Jersey, in 1903. The relationship between Merck & Company and E. Merck AG was severed when the United States entered the Great War. Merck divested its specialty chemical operations in 1995.

Friedrich Engelhorn (1821–1902) founded Badische Anilin- und Soda-Fabrik (BASF) in 1865 in Mannheim, state of Baden-Württemberg, Germany. The Mannheim gasworks produced tar as a byproduct, and Engelhorn used this tar to make synthetic aniline dyes. BASF became a major producer of other chemicals needed for dye works: sodium carbonate, sulfuric acid, and ammonia. These were also chemicals needed in larger quantities to produce explosives for German military use. BASF in 1925 was a founding member of the Interessen–Gemeinschaft Farbenindustrie monopoly (IG Farben), which cooperated with Adolf Hitler and the Nazi regime.

The World War II Allies dissolved IG Farben in 1945, but BASF survived, financially strong. In 2014, with annual chemical sales of $78.7 billion, BASF had been the world's largest chemical company for nine consecutive years.

Dye salesman Friedrich Bayer (1825–1880) and master dyer Johann Friedrich Weskott (1821–1876) formed the general partnership "Friedr. Bayer et comp." in 1863 in Barmen, Bergisches Land, Germany. The original objective of the company was the manufacture and sale of synthetic dyestuffs. Between 1881 and 1913, Bayer developed into a diversified chemical company with international operations. The Bayer chemical research laboratory developed many dyes and pharmaceuticals. Bayer aspirin became a commercial pharmaceutical product in 1899. In 1925, Bayer became a member of IG Farben. In 2014, with annual chemical sales of $28.1 billion, Bayer was the world's tenth largest chemical company.

Novartis was created in 1996 from the merger of Ciba-Geigy and Sandoz Laboratories, both Swiss companies with long histories of pharmaceutical chemical sales and manufacture. Ciba-Geigy was formed in 1970 by the merger of J. R. Geigy Ltd (founded in Basel by Johann Rudolf Geigy-Merian in 1758) and Chemische Industrie Basel (founded in Basel by Alexander Clavel-Oswald in 1859). Alfred Kern (1850–1893) and Edouard Sandoz (1853–1928) founded Chemiefirma Kern und Sandoz in 1886 to manufacture the dyes Alizarine Brilliant Blue and Auramine Yellow. Kern & Sandoz began production of saccharin in 1899, followed by a range of pharmaceuticals and other fine chemicals.

Eleuthère Irénée du Pont (1771–1834) founded E. I. du Pont de Nemours and Company in the United States in 1802, with funding and equipment from France. The company started at Eleutherian Mills, on the Brandywine Creek, near Wilmington, Delaware, just after du Pont fled the aftermath of the French Revolution. The company began as a gunpowder manufacturer; DuPont supplied half the gunpowder used by the Union Army during the American Civil War. DuPont established two of the first industrial research laboratories in the United States, investigating cellulose chemistry, lacquers, and related products. DuPont chemists synthesized Nylon in 1935. In 2014, with annual chemical sales of $29.9 billion, DuPont was the world's eighth largest chemical company.

Two highly respected American suppliers of chemical reagents of reliable purity were Baker and Mallinckrodt. John Townsend Baker (1860–1935) was born in Orange, New Jersey. He studied at Lafayette College in Easton, Pennsylvania, receiving a baccalaureate degree in chemistry in 1882 and the master's degree in 1885. By 1890, Baker, along with Lafayette classmate George P. Adamson, established the Baker and Adamson Chemical Company in Easton to sell chemical compounds. They were successful. In 1902, they sold their enterprise to the Allied Chemical Company in Pennsylvania, with the condition that neither Baker nor Adamson would create a rival business in Pennsylvania. Baker promptly founded the J. T. Baker Chemical Company in Phillipsburg, New Jersey. He marketed "Baker Analyzed" reagents, with the actual quantitative chemical analysis of each lot printed on the label.

Brothers Gustav Mallinckrodt (1840–1877), Edward Mallinckrodt (1845–1928), and Otto Mallinckrodt (1847–1876) founded G. Mallinckrodt Company in 1867. Their first factory was on land that had been purchased about 1840 in St. Louis, Missouri, by their father, Emil Mallinckrodt. Their enterprise quickly became a leading supplier of chemicals for the emerging photography industry. Edward incorporated Mallinckrodt Chemical Works in St. Louis in 1882 to manufacture fine chemicals for pharmaceutical products.

Western Reserve University

A friend and former colleague of Edward Williams Morley—Olin Freeman Tower (1872–1945), Hurlbut Professor of Chemistry at Western Reserve University, Cleveland, Ohio—visited the physical chemistry laboratory of Philippe-Auguste Guye at the University of Geneva. Tower and Guye discussed work then in progress on the composition of air. Tower wrote in 1912: "During a recent visit to Geneva, I was interested to learn that certain experiments which were then in progress in the chemical laboratory there, tended to confirm certain views, which were formerly held by Professor Morley." Albert Germann was working in Guye's laboratory at the time of Tower's visit. If Germann and Tower met and talked, then this probably would have been Albert Germann's first contact with Tower and with Western Reserve University. Such a conversation might be considered a de facto recruitment interview. There were to be many more Germann–Tower conversations—and eventually, collegial collaborations.

Another source of information about the Cleveland academic scene could have been J. Howard Mathews, director of Germann's M.Sc. research at Wisconsin. During a break in his doctoral research at Harvard, Mathews spent the 1906–1907 year as Instructor of Physical and Industrial Chemistry at Case Institute of Applied Science in Cleveland.

Western Reserve College opened in 1826 in Hudson, Ohio, the first collegiate institution in what is now northern Ohio. Twenty-six years earlier, Hudson had been in the Connecticut Western Reserve, part of the "land from sea to sea" granted to the Connecticut Colony in 1662 by Charles II (1630–1685), King of England, Scotland, and Ireland. This grant could be interpreted as including land now a part of the states of Ohio, Pennsylvania, Michigan, Indiana, Illinois, Iowa, Nebraska, Wyoming, Utah, Nevada, and California. Connecticut gradually relinquished land claims to Pennsylvania, to other states, and to Native Americans. Connecticut retained title to its Western Reserve in Ohio until 1800. Western Reserve College moved to Cleveland in 1882, and upgraded its status to Western Reserve University. The University and Case Institute of Technology (from 1880 to 1948, Case Institute of Applied Science) would merge in 1967 to form Case Western Reserve University. Western Reserve and Case campuses were physically adjacent before the merger.

The American Chemical Society designated Morley's research a National Historic Chemical Landmark in a ceremony in Cleveland on Thursday, September 14, 1995. The text of the commemorative plaque that marks the site of Morley's laboratory in Adelbert Hall on the campus of Case Western Reserve University reads:

> In his laboratory in the basement of this building, Edward W. Morley, Hurlbut Professor of Natural History and Chemistry from 1868 to 1906, carried out his research on the atomic weight of oxygen that provided a new standard to the science of chemistry. The accuracy of his analyses has never been superseded by chemical means. His great work, published in 1895, also gave important insight into the atomic theory of matter.

Professor Morley had retired from Western Reserve University before Albert Germann actively considered a faculty position at Western Reserve. Morley moved to West Hartford, Connecticut, in 1906. At that time, Albert Germann was still an undergraduate chemistry student at Indiana University. Yet the Morley aura was a significant influence drawing Germann to Western Reserve. A physical symbol of

Morley's distinguished physical-chemical research accomplishments was the equal-arm two-pan analytical balance that Morley modified for atomic-weight measurements and used in his Adelbert Hall laboratory at Western Reserve University. Germann acquired that balance. Decades later, he proudly displayed that historic balance in his laboratory at Nutritional Research Associates in South Whitley, Indiana. He pointed to holes drilled in the base of the balance to permit suspension of glass gas-containing globes from the balance pans.

Did Albert Germann apply for a faculty position at Western Reserve because the Chemistry Department had been the research home of Edward Williams Morley? Did Olin Freeman Tower actively recruit Albert Germann for his department? Did J. Howard Mathews influence Albert Germann to consider Cleveland? Regardless of the answers to these questions, the significant fact is: After Albert Germann spent a year in Germany at the Königlichen Friedrich-Wilhelms-Universität zu Berlin, he began a teaching career in Cleveland, centered at the Morley Chemical Laboratory of Western Reserve University.

In 1913, with a doctorate earned but not yet conferred, he became Instructor in Chemistry at The College for Women and at Adelbert College (for men), undergraduate colleges of Western Reserve University. His office and laboratory were in the new chemistry building—official name: "Morley Chemical Laboratory"—that had been constructed during the years between 1908 and 1910. The cornerstone of the Morley Chemical Laboratory was laid on the Adelbert College campus on Thursday, June 11, 1908. Chemistry laboratory director, Dr. Olin Freeman Tower, delivered an address. Dr. Tower at that time projected the construction cost to be at least $120,000, with an anticipated formal opening in the fall of 1909.

The three-floor collegiate-style gothic building was built of brick and concrete, with Indiana oolitic limestone trim. The first floor had two large laboratory rooms, classrooms, offices, a small research laboratory, darkrooms, a workshop, and a chemical storeroom. On the second floor were two large teaching laboratories, the main lecture auditorium (with adjoining room for preparing chemical demonstrations), a storage room, a small laboratory, a balance room, and offices. The third floor had additional recitation rooms, a laboratory for electrochemistry, and a library and reading room. The library included a collection of books assembled by Professor Morley and given by him to the University. Also on the third floor was space for the Department of Geology.

How did Ida and Albert Meet?

Albert remained an active member of St. John's Lutheran Church in Peru, and represented its youth group as a delegate to a Walther League convention in Detroit. There he met his future wife, Ida Helene Johanna Meinke (January 6, 1884–August 12, 1976).

Ida was born in Royal Oak Township, Oakland County, Michigan, daughter of Anna Maria Fasel and Henry Louis Meinike. Royal Oak Township, laid out in 1833, was a standard (6 mile × 6 mile) Congressional Township, with 36 one-mile-square sections of 640 acres each. The forty-acre Henry Meinike farm was in Section 24. Royal Oak, less than three miles west of the Meinike farm, was incorporated as a village in 1891. In 1900, Royal Oak village had a population of 468. The site of the Meinike farm is now within the city of Madison Heights (incorporated and chartered in 1955). The former farm is now developed. Lincoln and Dequindre streets border the farmland. A map of Royal Oak Township published in 1896 identifies the 40-acre parcel with the name "Henry Meinike." A map published in 1908 has the name "Henry Meinke." Family members dropped the second "i" and have used the shorter name since the turn of the century.

Ida probably began her formal education in a one-room school within walking distance of her home in School District No. 6. Later, she may have attended school in the village proper. Royal Oak had built a two-story wooden school building (replacing a log school building) in 1868. That building housed all grades until 1902.

Albert, now Dr. Germann, married Ida on Thanksgiving Day (Thursday, November 26) 1914, at the Royal Oak farm home of the bride's parents. It was 54 °F, windy, and cloudy in Royal Oak that autumn day. Ida and Albert lived in Cleveland for the next seven years (and later returned to Cleveland, as we shall see in Chapters 3, 4, and 5). They became the parents of four children: Luise Barbara Germann Pook [February 11, 1916–January 27, 2012; Cleveland (Ohio) East High School Class of 1933], Edith Germann Osborn [September 6, 1917–March 31, 1990; Cleveland East High School Class of 1935], Lucia May Germann Harley [May 28, 1920–January 12, 1998; South Whitley (Indiana) High School Class of 1938], and Albert Fredrick Ottomar Germann Jr. [born January 4, 1929; South Whitley High School Class of

1946]. Luise Barbara Germann adopted the name Barbara, probably to avoid confusion with her sister Lucia's name. A. F. O. Germann Jr. eventually adopted the name Albert Fredrick Ottomar Germann II. He was called "Bert" at South Whitley High School. At college, he became "Al" Germann.

All the children of Ida and Albert were born in Cleveland. They all attended public schools in Cleveland. Barbara, Edith, and Lucia attended the Addison Junior High School in Cleveland. Barbara entered Addison by transfer in September 1927 from the Lutheran St. John's Christian Day School in Peru, Indiana. Barbara, Edith, and Lucia each spent a year as students at St. John's. Later, in Chapter 4, we shall examine (at length) the interesting reasons for the period in Peru. In Chapter 3, we shall explain why Barbara began kindergarten in Palo Alto, California. Finally, in Chapter 5, we shall discover why Lucia and Albert Jr. became students at South Whitley High School.

With his Swiss diploma in hand, Albert Germann Sr. was promoted to Assistant Professor of Chemistry at Western Reserve University for the 1915–1916 academic year. He was then promoted to Associate Professor with tenure in 1921. Albert was also Professor of Chemistry at the Cleveland School of Nurses in 1918.

During summer sessions from 1915 through 1921, he was in charge of instruction in chemistry at the Cleveland Normal School. Cleveland Normal School, together with the Cleveland Board of Education and Western Reserve University, formed a three-institution consortium that offered courses from 1915 to 1920. The curriculum, designed for practicing teachers to qualify for reappointment, promotion, tenure, and especially salary increases, led to a baccalaureate degree. The consortium evolved into the Cleveland School of Education, which was accredited in 1922 and became affiliated with Western Reserve University. In addition to his extensive hands-on familiarity with instruction of students in the chemical laboratory, Albert had school teaching experience, both as a high school teacher at Bunker Hill and Reserve in Miami County, Indiana, and as a school administrator in Butler Township, Miami County. Being active in the evolution of Cleveland Normal School to accreditation as Cleveland School of Education, Albert gained practical insight into an accreditation process in which he was later to play a critical role at Valparaiso University.

Ida and Albert were married on November 26, 1914, five months after the assassination of Franz Ferdinand (Archduke of Austria and heir to the Austro-Hungarian throne) on June 28, 1914, in Sarajevo. The assassination led to the outbreak of warfare in Europe. Although the United States did not immediately enter the Great War, Congress anticipated involvement, and on May 18, 1917, authorized military conscription. Registration for the United States draft began on June 5, 1917, for men between the ages of 21 and 31; Albert was 31 in 1917. On September 12, 1918, registration was required for men between the ages of 18 and 45. There was automatic deferment for married men. The United States Selective Service System did not last long. Conscription ceased after the Armistice was signed on November 11, 1918. By March 1919, the local Selective Service Boards closed. All functions of the System ended in July 1919.

Frank Erhart Emmanuel Germann

Frank Erhart Emmanuel Germann was born in Peru on Tuesday, December 6, 1887, son of Mary Fredericke Mueller and Gustave Adolph Germann. Frank attended the Lutheran St. John's Christian Day School and then Peru High School, where he graduated in 1906. He was on the staff of the Peru High School yearbook, *Narcissus*. The *Narcissus* staff dedicated the 1906 yearbook to "Mr. Ross F. Lockridge, our esteemed former principal."

Ross Franklin Lockridge Sr. (October 26, 1877–January 12, 1952) was born in Miami County, attended Roann High School (Paw Paw Township, Wabash County), and graduated from Indiana University in 1900. Ross Lockridge taught history at Peru High School before becoming Principal. After leaving the faculty of Peru High School, he entered Indiana University Law School, receiving an LL.B. degree in 1907. He would later be known throughout the state as a popular speaker. He also became an historian of pioneer Indiana, especially of New Harmony, the utopian community downstream from Peru on the Wabash River. His son, Ross Franklin Lockridge Jr. (1914–1948), wrote a 1,066-page novel, *Raintree County*, published in 1948. The younger Lockridge set *Raintree County* in Straughn, Indiana (which he called Waycross), a small rural town on the National Road and the Pennsylvania Railroad, with a population of 275 in 1940 and 222 in 2010. *Raintree County* was the basis for a 1957 motion picture that starred Montgomery Clift, Lee Marvin, Agnes Moorehead, Nigel Patrick, Eva Marie Saint, Elizabeth Taylor, and Rod Taylor.

Ross Lockridge Sr. undoubtedly had a strong positive influence on both Frank and Albert Germann. A contemporary in Peru with whom they probably had no contact was Cole Albert Porter, born in Peru on June 9, 1891. His wealthy maternal grandfather, James Omar Cole, enrolled him in Worcester Academy (Worcester, Massachusetts) in 1905, so there was no high school overlap of Cole Porter and the Germann brothers within the Peru public school system. Cole Porter in 1909 entered Yale College, New Haven, Connecticut. He was an original member of the Whiffenpoofs at Yale, and was President of the Yale Glee Club. He wrote three hundred songs as an undergraduate, including persistent Yale football fight songs "Bulldog" and "Bingo Eli Yale." Among his many successful Broadway musicals were "Anything Goes" (1934), "Kiss Me, Kate" (1948), "Can-Can" (1952), and "Silk Stockings" (1955). In the list of classic Cole Porter tunes are "Begin the Beguine" and "In the Still of the Night."

No one could grow up in Peru at the turn of the century without being influenced by circus culture and flamboyance. Peru livery stable owner Benjamin E. Wallace (1847–1921) had opened his circus in 1884. Wallace purchased two hundred acres of land (near Peru, between the Wabash and Mississinewa rivers) in 1892 from descendants of Chief Francois Godfrey (1788–1840) of the Miami Nation. This land was used as the winter quarters of what would become the Hagenbeck–Wallace Circus, second-largest circus in America. Circus wagons were repaired and their carvings gold-leafed in the Peru winter quarters. A team of French Percheron draft horses drew each circus wagon. During the winter months in Peru, a thousand Percherons roamed the fields. Hundreds of exotic animals—elephants, giraffes, giant cats, and more—were housed and trained in numerous barns. The International Circus Hall of Fame, established in Peru by Wallace in 1892, still thrives.

According to the *Narcissus,* Frank as a senior would graduate from Peru High School with the highest number of course credits in his class. Immediately following his graduation, Frank began collegiate studies in summer school. He entered Indiana University in Bloomington on Thursday, June 21, 1906.

"For two years, following in about the same course pursued by his brother, he engaged in teaching school…. The country school teacher who was destined to become a Phi Beta Kappa Associate had his first teaching assignment in a rural area of Indiana. A year later, he taught fourth grade in Peru, Indiana." *Teachers' Roster for Miami, County, Indiana* listed Frank as teaching in Pipe Creek Township, Miami County, in 1906–1907. (Bunker Hill High School, where Albert Germann had taught, was in Pipe Creek Township.) In 1908–1909, Frank was listed as teaching fourth grade at Elmwood Elementary School in Peru.

He was awarded the degree of Bachelor of Arts in Physics by Indiana University on Wednesday, June 21, 1911. During his five years as an undergraduate, Frank was probably teaching in Miami County each year during the fall, winter, and spring short terms, taking courses in Bloomington each summer. To get a degree in five years, he somehow sandwiched other coursework at Indiana University into his school-teaching schedule.

Gamma of Indiana Chapter of Phi Beta Kappa elected Frank to membership in 1911 as he completed his senior year. This was the year when a Phi Beta Kappa chapter was installed at Indiana University; Frank Germann was a charter member of the chapter. When Gamma of Indiana Chapter was chartered, outstanding Indiana University alumni were also elected. Albert Germann and Ross Lockridge Sr. were among the alumni elected in 1911. Phi Beta Kappa (Φιλοσοφία Βίου Κυβερνήτης, "love of knowledge, the governor of life") is the nation's most prestigious collegiate academic honor society in the liberal arts and sciences.

Frank attended the Concordia Club, a Lutheran organization on the Indiana University campus.

The parallel paths followed by the Germann brothers sometimes satisfied criteria from their geometry books: "never converging, never intersecting." At Indiana University, their courses of study were similar, although they probably never enrolled in the same class at the same time. Chemistry and physics laboratories were in different campus buildings, although nearby on the "new campus" in Dunn's Woods. Frank was "following in about the same course pursued by his brother," and each brother chose to major in a physical science. After Albert had settled comfortably into the Chemistry Department, Frank needed to choose his academic major. Frank took a parallel (but largely nonintersecting) path in science. He majored in physics. He chose the Physics Department as his academic home, where he found two significant mentors. A decade later, in the State of Colorado, Frank moved from physics to physical chemistry.

Their paths did cross in 1910, when Frank took a three-credit undergraduate summer-session course, "Physical Chemistry," at the University of Wisconsin in Madison. The lecture course was taught by Professor Louis Kahlenberg, assisted by Instructor David Klein. David Klein had just completed a doctoral program with Louis Kahlenberg. The summer session began on June 27 and ended on August 5. During this time, Albert was also in Madison, completing work on his master's thesis.

Professor Kahlenberg approved Albert's M.Sc. thesis on Friday, August 5, 1910.

When Frank Germann matriculated as an undergraduate at Indiana University, the physics faculty was composed of Professor Arthur L. Foley; Associate Professor Rolla R. Ramsey; and Instructors Ryland Ratliff, Henry C. Brandon, and Thomas A. Chittenden. Arthur Foley was Head of the Department of Physics from 1897 to 1938. Both Foley and Ramsey had significant professional influence on Frank Germann's career.

Arthur Lee Foley (1867–1945) received the A.B. from Indiana University in 1890, and the Ph.D. in Physics from Cornell University in 1897. His doctoral dissertation, "Arc Spectra," reported his investigation of radiation from the electric arc discharge produced in a gap between two carbon electrodes when the electrodes are connected to a source of high-voltage, direct-current electricity. He also used copper electrodes to form an arc. He was interested throughout his career in radiation and wave phenomena of all sorts. As early as 1904, Foley was giving public demonstrations of radiation from radium. Instructor Ryland Ratliff investigated properties of the same "one-tenth of a gram of 'Curie' radium chloride." Ratliff reported his observations in 1905. At the same time, Foley was also investigating radio waves.

Foley continued research in radiation and waves. In 1917, he became the first recipient of a professorship in the Luther Dana Waterman Institute for Research at Indiana University. Arthur's later work focused on theories of sound amplification, leading to patents for the ideal shapes of horns for musical instruments and for the optimum placement of locomotive whistles. P. Blakiston's Son & Company, Inc. of Philadelphia published his college textbook, *College Physics*, in 1933. The third edition appeared in 1941.

Arthur Foley had important roles in building the new campus in Dunn's Woods. He was a member of the 1909 committee that recommended building a reservoir to deal with the University's chronic water shortage, and was architect and engineer for constructing the reservoir dam in 1910. He was architect and superintendent of construction for two power plants and connecting tunnels to supply steam, electricity, and telephone service to the new buildings. He was architect and superintendent of construction for the Wellhouse (1906) and for a 1907 addition to Maxwell Hall. He was superintendent of construction for Student Building (1906), the Library (1907), and Biology Hall (1910). He directed improvements in the acoustics of Assembly Hall in 1916–1917.

Rolla Roy Ramsey (1872–1955) received the A.B. in Physics from Indiana University in 1895. In his senior year, Ramsey was an assistant in the Physics Department shop. He then took a position as science teacher at Decatur (Indiana) High School during the 1895–1896 year. Decatur is east of Peru, 67 miles via the present-day highways U. S. 24 and 224. The next year, Ramsey returned to Bloomington to become a Laboratory Assistant in the Department of Physics and a graduate student in Physics during the 1896–1897 year. He received the A.M. degree in Physics from Indiana University in 1898. While writing his master's thesis during the 1897–1898 academic year, he held the position of Professor of Physics at Westminster College, New Wilmington, Pennsylvania, one of the first coeducational colleges in the United States. He then spent a year (1898–1899) as a Scholar in Physics during the formation of Clark University, Worcester, Massachusetts. Jonas Gilman Clark had founded the University in 1887. The formal opening of Clark (as the first all-graduate-studies institution in the United States) was on October 2, 1899, with research-focused departments of mathematics, physics, chemistry, biology, and psychology.

Ramsey moved to Cornell University in Ithaca, New York, and pursued doctoral studies there. He earned the Ph.D. in Physics from Cornell in 1901 with the dissertation "The Effect of Gravity and Pressure on Electrolytic Action." His research was under the direction of Edward Leamington Nichols (1854–1937). Edward Nichols and Ernest George Merritt (1865–1948) had founded the scholarly journal *Physical Review* at Cornell in July 1893, and continued as editors of the journal for thirty-three volumes. Nichols and Merritt were close collaborators, and both were senior members of the Cornell Department of Physics. *Physical Review* published Ramsey's doctoral dissertation.

Rolla Ramsey was absorbed in all aspects of radio throughout his career. He formed the Ramsey Publishing Company to print and distribute his books, *The Fundamentals of Radio* (1929) and *Experimental Radio* (1937). He initiated the first radio broadcasts in Bloomington, and in a 1927 demonstration sent a television image from a transmitter to a receiver at opposite ends of an Indiana University lecture hall. Ramsey was head of the World War I radio course at Indiana University, and introduced civilian instruction of radio into the United States Army.

We shall see in Chapter 2 that the years spent at Cornell by Arthur Lee Foley and by Rolla Roy Ramsey had a substantial impact on career choices made by Frank Germann.

Frank Follows Albert to Geneva

Albert Germann had traveled to Europe at the end of summer 1911 to begin graduate studies at the University of Geneva (Geneva, Switzerland). Frank followed a year later, enrolling in the Faculty of Sciences of the University of Geneva as a graduate student on Monday, October 30, 1911. Frank spent the next summer (from May 17, 1912 to August 6, 1912) with his brother at the University of Berlin. Frank enrolled at the University of Berlin as a chemistry student, and held a General Electric Fellowship.

The University of Geneva hired Frank Germann as Instructor in Physical Chemistry for the next two years (1912–1914). Frank's title was assistant en chimie théorique et technique. During much of this period, he was actively engaged in research in the physical chemistry laboratory, under the direction of Professor Philippe-Auguste Guye, chaire extraordinaire de chimie théorique et technique. Prof. Guye had also directed the doctoral research of Albert Germann at the University of Geneva.

An indication of that intense activity is the following list of research publications. These papers appeared in several of the most prestigious European journals of science, providing a wide international audience among chemists and physicists. The English translations of titles are by Frank.

F. E. E. Germann, "Eine Bestimmung der Dampfdruck- und Dichtskurven des Sauerstoffs und Konstruktion eines Apparates zur Bestimmung kritischer Daten" [A Determination of the Vapor Pressure and Density Curves of Oxygen, and Construction of an Apparatus for the Determination of Critical Data], *Physikalische Zeitschrift*, vol. 14 (1913), pp. 857–860.

M. Skossarewski und F. Germann, "Anordnung zur selbst-tätigen Zirkulation eines Gases in einem geschlossenen Kreis," *Angewandte Chemie*, vol. 27, Referatenteil zu Nr. 25 (March 27, 1914), p. 220.

M. Skossarewski et F. Germann, "Dispositif pour réaliser la circulation automatique d'un gaz dans un circuit fermé" [An Arrangement for Bringing About the Circulation of a Gas in a Closed Circuit], *Journal de Chimie Physique*, vol. 11 (1913), pp. 584–588; received February 15, 1913.

This paper includes two diagrams of the experimental apparatus.

Philippe-Auguste Guye et Frank-E.-E. Germann, "Analyse de très petites quantités de gaz; Application à l'analyse de l'air" [Analysis of Very Small Quantities of Gas; Application to the Analysis of Air], *Comptes Rendus Hebdomadaires des Séances de l'Académie des Sciences*, vol. 159 (1914), pp. 154–157.

Philippe-Auguste Guye und Frank-E.-E. Germann, "Einen Apparat zur Analyse ganz kleiner Gasmengen," *Zeitschrift für analytische Chemie (Fresenius' Journal of Analytical Chemistry)*, vol. 54, no. 5 (1915), pp. 263–264.

Philippe-Auguste Guye et Frank-E.-E. Germann, "Sur les gas retenus par l'iode et l'argent" [Concerning the Gases Retained by Iodine and Silver], *Comptes Rendus Hebdomadaires des Séances de l'Académie des Sciences*, vol. 159 (1914), pp. 225–229.

Philippe-Auguste Guye et Frank-E.-E. Germann, "Contributions à l'étude des causes d'erreur affectant les determinations des poids atomiques. IV. Méthode micro-analytique pour l'étude des gaz; Application à l'analyse de traces d'air. V. Des impuretes gazeuses continues dans l'argent considéré comme etalon auxiliaire de poids atomiques" [Contributions to the Study of the Causes of Error Affecting the Determinations of Atomic Weights. IV. Micro-analytical Methods for the Study of Gases; Applications to the Analysis of Traces of Air. V. Concerning Gaseous Impurities Contained in Silver Regarded as an Auxiliary Standard in Atomic Weight Determinations], *Journal de Chimie Physique*, vol. 14 (1913), pp. 195–243.

Frank completed his experimental research with Philippe-Auguste Guye by summer 1913. He had submitted some of his results for publication. The remaining work to complete requirements for the doctorate was writing—writing some more research papers, and writing his thesis. That writing could be accomplished anywhere, and so Frank came back to the United States with Albert. Albert joined the chemistry faculty of Western Reserve University in fall 1913. Frank went back to Indiana, and to Bloomington … but not to the Department of Physics.

Frank had a personal meeting with Indiana University President William Lowe Bryan (November 11, 1860–November 21, 1955; Vice-President from 1893 to 1902; President from 1902 to 1937) in Bloomington on Tuesday, December 9 or Wednesday, December 10, 1913. Frank had asked for this meeting: "I have a matter of very considerable importance to me, concerning which I would like to have your advice." Frank was on leave from the Department of Physical Chemistry of the University of Geneva, and was being offered a continuing position in that department. President Bryan encouraged Frank to accept the offer. While considering his professional future, Frank was prepared to begin a one-semester appointment at Indiana University, and to delay responding to the University of Geneva.

Frank joined the *Department of Romance Languages* at Indiana University for the second semester 1913–1914 as an Instructor of French. His salary was $500 for the semester. There were then four members of the Department of Romance Languages in the professorial ranks, and two instructors. Frank had taken courses in the Department during eight semesters (1907–1908 through 1910–1911) of his undergraduate years at Indiana University. He then strengthened his French language credentials during the time he spent at l'Université de Genève. Frank may have been a temporary replacement for Ruth Redfern Maxwell (1885–1962), Instructor in French; or for Frances Renshaw Latzke, Acting Instructor in French. Both women were graduate students, each a candidate for the A.M. degree at the close of the semester. Ruth Maxwell had an A.B. (1907) from Indiana University. Frances Latzke had an A.B. (1912) from Barnard College, New York City.

The semester as a teacher of French language later proved useful as an academic credential. It was cited years later when (in summer 1929) Frank was director of the "Residential Tour to Saint Servan" conducted by the New York School of Foreign Travel. From the tour brochure: "Professor Frank E. E. Germann, Docteur ès Sciences (Geneva, Switzerland), Department of Chemistry, University of Colorado; formerly of the staff of the French Department, University of Indiana."

That semester in Bloomington also provided informal opportunities (outside of the Department of Romance Languages) for Frank Germann to explore prospects for a long-term professional position. *The Arbutus by the Senior Class of Indiana University 1914* has two pages devoted to the 21-member Physics Club. Although most of the members were undergraduates, Arthur L. Foley, Rolla R. Ramsey, and F. E. Germann are also listed on the membership roll. Foley earned his Ph.D. in Physics from Cornell University in 1897; Ramsey earned his Ph.D. in Physics from Cornell University in 1901. Perhaps Foley's and Ramsey's familiarity with Cornell influenced Frank Germann's decision to apply for a Cornell faculty position in physics. In any case, Cornell hired Frank Germann as a physicist to begin teaching in the fall semester of 1914.

Frank spent summer 1913 in Switzerland. From a "local" item in the Fort Wayne, Indiana, *News* on Wednesday, December 3, 1913: "Mr. Frank E. E. Germann, formerly of Peru, Ind. is visiting with Professor and Mrs. E. J. Germann of South Wayne avenue. Mr. Germann has just returned from Geneva, Switzerland, where he has been a teacher of science and language for the past year, has accepted a position of teacher of French in Indiana university, at Bloomington, for the remainder of this year. Mr. Germann expects to return to Geneva next summer to continue his work as assistant professor of science in one of the largest universities of that country." Frank and E. J. Germann were cousins. Frank noted that he "studied at Lausanne and Neuchâtel in 1913." Both l'Université de Lausanne and l'Université de Neuchâtel are located in the heart of the French-speaking region of Switzerland, good places for him to have strengthened his credentials for teaching French at Indiana University in spring 1914.

Even though Switzerland maintained diplomatic neutrality during the run up to the Great War, Frank was prudent to return to the United States to write his doctoral thesis. Just after the spring semester closed at Indiana University, Archduke Franz Ferdinand was assassinated in Sarajevo, and the European war began. Switzerland fortified its boundaries. When the United States entered the conflict, both Germann brothers were employed in universities in the United States.

Frank completed all requirements for the doctorate, and he submitted a thesis that the University of Geneva published as a 62-page book. He received the title "docteur ès sciences physiques" on Thursday, January 21, 1915. Albert's degree from the same university, working in the same research laboratory, was "doctorat ès sciences physiques et chimiques."

Cornell University

Frank's initial appointment in the Department of Physics at Cornell University in 1914 was as Assistant in Physics. His highest academic degree at that time was the 1911 A.B. from Indiana University. Promotion to Instructor in Physics awaited the doctorate. His main teaching duties were in the laboratory of the general physics course for mechanical and electrical engineers. In alternate years, he taught either

"Electrolysis" or "Voltaic Cells and Storage Batteries." He was on the Cornell University faculty from 1914 to 1918.

When did Frank Germann first began to consider seriously a career move toward physical chemistry? He had a taste in 1910, when he took a summer-session course, "Physical Chemistry," taught by Louis Kahlenberg and David Klein at the University of Wisconsin. In 1914, the Physics Department at Cornell was not the place for any new person to explore professional ambitions in physical chemistry. The internal political situation in the physical sciences is simple to describe. The Chemistry Department in Morse Hall (not the Physics Department in Rockefeller Hall) was *the* home for physical chemistry at Cornell. Wilder Dwight Bancroft (1867–1953) and Joseph Ellis Trevor (1864–1941) were both professors in the Chemistry Department, each having achieved full-professor status in 1903. Each man considered himself a physical chemist. The two professors specialized in different areas of physical chemistry, but together they felt they had staked out the entire field. In 1896, Bancroft and Trevor had founded *The Journal of Physical Chemistry*, the first English-language journal of physical chemistry. Bancroft personally financed the new periodical, and was its owner for many years. Bancroft was a national leader in science. He was President of the American Chemical Society in 1910. There was no way that these influential men would make room for a third physical chemist anywhere in the university.

To make matters conclusive, a fire on Sunday, February 13, 1916, destroyed Bancroft's research equipment in Morse Hall. The fire compromised the structural integrity of the upper portion of Morse Hall irreparably. There was serious damage in the remaining chemical laboratories. No physical space was available on campus to accommodate chemical experimental research of another man. With the Great War looming, purchase of replacement scientific instruments from Europe was not going to happen. Frank Germann faced professional reality, and looked for another faculty position. The Colorado School of Mines announced two faculty openings—one in physics, another in electrical engineering. He applied for both. He was hired for both. Frank remained a physicist, but only for one more year.

The four years in Ithaca, however problematic professionally, were personally rewarding. Martha Minna Marie Knechtel and Frank Erhart Emmanuel Germann were married in Peru, Indiana, on Tuesday, July 25, 1916. It was 81 °F, windy, and cloudy in Peru that summer day. Perhaps it does not seem surprising that the couple chose Peru, Frank's hometown, for their wedding. However, the story of how Nebraska-born Martha Knechtel met Frank Germann is less obvious. The story brings Martha and Frank to Fort Wayne at the same time. The story also introduces people and themes having to do with governance of Lutheran institutions; we shall return to those people and themes in Chapter 4.

How did Martha and Frank Meet?

Martha Minna Maria Knechtel was born April 19, 1892, in Fremont, the county seat of Dodge County, Nebraska. Martha was the youngest child of Mary Ann (Anna) Schneider (1842–1935) and John Knechtel (1843–1906). John was a businessman, part owner of a retail mercantile store at 225 East First Street in Fremont. His store sold groceries and dry goods. Anna and John were married in 1869. Fremont was then a small town, with a population of 1,195 in 1870. The town was growing. Its population in 1880 was 3,013; in 1890, 6,747; in 1910, 8,718; in 1920, 9,592.

The Knechtel family was also growing. The couple had seven children (two died in infancy): Emma Friedericka Caroline (1871–1873), Edwin Edward Lloyd (1877–1940), Ida Helena Christina (1879–1957), Alfred John (1881–1916), Anna Olga Rosa (1884–1944), Hilda Magdalena Margaret (1889–1890), and Martha Minna Maria (1892–1966).

Edwin Edward Lloyd Knechtel. Martha's brother Edwin became a conductor for the Pullman Palace Car Company, operator of railway sleeping cars. Edwin worked out of St. Louis, Missouri. He married Della Paul, a native of Fort Wayne, Indiana, and they lived in St. Louis. After Edwin's death in September 1940, Della returned to Fort Wayne to live with her sister, Elsie Paul. Della was a member of the Emmaus Lutheran Church in Fort Wayne.

Ida Helena Christina Knechtel. Ida may have attended the Trinity German Lutheran School in Fremont. Established in 1884, Trinity was the oldest parochial school in Fremont. The school has continued to this day, now serving about two hundred kindergarten through eighth grade students. If Ida entered Trinity kindergarten at age five, her teacher would have been Gustav Jaeger. Probably coincidently, Ida's second marriage (in 1935) was to a Gustave Jaeger.

At age 19, Ida Knechtel's first marriage was to the 26-year-old Lutheran minister, Paul Peter Christian Stoeppelwerth. They were married in Dodge County, Nebraska, on Wednesday, July 6, 1898.

Paul Stoeppelwerth was born April 25, 1872, in Washington, Missouri. He graduated from the Lutheran Concordia College in Fort Wayne. The function of Concordia College was to prepare students for the Lutheran Concordia Seminary in St. Louis. Concordia Seminary, in turn, produced Lutheran ministers. Paul graduated from Concordia Seminary in 1895. Paul's first ministerial charge was for two years in Cincinnati, probably for a Lutheran congregation that no longer exists. In 1897, he accepted a pastoral call to the Missouri Synod St. Paul Lutheran Church in Amherst, Lorain County, Ohio, near Cleveland. He served the St. Paul parish until 1902. Then he became pastor of the Trinity German Lutheran Church (Missouri Synod, Indiana District) in Fort Wayne.

Early at Trinity, Rev. Stoeppelwerth became involved in the formation of "The Evangelical Lutheran Hospital Association of Fort Wayne, Inc." The Association incorporated on November 11, 1903, to build, organize, and operate the Fort Wayne Lutheran Hospital. He was appointed to the first Board of Directors of the Lutheran Hospital; he served as Vice-President of the Board. Both clergy and laity were involved in forming the Association and in supervising the operation of the hospital, but the articles of incorporation drew a distinct line between the Fort Wayne Lutheran Hospital and individual church congregations or specific synods.

Rev. Stoeppelwerth served Trinity German Lutheran Church in Fort Wayne from 1902 to November 1, 1914. Then he accepted a call to become pastor of St. John's Evangelical Lutheran Church in Peru, Indiana. He served the Peru congregation until 1928, when he retired to Fort Wayne because of failing health. Back in Fort Wayne, he joined the Redeemer Lutheran Church (Missouri Synod, English District). Paul Stoeppelwerth died at home in Fort Wayne of "complications" on December 12, 1931. Ida had accompanied Paul to Amherst, Ohio, then to Fort Wayne and Peru, and finally back to Fort Wayne. After Paul's death, Ida married Gustave Jaeger; in 1935, they were living in Milwaukee. Ida Helena Christina Knechtel (Stoeppelwerth) Jaeger died July 7, 1957, in Fort Wayne.

Paul had followed in the early footsteps of his older brother, Henry John Stoeppelwerth (1869–1934). Henry graduated from Concordia College in Fort Wayne in 1891 and from Concordia Seminary in St. Louis in 1893. In the months after graduating from the Seminary, Henry became the sole founding faculty member of St.

John's College, Winfield, Kansas. He taught Latin and history there for 41 years. It was a small school. Not until 1910 had the faculty grown to five members. John P. Baden, an influential and successful Winfield businessman, provided the initial funding for St. John's. Baden appears to have had personal control of design, location, and construction of the impressive stone classroom and administration building that bears his name and still maintains a dominant architectural presence in Winfield. Baden also dominated all other aspects of the institution. Nominal control was in a corporation (created February 20, 1893) and in a Board of Trustees, of which Mr. Baden was Chair. On May 10, 1893, "the property of the College" was presented to a local arm of the English Evangelical Lutheran Synod. The full significance of that gift is not clear, but the local Lutherans needed continuing financial support from J. P. Baden to sustain the College. Mr. Baden died March 3, 1900. In a meeting of delegates from throughout the greater Synod in 1908 in Fort Wayne, the Synod accepted substantial responsibility for the College.

St. John's College in its early years was a preparatory school for Concordia Seminary in St. Louis. On paper, St. John's was co-educational from its inception, although all its first graduates in 1898 were male. The school survived the Great War, the Great Depression, and World War II. It continued until 1986, having enrolled more than nine thousand students.

Henry Stoeppelwerth was intimately involved with practical difficulties inherent in an educational institution, nominally a creature of an association of churches, but actually financed and controlled by a single person. He had observed a better administrative model nearby in Fremont.

Lutheran minister P. Graef founded an orphanage in Fremont. At first, the orphaned children lived in the church parsonage. His congregation voted in 1892 to support the idea of constructing an orphanage building in Fremont. Wisely, the Fremont church decided not to act alone. Funds were solicited from a variety of sources. Some fourteen Lutheran congregations of the Nebraska district formed the "Lutheran Orphans' Home Society of Nebraska," a Lutheran organization without ties or allegiances to any specific congregation or, indeed, to any specific synod. The cornerstone was laid in fall 1892. The building was dedicated on Sunday, June 25, 1893. Celebration of the twenty-fifth anniversary of the institution was Monday, June 25, 1917, and the Reverend Professor Henry John Stoeppelwerth of Winfield was one of three visiting dignitaries officiating at the festivities. Henry had watched this organization survive and function. Its success was, in part, the result of prudent initial planning. The Home Society had a well-defined mission, and the Society was organized to circumvent political entanglements.

John Knechtel died September 22, 1906, in Fremont. His daughter Ida Stoeppelwerth traveled from Fort Wayne to be with her mother and the family for John's funeral and for his burial in Ridge Municipal Cemetery, 1761 West Linden Avenue, Fremont, Nebraska.

Olga (Anna Olga Rosa) Knechtel. Olga married Charles William Aumann in 1906, just about the time her father died. By 1913, Olga and Charles were living in Fort Wayne, where they were members of St. Paul's Evangelical Lutheran Church. Olga died September 1, 1944. Charles died February 10, 1952.

Martha Minna Maria Knechtel. Martha may have attended the Trinity German Lutheran School in Fremont for her elementary classes. She was just beginning her sophomore year at Fremont High School when her father died. She graduated from Fremont High School in 1909.

The Sophomore Class page in the Fremont High School 1907 yearbook has "a song that fits for every name." The song for Martha Knechtel was "The Maiden with the Dreamy Eyes." The chorus:

> There are eyes of blue,
>   There are brown eyes too,
> There are eyes of ev'ry size, and eyes of ev'ry hue,
>   But I surmise,
>   That if you are wise,
> You'll be careful of the maiden with the dreamy eyes.

In the Junior Writeups for Martha Knechtel in the 1908 yearbook:

> Both truth and sincerity are in her eyes,
>   To know her is to love her,
> In studies no one can succeed,
>   In getting marks above her.

Accompanying her senior photo in the 1909 yearbook is:

> Of all the bright marks,
> Of the school—she's the shark,
> Her average a hundred and one;
>   *She's* no pity to let,
>   For those you don't get,
> The good grades that she's always won.

At the graduation exercises, she delivered an oration, "The Mission of a Sunbeam:"

A sunbeam left its home of light on an errand of hope and kindness. It came with the first blush of morning, breaking, by its magic glow, the spell with which sleep had enchained the world. It painted the clouds with beauty, and gladdened the earth with its smile.

The trees wooed it to their embrace, and the rippling stream flowed softly, bearing it on its bosom. The flowers, whose delicate colouring was traced by its pencil, opened wide their petals to its life-giving ray. In the halls of wealth it shed a softer and richer glow. Its dimmed light struggled into the low-dwelling place of poverty, bearing to the despairing watcher there the boon of hope and peace. The little child looked up and smiled, as it paused to play with its golden curls. The tottering step of age grew firmer, as its silvery beam fell on its locks of grey. Everywhere it inspired joy. The gay and happy felt their pulses bound with more gladsome life. The sad and friendless were comforted by its peaceful influence.

At last, its mission ended, it returned again to its source. Its last bright rays were shed upon the evening clouds, gilding them with colours with which no painter's pencil can vie; while the earth lay calmed in its mellow radiance.

Would that our lives might be like sunbeams, that wherever we go we may cause joy and peace to spring in our pathway, and the blessing of hearts made glad by our presence to rest upon us! And when this short day of our earthly life shall close, and we pass away, may we leave behind us the bright light of our example to lessen the sorrows of life, and guide wayward man in the path to glory and to God!

As a senior, Martha was one of the twelve Fremont students in The Normal Training Class, each preparing to be a teacher. Martha probably attended classes at Fremont Normal School and Commercial Institute. The school's three-story brick building (1884, 1890) later became part of Midland College when, in 1919, Midland College moved to Fremont from Atchison, Kansas.

By 1914, Anna Knechtel and her daughter Martha had moved to Fort Wayne. Ida and Paul Stoeppelwerth were already living in Fort Wayne, where Paul had been pastor of the Trinity German Lutheran Church since 1902. Martha taught at Fort Wayne's James H. Smart Elementary School (at the corner of Smith Street and East Pontiac Street) in 1913–1914, 1914–1915, and 1915–1916. As was noted earlier, Frank Germann visited with Professor and Mrs. E. J. Germann in Fort Wayne in December 1913, just before Frank began a semester teaching French at Indiana University in Bloomington.

Paul Stoeppelwerth served Trinity German Lutheran Church in Fort Wayne until November 1, 1914, when he became pastor of St. John's Evangelical Lutheran Church in Peru. Martha and Frank were married in Peru on July 25, 1916. The Rev. Paul Stoeppelwerth officiated at the wedding of his niece-in-law.

This extended narrative does not directly answer the question "How Did Martha and Frank Meet?" Nevertheless, the narrative does place both young people in Fort Wayne at the same time.

After Martha and Frank were married, Anna Knechtel lived with Olga and Charles Aumann, Anna's daughter and son-in-law, in Fort Wayne. Anna died July 20, 1935. She was buried with her husband John and with their infant daughter Hilda, in Ridge Municipal Cemetery, Fremont, Nebraska.

Martha and Frank Germann had a son, Richard Paul Germann, born in Ithaca, New York, on April 3, 1918. Richard married Malinda Jane Plietz on December 11, 1942. Richard and Malinda's daughter, Cheranne Lee Germann, was born September 9, 1951; she died September 4, 2004.

Richard earned a B.A. in chemistry from the University of Colorado, and did graduate work at Western Reserve University and at Brown University, Providence, Rhode Island. He published a joint research paper with his father. Richard characterized himself professionally as a chemist and a chemical company executive; he held several positions in the chemical industry. He died in Norwalk, Ohio, January 15, 2007.

A daughter, Lois Marie, was born to Martha and Frank on June 30, 1921, in Boulder, Colorado. She began her study of violin and piano at an early age, and earned a baccalaureate degree (Class of 1939) and a master's degree in music at the University of Colorado. She often performed with the University of Colorado Orchestra, and throughout her life with chamber music groups. Lois Marie also earned a master's degree in psychology at the University of Colorado, and taught briefly at George Washington Carver Junior High School in Los Angeles.

Lois Marie married Horace Jones, Professor of Music and Violin at the University of Colorado. Horace Jones was the first Director of the University of Colorado Bands and the University Orchestra. They had a daughter Lorann and a son Frank. Horace retired in 1962, and the family moved to Ojai, California, into a home that Lois designed and whose stone walls she built herself. Horace died in 1984. Lois died February 20, 2013 in Ojai.

Sources and References for Chapter 1

Page 2, *Indiana in 1836 ...* Map drawn by Dr. E. V. Shockley. Dashed lines indicate proposed canals. Logan Esarey, *A History of Indiana from its Exploration to 1850* (Indianapolis: W. K. Stewart Co., 1915), p. 355.

Page 3, *Two thousand Native Americans remain ...* Estimate provided by Thomas Dunwoody, Executive Director, Circus Hall of Fame, 3076 East Circus Lane, Peru, Indiana. In 2014–2015, 1.0 percent of the students in the Peru Community Schools self-identified as "American Indian."

Page 3, *Coordinator of Miami Tribe Relations ...* Created from a recommendation of The Committee on Relationships between Miami University and the Miami Tribe of Oklahoma, http://miamioh.edu/_files/documents/about-miami/diversity/miami-tribe-relations/exec-summary.pdf, accessed April 19, 2015.

Page 4, *The Myaamia Center at Miami University ...* http://myaamiacenter.org, accessed April 19, 2015.

Page 4, *Town of Peru, on the banks of the Wabash River ...* Arthur L. Bodurtha, ed., *History of Miami County Indiana: A Narrative Account of Its Historical Progress, Its People and Its Principal Interests* (Chicago: Lewis Publishing Company, 1914), vol. I, pp. 162, 163, 167–173.

Page 4, *Sewers were put in later ...* "At the close of 1913 [Peru] had eleven main lines and thirty-five laterals, and several new lines were under construction." Bodurtha, op. cit., p. 173. The first sewers emptied directly into the Wabash River. A sewage treatment plant was planned in 1938 (Public Works Administration Docket Indiana 1277-F), and constructed in 1939–1940.

Page 4, *the first electrically lighted city in the world ...* At 8:00 p.m. on March 31, 1880, four carbon-arc lamps atop the Wabash County Courthouse were the first public demonstration of the lighting sys-

tem of Charles Francis Brush (1849–1929). A week later, the Wabash City Council voted to purchase the Brush system. "The Electric Light; The City Council More than Satisfied with the Test; They Formally Accept the Light and Pay For It," *Wabash Weekly Plain Dealer*, Friday, April 9, 1880.

Page 4, *had a macadam surface ...* This roadway surface, developed and popularized by Scotsman John Loudon McAdam (1756–1836), had been used in building the National Road. Construction of the National Road began in 1811 at Cumberland, Maryland. The Road reached Indianapolis in 1830.

Page 7, *a general and uniform system of Common Schools ...* Article 8. Education; Section 1. Common School System.

Page 7, *Wabash College faculty member...* The school was called Wabash Manual Labor College and Teacher's Seminary when Caleb Mills joined the faculty. Its campus has always been in Crawfordsville, Indiana. Wabash has always been a college for male students.

Page 7, *only classroom technology needed ...* If individual desks were available in the classroom, penmanship was taught. The first penmanship text recommended for Indiana schools was Jesse Wentworth Payson, Seldom Dunton, and William M. Scribner, *Payson, Dunton, & Scribner's Combined System of Rapid Penmanship* (Boston: Crosby, Nichols & Co., 1855). The most popular textbook a decade later was Henry Caleb Spencer and Platt Rogers Spencer, *Spencerian Key to Practical Penmanship* (New York: Ivison, Phinney, Blakeman, & Company; Chicago: S. C. Griggs; Philadelphia: J. B. Lippincott & Company; 1866). The Spencerian Steel Pen Company was formed in 1858 as a subsidiary of Ivison Phinney Publishing Company. An earlier book was for prospective clerks and secretaries: Platt Rogers Spencer and Victor Moreau Rice, *Spencer & Rice's System of Business Penmanship: Containing a Full*

Series of Copies, Rules, and Explanations, Carefully Prepared for the Counting-House and Schools, and Youth Fitting for Business Transactions (Geneva, Ashtabula County, Ohio: P. R. Spencer, 1848).

Page 8, *The textbooks recommended in 1853* ... Richard Gause Boone, "The School Law of 1852," chap. 9, *A History of Education in Indiana* (New York: D. Appleton and Company, 1892), p. 267.

Page 8, *The Cincinnati firm of Truman and Smith* ... http://www.ohiohistorycentral.org/w/Winthrop_ Smith, http://www.ohiohistorycentral.org/w/Joseph _Ray, http://www.ohiohistorycentral.org/w/William _H._McGuffey, accessed August 4, 2015. Truman and Smith was the most successful Midwestern publisher of common-school textbooks, but it was not the first American publisher of school readers. For example, J. and J. W. Prentiss (Keene, New Hampshire) in 1833 published *A Selection of Reading Lessons for Common Schools* (87 selections, 315 pages), "designed to be used after *Easy Lessons in Reading, American Popular Lessons,* and *Boston Reading Lessons.*"

Page 9, *the first state to make the* township *the school unit* ... Boone, op. cit., p. 148. *See also* Ross Franklin Lockridge, "The Hoosier Township Trustee," *in* Mark R. Gray, compiler, *Historical Resumé of the Indiana State Association of Township Trustees* (Indianapolis: Indianapolis Commercial Printing and Publishing Company, 1930), p. 27.

Page 9, *managed by elected township trustees* ... In 1852, there were three elected trustees in each township. "Then in 1859 the trusteeship was by a legislative act of that year consolidated into a single office to be held by one man elected annually for a term of one year. Thus the township was finally perfected as the local unit of government. It constituted almost a little republic within a republic of which the trustee was the responsible head. From that day to this [1930] the township trustee has been the unquestioned official embodiment of local government in this important territorial unit." Lockridge, op. cit., p. 28.

Page 9, *A typical township trustee* ... In 1930: "Of the trustees now in office, practically all have received their entire education in the common schools.... Since the trustees serve very largely in agricultural communities, it is natural that a very large proportion of them should be farmers... They are nearly always men of mature years.... Although women have been eligible to the office of township trustee and to all other school offices in Indiana for nearly fifty years, only a few women have held this position." Lockridge, op. cit., pp. 44–46, p. 51.

Page 9, *Indiana was chosen by outside, well-funded groups* ... Beth Sylvester Edwards, "Hoosier Schoolmaster, 1920–1940: A Case Study in Rural Elementary Education in South Central Indiana," *Indiana Magazine of History,* vol. 93, no. 3 (September 1997), pp. 244–270; James H. Madison, "John D. Rockefeller's General Education Board and the Rural School Problem in the Midwest, 1900–1930," *History of Education Quarterly,* vol. 24, (Summer 1984), pp. 181–199.

Page 10, *consolidate into county-unit schools* ... Information about township-unit versus county-unit controversies is taken from Ellwood Paterson Cubberly, *Rural Life and Education: A Study of the Rural-School Problem as a Phase of the Rural-Life Problem* (Boston: Houghton Mifflin, 1914); George Washington Knorr, *Consolidated Rural Schools and Organization of a County System* (Washington: Government Printing Office, 1910); and Chester C. Diettert, North Judson (Indiana) High School, "The County-Unit System of School Organization," *The Elementary School Journal,* vol. 27, no. 3 (November 1926), pp. 209–211.

Page 11, *Witter published his own* ... Conrad Witter, *Der deutsch-amerikanische Elementarschüler, oder, Die ersten Anschauungs-, Lese-, Schön- und Rechtschreibeübungen, methodisch und streng stufenweise bearbeitet: eine wohlfeile handfibel mit Druck- und Schreibschrift, mit Lesestucken und Bildern* (St. Louis: Conrad Witter, 1862); Conrad Witter, *Der deutsch-amerikanische Leseschüler, oder, Die zweiten Anschauungs-, Lese- und Rechtschreibe-Uebungen in kurzen, mustergültigen, poetischen und prosaischen Lesestücken, methodisch und streng stufenweise bearbeitet: ein allgemeines zweites Lesebuch mit Sil-ben-Abtheilungen und Holzschnitten* (St. Louis: Conrad Witter, 1863); Conrad Witter, *Witters drittes Lesebuch für deutsch-amerikanische Schulen Schlussstufe,* Third German Reader, copyright 1861 (St. Louis: Verlag der Conrad Witter'schen Schulbuchhandlung, stereotype edition 1863, http://catalog.hathitrust.org/api/volumes/oclc/25290339.html.)

Page 11, *targeted to German classes in public schools … For example,* Conrad Witter, *Witter's New Third German Reader for Public Schools: A Collection of Graded Pieces in Prose and Verse, with Copious Vocabularies* (St. Louis: Conrad Witter, 1881), 326 pages.

Page 11, *Witter faced a formidable competitor …* Van Antwerp, Bragg and Company announced *Deutsches erstes [–fünftes] Lesebuch für amerikanische Schulen* and *Deutsch Fibel nach der analytisch-synthe-tischen Schreiblesemethode: Für amerikanische Schulen.* The competition became even greater in 1890 when American Book Company was formed by consolidation of Van Antwerp, Bragg and Company; Ivison, Blakeman and Company; A. S. Barnes & Company; and D. Appleton and Company.

Page 11, *the first elementary school …* "The Lutheran Schools," http://thelutheranschools.org, accessed December 2, 2013.

Page 13, *Anne-Thérèse Guérin (1798–1856) …* Anne-Thérèse entered the congregation of the Sisters of Providence of Ruillé-sur-Loire, France, and was given the religious name Sister St. Théodore. She professed first vows September 8, 1825, and perpetual vows on September 5, 1831. In July 1840, Sister St. Théodore and five companions (Sister Olympiade Boyer, Sister Saint Vincent Ferrer Gagé, Sister Basilide Sénéschal, Sister Mary Xavier Lerée, and Sister Mary Liguori Tiercin) left France and traveled to the dense forests of the State of Indiana. On October 22, 1840, Sister St. Théodore and her companions arrived in Saint Mary-of-the-Woods, Indiana, an unincorporated community in Sugar Creek Township, northwestern Vigo County, a few miles northwest of Terre Haute. They founded a new order, separate from that in France. Guerin became known as Sister Mother Theodore, the Superior of the Sisters of Providence of Saint Mary-of-the-Woods. The sisters started a novitiate for the Sisters of Providence, and also St. Mary's Academy for Young Ladies. Mother Theodore was canonized and made a Saint in the Roman Catholic Church in October 2006.

Page 13, *Most (except Indiana University, Indiana State Normal School, and Purdue University) had explicit religious roots …* Note however that Reverend Andrew Wylie, Reverend William Daily, and Reverend Lemuel Moss were the first, third, and sixth presidents of Indiana University. "History of IU Presidents," http://www.iu.edu/leadership/past-presidents.shtml, accessed January 1, 2014. Before Indiana University had a President, its only instructor was Presbyterian minister Baynard Rush Hall. Wikipedia states that David Starr Jordan in 1885 became the first Indiana University president who was not an ordained minister, http://en.wikipedia.org/wiki/David_Starr_Jordan, accessed January 1, 2014.

Page 13, *The examples cited are unique neither … See, for example,* Allen Ezell and John Bear, *Degree Mills: The Billion-Dollar Industry That Has Sold Over a Million Fake Diplomas* (Amherst, New York: Prometheus Books, 2005); and Robert H. Reid, *American Degree Mills: A Study of Their Operations and of Existing and Potential Ways to Control Them* (Washington: American Council on Education, 1959).

Page 14, *had scarcely been imagined …* A north–south road (the Michigan Road) from Lake Michigan to the Ohio River was built in the 1830s and 1840s. It crossed the Wabash and Erie Canal west of Peru. Construction of an east–west road (the National Road) was begin in Cumberland, Maryland, in 1811. It reached Indianapolis in the 1830s. Neither road was of assistance to travelers between Van Wert and Peru in 1877. See map on page 2.

Page 14, *Thomas Jefferson's plan …* In 1784, Jefferson proposed land division into rectangles. The Land Ordinance of 1785, adopted by the United States

Congress of the Confederation on May 20, 1785, defined the standard township as a square with sides six miles long, the sides running due north and south, or due east and west.

Page 15, *Standard Cabinet Manufacturing Company ... Peru City Directory* (1895).

Page 15, *Jacob Theobald married Mary Shireman ...* Obituary, "Death of Jacob Theobald," *Peru Republican*, March 24, 1916, p. 6. "Peru Township," *History of Miami County* (Chicago: Brant and Fuller, 1887), http://debmurray.tripod.com/miami/miabioref-9.htm, accessed January 24, 2016. "Miami County Indiana Biographical Sketches," http://genealogytrails.com/ind/miami/bios.htm, accessed January 24, 2016.

Page 15, *Ernst Gerhard Wilhelm Keyl (1804–1872)* ... Johann Friedrich Köstering, *Leben und Wirken des Ehrw. Ernst Gerhard Wilh. Keyl* (St. Louis: Concordia, 1882), pp. 142–143.

Page 16, *then accepted a call from Trinity Lutheran Church ...* From the hundred-year anniversary booklet (1981) of Trinity Lutheran Church; photocopies of pages supplied by Ruth Guthman, Trinity Church office assistant, February 13, 2013.

Page 17, *Edwin Jacob Germann (1869–1942) ...* Obituary, "E. J. Germann, Musician, Dies," *Fort Wayne Journal Gazette*, Monday, March 30, 1942, p. 9, col. 1.

Page 18, *St. John's Christian Day School in Peru ...* "History," St. John's Lutheran Church, http://www.stjohnsperu.org/History.html, accessed February 9, 2013: "St. John's school contained grades K–8 for many years, adding preschool classes in the early 1990s. In 1991 the Base Realignment and Closure Commission selected Grissom AFB, Bunker Hill, IN, for realignment to the Reserves. Consequently, the 305th was inactivated. With inactivation scheduled for October 1994, the PACCS mission and EC-135 aircraft were eliminated in May 1992, as the aircraft and crews were reassigned. In July 1993, the air refueling mission and the KC-135s of the 70th and 305th Air Refueling Squadrons were transferred, leaving the 305th with no flying mission. St. John's school suffered a loss of students,

which led to, first, closing grades 7-8, and finally only maintaining a Kindergarten and preschool. Unable to be supported financially, these closed in 2006. In 2008, a building utilization committee was formed to consider uses for the empty classrooms. A decision was made to open a daycare and preschool. It opened in August 2009 and by 2012 had an enrollment of about 50 children."

Page 18, *The library continues ...* The city later built an addition to accommodate expansion. A $1,200,000 renovation (of the original building and the addition) throughout the 2015 year required temporary relocation of books and services to 12 Broadway Plaza.

Page 18, *the first yearbook published by the school ...* The Peru Public Library has a complete collection of the school yearbooks.

Page 19, *everlasting fame as debater or orator ...* Chemistry students are often advised that a *laboratory* is a workplace (a labor-atory), not a place for distracting talk (lab-oratory).

Page 19, *served as township principal ...* Arthur L. Bodurtha, ed., *History of Miami County Indiana: A Narrative Account of Its Historical Progress, Its People and Its Principal Interests* (Chicago: Lewis Publishing Company, 1914), vol. II, p. 456.

Page 19, *Some twenty-first century educational critics deplore ...* See, for example, Amy E. Slaton and Donna M. Riley, "The Wrong Solution for STEM Education," *Inside Higher Ed, Weekly Liberal Education News Watch*, American Association of Colleges and Universities (July 8, 2015).

Page 20, *from an iron-bound, oaken bucket ...* Samuel Woodworth (1784–1842) wrote in 1817 about the ubiquitous bucket over the well:

> How dear to this heart are the scenes
>   of my childhood,
> When fond recollection presents them
>   to view!
> The orchard, the meadow, the deep-
>   tangled wild-wood,

And every loved spot which my
infancy knew!

The wide-spreading pond, and the mill
that stood by it,

The bridge, and the rock where the
cataract fell,

The cot of my father, the dairy-house
nigh it,

And e'en the rude bucket that hung in
the well—

The old oaken bucket, the iron-bound
bucket,

The moss-covered bucket which hung
in the well.

Page 20, *sanitary standards for outdoor toilets* … The Works Progress Administration designed and built privies that met uniform (and new) Federal sanitary standards. Between 1933 and 1945, 2,309,239 Federally subsidized privies were built and installed in the United States. Ronald S. Barlow, *The Vanishing American Outhouse: A History of Country Plumbing* (El Cajon, California: Windmill Publishing Company, 1989), pp. 21–24.

Page 20, *teach in the public schools for a few years before moving on* … For example, we shall note later in this chapter that Ross Franklin Lockridge Sr., after teaching history at Peru High School and then becoming Principal, returned to Indiana University, earned an LL.B. degree in 1907, and became a lawyer. Two decades later, scenarios were often similar. Illustrative examples can be found within the eight-person faculty of the South Whitley (Indiana) High School in 1922–1923:

Principal *Leigh Lavon Hunt* (1900–1975), Columbia City High School Class of 1917, had just graduated from Indiana University with an A.B. degree in Economics. In 1922, while teaching at South Whitley, "he entered law practice" in Fort Wayne. At his death on February 24, 1975, he was senior member of the law firm of Hunt, Suedhoff, Borror, Ellbacher, and Lee in Fort Wayne.

Science teacher *Delmar F. Mitzner* (1900–1977), a

graduate of Wanatah High School in LaPorte County, was working his way through a chemistry major at Valparaiso University. He held the position of Assistant in Chemistry at Valparaiso from 1921 to 1923, took courses in the summer sessions, and taught at South Whitley during fall, winter, and spring. Delmar Mitzner graduated from Valparaiso on Wednesday, August 15, 1923, with a B.S. degree. Ruth Pinney and Delmar F. Mitzner were married in Wanatah on Thanksgiving, November 29, 1923. With his college diploma in hand, he was promoted to South Whitley High School Principal for 1923–1924.

Music teacher *Forrest Eugene Albert* was a graduate of Culver High School, Culver, Marshall County, Indiana. He had previously taught 3½ years in elementary schools. He matriculated at Indiana University in June 1921, attended summer school before joining the faculty at South Whitley, and continued studies at I.U. through August 1928, majoring in music. He did not complete a degree at I.U., but instead enrolled in the four-year Bachelor of Music Education program at Northwestern University, Evanston, Illinois. He received the degree of Bachelor of Music Education in 1933. He continued in a graduate program, receiving the degree of Master of Music in 1938 at Northwestern with the dissertation "Curriculum Practices in Music in Senior High School." He also studied at the European School of Music in Atlanta, Georgia, and in the Paul J. Christiansen Choral School. In 1945, he joined the faculty of Pikeville College, Pikeville, Kentucky, where he taught music until his retirement in 1957. The Pikeville yearbook, *The Highlander*, was dedicated to Forrest Albert in 1958.

Home Economics teacher *Celia Opal Carson* (1896–1954), a graduate of Colfax High School, Colfax, Perry Township, Clinton County, Indiana, attended Indiana State Normal School, and would earn the B.S. degree in Home Economics from Indiana University in 1927. She had taught in Colfax elementary school, Kirkland High School (1919–1920), and Hope High School before South Whitley. In 1930, she was a Textile and

Clothing Instructor in a junior high school in Englewood, Colorado. She did not marry. She did not survive her parents; all were buried in Plainview Cemetery, Colfax.

French and English teacher *Olive Blossom Perkins* (1897–1978) was a graduate of Decatur High School in Decatur, county seat of Adams County, Indiana. She had graduated from Indiana State Normal School, Terre Haute, in 1921 with an A.B. degree. She strengthened her language credentials by summer study at Middlebury College, Middlebury, Vermont, in 1924, and at the University of Wisconsin, Madison, in 1925. Olive Perkins joined the faculty of South Side High School in Fort Wayne in 1924, and was a French and Spanish teacher at South Side until her retirement. She did not marry.

Manual Training teacher *Dennis O. Wright*, a graduate of Eminence High School in Eminence (an unincorporated community in Adams Township, Morgan County, Indiana), was taking summer courses at Indiana State Normal School, Terre Haute. He would receive the B.S. degree from Indiana State Normal School in 1929. In 1930, he was still teaching in South Whitley, but his field had changed its name to Industrial Arts.

Sources: Senior Class of South Whitley High School, *The Reflector*, vol. 6, 1923, pp. 10–11; vol. 7, 1924, p. 39; and *The Highlander* (Pikeville College), 1945–1958. Emails November 3, 2015 from Dina Kellams, Indiana University Archivist; October 29, 2015, from Madeline Hamilton, Student Assistant, Valparaiso University Archives; November 9, 2015, from Becky Marangelli, Archives Specialist, Ball State University; November 16, 2015, from Dennis Vetrovec, Special Collections–University Archives, Cunningham Memorial Library, Indiana State University, Terre Haute; December 2, 2015, from Corey Scott, Principal of Eminence Junior–Senior High School, Eminence, Indiana; December 9, 2015, from Edna Fugate, CA, Archivist/Reference Librarian, University of Pikeville; December 10, 2015, from Janet C. Olson, Assistant University Archivist, Northwestern University Libraries. *Also,* Obituaries:

Leigh Hunt, Fort Wayne *Journal Gazette*, Wednesday, February 26, 1975, p. 12C, col. 1; Olive Blossom Perkins, Fort Wayne *Journal Gazette*, Thursday, October 5, 1978, p. 5C, col. 5; and Olive Blossom Perkins, *Decatur* [Indiana] *Daily Democrat*, Thursday, October 5, 1978. *And,* for the grave of Celia Opal Carson, http://www.findagrave.com/cgi-bin/fg.cgi?page=gr&GRid=70699190, accessed December 9, 2015.

Page 20, *married woman to be hired to teach* … This was not a matter of statute. The local township trustee (or in a town, the School Board) and the school superintendent had discretion in the hiring. For an exception to the general practice: Alvin R. Fleck, Superintendent of the South Whitley, Indiana, Schools (1922–1925), and School Board members George Talbert, Otis Plattner, and Addie Bollinger, hired Leigh Lavon Hunt as high school principal and his wife Mary Ruth Van Natta Hunt as high school teacher of English and Latin. Both taught in the Calhoun Street School in South Whitley in 1922–1923. *The Reflector*, op. cit., pp. 7 and 10. For verification that they were husband and wife, see the marriage record of their daughter Ellen Van Natta Hunt to William Lee Wilks on September 5, 1952 [Allen County (Indiana) Marriage Records, page 143:295; Allen County Genealogical Society of Indiana, http://www.acgsi.org/marriage/, accessed October 25, 2015].

Page 20, *Thomas Charlton Van Nüys (1844–1898)* … Thomas Charlton Van Nüys (March 24, 1844–August 1, 1898) was born in Pleasant Township, Switzerland County, Indiana. Switzerland County is in extreme southeastern Indiana, on the Ohio River. He graduated from the Medical College of Ohio in Cincinnati (since 1896, a part of the University of Cincinnati), with an M.D. degree in 1867. He practiced medicine in Evansville, Indiana, for two years. From spring 1869 to 1871, he worked in Germany with Oskar Matthias Eugen Liebreich (1839–1908) at the Pathological Institute of Berlin University. Dr. Liebreich had just discovered the narcotic effect of chloral hydrate. [*see* Oscar Liebreich, *Das Chloralhydrat; ein neues Hypnoticum und*

Anaestheticum und dessen Anwendung in der Medicin (Berlin: Otto Müller, 2nd ed., 1869).] When Van Nüys returned to America in 1871, he joined the new faculty of the Medical College of Evansville (chartered in 1849, suspended in 1854, reorganized in 1871, extinct in 1884). From 1873 to 1874, Van Nüys worked with analytical chemist Carl Remigius Fresenius (1818–1897) at his Chemische Laboratorium Fresenius in Wiesbaden, Prussia. Fresenius in 1862 had founded the world's first journal of analytical chemistry, *Zeitschrift für analytische Chemie,* which he edited until his death. Van Nüys joined the Indiana University faculty as Professor of Chemistry in June 1874. He married Mary Elizabeth (Lizzie) Hunter on December 28, 1875. They had two children: Fresenius, born 1876; and Morton Hunter, born 1879. In 1876, he was back in Europe, working with organic chemist Wilhelm Rudolph Fittig (1835–1910) at the Kaiser-Wilhelm-Universität in Strasbourg. This was a time of rapid expansion of the university, and Fittig was called upon to design modern laboratories for a new chemistry building. Van Nüys was thirty-three when he returned to Bloomington in 1877 as Professor of Chemistry and Head of the Chemistry Department. His most important publication was the book *Chemical Analysis of Healthy and Diseased Urine: Qualitative and Quantitative* (Philadelphia: P. Blakiston, Son & Co., 1888), 187 pages. He also wrote *Report on the Waters of the Indianapolis Water Works Co. and of White River, together with Analyses of the Same: Made to the Board of Health of the City of Indianapolis* (Indianapolis: Journal Company, 1881), 22 pages. He retired from Indiana University in 1895. The family moved to Charlottesville, Virginia. Fresenius and Morton both graduated from the University of Virginia (Charlottesville) with B.A. degrees on June 15, 1898. Fresenius began graduate studies in Botany at the University of Virginia, and eventually became a physician in Boston. Morton became a lawyer in Seattle. Thomas Charlton Van Nüys died in Charlottesville, Virginia, less than two months after his sons graduated from college. He was buried in the University of Virginia Cemetery. His wife returned to Bloom-

ington, studied law, and received the LL.B. degree from Indiana University in 1894. Barbie Selby, University of Virginia Library, supplied biographical information by email on November 30, 2015.

Page 21, *students reported that ... The Arbutus by the Senior Class of Indiana University 1894,* p. 41.

Page 21, *Not all of these faculty members were in residence in Bloomington at the same time ...* Robert Edward Lyons, "The History of Chemistry at Indiana University, 1829–1931," *Indiana University News-Letter,* vol. 19, no. 8, ii + 44 pp. (March 1931); Harry G. Day, *The Development of Chemistry at Indiana University, 1829–1991* (Bloomington, 1992), viii + 668 pp.; "Bibliography of Publications by Present Members of the Faculty of the Graduate School, and of Students since January 1904, by Departments," *Indiana University Studies,* vol. 8, study no. 50 (September 1921), pp. 17–133, Chemistry Department, pp. 27–39.

Page 21, *He began experimental research ...* T. C. Van Nüys and R. E. Lyons, "A Method for the Estimation of Albumin in Urine," *American Chemical Journal,* vol. 12, no. 5 (submitted March 1890, published May 1890), pp. 336–351; T. C. Van Nüys and R. E. Lyons, "Carbon Dioxide In Urine," *American Chemical Journal,* vol. 14, no. 1 (January 1892), pp. 14–19.

Page 22, *Ph.D. from the University of Heidelberg ...* Robert Edward Lyons, *Über die Phenylverbindungen von Schwefel, Selen und Tellur, Inaugural-Dissertation* (Heidelberg: J. Hörning, 1894), 33 pages.

Page 22, *Louis Sherman Davis ... Indiana University Bulletin,* vol. 2, no. 2 (September 1904), p. 10. He was the author of a high-school textbook, *Chemistry for Schools* (Chicago: Scott, Foresman and Company, 1904). He and Robert Lyons collaborated in writing two college textbooks: *The Qualitative Analysis of Inorganic Bodies in which the More Common Bases and Acids are Represented* (Anderson, Indiana: Herald Print, 1897 and 1900), and *A Manual of Toxicological Analysis* (Anderson: Morning Herald Print, 1899). Both books were used in their own courses, in some cases in manuscript form before publication. His inaugural dissertation, dealing with alkaloids from lupins, was *Ueber die Alkaloide der Samen von Lupinus albus und Lupinus angustifolius* (Marburg, 1896).

Page 23, *Oliver W. Brown* ... Fay Kenoyer Daily, Obituary, "Oliver W. Brown, Vermillion, Grove, Illinois, June 25, 1873–Bloomington, Indiana, April 20, 1967," *Proceedings of the Indiana Academy of Science*, vol. 77 (1967), pp. 37–38.

Page 22, *University Vice-President William Lowe Bryan* ... Bryan had been Vice-President since 1893. He became President in 1902, and served until 1937.

Page 23, *Mary Bidwell Breed* ... Biographical information from her entry in *Who's Who in America;* from the faculty record sheet that she prepared for the Margaret Morrison Carnegie College; from Mary R. S. Creese and Thomas M. Creese, *Ladies in the Laboratory? American and British Women in Science, 1800-1900: A Survey of Their Contributions to Research* (Lanham, Maryland: Scarecrow Press, 1998), pp. 258–259; from Jo Ann Fley and George R. Jaramillo, "Mary Bidwell Breed: The Educator as Dean," *The Journal of the National Association of Women Deans, Administrators & Counselors*, vol. 42, no. 2 (Winter 1979), pp. 45–50; and from information supplied by Molly Tighe, Archivist & Public Service Librarian, J. K. M. Library, Chatham University; Evan McGonagill, Assistant Director, The Albert M. Greenfield Digital Center for the History of Women's Education, Bryn Mawr College; Dina M. Kellams, Director of the Indiana University Office of University Archives; Gary Cox, University Archives, University of Missouri; and Julia Corrin, University Archivist, Carnegie Mellon University.

Page 23, *Mary Breed attended Pennsylvania Female College* ... *Fifteenth Annual Catalogue, Pennsylvania Female College* (1885–1886), p. 13; *Sixteenth Annual Catalogue, Pennsylvania Female College* (1886–1887), p. 11; *Seventeenth Annual Catalogue, Pennsylvania Female College* (1886–1887), p. 11; *Eighteenth Annual Catalogue, Pennsylvania Female College* (1887–1888),

p. 9; *Nineteenth Annual Catalogue, Pennsylvania Female College* (1888–1889), pp. 10, 21.

Page 24, *Chemical Section of the Franklin Institute* ... The Franklin Institute of the State of Pennsylvania for the Promotion of the Mechanic Arts was founded by Samuel Vaughan Merrick and William H. Keating on February 5, 1824. Mary Breed's paper was published as Mary Bidwell Breed, "On Phenolphthalein and Methylorange as Indicators," *Journal of the Franklin Institute*, vol. 135 (1893), pp. 312–316.

Page 24, *quantitative analysis of palladium diammonium chloride* ... Edward H. Keiser and Mary B. Breed, "The Atomic Weight of Palladium," *American Chemical Journal*, vol. 16 (1894), pp. 20–28. Submitted October 1893.

Page 24, *These experiments involved chemical reactions* ... Edward H. Keiser and Mary B. Breed, "The Action of Magnesium upon the Vapors of the Alcohols and a New Method of Preparing Allylene," *Journal of the Franklin Institute*, vol. 139 (April 1895), pp. 304–309; read at the stated meeting of the Chemical Section of the Franklin Institute, held December 18, 1894.

Page 24, *she became a private student* ... Such an arrangement was not unusual when the student was strongly motivated. Viktor Meyer, as a teenager, went to Heidelberg to work for a year as a private student under Robert Wilhelm Eberhard Bunsen (1811–1899). Meyer then received his doctorate in 1867 from the Ruprecht-Karls-Universität Heidelberg.

Page 24, *While finishing her doctorate, she served* ... *Twenty-eighth Annual Catalogue, Pennsylvania College for Women* (1897–1898), pp. 6, 22–23; *Twenty-ninth Annual Catalogue, Pennsylvania College for Women* (1898–1899), p. 6.

Page 25, *Frank Curry Mathers* ... "Frank C. Mathers, ECS President 1940–1941," The Electrochemical Society, http://www.electrochem.org/dl/hc/presidents/mathers.htm, accessed September 13, 2014.

Page 26, *The textbook used in the beginning chemistry* … *Indiana University Catalogue, Register 1900–1901, Announcements 1901–1902* (Bloomington: May 1901), p. 130.

Page 26, *"Ira Remsen was for many years* … Quotation from the second paragraph of William Albert Noyes and James Flack Norris, "Biographical Memoir of Ira Remsen," *Biographical Memoirs of the National Academy of Sciences* (Washington: National Academy of Sciences, vol. 14, presented to the Academy 1931), pp. 205–257.

Page 26, *Remsen was the author* … Textbooks by Ira Remsen: *The Principles of Theoretical Chemistry, With Special Reference to the Constitution of Chemical Compounds* (Philadelphia: Lea Bros and Company, 1876); five editions; German and Italian translations. *An Introduction to the Study of Organic Chemistry* (Boston: Ginn and Heath, 1885); German, French, Russian, and Japanese translations; fifth edition and revision (1922) by W. R. Orndorff in collaboration with Remsen. *Introduction to the Study of Chemistry* (New York: Henry Holt, 1886); eight editions; German, French, Russian, Finnish, Polish, Chinese, and Japanese translations. *The Elements of Chemistry* (New York: Henry Holt, 1888); translated into German. *Inorganic Chemistry* (New York: Henry Holt, 1889); five editions; translated into German. *A Laboratory Manual* to accompany *The Elements of Chemistry* (New York: Henry Holt, 1889); translated into German. *Chemical Experiments* to accompany *Introduction to the Study of Chemistry* (New York: Henry Holt, 1895); three editions. *A College Text-Book of Chemistry* (New York: Henry Holt, 1901); second edition, 1912.

Page 26, *Indiana Medical College* … Indiana Medical College in Indianapolis (1869–1878). It merged with the College of Physicians and Surgeons of Indiana (1874–1878) to form the Medical College of Indiana (1878–1905), forerunner of the Indiana University School of Medicine, http://library.medicine.iu.edu/special-collections-and-services/history-of-medicine/medicine-in-indiana/, accessed September 23, 2015.

Page 27, *Wiley was offered the position of Chief Chemist* … Quotation from "Harvey Washington Wiley, M.D." U. S. Food and Drug Administration Commissioner's Page, http://www.fda.gov/about-fda/commissionerspage/ucm113692.htm, accessed March 16, 2015.

Page 27, *Richard Dale Owen (1810–1890)* … Samantha Norling, "Richard Owen, Colonel of the 60th Indiana Volunteers," http://www.in.gov/idoa/2783.htm, accessed September 11, 2014.

Page 27, *the utopian community of New Harmony* … The Harmonie Society founded its utopian community, Harmonie, there in 1814. Rev. Johann Georg Rapp (1757–1847), a charismatic Lutheran dissenter from Germany, led the Harmonie Society. Rapp sold the settlement in 1825 to Robert Owen. *See* http://www.newharmony-in.gov/about_new_harmony.php, accessed September 21, 2014. *See also* "An Introduction to Posey County, Its History and Its Court Records: Harmonie Indiana," http://www.in.gov/icpr/2755.htm, accessed September 21, 2014.

Page 27, *Anderson's Institution in Glasgow* … Anderson's Institution was founded in 1796. Its name changed to Anderson's University in 1828, and then to Anderson's College in 1877. It is now a part of the University of Glasgow.

Page 28, *As early as 1865, technological innovations* … Swiss chemist Jules Piccard (1840–1933) described a vacuum filtration apparatus that employed a water aspirator: J. Piccard, "Eine wesentliche Beschleunigung des Filtrationsgeschäftes," *Fresenius' Zeitschrift für analytische Chemie*, vol. 4 (1865), pp. 45–48. Cited in William B. Jensen, "The Origins of the Hirsch and Büchner Vacuum Filtration Funnels," *Journal of Chemical Education*, vol. 83, no. 9 (September 2006), p. 1283. The water aspirator is a practical application of the Venturi effect, named after Italian physicist Giovanni Battista Venturi (1746–1822).

Page 28, *William Lowe Bryan in 1909 appointed a faculty committee* … John W. Cravens, "Buildings on the Old and New Campuses of Indiana University,"

Indiana University Alumni Quarterly, vol. 9, no. 1 (January 1922), pp. 317–319.

Page 28, *Water aspirators were used for vacuum filtrations* ... Thirteen models of water aspirator filter pumps, one similar to Piccard's 1865 device, another similar to the Fisherbrand™ Airejector™ Aspirator Pump advertised in 2014, were listed for sale in 1910. "Price List of Chemical and Bacteriological Apparatus and Assayers' Supplies," E. H. Sargent & Company (Chicago, 1910), pp. 5–6. An inexpensive water aspirator could be installed (by hand) over any sink that had a threaded water faucet. In at least one nineteenth-century student chemistry laboratory (in Stoddard Hall, Smith College, Northampton, Massachusetts), the drainage system could not accommodate as much wastewater as was delivered by simultaneous operation of all installed aspirators.

Page 28, *Hirsch and Büchner filter funnels* ... R. Hirsch, "Ueber eine Vorrichtung zum Filtriren," *Chemiker Zeitung,* vol. 12 (1888), p. 340. E. Büchner, "Filtration vermittelst des Dr. R. Hirsch'schen Patent-Trichters," *Chemiker Zeitung,* vol. 12 (1888), p. 1277. Cited in Jensen, "The Origins of the Hirsch and Büchner Vacuum Filtration Funnels," op. cit.

Page 28, *Gooch crucibles* ... Frank Austen Gooch (1852–1929) invented the Gooch crucible, first described by him in 1879–1880. It was used with a vacuum filter flask in quantitative chemical analysis to collect precipitates that were then dried and weighed. F. A. Gooch, "On a New Method for the Separation and Subsequent Treatment of Precipitates in Chemical Analysis," *American Chemical Journal,* vol. 1 (1879–1880), pp. 317–323. "Presented to the American Academy of Arts and Sciences. Communicated by the Author."

Page 28, *It has been estimated* ... Emily S. Tozzi and Armenn I. Malazian, "Laboratory Vacuum Pump Buyers' Guide," Labcompare: Online Buyer's Guide for Laboratory Equipment and Supplies, posted Thursday, July 12, 2012; http://www.labcompare. com/10-Featured-Articles/116935-Laboratory-Vacuum-Pump-Buyers-Guide, accessed August 19, 2015. Concerns about excessive water usage and about disposal of the resultant wastewater eventually prompted many chemical laboratories to curb reliance on water aspirators. For example, the organic chemistry teaching laboratories at the University of Colorado Boulder in 2015 were equipped with mechanical vacuum systems to supplement water aspirators, and students were encouraged to use the mechanical system whenever possible. "Vacuum Systems," *Organic Chemistry at CU Boulder* (updated August 11, 2015), http://orgchem. colorado.edu/Technique/Procedures/Vacuum/Vacuum.html, accessed August 19, 2015.

Page 29, *Samuel Brown Wylie (1854–1890)* ... Samuel Brown Wylie was the son of Theophilus Adam Wylie (1810–1895). T. A. Wylie was appointed in 1837 to teach natural philosophy and chemistry at Indiana College in Bloomington. Excluding 2½ years on the faculty of Miami University, T. A. Wylie was on the Indiana faculty for forty-eight years. T. A. Wylie was a cousin of Indiana University President Andrew Wylie. *See* "About the Wylie House: Theophilus Adam Wylie," Wylie House Museum, Indiana University Libraries, http://www.iub.edu/~libwylie/theowylie.html, accessed September 21, 2014.

Page 29, *first Indiana University Ph.D. in Chemistry* ... *Newsletter: Association of Indiana University Chemists,* vol. 18 (1970), p. 1. Dr. Carrick would be a member of the faculty of North Dakota Agricultural College (Fargo) for two decades, serving as Professor of Industrial Chemistry and Dean of the School of Chemical Technology. He joined the faculty of the Department of Chemical Engineering at the University of Michigan (Ann Arbor) as Professor of Chemical Engineering in 1945. "A Century of Chemical Engineering at the University of Michigan," http://um2017.org/2017_Website/Chemical_Engineering_files/*Wilkes%20Chemical%20Engineering%20History%20copy.pdf, accessed January 8, 2014; http://um2017.org/faculty-history/faculty/leo-l-carrick/memoir, accessed January 8, 2014.

Page 29, *research on a mercurous perchlorate voltmeter* ... *A Bibliography of Theses Submitted to Indiana University for Advanced Degrees 1883–1927*, p. 21: "Department of Chemistry, Master of Arts. 1910. Germann, Albert Frederick Ottomar. The mercurous per-chlorate voltameter." Frank C. Mathers and Albert F. O. Germann, "Studies on Perchloric Acid: Mercurous Perchlorate Voltameter," *Indiana University Studies*, vol. 1, no. 5, pp. 41–49 (Bloomington, Indiana: The University, 1910); "From a thesis presented to the faculty of Indiana university for the degree of master of arts, by Albert F. O. Germann, 1910." In that 68-page issue of *Indiana University Studies* were eight research papers by Indiana University faculty. Four were by Frank Mathers; two of his were publications of master's theses.

Page 30, *Chemisches Zentralblatt* ... *Chemisches Zentralblatt* (1830 to 1969) began as *Pharmaceutisches Zentralblatt* in 1830, was renamed *Chemisch Pharmaceutisches Zentralblatt* in 1850, and became *Chemisches Zentralblatt* in 1856.

Page 30, *Abstracts Section* ... The Chemical Society of London was formed in 1841. Queen Victoria granted the Society a Royal Charter for the general advancement of chemical science. From 1849 to 1862, the Society published the *Quarterly Journal of the Chemical Society*, and then the *Journal of the Chemical Society*. Beginning in 1878, the *Journal* was published in two sections: *Journal of the Chemical Society, Transactions* and *Journal of the Chemical Society, Abstracts*. The "Abstracts" section disappeared in 1925 when its American competitor, *Chemical Abstracts*, became more inclusive of international publications in a wider range of chemical sciences.

Page 30, *An author could submit an order* ... It was difficult to estimate the number of reprints that might be needed. An order for 1,100 reprints was submitted in 1949 for a paper [James W. Hensley, Arthur O. Long, and John E. Willard, "Reactions of Ions in Aqueous Solution with Glass and Metal Surfaces," *Industrial and Engineering Chemistry*, vol. 41, no. 7 (July 1949), pp. 1415–1421] by James

Hensley, one of Frank Germann's graduate students. Letter, dated September 1, 1949, to James W. Hensley from John E. Willard; copy supplied by David G. Null, Director of the University Archives, University of Wisconsin–Madison.

Page 30, *when she was a chemistry graduate student in 1895* ... Mary Bidwell Breed, '94, "Scientific Pastures New," *The Lantern* (Bryn Mawr College Literary Magazine), vol. 5 (June 1895), pp. 12–20.

Page 31, *It is not physical chemistry any more than it is chemical physics* ... A prominent physical chemist from Indiana engineered the editorial separation of physical chemistry and chemical physics. Harold Clayton Urey (April 29, 1893–January 5, 1981; Nobel laureate in Chemistry 1934) in 1933 was the first editor of the *Journal of Chemical Physics*. He remained editor until 1941, the year he entered the top-secret wartime Manhattan Project that was developing a nuclear weapon. Urey was born in Walkerton, Lincoln Township, St. Joseph County, Indiana, a town then with a population less than a thousand persons. He completed the course of study in a rural district school in Lake County, Indiana, and then attended Kendallville High School, graduating in 1911. A copy of his high school transcript was supplied on December 30, 2015, by Ann W. Linson, Superintendent, East Noble School Corporation, Kendallville, Indiana. He entered Earlham College, Richmond, Indiana, and was a student there for three months during the 1911–1912 year. He obtained a teacher's license from Earlham. "Directory," *The Earlham College Bulletin*, vol. 13, no. 5 (August 1916), p. 170; reference supplied by Jenny C. Freed, Earlham College Archives. He then taught in single-teacher schools in Indiana and in Montana. An account of his life, written for a young-adult audience, is Alvin Silverstein and Virginia Silverstein (with the cooperation of Harold Urey), *Harold Urey: The Man Who Explored from Earth to Moon* (New York: John Day Company, 1970). His wide ranging scientific accomplishments are described in James R. Arnold, Jacob Bigeleisen, and Clyde A. Hutchison Jr., "Harold Clayton Urey, 1893–1981," *Biographical Mem-*

oirs of the National Academy of Sciences (Washington: National Academy of Sciences, 1995), pp. 363–411.

For an interpretation of the separation of the two disciplines in Germany, Great Britain, the United States, and Japan, see Jeremiah James, "From Physical Chemistry to Chemical Physics, 1913–1941," *Proceedings of the International Workshop on the History of Chemistry 2015 Tokyo*, paper 25 (March 4, 2015), pp. 183–191, http://kagakushi.org/iwhc2015/papers/25. JamesJeremiah.pdf, accessed March 1, 2016.

Page 31, *Mathews, who was to be a mentor of Albert Germann* … An excellent source of information about the history of chemistry at the University of Wisconsin is Aaron J. Ihde, *Chemistry, as Viewed from Bascom's Hill: A History of the Chemistry Department at the University of Wisconsin in Madison* (Department of Chemistry, University of Wisconsin–Madison, 1990), xvi + 688 pages.

Page 31, *double-wall Dewar glass vacuum flask* … Scottish chemist and physicist James Dewar (1842–1923) invented the vacuum flask. By 1909, The American Thermos Bottle Company of Brooklyn, New York; Thermos Limited of Tottenham, England; and Canadian Thermos Bottle Company Ltd. of Montreal, Canada, were marketing this double-wall glass flask (the thermos bottle) with a partial vacuum between silvered-glass walls.

Page 32, *master's thesis was typewritten* … The University of Wisconsin library archives supplied a photocopy of the typewritten thesis.

Page 32, *the text was set in type and published* … J. Howard Mathews and A. F. O. Germann, "The Use of a Dewar Flask in Measurements of Heats of Neutralization," *Journal of Physical Chemistry*, vol. 15, no. 1 (1911), pp. 73–82. Submitted October 1910.

Page 32, *directions he had mimeographed* … Among his many inventions, Thomas Alva Edison received patents for the fundamental features of the mimeograph in 1870 and 1880. Albert B. Dick (1856–1934) obtained license to exploit Edison's printing patents, coined the word "mimeograph," and formed the A. B. Dick Company in 1883 to produce inexpensive machines that revolutionized the office printing world. There was a mimeograph in the Chemistry Department administrative office, as well as a typewriter with a lever that permitted the inked ribbon to be raised out of the way, so that a mimeograph stencil could be cut.

Page 32, *with added authors from the Wisconsin chemistry faculty* … By the time the sixth edition was published in 1962, Professors Robert Arnold Alberty (June 21, 1921–January 18, 2014) and Charles Daniel Cornwell (born December 27, 1924; Professor Emeritus, University Wisconsin, 1995) had been added to the list of authors. McGraw-Hill published all editions.

Page 33, *pumping station whose origins dated from 1876* … C. I. King, "The New Water Storage System for the University of Wisconsin," *The Wisconsin Engineer*, vol. 8, no. 4 (June 1904), pp. 225–230. In 1928, the pumping station supplied 850,000 gallons of lake water per day to the campus; M. J. O'Laughlin, "The University's Water Supply: A Description of the University Pumping Station, giving Details of the Extensive System of Mains and Features of its Operation," *The Wisconsin Engineer*, vol. 33, no. 1 (October 1928), pp. 9, 34, 36. As late as 1965, lake water accounted for 51% of the water used on campus. Information and references supplied by David G. Null, Director of University Archives, University of Wisconsin–Madison.

Page 33, *redistilled from an alkaline permanganate solution* … Dating back at least to the experimental research of Belgian analytical chemist Jean Servais Stas (1813–1891), methods were developed to produce ultrapure water. Stas, in the course of his determinations of atomic weights, redistilled water from an alkaline solution of manganate. Friedrich Wilhelm Georg Kohlrausch (1840–1910) improved Stas's methods to obtain "conductivity water" for his studies of ions in solution. By the turn of the century, redistillation from alkaline permanganate solutions was common. *See discussion in* William Robert Bousfield, "The Purification of Water by Continuous Fractional Distillation," *Journal of the Chemical Society, Transactions*, vol. 87, paper no. 75 (1905), pp. 740–747.

Page 34, *"During Mathews' first year* ... Aaron J. Ihde, manuscript prepared for *Chemistry, as Viewed from Bascom's Hill: A History of the Chemistry Department at the University of Wisconsin in Madison*, p. XIV-31. Manuscript kindly provided to the author by Professor Ihde. Much of the information in the quotation was obtained in an interview (March 8, 1969) with J. Howard Mathews by Sheldon J. Kopperl, doctoral student of Professor Ihde. Very similar information appears in the published book, Ihde, *Chemistry*, op. cit., p. 252.

Page 34, *Richards had a great deal of experience* ... Ihde manuscript, ibid., p. XIV-33. Published book, Ihde, *Chemistry*, op. cit., p. 253.

Page 34, *Josiah Parsons Cooke (1827–1894)* ... Cooke "can fairly be described as the first [American] university chemist to do truly distinguished work in the field of chemistry," I. Bernard Cohen, "Some Reflections on the State of Science in America during the Nineteenth Century," *Proceedings of the National Academy of Sciences of the United States of America*, vol. 45, no. 5 (May 1959), pp. 666–677; quotation on p. 672.

Page 35, *During the Scientific Revolution* ... Not every historian supports the concept of an eighteenth-century scientific revolution. *See, for example,* Ursula Klein, "A Revolution That Never Happened," *Studies in the History and Philosophy of Science*, vol. 49 (2015), pp. 80–90; Robert Siegfried, "The Chemical Revolution in the History of Chemistry," *Osiris*, vol. 4 (1988), pp. 34–50.

Page 35, *would later nominate Guye five times* ... Giorgio Nebbia and George B. Kauffman, "Prophet of Solar Energy: A Retrospective View of Giacomo Luigi Ciamician (1857–1922), the Founder of Green Chemistry, on the 150th Anniversary of His Birth," *The Chemical Educator*, vol. 12, no. 5 (2007), pp. 362–369, citing E. Crawford, compiler, *The Nobel Population 1901–1950: A Census of the Nominators and Nominees for the Prizes in Physics and Chemistry* (Tokyo: Universal Academy Press, 2002).

Page 35, *Guye would be awarded the Davy Medal* ... https://royalsociety.org/awards/davy-medal/, accessed February 19, 2015. Listing, from 1877.

Page 36, *MM. Arni et Bell, des Drs G. Baume, A. F. O. Germann et de Mlle Gillay* ... Ettore Cardoso, "Revision des Constantes Critiques des Gaz Liquéfiables," *Archives des Sciences Physiques et Naturelles*, vol. 34, pp. 20–31 (1912). The cited article describes the apparatus and the experimental methods used by members of this research group to determine the critical temperatures of C_2H_4, N_2O, H_2S, CO_2, C_2N_2, NH_3, and HCl.

Page 36, *thermodynamic properties of mixtures* ... Georges Baume and Albert-F.-O. Germann, "Courses de fusibilité des mélanges gazeux: systèmes oxoniens formés par l'acétylène, l'oxyde azotique et l'oxyde de méthyle," *Comptes Rendus Hebdomadaires des Séances de l'Académie des Sciences*, vol. 153 (1911), pp. 569–571.

Page 36, *Edward Williams Morley (1838–1923)* ... *See* Edward W. Morley, *On the Densities of Oxygen and Hydrogen and On the Ratio of their Atomic Weights* (Washington: Smithsonian Institution publication no. 980, 1895); *Smithsonian Contributions to Knowledge*, vol. 29, art. 2, 117 pages. *See also* Howard Raymond Williams, *Edward Williams Morley: His Influence on Science in America* (Easton, Pennsylvania: Chemical Education Publishing Company, 1957). Howard Williams taught chemistry at Western Reserve Academy, Hudson, Ohio, at the original site of Western Reserve College. *See further* Olin Freeman Tower, "Edward Williams Morley," *Science* (New Series), vol. 57, no. 1476 (April 13, 1923), pp. 431–434. Prof. Tower served with Prof. Morley on the Western Reserve University faculty. *In addition, a recent book,* Ralph Richard Hamerla, *An American Scientist on the Research Frontier: Edward Morley, Community, and Radical Ideas in Nineteenth-Century Science* (Dordrecht, Netherlands: Springer Academic Publishing, 2006). Richard Hamerla completed his Ph.D. at Case Western Reserve University in 2000.

Page 36, *Hurlbut Professor of Natural History and Chemistry* ... The Hurlbut Professorship was created in 1865 by a gift from Cleveland lawyer, banker, and railroad executive Hinman Barrett Hurlbut (1819–1884) to Western Reserve College in Hudson, Ohio. The first to hold a Hurlbut Chair was John Lang Cassels (1808–1879), a founder of Cleveland Medical College. Cassels' title from 1865 to 1869 was Lecturer in the Hurlbut Professorship of Chemistry and Natural History. In 1868, Edward Williams Morley was named Hurlbut Professor of Natural History and Chemistry. He continued to occupy the Hurlbut Chair when the College moved to Cleveland in 1882, and thereafter until his retirement in 1906. The professorship was renamed in 1907 with the appointment of Olin Freeman Tower as Hurlbut Professor of Chemistry. Tower retired in 1942 with the title Hurlbut Professor of Chemistry Emeritus, a title that he retained until his death. Helen Conger, Case Western University Archivist, supplied information by email on December 18, 2015.

Page 36, *Morley has been credited*... Frederick Clayton Waite, *Western Reserve University, The Hudson Era: A History of Western Reserve College and Academy at Hudson, Ohio, from 1826 to 1882* (Cleveland: Western Reserve University Press, 1943), p. 370.

Page 36, *determined by reference to hydrogen* ... There was no consensus on a single definition of an atomic weight scale, and not every scientist used hydrogen as the standard. Wilhelm Ostwald and some other contemporaries proposed a scale with the atomic weight of oxygen defined as exactly 16.000....

Page 37, *that there were isotopes of hydrogen, oxygen* ... George B. Kauffman, "Celebrating the Isotope," *Chemical & Engineering News*, vol. 91, no. 48 (December 2, 2013), pp. 30–31.

Page 38, *It was not until 1929 that* ... W. F. Giauque and H. L. Johnston, "An Isotope of Oxygen, Mass 18. Interpretation of the Atmospheric Absorption Bands," *Journal of the American Chemical Society*, vol. 51, no. 5 (May 1929), pp. 1436–1441; W. F. Giauque and H. L. Johnston, "An Isotope of Oxygen, Mass 17, in the Earth's Atmosphere." *Journal of the American Chemical Society*, vol. 51, no. 12

(December 1929), pp. 3528–3534.

Page 38, *His sixty-three-page doctoral thesis* ... Albert-F.-O. Germann, *Révision de la densité de l'oxygène, contribution à la détermination de la densité l'air à Genève*, Thèse No. 514 (Genève: Imprimerie Albert Kündig, 1913).

Page 38, *published a shorter version* ... Albert-F.-O. Germann, "Révision de la densité de l'oxygène, contribution à la détermination de la densité l'air à Genève," *Journal de Chimie physique*, vol. 12 (1914), pp. 66–108 [Mémoire reçu le 1ᵉʳ juillet 1913.].

Page 39, *Carl Zeiss ranked number ten internationally* ... *Chemical & Engineering News*, vol. 91, no. 17 (April 29, 2013), p. 11.

Page 40, *with annual chemical sales of $78.7 billion* ... Alexander H. Tullo, "Global Top 50," *Chemical & Engineering News*, vol. 93, no. 30 (July 27, 2015), pp. 14–21.

Page 40, *Friedr. Bayer et comp.* ... Alex Scott, "150 Years of Invention: Bayer Celebrates Its Spirit of Innovation and Ponders How to Apply It Next," *Chemical & Engineering News*, vol. 91, no. 23 (June 10, 2013), pp. 18–19.

Page 40, *Bayer was the world's tenth largest* ... Tullo, loc. cit.

Page 40, *DuPont was the world's eighth largest* ... Tullo, loc. cit.

Page 41, *Tower wrote in 1912* ... Olin F. Tower, "Is the Proportion of Oxygen in the Air Constant?" *Western Reserve Bulletin*, New Series, vol. 15, no. 8 (November 1912), pp. 158–165. Because the *Bulletin* was a Western Reserve University publication, it seems likely that any delay between writing and publication was less than eleven months.

Page 42, *National Historic Chemical Landmark* ... *Research on the Atomic Weight of Oxygen by Edward W. Morley: A National Historic Chemical Landmark* (Cleveland, Ohio, September 14, 1995: American Chemical Society, Division of the History of Chemistry, and the A.C.S. Office of Public Outreach). Adelbert Hall (2040 Adelbert Road at

Euclid Avenue) is the oldest building on campus. Built in 1881–1882, the building housed the Chemistry Department (and most other offices of the institution) until Morley Chemical Laboratory opened in 1910. Fire gutted the building on Sunday, June 23, 1991. Rebuilding Adelbert Hall took two years at a cost of 12.4 million dollars. It now serves as the College Administrative Building. http://blog.case.edu/archives/2011/06/23/adelbert_hall_burns_20_years_ago, accessed August 21, 2014.

Page 43, *Dr. Tower at that time projected the construction cost* ... The actual cost was $143,332. Chemistry and Geology moved into the building in 1910. The Chemistry Department was the primary occupant from 1925 to 1949. http://www.case.edu/its/archives/Buildings/morche.htm, accessed August 21, 2014.

Page 43, *The three-floor collegiate-style gothic building* ... "The Morley Chemical Laboratory of Western Reserve University," *Science* (New Series), vol. 29, no. 731 (January 1, 1909), p. 25.

Page 44, *Henry Meinike farm was in Section 24* ... "Map of Royal Oak Township," *Illustrated Atlas of Oakland County Michigan* (Racine, Wisconsin: Kace Publishing Company, 1896), p. 45.

Page 44, *A map published in 1908* ... "Map of Royal Oak Township," *Standard Atlas of Oakland County Michigan* (Chicago: Geo. A. Osle & Company, 1908), p. 64.

Page 44, *a two-story wooden school building* ... "Dates in Royal Oak Schools History," The Royal Oak Historical Society, http://www.royaloakhistoricalsociety.com/schoolhist.html, accessed April 6, 2013.

Page 45, *promoted to Associate Professor with tenure* ... A short history of academic tenure, viewed in a twentieth-century context, is Clark G. Ross, "Toward a New Consensus for Tenure in the Twenty-First Century: How Shall We Understand Tenure Today?," *Academe*, vol. 101, no. 3 (May–June 2015).

Page 46, *He was on the staff* ... 1905 *Narcissus* yearbook. Copy in the Peru Public Library.

Page 46, *Ross Franklin Lockridge Sr. (October 26, 1877–January 12, 1952)* ... "Historical Sketch," Ross F. Lockridge Papers, 1938-1948, Collection #: M 618 (Indiana Historical Society—Manuscripts & Archives, http://www.indianahistory.org/our-collections/collection-guides/ross-f-lockridge-papers-1938-1948.pdf, accessed April 23, 2013). Obituary, Fort Wayne *Journal Gazette*, January 14, 1952, p. 1.

Page 46, *throughout the state as a popular speaker* ... *For example*, Ross Lockridge Sr. spoke in South Whitley, Indiana, on Saturday, December 4, 1937, before five hundred persons at the centennial observance of the town's first school, Springfield Academy. Former Whitley County School Superintendent A. R. Fleck presented a stone monument, marking the site of the school building. That monument can still be seen in front of the entrance to Shindigz. We shall see more of South Whitley in Chapter 5.

Page 46, *He also became an historian* ... Ross Lockridge Sr. was author of *How Government Functions in Indiana* (Indiana supplement to Thomas Harrison Reed's *Form and Functions of American Government*), (Yonkers-on-Hudson, N.Y.: World Book Company, ©1918); *George Rogers Clark, Pioneer Hero of the Old Northwest* (World Book Company, 1927); *A. Lincoln* (World Book Company, 1930); *La Salle* (World Book Company, 1931); *The Old Fauntleroy Home* (New Harmony Memorial Commission, 1939); *The Labyrinth, A History of the New Harmony Labyrinth, Including Some Special Study of the Spiritual and Mystical Life of its Builders, the Rappites, and a Brief Survey of Labyrinths Generally* (New Harmony Memorial Commission, 1941); *Theodore F. Thieme, A Man and His Times* (Los Angeles: Haynes Corporation, 1942); *The Story of Indiana* (Oklahoma City: Harlow Publishing Corporation, 1951; adopted 1951 as an Indiana eighth-grade textbook).

Page 46, *Ross Franklin Lockridge Jr. (1914–1948)* ... Ross Lockridge Jr., *Raintree County: which had no boundaries in time and space, where lurked musical and strange names and mythical and lost peoples, and which was itself only a name musical and strange* (Boston: Houghton Mifflin Company, 1948).

Page 47, *Hagenbeck–Wallace Circus* ... Information supplied by Thomas Jefferson Dunwoody, Executive Director, Circus Hall of Fame, 3076 East Circus Lane, Peru, Indiana.

Page 47, *For two years, following in about the same course* ... Quotation from Arthur L. Bodurtha, ed., *History of Miami County Indiana: A Narrative Account of Its Historical Progress, Its People and Its Principal Interests* (Chicago: Lewis Publishing Company, 1914), vol. II, p. 456. *See also* the introductory note (by A. J. Buehner, editor) to article: Frank E. E. Germann, "The 'Parity Law' of Nuclear Physics Challenged," *The Lutheran Scholar*, vol. XIV, no. 4 (October 1957), pp. 571–577.

Page 48, *Gamma of Indiana Chapter of Phi Beta Kappa* ... Email December 11, 2013, from Laura Hartnett, Coordinator of Administration, The Phi Beta Kappa Society, Washington, D.C.

Page 48, *laboratories were in different campus buildings* ... Physics was taught in Owen Hall. Chemistry was taught in nearby Wylie Hall. Owen Hall and Wylie Hall were constructed in 1884, the first two buildings on the "new campus" in Dunn's Woods.

Page 48, *Their paths did cross in 1910* ... Office of the Registrar, University of Wisconsin–Madison, email May 26, 2015.

Page 48, *David Klein had just completed a doctoral program* ... Klein's Ph.D. thesis was "The Influence of Organic Liquids upon the Interaction of Hydrogen Sulphide and Sulphur Dioxide," *Journal of Physical Chemistry*, vol. 15, no. 1 (January 1912), pp. 1–19. He was quickly promoted to Assistant Professor, and he stayed at Wisconsin until 1914. In 1920, he joined Wilson Laboratories in Chicago. He later became President of Wilson Laboratories.

Page 49, *His doctoral dissertation, "Arc Spectra,"* ... Arthur L. Foley, *Physical Review* (Series I), vol. 5 (September 1897), pp. 129–151. His research was

under the direction of Edward Leamington Nichols. Nichols would also direct the research of Rolla Roy Ramsey at Cornell a few years later.

Page 49, *As early as 1904* ... *Hickman* (Kentucky) *Courier*, vol. 38, no. 51 (January 22, 1904), p. 1.

Page 49, *Ryland Ratliff investigated properties* ... Ryland Ratliff, "Effect of Radium on Electrolytic Conductivity," *Proceedings of the Indiana Academy of Science* (1905), pp. 109–114.

Page 49, *Foley was also investigating radio waves* ... Arthur L. Foley, "On the Use of Nickel in the Core of the Marconi Magnetic Detector," *Physical Review* (Series I), vol. 18, no. 5 (1904), pp. 349–354.

Page 49, *Luther Dana Waterman Institute for Research* ... Indianapolis physician and Indiana University School of Medicine Professor Emeritus Luther Dana Waterman (November 21, 1830–June 30, 1918) in 1915 donated property worth $100,000 to Indiana University for "the establishment and permanent maintenance of an Institute for Scientific Research." It was the largest gift for scientific research that had been made to the University. An 1853 graduate of the Medical College of Ohio at Cincinnati, Dr. Waterman was a charter organizer of the Indiana Medical College; he taught there for several years. In 1878, he was President of the Indiana Medical Society.

Page 49, *The third edition appeared in 1941* ... A reviewer of his 1937 second edition wrote: "A textbook that has received almost unanimous approval requires little alteration. The second edition of Foley's *College Physics* shows very few changes in content or order." *School Science and Mathematics*, vol. 37, no. 7 (October 1937), p. 874.

Page 49, *Arthur Foley had important roles in building* ... John W. Cravens, "Buildings on the Old and New Campuses of Indiana University," *Indiana University Alumni Quarterly*, vol. 9, no. 1 (January 1922), pp. 307–319.

Page 50, *published Ramsey's doctoral dissertation* ... Rolla Roy Ramsey, *Physical Review* (Series I), vol. 13 (May 1901), pp. 1–30.

Page 51, *enrolling in the Faculty of Sciences* ...
Dominique Torrione-Vouilloz, Archives administratives et patrimoniales, l'Université de Genève, email May 12, 2015.

Page 51, *list of research publications* ... Faculty record sheet, prepared by Frank Germann for the University of Colorado. Copy supplied by Archives, University of Colorado at Boulder Libraries.

Page 52, *William Lowe Bryan (November 11, 1860–November 21, 1955...* Letter, dated December 5, 1913, from Frank E. E. Germann to President W. L. Bryan. Response letter, dated December 6, 1913. Indiana University President's Office Correspondence, 1913–1937: Germann, Frank E. E. Reference to this internet file kindly provided by Dina Kellams, Associate Archivist, Indiana University, January 31, 2014. Bryan was born William Julian Bryan in Monroe County, Indiana. In 1889, he married Charlotte Lowe, and replaced his middle name with his wife's maiden name.

Page 53, *His salary was $500...* Letter, dated July 8, 1914, from Frank E. E. Germann to U. H. Smith, Treasurer, Indiana University. I. U. President's Office, loc. cit.

Page 53, *There were then four members* ... Email from Dina Kellams, Associate Archivist, Indiana University, January 14, 2014. The faculty were: Albert F. Kuersteiner, Professor of Romance Languages; George D. Morris, Associate Professor of French; Charles A. Mosemiller, Associate Professor of Romance Languages; Jotilda Conklin, Assistant Professor of French; Ruth R. Maxwell, Instructor in French; and Frances R. Latzke, Acting Instructor in French.

Page 53, *Frank had taken courses* ... Email from Roberta Roberts-Cradick, Records Services Assistant, Indiana University Office of the Registrar, January 15, 2014.

Page 53, *Both women were graduate students* ... "Register of Graduates 1830-1916," *Indiana University Bulletin*, vol. 15, no. 12 (December 1917). http://www.archive.org/stream/registerofgraduaooindi/registerofgraduaooindi_djvu.txt, accessed January 14, 2014.

Page 53, *From the tour brochure* ... Copy of the tour brochure was supplied by Archives, University of Colorado at Boulder Libraries.

Page 54, *studied at Lausanne and Neuchâtel* ... Undated newspaper clippings provided by Archives, University of Colorado at Boulder Libraries. Frank did not register formally as a student at the University of Neuchâtel between 1911 and 1914. Aronne Watkins, Unine Librarian, Université de Neuchâtel; Y. Fischer, Service d'immatriculation, Université de Neuchâtel.

Page 54, *submitted a thesis* ... Frank-E.-E. Germann, *Recherches sur les gaz retenus par l'argent métallique. Formation du chlorure de nitrosyle. Microanalyse des gaz.* [Investigations of the Gases Retained by Metallic Silver. Formation of Nitrosyl Chloride. Microanalysis of Gases], Université de Genève doctorat ès sciences physiques et chimiques Thèse No. 545 (Genève: Imprimerie Albert Kündig, 1915).

Page 54, *He received the title* ... Dominique Torrione-Vouilloz, Archives administratives et patrimoniales, l'Université de Genève, email May 12, 2015.

Page 56, *John was a businessman* ... *Illustrated Biographical Album of Northeastern Nebraska* (Omaha: National Publishing Company, 1893), p. 286.

Page 57, *Paul Stoeppelwerth was born April 25, 1872* ... Obituary of the Rev. Paul Stoeppelwerth, *Fort Wayne News-Sentinel*, December 12, 1931, p. 1.

Page 59, "*The Maiden with the Dreamy Eyes*" ... Sheet music: "The Maiden with the Dreamy Eyes," as sung by Anna Held in "The Little Duchess," direction of Florence Ziegfeld Jr. Words by James Weldon Johnson. Music by Bob Cole. New York: Jos. W. Stern & Company, 1901.

Page 60, *The Mission of a Sunbeam* ... *The Christian Miscellany, and Family Visiter*, Second Series, vol. IX. (London: John Mason, 1863), p. 219. This oration appeared as a poem in *The Home-maker: An Illustrated Monthly Magazine*, vol. ix, no. 1 (October 1892), p. 50. The oration and the poem may have been inspiration for the popular children's hymn "I'll be a Sunbeam" ("Jesus Wants Me for a Sunbeam"), with lyrics by Nellie Talbot and tune composed in 1900 by Edwin Othello Excell (1851–1921). Excell was an influential composer and music publisher, perhaps best remembered for his 1909 arrangement of John Newton's "Amazing Grace."

Page 61, *The Normal Training Class ... The Rustler Annual, 1907* (Published by the Students of Fremont High School); *The F. H. S. Annual, 1907–1908* (Fremont, Nebraska: Fremont High School); *The F. H. S. Annual, 1908–1909* (Fremont, Nebraska: Fremont High School).

Page 61, *Martha taught at Fort Wayne's James H. Smart Elementary School ...* Entries in *Fort Wayne City and Allen County Directory* (Fort Wayne: R. L. Polk), vol. 42 (1915); vol. 43 (1916). The school was named for James Henry Smart (1841-1900). Smart was primarily homeschooled, but he did attend high school in Concord, New Hampshire, at age 12. At age 17, after being employed as a bookkeeper, he returned to Concord High School as a temporary teacher. He then taught in Sanbornton, New Hampshire, and was a school administrator in Toledo, Ohio. He became Superintendent of the Fort Wayne Public Schools at age 25. He was elected Indiana State Superintendent of Public Instruction in 1874, and held that office for six years. He became the fourth President of Purdue University on August 23, 1883. Purdue University Libraries, Archives and Special Collections, http://www4.lib.purdue.edu/archon/?p=creators/creator&id=75, accessed January 8, 2016.

Page 61, *Trinity German Lutheran Church ...* St. Paul's Evangelical Lutheran Church, established in 1837, is Fort Wayne's oldest Lutheran church. It was one of the founding congregations of The Lutheran Church–Missouri Synod (LC–MS). St. Paul's is the "Mother Church" for many Fort Wayne Lutheran congregations, including Trinity German Lutheran Church (now Trinity Evangelical Lutheran Church LC–MS). The present Fort Wayne Trinity English Evangelical Lutheran Church (originally called English Evangelical Lutheran Church of the Holy Trinity) was founded

in 1846. It was the first English-speaking Lutheran church in northeastern Indiana. It now belongs to the Indiana–Kentucky Synod of the Evangelical Lutheran Church in America (ELCA). *See* Mildred L. Burger, *Short History of the Lutheran Church–Missouri Synod in Fort Wayne, Indiana* (Fort Wayne: Fort Wayne Public Library, 1967).

Another connection between Fremont and Fort Wayne involves Rev. Herman Ludwig August Lange (January 5, 1864–November 29, 1938.). "August Lange was born ... in St. Louis, Missouri. He attended Concordia College, Ft. Wayne before graduating from Concordia Seminary, St. Louis in 1886. He served as pastor in Freemont [sic], Nebraska (1886 to 1891), assistant pastor in Chicago (1891 to 1894), and pastor in St. Louis (1894 to 1896). He then assumed pastoral charge of [probably "became an assistant pastor at" (see next reference)] St. Paul's Evangelical Lutheran Church in Fort Wayne, Indiana, organizing it [probably "organizing a new congregation"] as Concordia Evangelical Lutheran Church from 1900 to 1922." http://www.lutheranhistory.org/collections/search2.asp, searched for "August Lange," accessed September 13, 2014. *See also the complementary information:* "On August 6, 1899, the eastern district and membership of St. Paul's Lutheran Church resolved to organize as an independent congregation. By mid-September they had chosen a spot on North Anthony (then called Walton Avenue) and Alliger. That October they organized under the name of Concordia Evangelical Lutheran Church. In January of 1900, they called the Rev. August Lange, an assistant pastor at St. Paul's who had been serving in this area. In 1904, a separate church building was dedicated. By then the school had four classrooms. In 1913, the congregation found it necessary to build a large annex to the school. The church built at the time has continued to serve as the worship center for the congregation. However, in 1960, the congregation built a spacious, modern school on Lake Avenue extended. A home on the property when it was purchased serves as the parsonage. Sunday services are held at both locations. Pastors of Concordia: August Lange 1900–1922; Walter Klausing 1922–1955; Osmar Lehenbauer 1955 to the present." Mildred L. Burger, *Short History of the Lutheran Church–Missouri Synod in Fort Wayne, Indiana* (Fort Wayne: Fort Wayne Public Library, 1967), pp. 30–32.

Page 61, *officiated at the wedding of his niece-in-law* ... Marriage Records, book C-20, page 505, Office of the Miami County Clerk, Peru, Indiana.

Page 61, *buried with her husband John ... Ridge Cemetery Index* (Fremont, Dodge County, Nebraska), http://www.rootsweb.com/~nedodge/tombstone.htm, accessed February 24, 2013. Copyright 2000 by Clarabelle Mares, Eastern Nebraska Genealogical Society, P. O. Box 541, Fremont, NE 68026. Used by permission.

Page 61, *Martha and Frank Germann had a son ... Who's Who in America*, 47th edition (1992–1993), p. 1228. Obituary, *Norwalk* (Ohio) *Reflector,* http://www.norwalkreflector.com/obituaries?page=329, accessed April 2, 2013.

Page 61, *published a joint research paper with his father* ... Frank E. E. Germann and Richard P. Germann, "Line Coordinate Representation of Solubility Curves," *Industrial and Engineering Chemistry,* vol. 36, no. 1 (January 1944), pp. 93–96.

Page 62, *A daughter, Lois Marie* ... "Lois 'Cookie' Jones," Obituary, *Santa Barbara* (California) *News-Press,* March 20–24, 2013; "Lois Jones," Obituary, *Boulder* (Colorado) *Daily Camera,* May 1, 2013.

MENDELÉEFF'S TABLE I.

SERIES.	GROUP I. — R_2O.	GROUP II. — RO.	GROUP III. R_2O_3.	GROUP IV. RH_4, RO_2.	GROUP V. RH_3, R_2O_5.	GROUP VI. RH_2, RO_3.	GROUP VII. RH, R_7O_7.	GROUP VIII. — RO_4.
1	H = 1							
2	Li = 7	Be = 9.1	B = 11	C = 12	N = 14	O = 16	F = 19	
3	Na = 23	Mg = 24.4	Al = 27	Si = 28	P = 31	S = 32	Cl = 35.5	Fe = 56, Ni = 58.5,
4	K = 39.1	Ca = 40	Sc = 44	Ti = 48.1	V = 51.2	Cr = 52.3	Mn = 55	Co = 59.1, Cu = 63.3.
5	(Cu) = 63.3	Zn = 65.4	Ga = 69.9	Ge = 72	As = 75	Se = 79	Br = 80	Rh = 103, Ru = 103.8,
6	Rb = 85.4	Sr = 87.5	Y = 89	Zr = 90.7	Cb = 94.2	Mo = 95.9	— = 100	Pd = 108, Ag = 107.9.
7	(Ag) = 107.9	Cd = 112	In = 113.7	Sn = 118	Sb = 120.3	Te = 125.2	I = 126.9	
8	Cs = 132.9	Ba = 137	La = 138.5	Ce = 141.5	Di = 145	—	—	— —
9	(—)	—	—	—	—	—	—	Ir = 193.1, Pt = 194.8,
10	—	—	Yb = 173.2	—	Ta = 182.8	W = 184	—	Os = 200, Au = 196.7.
11	(Au) = 196.7	Hg = 200.4	Tl = 204.1	Pb = 206.9	Bi = 208	—	—	— —
12	—	—	—	Th = 233.4	—	U = 239	—	— —

NATURAL SYSTEM OF THE ELEMENTS. (LOTHAR MEYER.)

	A I. B	A II. B	A III. B	A IV. B	A V. B	A VI. B	A VII. B	VIII
HYDROGEN, H = 1.01.								
	Li, 7.03	Be, 9.1	B, 11	C, 12	N, 14.04	O, 16	F, 19	
	Na, 23.05	Mg, 24.36	Al, 27.1	Si, 28.4	P, 31	S, 32.06	Cl, 35.45	
	K, 39.15	Ca, 40	Sc, 44.1	Ti, 48.1	V, 51.2	Cr, 52.1	Mn, 55	Fe, 56, Co, 59, Ni, 58.7
	Cu, 63.6	Zn, 65.4	Ga, 70	Ge, 72	As, 75	Se, 79.1	Br, 79.96	
	Rb, 85.4	Sr, 87.6	Y, 89	Zr, 90.7	Cb, 94	Mo, 96		Ru, 101.7, Rh, 103, Pd, 106
	Ag, 107.93	Cd, 112.4	In, 114	Sn, 118.5	Sb, 120	Te, 127	I, 126.85	
	Cs, 133	Ba, 137.4	La, 138	Ce, 140	[Di, 142.1]			
		E, 166	Yb, 173		Ta, 183	W, 184		Os, 191, Ir, 193, Pt, 194.8
	Au, 197.2	Hg, 200.3	Tl, 204.1	Pb, 206.9	Bi, 208.5			
				Th, 232.5		U, 239.5		
	1 [2, 3]	2 [1]	3 [1]	4 [2]	5 [3]	6 [2]	7 [1]	8 [2, 3, 4]

Periodic Law in 1901

II.
Colorado: the School of Mines, and then the University

THE WORLD would never be the same again. On Sunday, March 1, 1896, French physicist Antoine Henri Becquerel (1852–1908) made some unexpected observations. The next day he attended the weekly meeting of the Academy of Sciences in Paris, and reported those observations by reading a paper: "On the Invisible Rays Emitted by Phosphorescent Bodies." He had discovered the phenomenon of natural radioactivity. His discovery and its implications dominated subsequent experimental and theoretical activities of physicists at the turn of the century as they studied radiation of all sorts, wave phenomena of all sorts, and radioactivity from many sources.

When Frank Germann entered Indiana University as a freshman in 1906, the senior member of the five-person Indiana University physics faculty was Professor Arthur Lee Foley (1867–1945). Foley had received the Ph.D. in physics from Cornell University in 1897, with experimental research on the spectrum of radiation from electric arcs. He completed his doctorate just about a year before Marie Skłodowska-Curie, Pierre Curie, and Gustave Bémont announced (November 1898 in Paris) their discovery of radium. Seizing an opportunity to popularize a new scientific phenomenon, as early as 1904 Dr. Foley was giving (in at least two states) spectacular public demonstrations of radiation from radium. He demonstrated some effects of the radiation by using the spinthariscope, invented by Sir William Crookes in 1903.

Foley's demonstrations were in a long tradition of scientists communicating science in a dramatic fashion to a wide community. On Saturday, April 25, 1801, Humphry Davy (1778–1829) gave a public lecture on "Galvanism" at the Royal Institution in London. This opened his first series of popular demonstration-lectures, a series that lasted until June. Almost five hundred attended his June lecture. Davy's many lectures over the next decade included always spectacular and sometimes dangerous chemical and physical demonstrations, as well as reliable new scientific information. Harold Hartley has written that Davy was "the first great popular scientific lecturer." Davy's choice of successor lecturer was Michael Faraday (1791–1867). Faraday's famous and entertaining Christmas Lectures for Young People at the Royal Institution between 1827 and 1860 were designed to present science to the public and to the younger generation. Faraday's demonstrations drew capacity audiences. His protégé and successor at the Royal Institution, John Tyndall (1820–1893), continued public lectures in the format of theatrical lecture-table demonstrations from 1853 to 1885. Often there was a series of a dozen weekly lectures. Sometimes afternoon programs were aimed toward youngsters. Sometimes evening programs were performances for London sophisticates. Audiences of 250 persons were typical. Peter Guthrie Tait (1831–1901) popularized his abstract theories about vortex atoms in the æther with fascinating lecture demonstrations of smoke rings, smoke rings that he would entangle and knot in the air to model the formation of molecules.

The tradition has continued. Huntington (Indiana) science teacher Eiffel G. Plasterer (1899–1989; DePauw University Class of 1924) spent fifty-five years demonstrating the art, geometry, and science of soap bubbles to enthusiastic audiences throughout Indiana, as well as on television as a guest of late-night host David Letterman. American Chemical Society President (2012) and University of Wisconsin Chemistry Professor Bassam Z. Shakhashiri (born 1939) has given more than a thousand chemical demonstrations to students and their teachers (including eight Christmas lectures, in the spirit of Michael Faraday, on Wisconsin Public Television). Shakhashiri throughout his career has been an advocate for safe and pedagogically effective classroom chemistry demonstrations, and has published several handbooks of chemical demonstrations for teachers.

One fictional lecture series in 1910 was prophetic. Herbert George Wells (1866–1946) described that imagined course of afternoon lectures on radium and radioactivity. A Professor Rufus gave the lectures in Edinburgh. Professor Rufus held up a bottle with fourteen ounces of uranium and traces of radium. "In this bottle, ladies and gentlemen, in the atoms in this bottle there slumbers at least as much energy as we could get by burning a hundred and sixty tons of coal. If at a word, in one instant I could suddenly release that energy here and now it would blow us and everything about us to fragments; if I could turn it into the machinery that lights this city, it could keep Edinburgh brightly lit for a week." The detailed prophesy (with prescient dates) was the substance of H. G. Wells, *The World Set Free* (London: Macmillan, 1914; New York: E. P. Dutton & Company, 1914).

Professor Arthur Foley probably performed lecture demonstrations with radium in his Indiana University physics classes attended by Frank Germann between 1906 and 1911. Frank Germann and Arthur Foley were together again in 1914 as members of the Indiana University Physics Club. A typical activity of such a club would have been student and faculty presentations. The latest research on radioactivity was of great interest to all physical scientists in spring 1914. Maybe someone gave a book review of *The World Set Free*.

The first elemental radium ever isolated was from industrial waste. The waste came from pitchblende ore that had been mined in Joachimsthal, Bohemia (now Jáchymov in the Czech Republic), and then mechanically and chemically processed to extract uranium. Local artisans used uranium compounds to produce colored pottery glazes and colored glassware. The Joachimsthal mines were the only known sources of uranium, an element then with few commercial uses other than as a colorant for ceramics.

Marie Skłodowska-Curie performed the laborious and hazardous chemical separation of radium from chemically similar elements in these residual Joachimsthal ore tailings. Scientists soon discovered that all uranium ores, wherever mined, contain radium. Further research demonstrated that radium is one of the "daughter" products of the radioactive disintegration of the most abundant uranium isotope, ^{238}U. But eager mineral prospectors did not wait until that complex radioactive decay scheme was elucidated in science laboratories.

Gold had been reported in 1859 in the Pike's Peak region of what is now Colorado. Prospectors rushed to stake mineral claims. The most persistent prospectors located veins of minerals that, it eventually turned out, sometimes had immense eco-

nomic value beyond nuggets of gold. For our story, the significant mineral is carnotite, a yellow radioactive substance that contains vanadium oxides, hydrates of
potassium salts of uranium and vanadium [such as $K_2(UO_2)_2(VO_4)_2 \cdot 3H_2O$)], and
commercially significant quantities of radium. Carnotite was discovered in Montrose
County, Colorado, in 1898. Its value as a source of radium was quickly recognized.
For the next decade, Colorado was a center of the world's radium production.

Frank joined the physics faculty at Cornell University in fall 1914. Having been
exposed intellectually to radium throughout his academic life, he now saw that specialization on radium chemistry could be a career opportunity. However, radium
itself would not be his immediate experimental focus. Laboratory facilities in the
Cornell Physics Department were not suitable for safe manipulation of radium and
its compounds. Purchase of quantities of radium sufficient for chemical research
would not have been financially feasible. Frank saw a realistic option. The closely
related field of uranium chemistry promised a practical entry into the field.

In addition to his teaching duties at Cornell, Frank held a part-time fellowship
as a Carnegie Research Associate. This fellowship gave him modest funding to begin
research on uranium chemistry. The research fellowship also gave him an academic
justification for spending time in the laboratory away from his teaching commitments. Andrew Carnegie (1835–1919), perhaps the wealthiest man in the world
early in the twentieth century, had directed much of his early personal philanthropy
to constructing public libraries and to purchasing church organs. Peru, Indiana,
received a Carnegie grant in 1901 for constructing the public library building that
still stands in the center of the city at 102 East Main Street. Frank's fellowship at
Cornell was among the first Carnegie small research grants to individual scientists.
When Frederick Paul Keppel (1875–1943) became President of the Carnegie Corporation in 1923, colleges and universities began to receive institutional grants. As
we shall see, Frank Germann's sabbatical leave from the University of Colorado in
1925–1926 was funded by a more substantial grant from the Carnegie Corporation.

Frank conducted experimental studies of the thermal properties—the cooling
and warming properties—of the substance uranium nitrate. By analyzing his experimental temperature-versus-time data, he found evidence for a previously unknown
inorganic compound: the iscositetrahydrate of uranium nitrate, $UO_2(NO_3)_2 \cdot 24H_2O$.
A hydrate of a salt contains chemically-bound water. These experiments required

only equipment and laboratory space readily available to him within the Cornell University Physics Department. He read the numerical data directly from a thermometer and from a clock. He recorded temperatures and times by hand on the pages of a bound laboratory notebook. Uranium salts are radioactive, but his experiments did not entail the much higher personal radiation risks of handling quantities of pure radium compounds.

The evidence for the chemical compound $UO_2(NO_3)_2 \cdot 24H_2O$ came from Frank Germann's physical chemical interpretations of his physical chemical experiments. However, he was a member of the Cornell *Physics* Department, and he chose to present his experimental results and his conclusions at the Rochester (New York) meeting of the American *Physical* Society in 1917. Two of his senior colleagues in the Physics Department (Edward Leamington Nichols and Ernest George Merritt) were the founders and were still the editors of the journal *Physical Review*. Frank Germann chose to submit his results and conclusions for publication in *Physical Review*. That seemed like good politics. Frank had begun to see himself as a physical chemist, but his academic appointment and his academic degrees were in physics. Politically and philosophically, Frank Germann was finding physics an uncomfortable fit. It would be a few years before Frank Germann found a congenial home in a chemistry department. First, there would be an interlude at the Colorado School of Mines.

Colorado School of Mines

Frank became convinced for pragmatic reasons that his career as a physical chemist could not flourish at Cornell. He was a junior member of the Physics Department, where the senior members were influential members of the American physics fraternity. They were unlikely to view favorably a newcomer's collaboration with chemists. Wilder Dwight Bancroft and Joseph Ellis Trevor (both senior members of the Chemistry Department) dominated physical chemistry at Cornell. Even if Bancroft and Trevor had been inclined to encourage Frank Germann as an interdepartmental colleague, the destructive Morse Hall fire on February 13, 1916, removed any possibility of shared research space, let alone shared experimental apparatus.

When Frank discovered that the state-supported Colorado School of Mines in

Golden had two open faculty positions, he applied for both. He was accepted for both. He was hired as Associate Professor of Physics and Electrical Engineering at a salary of $1,800 per year. The joint appointment in the Department of Physics and in the Department of Electrical Engineering was for one calendar year: September 1, 1918, to August 31, 1919.

The Germann family moved across the continent from Ithaca, New York, to Golden, Colorado. It is hard to exaggerate the difference between Ithaca and Golden, or the contrast between Cornell University and the Colorado School of Mines. Golden was originally a mining camp, but its name did not come from the metallic element. The city was named for prospector Thomas L. Golden, a man active in the Pike's Peak gold rush. The city of Golden had been capital of the Colorado Territory from 1862 until 1867. Its population was steady: 2,477 in 1910, 2,481 in 1920. The population of Ithaca was greater and growing: 14,802 in 1910, 17,004 in 1920.

The School of Mines traces its history back to June 11, 1866, when the newly conse-crated Episcopal Bishop George Maxwell Randall (1810–1873), "Missionary Bishop of Colorado and Parts Adjacent," arrived in Golden. Bishop Randall had bold, long-range plans for a university in Golden. As two first steps, he founded the Jarvis Hall Collegiate School in 1870, followed by the Matthews Hall Episcopal Theological School in 1872. The School of Mines opened in 1873 under the auspices of the Epis-copal Church. Its present status as a public institution came on March 14, 1876, when the Colorado Territorial Legislature provided funds to establish Colorado School of Mines in Golden, the University of Colorado in nearby Boulder, and the Colorado Agricultural College (now Colorado State University) in Fort Collins. We shall learn much more about each of the three schools.

It was a three-member Germann family making the move. Richard was born on Wednesday, April 3, 1918, and was almost five months old when Frank's formal duties began at the School of Mines. The United States had entered the Great War, and wartime restrictions and military priorities complicated the transcontinental journey. The family probably travelled by rail to Fort Wayne, where Martha's mother was living. Frank's parents and many relatives were living near Fort Wayne, and eve-rybody wanted to see baby Richard. The next leg of the trip was to Chicago. In Chi-cago, they changed railroads for the long ride west.

Forty-one years earlier, another family of three had made a similar trip. Joseph Addison Sewall, with his two daughters Jane and Lucinda, had travelled by train from Normal, Illinois, to Chicago, and then west to Boulder, Colorado. Sewell was leaving his professorship at Illinois State Normal University to become the first President of the University of Colorado in Boulder. "Not the whole family, only father, Lucinda and I," wrote Joseph's daughter Jane. "It had been decided that we should go as an advance guard to our new home, giving Mother, with Ann to help her with the little children, a few weeks more time to finish the moving and the packing." We shall return to the Sewall family soon.

The two advertised faculty openings at the Colorado School of Mines were to fill vacancies created by two faculty leaves of absence granted by the School of Mines for the 1918–1919 academic year—leaves for Claude Cornelius van Nuys, B.S., E.M., A.M., Professor of Physics; and for William Jonathan Hazard, E.E., Professor of Electrical Engineering. Frank Germann replaced both men for the year. Neither van Nuys nor Hazard returned to the School of Mines faculty after his leave of absence. The appointments for the next year (1919–1920) were new hires: Arthur Emmons Bellis, A.B., M.S., Professor of Physics; and Arlington P. Little, B.S., E.E., Professor of Electrical Engineering. The appellation E.E. probably signifies the degree "Engineer of Electricity," awarded upon the completion of freshman and sophomore courses in electrical engineering. E.M. signifies a two-year degree "Engineer of Mines." With a doctorat ès sciences physiques from the prestigious University of Geneva, and four years of experience on the Cornell University faculty, Frank Germann had significantly stronger academic and professional credentials than either his immediate predecessors or his immediate successors.

Frank joined a small faculty at Colorado School of Mines. There were fifteen persons (including Frank) with titles indicating teaching responsibilities. Two were in chemistry, one in physics, two in geology and mineralogy, two in mathematics, six in mining, metallurgy, electrical engineering, and civil engineering, one in mining law, and one in modern languages. Frank Germann was senior professor in the Department of Electrical Engineering, but he had no teaching assignments in that department. Joseph William Gray, Assistant Professor of Electrical Engineering, taught the Electrical Engineering courses.

In the Physics Department, Joseph Gray assisted in "General Physics" laboratory each semester. Frank Germann had all other departmental teaching responsibilities. In the first semester: "General Physics" lectures, "Analytical Mechanics" lectures, "Electron Theory and Radioactivity" lectures, "Electrical Measurements" laboratory, "Chemical Physics" lectures, and "Electrolytes and Electrolysis" lectures. In the second semester: "General Physics" lectures, "Alternating Currents" laboratory, "Primary and Reversible Batteries" lectures, and "Chemical Physics" laboratory. Frank had previous experience teaching engineers. His main teaching duties at Cornell from 1914 to 1918 had been in the laboratory section of the general physics course taken by mechanical and electrical engineers. It appears that Frank Germann had all the administrative responsibilities within the two departments at the School of Mines, although the organizational structure of the entire institution seems to have been ill defined.

This heavy teaching schedule did not leave time for laboratory research. However, Frank did have the opportunity for on-campus meetings with two special visiting lecturers. Philip E. Argall (1854–1922), expert on the cyanide process for gold extraction and a consulting metallurgist from nearby Denver, spoke to faculty and students on "The Flotation Process." Fred Carroll (Colorado Commissioner of Mines, Denver) spoke on "Oil Flotation of Ores." Frank later (in 1921 and 1923) published papers on this subject.

The Alumni Association of the Colorado School of Mines had suspended publication of its periodical (*The Colorado School of Mines Magazine*) during the Great War. After the Armistice was signed on November 11, 1918, the Alumni Association decided to resume publication. That first restart issue, dated January 1919, contained a detailed exposition of "Radioactivity and Radioactive Transformations," as well as details of "Methods of Determining the Radium Content of Minerals," each by the School of Mines newly-appointed professor Frank Germann. Frank was ready with material for eleven printed pages on radium. He had only a few weeks between the Alumni Association's decision to resume publication and the printer's deadline. In addition, this was during his busy end-of-semester examination schedule and Christmas-time activities. Frank evidently had been thinking about radioactivity and radium for some time, and he must have written drafts of these two manuscripts earlier, probably at Cornell as he contemplated his career change. These drafts had also provided lecture notes for his first-semester School of Mines course "Electron Theory and Radioactivity."

The physical facilities at the School of Mines were inadequate for any experiments that could have furthered Frank's research. The home of the Physics Department was in a three-building complex (sections built in 1880, 1882, and 1890) called the Hall of Chemistry. Typical of academic chemistry buildings built in this era, it contained an office and private laboratory for the senior professor of chemistry, as well as a chemical lecture hall (with a lecture bench designed for chemical demonstrations, including a chemical-resistant tabletop, with piped-in and wired-in utilities), a chemical storeroom, and several general-purpose classrooms. The teaching laboratory for physics courses was in this building complex. There was only minimal office space for other chemistry faculty and for physics faculty. The School of Mines barely had a graduate program; just two graduate students enrolled in 1918–1919.

There were severe systemic and personal administrative problems within the Colorado School of Mines. Victor Clifton Alderson (born 1862) was President, with an overt agenda that catered to the shale oil industry. Alderson was initially hired in 1903 as Principal Professor (then the title for the President of the School of Mines). Before coming to the School of Mines, he had been Dean of Engineering and Acting President of the Armour Institute of Technology in Chicago. "Upon coming to Mines, Dr. Alderson became very interested in the oil shale deposits in Western Colorado and became active in working with the oil shale interests there. The Board of Trustees became concerned with this outside work, as they believed the President should devote his full time efforts to CSM. This, along with Dr. Alderson's history of friction between him and the students, faculty, and Board of Trustees, caused the Board to fire him in 1913." Brief presidential stints by William G. Haldane (1913), William B. Phillips (1915), and Howard C. Parmelee (1916) followed. Then the Board of Trustees hired Victor Clifton Alderson again, this time beginning in the 1917–1918 academic year.

President Alderson continued his vigorous activities involving oil shale, activities both outside and inside the School of Mines. He organized an Oil Shale Symposium with the American Mining Congress in 1918, and published the first in a series, *The Oil Shale Industry,* under the auspices of the School of Mines. Within two years, he had several other members of the small faculty engaged with him in oil-shale promotion and shale-oil research. In 1923, President Alderson was dismissed for the second time.

Frank Germann wrote on March 27, 1919, to Indiana University President William Lowe Bryan about the situation with School of Mines President Alderson: "[I] have just informed the President that no money could induce me to stay, as I learned that he takes student's words and town gossip as his guide in retaining or discharging men. Until just recently I had refused to believe the tales told on him, but now I have the proof first hand and largely from his own mouth. Some of the best men here are leaving for the same reason that I am, among them the head of the Geology Dept. I feel it my duty to tell you and anyone else to whom he might write for applicants, that a young man would make a great mistake to come here, unless he were of the caliber of a high school teacher, as nearly all of his men are that he retains. They are men who know little if anything beyond what they have to teach. Professor Gray, my assistant, is leaving with me."

Frank was far from alone in his assessment of problems in the President's Office at the School of Mines. The report of an investigation by the American Association of University Professors found that President Alderson dismissed "strong teachers of professional rank and of long service ... without charges, hearing, or adequate warning; that he lowered the standards of scholarship ... by compelling members of the faculty to change the grades of students, especially of those who had influential relatives." This was one of the early institutional investigations by the American Association of University Professors, an organization founded in 1915 by Arthur Oncken Lovejoy (1873–1962) and John Dewey (1859–1952) to investigate and then publically report on questions of academic freedom and academic tenure in universities and colleges. Since its inception, the A.A.U.P. has played a significant role in American higher education by developing professional standards and procedures that maintain quality in education, and by conducting investigations of reported infractions. The effective action taken by the A.A.U.P. at the School of Mines was influential in getting Frank involved with the A.A.U.P. He stayed involved for the rest of his life. As a national councilor, he later installed an A.A.U.P. chapter at Colorado School of Mines.

The University of Colorado

The year as a physicist at Colorado School of Mines gave Frank Germann an incentive to change institutions and the opportunity to change academic fields. He explored the prospects of a faculty appointment in *chemistry* at the University of Colorado in Boulder, less than twenty miles away. By spring 1919, Frank may have obtained assurance of an appointment in physical chemistry at the University. The University must have been aware of the impending resignation of Harry Alfred Curtis (1884–1963), Professor of Physical Chemistry, from the University faculty. Frank sent his own resignation, dated March 31, 1919, to the Board of Trustees of the School of Mines. The Board accepted his resignation, to take effect August 31, 1919.

Frank's appointment at the University of Colorado was as Associate Professor of Chemistry for the 1919–1920 academic year. He was promoted to the rank of Professor of Chemistry within a year. His next "promotion" by the University was to Professor Emeritus in 1956.

The professional career of Frank Erhart Emmanuel Germann moved into a stable phase in 1919. What was also happening in 1919?

Woodrow Wilson was President of the United States. Indiana's Thomas Riley Marshall was Vice-President. The Treaty of Versailles was signed on June 28, 1919. Albert Germann was on the faculty of Western Reserve University. Albert had been promoted to Assistant Professor of Chemistry for the 1915–1916 academic year, and would be promoted to Associate Professor with tenure in 1921. Henry Baker Brown, President of Valparaiso University (see Chapter 4), had died on September 16, 1917. Acting-President Oliver Perry Kinsey (who, with Brown, had been co-proprietor of Valparaiso University) retired to Florida in May 1919. Flamboyant and charismatic Robert E. Hicks was in Chicago, publishing his new magazine. Hicks would return to South Whitley (see Chapter 5) to buy the Atoz Printing Company at a bankruptcy price in spring 1921. The sixteenth through forty-fourth states ratified the 18th Amendment to the Constitution in January 1919, prohibiting manufacturing, transportation, and sale of alcoholic beverages. On June 4, 1919, Congress passed a Constitutional Amendment guaranteeing American women the right to vote; the Amendment would be ratified August 18, 1920.

The University of Colorado was in the midst of a major transition that would continue for a half century. During the 1919–1920 academic year, a third of its 170-member faculty were in the School of Medicine. With much political controversy, the medical school was gradually moving from Boulder to Denver, the state capitol. By 1925, most of the medical faculty would be on the new School of Medicine campus, a quadrangle of four brick buildings on Ninth Avenue and Colorado Boulevard in Denver. As early as 1912, an Extension Division of the University of Colorado was functioning in Denver. The Extension Division slowly grew. It would become the University of Colorado–Denver Center in 1964, and then the University of Colorado at Denver in 1973.

Frank Germann joined a nine-member faculty in the Department of Chemistry on the original Boulder campus. The senior member was Dr. John Bernard Ekeley (1869–1951), Professor of Chemistry and Head of the Department of Chemistry. Frank as Associate Professor was second in seniority by rank. The other members of the Department were:

> Paul M. Dean, Ph.D., Assistant Professor
> Charles F. Poe, A.M., B.S. (Phar.), Instructor
> Horace B. Van Valkenburgh, M.S., Instructor
> Benjamin D. Cornell, A.M., Instructor
> Eva M. Baum, A.B., Instructor
> William Warren Howe, A.B., Instructor
> Emmett B. Carmichael, A.B., Instructor

The three men who constituted the senior chemistry faculty in 1919–1920 were to lead the Department of Chemistry for many years. John Ekeley retired in 1937. Paul Dean retired in 1953. Frank Germann retired in 1956. A fourth man, Charles Poe, would become the University's second Dean of Pharmacy in 1946, and then serve as Dean until his retirement from the University in 1956. A great deal can be inferred about the collegial atmosphere within the Chemistry Department from the several biographical sketches that follow in this chapter.

Several promotions took effect for the 1920–1921 academic year, resulting in the following faculty, listed in order of rank, and within each rank, in order of appointment:

John Bernard Ekeley, Professor
Frank E. E. Germann, Professor
Paul M. Dean, Associate Professor
Charles F. Poe, Assistant Professor
Horace B. Van Valkenburgh, Assistant Professor
Benjamin D. Cornell, Instructor
Eva M. Baum, Instructor
Emmett B. Carmichael, Instructor

Instructor Eva M. Baum died on November 26, 1921. The University funded eight Assistant in Chemistry positions for the 1921–1922 academic year, providing paid student teaching assistantships to support an expanding graduate program. The Department of Chemistry for 1921–1922, including the Assistants in Chemistry, was composed of:

John Bernard Ekeley, Professor
Frank E. E. Germann, Professor
Paul M. Dean, Associate Professor
Charles F. Poe, Assistant Professor
Horace B. Van Valkenburgh, Assistant Professor
Benjamin D. Cornell, Instructor
Emmett B. Carmichael, Instructor
Glen Wakeham, B.S., Instructor in Piano and Assistant in Chemistry
Dwight A. Cummings, A.B., Assistant in Chemistry
Inez Y. Riffe, A.B., Assistant in Chemistry
Emmet C. Rogers, B.S., Assistant in Chemistry
Margaret V. Smith, A.B., Assistant in Chemistry
Margaret Swisher, B.S. (Phar.), Assistant in Chemistry
Ralph N. Traxler, A.B., Assistant in Chemistry
Kenyon C. Vail, B.S. (Ch.E.), Assistant in Chemistry

John Bernard Ekeley

John Bernard Ekeley was born on January 1, 1869, in Örebro län, a county in central Sweden. His early education was in Omaha, Nebraska. He received the A.B. (1891) and A.M. (1893) degrees from Colgate University, Hamilton, New York. John Ekeley then began teaching science, becoming Science Master at St. Paul's School, Garden City, Long Island, New York. St. Paul's, an Episcopal boys college preparatory and science boarding school, opened in 1879 in a new building, the gift of the widow of multi-billionaire businessman Alexander Turney Stewart (1803–1876), founder of Garden City. While teaching at St. Paul's, Ekeley wrote and published a detailed illustrated laboratory manual for high school chemistry classes. Chemical laboratory instruction in schools was new in much of America. In Chapter 1, we wrote that Edward Williams Morley introduced "the laboratory method of chemistry instruction" at Western Reserve College in September 1869, perhaps the first such course in any western college. Also in Chapter 1, we noted that Harvey Washington Wiley taught Indiana's first laboratory course in chemistry in 1873 at a medical school.

John Ekeley then went to Europe for advanced studies in chemistry, working with Albert Edinger (1865–1914) at the Albert Ludwig University of Freiburg in Breisgau, Baden-Württemberg, Germany. Ekeley earned the Ph.D. degree from Albert Ludwig University in 1902. His thirty-three-page inaugural dissertation was published as *Uber die Einwirkung von Halogenschwefel auf Paratoluchinolin* (Freiburg im Breisgau: Speyer & Kaerner, 1902). Immediately after becoming Dr. Ekeley, John joined the faculty of the University of Colorado as Professor of Chemistry and Head of the Department of Chemistry. John Ekeley, third man to head the Chemistry Department, was the first to devote full-time energies to the post. He was founder of the modern Department of Chemistry at the University, and remained Head of the Department for thirty-five years. He retired in 1937.

Chemistry had a strong presence at the University of Colorado from the very beginning of the institution. The University of Colorado opened on Wednesday, September 5, 1877, with two instructors, forty-four students, and one building. Joseph Addison Sewall, the first President of the University and one of its two instructors, presided at the opening ceremonies. *Sewell was a chemist.* He had been recruited from Illinois State Normal University (now Illinois State University) in Normal, Illinois, where he had been a member of the faculty for sixteen years.

Joseph Addison Sewall (1830–1917) was born in Scarborough, Maine. His father was a physician. Joseph graduated from the Biddeford (Maine) High School. He interned with his father and read medicine in Maine, then established an independent medical practice in Bangor about 1852. After two years, the young man moved west to Illinois, where he taught school in Princeton (Bureau County). He established a drug store in the small village of Tonica (LaSalle County). He may have practiced medicine in Tonica as an adjunct to his service as the village pharmacist and the community's only mercantile chemist. Nearby, at a railroad junction just north of Bloomington (McLean County), Illinois State Normal University was being founded.

Charles Edward Hovey (1827–1897), a native of Vermont, was the first Principal of the new Normal University. He met with Joseph Sewall in Bloomington in 1858. Hovey was actively recruiting faculty, and he offered Sewall a position. Sewall, whose slim résumé included skimpy stints in medicine, pharmacy, and classroom teaching, would be expected to teach all the natural sciences at the university level envisioned by Hovey. The details of their conversations are lost, but Hovey "sent Dr. Joseph Addison Sewall to Harvard so that the physician could prepare to teach 'agricultural chemistry'…" Published references to Joseph Addison Sewall often include the appellation "Dr.," but there is no documentary evidence that he ever earned a doctorate. During the next two years, Sewall attended classes and lectures at the Sheffield Scientific School of Yale University in New Haven, Connecticut, and at the Lawrence Scientific School of Harvard University in Cambridge, Massachusetts.

Sheffield Scientific School was founded as Yale Scientific School in 1847 by chemists John Pitkin Norton (1822–1852) and Benjamin Silliman Jr. (1816–1885), with encouragement from Benjamin Silliman Sr. (1779–1864). The senior Silliman (Yale A.B., 1796; Yale A.M. 1799), one of the first American professors of science, had been appointed in 1802 to Yale's new professorship of "chymistry and natural history." His first classroom laboratory—"the world's first teaching laboratory for modern chemistry"—was built mostly underground as part of the Old Brick Row in the middle of what is now Yale's Old Campus quadrangle. In July 1818, he founded the *American Journal of Science*, the oldest scientific journal in the United States.

Although technically retired from the Yale faculty, the senior Silliman was still giving lectures on geology when Sewall was in New Haven. The school was renamed in 1861 in recognition of gifts from New Haven philanthropist Joseph Earl Sheffield (1793–1882). The Sheffield Scientific School and the Yale College Academic Department were separate entities until 1945.

Lawrence Scientific School at Harvard University was founded in 1847 with a gift from Massachusetts industrialist Abbott Lawrence (1792–1855). Among the prominent scientists associated with Lawrence Scientific School when Sewall was in Cambridge were Asa Gray (1810–1888), enthusiastic advocate of the ideas of Charles Darwin and perhaps the foremost American botanist of the century; paleontologist Jean Louis Agassiz (1807–1873), renowned director of Harvard's Museum of Comparative Zoology and a lifelong opponent of Charles Darwin's theories of evolution; and Eben Norton Horsford (1818–1893), a student of German organic chemist Justus von Liebig. Horsford was co-founder of the Rumford Chemical Works, and creator of the present formulation of baking powder. It was not unusual for a student to attend classes without being a candidate for a degree; in 1859, sixty-two students were enrolled in Lawrence Scientific School, but only nine degrees were awarded. Lawrence Scientific School and Harvard College were separate entities until 1906.

Sewall returned to Illinois in 1860, and joined the faculty of Illinois State Normal University as Professor of Natural Sciences, at an annual salary of $1,500. In 1862, he was in complete charge of instruction in science. His colleague John Wesley Powell (1834–1902), although not officially a member of the faculty, lectured in science courses and was the prime mover in expanding the collections of the Illinois State Natural History Museum, housed on campus. Both Sewall and Powell served terms as Curator of the Museum. Powell was to achieve prominence by leading an 1869 expedition that included the first scientific exploration of the Grand Canyon. Powell was director of the United States Geological Survey from 1881 to 1894.

New England native Joseph Addison Sewall had made the adventuresome trek west to Illinois when he was 24. He made an equally adventuresome move further west at age 47 when he left Illinois in 1877 to become the first President of the University of Colorado. He returned briefly to Illinois in June 1879 to receive an honorary Ph.D. from Knox College, Galesburg, Illinois. Former President Albert Hurd (1823–1906), who was still on the Knox faculty as Professor of Chemistry and Physical Science, probably nominated Sewall for the degree. It was the first Ph.D. awarded by Knox College. It was the first doctorate for Joseph Addison Sewall.

Sewall, when President of the University of Colorado, also occupied the Chair of Chemistry. Ten years later (in 1887), when Sewall was replaced in the presidency by Horace Morrison Hale, Sewall was replaced in the Chair of Chemistry by Charles Palmer.

Charles Skeele Palmer (1858–1939), second Head of the Department of Chemistry at the University of Colorado, was born in Danville, Illinois. He attended Chicopee (Massachusetts) High School, and then nearby Amherst College, Amherst, Massachusetts, earning the B.A. degree in 1879 and then the M.A. in 1882. He taught in Massachusetts public schools in West Warren, Florence, and North Andover from 1879 to 1884. Palmer entered the doctoral program in chemistry at The Johns Hopkins University in Baltimore in 1884. He was a Graduate Fellow in Chemistry in 1885–1886. His research was with Ira Remsen (1846–1927), and he received the Ph.D. in 1886 with the dissertation "On Benzoyl-phenyl-sulph-imide and Its Derivatives." He worked for the next year at G. & C. Merriam Company of Springfield, Massachusetts, at the time when George and Charles Merriam were preparing their first edition of *Webster's International Dictionary* (1890).

Charles Palmer went west in 1887 to become Professor of Chemistry at the University of Colorado. He was granted a leave of absence for 1892–1893 to study at the University of Leipzig (Universität Leipzig, founded in 1409) with physical chemist Wilhelm Friedrich Ostwald (1853–1932; Nobel laureate 1909).

He resigned from the University of Colorado in July 1902, and was appointed Principal (President) of the Colorado School of Mines in fall 1902. "This was during a period of student and faculty unrest. Palmer, along with most of the faculty, was removed from office by the Board of Trustees in Spring 1903. Palmer was succeeded by Victor Alderson." We have already discussed Frank Germann's unpleasant interactions with Victor Alderson at the School of Mines.

John Bernard Ekeley joined the University of Colorado faculty in 1902. He was the third Head of the Department of Chemistry. The University was still small. There were 510 collegiate students and 105 members of the faculty and staff. Finances were perennially perilous. For several years, John Ekeley was the only member of the Chemistry Department with a doctorate, the only member of the Chemistry Department in the professorial ranks. For example, in 1905–1906 the Chemistry Department consisted of Professor Ekeley and three assistants. Two of his assistants had only B.A. degrees, and the third (with no academic degree) probably was an undergraduate. Ekeley was the lecturer and discussion leader in every chemistry course—general, analytical, organic, physical, and more. He alone determined the curriculum, and he alone was responsible for the content of the practical laboratory courses. He was also the only institutional advocate for funding chemistry facilities—space, supplies, equipment, and personnel.

In spite of the heavy teaching and administrative responsibilities, John Ekeley found time and enthusiasm for experimental research on a wide range of subjects. He submitted at least five research reports to the new *University of Colorado Studies,* including a paper in the inaugural volume. *University of Colorado Studies* was distributed free to many college and university libraries in exchange for receiving similar publications from the recipient institutions. He also submitted a lengthy article to the *University of Colorado Journal of Engineering.*

From the perspective of a non-chemist, his most interesting research report was on quantitative analyses of arsenic in the organs of a human cadaver. He wrote: "Some years ago the writer made a very complete chemico-legal examination of the organs of G...... R......, who had died from the effects of arsenic, criminally administered. The results of the analyses appeared at the time in a publication of local circulation. The writer is not aware of any other investigation carried out to such an extent upon the body of a person *known to have died from arsenic poisoning.* It is therefore desirable that the results of this investigation find their way into the literature of arsenical poisoning."

John Ekeley also found time to write another book, *A Laboratory Manual of Inorganic Chemistry* (New York: John Wiley & Sons, 1912). John Wiley published this lab manual to accompany its popular text, *A Text Book of Inorganic Chemistry* by Arnold Frederick Holleman. Dr. Ekeley was identified on the title page as John B. Ekeley, Ph.D., Sc.D., recognition that Colgate University had awarded him an honorary Doctor of Science degree (Sc.D., *Scientiæ Doctor honoris causa*) in 1911.

John Ekeley initiated the graduate program in the Department of Chemistry. One of his first graduate students, Paul Marshall Dean (born 1885), received a master's degree in chemistry from the University of Colorado. His thesis, as deposited in the University Library, was a bound offprint of a published article: John B. Ekeley and Paul M. Dean, "The Action of Acetic Anhydride on Some Benzylidene Anthranilic Acids," *Journal of the American Chemical Society*, vol. 34, no. 2 (February 1912), pp. 161–164. The library catalogued the thesis with the description "M.S. University of Colorado 1912." Dean entered the doctoral program at the University of Illinois, studying under the direction of Clarence George Derick (1883–1980). In his 1916 Ph.D. thesis ("The Scale of Influence of Substituents in Paraffin Monobasic Acids. The Phenyl Radical"), he included the following biographical note on page 67: "The writer received the Bachelor of Arts degree from the University of Colorado in 1908. During the year 1908–1909, he taught in the High School at Golden, Colorado. The following year he held the position of chemist at the plant of the Western Chemical Manufacturing Company in Denver, Colorado. In the fall of 1910, he entered the Graduate School of the University of Colorado, receiving the Master of Arts degree in the spring of 1911. From the fall of 1911 until the present time, the writer has been Instructor in Chemistry in the University of Colorado. From the spring of 1914 until the fall of 1915, he studied Chemistry in the University of Illinois." Paul Dean rapidly rose through the ranks in the University of Colorado Department of Chemistry, becoming Assistant Professor in 1917, Associate Professor in 1920, and Professor in 1923. He served as Head of the Department of Chemistry from 1943 until his retirement in 1953. Paul Dean was Assistant Professor when Frank Germann joined the Department.

Charles Franklin Poe (1888–1970) was Instructor of Chemistry when Frank Germann joined the faculty. Poe was born in Golden, Colorado. He received both the B.A. and A.M. degrees in Chemistry from the University of Colorado in 1911. His master's thesis was "A Study of Boulder's Milk Supply with the View of Establishing a Bacterial Standard." In 1913, the University organized a separate School of Pharmacy on the Boulder campus, and in 1914 awarded its first B.S. degree in Pharmacy to Charles Poe. At the same, Poe received the Ph.C. (Pharmaceutical Chemist) degree. During the Great War, he served two years as a Captain in the armed forces. After the War, he joined the chemistry faculty of the University of Colorado: in 1919–1920, he was Instructor of Chemistry; in 1920–1921 and 1921–1922, he was Assistant Professor of Chemistry. He entered a doctoral program in the Department of Chemistry at Cornell University in 1924, and took a year leave of absence from the University of Colorado in 1925–1926. Cornell awarded him the Ph.D. degree on September 25, 1926. His doctoral thesis was "Study of Media for the Production of Bacterial Fluorescence."

In 1946, Charles Poe became the University's second Dean of Pharmacy. By then, the School of Pharmacy had become the College of Pharmacy. He served as Dean until his retirement from the University in 1956.

Another member of the Chemistry Department when Frank Germann arrived was Horace Bulle Van Valkenburgh II. He was born February 3, 1883, in Warren, the county seat of Bradley County, Arkansas. Warren had a population of 301 in 1880. He was son of Sally Catherine Smith and Horace Bulle Van Valkenburgh. In 1901, the junior Van Valkenburgh entered the University of Arkansas (Fayetteville), where he was Associate Editor of *The Cardinal* (the school yearbook, later named *The Razorback*), President of the Mathetian Literary Society, Class Treasurer, and a varsity football player. He received the B.S. degree in 1905. He and his wife (née Beulah Williams, also a 1905 graduate of the University of Arkansas) then spent time in China as missionary volunteers for the Southern Presbyterian Church. A son, Horace Bulle Van Valkenburgh III, was born in China on July 15, 1908.

After their return to Fayetteville, Horace entered the graduate program of the University of Arkansas (where a new chemistry building had been built in 1905), earning the M.S. degree in Chemistry in 1912. His two-part analytical chemistry thesis: "The Adsorption of Iron by Strontium Sulphate Precipitates. Potassium Chlorate as a Standardizing Substance for Solutions of Alkali." He was appointed Instructor in the University of Colorado Chemistry Department in 1917, and was promoted to Assistant Professor in 1920.

Perhaps Van Valkenburgh's most famous student was John Christian Bailar Jr. (1904–1991). Bailer's parents—Rachel Ella Work and John C. Bailer Sr.—were said to have been "the first married couple to enrol in and graduate from the University of Colorado." John Sr. was Instructor of Chemistry at the School of Mines in Golden in 1904, and by the 1920s had become a senior research chemist at Great Western Sugar Company in Denver. John Jr. was born in Golden. He attended the University of Colorado, joined Alpha Chi Sigma (the national chemistry fraternity), and received the B.A. degree in 1924 and the M.A. degree in 1925. His graduate research, directed by Van Valkenburgh, resulted in Bailar's first scholarly publication. Bailer was to publish almost three hundred more papers and several books. After receiving his Ph.D. at the University of Michigan, he joined the faculty of the University of Illinois at Urbana–Champaign. Bailar remained at Illinois for sixty-three years, receiving many national and international awards, especially in inorganic coordination chemistry.

Van Valkenburgh entered the Graduate School of the University of Chicago on September 30, 1922, and enrolled in coursework during five academic quarters: Autumn 1922, Winter 1923, Spring 1923, Summer 1925, and Summer 1926. His doctoral research was with Hermann Irving Schlesinger (1882–1960), Professor of Chemistry. He presented his results in two papers, and in his two-part doctoral thesis: "I. Ferrous Nitroso Compounds. II. The Structure of Ferric Thiocyanate and the Thiocyanate Test for Iron." He received the Ph.D. degree from the University of Chicago on June 10, 1930.

An Office, a Lab, and a Research Group

When Frank Germann came to the University of Colorado campus, the Department occupied the three-story Chemistry Building. Teaching laboratories for organic and physiological chemistry, for food analysis, and for water analysis were in the basement. On the ground floor were the balance room and a sample-combustion room, as well as teaching laboratories for introductory inorganic chemistry, qualitative analytical chemistry, and quantitative analytical chemistry. Teaching laboratories for physical chemistry, advanced analytical chemistry, and gas analysis were on the top floor.

Also on the top floor was an auditorium with seating for 250 students. The lecture desk was designed for chemical demonstrations, fitted with a chemical-resistant surface, and supplied with water, gas, suction pumps, electricity, and an exhaust system to remove fumes and noxious gases. Adjacent to this main lecture hall was a room for storage of chemicals and apparatus for lecture demonstrations, and for preparation of demonstrations just before class. Close to the lecture hall were the chemistry library, and Professor Ekeley's study and private laboratory. Frank Germann's private laboratory was on the ground floor.

Finally having appropriate chemical laboratory facilities at his disposal, Frank began to plan his own experimental research involving the chemistry of radium. The first chemical step used by Marie Skłodowska-Curie in separating radium from pitchblende was removal of barium compounds from the ore. Radioactivity followed the barium, indicating that barium and radium have similar chemical properties. In Switzerland, Frank had studied the adsorption of gases on elemental iodine and silver. Frank decided to investigate aspects of radium chemistry by studying another adsorption phenomenon—the adsorption from solution of radium cations onto surfaces of solid barium sulfate. [A cation is a chemical species with a positive charge. A radium cation in a solution of radium bromide ($RaBr_2$) is Ra^{+2}.] To give the radium cations uniform three-dimensional surfaces for adsorption, Frank prepared very small particles of freshly precipitated barium sulfate.

He was interested in applying newly developed physical chemical theories of adsorption phenomena and surface chemistry to interpret his experimental data. Practical implications for the local mining industry also influenced his choice of research topic. Frank observed: "The study of this particular case is of considerable importance in the commercial refining of radium." These experiments were very important to Frank. Frank felt that they should be conducted both carefully and expeditiously. He did not assign the laboratory work to inexperienced students who had other time commitments. He did the experiments himself, and submitted the research results for publication on May 2, 1921. This time, he submitted his paper to a *chemical* journal.

Frank determined the radium concentration in a solution by measuring the radioactivity of "radium emanation" captured from above the heated solution. "Radium emanation" (a name no longer used) is the gas radon, a radioactive "noble element" with the symbol Rn and atomic number 86. Herman Schlundt and Richard B. Moore at the University of Missouri had described this analytical procedure in 1905. Frank Germann later (in 1924) published details of his own adaptation of the emanation method.

Arriving at the University of Colorado as a physical chemist, Frank quickly established his own physical chemistry research group. During his thirty-seven years on the faculty, Frank would supervise the research of at least twenty-three students who then completed the requirements for graduate degrees at the University. His research students came from diverse backgrounds, and their subsequent careers were varied. Biographical snapshots of several of those students are included in this chapter. We begin with Ralph Traxler.

The Chemistry of Photography

Frank gave an experimental project (adsorption of elemental iodine on solid silver iodide crystals) to his first graduate student, Ralph Newton Traxler.

Ralph Traxler was born in Lamar, the county seat of Prowers County, Colorado, in 1897. Lamar had a population of less than a thousand when Ralph was born. His father was a lawyer. The family lived at 503 South Third Street, between Pearl Street and Parmenter Street, within walking distance of both the courthouse and the school. Ralph attended Lamar High School, where he was President of his Freshman Class, an editor of the school yearbook (*The Harbinger*), and a member of the Debate Club. He gave the Senior Class Oration on Thursday, May 25, 1916, as part of his Lamar High School graduation activities. He entered the University of Colorado, took a leave of absence to serve in the Army during the Great War, and then returned to the University of Colorado to complete a major in chemistry. He received the A.B. degree in June 1920. After working in an industrial research laboratory, he returned to the University of Colorado, where he was appointed Assistant in Chemistry for the 1921–1922 year.

Traxler's project may have initially seemed to be only a variation on Germann's theme of adsorption of radium on barium sulfate. It was based on Wilder Bancroft's "Problem 54 in Colloid Chemistry," in turn derived from observations by the pioneer photography chemist Matthew Carey Lea (1823–1897). Germann and Traxler submitted a research report on July 25, 1921, to the *Journal of the American Chemical Society;* this paper was the basis for Traxler's thesis for the M.A. degree in June 1922. Ralph Traxler continued experimental research on iodine chemistry with Frank Germann during summers after receiving the M.A. One joint paper published in 1925 pursued Bancroft's Problem 53. Another paper published in 1927 reported the chemical synthesis and characterization of iodides of phosphorus. Traxler also took summer-school graduate courses in physics at the University of Colorado.

After receiving the M.A. degree, Ralph Traxler married Mabel Barnett. They moved to Highland, Kansas, where Ralph taught science at Highland High School for the 1922–1923 year. He then was Professor of Chemistry and Physics at Highland College during the 1923–1924 academic year. A son, Ralph N. Traxler Jr. (1923–2001), was born in Highland.

Frank Germann had taken a summer-school course in physical chemistry in 1910 from Professor Louis Kahlenberg at the University of Wisconsin in Madison. Probably on the advice of Frank, Ralph Newton Traxler entered the graduate program of the University of Wisconsin in 1924 to work with Louis Kahlenberg. Traxler received the Ph.D. in Chemistry from Wisconsin in 1926 with research on osmosis. Dr. Traxler then joined the faculty of Macalester College, Saint Paul, Minnesota, as Associate Professor of Chemistry. He was at Macalester for just the 1926–1927 academic year, but was on campus long enough to conduct experimental studies on the rate of osmosis, and to supervise undergraduate research by Harry N. Huntzicker. After Macalester, Traxler worked in research laboratories in New Jersey and at Port Neches, Texas. Their other son, Richard Warwick Traxler (1928–2010), was born in New Orleans. In 1951, Ralph was Director of Asphalt Research at the Texas Company (after May 1959, Texaco, Incorporated), and President of the Society of Rheology. He became a recognized authority on the chemistry and physics of bituminous pavement materials.

After three decades in industrial research, Traxler accepted an appointment to the Texas Transportation Institute on February 1, 1959. The appointment was as Research Engineer in the Asphalt Technology Department, located on the campus of the Agricultural and Mechanical College of Texas in College Station. He was also appointed Professor of Chemistry and Professor of Civil Engineering at the College. In 1963, the College was renamed Texas A&M University, with the logotype A&M considered only an historical symbol, no longer standing for "Agricultural and Mechanical." During his years at A&M, Traxler wrote a major book on asphalt and was author or co-author of several publications related to asphalt. He retired from the Institute on August 31, 1975.

Matthew Carey Lea's published research reports led to a series of experiments in the Germann laboratory on the chemistry of photography. From the beginnings of photography until the late twentieth century, capture of an optical image was a chemical phenomenon. Making the captured image permanent was an early chemical research challenge of immense practical importance. Johann Heinrich Schulze (1687–1744) observed that silver nitrate and silver chloride, both white crystalline substances when pure and kept in the dark, change color when exposed to light. In about 1724, he was able to capture a fleeting image using silver salts. Schulze was not able to make his images permanent.

Louis-Jacques-Mandé Daguerre (1787–1851) in 1839 announced the daguerreotype. William Henry Fox Talbot (1800–1877) in 1841 announced the calotype. Frederick Scott Archer (1813–1857) invented the collodion wet plate process in 1848. The daguerreotype process, the calotype process, and the collodion wet plate process involve production of an invisible latent image when silver salts are exposed to light. In each case, the latent image can then be made permanent by chemical development.

Richard Leach Maddox (1816–1902), a contemporary of Matthew Carey Lea, in 1871 described his new method of coating glass plates with a gelatin emulsion in which microscopic crystals of a silver halide were imbedded. After exposure to light in a camera, the emulsion held the invisible latent image. That image could be made visible by a chemical development process that converted sensitized silver salts into black grains of metallic silver. The unsensitized silver salts were then washed away. Although the latent image was unstable, the metallic silver image was permanent.

Before this "dry emulsion method" became available, professional photographers carried portable laboratory equipment and chemicals with their cameras into the field. The photographers were, of necessity, practicing chemists wherever they shot their photos. The dry emulsion plates permitted the "wet chemistry" to be postponed, performed later in a dark room.

George Eastman (1854–1932) finally removed the skilled chemist from active involvement in popular photography. Eastman invented and patented a dry-plate emulsion-coating machine. In 1884, the Eastman Dry Plate and Film Company began to produce dry emulsion on rollable film. He coined the word "Kodak," and formed the Eastman Kodak Company in 1892. By 1900, he had introduced the Brownie camera that even a child could use. Many such innovations transformed photography into an enterprise in which the fundamental operations gave generally predictable results. However, much mystery continued to surround photographic processes. In the 1920s, persistent mysteries involved the fundamental nature of the latent photographic image, and the reasons for photosensitivity of silver halides.

Matthew Carey Lea was given explicit credit for inspiring Ralph Traxler's first research project. The cited Lea paper recorded the experimental observation that "silver iodide has the property of taking up and retaining small portions of iodine." However, Lea's paper was largely concerned with photosensitivity of silver halides. Doctoral student Malcolm Cleveland Hylan, in the Germann laboratory, was investigating that photosensitivity, fundamental to understanding the chemical nature of silver-halide photography. His Ph.D. thesis in 1923 was "Adsorption in Photography," and there were three joint research publications (Germann and Hylan) on silver halides in photography.

Malcolm Cleveland Hylan (September 29, 1896–December 15, 1944) was born in Westboro, Massachusetts, son of Lillian Rice and Rev. Albert Hylan. He was salutatorian of Medfield, Massachusetts, High School, where he graduated in a class of seven on Thursday, June 18, 1914. He received the degree of Bachelor of Philosophy (Ph.B.) from Brown University, Providence, Rhode Island, in the Class of 1918. He served as Lt. Colonel (Ordnance) in the Great War. After the War, he returned to Brown to earn the M.A. degree in 1920. After receiving his doctorate with Frank Germann, Dr. Malcolm Hylan stayed in Boulder. He later joined the Department of Physics at the University of Colorado, where he continued research on the photographic latent image. Hyland worked with physicist Julian M. Blair. At about the same time, Germann and Blair were collaborating with Thomas Howard James in studies of the latent image.

Dzu-Kun Shen and Thomas Howard James, two of Frank Germann's doctoral students, concentrated on investigations of the latent image in black-and-white silver halide photography. The silver halides investigated in Germann's laboratory were silver bromide (AgBr) and silver iodide (AgI). Shen's Ph.D. thesis in 1928 was "Photographic Sensitivity and the Latent Image." James' Ph.D. thesis in 1935 was "The Nature of the Latent Photographic Image from a Theoretical and Experimental Point of View." James' M.A. thesis, also completed in 1935, was "The Influence of Salts upon Intermittent Photographic Exposures."

Shen came to the University of Colorado from Lehigh University, Bethlehem, Pennsylvania, where he received the Master of Science degree in June 1923. He had entered Lehigh University in 1921–1922 from Hankow, China. "Shen spent four years at Chili Technical College, Tientsin, China, graduating in 1915 with the honor of having been head of his class every year. He continued his good work at Hanyang Arsenal, China, where he worked as a chemist until sent to Washington in 1921 as a member of the Chinese Delegation to the Disarmament Conference."

Research with Frank Germann was James' introduction to experimental and theoretical photographic chemistry. It was the beginning of his illustrious scientific career. Thomas Howard James (November 7, 1912–August 24, 2000) was born in Boulder. He graduated with a B.A. in Chemistry from the University of Colorado in 1932. He then began graduate studies on the chemistry of photography with Frank Germann, earning M.A. and Ph.D. degrees in 1935. James joined the research laboratories of Eastman Kodak Company, Rochester, New York, in January 1936, and became Department Head of Kodak's Phototheory Laboratory in 1972. He retired from Kodak in 1977. During his years at Kodak, he also taught courses in photographic theory at the University of Rochester and at Rochester Institute of Technology. He summarized his many patents as involving photographic developing agents, developer compositions, photographic emulsions, and sensitization by hydrogen. James made major contributions to elucidating the kinetics and chemical mechanisms of photographic development. He was an author of 150 scientific papers.

In 1977, Thomas Howard James received the second Lieven-Gevaert Award, sponsored by the Agfa Corporation, recognizing his outstanding contributions in the field of silver halide photography. Edwin Herbert Land (1909–1991), inventor of Polaroid film and co-founder of the Polaroid Corporation, had received the first award. James received the Raymond C. Bowman Award of the Society for Imaging Science and Technology in 1986. He also received the President Louis-Alphonse Davanne Medal of the Société française de photographie, and the Progress Medal and the Henderson Medal of the Royal Photographic Society of Great Britain. James was an author of several books on photographic theory, and editor of the journal *Photographic Science and Engineering*.

A Sabbatical, the Ku Klux Klan, and Cornell

The University of Colorado granted Germann a sabbatical leave of absence for the 1925–1926 academic year. If the informal practice in Colorado were to count years of service within the entire Colorado higher education system, then this would have been a year leave of absence granted after six years of teaching. Such a practice would have been in general accord with prevailing faculty plans at other institutions, although details varied widely (then as now) across the spectrum of colleges and universities. Frank was familiar with sabbatical leaves. Cornell University had a long-standing sabbatical plan (instituted in 1885), but Frank did not stay the requisite six years at Cornell.

The University of Colorado policy in 2014 is that a "sabbatical is a privilege granted by the University for the advancement of the University, subject to the availability of resources." In 1925–1926, "availability of resources" was problematical because of Ku Klux Klan involvement in state legislation directed at the University, and attempted involvement by the Ku Klux Klan in University administration.

Physician John Galen Locke (1873–1935) was Grand Dragon of the Colorado Ku Klux Klan. He operated from headquarters in the basement of his private hospital in Denver. He organized a disciplined and largely invisible Colorado political primary election campaign in 1924 that placed Klan candidates in strong positions for the general election. Grand Dragon John Galen Locke handpicked gubernatorial candidate Clarence Joseph Morley (1869–1948). It was a landslide for the Klan in the 1924 election. The Klan elected the Governor, the Lieutenant Governor, the Secretary of State, a majority in the House, a substantial bloc in the Senate, and both United States Senators—Rice William Means and Lawrence Phipps.

Under instructions from Grand Dragon Locke, Governor Morley ordered University of Colorado President George Norlin (1871-1942) to dismiss all Catholics and all Jews from the University faculty. President Norlin refused. Rebuffed Klansmen in the House were not able to organize to force President Norlin to acquiesce. They did succeed in adjourning the deadlocked General Assembly before the University funding appropriation for the 1925–1926 academic year could be voted. It was a classic do-nothing legislature. Only a few bills passed the General Assembly, including one forbidding picking Colorado Blue Columbine (the state flower, *Aquilegia coerulea*), another allowing counties to kill prairie dogs, and a third authorizing convicts to manufacture automobile license plates in prison.

The political influence of the Ku Klux Klan in Colorado had risen unexpectedly. The Klan's power peaked with the election in November 1924. Its political power in the state was extremely short lived. The Klan had won the 1924 Colorado election, but it could not govern.

President George Norlin, loyal to the University and its ideals, successfully resisted the Klan's attacks. Norlin, a Greek scholar, had joined the University of Colorado faculty in 1899. He was Acting President in 1917. He became President in 1919, and was to serve as President for twenty-two years. The President must have been pleased when Frank Germann informed him that the Carnegie Corporation was funding his 1925–1926 sabbatical leave. The University did not have to pay Frank's salary during this financially troubled year. Carnegie Corporation had helped President George Norlin through the Klan-manufactured crisis.

Frank Germann spent the 1925–1926 sabbatical year in Ithaca, New York, with Martha, seven-year-old Richard, and three-year-old Lois Marie. Frank was back again at Cornell University, this time in the Chemistry Department. Also on leave from the University of Colorado Chemistry Department that year was Charles Franklin Poe, who spent the year at Cornell studying bacterial fluorescence and completing work on his Ph.D. thesis. Charles had married Frances Elizabeth Woland (1892–1967) on June 27, 1913. They had three children: Emily E., Alice L., and Frances E. The Poe sisters were about the same ages as the Germann children. Perhaps the entire Poe family spent the year in Ithaca with the Germann family.

Albert Germann was 350 miles away in Cleveland in 1925, having become Research Director of Laboratory Products Company. There may have been an opportunity for cousins Barbara, Edith, Lucia, Richard, and Lois to visit during the school year, but probably the opportunities came during summers 1925 and 1926 in Indiana when the Germann clan gathered as Martha, Frank, Richard, and Lois passed through Fort Wayne and Peru. By the end of summer 1926, Albert had become Professor of Chemistry and Head of the Department of Chemistry at Valparaiso University, and Ida and the girls had moved to 123 West 3rd Street in Peru. More about that in Chapter 4.

Frank described the facilities available for his sabbatical research as including "splendidly equipped laboratories," a very different description than he would have given during his 1914 to 1918 years at Cornell. Then he was in the Physics Department in Rockefeller Hall. A devastating fire during the winter of 1915–1916 had almost razed Morse Hall, the Cornell chemical laboratory building. In the intervening years, a new chemistry building had been designed and constructed, funded with a gift of $1,500,000 from New York financier and philanthropist George

Fisher Baker (1840–1931). The Baker Laboratory was dedicated in 1923. The building included a spacious (22 ft × 35 ft) third-floor laboratory room reserved for visiting research chemists.

The visiting-chemists laboratory room was near several spectroscopy laboratories, with "state-of-the-art instrumentation" that had been purchased as part of the George Fisher Baker gift. "State of the art" in 1925 implied precision optical components. Emission spectra were captured directly on photographic media—photosensitive paper, emulsion-coated film, or emulsion-coated glass plates. The data were obtained in the dark or under subdued red light, and then made permanent by developing the media in a photographic darkroom. Electronic instrumentation was in the future. Mechanical pen-and-paper recorders for acquiring spectroscopy data directly from chemical experiments did not become available for another quarter century. It would be a half century before even primitive digital computer technology became common-place in physical chemistry laboratories. Physical chemistry laboratory records in 1925 were numerical data, procedure descriptions, and experimental observations. These records were written by hand (or drawn by hand) on the paper pages of bound note-books, supplemented for spectroscopy experiments with photographic images.

Fluorescence and Phosphorescence

Frank's sabbatical research plan was to study the fluorescence of platinum cyanides. He intended to emphasize practical applications related to platinum-containing ores. Spectroscopy instrumentation was essential for design of his fluorescence experiments and for subsequent fluorescence measurements.

Graduate students at Colorado later extended Frank's sabbatical research on the chemistry of platinum compounds and other cyanides. Derk Vivian Tieszen studied the salt sodium platinocyanide. Oscar Brauer Muench devised a method for the quantitative chemical analysis of hydrates of platinocyanate salts. Charles LeRoy Gibson studied the "dark reaction" that follows irradiation of certain copper cyanides.

Derk Vivian Tieszen (October 19, 1894–January 22, 1960) was born into a large Mennonite family on a farm in Rosefield Township, northwest of Marion Junction, Turner County, South Dakota. Marion Junction was a small village on the Chicago,

Milwaukee and St. Paul Railroad, at a branch of the C. M. & S. P. R. to Running
Water. He was one of thirteen children of Helena Deckert (1859–1948) and the Rev.
Derk P. Tieszen (1859–1946); ten of their children survived into adulthood. His
paternal grandparents were among 598 Mennonites who emigrated from the
Molotschna Colony in Ukraine, arriving in New York aboard the SS *Cimbria* on
August 27, 1874. Twenty-six children and grandchildren of Peter Tieszen (1789–
1873) departed the steamship, went west, and settled in Rosefield Township. By
1954, descendants in the United States of those Tieszens numbered at least 1,174.
Helena Deckert was the daughter of Maria Schartner and Wilhelm Deckert. The
Deckert family emigrated from Karlswalde, Wolhynia, Russian Poland, arriving in
New York aboard the SS *Suevia* on November 12, 1875. Helena Deckert and Derk
P. Tieszen were married Saturday, December 4, 1880.

Derk Vivian Tieszen was born in a sod house near the Tieszen Mennonite
Church (now Bethesda Mennonite Church). German was spoken in his home, in his
church, and in the one-room, one-teacher Dick School that he, his siblings, and
many cousins attended for grades one through eight. Unlike one-room schools in
forested regions of the upper Midwest, where local cordwood for heating was available just for the splitting, the Dick School was heated with a coal stove. After eighth
grade, Derk enrolled in the Academic Course of the Mennonite Freeman Academy
in Freeman, thirteen miles from Marion Junction. His father served as a member of
the Board of Directors of Freeman Academy. At his 1920 graduation, Derk received
a high school diploma from the Academy.

Derk then studied for two years at Bethel College, North Newton, Kansas.
Bethel College is the oldest Mennonite college in North America. He transferred to
Yankton College, Yankton, South Dakota, for his junior and senior years. Yankton
College had its own radio station, 9YAK, and Derk was a member of the Radio Club.
He was also on the staff of the yearbook, *The Greyhound*. He received the B.A. degree
in Physical Science on Wednesday, June 11, 1924.

Immediately after graduating from Yankton College, Derk Tieszen began graduate studies at the University of Chicago, taking courses during summers 1924 and
1925. During fall, winter, and spring, from 1924 to 1927, he taught science at Holdrege High School, Holdrege, Nebraska. Holdrege, the county seat of Phelps County,
had a population of about 3,200. Then he received a graduate Assistantship in Chem-

istry at the University of Colorado. His research with Frank Germann on sodium platinocyanide [$Na_2Pt(CN)_4$] earned him the M.A. degree in 1928.

Derk held a replacement faculty position at Goshen College, Goshen, Indiana, for two academic years: 1928–1929 and 1929–1930. Although Bethel College is older than Goshen College, Goshen was the first Mennonite school of higher education in North America to confer a four-year degree. At Goshen, he taught physical science, including courses in chemistry, physics, and earth sciences. He also taught "The Teaching of Physical Science." On Tuesday, June 4, 1929, he married Merle Wilson (1894–1960) of Lincoln, Nebraska; she had been the physical education teacher at Holdrege High School in 1925.

Abram Royer Brubacher (1870–1939), President of The New York State College for Teachers in Albany, recruited Tieszen to join his faculty. Brubacher had been President since 1915, and would serve in that office until his death. He was born in Schaefferstown, Lebanon County, Pennsylvania. He married Rosa M. Haas in Shamokin, Pennsylvania, in 1897. Their son John Seiler Brubacher (1898–1988) boasted that he was a descendant of Pennsylvania Mennonites. President Brubacher had contacts at Mennonite Goshen College who told him about Derk Tieszen, a man with strong science credentials, experience in teaching high school, and an interest in pedagogy. Brubacher hired Tieszen for the 1930–1931 year, and encouraged him to earn a doctorate.

Derk entered the graduate program in chemistry at The Ohio State University (Athens, Ohio). He was awarded the Ph.D. by Ohio State in 1945 with the thesis "Mono-Alkylation of Starch." He retired from The New York State College for Teachers because of ill health in July 1959, having spent twenty-eight years on the faculty. He died January 22, 1960, and was buried in the Tieszen Cemetery of the Bethesda Mennonite Church in Rosefield Township. The College established the Derk V. Tieszen Award, still given "to a senior chemistry major on the basis of demonstrated achievement in chemistry, physics, and mathematics, plus potential as a research worker and teacher of chemistry at an advanced level." In 1962, the College became one of the four centers of the new State University of New York. Its name is now The University at Albany.

Oscar Brauer Muench (1891–1953), son of Louisa and Theodore Muench, was born in Washington, the county seat of Franklin County, Missouri. Washington had a population of about 28,000 when he was born, about 36,000 when he died. Oscar grew up in a house, built by his parents, at 202 West Fifth Street in Washington. His great-grandfather, Friedrich Muench (1799–1881), had been a Lutheran pastor in Nieder Gemünden, Hessen, Germany. In 1834, Friedrich Muench was a leader of the Gießener Auswanderungs gesellschaft (Gießen Emigration Society to the New World) with plans to create a democratic German state in America. According to his descendants, Friedrich played a notable role in Missouri politics at the time of the Civil War, when he served in the Missouri legislature, pushed for emancipation, and helped keep Missouri in the Union.

Oscar Muench graduated from Washington High School in 1909. He then entered the College of Arts and Science of the University of Missouri in Columbia, and received the A.B. degree on September 20, 1913. Oscar continued at his alma mater and began graduate study in chemistry at the University of Missouri, receiving the A.M. degree in 1915 with the dissertation "The Microscopic Examination and Chemical Analysis of Some Pieces of Iron." He was appointed Assistant in Chemistry at the University of Missouri immediately after receiving his A.M. degree. He married Florence A. Bowers (1891–1979). A son Joseph was born in 1921 in Lexington, Missouri, a hundred miles west of Columbia.

Oscar remained associated with the University of Missouri for more than a decade, at the same time pursuing doctoral research at the University of Colorado with Frank Germann. Muench received the Ph.D. from the University of Colorado in June 1928, with the thesis "Lithium Platinocyanide and a Micro Method for the Quantitative Determination of its Hydrates." Muench and Germann continued to collaborate. Five years later, they published "Studies on the Physical and Chemical Properties of the Platinocyanides. I. The Hydrates of Lithium Platinocyanide," *Journal of Physical Chemistry*, vol. 33, no. 3 (1933), pp. 415–423.

Muench also maintained active contact with Professor Herman Schlundt at the University of Missouri. In 1931–1932, Muench spent several months in Schlundt's laboratory, analyzing uranium-containing minerals as part of a project to measure absolute geologic time. He joined the faculty of New Mexico Highlands University, Las Vegas, in August 1928, as Professor of Physics and Chemistry with a salary of $3,000. His title varied over the years from Professor of Physical Sciences to Professor of Chemistry, and he had stints as Head of the

Department. These were rocky years for the University. Muench was President of the Southwestern and Rocky Mountain Division of the American Association for the Advancement of Science in 1949–1950. He retired from New Mexico Highlands on June 21, 1952, as Professor Emeritus of Chemistry. He died a few months later. He was buried in the Wildey Odd Fellows Cemetery in Washington, where Florence would also be buried twenty-six years later.

Charles LeRoy Gibson (1911–December 8, 1944) was born in Clovis, New Mexico, a town created by the Atchison, Topeka and Santa Fe Railway in 1906. The family moved 250 miles west to Belen, New Mexico, a town that had become important to the A. T. & S. F. when the Belen Cutoff was constructed to facilitate transcontinental rail travel. Charles went to school in Belen, and graduated from Belen High School in 1928. In 1929, he entered the University of New Mexico in nearby Albuquerque, where he majored in chemistry and mathematics.

Gibson received the Chester T. French Medal for Scholarship, presented to the graduating senior with the highest academic record in the last two years of college. He also was inducted into Phi Kappa Phi, one of the nation's oldest collegiate academic honor societies, and Kappa Mu Epsilon, a national collegiate mathematics honor society founded in 1930. He was not elected to Phi Beta Kappa, because the University of New Mexico Chapter was not chartered until 1965. In a letter to University of New Mexico President James Fulton Zimmerman on May 18, 1942, Frank Germann wrote: "I proposed his [Charles LeRoy Gibson's] name for election to the honor society Phi Beta Kappa and am pleased to say he was elected last week. Very few people are elected to the society on obtaining the Ph.D. degree, but he is one of the few thoroughly worthy of it." Frank was a charter member of Gamma of Indiana Chapter of Phi Beta Kappa, elected in 1911 as he completed his senior year at Indiana University.

Charles Gibson received the B.S. degree from the University of New Mexico in June 1933. During his senior year, he had decided to explore a career in Education. He elected "Principles of Secondary Education," "City School Administration," and "Problems of the Teaching Profession" in his final semester. Charles then began graduate study in the Department of Education in summer 1933, taking the courses "Philosophy of Education" and "Research Methods of Education," as well as two credits of directed research. Belen High School hired Charles Gibson to teach mathematics during the 1933–1934 school year at a salary of $1,000 for ten months.

Sometime during 1933–1934, Charles' early interest in chemistry was rekindled. The opportunities for graduate study in chemistry at the University of New Mexico then were limited. The department was small. Laboratory equipment and supplies were minimal. He formulated his two-fold professional advancement plan. He obtained an appointment as Assistant in Chemistry at the University of New Mexico, at a salary of $900 for nine months, to start in September 1934. And he entered the chemistry graduate program of the University of Colorado, beginning in June 1934. At New Mexico, he taught in the General Chemistry laboratory and in the Physical Chemistry laboratory. At Colorado, he began experimental photochemical research with Frank Germann.

He received the M.S. degree in 1936 from the University of Colorado. His master's research was published as Frank E. E. German and Charles LeRoy Gibson, "Studies on the Reactions of the Leucocyanides of the Triphenylmethane Dyes. I. The Mechanism of the Dark Reaction Following the Photolysis of Malachite Green Leucocyanide," *Journal of the American Chemical Society*, vol. 62, no. 1 (1940), pp. 110–112. With his M.S. degree in hand, he was promoted to Instructor of Chemistry at the University of New Mexico. His salary was $1,800. He continued research on copper chemistry with Frank Germann, receiving the Ph.D. in 1941. Dr. Gibson was promoted to Assistant Professor of Chemistry in 1942. His salary rose to $2,400.

In 1940–1941 and in 1941–1942, the University of New Mexico Chemistry Department was composed of John Dustin Clark (born 1882; Stanford Ph.D. 1914), Veon Carter Kiech (April 19, 1904–April 1984; New Mexico B.A. 1924, Stanford A.M. 1928, Stanford Ph.D. 1932), and Charles LeRoy Gibson. Gibson collaborated with Veon Kiech to write *Laboratory Manual for General Chemistry* (Albuquerque: University of New Mexico Press, 1939, 1941, 1943; 143 pages). This book was their laboratory textbook in "Chemistry 1."

Charles Gibson was promoted to Associate Professor of Chemistry with tenure for the academic year 1944–1945. He died at the age of 33 on December 8, 1944. In 1945, his widow established the Charles LeRoy Gibson Trust Fund to provide income for the Charles Leroy Gibson Endowed Scholarship, awarded annually to the outstanding senior student who majored or minored in chemistry.

It would be more than a decade before the fluorescence of platinum cyanides could be studied quantitatively at the University of Colorado. This phase of Frank Germann's research program awaited major improvements in instrumentation.

Chemists in 1925 conducted their fluorescence experiments by exposing a sample to their best source of "excitation light" of a single wavelength ("monochromatic light"), and then measuring or estimating the intensity of light (of a longer wavelength) emitted when the sample fluoresced. They obtained monochromatic excitation light by passing light (perhaps from an intense mercury-vapor lamp or from an electric arc formed between two carbon electrodes) through a glass filter that (ideally) transmitted only light of the desired wavelength. Another filter excluded the excitation light and permitted transmission of only the emitted light. In practice, chemists usually had to be satisfied with a narrow band of excitation wavelengths rather than light of a single wavelength.

Analysis of the fluorescence spectrum of a sample could be laborious. In a perfect experiment, one should examine the consequences of monochromatic exciting radiation, with individual experiments at single wavelengths selected throughout a wide range of wavelengths. In practice, only a few satisfactory excitation light sources were available. To analyze the emission spectrum, the fluorescent radiation was passed through a combination of filters, or through a prism, or through a transmission diffraction grating. A prism or a grating yielded a series of spectral lines that could be recorded photographically. The more intense the radiation of a particular wavelength, the darker the line. The wavelength of each line could be determined with precision, but the intensity determination was at best semiquantitative.

When James Hensley (one of Frank's graduate students at Colorado) fifteen years later extended the research that Frank began at Cornell, Hensley constructed his own fluorometer. He measured the emitted light intensity electronically with a glass-enclosed photoelectric tube. One compact instrument of similar design was the Coleman filter fluorometer; it became commercially available in the 1940s. The Coleman instrument had a mercury-vapor lamp for excitation and a photomultiplier tube for detection.

James William Hensley (March 5, 1915–June 24, 1975) was born in Denver, Colorado. He graduated in 1937 from the New Mexico College of Agriculture and Mechanic Arts (since 1960, New Mexico State University), Las Cruces, New Mexico, with a Bachelor of Science degree in Chemical Engineering. He became a graduate student at the University of Colorado, worked with Frank Germann, and received the

M.S. degree in Chemistry in 1939 with the thesis "A Method of Capillary-Fluorescence Analysis." This graduate research resulted in two publications: Frank E. E. Germann and James W. Hensley, "Quantitative Capillary Luminescence Analysis," *Journal of Physical Chemistry,*" vol. 44, no. 9 (September 1940), pp. 1071–1081; and Frank E. E. Germann and J. W. Hensley, "A Direct Vision Fluorometer," *University of Colorado Studies. Series D. Physical and Biological Sciences,* vol. 1, no. 1 (March 1940), pp. 37–41.

Hensley joined the J. B. Ford Company of Wyandotte, Michigan, in 1939 as a member of the research staff. Captain John Baptiste Ford (1811–1903) had created the Michigan Alkali Company in Wyandotte to produce soda ash (Na_2CO_3). He then formed the J. B. Ford Company to use the soda ash to manufacture soaps and other cleaning agents. BASF purchased Michigan Alkali Company and the J. B. Ford Company in 1969. The merged concern was named BASF Wyandotte.

On December 8, 1941, the United States Congress declared war on the Empire of Japan. The next month, James Hensley was called to active duty in the United States Chemical Warfare Service. He served at Edgewood Arsenal, and in North Africa, in Italy, and in the Philippines. He returned to civilian research in 1946.

The Ford Company sent Hensley to Madison, Wisconsin, to work (on applications of radioactive tracers in studies of detergency) with nuclear chemist John E. Willard (1908–1996) at the University of Wisconsin. Willard had been involved with the Manhattan Project, including the first weighing of plutonium, the first human-made ("artificial") element. Hensley enrolled as a doctoral candidate in the Graduate School, but his primary objective was to develop research skills. He published two research papers with John Willard.

Upon returning from Madison, Hensley at BASF Wyandotte established the first laboratory devoted to investigation of cleaning problems by radioactive-tracer techniques. He took early retirement due to health problems in 1974. He died June 24, 1975, at Wyandotte, Michigan, and was buried in Denver, Colorado.

Graduate students Ray Alan Woodriff and Robert George Rekers in Germann's Colorado laboratory continued investigations of fluorescence into the 1940s. This research was supported in part by a grant to Frank Germann from the United States Office of Naval Research. His was one of the first research grants to an individual chemist after O.N.R. was authorized by Congress and approved by President Harry S. Truman on August 1, 1946.

Ray Alan Woodriff (January 9, 1909–March 1, 1983) was son of Violet T. and Alan Woodriff. Ray had two brothers, George Leslie and Alvin. The boys grew up on the family cattle ranch near Wetmore, Custer County, Colorado. They learned reading, writing, and arithmetic in a one-room school, travelling from home each day on horseback. Ray attended Florence High School in Florence, Fremont County, Colorado, eleven miles north of Wetmore. Wetmore and Florence are on the semi-arid high deserts of southern Colorado. There were fewer than 2,000 people in all of Custer County in 1910; by comparison, the City of Florence had a population of 2,712 in 1910.

Ray attended Colorado Agricultural College (from 1935 to 1957, Colorado State College of Agriculture and Mechanic Arts; now Colorado State University) in Fort Collins for one year. He then transferred to the University of Colorado where he received the B.S. degree on Monday, June 12, 1933. He entered the graduate school of Oregon State Agricultural College in Corvallis (after 1937, Oregon State College; since 1961, Oregon State University) on October 20, 1933. He received the M.S. degree from Oregon State on June 6, 1935, with the thesis "Allison's Method of Magneto-Optic Analysis." His research project was a disappointment. He attempted to set up an Allison magneto-optic apparatus, but the apparatus proved to be unreliable as an analytical tool.

In college, Ray met Margaret Ruby Oswald (March 20, 1910–August 3, 1999). Margaret grew up on the Oswald family ranch several miles from Kit Carson, "a little town on the Eastern Plains" in Cheyenne County, Colorado. The population of Kit Carson was 233 in 2010. She attended a one-room school until sixth grade, travelled daily on horseback to junior high school, and then boarded in Kit Carson for high school where she graduated as valedictorian. She attended the University of Colorado, graduating with a bachelor's degree. Margaret and Ray married on Monday, August 1, 1938.

In 1939, Ray joined the faculty of Montana College of Agriculture and Mechanic Arts (since 1965, Montana State University) in Bozeman as Instructor of Chemistry. He took a three-year leave for doctoral study with Frank Germann at the University of Colorado, earning the Ph.D. in 1942 with the thesis "Investigation by an Improved Method of the Wavelengths of Fluorescence of Lead Tungstate–Calcium Tungstate Mixtures Excited by Various Wave Lengths of Ultraviolet Light." Calcium tungstate, $CaWO_4$, was once used in imaging screens for fluoroscopic medical x-ray examinations and in shoe-fitting fluoroscopes found in many retail shoe stores from the 1920s until the 1950s.

Ray returned to Montana College of Agriculture and Mechanic Arts. Now *Doctor* Woodriff, he was promoted to Assistant Professor of Chemistry in 1944, to Associate Professor in 1948, and to Professor in 1954. Ray Woodriff and Frank Germann continued to collaborate, publishing joint papers on fluorescence in 1944 and 1946. Woodriff spent many summers from 1958 to 1968 at Idaho laboratories of the Atomic Energy Commission and Argonne–West. Even after his formal retirement, he continued to be involved with the Chemistry Department of Montana State University. His handwriting became a bit shaky, but he was still signing doctoral examination documents as late as 1975. The Ray Woodriff Award was established in his honor to recognize imagination, independence of thought, and creativity by Montana State University undergraduates, especially in analytical chemistry.

Robert George Rekers (February 1, 1920–May 10, 1995) was born in Rochester, New York. For twenty-seven years, it seemed that he was going to stay close to his birthplace. He attended the public schools of Rochester. He attended the University of Rochester from 1938 to 1942, earning the B.S. degree in Chemistry. He then joined the staff of the Hawk Eye Works of Eastman Kodak Company in Rochester, advancing from Analytical Chemist to Process Control Group Leader between 1942 and 1947. While employed at Eastman Kodak, Rekers enrolled in the War Training Program (Engineering Science and Management, Optics and Optical Devices) at the University of Rochester. He also took evening courses in organic chemistry.

Then Robert Rekers went west. He joined Frank Germann's research group at the University of Colorado in 1947. He became Research Assistant and then Research Fellow. For the academic year 1950–1951, he replaced Assistant Professor Kenneth A. Gagos (on sabbatical leave) as instructor in the "Physical Chemistry Laboratory" course, so Rekers and Germann were collaborating in teaching undergraduate physical chemistry for the year. Rekers was awarded the Ph.D. in 1951 with the thesis "An Investigation of the Fluorescence of Certain Organic Compounds in Dilute Solution." His Ph.D. major was Physical Chemistry, with minors in Analytical Chemistry and Applied Mathematics.

In 1951, Dr. Rekers joined the staff of the Michelson Laboratory at the United

States Naval Ordnance Test Station, Inyokern, China Lake, California, where he became Head of the Spectroscopy Section, Physical Chemistry Branch, Chemistry Division of the Research Department. During the years when he was at the Michelson Laboratory, he took courses in the Extension Program of the California Institute of Technology.

Rekers joined the faculty of Texas Technological College (since 1969, Texas Tech University) in Lubbock, Texas. He was appointed in 1955 as Assistant Professor of Chemistry. He was granted tenure on September 16, 1959, and was promoted to Associate Professor in 1961. At Texas Technological College, he was active in the Water Resources Center. He was a guiding force in planning a new chemistry building, and the subsequent extensive renovation of the old chemistry building. He retired in 1986.

Elmer Russell Alexander (February 19, 1902–August 1, 1987) in Frank Germann's research group was looking at phosphorescence. Phosphorescence differs experimentally from fluorescence by a difference in the time scale. A material is phosphorescent if there is a significant time lapse between excitation and emission. Alexander's 1949 Ph.D. thesis was "Ethylene Borate and Similar Borate Glasses as Media for Investigating Phosphorescence of Organic Compounds." His graduate research in physical chemistry with Frank Germann was at the middle of his long and wide-ranging academic career.

Elmer Russell Alexander, son of Magnolia Tate (1887–1924) and Elmer Russell Alexander Sr., was born in Grant Township, Antelope County, Nebraska. The nearest settlement on this sparsely populated prairie farmland was St. Clair Post Office. If his family remained close to his birthplace, his first formal education would have been in a one-teacher district school. The family moved to a farm near Greeley, Colorado, and Elmer Jr. entered Greeley High School, graduating in May 1919. That fall, he entered the Colorado State Normal School in Greeley. He received his "life certificate (two-year course)" on Wednesday, June 14, 1922, providing him credentials for teaching positions as he continued his formal education. While he was attending Colorado State Normal School, the institution changed its name to Colorado State Teachers College. In 1935, it was Colorado State College of Education; after 1957, Colorado State College; since 1970, University of Northern Colorado. In college, Alexander was a heavyweight wrestler, he played football, and was a member of the Student Council and the Science Club. His Senior Class Yearbook prophesy:

"Another Alexander, who weeps because he has no more worlds to conquer." There were to be more worlds in Elmer's future. He received the A.B. degree in Education on August 21, 1924. He then received the A.M. degree in Education from Colorado State Teachers College on August 24, 1929.

Elmer Alexander taught school and was a high school principal. During summers 1930 and 1936, he attended graduate classes at Columbia University in the City of New York. Teachers College Columbia is the oldest graduate school of education in the United States; in 1930, it was probably the largest and the best. Then he spent an academic year at Columbia, enrolled from September 1937 to May 1938. He did not graduate from Columbia University.

In September 1931, Elmer Alexander joined the faculty of East Texas State Teachers College in Commerce, Hunt County, Texas. Hunt County is part of the temperate grassland ecoregion called the Texas blackland prairies. He was to remain on the East Texas faculty until 1948. There he taught courses in General Science, Physics, and Chemistry. From 1931 to 1942, he was in the Training School Department. In different years, Elmer had the title of "Supervising Teacher Senior High School" or "Supervising Teacher Junior High School." He took leaves of absence in summer 1936 and for the academic year 1937–1938 to attend Teachers College Columbia. From June 5, 1941 to August 29, 1941, he was enrolled in the Graduate school of the University of Texas in Austin.

From 1942 to 1948, Elmer Alexander remained nominally on the East Texas faculty but he may have had no teaching responsibilities. For part of that time, he was in Boulder and active in Frank Germann's research group. Alexander submitted his Ph.D. thesis in 1949. With a doctorate from the University of Colorado assured, Texas Christian University in Fort Worth, Texas, hired him in their Department of Chemistry in September 1948. He was Professor of Chemistry in 1957. He had been a member of the Texas Christian chemistry faculty for twenty-two years when he retired in 1970.

State-of-the-art instrumentation for fluorescence measurements advanced dramatically in 1955. Robert L. Bowman (1916–1995) constructed a prototype spectrophotofluorometer at the National Institutes of Health in Bethesda, Maryland. Bowman's instrument permitted the wavelength of the exciting radiation to be varied continuously, in both the visible and the ultraviolet regions. It allowed the full visible-

and ultraviolet-spectrum of emitted radiation to be observed and recorded automatically on paper charts with a mechanically driven pen. The American Instrument Company in nearby Silver Spring, Maryland, made the commercial instrument. The first AMINCO–Bowman spectrophotofluorometer was introduced in 1956.

From Duboscq to Beckman and Cary: A Revolution in Instrumentation

What instrumentation was available in 1925 in the new spectroscopy laboratories of Cornell's Baker Laboratory for measuring the optical absorbance of liquids? Such measurements had been used in quantitative chemical analysis laboratories for many decades. The Baker Laboratory certainly had a Duboscq colorimeter. Instrument maker Louis Jules Duboscq (1817–1886) and Parisian chemistry teacher Charles Mène described the colorimeter at l'Académie des Sciences in 1868. The instrument permitted the intensity of light transmitted through a solution of known concentration to be compared visually with the intensity of light transmitted through a solution of unknown concentration of the same colored substance. Two identical glass plungers dipped into the two solutions in separate cups. One plunger was raised or lowered until the transmitted light through the two plungers had the same intensity when viewed side-by-side with a split-screen eyepiece. The chemist then calculated the ratio of solute concentrations as the inverse ratio of the lengths of light paths through the two solutions.

Because matching light intensity in the split-screen field depended on a human eye, the Duboscq colorimeter necessarily restricted measurements to visible light. It would be seventy years before the practical chemical color scale could be extended beyond the visible spectrum, into the ultraviolet and the infrared.

Duboscq colorimeters were manufactured and sold by Louis Jules Duboscq, and then (through the 1920s) by his Paris firm's successor, Ph. Pellin, Ingeniur des Arts et Manufactures. Modifications of the instrument were still being produced by various optical companies in the United States (and sold by the leading scientific apparatus companies) until the early 1950s.

Photoelectric detectors did not appear in colorimeters until after Frank Germann's sabbatical year. The first imaginative attempts seem amateurish in retrospect. Stanley P. Reimann at the Research Institute of The Lankenau Hospital (Philadelphia) in 1926 clamped an argon-filled glass photoelectric cell, a Duboscq sample cup, and an ordinary household incandescent light bulb onto a laboratory ring stand. The concept was innovative; his physical rendition as portrayed in his published paper was crude. He claimed: "The personal factor of color comparisons is absolutely eliminated. A child can operate the instrument."

Charles Sheard and Arthur H. Sanford at the Mayo Clinic in Rochester, Minnesota, described a much more sophisticated instrument in 1928. They used an automobile headlight bulb as the light source, and a light-sensitive cesium-coated film as the photodetector. Over the next two years, they reported modifications and improvements. Charles Sheard applied for United States patent rights, with assignment to The American Society of Clinical Pathologists.

Glenn Austin Millikan (1906–1947) in 1933 described the use of a copper–copper-oxide detector for a colorimeter that he designed for a chemical kinetics experiment. He used his colorimeter to observe the rate of chemical conversion (and corresponding color change) of oxyhemoglobin to reduced hemoglobin in solution.

Kenneth A. Evelyn in 1936 described a colorimeter with a blocking-layer photocell, with a set of optical filters to select a limited range of wavelengths, and with a flashlight bulb as the light source. He filed for a patent on March 7, 1938, and received U. S. Patent 2,193,315 on March 12, 1940. The Evelyn instrument was the first commercial electronic colorimeter that a fledging analytical chemist could operate reliably. Evelyn colorimeters were in widespread use in chemical and biochemical research laboratories and in teaching laboratories throughout the 1940s and 1950s. Still, many traditional chemists considered the visual Duboscq colorimeter to be a more versatile and useful instrument for colorimetric chemical analysis.

If the Evelyn colorimeter had been available a decade earlier, then the doctoral research of Frank Germann's student, Norman Jackson Harrar, might have included quantitative visible absorption spectra of solutions. Instead, Harrar recorded and published qualitative visual observations of colors—green, yellow, orange, and red. Obtaining quantitative data with the Evelyn instrument would have required much more laboratory time, but probably would not have changed the conclusions of his studies.

In 1940, Howard H. Cary (1908–1991) at National Technical Laboratories in

California (manufacturer of the Beckman pH meters; see Chapter 3) began to design a colorimeter that would function in the ultraviolet. His first instruments used a vacuum-tube photo-detector. He used the Beckman pH meter to serve both as the electronic amplifier and also as the analog readout of light intensity. The first commercial model of the Model D spectrophotometer (soon to evolve into the popular Beckman DU) was demonstrated at Massachusetts Institute of Technology (Cambridge, Massachusetts) in July 1941. The Beckman DU and its successors revolutionized the world of chemical absorption spectrophotometry. This revolution came a generation too late for Frank Germann's laboratory.

A second dramatic change occurred when automated pen-and-ink recording replaced the manual recording of instrument readings. The automated recorder graphed absorbance versus wavelength (or absorbance versus time for a reacting chemical system) as a smooth line that connected successive data-points. A spectrum that took a day to record by hand could be drawn on a paper chart by an automated recorder in a few minutes. Mellon Institute in Pittsburgh purchased the first practical commercial recording spectrophotometer (the Cary 11) in April 1947. The Cary 11 found immediate use in chemical kinetics. Without human intervention, the instrument could plot graphs of absorbance versus time for reactions with half-lives of only a few minutes.

Physical chemists whose professional careers spanned the transformation from visual colorimetry to automated spectrophotometry heralded (as progress) the resultant quantification of laboratory data and the ability to obtain much more data per hour in the laboratory. For others, however, the abstractness of graphs of optical absorbance versus wavelength emphasized an increasing separation of laboratory research from ordinary human experience. Most persons perceive colors as actual properties of matter. Absorption spectra of solutions are at least one step removed from human perception and experience.

Norman Jackson Harrar (January 7, 1902–October 16, 1941), who before the advent of commercial spectrophotometers had characterized solutions by their colors from green to red, was born in Philadelphia. He graduated from the Academy at Westinghouse in Pittsburgh, and then attended the School of Chemistry of the University of Pittsburgh, earning the B.S. degree in 1922. He was Instructor in Chemistry at Colorado Agricultural College (after 1935, Colorado State College of

Agriculture and Mechanic Arts; since 1957, Colorado State University) in Fort Collins from 1924 to 1926. He then entered the graduate program of Pennsylvania State College (since 1953, The Pennsylvania State University) in College Station, where he was awarded the M.S. degree in 1928. When he came back west to the University of Colorado, he worked with Frank Germann, receiving the Ph.D. degree in 1930. After two years as Assistant Professor of Chemistry at Washington and Lee University, Lexington, Virginia, Dr. Harrar joined the faculty of Franklin College, Franklin, Indiana. From 1932 until his premature death from pneumonia in 1941, he was Professor and Head of the Department of Chemistry at Franklin College.

An Adventure in Europe

The Germann family had an adventure in Europe during summer 1929. Richard Paul was eleven years old and Lois Marie was seven. Frank was director of a "Residential Tour to Saint Servan (St. Malo)," conducted by the School of Foreign Travel, Inc. Martha was "Counsellor of Women" for the tour. The group sailed from New York on the SS *Statendam* on June 29, spent July 7 to July 12 in Paris, and then took up residence from July 13 to August 5 in the town of Saint Servan in Brittany. The tour brochure pointed out that Frank had been a member of the French faculty at Indiana University and had published in French periodicals, and that Martha was "a student of French." A course was offered in "Elementary French," taught by Frank, as well as a course in "Intermediate French," taught at the Université de Rennes. Members of the group could return on the SS *Rotterdam* from Boulogne-sur-Mer (sailing on August 8) or could opt (for an additional $100) for sightseeing in Cologne, Brussels, and London, then sailing on the SS *New Amsterdam* from Southampton on August 14. Either voyage to New York took nine days.

Subterranean Carbon Dioxide

Omer Holman, editor of *The Peru* [Indiana] *Republican* newspaper, wrote to Albert Germann in summer 1946, requesting a thousand-word autobiographical sketch. It is likely that Omer Holman also sent the same request to Frank. In any case, the files of the Miami County Historical Society contain what appear to be slightly augmented versions of the two requested sketches. It is an indication of the importance Frank attached to a single aspect of his research career that he devoted more than a third of his sketch to his new method of producing dry ice (solid carbon dioxide) from gas mixtures. He had reported the method in a talk before a Denver meeting of the American Chemical Society, Division of Industrial and Engineering Chemistry, in August 1932. He published details of the method in February 1933. Science Service, in its *Science News-Letter* for Saturday, December 23, 1933, cited Frank's method as among the impressive array of achievements in science in 1933. Also listed in those 1933 science achievements were the first solo flight around the world (by Wiley Post), discovery of the positron by Carl Anderson at California Institute of Technology, development of the iconoscope (a television receiver with no moving mechanical parts) at Radio Corporation of America, and the beginning of construction of the world's largest suspension bridge across the Golden Gate at San Francisco. The American Chemical Society, in its *Industrial and Engineering Chemistry News Edition* for Wednesday, December 20, 1933, cited Frank's method as among the thirty-six "High Points in Chemistry" for 1933.

Frank continued to pursue his interest in exploiting sources for pure carbon dioxide. As President of the Southwestern Division of the American Association for the Advancement of Science, he addressed the Division at its April 27, 1938, meeting in Albuquerque, New Mexico, on "The Occurrence of Carbon Dioxide, with Notes on the Origin and Relative Importance of Subterranean Carbon Dioxide." The journal *Science* published his speech that summer. His graduate student Herbert Wilmot Ayres submitted a thesis, "The Hydrolytic Dissociation of Oolitic Limestone," for the M.A. degree in 1939. This research was presented under the title "The Origin of Underground Carbon Dioxide" at the Eighteenth Colloid Symposium at Cornell University, June 19–21, 1941, and published in the *Journal of Physical Chemistry*. "CO_2 Gas Wells May Yield 'Air Fertilizer' For Crops" was the headline for a *Science News-Letter* story (vol. 34, no. 7, Saturday, August 13, 1938, p. 107) that profiled Frank Germann's ideas about capturing carbon dioxide from underground sources, converting the gas to a solid for economical transport, and then using the gas agriculturally to increase plant growth. The concept of capturing carbon dioxide and then converting it, in a cost-effective manner, to commercially valuable commodities has recently been revived by researchers at Stanford University, the University of Delaware, Princeton University, the University of Messina in Italy, and the technology company DNV in Høvik, Norway.

Herbert Wilmot Ayres (1914–1989) came from an academic family. He was born in Berkeley, California, son of Dr. Arthur Ayres. Dr. Arthur Ayres died in 1918, and young Herbert was taken to Upland, Jefferson Township, Grant County, Indiana, to live with his paternal grandparents, Mary Etta Higgins and Bert Wilmot Ayres. Bert W. Ayres (A.M., Ph.D., LL.D.) was Professor of Philosophy and Vice-President of Taylor University in Upland. He served as Acting President of the University in 1903–1904 and again in 1922. When the Zondervan Library was built on campus in 1986, the former library building was named Ayres Hall in his honor. Ayres Hall now houses a lecture auditorium and administrative offices.

Herbert Ayres graduated from Jefferson Township High School in 1932, and then entered Taylor University. He was President of his Freshman Class and his Junior Class, and was a member of the Philalethean Literary Society and the Eurekan Debating Club. He was on the staff of *Echo,* the student newspaper; and the yearbook, *The Gem: A Diary of Student Life at Taylor.* He was Editor-in-Chief of *The Gem 1936* in his Senior Year. Herbert studied chemistry with Dr. George Harlowe Evans, and graduated with a chemistry major in 1936, receiving the B.A. degree *magna cum laude.*

Herbert Ayres then went west to the University of Colorado. His graduate research had a Hoosier aspect. Oolitic, a small southern Indiana town, is the site of some of the largest oolitic limestone quarries in the world. His research on the chemistry of oolitic limestone was directed by Frank Germann. His 1939 M.A. degree from the University of Colorado provided the credentials needed for Ayres to be hired as an analytical chemist by the United States Food and Drug Administration. He served for thirty-four years as an FDA chemist, investigator, inspector, and compliance officer. He was Counselor of the Philadelphia Section of The Institute of Food Technologists, the largest food science organization in the world. He was also Secretary of the Central Atlantic States Association of Food and Drug Officials. Herbert Ayres retired in 1974.

Frank Germann continued to direct the research of graduate students at the University of Colorado. They were a diverse group of men. Their experiments ranged over the fields of inorganic chemistry, analytical chemistry, and physical chemistry. The names of his research students, with their thesis and publication titles, are listed in Appendix A. Biographical sketches of some of his students are included in this chapter, indicating how graduate study with Frank Germann fit into the life of each. Here is a sketch about Paul Frey, a man who became a physical chemist as a student of Frank Germann and who later became an influential writer of chemistry textbooks.

Paul Reheard Frey (April 30, 1902–May 12, 1993) was born in Schuylkill, Pennsylvania. He attended Wrightsville (Pennsylvania) High School, and then Albright College in the borough of Myerstown, Pennsylvania. (In 1928, Albright College at Myerstown and Schuylkill College merged to become Albright College at Reading.) He matriculated at Albright College in September 1918, and graduated on Wednesday, June 14, 1922. He took many courses in education; his concentration was chemistry. He was a member of the Neocosmian Literary Society. He probably taught school for a few years.

In 1927, Paul Frey went west to the University of Colorado. He became an Assistant in Chemistry and a graduate student in physical chemistry in the research group of Frank Germann. The University of Colorado awarded Frey the M.S. degree in Chemistry in 1930, with the thesis "Determination of the Hydrates of Uranyl Nitrate and the Description of Some of Their Properties."

From 1930 to 1933, he was on the faculty of York College, York, Nebraska. York College was a small institution, with 222 collegiate students in 1930 and 246 students in 1933. Also under the same academic umbrella were York Academy (a high school), York Business College, and York Conservatory. Frey took graduate courses at the University of Nebraska at Lincoln, from September 1933 to September 1934, and then entered a doctoral program at Oregon State Agricultural College (after 1937, Oregon State College; since 1961, Oregon State University) in Corvallis. He earned the Ph.D. from Oregon State in 1936 with Professor Earl C. Gilbert. Frey's physical-chemical thesis was "Electric Moment Studies of a Series of Related Hydrazine Derivatives."

Dr. Frey joined the faculty of Colorado State College of Agriculture and Mechanic Arts (since 1957, Colorado State University) in Fort Collins as Instructor of Chemistry for 1937–1938. By 1939–1940, he was co-teaching "Physiological Chemistry with lab." That course was to evolve over the years to become "Biochemistry (Home Economics) with lab" and then "Biochemistry I, II, and III" as well as "Biological Preparations." His teaching assignments also usually included "Physical Chemistry with lab." He was promoted to Assistant Professor of Chemistry, and then in 1942 to Associate Professor. As early as 1944, Frey was also on the staff of the Colorado Agricultural Experiment Station, the on-campus land-grant component of the College. In 1954–1955, he was Professor of Chemistry and Experiment Station Chemist.

Paul Frey received the National Council Citation Award from Albright College in 1980 "for his excellence as a teacher and as a writer of a long list of books in the field of chemistry." In 1938, he wrote the book *An Outline of Mathematics and Problems for Students of General Chemistry*. It proved to be a popular addition to the Barnes and Noble *College Outline* series. The seventh edition, *Chemistry Problems and How to Solve Them*, was published in 1969, and an eighth edition was in print in 1985. He published another book, *Metric America: Math and Measures* (Indianapolis: Bobbs-Merrill, 1980). His most influential textbook was *College Chemistry* (Englewood Cliffs, New Jersey: Prentice-Hall, 1952, 1958, 1965). A trimmed version was *Essentials of College Chemistry* (Prentice-Hall, 1960). He collaborated with Wendell Bernard King to produce a companion *Laboratory Manual for College Chemistry*, also published by Prentice-Hall. Frey, together with other members of the Chemistry Department (including Wendell Bernard King and Wesley Emerson Pyke), in the 1940s produced an annual mimeographed study guide, keyed to the Colorado State College of Agriculture and Mechanic Arts "General Chemistry" course syllabus. By 1952, it had become *General College Chemistry: A Study Guide* (Dubuque, Iowa: W. C. Brown Company). His *alma mater* Albright College awarded him an honorary doctor of science degree (*Scientiæ Doctor honoris causa*) in 1984.

A New Scholarly Journal

Paul Frey's Master of Science thesis incorporated material that had first been reported in print in the inaugural issue of *The Journal of the Colorado-Wyoming Academy of Science*. Frank Germann was instrumental in establishing the *Journal*, which has continued irregular publication into the twenty-first century. He and his students wrote five more articles for the first volume. The Colorado-Wyoming Academy of Science had been established in 1927. Frank Germann was a member of its seven-member Committee of Organization, which first met November 25–26, 1927 (the Friday and Saturday after Thanksgiving), at the University of Wyoming in Laramie. He was a member of the Executive Committee of the Academy from 1927 to 1930, and was President in 1930–1931. The Academy's *Journal* began publication in 1929, with Frank Germann as the editor.

The Journal of the Colorado-Wyoming Academy of Science is representative of a long tradition of periodicals created for publication of scholarship when access to established academic journals seemed available only to a favored few. We noted in Chapter 1 that Frank C. Mathers and Albert F. O. Germann published a portion of Albert Germann's 1910 M.A. thesis in a 68-page issue of *Indiana University Studies* (vol. 1, no. 5) that included eight research papers by Indiana University faculty and graduate students. Frank Germann, together with one of his current graduate students and with a former graduate student, helped initiate Series D (Physical and Biological Sciences) of the *University of Colorado Studies* by submitting papers to volume 1 (1940). *University of Colorado Studies* had begun in 1902, with John Ekeley contributing a paper to its initial volume. We noted earlier in this chapter that Ralph N. Traxler's doctoral research was published in *Transactions of the Wisconsin Academy of Sciences, Arts, and Letters*, vol. 28 (1933), pp. 275–290. We shall see in Chapter 3 that M.A. research of Harold Simmons Booth (a graduate student of Albert Germann) was published in *The Bulletin of Western Reserve University*, vol. 19, no. 8 (1916), pp. 45–54; and also that undergraduate chemist Hamilton P. Cady reported "a new explosive compound" in *The Kansas University Quarterly*, vol. 6, series A, no. 2 (April 1897), pp. 71–75. In Chapter 4, we note that seven publications of the botanical research of Louis Frederick Heimlich from 1914 to 1927 appeared in the *Proceedings of the Indiana Academy of Sciences*, and that the doctoral thesis of Frank Elliott was published in *The Ohio Journal of Science*, vol. 30, no. 1 (January 1930), pp. 1–22. The pragmatic tradition continues, with many colleges and universities in the twenty-first century publishing scholarly documents, ranging from senior honors theses to faculty research, in open digital repositories such as Dspace, freely accessible to the interested public via the internet.

Several prestigious research journals, now supported by major scientific societies, had analogous origins. Edward Leamington Nichols and Ernest George Merritt founded the journal *Physical Review* at Cornell University in July 1893, and continued to edit the journal for thirty-three volumes. Frank German submitted results of his Cornell research to *Physical Review* in 1917 and 1922. Wilder Bancroft and Joseph Trevor (with Bancroft's personal funding) founded *The Journal of Physical Chemistry* three years later at Cornell in 1896, at least in part to provide a vehicle for publishing their own research without external editorial or reviewer restrictions. Yale chemist Benjamin Silliman Sr. (1779–1864) in 1818 founded the *American Journal of Science*, America's oldest scientific periodical still in publication. It was often called *Silliman's Journal* throughout its first hundred years; editorship remained in the Silliman family until 1926. Justus von Liebig (1803–1873), characterized in Chapter 3 as the father of organic chemistry, considered one major chemistry journal to be almost one of his children. The journal had several titles, beginning in 1832 as *Annalen der Pharmacie*, then *Justus Liebig's Annalen der Chemie und Pharmacie*. It continued publication until 1997, when it was absorbed into the *European Journal of Organic Chemistry*. Even after Liebig's death, the journal was widely known as *Liebig's Annalen*. Nichols, Merritt, Bancroft, Trevor, Silliman, and Liebig sought "peer review" by their friends and colleagues of some submitted articles, but each reserved his own right of editorial discretion. *Zeitschrift für physikalische Chemie, Stöichiometrie und Verwandtschaftslehre* was founded in February 1887 in Leipzig by Friedrich Wilhelm Ostwald (1853–1932; Nobel laureate 1909) and Jacobus Henricus van 't Hoff (1852–1911; Nobel laureate 1901). Ostwald and van 't Hoff assembled a prestigious editorial advisory board from Europe and the United States, but the two founders were the actual editors, and they made the decisions about which papers (and whose papers) would be printed. Ostwald was listed as an editor for a hundred volumes of the journal from 1887 to 1922.

The world's first scientific journal was *Philosophical Transactions*, founded in February 1665 by Henry Oldenburg (abt 1619–1677), the first Secretary of the Royal Society of London. The journal was owned and edited by Oldenburg until his death. It was always associated with the Royal Society, and in 1752 the Royal Society assumed financial responsibility. The journal continues, with celebration in 2015 of its 350th year of continuous publication.

Another form of publication, extremely important for advancing the quality of hands-on education in the sciences (but often not recognized by university deans as "true academic scholarship"), was the creation of mimeographed student instructions for individual experiments in teaching laboratories. At the University of Wisconsin, this effort in physical chemistry focused on creation of a book to provide tested and standardized protocols applicable at many colleges and universities; Albert Germann contributed to that effort as a graduate student. Scientific instrument companies often marketed apparatus designed for specific experiments in this book. It is revealing that the Chemistry Research Library at Wisconsin failed to collect successive editions of the Chemistry Department's own *Experimental Physical Chemistry*. The chemistry librarians apparently did not consider this widely adopted textbook to be a *research* publication. It required a twenty-first century plea in the alumni magazine *Badger Chemist* for fill-in copies of *Experimental Physical Chemistry* to complete the library's neglected collection. At Colorado, Frank Germann created a system of individualized "handouts" or "lab separates"—usually mimeographed when first written, then often commercially printed after successive versions had evolved. With a hole punch for sheets of paper, a student could keep a semester of lab protocols collated in a ring binder. Frank Germann called each year's collection *The University of Colorado Laboratory Manual of Physical Chemistry*, and included this manual in his list of scholarly publications. The widespread practice continued in many institutions. Copy production was transformed successively from mimeographs, to hectographs and spirit duplicators, then to multi-lithographs, photocopiers, and finally to ink-jet or laser printers interfaced with computers.

We noted earlier in this chapter that Charles Gibson and Veon Kiech wrote the in-house *Laboratory Manual for General Chemistry* as their laboratory textbook in "Chemistry 1" at the University of New Mexico. Their *Manual* was printed, with biennial revisions, in Albuquerque by the University of New Mexico Press. At Colorado State College of Agriculture and Mechanic Arts, Paul Frey collaborated with other members of the Chemistry Department in the 1940s to produce an annual mimeographed study guide, keyed to their "General Chemistry" course syllabus. By 1952, it had morphed into *General College Chemistry: A Study Guide*, commercially published by W. C. Brown Company.

The University of Colorado Laboratory Manual of Physical Chemistry was co-authored by Frank Germann and Kenneth A. Gagos. Kenneth A. Gagos supervised the physical chemistry laboratory at the University of Colorado for most of the years from 1924 until his retirement in 1964. He received a sabbatical leave of absence in 1950–1951, replaced for the year by Robert George Rekers, a doctoral student of Frank Germann.

Kenneth A. Gagos (April 5, 1896–May 29, 1995) was born in Armenia, son of Azniv Beldoian and Mamprey Avedis Gagossian. Kenneth had seven siblings. It seems probable that Kenneth was the only child in the family who survived the Armenian Genocide. Kenneth served in the United States Army Signal Corps during the Great War. After the War, he attended Stanford University, receiving the A.B. degree in 1923. He then became a graduate student of Albert Germann at Stanford, studying the chemistry of aluminum chloride and calcium in liquid phosgene. Kenneth Gagos received glass-blowing instruction from Albert Germann, who prided himself on his ability to "work glass in the flame." After receiving the A.M. degree in chemistry from Stanford in 1924, Gagos joined the Chemistry Department of the University of Colorado. In addition to supervising the physical chemistry laboratory, he also taught classes in glass blowing. He held the rank of Assistant Professor. He worked with Frank Germann on several projects. Gagos also collaborated with members of the departments of Physics and Geology, and published a joint paper with a member of the Frank Germann research group.

We noted that Frank Germann and two students helped initiate Series D (Physical and Biological Sciences) of the *University of Colorado Studies* by submitting papers to volume 1. The students were James William Hensley (a biographical sketch appeared earlier) and Charles Franklin Metz.

Charles Franklin Metz (September 23, 1904–February 10, 1974) was born near the crossroads settlement of Deerfield, Ward Township, Randolph County, Indiana, near the Mississinewa River. Deerfield is seven miles north of Winchester, the county seat. He attended the Saratoga School in Ward Township, next the neighboring Jefferson Township School, and then Winchester High School, graduating with a class of twenty-four students in May 1922. By high school, he had decided to go west; his 1922 Class Prophesy projection for fifty years in the future: "he looks like a cowpuncher from the West with a 45-Colt on each hip."

The school system in Randolph County was changing dramatically in the early years of the twentieth century, change led by Leotis (Lee) Lincoln Driver (1867–1960). Driver was a district schoolmaster in Randolph County, then Principal of

Winchester High School, and (from 1907 to 1919) Randolph County Superintendent of Schools. As County Superintendent, he presided over the closing of more
than a hundred single-teacher district schools, and the opening of twenty multi-
room consolidated schools. Active in the national Country Life Movement, he
touted Randolph County as a model for rural school consolidation. One of the goals
of the Country Life Movement was to make rural life more attractive, so that young
people would not leave home for more attractive lives elsewhere.

Charles Metz did leave home. He was driven by a bold desire to get an education. He went west, and entered the South Dakota School of Mines (since 1943,
the South Dakota School of Mines and Technology) in Rapid City on Saturday,
September 16, 1922. He received the B.S. degree in Chemical Engineering on
Tuesday, June 1, 1926. He then went to Boulder, Colorado, where the University of
Colorado appointed him Assistant in Chemistry. He joined Frank Germann's
graduate research group. His research was a thermodynamic study of the silver
iodide–lead iodide system. The University of Colorado awarded him the M.S.
degree in Chemistry in 1928.

Park College, Parkville, Missouri, hired him in 1928 as Instructor of Chemistry and Physics. Park promoted him to Associate Professor of Chemistry and
Physics in 1931. Park College granted him a leave of absence for the 1935–1936
academic year to complete requirements for the Ph.D. in Chemistry. He was a
graduate student again with Frank Germann at the University of Colorado. This
time he held a Research Fellowship at Colorado while he conducted instrumental
chemical experiments, measuring magnetic double refraction. He was awarded the
Ph.D. in 1936. Charles Metz considered Frank Germann to be a great friend as
well as a fine professor.

Dr. Metz joined the faculty of the Colorado State College of Agriculture and
Mechanic Arts (Colorado A&M; since May 1, 1957, Colorado State University) in
Fort Collins, beginning in 1938 as Assistant Professor of Chemistry. He taught
"Physical Chemistry," "Physical Chemistry Laboratory," and "Physical and Histori-
cal Geology." From 1938 to 1943, Charles Franklin Metz and Paul Reheard Frey,
previous doctoral students of Frank Germann, were colleagues together in the
Chemistry Department of Colorado State A&M.

The Colorado State A&M *Catalogue* and the *Directory* disguise the activities and the home address of Dr. Metz in 1943 and subsequent years. These official (and public) University publications indicate that he was promoted to Associate Professor, that he became an Associate Chemist at the Colorado Agricultural Experiment Station, that he was given a leave of absence, and that his home continued to be at 631 West Myrtle Street in Fort Collins, a block north of campus. In fact, Metz had been surreptitiously recruited to Los Alamos, New Mexico, to become part of a United States Army program with the codename "Development of Substitute Materials." It turned out that this was part of the Manhattan Project, the secret wartime Federal research program for developing nuclear weapons. Charles F. Metz and his family moved in 1943 to Los Alamos. His son, Charles V. Metz, recalled aspects of his high school years (during the development of "the bomb") in Los Alamos during a September 16, 2006, interview (Lynnette Baughman, "Chuck Metz: Young Pioneer of the Manhattan Project," *Los Alamos History; Community History, Global Connections*, www.losalamoshistory.org/chuck_metz.htm, accessed January 29, 2015).

Charles F. Metz hired on as a scientist at the Los Alamos National Laboratory (managed by the University of California) in May 1944. He was one of the twelve scientists who conducted the world's first firing of a nuclear weapon, the "Trinity" test on New Mexico's Alamogordo Bombing and Gunnery Range, 210 miles south of Los Alamos, on Monday, July 16, 1945. On Monday, August 6, 1945, a nuclear bomb was detonated over Hiroshima, Japan. Later that week, on Thursday, August 9, 1945, a nuclear bomb was detonated over Nagasaki, Japan. Japan surrendered on Tuesday, August 14, 1945. Charles F. Metz resigned from the Los Alamos National Laboratory that month.

Charles V. Metz has written: "Both of us were employed by the U of Cal during the war and until my father retired. I had left the Lab in 1948 for school at the U of New Mexico. I still worked with the Lab in the Overseas Test Division when there was a big test going on. I was recalled to US Force duty and from that point forward I was a fighter Pilot until I retired in the Late 60's."

Charles F. Metz was rehired in March 1946 as Group Leader of CMR-1, the Analytical Chemistry Group at the Los Alamos National Laboratory. In September 1956, CMR-1 became CMB-1 (same group, same function, different acronym). He retired as CMB-1 Group Leader in April 1972. At CMR-1 and CMB-1, he became an expert in the analytical chemistry of plutonium. Many of his research reports were kept secret by the Federal Government, although some have been declassified and are available via internet Google Scholar searches. Fifty years after his high school graduation, he had emerged as a nuclear scientist from the West with a much more lethal weapon in his portfolio than "a 45-Colt on each hip."

Frank Germann was a member of Phi Lambda Upsilon, a national chemistry honor society founded at the University of Illinois in March 1899. It is likely that Frank was influential to establishing the Alpha Sigma chapter of Phi Lambda Upsilon at the University of Colorado in 1950. He was also a member of Alpha Chi Sigma, a national chemistry fraternity organized at the University of Wisconsin in 1902 by eight chemistry undergraduate majors. One of the eight organizers was Joseph Howard Mathews, the chemist who (in 1909–1910) was Albert F. O. Germann's graduate research advisor at Wisconsin. By 1910, Mathews held the title of G.M.A. (Grand Master Alchemist) of the Alpha Chapter. Eta Chapter of Alpha Chi Sigma was formed at the University of Colorado in 1908. Frank Germann contributed an article, "New Fields for Scientists," to the fraternity's quarterly, *The Hexagon of Alpha Chi Sigma*, vol. 15 (1925), pp. 465–467. By 2013, the Eta Chapter had become inactive.

Frank delivered an address ("Research: The Price of Progress") on Friday, March 15, 1929, to the Delta Epsilon Honorary Scientific Society at Colorado College, a private liberal arts college in Colorado Springs. The faculty had organized Delta Epsilon during the college year 1920–1921. The faculty asserted that Delta Epsilon at Colorado College was the first of its kind in the United States, and that other colleges similar to Colorado College were "considering organization." Few, if any, did more than consider. Delta Epsilon was active at Colorado College until at least 1972.

He was also a member of the Lutheran Academy for Scholarship (Academia Lutherana Philosophiæ), an interdisciplinary association organized in March 1942 in Chicago. Membership was by invitation. Frank contributed an article ("The 'Parity Law' of Nuclear Physics Challenged") to the Academy quarterly, *The Lutheran Scholar*, in 1957.

Throughout his professional life, Frank was a member of the American Chemical Society. He was Vice-President of the Colorado Section in 1933, President from 1934 to 1936, and a member of the Council from 1936 to 1938. He published articles in several A.C.S. journals: *Journal of the American Chemical Society, Journal of Physical Chemistry, Industrial and Engineering Chemistry, Chemical and Engineering*

News, and *Journal of Chemical Education.* The Society was formed at the College of Pharmacy of the City of New York on April 6, 1876. It is the premiere scientific society that supports inquiry in all the fields of chemistry and chemical engineering.

Changing of the Guard

Professor John Ekeley, who had been Head of the Department of Chemistry for thirty-five years, retired in 1937. He was replaced by biochemist Reuben Gilbert (Gus) Gustavson (April 6, 1892–February 23, 1974), then Professor of Chemistry and Chair of the Department of Chemistry at the University of Denver.

The appointment of Gus Gustavson brought a prolific researcher into the leadership of the Department. He had published twelve research papers during the 1930–1931 year, and three to five papers each succeeding year at the University of Denver. It was surely the intent of the administration to use this appointment to bring national attention to the University of Colorado as an up-and-coming center for chemical research. As we shall see, World War II was to delay this effort, at least with respect to research by Gus Gustavson.

The appointment of a biochemist to head the Department of Chemistry foreshadowed an evolutionary change in the focus of the department toward biochemistry. In 1923, Frank Germann signed a publication [Frank E. E. Germann and Malcolm C. Hylan, "Dispersity of Silver Halides in Relation to Their Photographic Behavior," *Science,* (New Series), vol. 58, no. 1504 (October 26, 1923), pp. 332–333] as a contribution from the "Department of Theoretical and Physical Chemistry of the University of Colorado." Gus Gustavson's tenure was too short for him to transform the Department from a physical slant to a biological slant, but the transformation eventually did occur. In 1978, the Department hired biochemist Thomas Robert Cech (born December 8, 1947). Cech was to share the 1989 Nobel Prize in Chemistry with Sidney Altman (born May 7, 1939) for their discovery of catalytic properties of ribonucleic acid. In 1986, a semi-independent Biochemistry Division was established within the Department. By 2014, the name had become the "Department of Chemistry and Biochemistry."

Gus Gustavson was a son of Colorado and of Denver. The University of Denver traces its history back to the formation of Colorado Seminary in Denver by Methodist John Evans (1814–1897) in 1864. Evans was the second governor of the Colorado Territory. He was also one of the nine men who founded Northwestern University in 1850, above a hardware store on Lake Street in Chicago, under the patronage of the Methodist Episcopal Church. The private Colorado Seminary, with strong ties to the Methodist Episcopal Church but without secure funding, closed after a few years. The Seminary reopened as the private University of Denver in 1880. It granted its first diploma in 1884.

Reuben Gilbert Gustavson was born in Denver, son of Hildegard Charlotte Silen and James Gustavson. He attended Denver West High School, and then received the A.B. degree in 1916 and the A.M. degree in 1917 from the University of Denver. From 1917 to 1920, he was a member of the faculty of Colorado Agricultural College (after 1935, Colorado State College of Agriculture and Mechanic Arts; since May 1, 1957, Colorado State University) in Fort Collins. In 1920, he joined the University of Denver faculty as Assistant Professor of Chemistry. At the same time, be began graduate work at the University of Chicago. He was awarded the Ph.D. by the University of Chicago in 1925 with the dissertation "A Biochemical Study of the Female Sex Hormone." Promotion to Associate Professor at the University of Denver came in 1926, followed by elevation to Professor of Chemistry in 1927.

Much was happening in the University of Colorado and in the world as the decade of the 1940s dawned. The events in the world had transformational effects at the University. George Norlin, President of the University of Colorado since 1919, retired on July 1, 1939. Germany invaded Poland on September 1, 1939. Robert Stearns became President of the University on September 8, 1939. The Imperial Japanese Navy attacked the United States naval base at Pearl Harbor, Hawaii, by air on Sunday, December 7, 1941. Reuben Gustavson, continuing as Head of the Department of Chemistry, became Dean of the Graduate School for the year 1942–1943, placing him in line for a higher administrative role. On September 25, 1942, President Stearns took a leave of absence to serve in the Army Air Forces School of Applied Tactics at Orlando, Florida. On August 21, 1943, President Stearns was granted an indefinite leave from the University to become Operations Chief of the Analysis Division, 13th Air Force. At that time, Dean Reuben Gustavson was promoted to become Acting President of the University of Colorado. Paul Dean became

Head of the Department of Chemistry in August 1943; Dean continued as Head of the Department until his retirement in 1953. Victory-in-Europe Day (V-E Day) was Tuesday, May 8, 1945. President Stearns returned to campus and to the presidency. Acting-President Gustavson resigned from the faculty, effective July 1, 1945.

Reuben Gustavson had been Acting President for less than two years. Those years were turbulent on campus.

Harry Bridges (1901–1990), militant leader of the International Longshore and Warehouse Union, was invited to campus for a speech on Thursday, March 16, 1944. His announced topic was "Labor and Political Action." The Boulder Post of the American Legion protested with vigor. An American Legion national committeeman from Denver called for the University Regents to determine the advisability of retaining Gustavson. Gustavson stood up for freedom of speech at the University, but he was supported by only the narrowest margin (three votes to two) by the Board of Regents.

A year later, a similar freedom-of-speech issue arose. Frances Perkins (1880–1965), retiring in 1945 as the longest serving United States Secretary of Labor (and the first woman appointed to a Presidential Cabinet), was scheduled to speak on campus. She had played a central role in enactment and implementation of President Franklin Roosevelt's domestic agenda. She had been a powerful voice in helping labor unions gain political power. Again, there was heavy pressure to prevent her appearance. Again, Gustavson effectively resisted that pressure. He was quoted as believing "that social, economic and political problems could and should be treated as matter-of-factly and as dispassionately as a chemical problem."

Gustavson became an energetic administrator. He had left the classroom and the chemistry research laboratory in 1942 to become Dean and then Acting President. After resigning from the Colorado faculty in summer 1945, he accepted simultaneous administrative appointments as Vice-President and Dean of Faculties at the University of Chicago. He had been a visiting professor at Chicago in 1929, and earlier had been a graduate student there from 1920 to 1925. He was associated with the Metallurgical Laboratory at the University of Chicago, and was a member of the Board of Governors of nearby Argonne National Laboratory, as part of the Manhattan Project. His 1974 obituary divulges that he was "a participant in the birth of the atomic bomb." He had a major role in 1945 at the University of Chicago in reorganizing science teaching and research after the stressful period when the non-military open-campus pursuits of undergraduate and graduate science education had to be isolated from, and often subordinated to, intensive secret research and development activities on the Chicago campus and at Argonne labs.

If Frank Germann were involved in any way with the Manhattan Project, he kept such connections private. Germann's professional interest in uranium chemistry dated from before the First World War, a fact known by Gus Gustavson. However, the legendary compartmentalization of research in this massive government project, together with extraordinary security protocols, suggest that any relevant conversations between Germann and Gustavson will remain undiscovered. We have noted that Germann's student Charles Franklin Metz had a significant role in the Manhattan Project, beginning in 1943, and that Germann's student James William Hensley had at least second-hand relationships with the Manhattan Project.

Gustavson's administrative work at the University of Chicago was followed by the Chancellorship of the University of Nebraska at Lincoln. He was Chancellor from 1946 to 1953.

Ford Foundation, in fall 1952, provided staff and funding to establish Resources for the Future, Incorporated, a non-profit organization based in Washington, D.C. They recruited biochemist Reuben Gustavson, anticipating that Resources for the Future would focus on the physical and biological sciences. In November 1952, Gustavson became a Director of Resources for the Future. In June 1953, he was elected President and Executive Director.

In November 1953, economist Joseph Lyman Fisher (1914–1992) was named Associate Director. Fisher's appointment signaled a shift in emphasis toward the social sciences. Gustavson remained at the head of the organization until 1959, but was unhappy with the change of focus away from the natural sciences. He retired on Monday, August 31, 1959, replaced on Tuesday by Joseph Fisher. Gustavson "often said later that he might not have taken the job if he had known where it would lead him."

The next day Gustavson began an eleven-year stint at the University of Arizona in Tucson. He held the title "Professor of Chemistry" throughout his years at Arizona, complemented by such additional titles as "Advisor on Television and Science Education," "Presidential Advisor," and "Professor of the History of Science." He was age 67 when he moved to Tucson. It probably had been seventeen years since he had taught a laboratory course. At Tucson he was a valuable advisor to administrators and to younger scientists, but it is unlikely that he spent much time in laboratory instruction.

Professional Leadership Roles

Frank Germann had active leadership roles in several professional organizations, roles that extended through the years of World War II and beyond. He had been President of the Southwestern and Rocky Mountain Division of the American Association for the Advancement of Science from 1936 to 1938, and was Executive Secretary-Treasurer from 1940 until 1956. The American Association for the Advancement of Science, the first national organization to promote all aspects of science and engineering, was formed in 1848. Inactive during the Civil War, it was resurrected in 1866. Frank submitted several research papers to *Science,* the weekly journal of the A.A.A.S. His former doctoral student, Oscar Brauer Muench, was President of the Southwestern and Rocky Mountain Division in 1949–1950.

Frank was also very involved in the work of the American Association of University Professors, an organization (founded in 1915) that has vigorously promoted the concepts of academic freedom and of shared governance (sharing by faculty, by administration, and by trustees) in academic institutions. His experience in 1919 with the flawed administration of President Victor Clifton Alderson at the Colorado School of Mines probably spurred his initial interest in the work of the Association. Frank was President of the University of Colorado Chapter from 1928 to 1930, and became a Regional Director in 1936. He was a member of the A.A.U.P. Council of thirty-eight persons that conducted national business during a World War II governmental ban against large conventions. As an A.A.U.P. Councilor, he installed (in October 1945) a Chapter of the Association at Colorado School of Mines, where he had been a faculty member in 1918–1919.

In 1940, Frank was elected to a three-year term as Secretary of the Western District of Phi Beta Kappa. He was elected President of the Western District in 1946. He had become a member of Phi Beta Kappa in 1911 when he earned the A.B.

degree at Indiana University. He was a charter member of the Indiana University Chapter. The Phi Beta Kappa honor society was founded at the College of William and Mary on December 5, 1776. It is the oldest academic honor society in the United States for the liberal arts and sciences.

Frank was a member of the Society of the Sigma Xi, an international honor society of research scientists and engineers. Sigma Xi was founded in 1886 to honor excellence in scientific investigation, and to encourage a sense of companionship and cooperation among researchers in all fields of science and engineering. He was President of the University of Colorado Sigma Xi Chapter during the 1926–1927 academic year. He gave a lecture—"Discovery of Properties of Ortho- and Para-Hydrogen"—to the Chapter on December 6, 1929. He also offered a "speech after dinner" at the June 6, 1924, Chapter initiation banquet.

He maintained memberships in several European scientific organizations, including Association des Chimistes de Genève, Société Suisse de Chimie, Société Française de Physique, and Société de Chimie Physique.

Retirement

After he retired from the University of Colorado on June 30, 1956, Frank Germann joined the research staff of the National Bureau of Standards–Boulder where he had an office. The United States National Bureau of Standards, headquartered in Gaithersburg, Maryland, was founded March 3, 1901. It was the first physical-science research laboratory operated by the Federal government. Among its initial responsibilities was to be custodian of the primary United States radium standard, a sample used by N.B.S. for calibrating radium and radon preparations. Boulder became home of "the western campus" of the National Bureau of Standards. Frank was officially at N.B.S. from 1956 to 1966, and he collaborated with others there until at least 1970. In 1962, the University and N.B.S. formed the Joint Institute for Laboratory Astrophysics in Boulder, and constructed an impressive research facility in the center of the University campus. N.B.S. changed its name in 1988, becoming the National Institute of Standards and Technology (NIST). N.B.S. (with three periods) was always called by its initials; NIST (with no periods) was pronounced as one syllable.

Throughout his life, Frank enjoyed translating materials to and from French and German for his friends and colleagues. In addition, he translated documents for the Bureau of Mines (United States Department of the Interior) when he was on the staff of the National Bureau of Standards–Boulder.

Martha and Frank took advantage of retirement freedom to travel, both in the United States and abroad. During winter 1956, they vacationed in the small town of Anna Maria on Anna Maria Island, a barrier island off the coast of Manatee County, Florida. Anna Maria Island is due west of Bradenton and Bradenton Beach. Martha and Frank spent summer 1958 in Europe; they showed their 35 mm Kodachrome slides of "Gardens of Switzerland and Holland" at a January 1959 meeting of the Boulder Garden Club. They took a forty-two-day cruise of the South Pacific, sailing aboard the Matson luxury ocean liner SS *Monterey*. The cruise left from San Francisco, with outbound calls at Los Angeles, Tahiti, Auckland, and Sydney, and inbound calls at Auckland, Suva, Pago Pago, and Honolulu.

Travelling and vacationing were enjoyable, but Boulder was home. Martha Germann was a long-time member of the Boulder Garden Club. One of her favorite neighborhood projects was landscaping a 4,000 ft² triangle at the end of Sunset Boulevard in Boulder. To begin the work, the thin layer of topsoil was removed. Then a big surprise! Underneath the topsoil was an impermeable caliche layer, four to eighteen inches thick. Caliche is a cement-like deposit, mostly calcium carbonate. This hardpan prevented rainwater from draining properly, and severely limited the volume of soil available for plant roots. Martha delegated to Frank the task of using a pickaxe and a sledge to chop a hole through the caliche for each landscape plant.

Martha's plan was to have changing color throughout the year. She included low red and green barberry, golden creeping Pfitzer's juniper, bird cherries, and roses. In front of a gray-green Burkii juniper, she placed groupings of purple, pink, and white Rose of Sharon hibiscus, as well as gladioli and day lilies. In the back was a taller gray upright Colorado juniper, surrounded by four low-spreading green junipers. A *Boulder Daily Camera* newspaper columnist described the triangle as "truly a gem of a beauty spot."

The plantings in the triangle were important to Martha as long as she was physically able to take an active part in their care, and she found comfort in that beauty spot during her final extended illness. She died on Wednesday, December 21, 1966.

Frank was later instrumental in having the triangle accepted as part of Sunset Park by the Boulder Parks Department. In March 1972, the metal letter "G" (which had formerly been displayed on the chimney of the Germann home at 1800 Sunset Boulevard) was placed in the park as a memorial to Martha. Frank, who had moved to Ventura, California in 1970, was present for the March 1972 ceremony.

Frank moved into a retirement apartment in Ventura to be near his daughter and son-in-law, Lois Marie and Horace Jones, in Ojai, California. Frank died in Ojai on Wednesday, February 27, 1974. He was buried next to Martha in Mountain View Memorial Park, Boulder.

Sources and References for Chapter II

Page 82, *Periodic Law* ... The Periodic Table, as presented to students in beginning chemistry at Indiana University in the first decade of the 20th century. From "Natural Classification of the Elements.—The Periodic Law," Chapter XI in Ira Remsen, *A College Text-Book of Chemistry* (New York: Henry Holt and Company, 1901), pp. 174, 177. Compare with a Periodic Table in any 21st-century chemistry book.

Page 83, *On the Invisible Rays* ... Becquerel, Antoine Henri, "Sur les radiations invisibles émises par les corps phosphorescents," *Comptes Rendus Hebdomadaires des Séances de l'Académie des Sciences*, vol. 112, pp. 501–503 (séance of March 2, 1896). *See also* William G. Myers, "Becquerel's Discovery of Radioactivity in 1896," *Journal of Nuclear Medicine*, vol. 17, no. 7, pp. 579–582 (1976).

Page 83, *His discovery and its implications dominated* ... "There has been a revolution in the physical science of today ..." These words opened an article by Professor Arthur L. Foley, "Recent Developments in Physical Science," *Popular Science Monthly*, vol. 77 (November 1910), pp. 447–456.

Page 83, *their discovery of radium* ... Note by M. P. Curie, Mme. P. Curie, and M. G. Bémont, presented by M. Becquerel, "Sur une Nouvelle Substance Fortement Radioactive, Contenue dans la Pechblende [On a New Substance, Strongly Radioactive, Contained in Pitchblende]," *Comptes Rendus Hebdomadaires des Séances de l'Académie des Sciences*, vol. 127 (1898), pp. 1215–1217.

Page 84, *Humphry Davy (1778–1829)* ... Richard Holmes, *The Age of Wonder: How the Romantic Generation Discovered the Beauty and Terror of Science* (New York: Pantheon Books, 2008); *see* chaps 6–9: "Davy on the Gas," "Dr Frankenstein and the Soul," "Davy and the Lamp," and "Sorcerer and Apprentice." David Knight, *Humphrey Davy: Science & Power* (Oxford: Blackwell Publishers, 1992).

Harold Hartley, *Humphry Davy* (London: Thomas Nelson and Sons, 1966). Anne Treneer, *The Mercurial Chemist: A Life of Sir Humphry Davy* (London: Methuen & Company, 1963). Thomas Edward Thorpe, *Humphry Davy: Poet and Philosopher* (New York: Macmillan & Company, 1896).

Page 84, *the first great popular scientific lecturer* ... Hartley, op. cit., p. 45.

Page 84, *Christmas Lectures for Young People* ... Michael Faraday, *The Chemical History of a Candle: With a Facsimile Reproduction of Faraday's Manuscript Lecture Notes from Royal Institution MS F4 J21* (Oxford: Oxford University Press, 2011 Sesquicentenary edition, Frank A. J. L. James, editor).

Page 84, *His protégé and successor* ... Jill Howard, "Physics and Fashion: John Tyndall and His Audiences in Mid-Victorian Britain," *Studies in History and Philosophy of Science*, Part A, vol. 35A, no. 4 (December 2004), pp. 729–758. *See also* Arthur Stewart Eve and Clarence Hamilton Creasey, *Life and Work of John Tyndall* (London: Macmillan, 1945).

Page 84, *lecture demonstrations of smoke rings* ... Cargill Gilston Knott, *Life and Scientific Work of Peter Guthrie Tait* (Cambridge, England: Cambridge University Press, 1911), p. 68; P. G. Tait, *Lectures on Some Recent Advances in Physical Science* (London: Macmillan, 1876), p. 291.

Page 84, *science teacher Eiffel G. Plasterer* ... Eiffel G. Plasterer, "The Educational Use of Soap Bubbles," *School Science and Mathematics*, vol. 44, no. 5 (1944), pp. 462–466.

Page 84, *several handbooks of chemical demonstrations* ... Bassam Z. Shakhashiri, *Chemical Demonstrations: A Handbook for Teachers of Chemistry* (Madison: University of Wisconsin Press; vol. 1, 1983; vol. 2, 1985; vol. 3, 1989; vol. 4, 1992; vol. 5, 2011).

Page 86, *Purchase of quantities of radium* ... In 1920,

a gram of radium cost $100,000. Fund raising led by Marie Meloney made possible a gift of a gram of radium for Marie Curie's research. President Warren Gamaliel Harding presented the radium (in a lead box) to her in 1921 at the White House. http://www.aauw.org/article/when-marie-curie-needed-radium/, accessed July 6, 2014.

Page 87, *Germann chose to present his results and* ... Frank E. E. Germann, "A New Hydrate of Uranium Nitrate: Uranium Nitrate Icositetrahydrate," abstract of a paper presented at the Rochester meeting of the American Physical Society, October 26 and 27, 1917, *Physical Review* (Second Series), vol. 11, no. 3 (1918), pp. 245–246; submitted October 11, 1917. Details of this research, based on experiments conducted at Cornell, were later published in papers submitted from the University of Colorado: Frank E. Germann, "Thermal Analysis at Low Temperatures," *Physical Review* (Second Series), vol. 19, no. 6 (1922), pp. 623–628; and Frank E. E. Germann, "A New Hydrate of Uranyl Nitrate," *Journal of the American Chemical Society*, vol. 44 (1922), pp. 1466–1469.

Page 88, *He was accepted for both* ... Minutes, Colorado School of Mines Board of Trustees, August 13, 1918.

Page 89, *wrote Joseph's daughter Jane* ... Vivid recollections of the trip, and the arrival of the Sewall family at their new home in the only building on campus, are given by Jane Sewall in her delightful book, *Jane, Dear Child* (Boulder: University of Colorado Press, 1957).

Page 89, *two faculty leaves of absence* ... *Quarterly of the Colorado School of Mines*, vol. 14, no. 1 (1919) [Catalogue Edition], p. 9. This issue also contained a listing of graduate students and special lecturers, a description of the Hall of Chemistry, and information about the School of Mines E.M. degree.

Page 89, *Neither van Nuys nor Hazard returned* ... *Quarterly of the Colorado School of Mines*, vol. 15, no. 1 (1920) [Catalogue Edition], p. 9.

Page 89, *There were fifteen persons* ... Listing of faculty in *Colorado School Directory* (Colorado

Department of Education: 1919), pp. 16–17.

Page 90, *published papers on this subject* ... Frank E. Germann, "The Flotation Process—Its Present Status and Future Possibilities," *The Colorado Manufacturer and Consumer* (Colorado Manufacturers and Merchants Association), vol. 6 (1921), p. 18. "The Flotation Process—Its Present Status and Future Possibilities," *The Colorado Engineer* (University of Colorado), vol. 18, no. 2 (January 1923), pp. 69, 88.

Page 90, *eleven printed pages on radium* ... Dr. Frank E. E. German, "Radioactivity and Radioactive Transformations," *The Colorado School of Mines Magazine* (Golden: Alumni Association of the Colorado School of Mines), vol. 9, no. 1 (January 1919), pp. 1–8. Dr. Frank E. E. German, "Methods of Determining the Radium Content of Minerals," *The Colorado School of Mines Magazine*, vol. 9, no. 1 (January 1919), pp. 8–11. This was the first issue after publication had been suspended during the Great War.

Page 91, *Upon coming to Mines* ... James H. Gary, "Historical Overview of the Colorado School of Mines Oil Shale Symposia" (26th Oil Shale Symposium, Colorado School of Mines, October 16–October 19, 2006).

Page 91, *published the first in a series* ... Victor Clifton Alderson, *The Oil Shale Industry* (Golden: Colorado School of Mines, 1918; *School of Mines Quarterly*, vol. 13, no. 2), 30 pages.

Page 92, *Frank Germann wrote* ... Letter dated March 27, 1919, from Frank E. E. Germann to President Wm. L. Bryan. President Bryan replied: "I shall be very glad to extend assistance to you in securing a place where the conditions will be more favorable." Indiana University President's Office Correspondence, 1913–1937: "Germann, Frank E. E." Dina Kellams, Associate Archivist, Indiana University, on January 31, 2014, provided the reference to this correspondence. It was accessed online via the finding aid: http://purl.dlib.indiana.edu/iudl/findingaids/archives/InU-Ar-VAA8687.

Page 92, *The report of an investigation* ... Quotation from "Colorado School of Mines," *Mining and*

Scientific Press, September 11, 1920, pp. 369–370.

Page 93, *impending resignation of Harry Alfred Curtis (1884–1963)* ... Harry Alfred Curtis (1884–1963), B.S. (Ch.E.), Ph.D., Professor of Physical Chemistry, was a former student of John Bernard Ekeley, and was to have a brilliant career beyond Colorado. Curtis is listed on the faculty roster for 1919–1920, with the notation "Resigned October 10, 1919." *Catalogue, 1919–1920; University of Colorado Bulletin* (vol. 20, no. 4, General Series no. 153; Boulder: April 1920), p. 17. From "Personal Items," *Chemical Age* (vol. 1, no. 3, August 10, 1919), p. 140: "Dr. Harry A. Curtis has been appointed Professor of Chemistry at Northwestern University. Dr. Curtis left his duties at the University of Colorado to take part in the Mexican Campaign in 1916. He was one of the first chemists to enlist after the war with Germany was declared and has served in the Nitrate Development Division of the Chemical Warfare Service." Born in Sedalia, Colorado, Curtis earned the B.S.C.E. (1908) and M.A. (1910) degrees from the University of Colorado, and the Ph.D. (1914) from the University of Wisconsin. Excepting leaves for doctoral study and for military service, Curtis held appointments at the University of Colorado from 1906 to 1920: Chemistry Stock Room Assistant, 1906–1907; Assistant in Chemistry, 1907–1908; Instructor in Chemistry, 1908–1912; Assistant Professor in Chemistry, 1912–1915; Professor of Physical Chemistry, 1915–1920. In 1907–1908, students Harry Alfred Curtis and Paul Marshall Dean, together with Professor John Bernard Ekeley, were members of the Chemical Society of the University of Colorado, an organization for students of chemistry and chemical engineering. For the B.S. degree in chemical engineering, Curtis submitted the thesis "A Study of Boulder Natural Gas." For the M.A. degree in electrical engineering, he submitted the thesis "Rapid Electrolytic Methods Applied in Analysis of Western Ores." For the Ph.D. degree in academic physical chemistry, he submitted reprints of research articles on "The Photolysis of

Potassium Iodate" and "The Photochemical Decomposition of Hydrogen Peroxide," published jointly with his advisor J. Howard Matthews in the *Journal* of *Physical Chemistry*, vol. 18, pp. 166–178, 521–537, 641–652. Sources: library catalogs of the University of Colorado and the University of Wisconsin; Dina C. Carson, "Faculty, Staff and Administrators of the University of Colorado, 1877–1921," *Boulder Genealogical Society Quarterly*, vol. 43, no. 1 (February 2011), pp. 39–46; *The 1908 Coloradoan* (vol. 8, 1907), pp. 27, 85, 146, 255. Harry Alfred Curtis and George Dyke Kendall Jr. in 1908 were the first two recipients of the degree of Bachelor of Science in Chemical Engineering from the University of Colorado. Byron E. Lauer and Therese Morrison, *A History of the Department of Chemical Engineering at the University of Colorado from its beginning in 1904 until August 1962* (Boulder: Department of Chemical Engineering at the University of Colorado, 1962), p. 10. Mrs. Curtis donated her husband's papers in 1964 to establish the Harry Curtis Collection, MS.0323, University of Tennessee Libraries, Knoxville, Special Collections; the internet address for the finding aid is http://dlc.lib.utk.edu/spc/view?docId=ead/0012_000285_000000_0000/0012_000285_000000_0000.xml;query=.

Harry Alfred Curtis became the first Chairman of the Department of Chemical Engineering at Yale University, appointed for the 1922–1923 year. His office and laboratories were in the new Sterling Chemistry Laboratory, built in 1923 with funds bequeathed by John William Sterling (1844–1918), Yale Class of 1884. "Professor Curtis served as Chairman until 1931 and then left Yale to continue a distinguished career as director of research for a major oil company and later as Dean of Engineering at the University of Missouri and a member of the Board of Governors of the Tennessee Valley Authority," Charles A. Walker, "CHE at Yale," *Chemical Engineering Education* (Summer 1982), pp. 102–106; http://ufdc.ufl.edu/AA00000383/00075/8x, accessed December 3, 2015.

Curtis was awarded honorary doctoral degrees by

the University of Wisconsin (1937) and the University of Louisville (1948), the Norlin Medal of the University of Colorado (1930), the Nathan W. Dougherty Award of the University of Tennessee (1959), the University of Missouri Engineering Honor Award (1963), and the Distinguished Engineering Alumni Award of the University of Colorado posthumously in 1966. http://www.colorado.edu/engineering/deaa/cgi-bin/display.pl?id=2, accessed September 2, 2014; http://www.engr.utk.edu/give/awards_engineering.html, accessed December 3, 2015.

Page 93, *The Board accepted his resignation* ... Minutes, Colorado School of Mines Board of Trustees, April 24, 1919.

Page 94, *in the midst of a major transition* ... A twenty-first century view of the transition is Jarett Zuboy, *The Road to Independence and Beyond: Commemorating the 40th Anniversary of the University of Colorado Denver, 1973–2013* (Denver: University of Colorado Denver, September 2013).

Page 94, *a third of its 170-member faculty* ... A listing of the faculty (with rank, degrees, and department) of the University of Colorado–Boulder is given in *Colorado Educational Directory, School Year 1919–1920* (Boulder: State Superintendent of Public Instruction, 1919), pp. 18–21.

Page 94, *joined a nine-member faculty* ... *Catalogue, 1919–1920*, op. cit.

Page 94, *Several promotions took effect* ... *Catalogue, 1920–1921; University of Colorado Bulletin* (vol. 21, no. 3, General Series no. 168; Boulder: March 1921), pp. 15–22.

Page 95, *Eva M. Baum died on November 26, 1921* ... Eva M. Baum (1892–1921) was the daughter of Anna (1873–1949) and John F. Baum (1867–1945). Eva was buried in the Gypsum Hill Cemetery, Salina, Kansas. http://www.findagrave.com/cgi-bin/fg.cgi?page=gr&GRid=83743313, accessed September 2, 2014.

Page 95, *The Department of Chemistry for 1921–1922* ... *Catalogue, 1921–1922; University of Colo-*

rado Bulletin (vol. 22, no. 3, General Series no. 180; Boulder: March 1922), pp. 60–63.

Page 96, *John Bernard Ekeley was born* ... "John B. Ekeley," http://www.findagrave.com/cgi-bin/fg.cgi?page=gr&GRid=15159085&ref=wvr, accessed September 3, 2014.

Page 96, *laboratory manual for high school chemistry* ... John Bernard Ekeley, *An Elementary Experimental Chemistry* (New York: Silver, Burdett & Company, 1900), xii + 252 pages. Silver, Burdett & Company, founded in 1888, was a leading school textbook publisher in the first half of the twentieth century.

Page 96, *working with Albert Edinger* ... *See* Albert Edinger und John B. Ekeley, "Ueber die basischen Eigenschaften des Schwefels" [About the Basic Properties of Sulfur], *Berichte der Deutschen chemischen Gesellschaft*, vol. 35, no. 1 (January–March 1902), pp. 96–98. *See also* Alb. Edinger und John B. Ekeley, "Ueber die durch Einwirkung von Chlorschwefel auf aromatische Amine entstehenden Dithioniumbasen und Halogensubstitutionsprodukte" [Action of Sulphur Chloride on Aromatic Amines], *Journal für praktische Chemie*, vol. 174 (New Series vol. 66), no. 2 (August 28, 1902), pp. 209–230.

Page 96, *The University of Colorado opened* ... William E. Davis, *Glory Colorado! A History of the University of Colorado, 1858–1963* (Boulder: Pruett Press, 1965), pp. 23–27. This book has no index. Printing type of the 798 pages of text and the front matter was probably electrotyped. In the years between 1998 and 2007, an index was prepared. A sequel (*Glory Colorado! A History of the University of Colorado, 1963–2000*) was written by William E. Davis. Using the original electrotype plates and incorporating the new index, the 1965 book was reprinted and issued as Volume I of a two-volume set with the title *Glory Colorado!* Because the original plates were used unchanged for the second printing, pagination remained the same and identical citations can be made to either printing. No publisher or printer is given for the two-volume set.

Page 97, *Joseph Addison Sewall (1830–1917)* … Davis, *Glory Colorado!*, vol. 1, op. cit., pp. 23–28. *See also* Helen E. Marshall, *Grandest of Enterprises: Illinois State University, 1857–1957* (Normal, Illinois: Illinois State University History Book, Book 4, 1956), http://ir.library.illinoisstate.edu/isuhistory-book/4, pp. 78, 92, 109, 118, 127, 130; accessed December 18, 2015. *See further,* John R. Freed, *Educating Illinois: Illinois State University, 1857–2007* (Normal, Illinois: Illinois State University, 2009), http://ir.library.illinoisstate.edu/cgi/viewcontent.cgi?article=1000&context=eil, Chapter 2, "The State University of Illinois, 1857–1867," especially pp. 55–56, 60–61; accessed December 18, 2015. Jenna Self, Archives Assistant, Illinois State University, supplied references to the Marshall and Freed books. An account of the early years of the University of Colorado is John W. Horner (William A. Weber, editor), *Colorado University: The Austere Years (The Story of Its First Quarter Century)* (Boulder: University of Colorado, 2014). Joseph's daughter Jane Sewall in her appealing and insightful book, *Jane, Dear Child* (Boulder: University of Colorado Press, 1957), records first-hand impressions of the arrival of the Sewall family in Boulder, the first Commencement in 1885, and the move of the family from quarters in Old Main into the new President's House. The "Forward" is by Robert L. Stearns, sixth President of the University of Colorado (1939–1953). A fourteen-page tribute (that relies heavily on secondary sources) is Nolie Mumey, P.M., *Joseph Addision Sewall (1830–1917): Pioneer Physician, Educator and the First President of the University of Colorado*, written in September 1959 for the *Journal of Medical Education* of the College of Medical Evangelists, Los Angeles, and reprinted from the *1966 Brand Book* of the Denver Posse of The Westerners.

Page 97, *read medicine in Maine* … William E. Davis has written that Sewall "graduated from Massachusetts Medical School [predecessor of Harvard Medical School] in 1852 with the degree of M.D." Davis, *Glory Colorado!*, vol. 1, op. cit., p. 24. *See, however:* "Although I have seen a published

reference to Joseph Addison Sewall's 1852 medical degree from Harvard, I can find no indication that he ever received such a degree, nor that he ever was a matriculant at the Medical School during this period." Email, January 12, 2015, from Jack Eckert, Public Services Librarian, Center for the History of Medicine, Francis A. Countway Library of Medicine, Harvard Medical School.

Page 97, *"sent Dr. Joseph Addison Sewall to Harvard* … Freed, op. cit., p. 55.

Page 97, *there is no documentary evidence* … The Reference Staff of the Harvard University Archives reported (emails January 9 and 12, 2015) that a search of their collections, including the *Quinquennial Catalogue*, the *Tolman Index to University Records*, the *Annual Reports*, and the *General Catalogue*, revealed no information regarding Joseph Addison Sewall or any connection to the University.

Page 97, *Benjamin Silliman Jr. (1816–1885)* … A well-documented paper that places Benjamin Silliman Jr. in the context of early American chemical research is Martin D. Saltzman, "Benjamin Silliman Jr.'s 1874 Papers: American Contributions to Chemistry," *Bulletin of the History of Chemistry*, vol. 36, no. 1 (2011), pp. 22–34.

Page 97, *"the world's first teaching laboratory* … Quotation from Kevin Adkisson, "How Science Was Built: 1701-1900," *Yale Scientific Magazine* ("the nation's oldest college science publication"), vol. 83, no. 3 (October 2, 2010). The credibility of this assertion depends, in part, on the definition of "modern chemistry."

Page 97, *In July 1818, he founded* … The original title was *The American Journal of Science, More Especially of Mineralogy, Geology, and the Other Branches of Natural History; Including also Agriculture and the Ornamental as well as Useful Arts.* Reproduction of the title page of volume 1, Richard Conniff, "How Science Came to Yale," *Yale Alumni Magazine*, vol. 78, no. 4 (March/April 2015), pp. 46–52.

Page 98, *It was not unusual for a student* … *Catalogue of Graduates of the Lawrence Scientific School of*

Harvard University, 1851–1895 (Cambrdige: 1896), pp. 7–8, 24.

Page 98, *honorary Ph.D. from Knox College* … Maryjo McAndrew, Senior Archive Assistant, Knox College, email, January 12, 2015.

Page 99, *Charles Skeele Palmer (1858–1939)* … Christina E. Barber, Deputy Archivist, Amherst College; and James Stimpert, Senior Reference Archivist at Sheridan Libraries, The Johns Hopkins University, supplied biographical information. *See also* Davis, *Glory Colorado!,* vol. 1, op. cit., pp. 58, 92.

Page 99, *"This was during a period of student* … Lisa Dunn, Reference Department, Arthur Lakes Library, Colorado School of Mines, email January 9, 2015.

Page 100, *the third (with no academic degree)* … Employing undergraduate students as teaching assistants in chemistry laboratories was not unique to the early years of the University of Colorado. The pattern has continued at institutions throughout the United States, and into the twenty-first century. For example, in 2012 the Chemistry Department of the University of Colorado–Denver formalized the practice, initiating an end-of-summer "boot camp" to train undergraduate teaching assistants for general chemistry and organic chemistry laboratories. Celia Henry Arnaud, "Boot Camp Prepares Undergraduates to Teach Lab Sections," *Chemical & Engineering News,* vol. 92, no. 39 (September 29, 2014), p. 41.

Page 100, *five research reports* … John B. Ekeley, "On the action of the Halogens and the Sulphur Halides upon Paratoluqinoline," *University of Colorado Studies,* vol. 1, no. 2, 1902; John B. Ekeley, "On a Dihydro-Quinoxaline from Orthophenilene-Diamine and Mesityloxide," *University of Colorado Studies,* vol. 2, no. 2, 1904; John B. Ekeley, "On a New Alpha-Dihydroquinoxaline," *University of Colorado Studies,* vol. 3, no. 3, 1906; John B. Ekeley, "The Composition of Some Colorado Tungsten Ores," *University of Colorado Studies,* vol. 6, no. 2, 1909; John B. Ekeley, "The Electrochemistry of the Solution of Gold in Potassium Cyanide," *University of Colorado Studies,* vol. 6, no. 3, 1909.

Page 100, *a lengthy article* … John B. Ekeley, "The New Proposed Coal Mining Law for Colorado," *University of Colorado Journal of Engineering,* no. 7 (May 1911), pp. 24–35.

Page 100, *arsenic in the organs of a human cadaver* … John B. Ekeley, "On the Distribution of Ante-Mortem Administered Arsenic in the Human Cadaver," *Journal of the American Chemical Society,* vol. 35, no. 4 (April 1913), pp. 483–485.

Page 100, *to accompany its popular text* … This English version was translated by Hermon Charles Cooper from Arnold Frederik Holleman, *Lehrbuch der anorganischen Chemie für Studierende an Universitäten und technischen Hochschulen* (Leipzig: Veit & Comp., 1900).

Page 100, *Colgate University had awarded him* … *Science* (New Series), vol. 34, no. 867 (August 11, 1911), p. 178.

Page 101, *Charles Franklin Poe (1888–1970)* … Davis, *Glory Colorado!,* vol. 1, op. cit., pp. 533–534. Doug Petersen, Registrar's Office, Cornell University, supplied additional information in an email on December 23, 2014. Charles was born February 15, 1888, son of Christie Stokes Hoagland and Jefferson Quigley Hall. Mr. Hall died of pneumonia when Charles was very young. When his mother married Samuel S. Poe, Charles was given the surname Poe. *See* http://www.findagrave.com/cgi-bin/fg.cgi?page=gr&GRid=65231985, accessed December 18, 2015.

Page 102, *Study of Media for the Production of Bacterial Fluorescence* … The thesis in the Cornell University Library is a bound copy of two reprints: Frederick Raymond Georgia and Charles Franklin Poe, "Study of Bacterial Fluorescence in Various Media. I. Inorganic Substances Necessary for Bacterial Fluorescence," *Journal of Bacteriology,* vol. 22, no. 5 (November 1931), pp. 349–361; and Frederick Raymond Georgia and Charles Franklin Poe, "Study of Bacterial Fluorescence in Various Media. II. The Production of Fluorescence in Media Made from Peptones," *Journal of Bacteriology,* vol. 23, no. 2 (February 1932), pp. 135–145.

Page 102, *Horace Bulle Van Valkenburgh II ... The Cardinal* (University of Arkansas, 1905), p. 30. Copy supplied by Amy L. Allen, University Archivist, University of Arkansas Libraries.

Page 102, *spent time in China as missionary volunteers* ... "Sailed Volunteers for 1907," *The Intercollegian*, vol. 30 (March 1908), p. 147.

Page 102, *were said to have been* ... George B. Kauffman, "Éloge: John C. Bailar, Jr. (1904–1991), *Journal of Coordination Chemistry*, vol. 28, issue 3–4 (1993), pp. 183–189.

Page 102, *first scholarly publication* ... H. B. Van Valkenburgh and John C. Bailar Jr., *Journal of the American Chemical Society*, vol. 47, no. 8 (August 1925), pp. 2134–2137.

Page 103, *Van Valkenburgh entered the Graduate School* ... Peter Lido, Reference Assistant, the University of Chicago Library, email February 18, 2015.

Page 103, *He presented his results in two papers* ... H. I. Schlesinger and H. B. Van Valkenburgh, "Ferrous Nitroso Compounds," *Journal of the American Chemical Society*," vol. 51, no. 5 (May 1929), pp. 1323–1331; H. I. Schlesinger and H. B. Van Valkenburgh, "The Structure of Ferric Thiocyanate and the Thiocyanate Test for Iron," *Journal of the American Chemical Society*, vol. 53, no. 4 (April 1931), pp. 1212–1216.

Page 103, *the three-story Chemistry Building* ... *Catalogue, 1919–1920*, op. cit., p. 52.

Page 103, *chemical-resistant surface* ... The likely chemical-resistant materials for the lecture desktop, as well as for laboratory work surfaces throughout the Chemistry Building, were either soapstone or carbonized wood. Both materials performed well in many other laboratories for decades. Typically, such laboratory work surfaces were at least 1¼ inch thick. A major supplier of quarried soapstone laboratory tabletops was the Albemarle Soapstone Company, formed in 1883 by James H. Serene and Daniel J. Carroll in Schuyler, Virginia. They called their product "Alberene stone." The wood used for tabletops was often maple or birch. A recipe for carbonizing and staining wood is given by C. R. Hoover, "Laboratory Table-Top Materials," *Industrial and Engineering Chemistry*, vol. 15, no. 6 (June 1923), 569–570. Hoover cites (and reprints) a similar recipe from *N.B.S. Circular 69* (Washington: United States National Bureau of Standards), p. 53.

Page 104, *adsorption of gases on elemental iodine and silver* ... Philippe-Auguste Guye et Frank-E.-E. Germann, "Sur les Gas Retenus par l'Iode et l'Argent" [Concerning the Gases Retained by Iodine and Silver], *Comptes Rendus Hebdomadaires des Séances de l'Académie des Sciences*, vol. 159 (1922), pp. 225–229; Philippe-Auguste Guye et Frank-E.-E. Germann, "Contributions à l'Étude des Causes d'Erreur Affectant les Determinations des Poids Atomiques. IV. Méthode Micro-analytique pour l'Étude des Gaz; Application à l'Analyse de Traces d'Air. V. Des Impuretes Gazeuses Continues dans l'Argent Considéré Comme Etalon Auxiliaire de Poids Atomiques" [Contributions to the Study of the Causes of Error Affecting the Determinations of Atomic Weights. IV. Microanalytical Methods for the Study of Gases; Applications to the Analysis of Traces of Air. V. Concerning Gaseous Impurities Contained in Silver Regarded as an Auxiliary Standard in Atomic Weight Determinations], *Journal de Chimie Physique*, vol. 14 (1913), pp. 195–243.

Page 104, *newly developed physical chemical theories ... For an example, see* Irving Langmuir, "The Adsorption of Gases on Plane Surfaces of Glass, Mica and Platinum," *Journal of the American Chemical Society*, vol. 40, no. 9 (September 1918), pp. 1361–1403. Irving Langmuir (1881–1957) received the Nobel Prize in Chemistry in 1932 for his pioneering work in the physical chemistry of surfaces.

Page 104, *Frank observed* ... Frank E. E. Germann, "Adsorption of Radium by Barium Sulfate," *Journal of the American Chemical Society*, vol. 43 (1921), pp. 1615–1621.

Page 104, *he submitted his paper to a* chemical *journal ... Journal of the American Chemical Society*.

Page 104, *"radium emanation"*... Herman Schlundt and Richard B. Moore, "Radio-activity of Some Deep Well and Mineral Waters," *Journal of Physical Chemistry*, vol. 9 (1905), pp. 320–332; Frank E. E. Germann, "The Emanation Method for Radium," *Science* (New Series), vol. 59, no. 1528 (April 11, 1924), pp. 340–341. A twenty-first century student experiment to measure the concentration of radon has been described by J. A. Tripp, *Laboratory Manual* to accompany *Chemistry in Context* (New York: McGraw-Hill, 7th edition, 2012), pp. 141–148; cited by Sheila Adamus Liotta, "An Experiment to Accompany the Study of Nuclear Chemistry: The Measurement of Radon," *NEACT* [New England Association of Chemistry Teachers] *Journal*, vol. 29 (Fall 2014), pp. 1–3.

Page 104, *radon, a radioactive "noble element"* ... The six noble gases that occur in nature are helium, neon, argon, krypton, xenon, and radon. These elements were called "inert gases" until 1962, because there was no known chemistry involving them. Then Neil Bartlett (1932–2008) reported the synthesis of the compound xenon hexafluoroplatinate. Bartlett subsequently synthesized other xenon compounds. Compounds of other noble gases have since been reported.

Page 105, *Ralph Newton Traxler* ... *University of Colorado Bulletin*, vol. 22, no. 3, General Series no. 180 (Boulder: March 1922), pp. 60-63. *The Harbinger*, Lamar High School Annual Yearbook, 1915 and 1916; and the 1916 Lamar School Census Book; copies of relevant pages were provided by Dave Tecklenburg, Superintendent, Lamar Re-2 School District. Information was also provided by Jeri Bonnes, Transcript Coordinator, Office of the Registrar, University of Colorado Boulder; by Betty Forney, Highland Community College, and by Principal Chris Lackey, Doniphan West High School, Highland, Kansas.

Page 105, *Problem 54 in Colloid Chemistry* ... Wilder D. Bancroft, *Research Problems in Colloid Chemistry*, reprint and circular series, no. 13 (Washington: National Research Council, 1921), 54 pages.

Page 105, *pioneer photography chemist Matthew Carey Lea* ... M. Carey Lea, "On Photobromide and Photoiodide of Silver," *American Journal of Science* [*Silliman's Journal*], vol. 33, article 48, (June 1887), 6 pages; M. C. Lea, *A Manual of Photography: Intended as a Text Book for Beginners and a Book of Reference for Advanced Photographers* (Philadelphia: Benerman and Wilson, 1868). Biographies: Laszlo Takacs, "M. Carey Lea, the Father of Mechanochemistry," *Bulletin of the History of Chemistry*, vol. 28, no. 1 (2003), pp. 26–34; George F. Barker, "Matthew Carey Lea (1823–1897)," *Biographical Memoirs of the National Academy of Sciences* (Washington: National Academy of Sciences, 1903), pp. 155–205.

Page 105, *Germann and Traxler submitted a research report* ... Frank E. E. Germann and Ralph N. Traxler, "Adsorption of Iodine by Silver Iodide," *Journal of the American Chemical Society*, vol. 44, no. 3 (1922), pp. 460–464; Ralph N. Traxler and Frank E. E. Germann, "The Action of Red Phosphorus on Iodine in Organic Solvents," *Journal of the American Pharmaceutical Association*, vol. 14, no. 6 (June 1925), pp. 476–477; Ralph N. Traxler and Frank E. E. Germann, "The Decolorization of Carbon Disulphide Solutions of Iodine by Red Phosphorus," *Journal of Physical Chemistry*, vol. 29, no. 9 (1925), pp. 1119–1124; Frank E. E. Germann and Ralph N. Traxler, "Preparation and Melting Points of Pure Di- and Tri-Iodide of Phosphorus," *Journal of the American Chemical Society*, vol. 49, no. 2 (February 1927), pp. 307–312.

Page 105, *Professor of Chemistry and Physics* ... Faculty section, *Trail Blazer*, Highland College Yearbook (1924). Copy supplied by Penny Donaldson, Library Director, Highland Community College, February 9, 2016.

Page 106, *Ph.D. in Chemistry from Wisconsin* ... Ralph Newton Traxler, "The Osmotic Permeability of Living Plant Membranes," University of Wisconsin Ph.D. dissertation, 1926; Louis Kahlenberg and Ralph N. Traxler, "The Osmotic Permeability of Living Plant Membranes," *Transactions of the Wisconsin Academy of Sciences, Arts, and Letters*, vol.

28 (1933), pp. 275–290; Louis Kahlenberg and Ralph Traxler, "On the Passage of Boric Acid and Certain Salts into Fruits and Vegetables," *Plant Physiology,* vol. 2, no. 1 (January 1927), pp. 39–54.

Page 106, *Dr. Traxler then joined the faculty of Macalester College* ... Information supplied by Ellen Holt-Werle, Archivist, Dewitt Wallace Library, Macalester College.

Page 106, *conduct experimental studies on the rate* ... Ralph N. Traxler, "The Effect of Temperature on Rate of Osmosis," *Journal of Physical Chemistry,* vol. 32, no. 1 (January 1927), pp. 127–141.

Page 106, *undergraduate research by Harry N. Huntzicker* ... Ralph N. Traxler and Harry N. Huntzicker, "Influence of the Presence of a Solute on Rate of Osmosis," *Journal of Physical Chemistry,* vol. 39, no. 3 (January 1935), pp. 431–435.

Page 106, *Port Neches, Texas* ... The patent application of Joseph W. Romberg and Ralph N. Traxler for "Asphalt Cutbacks" on July 6, 1949, gave their address as Port Neches, Texas. The patent (US 2661300A) was assigned to the Texas Company.

Page 106, *Director of Asphalt Research at the Texas Company* ... "The Society of Rheology," *Physics Today,* vol. 4, no. 10 (October 1951), pp. 24–25. The Society in 1929 defined the word "rheology" as "the science of deformation and flow of matter."

Page 106, *Traxler accepted an appointment* ... Shannon Turner, Assistant to the Executive Associate Director, Texas A&M Transportation Institute, email February 16, 2015.

Page 106, *Traxler wrote a major book* ... Ralph Newton Traxler, *Asphalt: Its Composition, Properties, and Uses* (New York: Reinhold Publishing Corporation, 1961), 294 pages.

Page 106, *was author or co-author of several publications* ... For example, Ralph Newton Traxler and Frank L. Carter, *Oxygen Consumption by Asphalt Films and Resulting Viscosity Changes* (College Station: Texas Transportation Institute, 1967); Ralph Newton Traxler, Frank H. Scrivner, and William E. Kuykendall, *Loss of Durability in Bituminous Pavement Surfaces—Importance of Chemically Active Solar Radiation* (College Station: Texas Transportation Institute, 1971); Douglas Bynum and Ralph N. Traxler, *Performance Requirements of High Quality Flexible Pavements* (College Station: Texas Transportation Institute, 1969); Ralph Newton Traxler, *Use of Additives to Retard Hardening of Asphalts by Actinic Solar Radiation* (College Station: Texas Transportation Institute, 1972); Ralph N. Traxler, *Viscosity of Asphalt Cement from a Construction Standpoint* (College Station: National Bituminous Concrete Association, 1963); Ralph N. Traxler, *Stiffness of Asphalt Cements Evaluated by Compression* (College Station: Texas Transportation Institute, 1968); Ralph N. Traxler, *Hardening of Asphalt Cements by Exposure to Ultraviolet and Short Wave Length Visible Light* (College Station: Texas Transportation Institute, 1968); Ralph N. Traxler, *Retardation of Asphalt Hardening by Chemical Additives* (College Station: National Bituminous Concrete Association, 1964); Ralph N. Traxler, *Best Temperature to Measure Viscosity for Evaluation of Asphalt Durability in Service* (College Station: Texas Transportation Institute, 1968); Ralph N. Traxler, *Research in Asphalt Quality Control* (College Station: Texas Transportation Institute, 1960); Ralph N. Traxler, *Hardening of 85–100 Penetration Asphalt Cements During Service in Pavement* (College Station: Texas Transportation Institute, 1965); Ralph N. Traxler, *Hardening of Paving Asphalts and Relation to Composition* (College Station: Texas Transportation Institute, 1961); Ralph N. Traxler, *Viscosity and Industrial Asphalt Index of Samples of Asphalt Cement* (College Station: National Bituminous Concrete Association, 1964).

Page 107, *Richard Leach Maddox* ... R. L. Maddox, "An Experiment with Geltino-Bromide," *British Journal of Photography,* vol. 18, no. 592 (September 8, 1871), pp. 422–423.

Page 108, *was investigating that photosensitivity* ... Frank E. E. Germann and Malcolm C. Hylan, "Dispersity of Silver Halides in Relation to Their Photographic Behavior," *Science,* (New Series), vol. 58, no. 1504 (October 26, 1923), pp. 332–

333; Frank E. E. Germann and Malcolm C. Hylan, "The Photographic Sensitiveness of Silver Iodide," *Journal of the American Chemical Society*, vol. 45, no. 11 (November 1923), pp. 2486–2493; Frank E. E. Germann and Malcolm C. Hylan, "Dispersity of Silver Halides in Relation to Their Photographic Behavior," *Journal of Physical Chemistry*, vol. 28, no. 5 (1924), pp. 449–456. The 1923 paper in *Science* was signed as a contribution from the "Dept. of Theoretical and Physical Chemistry, University of Colorado."

Page 108, *Malcolm Cleveland Hylan (September 29, 1896–December 15, 1944) ... Annual Report of the School Committee and the Superintendent of Schools* (Town of Medfield: December 31, 1914). *The Catalogue* (Providence: Brown University, vol. 13, no. 5, December 1916). *The Catalogue* (Providence: Brown University, 1920–1921).

Page 108, *later joined the Department of Physics ...* Obituary, "Ellen Hyland Clark," *The White Mountain Independent*, Show Low, Arizona, August 5, 2014, http://www.estesparknews.com, posted August 7, 2014. Obituary, "Bruce H. Hylan," *The Washington Post*, February 16, 2011. Mary Alice Hartley (1900–1988) and Malcolm Cleveland Hylan had four children: June, Ann, Bruce, and Ellen.

Page 108, *research on the photographic latent image ...* Julian M. Blair and Malcolm C. Hyland (Department of Physics), "The Intermittency Effect in Photographic Exposure," *Journal of the Optical Society of America*, vol. 23, no. 10 (1933), pp. 353–358; Julian M. Blair and Malcolm C. Hyland (Department of Physics), "The Fading of the Latent Photographic Image on Standing," *Journal of the Optical Society of America*, vol. 25, no. 8 (1935), pp. 246–248.

Page 108, *Dzu-Kun Shen ...* Frank E. E. Germann and Dzu-Kun Shen, "Studies in Photography. I. The Nature of Sensitivity and the Latent Image," *Journal of Physical Chemistry*, vol. 33, no. 6 (1929), pp. 864–872; Frank E. E. Germann and Dzu-Kun Shen, "Studies in Photography. II. The Rôle of Sen-

sitizers in Photography and the Latent Image," *Journal of Physical Chemistry*, vol. 33, no. 10 (1929), pp. 1583–1592; Frank E. E. Germann and D. K. Shen, "The Relation between Photographic Reversal and the Sensitivity of the Silver Halide Grain," *Journal of Physical Chemistry*, vol. 35 (1931), pp. 93–99.

Page 108, *Thomas Howard James ...* T. Howard James, F. E. E. Germann and Julian M. Blair, "The Influence of Salts on Intermittent Photographic Exposures," *The Journal of the Colorado-Wyoming Academy of Science*, vol. 1, no. 6 (1934), p. 17; T. Howard James, F. E. E. Germann and Julian M. Blair, "The Action of Water on the Latent Photographic Image," *Journal of Physical Chemistry*, vol. 38, no. 9 (December 1934), pp. 1211–1216; T. Howard James, F. E. E. Germann and Julian M. Blair, "Action of Water on the Latent Photographic Image," *The Journal of the Colorado-Wyoming Academy of Science*, vol. 1, no. 6 (1934), p. 20.

Page 108, *where he received the Master of Science ... Alumni Bulletin of Lehigh University*, vol. 10, no. 9 (June 1923), p. 23.

Page 108, *Shen spent four years ... Epitome Yearbook, Class of 1924* (Lehigh University), p. 132.

Page 109, *Chinese Delegation ...* "Invitations to the Conference," *Conference on the Limitations of Armament*, 67th Congress, 2d Session, Senate Document No. 126, read February 3, 1922 (Washington: Government Printing Office, 1922), p. 30. http://hdl.handle.net/2027/hvd.32044009979568, accessed December 18, 2015.

Page 109, *Thomas Howard James (November 7, 1912–August 24, 2000) ... Who's Who in Science and Engineering*, accessed via the *Marquis Who's Who* internet database. Additional information was supplied by Xi Gao, Office of the Registrar, University of Colorado Boulder. *See also,* Annabel A. Muenter, "In Memoriam: Thomas Howard James, 1912–2000," *Journal of Imaging Science and Technology*, vol. 45, no. 1 (January/February, 2001), p. iii.

Page 109, *several books on photographic theory ...* Thomas H. James, *The Theory of the Photographic*

Process (New York: Macmillan, 3rd edition 1969, 4th edition 1977); George Clinton Higgins and Thomas Howard James, *Fundamentals of Photographic Theory* (New York: John Wiley, 2nd edition 1949); Burt Haring Carroll, George Clinton Higgins, and Thomas Howard James, *Introduction to Photographic Theory: The Silver Halide Process* (New York: John Wiley, 1980).

Page 109, *Such a practice would have been in general accord* ... Walter Crosby Eells, "The Origin and Early History of Sabbatical Leave" (*AAUP Bulletin*, American Association of University Professors), vol. 48, no. 3 (September 1962), pp. 253–256.

Page 110, *University of Colorado policy in 2014* ... "Policy 5A: Approval of Sabbatical Assignments," http://www.cu.edu/regents/policy-5a-approval-sabbatical-assignments, accessed February 23, 2014.

Page 110, *Colorado Ku Klu Klan* ... Robert Allen Goldberg, *Hooded Empire: The Ku Klux Klan in Colorado* (Urbana: University of Illinois Press, 1981). *See especially* chap. 4, "Triumph at the Polls;" and chap. 5, "Under Invisible Rule."

Page 110, *dismiss all Catholics and all Jews* ... CU Heritage Center, "President George Norlin," http://cuheritage.org/exhibits/presidents/president-george-norlin/, accessed February 23, 2014.

Page 111, *Frances Elizabeth Woland (1892–1967)* ... http://www.findagrave.com/cgi-bin/fg.cgi?page=gr&GRid=65231985, accessed December 18, 2015.

Page 111, *Frank described the facilities* ... Newspaper interview; undated clipping supplied by Archives, University of Colorado Libraries.

Page 111, *a new chemistry building had been designed and constructed* ... Louis Munroe Denis (1863–1936), Professor of Inorganic Chemistry, *The Baker Laboratory of Chemistry at Cornell University: A Description* (Ithaca: Cornell University, 1923), 53 pages.

Page 112, *Mechanical pen-and-paper recorders* ... Pen-and-paper chart recorders for monitoring temperature and pressure were being used before the Great War for some industrial operations. Several such recorders were advertised in the *Chemical Engineering Catalog* (New York: The Chemical Catalog Company, Inc., 1916 edition), including devices sold by The Brown Instrument Company, Philadelphia (page 115); The Foxboro Company, Inc., Foxboro, Massachusetts (page 162); Wm. Gaertner & Company, Chicago (page 165); and Thwing Instrument Company, Philadelphia (page 265). Experimental physiology and pharmacology laboratories used kymographs to record blood pressure and muscle contractions as a function of time. A mechanical kymograph was invented in 1847 by Carl Ludwig (1816–1895). For a century, recordings were made on smoked paper affixed to a rotating metal drum. The recorded data were made permanent by fixing the smoked tracings with an alcoholic solution of shellac. *See* Gurudas Khilnani, Rekha Thaddanee, and Ajeet Kumar Khilnani, "The Smoked Drum," *Indian Journal of Pharmacology*, vol. 45, no. 6 (November–December 2013), pp. 643–645.

Page 112, *Graduate students at Colorado later extended* ... Derk Vivian Tieszen, "Sodium Platinocyanide," M.A. thesis, 1928; Oscar Brauer Muench, "Lithium Platinocyanide and a Micro Method for the Quantitative Determination of its Hydrates," Ph.D. thesis, 1928; Frank E. E. Germann and O. B. Muench, "Studies on the Physical and Chemical Properties of the Platinocyanides. I. The Hydrates of Lithium Platinocyanide," *Journal of Physical Chemistry*, vol. 33, no. 3 (1933), pp. 415–423.

Page 112, *Derk Vivian Tieszen (October 19, 1894– January 22, 1960)* ... Biographical information was supplied by Vicki Schardin, Administrative Secretary, Marion High School, Marion, South Dakota; Vernetta Waltner, Development Director, Freeman Academy; John D. Thiesen, Archivist and Co-Director of Libraries, Mennonite Library and Archives, Bethel College; Joe Springer, Curator, Mennonite Historical Library, Goshen College; and Judi Olson, Yankton College Staff. [Yankton College closed in December 1984, but it maintains a "College Without Walls" presence in downtown Yankton.] John D. Thiesen provided the reference to an obituary of Dr. Derk Vivian Tieszen [*Mennonite Weekly Review* (Newton, Kansas), February 11, 1960, p. 8; https://mla.bethelks.edu/mediawiki/index.php/Tieszen,_Derk_V._(1894-1960), accessed December 18, 2015.] The emigration from Ukraine and the settlement in Rosefield Township are described in John David Unruh, *The Derk Tieszen Story* (Freeman, South Dakota: Pine Hill Press, 1975), 20 pages saddle-stitched; photocopy from the Mennonite Library & Archives, North Newton, Kansas.

Page 113, *Tieszen descendants numbered at least 1,174* ... David Derk Tieszen, *History and Record of The Tieszen Family* (Marion, South Dakota: 1954), 123 pages.

Page 113, *one-room, one-teacher Dick School* ... "Rural Schools in Northwest Turner County," *in* Marion Centennial Book Committee, *A Tale of Three Cities: Marion, Monroe & Dolton* (Freeman, South Dakota: Pine Hill Press, 1979), pp. 146–154.

Page 113, *Bethel College is the oldest Mennonite college* ... Bethel College was founded in 1886, although it was not until September 20, 1893, that the first campus building was dedicated; then the first classes were held. It was originally a two-year school. The Bethel four-year curriculum was introduced in 1911. Goshen College in Indiana was founded in 1894 as the Elkhart Institute Association. The Goshen four-year curriculum was introduced in 1908.

Page 114, *she had been the physical education teacher* ... *The Holdrege Duster* (Holdrege, Nebraska: Holdrege High School), vol. 5, no. 11 (March 31, 1925), p. 1. https://ia800500.us.archive.org/33/items/HoldregeDusterStudentNewspaper1925-1926/HoldredgeDusterStudentNewspaper1925-1926.pdf, accessed November 6, 2015.

Page 114, *Abram Royer Brubacher (1870–1939)* ... Brubacher graduated in 1893 from Phillips–Andover Academy, Andover, Massachusetts, and then received the B.A. degree from Yale College. After teaching for two years at Williston Academy, Easthampton, Massachusetts, he returned to Yale in 1899 for graduate studies in Greek. He received the Ph.D. in 1902. He successively was Principal of Gloversville High School, Gloversville, New York, and Principal in Schenectady, New York. From 1908 until 1914, he was Superintendent of Schools in Schenectady. Then he became President of the New York State College for Teachers at Albany. James Sullivan, ed., *The History of New York State Biographies*, Part 16 (New York: Lewis Historical Publishing Company, Inc., 1927), pp. 90–91.

Page 114, *Oscar Brauer Muench (1891–1953)* ... Information supplied by Jackie Hawes, Director, Washington Public Library, Washington, Missouri; Lynn E. Gates, Head of Archives, Thomas C. Donnelly Library, New Mexico Highlands University; Gary Cox, University Archives, University of Missouri; Lori Asher, Office Support Staff, Registrar's Office, University of Missouri; and Julie Bell, Assistant to the Superintendent, School District of Washington, Missouri. *See also* Karen Cernich, Feature Editor, "Remembering When," an interview with 90-year-old Joseph Muench, son of Florence and Oscar Muench, posted August 11, 2012, on *eMissourian.com*, the online version of *The Missourian* (Washington, Missouri), http://www.emissourian.com/features_people/feature_stories/article_cee96d99-8729-5cb9-947c-c129cec9547c.html?mode=jqm, accessed November 7, 2015. *See further,* Muench Family Association internet website, http://www.muenchfamilyassociation.com.

Page 116, *Charles LeRoy Gibson (1911–December 8, 1944)* ... "Faculty Record" prepared by Dr. Gibson on December 12, 1938; miscellaneous correspondence (including an exchange of letters between University of New Mexico President J. F. Zimmerman and Frank Germann); and information about the Charles LeRoy Gibson Trust Fund: copies supplied by Ms. Terry Gugliotta, University of New Mexico Archivist, and Judith Davenport, UNM Foundation. Information about the University of New Mexico Chapter of Phi Beta Kappa was supplied by Richard Willis Holder, Professor of Chemistry and President, Alpha of New Mexico Phi Beta Kappa.

Page 118, *Hensley constructed his own fluorometer* ...

Frank E. E. Germann, and J. W. Hensley, "A Direct Vision Fluorometer," *University of Colorado Studies. Series D. Physical and Biological Sciences,* vol. 1, no. 1 (March 1940), pp. 37–41.

Page 118, *Coleman filter fluorometer* ... Sidney Udenfriend, "Recollections: Development of the Spectrophotofluorometer and Its Commercialization," *Protein Science,* vol. 4, (1995), pp. 542–551.

Page 118, *James William Hensley (March 5, 1915–June 24, 1975)* ... Biographical information was supplied by David G. Null, Director, University Archives, University of Wisconsin–Madison; and Janet Garrett, Office of the Registrar, University of Colorado Boulder. Very informative is a scan of an obituary; that document had been prepared by BSAF Wyandotte on June 24, 1975, and a copy had been sent by Hensley's mother to Professor John E. Willard.

Page 119, *the first weighing of plutonium* ... Glenn T. Seaborg, *Recollections and Reminiscences at the 25th Anniversary of the First Weighing of Plutonium* (University of Chicago: September 10, 1967), pp. 25–26; http://www.osti.gov/accomplishments/documents/fullText/ACC0071.pdf, accessed January 28, 2015.

Page 119, *two research papers with John Willard* ... James W. Hensley, Arthur O. Long, and John E. Willard, "Reactions of Ions in Aqueous Solution with Glass and Metal Surfaces," *Journal of the American Chemical Society,* vol. 70, no. 9 (September 1948), pp. 3146–3147; James W. Hensley, Arthur O. Long, and John E. Willard, "Reactions of Ions in Aqueous Solution with Glass and Metal Surfaces," *Industrial and Engineering Chemistry,* vol. 41, no. 7 (July 1949), pp. 1415–1421.

Page 120, *Ray Alan Woodriff (January 9, 1909–March 1, 1983)* ... Information supplied by Heather Hultman, Certified Archivist, Special Collections Library, Montana State University; Geoff Somnitz, Lead Student Archivist, Special Collections and Archives, Oregon State University Library; and Jeri Bonnes, Transcript Coordinator, Office of the Registrar, University of Colorado Boulder. *See also*

"Veteran chemist Ray Woodriff dies at age 71," *Bozeman* [Montana] *Daily Chronicle,* Wednesday, March 2, 1983, p. 1; Obituary, loc. cit., p. 2.

Page 121, *Ray Woodriff and Frank Germann continued to collaborate* ... Frank E. E. Germann and Ray Woodriff, "Cross-Prism Investigation of Fluorescence," *The Review of Scientific Instruments,* vol. 15, no. 6 (June 1944), pp. 145–149; Frank E. E. Germann and Ray Alan Woodriff, "Energy Distribution in Fluorescence," *The Journal of the Colorado-Wyoming Academy of Science,* vol. 3 (1946), p. 17.

Page 121, *Robert George Rekers (February 1, 1920–May 10, 1995)* ... Melissa S. Mead, John M. and Barbara Keil University Archivist, University of Rochester, supplied information about his attendance at the University of Rochester. Randy Vance, Reference Librarian, Southwest Collection/Special Collections Library, Texas Tech University, supplied a summary of his employment at Texas Tech, as well as a five-page curriculum vitae prepared about 1970 by Professor Rekers.

Page 122, *During the years when he was at the Michelson Laboratory* ... Among the courses were "Modern Physics for Engineers," 1952; "Modern Mathematics for Engineers," 1953.

Page 122, *he was active in the Water Resources Center* ... *See, for example,* Dan M. Wells, Ellis W. Huddleston, and Robert G. Rekers, "Concentrations of Pollutants in Agricultural Runoff," paper no. 70102 of the "Water Resources Bulletin," *Journal of The American Water Resources Association,* vol. 7, no. 1 (1971), pp. 124–132.

Page 122, *He was a guiding force in planning* ... *The Test Tube: The Chemistry Department Newsletter* (Texas Tech University): 1983, p. 7; 1985, p. 2.

Page 122, *Elmer Russell Alexander (February 19, 1902–August 1, 1987)* ... Biographical information was supplied by Jay Trask, Head of Archival Services, James A. Michener Library, University of Northern Colorado; Lisa Peña, Special Collections Librarian, Mary Couts Burnett Library, Texas Christian University; Bill W. Santin, Registrar Services Associate,

Columbia University; Richard Gilreath, Reference Intern, Dolph Briscoe Center for American History, University of Texas; and Andrea Weddle, Head of Special Collections and Archives, James Gee Library, Texas A&M University–Commerce.

Page 123, *He was Professor of Chemistry in 1957* ... Texas Christian University, *Horned Frog Yearbook* (Fort Worth, Texas: 1957), p. 27.

Page 123, *Robert L. Bowman (1916–1995)* ... National Institutes of Health, Stetten Museum, "The AMINCO–Bowman SPF." http://history. nih.gov/exhibits/bowman/HSfluor.htm, accessed February 6, 2014.

Page 124, *had been used in quantitative chemical analysis* ... Karl Vierordt, "Die Anwendung des Spektralapparates zur Photometrie der Absorbtionsspectren und zur quantitativen chemischen Analyse" (Tubingen: 1873). Cited as a "description of what must be the first spectrophotometer" by M. G. Rinsler, "Spectroscopy, Colorimetry, and Biological Chemistry in the Nineteenth Century," *Journal of Clinical Pathology*, vol. 34 (1981), pp. 287–291.

Page 124, *described the colorimeter* ... J. Duboscq et Ch. Mène, "Nouveau colorimètre pour l'analyse des matières tinctorioles au point de vue commerciel," *Comptes rendus hebdomadaires des séances de l'Académie des sciences*, vol. 67 (1868), pp. 1330–1331. *See also* Deborah Jean Warner, "The Duboscq Colorimeter," *Bulletin of the Scientific Instrument Society*, no. 88 (2006), pp. 68–70.

Page 124, *Modifications of the instrument* ... Bausch & Lomb Optical Company, Rochester, New York, advertised their own Duboscq colorimeters, with 40 mm, 50 mm, and 100 mm plungers, in the *Chemical Engineering Catalog* (New York: The Chemical Catalog Company, Inc., 1922 edition), page 324. The "Duboscq Leitz" colorimeter, equipped with 100 mm plungers, was advertised in the same catalog (on page 621) by E. Leitz, Inc., New York. *See also* William B. Jensen, "Colorimeters," *Oesper Museum Booklets on the History of Chemical Apparatus*, no. 4, (University of Cincin-

nati: 2014), https://drc.libraries.uc.edu /handle/2374.UC/733810, accessed April 27, 2015.

Page 124, *Photoelectric detectors did not appear* ... Stanley P. Reimann, "The Photo-Electric Cell as a Colorimeter," *Scientific Proceedings: Proceedings of the Society for Experimental Biology and Medicine*, vol. 23, paper no. 3039 (April 21, 1926), pp. 520–523.

Page 125, *a much more sophisticated instrument* ... Charles Sheard and Arthur H. Sanford, "A Photo-Electric Hemoglobinometer: Clinical Applications of the Principles of Photo-Electric Photometry to the Measurement of Hemoglobin," *The Journal of Laboratory and Clinical Medicine*, vol. 14 (1929), pp. 558–574; read before the American Society of Clinical Pathologists, Minneapolis, Minnesota, June 9, 1928. Charles Sheard and Arthur H. Sanford, "A Photo-Electrometer with One Stage Amplification as Applied to the Determination of Hemoglobin," *Journal of the American Medical Association*, vol. 93, no. 25 (December 21, 1929), pp. 1951–1957. Charles Sheard and Arthur H. Sanford, "The Determination of Hemoglobin with the Photoelectrometer," *The Journal of Laboratory and Clinical Medicine*, vol. 15 (1930), pp. 483–489; read before the American Society of Clinical Pathologists, Portland, Oregon, July 1929. The instrument was modified and improved over the next decade. By 1941, a commercial version, the Cenco–Sheard Spectrophotelometer, was being sold by the Central Scientific Company of Chicago; *see* William B. Jensen, "Spectrophotometers," *Oesper Museum Booklets on the History of Chemical Apparatus*, no. 6, (University of Cincinnati: 2014), pp. 7–8, 23, https://drc.libraries.uc.edu/handle/2374. UC/733810, accessed April 27, 2015.

Page 125, *Glenn Austin Millikan (1906–1947)* ... G. A. Millikan, "A Simple Photoelectric Colorimeter," *Journal of Physiology*, vol. 79 (1933), pp. 152–157.

Page 125, *Kenneth A. Evelyn in 1936* ... Kenneth A. Evelyn, "A Stabilized Photoelectric Colorimeter with Light Filters," *Journal of Biological Chemistry*, vol. 115 (1936), pp. 63–75. For more on the Evelyn colorimeter and contemporary instruments, see William B. Jensen, "Filter Photometers," *Oesper Museum Booklets on the History of Chemical Apparatus*, no. 5, (University of Cincinnati:, 2014), https://drc.libraries.uc.edu/handle/2374.UC/733810, accessed April 27, 2015.

Page 125, *Still, many traditional chemists* ... Ralph H. Müller, "Photoelectric Methods in Analytical Chemistry," *Industrial and Engineering Chemistry, Analytical Edition*, vol. 11, no. 1 (January 15, 1939), pp. 1–17, with extensive bibliography. *See* "Choice of Instrument," p. 12.

Page 125, *qualitative visual observations of colors* ... "A Study of the Iron Compounds of Certain Organic Acids," University of Colorado Ph.D. thesis, 1930; Norman J. Harrar and Frank E. E. Germann, "A Study of Organic Acid Iron Solutions. I. Concentrations and Colors," *Journal of Physical Chemistry*, vol. 35, no. 6 (1931), pp. 1666–1673; Norman J. Harrar and Frank E. E. Germann, "A Study of Organic-Acid Iron Solutions. II. Colloidal Properties," *Journal of Physical Chemistry*, vol. 35, no. 8 (1931), pp. 2210–2218; Norman J. Harrar and Frank E. E. Germann, "A Study of Organic-Acid Iron Solutions. III. Complex-Colloid Equilibrium," *Journal of Physical Chemistry*, vol. 36, no. 2 (1932), pp. 688–695.

Page 125, *Howard H. Cary (1908–1991)* ... A. O. Beckman, W. S. Gallaway, W. Kaye, and W. F. Ulrich, "History of Spectrophotometry at Beckman Instruments, Inc.," *Analytical Chemistry*, vol. 49, no. 3 (March 1977), pp. 280A–300A. *See also* H. H. Cary and A. O. Beckman, "A Quartz Photoelectric Spectrophotometer," *Journal of the Optical Society of America*, vol. 31 (1941), pp. 682–689; and Robert D. Simoni, Robert L. Hill, Martha Vaughan, and Herbert Tabor, "A Classic Instrument: The Beckman DU Spectrophotometer and Its Inventor, Arnold O. Beckman," *The Journal of Biological Chemistry*, vol. 278, no. 49 (December 5, 2003), pp. 79–81.

Page 126, *Mellon Institute in Pittsburgh purchased* ... Introduction to *Varian Cary 50 Series Spectropho-tometer* sales brochure, circa 1999, http://www.nist.gov/ncnr/upload/E136uvvis.pdf, accessed January 18, 2015.

Page 126, *Norman Jackson Harrar (January 7, 1902–October 16, 1941)* ... Obituary, Frank E. E. Germann, "Norman Jackson Harrar: January 7, 1902–October 16, 1941," *Science* (New Series), vol. 94, no. 2448 (November 28, 1941), pp. 507–508. *See also: The 1922 Owl* (The Yearbook of the University of Pittsburgh, vol. 16, 1922), pp. 28, 37, 244.

Page 127, *Residential Tour to Saint Servan* ... A copy of the tour brochure was supplied by Archives, University of Colorado at Boulder Libraries.

Page 128, *details of the method in February 1933* ... Frank E. E. Germann, "Solid Carbon Dioxide from Flue Gas by Application of Joule–Thomson Effect," *Industrial and Engineering Chemistry*, vol. 25, no. 2 (February 1933), pp. 150–152.

Page 128, *Science Service* ... Journalist Edward W. Scripps and zoologist William Emerson Ritter, collaborating with the American Association for the Advancement of Science, the National Academy of Sciences, and the National Research Council, founded Science Service in 1921 with the goal of informing the press and the public of scientific achievements. The next year, Science Service initiated *Science News-Letter*, renamed *Science News* in 1966. In 2008, Science Service became the Society for Science & the Public.

Page 128, *among the impressive array of achievements* ... "Science Marches On: Science Review of the Year," *Science News-Letter*, vol. 24, no. 663 (Saturday, December 23, 1933), pp. 403–416.

Page 128, *the thirty-six "High Points in Chemistry" for 1933* ... "The year 1933 in Review: High Points in Chemistry," *Industrial and Engineering Chemistry News Edition*, vol. 11, no. 24 (Wednesday, December 20, 1933), p. 361.

Page 128, *he addressed the Division* ... Frank E. E. Germann, "The Occurrence of Carbon Dioxide, With Notes on the Origin and Relative Importance of Subterranean Carbon Dioxide." *Science*, vol. 87, no. 2267 (June 10, 1938), pp. 513–521.

Page 128, *Eighteenth Colloid Symposium at Cornell University* ... Frank E. E. Germann and Herbert W. Ayres, "The Origin of Underground Carbon Dioxide," *Journal of Physical Chemistry*, vol. 46, no. 1 (January 1942), pp. 61–68.

Page 129, *has recently been revived* ... Mitch Jacoby, "The Hidden Value of Carbon Dioxide," *Chemical & Engineering News*, vol. 91, no. 26 (July 1, 2013), pp. 21–22.

Page 129, *Herbert Wilmot Ayres (1914–1989)* ... "Wendell W. Ayres, M.D.," *in* Charles Roll, *Indiana: One Hundred and Fifty Years of American Development* (Chicago: Lewis Publishing Company, 1931), vol. 3.

Page 129, *and then entered Taylor University* ... Information supplied by Ashley Chu, Taylor University Archivist, and Emily MaGee, Archives Assistant.

Page 129, *He served for thirty-four years* ... "Herbert W. Ayres: Retired Food and Drug Officer," Obituary, *Marin Independent Journal* (Marin County, California), October 11, 1989, sec. B, p. 2.

Page 130, *Paul Reheard Frey (April 20, 1902–May 12, 1978)* ... Biographical information supplied by Sidney Garth Dreese, College Archivist, F. Wilbur Gingrich Library, Albright College; Hope Glenn, Archivist, Special Collections and Archives Research Center, Oregon State University Library; and Vicky Lopez-Terrill, Archives and Special Collections, Morgan Library, Colorado State University. Information about York College in the years from 1930 to 1933 is from Dale R. Larsen, "A History of York College," doctoral thesis, University of Nebraska Teachers College, accessed via the York College internet website.

Page 130, *Professor Earl C. Gilbert* ... A chemistry building, constructed in 1939, was later named Gilbert Hall in honor of Earl C. Gilbert, who had been on the faculty since 1917. He was head of the Chemistry Department from 1940 to 1956. Paul Frey's Chemistry Ph.D. was one of the first

awarded by Oregon State University; the first doctoral degree in chemistry at Oregon State University was in 1935. "Chemistry Department Records," http://scarc.library.oregonstate.edu/coll/rg098/biographicalnote.html, accessed February 9, 2015. Earl Gilbert earned his doctorate in 1922 from the University of Chicago, with research under the direction of Julius Stieglitz (1867–1937). For a detailed biography of Stieglitz, see William Albert Noyes, "Biographical Memoir of Julius Stieglitz, 1867–1937," *Biographical Memoirs of the National Academy of Sciences* (Washington: National Academy of Sciences, vol. 21, 1939), memoir 7, pp. 155–205.

Page 131, *the inaugural issue* ... Frank E. E. Germann and Paul Reheard Frey, "The Hydrates of Uranyl Nitrate, Their Respective Vapor Pressures and Relative Stability of the Lower Hydrate," *The Journal of the Colorado-Wyoming Academy of Science*, vol. 1 (1929), p. 54.

Page 131, *five more articles* ... Frank E. E. Germann and Odon S. Knight, "Vapor Pressure–Temperature Data Represented by Line Co-ordinate Charts," *The Journal of the Colorado-Wyoming Academy of Science*, vol. 1, no. 6 (1934), p. 14; T. Howard James, F. E. E. Germann, and Julian M. Blair, "The Influence of Salts on Intermittent Photographic Exposures," *The Journal of the Colorado-Wyoming Academy of Science*, vol. 1, no. 6 (1934), p. 17; T. Howard James, F. E. E. Germann, and Julian M. Blair, "Action of Water on the Latent Photographic Image," *The Journal of the Colorado-Wyoming Academy of Science*, vol. 1, no. 6 (1934), p. 20; J. J. Coleman and Frank E. E. Germann, "The Heat of Formation of Binary Liquid Solutions from Their Liquid Components," *The Journal of the Colorado-Wyoming Academy of Science*, vol. 1, no. 6 (1934), p. 15; Frank E. E. Germann and Dzu-Kun Shen, "Sensitization and Desensitization of Silver Iodide," *The Journal of the Colorado-Wyoming Academy of Science*, vol. 1 (1929), p. 25.

Page 132, *submitting papers to volume 1 (1940)* ... The papers were Frank E. E. Germann and J. W.

Hensley, "A Direct Vision Fluorometer," *University of Colorado Studies. Series D. Physical and Biological Sciences*, vol. 1, no. 1 (March 1940), pp. 37–41; Frank E. E. Germann and Charles F. Metz, "Magnetic Double Refraction," *University of Colorado Studies. Series D. Physical and Biological Sciences*, vol. 1, no. 2 (October 1940), pp. 71–103. Germann also submitted another paper: F. E. E. Germann, "A History of the Development of Capillary Analysis and of Capillary Luminescence Analysis," *University of Colorado Studies. Series D. Physical and Biological Sciences*, vol. 1, no. 1 (March 1940), pp. 7–14.

Page 133, *Frank German submitted results ...* Frank E. E. Germann, "A New Hydrate of Uranium Nitrate: Uranium Nitrate Icositetrahydrate," *Physical Review* (Second Series), vol. 11, no. 3 (1918), pp. 245–246; submitted October 11, 1917. Frank E. Germann, "Thermal Analysis at Low Temperatures," *Physical Review* (Second Series), vol. 19, no. 6 (1922), pp. 623–628.

Page 133, *The world's first scientific journal ...* Julie McDougall-Waters, Noah Moxham, and Aileen Fyfe, *"Philosophical Transactions: 350 Years of Publishing at the Royal Society (1665–2015),"* https://royalsociety.org/~/media/publishing350/publishing350-exhibition-catalogue.pdf.

Page 134, *With a hole punch for sheets of paper ...* Friedrich Soennecken (1848–1919) may have invented the paper punch and the ring binder system about 1886. He was certainly influential in popularizing this method of organizing documents via his own office-supply firm.

Page 135, *He received a sabbatical leave of absence ...* Curriculum vitae of Robert George Rekers, supplied by Randy Vance, Reference Librarian, Southwest Collection/Special Collections Library, Texas Tech University.

Page 135, *Kenneth A. Gagos (April 5, 1896–May 29, 1995) ...* In 1924, Bertha Evelyn Redfield and Kenneth A. Gagos built a one story "vernacular wood frame" house at 1602 Baseline Road, Boulder, CO 80302. From a 1992 interview: "Kenneth A. and Bertha E. Gagos, the original owners, still reside in the house. Gagos was an assistant professor in the chemistry department at C. U. who organized and oversaw the laboratory, and co-authored a manual entitled 'Experimental Physical Chemistry.' He retired in 1964," Colorado Historical Society, Office of Archaeology and Historic Preservation, 1300 Broadway, Denver, Colorado 80203, *Historic Building Inventory Record: Boulder Survey of Historic Places, 1992*, http://www.boulderlibrary.org/cpdfs/780_Baseline_1602.pdf, accessed August 31, 2014.

Page 135, *Kenneth served in the United States Army Signal Corps ...* "Obituaries, 1920s," *Stanford Magazine* (March/April 1997).

Page 135, *He worked with Frank Germann ... For example,* Frank E. E. Germann, K. A. Gagos, and C. A. Neilson, "Improved Apparatus for Quantitative Estimation of Helium in Gases," *Industrial and Engineering Chemistry, Analytical Edition*, vol. 6, no. 3 (May 1934), pp. 215–217.

Page 135, *collaborated with members of the departments ...* James W. Broxon, "The Residual Ionization in Nitrogen at High Pressures," *Physical Review*, vol. 38, no. 9 (November 1, 1931), pp. 1704–1708 [Gas was analyzed by Kenneth Gagos, who estimated the accuracy of his results.]; Robinson P. Lockwood, "Role of Cap Rock in Oil Accumulation," *Bulletin of the American Association of Petroleum Geologists*, vol. 17, no. 6 (June 1933), pp. 713–731 ["indebted to ... K. A. Gagos ... for his skillful construction of the glass apparatus."].

Page 135, *joint paper with a member ...* A. R. Ronzio and K. A. Gagos, "An Improvement in the Victor-Meyer Method," *Journal of Chemical Education*, vol. 9, no. 10 (October 1932), pp. 1827–1828. Viktor Meyer (1848–1897) invented a widely used apparatus for determining the molecular weight of a volatile liquid.

Page 135, *Charles Franklin Metz (September 23, 1904–February 10, 1974) ...* Biographical material was supplied by Jana Barnes, Director, and Judy Stevick, Library Assistant, Winchester Community Library, Winchester, Indiana; Janet L. Taylor,

Devereaux Library, South Dakota School of Mines and Technology; Carolyn Elwess, Archivist, Park University, Parkville Campus Library; Vicky Lopez-Terrill, Archives and Special Collections, Morgan Library, Colorado State University; Alan Brady Carr, Historian, Los Alamos National Laboratory; and Charles V. Metz, Capt. USAF, personal communication, April 18, 2015. *See also* Obituary, "Dr. Charles Metz," *News-Gazette* (Winchester, Indiana), Wednesday, February 13, 1974, p. 7; and biographical entry, *Randolph County, Indiana, 1818-1990* (Winchester, Indiana: Historical & Genealogical Society of Randolph County, Indiana, 1991), p. 579.

Page 135, *change led by Leotis (Lee) Lincoln Driver (1867–1960)* ... Text of historical marker at the Driver Middle School, 130 South 100 East, Winchester, Indiana, http://www.in.gov/history/markers/LeeLDriver.htm, accessed February 23, 2015. *See also* David B. Danbom, "Rural Education Reform and the Country Life Movement, 1900–1920," *Agricultural History*, vol. 53, no. 2 (April 1979), pp. 462–474.

Page 136, *M.S. degree in Chemistry in 1928* ... His thesis was "The Phase Diagram of the System Silver Iodide–Lead Iodide."

Page 136, *Park College granted him a leave of absence ... Hardrock*, mimeographed publication of alumni of South Dakota School of Mines, vol. 2, no. 1 (December 1935), p. 2.

Page 136, *He was awarded the Ph.D. in 1936* ... His thesis was "The Effect of Concentration on the Magnetic Double Refraction of Some Organic Salts."

Page 136, *a great friend as well as a fine professor* ... The source of this judgement is Charles V. Metz, personal communication, April 18, 2015.

Page 137, *Charles V. Metz has written* ... Charles V. Metz, personal communication, April 18, 2015.

Page 138, *active at Colorado College until at least 1972* ... Information about Delta Epsilon was supplied by Jessy Randall, Curator and Archivist, Colorado College Special Collections.

Page 138, *Lutheran Academy for Scholarship* ... Roger Beese, "The First Quarter Century," *The Lutheran Scholar*, vol. 26, no. 2 (April 1969), pp. 28–32.

Page 138, *Frank contributed an article* ... Frank E. E. Germann, "The 'Parity Law' of Nuclear Physics Challenged," *The Lutheran Scholar*, vol. 14, no. 4 (October 1957), pp. 571–577.

Page 139, *Reuben Gilbert (Gus) Gustavson (April 6, 1892–February 23, 1974)* ... Much biographical information came from a history of the University of Denver Department of Chemistry and Biochemistry, written by Dr. Bernie Spilka, Professor Emeritus at the University of Denver: https://portfolio.du.edu/downloadItem/123321, reference supplied by Katherine Crowe, Curator of Special Collections and Archives, University of Denver Libraries. Jill Rittersbacher, Archives Assistant, Special Collections and Archives, University of Denver Libraries, supplied copies of a biographical note, a memorial minute, and newspaper obituaries of Dr. Gustavson and his wife Edna Marie Carlson. *See also* "Reuben Gilbert Gustavson," *Who Was Who in America*, accessed via the *Marquis Who's Who* internet database.

Page 140, *President Stearns took a leave of absence* ... Davis, *Glory Colorado!*, op. cit., pp. 459–465.

Page 141, *He was quoted as believing* ... Davis, *Glory Colorado!*, op. cit., p. 469.

Page 142, *Chancellorship of the University of Nebraska* ... Josh Caster, Archives Associate, University of Nebraska–Lincoln Libraries; email January 5, 2015.

Page 142, *provided staff and funding* ... John C. Rumm, Jennifer A. Mall, Peggy Dillon, *Resources for the Future, Incorporated: A Historical Chronology* (History Associates Incorporated, May 1999). Unpublished document; copy supplied by Chris Clotworthy, Librarian, Resources for the Future.

Page 142, *focus on the physical and biological sciences* ... Marion Clawson, *From Sagebrush to Sage: The Making of a Natural Resource Economist* (Washington: Ana Publications, 1987), p. 254. Citation from Rumm, et al., op. cit., p. 7.

Page 142, *Gustavson "often said later* ... Henry Jarrett, "A Brief History of RFF," *in* Henry Jarrett, et al., *Resources for the Future: The First 25 Years, 1952–1977* (Washington: Resources for the Future, 1977), p. 16.

Page 142, *eleven-year stint at the University of Arizona* ... Wendel Cox, Assistant Special Collections Librarian at the University of Arizona, kindly supplied a detailed summary of a Special Collections biographical file for Dr. Gustavson, as well as material from the University's annual reports.

Page 143, *Frank submitted several research papers* ... Among those papers were: Frank E. E. Germann and Malcolm C. Hylan, "Dispersity of Silver Halides in Relation to Their Photographic Behavior," *Science*, (New Series), vol. 58, no. 1504 (October 26, 1923), pp. 332–333; Frank E. E. Germann, "The Emanation Method for Radium," *Science* (New Series), vol. 59, no. 1528 (April 11, 1924), pp. 340–341; Frank E. E. Germann, "Cooperation in Research," *Science* (New Series), vol. 63, no. 1630 (March 26, 1926), pp. 324–327; Frank E. E. Germann, "Ceramic Pigments of the Indians of the Southwest," *Science* (New Series), vol. 63, no. 1636 (May 7, 1926), pp. 480–482.

Page 144, *the Society of the Sigma Xi* ... Information supplied by Jon Ann Joselyn, Secretary, University of Colorado Chapter of Sigma Xi, April 26, 2013.

Page 144, *joined the research staff* ... Two publications from his time at N.B.S.–Boulder: R. B. Stewart, F. E. E. Germann, and R. D. McCarty (National Bureau of Standards, Boulder Laboratories), "The Surface Tension of Hydrogen," N.B.S. Report 7616, United States Department of Commerce, National Bureau of Standards (October 1, 1962); L. A. Hall and F. E. E. Germann (Cryogenics Division, Institute for Basic Standards, National Bureau of Standards, Boulder, Colorado), "Survey of Electrical Resistivity Measurements on 8 Additional Pure Metals in the Temperature Range 0 to 273 K," N.B.S. Technical Note 365-1, 85 pages, Department of Commerce, National Bureau of Standards (August 1970).

Page 145, *he translated documents for the Bureau of Mines* ... *For example:* L. Holborn and J. Otto, "Über Die Isothermen von Stickstoff, Sauerstoff und Helium" [Isotherms of Nitrogen, Oxygen, and Helium], *Zeitschrift für Physik*, vol. 10 (1922), pp. 367–376 (in German). Translated by Dr. Frank E. E. Germann, National Bureau of Standards, Boulder, June 1964, into English. *And also:* L. Holborn and J. Otto, "Über die Isothermen Einiger Gase zwischen 400 Deg. und −183 Deg." [The Isotherms of Various Gases between 400 Deg. and −183 Deg.], *Zeitschrift für Physik*, vol. 33 (1925), pp. 1–12 (in German). Translated by Dr. Frank E. E. Germann, National Bureau of Standards, Boulder, June 1964, into English. From *Research and Technologic Work on Explosives, Explosions, and Flames: Fiscal Year 1967*, Explosives Research Center Information Circular 8387, Bureau of Mines, United States Department of the Interior, p. 10.

Page 145, *truly a gem of a beauty spot* ... Mrs. E. F. Crambilt Sr., "Germanns of Sunset Hill Set Example to Make Boulder a City Beautiful," *Boulder Daily Camera*, October 5, 1956.

Two-pan Analytical Balance

III.
Western Reserve, then to Stanford, and back to Cleveland

ALBERT GERMANN was appointed Instructor in Chemistry at the undergraduate College for Women of Western Reserve University (Cleveland, Ohio) in 1913. At the same time, he was appointed Instructor in Chemistry at Adelbert College, the Western Reserve University undergraduate college for men. He met his first classes at the beginning of the first semester of the 1913–1914 academic year.

As we have already seen (and as we shall see again), several United States colleges and universities at the time were making appointments at professorial ranks to persons whose academic credentials included only a few courses beyond high school. Western Reserve had professional standards that were more rigorous; a doctorate was required for appointment at Western Reserve above the rank of Instructor in the Chemistry Department. After the University of Geneva conferred the degree of doctorat ès sciences physiques et chimiques (on Thursday, January 15, 1914), Western Reserve University promoted Albert to the rank of Assistant Professor of Chemistry. The higher rank became effective for the 1915–1916 academic year. He was promoted to Associate Professor with tenure in 1921. Albert also held a joint appointment as Professor of Chemistry at the Cleveland School of Nurses in 1918.

Albert Germann joined Dr. Olin Freeman Tower (1872–1945) and Dr. Hippolyte Washington Gruener (1869–1961) on the Western Reserve chemistry faculties.

Olin Freeman Tower was born in Brooklyn, New York. He attended Wesleyan

University, Middletown, Connecticut, earning the A.B. degree in 1892 and the A.M. in 1893. He then went to Germany to study with physical chemist Friedrich Wilhelm Ostwald (1853–1932; Nobel laureate in Chemistry 1909) at Leipzig University, completing his doctorate in physical chemistry at Leipzig in 1895. His dissertation was "Studien über Superoxyd-Elektroden." Tower collaborated with Ostwald on three volumes of the second edition of *Lehrbuch der allgemeinen Chemie* (Leipzig: Wilhelm Engelmann, 1896–1906). Tower wrote a physical chemistry book, *The Conductivity of Liquids: Methods, Results, Chemical Applications and Theoretical Considerations* (Easton, Pennsylvania: Chemical Publishing Company, 1905). His analytical chemistry textbook, *A Course of Qualitative Chemical Analysis of Inorganic Substances* (Philadelphia: P. Blakiston's Sons & Company) went through six editions (1909, 1911, 1915, 1921, 1926, 1932).

Just after he completed his doctorate, Tower returned to Wesleyan as Assistant in Chemistry. He became a member of a new laboratory team in nutrition investigations, funded by the United States Department of Agriculture. He took part in a classic calorimetric experiment conducted by three Wesleyan faculty members—chemist Wilbur Olin Atwater (1844–1907), physicist Edward Bennett Rosa (1873–1921), and chemist Francis Guano Benedict (1870–1957). Atwater, Rosa, and Benedict built a large respiration calorimeter in Wesleyan's Judd Hall. The calorimeter had a chamber (with a 4 ft × 8 ft footprint) in which a human subject could be confined while measurements were made of temperature, oxygen consumed, and carbon dioxide produced. The object was to confirm thermodynamic predictions related to human metabolism. On Monday, March 16, 1896, Olin Freeman Tower was locked in the chamber. He spent the next five days as the human subject. Atwater used such thermodynamic data to formulate his Atwater diet that emphasized calories as the most important aspect of human nutrition.

In 1898, Tower was hired by Adelbert College as Instructor of Chemistry. At that time, Edward Williams Morley, Hurlbut Professor of Natural History and Chemistry, was the senior member of the Chemistry Department. Tower was promoted to Assistant Professor in 1901. Morley retired in 1906. Tower in 1907 became Hurlbut Professor of Chemistry, Head of the Department of Chemistry, and Director of the Chemistry Laboratories. The Olin Freeman Tower Prize for excellence in physical chemistry was established in his honor at Western Reserve.

Hippolyte Washington Gruener was born in New Haven, Connecticut. He studied chemistry at Yale in New Haven, conducting undergraduate research in the Kent Chemical Laboratory with analytical chemist Frank Austen Gooch (1852–1929). Gruener received the A.B. degree from Yale College in June 1891, and his research with Professor Gooch was published in "Silliman's Journal" in September 1891. He stayed at Yale for doctoral research with Frank Gooch. Gruener received the Ph.D. degree in June 1893, with the dissertation "The Reducing Action of Hydriodic Acid as Applied in Inorganic Analysis: With Special Reference to the Determination of Nitric Acid." He then spent two postdoctoral years at the Ludwig-Maximilians-Universität München in Munich and at the Friedrich-Wilhelms-Universität in Berlin.

In 1895, Gruener was hired by Adelbert College as Instructor of Chemistry. He rose through the ranks, and became Professor of Chemistry in 1907. He retired as Professor Emeritus in 1939. After 1939, he was on the chemistry faculty of the Flora Stone Mather College of Western Reserve. The Hippolyte Washington Gruener Prize for merit in chemistry was established in his honor at Western Reserve.

About 1920, Gruener made arrangements with New York publishers P. F. Collier and Harper & Brothers to publish both a chemistry textbook and also a chemistry book that would appeal to general readers. The popular chemistry book went through seven editions, surviving World War II. He and two younger faculty colleagues in the late 1930s wrote an organic chemistry textbook with accompanying laboratory manual.

The Department of Chemistry at Western Reserve was a small department in 1913. Members of the department had the primary responsibility for defining the chemistry curriculum, for selecting the courses to be offered, and for teaching those courses. By necessity, each member of the faculty lectured on a wide range of chemical subjects. Even more challenging was conducting laboratory courses on a similarly wide range of practical chemical techniques. To be effective and credible in the chemistry laboratory, an instructor must be able to demonstrate hands-on experimental techniques, and be able to respond quickly to unexpected situations. Albert experienced comparable classroom challenges less than a decade earlier when he was responsible for teaching diverse subjects at Bunker Hill and at Reserve in Miami County, Indiana.

The principal professional interests and specializations of Tower, Gruener, and Germann were in physical chemistry, analytical chemistry, general chemistry, and inorganic chemistry. If there were not enough courses within the Chemistry Department, chemistry students at Western Reserve could round out their major by electing courses in related departments, courses in physics, geology, and medical subjects. There were rich course offerings in organic chemistry and biochemistry in the Medical School. Compared to the small Chemistry Department, the Western Reserve University Medical School was huge.

Some of Albert Germann's first experimental research at Western Reserve extended his doctoral investigations. He continued precise gas-density measurements. He also made improvements in the specialized apparatus for handling gases. Albert was especially interested in evaluating sources of any systematic experimental errors involved in determining the density of oxygen, especially the density of oxygen from a variety of different sources. A fundamental problem in explaining all oxygen-density results, unknown to Germann and probably unknowable at the time, was the existence of a mass-18 isotope of oxygen. The fact that the relative abundance of isotopes ^{16}O and ^{18}O depends on the source (and thus the previous history) of oxygen samples was a still undiscovered factor, complicating interpretation of Germann's high-precision measurements. Experiments revealing the dependence of isotopic composition on the source of samples were first reported in the chemical literature two decades later.

Albert Germann, like his exemplar Edward Williams Morley and his mentor Philippe-Auguste Guye, made mass measurements with meticulously constructed mechanical equal-arm, two-pan balances. These balances permitted mass measurements whose precision has not been equaled after these balances went out of fashion in mid-20th century. When an experienced analytical chemist used such a balance in an isolated laboratory room free of vibration, with minimal air movement, and with temperature stabilization, when the chemist personally calibrated the set of working weights, made appropriate corrections for the buoyancy of ambient air (buoyancy affecting both the object being weighed and also the counterbalancing working weights), used *with patience* the time-consuming "method of swings" to locate the extent of "off-balance" with each weighing, and was diligent in arithmetically adding the *calibrated* values of the working weights, then the experimental data could be more precise and more reliable than similar measurements made routinely and much more rapidly today with single-pan electronic balances.

Setting up a new chemical laboratory often involves scrounging in storerooms, resurrecting old equipment for fresh uses. Germann observed: "At the Morley Laboratory, we have had some difficulty during the past few years in obtaining suitable glass for constructing apparatus for work with gases. Much of Pro. Morley's apparatus remains, but practically all of it devitrifies when the effort is made to work it in the flame." Germann found (and reported in two scientific publications) that repair of devitrified (crystallized) glassware can be accomplished by pretreatment of the glass with hydrofluoric acid, an aqueous solution of hydrogen fluoride (HF). Using this technique, his advanced students were able to construct their own apparatus by modifying old glassware, even when complex glass blowing was required. He considered competence in "working glass in the flame" a requirement for every advanced chemistry student. These were times when chemists of necessity fabricated much of their own apparatus, including specialized and sometimes intricate glassware.

Before the Great War, chemical laboratories in the United States were importing much of their specialized glassware from Germany. A major German source was Jenaer Glaswerk in Jena, Thuringia, where Friedrich Otto Schott (1851–1935) had invented borosilicate glass by 1893. The War cut off this traditional source of scientific glassware.

In Corning, New York, the Corning Glass Works before the War was manufacturing mainly glass chimneys for kerosene lamps, and colored glass lenses for railroad signal lights. In the 1890s, Corning had begun to manufacture glass tubing (including fine-bore drawn thermometer tubing) to compete directly with the Jenaer Glaswerk. In 1908, Corning developed a new glass formulation that contained lead, boric acid, and silica. Because the new glass had a very low thermal coefficient of expansion, it was resistant to expanding (and thus cracking or breaking) when heated. This borosilicate glass had properties ideal for many laboratory uses, especially for beakers and flasks in which liquids could now be heated safely over an open flame. The new glass was named CNX (Corning Non-eXpansion glass) or Nonex. Because of health concerns about the lead content, Corning was reluctant to promote Nonex for the consumer market. By the 1930s, Corning had developed an improved Nonex borosilicate glass without lead. The first household product using the new glass was a pie plate that could be used in a kitchen bake oven without shattering. That pie plate was the inspiration for the name Pyrex®.

Albert Germann was not content to restrict his laboratory activities to gas-density measurements. He organized a research group at Western Reserve to investigate freezing-point depression. Freezing-point depression is the phenomenon commonly exploited to make a slurry of common table salt, water, and ice cold enough to freeze ice cream. A similar effect occurs in water with other salts. The extent of temperature lowering in water depends on the concentration of the salt in the water, and also on the chemical nature of the particular salt.

The reason for conducting such cryoscopic experiments is that quantitative freezing-point depression data (temperature as a function of concentration, in a slurry in which the solution is in chemical, physical, and thermal equilibrium with the solid form of the solvent) can be interpreted to reveal the nature of the dissolved chemical species. Freezing point is a "colligative property" of a solution, a property that depends on the number of particles dissolved. If a solute dissolves as molecules, then there will be fewer particles in solution than would be expected if the solute were to dissociate into cations (ions with positive charge) and anions (ions with negative charge). Incomplete dissociation results in an intermediate number of particles. Sometimes the data can be interpreted to suggest more complicated solution chemistry, such as association of molecules and ions. The data may even reveal aspects of the structure of the solvent.

Albert Germann decided to extend investigations to solvents other than water. Germann's research group began to investigate the freezing-point depression produced by various compounds when dissolved in a particular non-aqueous solvent—liquid boron trifluoride (BF_3). This new solvent presented formidable experimental challenges. The freezing point of boron trifluoride is very low, -127 °C. The temperature range through which the compound is liquid is narrow; its boiling point (at atmospheric pressure) is -100 °C. A significant safety factor in planning the experiments is the high chemical reactivity and the extreme toxicity of boron trifluoride. The gas was said to have a pungent suffocating odor. Inhalation is likely to be fatal. A prudent chemist today would take the word of earlier investigators regarding its characteristic odor and the consequences of inhalation.

These cryoscopic experiments were explorations of the practicality of larger-scale studies of chemical systems in which boron trifluoride was the solvent. Results of preliminary studies were presented in four talks at the 60th National Meeting of the American Chemical Society in Chicago in September 1920. The talks were listed in the Division of Physical and Inorganic Chemistry program as:

> A. F. O. Germann and H. S. Booth. "I—The Cryoscopy of Boron Trifluoride Solutions: System with Hydrogen Sulfide."
> A. F. O. Germann and Vernon Jersey. "II—The Cryoscopy of Boron Trifluoride Solutions: System with Phosgene" (presentation with lantern slides).
> A. F. O. Germann and Wendell Phillips. "III—The Cryoscopy of Boron Trifluoride Solutions: Systems with Sulfur Dioxide and with Nitric Oxide" (presentation with lantern slides).
> A. F. O. Germann and Leland R. Smith. "IV—The Cryoscopy of Boron Trifluoride Solutions: System with Hydrogen Chloride" (presentation with lantern slides).

A fifth presentation by a member of the Germann research group was at a 1921 meeting of the American Chemical Society (Division of Physical and Inorganic Chemistry) in Rochester, New York: A. F. O. Germann and Marion Cleaveland, "The Cryoscopy of Boron Trifluoride Solutions—V. Systems with Methyl Ether and with Methyl Chloride."

In lecture halls today, many talks are illustrated with computer-generated Power-Point presentations. An appropriate computer and a display device are needed in the hall. In 1920, presenters at the Chicago A.C.S. meeting gave advance warning that they needed a lantern-slide projector and a projection screen in the room. The presenters brought their own 4" × 3¼" transparent glass lantern slides. A Cleveland photography studio could have prepared slides from the presenters' drawings or photographs. Some chemistry departments had equipment to make their own lantern slides.

Harold Simmons Booth (1891–1953) had already completed his doctoral program at Cornell. In September 1920, Booth had become a member of the Western Reserve chemistry faculty. Vernon Jersey (1898–1984) had received the A.B. in chemistry at the 1920 Adelbert College commencement, and in September had begun graduate research with Germann on phosgene. We shall soon have a lot to say about phosgene. Marion Cleaveland (1898–1975) had received the B.A. in chemistry from the College for Women in 1920. She would be awarded the M.A. in chemistry from Western Reserve University in 1921. Wendell Phillips was beginning his senior year at Adelbert College. He would be awarded the A.B. degree in 1921. Leland Roy Smith had received the A.B. degree from Adelbert College in 1920, and was beginning graduate studies at Western Reserve. He received the A.M. degree from Western Reserve University in 1921, and (according to Western Reserve records) received the A.M. degree from Harvard University in 1923. He later returned to Western Reserve to earn a B.S. degree in the School of Library Science in 1929.

Albert Germann was mentor to three Western Reserve graduate students who became professional chemists: Harold Simmons Booth, Vernon Jersey, and Marion Cleaveland.

Harold Booth was born in Cleveland on January 30, 1891. He graduated from Adelbert College in 1915 with an A.B. degree, and was elected to Phi Beta Kappa. His graduate research with Albert Germann was on the density of air in Cleveland. Booth received the M.A. in chemistry from Western Reserve in 1916. He then entered the chemistry graduate program at Cornell University, where he was a Henry Williams Sage Graduate Fellow (1917–1918) and a du Pont Fellow (1918–1919). During the 1917–1918 year, Frank Germann was a member of the Cornell Physics Department while Harold Booth was a graduate student in the Cornell Chemistry Department in a different building. Harold Booth received the Ph.D. from Cornell in 1919 with the dissertation "The Atomic Weight of Nitrogen." His advisor was Emile Monnin Chamot (1868–1950). Booth returned with his doctorate to Western Reserve to become a member of the faculty. Harold Booth had a distinguished career as an inorganic chemist at Western Reserve. He served as department chair. He was Editor-in-Chief of the inaugural volume (in 1939) of *Inorganic Syntheses,* a prestigious series that continues; volume 36 was published in 2014. He was promoted to Hurlbut Professor of Chemistry in 1947.

Vernon Jersey was born in Buffalo, New York, on September 1, 1898. He spent his formative years in Cleveland, and received the A.B., *cum laude*, in chemistry from Adelbert College of Western Reserve University in 1920. His graduate research, with Albert Germann, involved experimental studies of phosgene, a colorless gas with the simple molecular formula CCl_2O. Jersey was Assistant in Chemistry at Adelbert College and at the College for Women during the 1920–1921 year. He received the A.M. degree from Western Reserve in 1921. We shall hear a lot more about Vernon Jersey, later in this chapter and then again in Chapter 5.

There will be more about Marion Cleaveland, after an excursion into the treacherous realm of phosgene.

Phosgene

Phosgene enters our narrative at two different universities in two apparently independent ways. At Stanford University in 1918, graduate student William M. Schaufelberger obtained an appointment as a research assistant at Edgewood Arsenal in Maryland. At Edgewood, he measured vapor pressures of mixtures of phosgene and chlorine. Dr. Ralph E. Hall, a physical chemist whose earlier research experience included cryoscopy of aqueous salt solutions, directed Schaufelberger's experiments. At Western Reserve University during the 1920–1921 school year, graduate student Vernon Jersey studied solutions of phosgene and chlorine, obtaining cryoscopic evidence for ten different compounds, including chlorine octaphosgenate, $8COCl_2 \cdot Cl_2$. Albert Germann directed his research. Germann and Jersey observed that $8COCl_2 \cdot Cl_2$ in liquid phosgene is analogous to the octahydrate of chlorine in liquid water. Chlorine octahydrate ($8H_2O \cdot Cl_2$) is a bright yellow crystalline substance, sometimes called chlorine ice. When Albert Germann left Western Reserve and joined the chemistry faculty at Stanford University in 1921, he quickly formed a research group at Stanford to undertake experimental investigations of phosgene and chemical reactions in liquid phosgene.

John Davy [1790–1868; brother of chemist Sir Humphry Davy (1778–1829), discoverer of the elements barium, boron, calcium, potassium, and sodium] was the first person to synthesize phosgene. He generated phosgene by exposing a gaseous mixture of carbon monoxide (CO) and chlorine (Cl_2) to bright sunlight. Without implying anything about the molecular mechanism of the reaction or about the role of sunlight, we can be summarize Davy's synthesis as

$$CO + Cl_2 \rightarrow COCl_2$$

John Davy had the perogative of naming the new chemical compound. He coined its name from two Greek words. Davy wrote in 1812: "… it will be necessary to designate it by some simple name. I venture to propose that of phosgene, or phosgene gas; from φως, light, and γινομαι, to produce, which signifies formed by light …"

Davy reported: "Its odour was different from that of chlorine, something like that which one might imagine would result from the smell of chlorine combined with that of ammonia, yet more intolerable and suffocating than chlorine itself, and affecting the eyes in a peculiar manner, producing a rapid flow of tears and occasioning painful sensations." In the 21st century, few practicing chemists allow themselves to make such bodily contact with unfamiliar or unknown substances. It was not always thus.

Many chemists educated before 1900 knew (from personal experience) the characteristic and identifying tastes of many chemicals in their laboratories. Constantin Fahlberg (1850–1910) gave this account of his 1879 discovery of the taste of saccharin: "One evening I was so interested in my laboratory that I forgot about supper until quite late, and then rushed off for a meal without stopping to wash my hands. I sat down, broke a piece of bread, and put it to my lips. It tasted unspeakably sweet. I did not ask why it was so, probably because I thought it was some cake or sweetmeat. I rinsed my mouth with water, and dried my mustache with my napkin, when, to my surprise, the napkin tasted sweeter than the bread. Then I was puzzled. I again raised my goblet, and, as fortune would have it, applied my mouth where my fingers had touched it before. The water seemed sirup. It flashed upon me that I was the cause of the singular universal sweetness, and I accordingly tasted the end of my thumb, and found that it surpassed any confectionery I had ever eaten. I saw the whole thing at a glance. I had discovered or made some coal tar substance which outsugared sugar. I dropped my dinner, and ran back to the laboratory. There, in my excitement, I tasted the contents of every beaker and evaporating dish on the table. Luckily for me, none contained any corrosive or poisonous liquid."

Chemists knew from direct experience early in their careers many physiological effects of dangerous chemicals. Most had observed, for instance, that sodium hydroxide solutions remove protective layers of human skin and can induce bleeding. Some chemists actually ingested substantial quantities of laboratory reagents to study metabolic reactions. Johann Lewinski reported (in 1908) that men who ingested as much as twenty grams of sodium benzoate converted the chemical quantitatively to hippuric acid, which they then excreted in urine. H. D. Dakin confirmed Lewinski's observations in 1909. As late as the 1940s, an undergraduate organic chemistry laboratory exercise involved the same ingestion procedure, with students given weighed samples of sodium benzoate to swallow, and then graded on the yield of the hippuric acid they recovered from their urine.

Most chemists educated before 1950 knew the odors of the volatile chemicals that they used. The rotten-egg odor of the toxic hydrogen sulfide (H_2S), a gas routinely generated in the collegiate teaching laboratory for qualitative inorganic analysis until the 1970s, was familiar and expected. Students were told that they should get outside air when they could no longer smell the gas. On several campuses, visitors could locate the chemistry building simply by detecting the H_2S emanation. Entomologists used hydrogen cyanide "killing jars" when collecting insects. As late as the 1940s, Purdue University gave ten-year-old junior entomologists in Indiana 4-H clubs instructions for constructing their own cyanide killing jars, using ingredients that could be purchased from local pharmacists. If they were among the persons able to smell the gas, those fledgling entomologists knew first-hand the characteristic odor of lethal hydrogen cyanide (HCN).

The common names of several chemical compounds are based on taste or odor. Sugar of lead (lead acetate) is said to have a sweet taste, and has been implicated in accidental poisonings and in homicides for centuries. Among the most notorious odoriferous substances are amines appropriately named putrescine, $(NH_2)(CH_2)_4(NH_2)$, and cadaverine, $(NH_2)(CH_2)_5(NH_2)$. Ludwig Brieger (1849–1919) reported isolation of each from rotting flesh in 1885.

Most chemists educated before 1975 knew from experience the physical appearance of a wide range of chemicals. Many of those elements and compounds were freely available in containers (often transparent glass containers) on open reagent shelves in labs. For example, physical chemists made extensive use of metallic mercury throughout the twentieth century. Albert Germann used mercury as the working fluid in his thermometers, thermoregulators, manometers, and barometers, and as a component of his electrochemical cells. Chemists routinely purified contaminated mercury on the benchtop in their own laboratories. By the twenty-first century, many neophytes did not know why mercury metal was called quicksilver. Long-fiber asbestos was used in quantitative gravimetric analysis to collect precipitates in a Gooch crucible. Asbestos was also used as a heat-distributing coating on wire gauze to protect beakers from Bunsen burner flames, as a major component of an insulating board that protected benchtop surfaces from direct heat, and in asbestos gloves designed for safe handling of hot objects. The colorful compounds of nickel, copper, cobalt, chromium, and cadmium were on display on reagent shelves, and were routinely used in laboratory operations. Many artists had chemical workrooms where they mixed pigments and binders, creating paints with desired visual appeal, unfortunately often without sufficient regard for toxicity of the ingredients. Varieties of "waste chemicals" were routinely discarded down the drain. Within a generation, safety and environmental concerns (and laws) changed dramatically. Acceptable laboratory practice changed accordingly. The phrase "hands-on chemistry" acquired a figurative meaning.

Davy's wary description of the physiological properties of phosgene suggests that phosgene is not a benign substance. Davy had laboratory experience with many other substances that were far from benign. Davy did not warn readers of his 1812 paper that phosgene was especially hazardous, maybe even with the potential of being used as a weapon of warfare. Brothers Humphry and John Davy both worked with chlorine, but did not suggest possible military uses of chlorine gas. Both phosgene and chlorine did become deadly weapons in the Great War.

The first poison gas used in the War was xylyl bromide (bromomethyl-methyl-benzene, C_8H_9Br). Xylyl bromide is a powerful lachrymator, a tear gas. The German Ninth Army deployed xylyl bromide ineffectively against the Russian Second Army near the Polish village of Bolimów on January 31, 1915. The Germans tried another chemical. On April 22, 1915, in the Second Battle of Ypres, the German Army released chlorine gas against troops of the French 45th and 78th divisions. Chlorine turned out to be potent as a battlefield killer. It was even deadlier when mixed with phosgene. Germany used the phosgene–chlorine combination against the British at Wieltje, Belgium, on December 19, 1915. In September 1917, the Germans used sulfur mustard gas [bis-(2-chloroethyl) sulfide, $C_4H_8Cl_2S$] with deadly effect.

Vernon Jersey obtained phosgene for his experiments from the National Lamp Works of the General Electric Company, located in Nela Park, East Cleveland, Ohio, near the Western Reserve laboratories. (Nela is an acronym for National Electric Lamp Association.) National Lamp Works was testing various types of charcoal for use in gas masks; the idea was that activated charcoal might adsorb most of the phosgene from poisoned atmosphere before air was inhaled. Technical grade phosgene for Germann's later experiments at Stanford University was probably obtained from the United States Army Edgewood Arsenal in Maryland. Edgewood Arsenal produced phosgene, using only slight variations of Davy's original synthesis method.

Technical grade phosgene required careful and thorough purification before being used in physical chemical experiments. A 1923 paper (published by Albert Germann after he had moved to Stanford University) reported: "It is most important for the progress of the study of the properties of phosgene that a method be developed for the rapid and complete purification of the technical product. Work in this direction in cooperation with the chemical warfare service is in progress at the Stanford Laboratory." A 1925 paper acknowledgment: "Thanks are due the Chemical Warfare Service, for the generous supply of phosgene provided for this research." From another paper: "I wish to express my thanks to the Chemical Warfare Service for supplying the phosgene necessary for this investigation."

The United States Army created the Chemical Warfare Service in 1918. The Service was assigned responsibility for responding to chemical attacks. After the Armistice that year, there was pressure from President Woodrow Wilson and from the public to close the Chemical Warfare Service. Major General Amos Alfred Fries (1873–1963), Chemical Warfare Service Chief from 1920 to 1929, countered by enumerating peacetime achievements of the Service—protecting marine docks and waterfront structures, combating the boll weevil, protecting ship bottoms from marine organisms, and fumigating ships from foreign countries to combat typhus fever and bubonic plague.

General Fries carefully chose his examples of peacetime uses to make a persuasive case. There were significant economic and medical examples. The boll weevil (*Anthonomus grandis*), feasting on cotton buds and flowers, was devastating plantings in all cotton-growing regions of the United States in 1920. Typhus, caused by Rickettsia bacteria, is transmitted to humans by parasites such as fleas and ticks. Typhus had ravaged troops on the eastern front in the Great War, and the epidemic continued after the Armistice. In 1920, there were twenty million cases of typhus in Russia, and the peak of the epidemic had not been reached. There were still memories of the 1899 bubonic plague outbreak in Oahu, Hawaii, rumored to have been caused when rats (carrying infected fleas) fled cargo ships from China.

Similar tensions persist today between advocates of abolishing "chemical warfare agents" and proponents of exploring and exploiting useful properties of similar chemicals. Chlorine was shown to be an extraordinarily effective weapon of mass killing, but half of the commercial products produced by the chemical industry depend on chlorine chemistry. Over ninety percent of top-selling pharmaceuticals are made using chlorine, and most municipal domestic water in the United States is chlorinated. Phosgene, although now controlled by the International Organisation for the Prohibition of Chemical Weapons, is synthesized commercially in large quantities as a precursor in the manufacture of many economically important organic compounds. Apart from safety considerations, phosgene is simple to produce. Because of its toxicity, phosgene is often produced and consumed within the same industrial plant to avoid the hazards of transporting the compound.

Scientists at the Bureau of Mines within the United States Department of the Interior had been studying poisonous gases (such as those encountered in mineral mining operations) since the establishment of the Bureau in 1910. In February 1917, with active involvement in the War imminent and with ominous reports from Bolimów, Ypres, and Wieltje, the Bureau of Mines began to investigate improved gas masks for protecting military personnel. By June 30, 1917, the Bureau had expanded its research to include gases with potential for offensive warfare. In November 1917, Secretary of the Interior Franklin Knight Lane (1864–1921) appointed a blue-ribbon Advisory Board to provide expert guidance to the Director of the Bureau of Mines "on war problems." The Board included Edward Curtis Franklin (1862–1937; Professor of Chemistry at Stanford University), William Henry Nichols (1852–1930; one of the founders of the American Chemical Society), Charles Lathrop Parsons (1869–1954; Chief Mineral Chemist at the Bureau of Mines), William Hoskins (1862–1934; co-inventor of nichrome electrical resistance heating wire and the modern billiard-cue chalk), Henry Paul Talbot (1864–1927; Professor of Chemistry at the Massachusetts Institute of Technology), Francis Preston Venable (1856–1934; Professor of Chemistry at the University of North Carolina), Ira Remsen (1846–1927; founder in 1879 of the *American Chemical Journal* and its editor for 35 years; a member of the original faculty of The Johns Hopkins University), and Theodore William Richards (1868–1928; Professor of Chemistry at Harvard University; Nobel laureate 1914).

In December 1917, the Chemical Service was established as a unit of the United States Army. The Chemical Service was under the command of Lieutenant Colonel William Hultz Walker (1869–1934). Dr. Walker had been Professor of Industrial Chemistry at the Massachusetts Institute of Technology since 1894, and had founded the M.I.T. School of Chemical Engineering Practice. Lieutenant Colonel Walker was soon transferred to the Ordnance Department and placed in charge of Edgewood Arsenal, a large facility for manufacturing chemicals being constructed near Baltimore, Maryland. Chemical warfare research was removed from the Bureau of Mines in summer 1918 with creation of the Chemical Warfare Service. William Hultz Walker (promoted to Colonel Walker) was in charge of large-scale manufacturing of gases at Edgewood Arsenal. Through his service on the Bureau of Mines Advisory Board, Stanford University professor Edward Curtis Franklin learned of a research assistantship opportunity at Edgewood Arsenal for one of his chemistry students, William M. Schaufelberger.

William M. Schaufelberger was born July 24, 1896, in Hastings, Nebraska. His father, Frederick J. Schaufelberger, was a physician in Hastings. William graduated from Hastings High School in 1914, and matriculated at Stanford University in September 1914. He majored in chemistry in the chemical engineering curriculum, and received the A.B. degree (in Chemistry) in June 1918. He immediately transferred to the Graduate Division of the University, and continued his studies at Stanford as a candidate for the professional degree of Chemical Engineer. This program required a year of graduate study, and presentation of a thesis. University regulations permitted thesis research to be conducted at another institution. The Stanford Chemistry Department approved a proposal for Mr. Schaufelberger to carry out experimental work on phosgene in the chemical laboratory of Captain Ralph E. Hall C.W.S. at Edgewood Arsenal. Captain Hall was a physical chemist who had earned a Ph.D. from the University of Chicago.

While a graduate student in chemical engineering, Mr. Schaufelberger was on the instructional staff of the Stanford University Chemistry Department as a Teaching Assistant for the 1919–1920 year.

William M. Schaufelberger submitted his thesis, "Vapor Pressure of Phosgene–HCl Mixtures," in March 1920. Professor Franklin signed the thesis for the Chemistry Department. With permission of Colonel Walker, Edgewood Arsenal Chemical Laboratory released its Report No. 223 for incorporation into the thesis. Mr. Schaufelberger wrote his thesis at Stanford. He gave Stanford chemistry professor Stewart Woodford Young credit "for valuable assistance in writing this thesis." Professor Young probably directed two semesters of Schaufelberger's undergraduate experimental research in senior year (Special Studies Chemistry, laboratory course K). Stanford University awarded the degree of Chemical Engineer to William M. Schaufelberger in 1920.

It does not appear that Schaufelberger's experimental results on phosgene were ever published in a scientific journal. No documentation has been found to suggest that Albert Germann knew of Schaufelberger's phosgene research prior to Germann's arrival at Stanford. Germann certainly found out about it after his arrival.

Now we return to Marion Cleaveland.

Marion Cleaveland (March 31, 1898–December 23, 1975) was born in the village of Fredonia in Chautauqua County, the westernmost county in New York State. She received the degree of Bachelor of Arts in Chemistry from the College for Women of Western Reserve University in 1920, and was elected to Phi Beta Kappa. She was awarded the degree of Master of Arts in Chemistry from Western Reserve University in 1921. Western Reserve University did not require a thesis for a master's degree at that time. However, her graduate research was presented (as noted above) at a meeting of the American Chemical Society (Division of Physical and Inorganic Chemistry) in Rochester, New York, and reported in 1921 in the journal *Science* as a joint contribution of A. F. O. Germann and Marion Cleaveland.

From 1921 to 1922, she was Assistant in Chemistry at the College for Women of Western Reserve University. From 1922 to 1926, she was Instructor of Chemistry at the College for Women. She was a graduate student at Columbia University from 1926 to 1928, receiving the degree of Doctor of Philosophy in 1929 with the dissertation: "A Quantitative Study of the Influence of Certain Neutral Salts upon the Activity of Malt Amylase."

Marion Cleaveland returned to the Western Reserve faculty, appointed Instructor of Chemistry at the College for Women for the years 1928 to 1930. Dr. Cleaveland's promotion to Assistant Professor of Chemistry in 1930 coincided with the transformation of the College for Women into the Flora Stone Mather College of Western Reserve, and followed the awarding of the Ph.D. by Columbia University. She remained on the chemistry faculty of Flora Stone Mather College until 1946, and from 1944 to 1946 held a joint appointment as Assistant Professor of Chemistry at Adelbert College.

In 1925, Cleveland College opened in downtown Cleveland, founded "by Western Reserve University and Case School of Applied Science to provide education for adult learners." Case School of Applied Science was founded in 1880, the fourth American institution of higher learning to concentrate on a technical education, the first located west of the Appalachians. Case was rechristened Case Institute of Technology in 1947. It merged with Western Reserve in 1967 to form Case Western Reserve University. Marion Cleaveland taught a night course at Cleveland College in 1942 on the chemistry of fermentation. For many years, beginning in 1925, Harold Booth was Head of the Division of Physical Sciences of Cleveland College, in addition to being a member of the Western Reserve chemistry faculty. Marion Cleaveland married Norbert Adolph Lange (1892–1972), then a member of the Western Reserve chemistry faculty, on Thursday, April 18, 1946. The marriage was just after the death of his mother. "Marion Cleaveland, Sandusky, Ohio," is listed among the contributors to the 10th edition (1966) of the classic *Handbook of Chemistry*, compiled and edited by Norbert Lange. Marion Cleaveland kept her professional name after marriage to Norbert Lange, but did not remain on the faculty with him. Norbert died October 12, 1972. In his will, he created The Norbert A. and Marion Cleaveland Lange Trust of Sandusky (Ohio) Library, an endowment that supports cultural and educational programs for residents of Sandusky and Erie counties. Marion augmented the trust in 1974. She died December 23, 1975.

It is possible that Marion Cleaveland was a descendant of Moses Cleaveland (1754–1806), a surveyor who has been credited with founding the City of Cleveland (originally Cleaveland) while surveying the Western Reserve of Connecticut in 1796 for the Connecticut Land Company, of which he was a shareholder. Moses Cleaveland was born in Canterbury, Connecticut. He spent most of his life in Canterbury, where he was a lawyer and a representative of the town in the Connecticut General Assembly.

Theories of Solvent Systems

The Chemistry Department at Western Reserve was a congenial place. It was a small place. Olin Freeman Tower, Hippolyte Washington Gruener, and Albert Germann constituted the entire chemistry faculty until Harold Booth joined them for the 1919–1920 year. Albert's research interests were evolving. It appears that he was restless. He began to look beyond Cleveland, and particularly at Stanford University in Palo Alto, California.

Albert's brother Frank had made a cross-continent move from Ithaca, New York, to Golden, Colorado, in 1918. In Golden, Frank taught for one year as part of an even smaller faculty at Colorado School of Mines. There he was the only professor in *two* departments. It is difficult to imagine a smaller viable academic community. Frank found the School of Mines situation untenable, and quickly moved a few miles to Boulder and to the University of Colorado for the 1919–1920 academic year. Frank lived in Boulder for the rest of his professional career.

Jane Eliza Lathrop Stanford (1828–1905) and Amasa Leland Stanford (1824–1893) founded Stanford University in memory of their son, Leland Stanford Jr., who died of typhoid fever at the age of fifteen. They named the institution Leland Stanford Junior University. The first students enrolled October 1, 1891.

Railroad tycoon Leland Stanford Sr. had created the Palo Alto Stock Farm in 1876 for breeding and training trotters, horses that pulled sulkies in harness races. In 1882, Stanford bought adjacent land (Ayrshire Farm) from cattleman Peter Coutts. This farmland, together with land bought by Timothy Hopkins of the Southern Pacific Railroad, were the sites chosen for the new university and for the new Temperance Town of Palo Alto.

A large chemistry building, designed by San Francisco architect Clinton Day, opened in 1903 in the center of campus. Tall brick chimneys, through which laboratory fume hoods discharged their noxious gases, were integrated into the design of the neoclassical façade. The interior design was praised for excellent natural light provided by high ceilings, large windows, and three skylights. The massive April 18, 1906, California earthquake damaged the building. All those chimneys collapsed, and some outer walls were badly shaken, but the damage was small compared to the earthquake's effect on the nearby new campus gymnasium and the library building. Gym and library were demolished by the quake. The chemistry building was quickly rehabilitated. It was reoccupied by the Chemistry Department a few months later, in autumn 1906. Although concerns were expressed for decades about the quality of the rehabilitation, the building continued to be the home of chemistry until 1986.

The spacious physical facilities for teaching and research were an attraction, but not the overriding factor for Albert Germann. He wanted to expand his research on solvent systems. Albert thought that study of solvent systems was a research area in physical chemistry where he and his students could make significant contributions. He was drawn to Stanford by the early research accomplishments of Stanford chemistry professor Edward Curtis Franklin (1862–1937) in studying the ammonia solvent system. Albert had in mind complementary studies of the phosgene solvent system. He hoped for a collegial relationship with Professor Franklin.

In assessing a professional future at Stanford, Albert observed that the Stanford chemistry faculty was aging. There had been no new professorial appointments since 1906. Professor Emeritus John Mason Stillman (1852–1923), one of the fifteen founding faculty of the University and Executive Head of the Chemistry Department from 1891 to 1917, had retired after the 1917–1918 year. He had not been replaced. The chances for advancement through the ranks to a tenured position seemed actuarially good. Ernest Oertly, Instructor of Chemistry, died January 5, 1920, and had not yet been replaced.

Albert Germann decided to make the major move across the continent. He applied for a faculty position at Stanford. Maybe he resigned from Western Reserve; more likely, he requested and received a leave of absence, inasmuch as he had just been granted tenure. Albert F. O. Germann was listed as a member of the chemistry faculty in the Western Reserve *Catalogue* for 1922, even though he had joined the Stanford Chemistry Department as Assistant Professor of Chemistry in 1921.

The first quarter of the twentieth century were years of intense physical-chemical research and speculation about the nature of liquid solutions. Chemists in Europe and in America were devising new experimental methods to investigate solutions, and inventing a new vocabulary to describe chemical reactions in those solutions. Josiah Willard Gibbs (1839–1903) at Yale University had published a major treatise on thermodynamics in the 1870s. Gibbs laid out theoretical principles that would guide physical chemists during the next hundred years as they developed the concepts of Gibbs free energy, chemical potential, fugacity, activity, and activity coefficients, and applied these concepts to interpret chemical equilibria in solutions.

Albert Germann, like many of his contemporaries, was closely following this blossoming theoretical and experimental research. Albert intended to be a contributor, especially in the laboratory.

Liquid water (H_2O) was the first solvent examined in detail by physical chemists. Next was liquid ammonia (NH_3). Germann was initially attracted to boron trifluoride (BF_3) and phosgene (CCl_2O) as third and fourth solvent systems that might be susceptible to systematic study. At first, it appeared that he might be able to exploit both liquid boron trifluoride and also liquid phosgene. By 1921, he had settled on phosgene.

Edward C. Franklin at Stanford concentrated on liquid ammonia, but he was also learning about chemistry in liquid phosgene. As we have noted, Franklin K. Lane, Secretary of the Interior, had appointed Edward C. Franklin to the Advisory Board to the Director of the Bureau of Mines "on war problems." The scope of these war problems rapidly expanded to include chemical weapons. Phosgene gas was one of those potential weapons under active investigation, both in the United States and in Europe.

To provide some context, we shall examine the status of experimental investigations of solvent systems in the first quarter of the century. We begin with water.

In water, the simplest chemical descriptions involve the ultrafast reaction

$$H_2O \rightleftharpoons H^+ + OH^-$$

in which a molecule of water (H_2O) dissociates reversibly into two ions: a hydrogen cation (H^+) and a hydroxyl anion (OH^-). This reaction maintains dynamic chemical equilibrium among molecular water and the ions. From 1901 to 1938, chemist Søren Peder Lauritz Sørensen (1868–1939) was head of the Carlsberg Laboratory in Copenhagen. There he led pioneering investigations of proteins dissolved in water. From his viewpoint, a dissolved molecule is an acid if it contains a dissociable hydrogen ion; the molecule is a base if it can react with a hydrogen ion or if it can produce a hydroxyl ion. The molar concentration of hydrogen ions, a quantity symbolized by the composite symbol $[H^+]$, can have a numerical value greater than 10 moles/liter in concentrated acid solutions, lower than 10^{-14} moles/liter in strongly basic solutions, or anywhere in between. To simplify discussions of experiments in which the numerical value of $[H^+]$ can vary by more than fourteen powers of ten, Sørensen (in 1909) introduced the convenient pH scale, where the composite symbol pH is defined as

$$pH = -\log_{10}[H^+]$$

which is mathematically equivalent to

$$[H^+] = 10^{-pH}$$

On Sørensen's logarithmic scale (with acidity expressed in "Sorensen units" from 1 to 14), pH = 1 when $[H^+]$ = 10^{-1} moles/liter, and pH = 14 when $[H^+]$ = 10^{-14} moles/ liter. This scale spans the range of acidity and basicity ordinarily encountered in living systems, as well as the range of acidity and basicity ordinarily encountered by chemists investigating biomolecules dissolved in water. Laboratories throughout the world quickly adopted the Sørensen pH scale; it remains the standard way of expressing acidity in aqueous media.

For pH to be studied quantitatively in the laboratory, a device is needed to measure the concentration of hydrogen ions in solution. One device exploits the decomposition of hydrogen gas to yield hydrogen ions and electrons:

$$H_2 \rightleftarrows 2H^+ + 2e^-$$

This electrochemical reaction can be studied in an electrochemical cell by immersing a platinum electrode in a test solution, bubbling hydrogen gas over the platinum, and measuring the electrical potential between the platinum "indicating electrode" and a suitable "reference electrode." In some respects, this "hydrogen electrode" is an elegant way to measure pH, especially in the hands of a skilled electrochemist. However, the electrode's response to $[H^+]$ is easily compromised by the presence of proteins (and many other substances) in the test solution. Because its use requires a steady source of explosive hydrogen gas, the hydrogen electrode is not portable. For measurements except under ideal laboratory conditions, the hydrogen electrode is unreliable and impractical.

A very different indicating electrode was invented by Fritz Jacobus Haber (1868–1934; Nobel laureate 1918) and Zygmunt Aleksander Klemensiewicz (1886–1963).

This electrode was a fragile bulb made with very thin glass walls. Haber and Klemen-siewicz discovered that the electrical potential between two solutions separated by a glass membrane is due, at least in part, to the difference in the numerical value of [H$^+$] between the two solutions. They described this phenomenon in 1909. Fifteen years later, Walter S. Hughes built an instrument to compare the glass electrode with the hydrogen electrode. He found that, with careful calibration procedures, glass-electrode readings can be translated into hydrogen-electrode readings. Hughes' instrument simultaneously dipped both electrodes into the same test solution. He employed an equal but opposite electrical potential from dry cells (the applied volt-age regulated with a rheostat), and used a Kelvin quadrant electrometer to detect the rheostat setting at which this bucking potential was equal to the difference between the two electrodes. This was a "null-point" method.

It takes an experienced and patient electrochemist to make such measure-ments, using the delicate and temperamental Kelvin quadrant electrometer. A cru-cial advance in making pH measurements convenient was to employ the new technology of electronics. Lee de Forest (1873–1961) had invented a diode vac-uum tube in 1906 (the audion), and a year later a triode. The triode (with a grid, a filament cathode, and an anode, all sealed together within an evacuated glass tube) was used in 1921 by Kenneth H. Goode as a voltmeter (which drew no current) in what he called "a continuous-reading electrotitration apparatus." Goode's indicat-ing electrode was a glass membrane.

Hughes and Goode each had cannibalized components from other equipment to build their experimental apparatus. They then assembled components on laboratory bench tops, and connected the parts with jumbles of electrical cables. Such a device was clearly not portable. Each device was viewed by contemporaries (if viewed at all) for more than a decade as merely a scientific curiosity.

Arnold Orville Beckman (1900–2004) entered the story in the early 1930s. As Beckman tells it, a University of Illinois classmate (Glen Joseph, a chemist for the mar-keter of Sunkist fruit juices) sought Beckman's assistance in getting an accurate and rapid measure of the acidity of lemon juice. Beckman, then Dr. Beckman and an Assis-tant Professor of Chemistry at California Institute of Technology, offered to build an acidimeter for Dr. Joseph. Beckman developed a more rugged glass electrode. He used an improved vacuum-tube voltage-amplification circuit. He then connected all the components, and packaged the ensemble in a small wooden box. Glen Joseph liked the portable, reliable, and easy-to-operate acidimeter. He ordered a second.

Beckman made a fateful career choice. He resigned from the Cal Tech faculty, and formed National Technical Laboratories to improve, manufacture, and distribute what was soon to become the Beckman Model G pH Meter. In a wooden box with a carrying handle and a latch, the instrument was demonstrated at the national meeting of the American Chemical Society in 1935. Within a few years, the Model G was being used in just about every chemistry and biochemistry laboratory in the nation. The United States National Bureau of Standards began marketing pH standards for use in calibrating the Model G. Before his retirement in 1938 from the Carlsberg Laboratory, Søren Peder Lauritz Sørensen had seen his pH scale become the experimental touchstone for quantitative research in aqueous solution chemistry.

Although liquid water (the ubiquitous solvent for living systems) continued to be the solvent most studied by biochemists, the liquid ammonia solvent system was also being investigated in America at the beginning of the twentieth century. Chemist Edward Curtis Franklin (1862–1937), physicist Charles August Kraus (1875–1967), and Franklin's students Hamilton Perkins Cady (1874–1943), Gilbert Newton Lewis (1875–1946), and Orin Fletcher Stafford (1873–1941) began experimental studies of the ammonia system at the University of Kansas in 1896.

Franklin recalled that Cady, then an undergraduate in Franklin's quantitative analysis chemistry laboratory course, prepared a cobalt-ammine crystal and suggested "that liquid ammonia would probably be found to resemble water in its physical and chemical properties." The first ammonia experiments from Kansas were reported in the chemical literature by Cady alone in 1897. Cady graduated from the University of Kansas with an A.B. in 1897, and then began research at Cornell University with Wilder Dwight Bancroft. Bancroft was founder, owner, and (with Joseph Trevor) editor of the *Journal of Physical Chemistry*, first English-language research periodical in physical chemistry; Cady's paper appeared in the journal's first volume. After two years at Cornell, Cady returned to Kansas to continue research with Franklin. Cady received the Ph.D. from the University of Kansas in 1903, submitting the thesis "Concentration Cells in Liquid Ammonia."

Charles August Kraus from the University of Kansas Physics Department joined the research team. Franklin and Kraus investigated the solubilities of 175 salts in liquid ammonia. They then began the experiments needed for determining molecular weights of dissolved species. Olin Stafford's experimental research resulted in an A.M. thesis, "Reactions between Acid and Basic Amides in Liquid Ammonia Solution" (1902), and a publication with Franklin on chemical reactions in liquid ammonia. In that publication, the close analogies between liquid ammonia and liquid water were explored. Stafford and Franklin presented evidence for equilibria among the chemical species NH_2^-, NH_3, and NH_4^+. The analogous species in water can be written as OH^-, OH_2, and OH_3^+.

Chemist George Mann Richardson (1863–1902) was one of the original faculty of fifteen recruited in 1891 by David Starr Jordan (1851–1931), first president of Stanford University. Biologist Jordan had been President of Indiana University since 1885. When Richardson died July 26, 1902, President Jordan needed a promising research chemist to be Richardson's replacement. Jordan offered Edward Franklin an appointment at Stanford as Professor of Chemistry, with teaching responsibilities in organic chemistry. His former Kansas colleague, Vernon Lyman Kellogg (1867–1937), urged Franklin to accept the offer. Kellogg had taught entomology at the University of Kansas from 1890 to 1894, before accepting an appointment as Professor of Entomology at Stanford University in 1894.

Edward Franklin did accept the Stanford University offer, joining the faculty in 1903. Although hired as an organic chemist, and placed in charge of the undergraduate organic courses, Franklin focused his research on ammonia chemistry. A rising star, he appeared to have a promising future at Stanford. That promise was to be fulfilled at Stanford and nationally. His research publications and his books, *Reactions in Liquid Ammonia* and *The Nitrogen System of Compounds*, would bring him recognition as an innovative inorganic chemist and as a physical chemist. He would be awarded the William Henry Nichols Gold Medal, the nation's oldest award for chemistry, by the New York Section of the American Chemical Society in 1925. He would receive the Josiah Willard Gibbs Gold Medal of the Chicago A.C.S. Section in 1932. He would serve as President of the American Chemical Society, and would be elected to the National Academy of Sciences.

Water (H_2O) is a liquid at ordinary laboratory temperatures. It has a boiling point of 100 °C at one atmosphere pressure. These properties are consistent with the central role played by water in all living systems. These properties also make aqueous systems amenable to experiments under conditions of temperature and pressure that are convenient for human investigators. Ammonia (NH_3), another apparently simple molecule, has less convenient properties. It has a boiling point of −33 °C at one atmosphere, but it is a liquid at 15 °C at seven atmospheres pressure. Boron trifluoride (BF_3) has a boiling point of −100 °C at one atmosphere. Germann and his students had encountered enough experimental difficulties with boron trifluoride to leave this highly corrosive liquid, with an especially inconvenient boiling point, as a solvent for further study by others.

Another small molecule is phosgene (CCl_2O). A liquid with a boiling point of 8 °C at one atmosphere pressure, phosgene seemed worth investigating. Albert Germann had sought to emulate Franklin's methodology when he and Vernon Jersey studied the phosgene solvent system at Western Reserve University. No analytical methods analogous to the Haber–Klemensiewicz glass electrode seemed close at hand for ammonia, boron trifluoride, or phosgene solutions, but even the glass electrode had not yet proven itself. It would be fifteen more years before the Beckman Model G pH Meter demonstrated the practicality of the glass electrode for aqueous solutions. Electrodes that respond selectively to NH_3 or NH_4^+ would be even farther into the future.

When Albert joined the Stanford Chemistry Department in 1921 as an Assistant Professor, the chemistry faculty consisted of five Professors, one other Assistant Professor, and five Instructors.

Professor Robert Eckles Swain (1875–1961) joined the Department in 1902. Eckles was an able and active administrator. He enjoyed politics. He was a member of the Palo Alto City Council from 1912 to 1921, and Mayor of Palo Alto from 1914 to 1916. In 1921, he was Executive Head of the Department, and he would remain as Head of the Department until 1940. Eckles would also serve as Acting President of the University from 1930 to 1933 while President Ray Lyman Wilbur was United States Secretary of the Interior.

Professor Edward Curtis Franklin (1862–1937) joined the Department in 1903.

Professor Lionel Remond Lenox (1865–1927) joined the Department in 1892.

Professor John Pearce Mitchell (1880–1973) joined the Department in 1905, and was promoted to Professor for 1920–1921. He would be University Registrar from 1925 to 1945.

Professor Stewart Woodford Young (1869–1931) joined the Department in 1893.

Assistant Professor Albert Frederick Ottomar Germann (1886–1976) joined the Department in 1921.

Assistant Professor William Henry Sloan (1877–1950) joined the Department in 1906. Sloan studied with Friedrich Wilhelm Ostwald (1853–1932; Nobel laureate in Chemistry 1909) at Leipzig University, but never completed his doctorate.

Albert Germann's first teaching assignments were in first-year general chemistry. He shared lecture responsibilities with John Mitchell. He shared laboratory responsibilities with Mitchell and with instructor Norris Watson Rakestraw. Germann also offered a lecture course "Chemistry of Gases," and a laboratory course "Manipulation of Gases." "Manipulation of Gases" met "two or more afternoons" a week, and appears to have had an enrollment of two students in the winter term and one student in the summer term. These laboratory students likely constituted the core of his Stanford research group. His teaching assignments remained the same for the next three years.

When making his decision to come to Stanford, Albert Germann may have thought that two chemists (Franklin and Germann), using similar strategies to investigate two different chemical systems, could make Stanford a recognized competitor with Carlsberg for experimental and theoretical study of solvent systems. If Albert Germann had anticipated developing a productive and collegial relationship with Edward Franklin, then he may have been disappointed when he met Franklin in person. Read what reserved Chemistry Professor Eric Hutchinson (1920–2005; Stanford Chemistry Faculty 1949–1983) wrote about Franklin:

"To my regret I never knew that rare, engaging, and (if what I gather is true) infuriating person E. C. Franklin. If even half of the anecdotal material on Franklin is true, he must have been an extraordinary person. But since I cannot vouch for the authenticity of most of the Frankliniana, I have regretfully omitted it."

"Franklin possessed an iconoclastic nature, and he was given to what at times amounted to an over-frank expression of opinions. As mischievous as a child, in some respects, he nevertheless had a first-rate mind: on many occasions a shrewd question from Franklin deflated a seminar speaker carried away on the wings of hypotheses. Within the Department of Chemistry he generated untold anecdotes and legends."

Regardless of whether Edward Franklin would ever be inclined to share limelight with Albert Germann, Albert began at once to form his own research group to investigate the phosgene solvent system. Two chemistry graduate students (Charles Russel Timpany and Kenneth A. Gagos) and two graduate students in chemical engineering (Quimby W. Taylor and Dionisio Martinez Birosel) began experimental investigations of phosgene itself, and investigations of chemical reactions in liquid phosgene. An undergraduate, Glenn Hazel McIntyre, also joined the research group, conducting experiments on solutions of aluminum chloride in phosgene. Appendix B sets forth information about their research work, including resultant publications, Stanford degrees, and biographical sketches.

In addition to numerous joint publications with his students, Albert Germann was busy writing his own papers on solvent systems in general, on phosgene systems in particular, and on factors involved in designing new apparatus for his experiments. Both in the laboratory and at his desk, 1924 was a very productive year. Ten research publications resulted from this activity:

"Reactions in Phosgene Solutions. III. Reactions with Metallic Oxides, Sulfides, and Carbonates," *Science* (New Series), vol. 59 (May 30, 1924), p. 491.

"Reactions in Phosgene Solution. I," *Journal of Physical Chemistry*, vol. 28, no. 8 (August 1924), pp. 879–886.

"The Reactivity of Liquid Phosgene," *Science* (New Series), vol. 60, no. 1558 (November 7, 1924), p. 434. Presented at the Stanford University meeting of the Pacific Division of the American Association for the Advancement of Science, June 26, 1924.

"The Action of Chlorine on Mercury, *Journal of Physical Chemistry*, vol. 28, no. 11 (November 1924), pp. 1218–1220.

"The Conductivity of Phosgene Solutions of Aluminum Chloride at 25°, 0°, and −45°," *Science* (New Series), vol. 60, no. 1565 (December 26, 1924), pp. 595–596.

"Carbon Monoxide, a Product of Electrolysis," *Science* (New Series), vol. 61, no. 1568 (January 16, 1925), pp. 70–71.

"What is an Acid?" *Science* (New Series), vol. 61, no. 1568 (January 16, 1925), p. 71.

"Densities of Solutions of Aluminum Chloride in Liquid Phosgene," *Journal of Physical Chemistry*, vol. 29, no. 2 (February 1925), pp. 138–141.

"The Conductivity of Phosgene Solutions of Aluminum Chloride at
25°, 0°, and −45°," *Journal of Physical Chemistry,* vol. 29, no. 9 (September
1925), pp. 1148–1154.

"A General Theory of Solvent Systems," *Journal of the American Chemical Society,* vol. 47, no. 10 (October 1925), pp. 2461–2468.

Germann was exploring several electrochemical methods for studying chemistry in phosgene. The short note in *Science* and the longer paper in *Journal of Physical Chemistry* on conductivity in phosgene solution were preliminary investigations into the applicability of electrical conductivity as a tool for detecting new chemical solute species in phosgene. Studies of reactions of chlorine with mercury, and carbon monoxide produced by electrolysis, suggest that he was also investigating the use of the newly developed Heyrovský polarographic electrochemical technique. Heyrovský employed a "dropping mercury electrode," an innovation in which a fresh mercury electrode surface was continuously formed as mercury dropped from a glass capillary tube. Complications in Germann's experiments apparently involved decomposition of phosgene into chlorine and carbon monoxide at the electrode during attempts to perform polarographic experiments.

Germann was unable to discover an experimentally accessible analogue to the OH^-, OH_2, and OH_3^+ equilibria or to the NH_2^-, NH_3, and NH_4^+ equilibria. The thermodynamics of the water equilibria and of the ammonia equilibria favor facile reversible transfer of protons (hydrogen cations, H^+ ions) among a triad of stable species. For phosgene, he could write a chemical reaction on paper as

$$O=CCl_2 \rightleftarrows O=C-Cl^+ + Cl^-$$

The energetics of this hypothetical reaction are prohibitively unfavorable. The alternative reaction—decomposition of phosgene into chlorine and carbon monoxide gases—has the overwhelming advantage.

In his short paper "What is an Acid?" Germann was asking a fundamental question that still has no simple answer. The answers that serve well for students just beginning to learn about acids and bases apply only to aqueous solvent systems. Germann was looking for an answer that applied more widely. He explored this subject further in his longer paper, "A General Theory of Solvent Systems."

Albert Germann had directed an immense amount of intellectual energy toward his general theory of solvent systems during his years at Stanford University. In addition, the National Research Council invited Albert Germann to review the scientific literature relating to vapor pressures of organic compounds. His review, "Vapor Pressures and Orthobaric Densities above One Atmosphere, Two-Phase, Liquid–Vapor, Organic Compounds," appeared in the comprehensive *International Critical Tables of Numerical Data: Physics, Chemistry and Technology* (New York: McGraw-Hill Book Company), vol. III (1928), pp. 237–244. Among his qualifications for conducting this review was his participation in 1912 in a study led by Ettore Cardoso on critical constants of gases. Albert may have been considering study of vapor pressure of phosgene solutions as an experimental way to investigate phosgene as a solvent.

In an academic world where research and research publication counted a great deal, Albert at age 38 seemed poised for a successful career as a university scientist. He was to have a successful career as a scientist, but his future would not be at Stanford University. Surprisingly, his future would be unrelated to phosgene. Albert Germann decided to leave Stanford University, and he informed the University of that intention. His appointment for the 1924–1925 year was as *Acting* Assistant Professor, and he had a reduced teaching load.

Ida and Albert probably did not find Palo Alto to be the ideal place to raise their young family. Any significant Lutheran presence in Palo Alto would be in the future. It was not until 1925 that the California–Nevada District of the Lutheran Church–Missouri Synod called the Rev. Paul H. D. Lang to serve as a missionary to the Stanford University campus and to Palo Alto. Albert probably did not find the Stanford Department of Chemistry to be as congenial as he remembered the Western Reserve community. Ida and Albert Germann decided to return to familiar territory, and Albert decided to make a major professional career change.

The Germann family moved back to Cleveland. Although Edward Franklin and Albert Germann did not remain colleagues at Stanford University, Germann continued to admire Franklin's accomplishments. It is likely that former Western Reserve faculty member Germann, after returning to Cleveland, nominated Franklin for an honorary doctorate. Edward Curtis Franklin was awarded the degree D.Sc. *honoris causa* by Western Reserve University in 1926. In all probability, Albert Germann was host for the doctoral candidate at Commencement.

Laboratory Products Company

Returning to Cleveland in 1925, Albert Germann became Research Director of Laboratory Products Company. His move to leadership in Laboratory Products Company marked the first significant divergence in the career paths of Albert and Frank Germann. Frank had settled into the academic community of the University of Colorado, where he would flourish for the rest of his life. Albert did not forsake academia, but he redirected his research interests. His new direction involved Laboratory Products Company, a commercial enterprise that was also in the midst of redirecting operations.

What was Laboratory Products Company?

According to *The Encyclopedia of Cleveland History*, brothers William Otto Frohring and Paul R. Frohring "did groundbreaking laboratory work at the Laboratory Products Co. in Cleveland that produced the first ready-prepared infant formula." Remember the key (and carefully constructed) phrase: "produced the first ready-prepared infant formula." The phrase implies a truly fresh, unusual, and original approach to infant nutrition. Can this statement be factual? Who were the Frohring brothers? What was the Laboratory Products Company? What was to be the role of Albert Germann in the evolution of Laboratory Products Company?

To put these questions (and their partial answers) in context, we shall begin by examining a few milestones in the controversial history of "infant formula," leaving the reader to parse and evaluate the claim that the Frohrings "produced the first ready-prepared infant formula." Familiar product names emerge from this history: Mellin's, Nestlé, Horlick, Borden, Smucker, Pet, Eagle Brand, Lily Brand, Carnation, Meyenberg, Similac, Sealtest, and Formulac. Then we shall look at the S.M.A. Corporation (successor of Laboratory Products Company) and the Frohring brothers. The context, for Albert Germann, was a rapidly evolving chemical research focus at Laboratory Products Company, at S.M.A., and ultimately at Nutritional Research Associates. That evolution—from cow's milk, to infant formula, to vitamins, and eventually to carotene—was made possible by remarkable advances in analytical chemistry and biochemistry, accompanied by fundamental changes in methodologies of conducting nutritional research.

Chemists are likely to date the origins of infant formula from the work of Justus von Liebig (1803–1873), "revered in Germany as the father of organic chemistry." The end of the *eighteenth* century (the 1700s) had seen the birth of modern chemistry in Europe. Among the many research contributors were Joseph Black (1728–1799), Joseph Priestley (1733–1804), Henry Cavendish (1731–1810), Carl Wilhelm Scheele (1742–1786), Claude Louis Berthollet (1748–1822), Joseph Louis Proust (1754–1826), Antoine François, comte de Fourcroy (1755–1809), John Dalton (1766–1844), Humphry Davy (1778–1829), and especially Antoine-Laurent Lavoisier (1743–1794) and his wife Marie-Anne Pierrette Paulze (1758–1836). The end of the *nineteenth* century (the 1800s) saw the commercial and theoretical development of the sub-discipline of organic chemistry, the chemistry of carbon-containing compounds. Justus von Liebig contributed significantly to this research. He was also an active leader in supporting other organic chemists. He played a major role in communicating and popularizing their results.

Liebig observed in 1865: "For mothers who are deprived of the happiness of being able to breastfeed their own children, or lacking enough food to nourish her baby, the choice of a suitable diet is of great importance.... The simple laws of nutrition should determine this choice." Liebig compared data from the chemical analyses of human milk and cow's milk, and concluded that the significant differences in composition involved protein, sugar, and minerals. His goal was to produce a formula (a recipe) for converting cow's milk into a chemical equivalent of mother's milk. He hoped that his chemical equivalent would also be a nutritional equivalent of mother's milk.

The chemical composition data used by Liebig came from a "proximate analysis" of milk samples. Proximate analysis is a quantitative chemical determination of percentage composition in terms of various proximates, each proximate composed of closely related components. For foods, typical categories of proximates are water, protein, fat, carbohydrate, and ash. Quantitative analysis of a food for water may involve measuring the weight loss when the food is dried, for protein by determining the nitrogen content of a sample, for fat by extracting a sample with diethyl ether, for ash by burning the sample and weighing the residue. Sometimes, when all but one proximate have been determined, the remaining proximate is calculated arithmetically "by difference."

Liebig expressed his analytical data in terms of water, total protein, total fat, milk sugar, and ash. He asserted (without supporting analytical chemistry data) that the seeds of peas and beans (as well as the seeds of oats, wheat, barley, and rye) contain protein that is identical to the protein in milk. Analytical methods far superior to those available to Liebig would be developed by others during the next decades. Johan Gustav Christoffer Thorsager Kjeldahl (1849–1900) in 1883 published details of his method of quantitatively converting the nitrogen of nitrogenous substances (including proteins) into ammonia, which could then be titrated by traditional acid-base methods. Stephen Moulton Babcock (1843–1931) in 1890 reported his method of determining the fat content of milk. The Kjeldahl nitrogen method and the Babcock butterfat method each quickly became standard in analytical chemistry laboratories, and remained in widespread use throughout the twentieth century. However, analysis for total nitrogen gives no information about the relative amounts of individual amino acids in proteins. Analysis for total fat gives no information about relative amounts of individual fats. Routine analysis of a food protein for its composition in terms of individual amino acid constituents would await the development of chromatographic techniques in the last half of the twentieth century.

Liebig used legumes and grains as sources of added protein. Liebig prepared his first substitute milk by cooking wheat flour and malt flour in water, and then adding cow's milk. He added potassium carbonate (a base) to counteract acidity from the flours. He published this recipe (as he published many of his scientific papers) in a journal which some of his contemporaries considered to be Liebig's personal magazine of science: *Justus Liebig's Annalen der Chemie und Pharmacie*.

Liebig organized a commercial company for the production and distribution of his substitute milk. At first, Liebig sold the substitute as a liquid, ready for consumption. In 1867, a dried product was introduced to the European market as Liebig's Soluble Food for Babies. Within a year, it was being manufactured, advertised, and sold in London by the Liebig's Registered Concentrated Milk Company Ltd. In 1869, Liebig's Soluble Food for Babies was for sale in the United States.

Gustav Mellin in London replicated Liebig's published formula in 1866, and began selling his Mellin's Food for Infants and Invalids. By the early 1870s, he was exporting Mellin's Food to the United States. Mellin's Food was promoted as a science-based product: "Mellin's Food Method is a simple, practical, and accurate system for making any possible combination of Proteids, Fat, and Carbohydrates in a mixture for infant feeding." "Mellin's Food is a dry, soluble extract made from wheat and barley malt, and consists of maltose, dextrin, proteids, and salts. Mellin's Food is entirely free from unconverted starch and cane sugar. Mellin's Food is a preparation for the modification of fresh cow's milk." Mellin's Food was promoted to physicians by distributing free copies of such publications as *The Home Modification of Cow's Milk* (30 pages, 1899), *The Care and Feeding of Infants* (68 pages, 1900), and *The Mellin's Food Method of Percentage Feeding* (183 pages, 1908). Each was published in Boston by The Press of Mellin's Food Company.

James Horlick Jr. (1844–1921) worked for Mellin's Food Company in London. There he learned the practical details of how Mellin's processed wheat and barley. With his brother William Horlick (1846–1936) and their father James Horlick Sr. (1809–1879), Horlick experimented with variations of the Liebig and Mellin recipes. The Horlick laboratory was a small stone building in their home village, Ruardean in the Forest of Dean, Gloucestershire, England. William visited the United States in 1869, returned to England, and then immigrated to Wisconsin in 1872. A year later, James Jr. joined his brother, and they formed J. & W. Horlicks in Chicago to make their infant-food product. In 1882, William applied for a patent for a dry product that could be dissolved in cow's milk. He was granted U. S. Patent 278,967 on June 5, 1883, for "Granulated Food for Infants and Process for Preparing the Same." By then, the brothers were in business in Racine, Wisconsin. They called their dry powder Diastoid. In 1887, they changed the name to Horlick's Malted Milk.

Although originally marketed as an ingredient in infant food, the dry powder quickly found its way to soda fountains. When Horlick's powder was blended with milk and ice cream, the result was a malted milkshake, or simply a "malt." Soda Fountain® Malted Milk Powder, made in Wisconsin, is still available for sale in the United States, especially in Wisconsin.

Heinrich Nestle (1814–1890), a contemporary of Justus von Liebig, was also an important innovator in infant-formula development. The eleventh of fourteen children of Johann Ulrich Matthias Nestle and Anna-Maria Catharina Ehemann, Heinrich was born in Frankfurt am Main, Germany. He learned practical chemistry as a pharmacy apprentice, beginning when he was sixteen. As a young businessman, he became involved with numerous pharmaceutical, chemical, and agricultural enter-prises in Vevey, Switzerland, including the production of rapeseed oil (known in North America as canola oil) and nut oils, as well as carbonated mineral water and lemonade. His move to a French-speaking region of Switzerland coincided with his name change to Henri Nestlé.

Henri Nestlé and Anna Clémentine Thérèse Ehemant were married in 1860. Soon after their marriage, Henri became actively interested in infant nutrition. Anna, as daughter of a charity doctor, knew first-hand a great deal about infant mortality. Henri did not have to be reminded that seven of his siblings died before reaching adulthood.

Henri collaborated with Jean Balthasar Schnetzler (1823–1896) to formulate a substitute for mother's breast milk. Schnetzler was a biologist who had just com-pleted the Maître de sciences au collège de Vevey. Nestlé and Schnetzler combined cow's milk with sugar and chemically modified wheat flour. When dried, the powder could be stored without spoilage. The powder could be converted into an infant's drink simply by adding water. By 1867, *Farine Lactée Henri Nestlé* was being sold throughout Europe. By the 1870s, Nestlé Infant Food, made with malt, cow's milk, sugar, and wheat flour, was available in the United States.

The development of canned milk products had a major impact on infant nutri-tion. Gail Borden (1801–1874) received patents in 1856 for "a new and useful pro-cess or method of operation for concentrating and preserving milk." He heated milk at reduced atmospheric pressure. In this process, the milk was sterilized and a signif-icant amount of water was removed. The resulting condensed milk was marketed in a sealed metal can. After only limited financial success in promoting his product, Borden formed a partnership with New York financier Jeremiah Milbank. The com-bination of Milbank's influx of capital into the Borden-Milbank New York Con-densed Milk Company, the financial expertise of Milbank, and the demand for canned condensed milk from the Union Army during the American Civil War, made the enterprise a huge success.

The J. M. Smucker Company, successor in 2013 of the Borden-Milbank New York Condensed Milk Company, claims that "Eagle Brand® condensed milk was introduced in 1856 by Gail Borden to combat food poisoning and other illnesses related to lack of refrigeration and preservation techniques ... Additionally, Eagle

Brand Sweetened Condensed Milk was credited with significantly lowering the infant mortality rate in North America." The product remains for sale in 2014 in United States grocery stores.

Brothers George Ham Page (1836–1899), Charles A. Page, William B. Page, and David S. Page, together with their sister Julia M. Page, were raised in Dixon, Illinois. George and Charles went to Switzerland. In 1866, they built the first European milk condensary in Cham, Switzerland. It was an immediate success. They established factories throughout the continent and in England. The Page's Anglo-Swiss product was *sweetened* condensed milk. Sales to America were low because of heavy tariffs, so the enterprising Page family set up parallel operations in the United States. In 1888, the Page family opened the Anglo-Swiss Condensed Milk Company back home in Dixon. William was superintendent of the Dixon plant. After George's death, the Page family operations were sold to the Borden-Milbank New York Condensed Milk Company.

John Baptist Meÿenberg (1847–1914) was employed by the Page enterprise in Cham from 1866 to 1883. While working for the Pages, Meÿenberg conducted his own experiments, and developed a process for condensing and preserving milk without added sugar. He offered his process and his expertise to Anglo-Swiss, but the Pages were not interested. Meÿenberg resigned and moved to the United States. He looked (with little success) for financial backing in St. Louis, but found support just across the Mississippi River among merchants and professionals in Helvetia (now Highland), Madison County, Illinois. One of those supporters was Louis F. Latzer (November 11, 1848–March 27, 1924). Latzer had attended McKendree College (now McKendree University, the oldest university in Illinois, in nearby Lebanon, Illinois) in winter 1871–1872. He then attended Illinois Industrial University (now the University of Illinois, Champaign–Urbana) in 1872–1873. Illinois Industrial University had opened in 1868 with just fifty students. Louis Latzer was obliged to return to manage the family home farm when his father died, but Louis continued his scientific education with private lessons in chemistry and bacteriology from Helvetia physician Werner Schmidt.

The Helvetia Milk Condensing Company was formed on February 14, 1885, with Meÿenberg, Latzer, and John Wildi the principal investors. During his short stay in St. Louis, Meÿenberg had filed patent applications for "Apparatus for Preserving Milk" and for "Process of Preserving Milk." After moving to Helvetia, he filed for a patent for "certain new and useful improvements in Processes of Preserving Milk." From Meÿenberg's viewpoint, the operations in Helvetia were a disaster. His steam sterilizer exploded in July 1885. Much of the milk canned in early 1886 spoiled. Meÿenberg left the company in August 1886. Louis Latzer took charge of the Helvetia Milk Condensing Company, and Latzer became successful by anybody's standards. Helvetia became the Pet Milk Company in 1922. A newspaper feature article estimated the wealth of Louis Latzer at $5,000,000 when he died, and the wealth of John Wildi's widow at $3,520,000. After the death of Louis Latzer, his son John became president. John headed the company until his death in 1952.

Meÿenberg became an itinerant organizer of canned-milk companies. His next enterprise was in Monroe, Wisconsin. The brand name was Monroe. Then came Columbia Brand milk in Elgin, Illinois. Perhaps Meÿenberg became acquainted with James A. Whitaker, a Chicago wholesale grocer, who in 1887 founded the city of Buena Park in Orange County, California. In any case, John Meÿenberg moved to California and formed a company in Buena Park that produced Lily Brand cream.

By 1899, John Meÿenberg was assisting the grocer Elbridge Amos Stuart (1856–1944) and the grocer Thomas E. Yerxa (1851–1916) in rescuing Ezra Meeker's bankrupt plant (in Kent, Washington) for making sweetened condensed milk. They incorporated their business as Pacific Coast Condensed Milk Company on December 31, 1900. Meÿenberg continued his own research, and filed a patent application on July 20, 1900, for a "Process of Making Substitutes for Mothers' Milk." By 1910, Stuart was obtaining milk from his herd of Holstein cows in Tolt, Washington. These were the "contented cows" for his Carnation Brand canned milk. The red carnation symbol proved to be more popular with shoppers than the white lily symbol of Lily Brand cream. The town of Tolt changed its name to Carnation, and President Stuart presided over a business that eventually had more than twenty plants processing milk from a hundred and fifty thousand contented cows. Nestlé acquired the business in 1985. Nestlé was selling Carnation® Infant Formula and Carnation® Sweetened Condensed Milk in United States grocery stores in 2014. It has been a challenge for shoppers to track the flower logos. In 2014, Carnation product labels displayed a triplet of carnations: a red, a pink, and a white. And Borden in 2014 was marketing Magnolia Brand sweetened condensed milk, with white flowers on the label.

The Meÿenberg name did not disappear from the milk industry, although the umlaut did vanish. John P. Meyenberg, son of John Baptist Meÿenberg, started to process goat milk in California. "It was in 1934 that Harold Jackson discovered Meyenberg while searching for a milk alternative. His son, Robert, was sensitive to cow milk, yet it turned out the boy could drink highly-digestible goat milk. Gladdened by this turn of events, Harold decided to buy the company. Today, that same young boy with the milk allergy or milk intolerance now owns and operates Meyenberg. Robert Jackson, and his wife Carol, have worked together to grow Meyenberg into the largest manufacturer of goat milk products in the nation."

Alfred Willson Bosworth (February 1, 1879–June 8, 1963) developed what has been called "the first commercial milk-based infant formula." Bosworth was born in Warren, Rhode Island. His ancestors came to Hingham, Massachusetts in 1635 from England, and then settled in Bristol, Massachusetts. The towns of Bristol and Warren became part of Rhode Island in 1746. He graduated from English High School in Boston. English High School had opened in 1821; the school claims to be "the oldest public high school in the United States." He earned a B.S. degree from Rhode Island College (now the University of Rhode Island) in Providence in 1899.

Upon graduation from college, Alfred Bosworth became an Assistant Chemist at the Rhode Island Agricultural Experiment Station in Kingston. Established in 1888, the Experiment Station was conducting research in food production, food processing, nutrition, agriculture, and natural resource management. Bosworth was on the staff of the Rhode Island Agricultural Experiment Station from 1899 to 1904.

Then, after a year at the United States Department of Agriculture, Alfred Bosworth in 1905 accepted a position as an Assistant Chemist at the New York Agricultural Experiment Station in Geneva. Bosworth worked under the leadership and tutelage of Lucius Lincoln Van Slyke (January 6, 1859–September 30, 1931). A year later, he was promoted to Associate Chemist. He continued at Geneva until 1916.

L. L. Van Slyke was already recognized as a distinguished analytical chemist and dairy chemist. Van Slyke had become Chief Agricultural Chemist at the New York Agricultural Experiment Station in 1890. He was to serve in that capacity until his retirement in 1929. He was also Professor of Dairy Chemistry at the Geneva campus of the New York College of Agriculture of Cornell University. In addition to many research reports, Van Slyke published a major book on chemical analysis of dairy products; it went through three editions. He also published textbooks for cheese making, and books on plant fertilizers. He was a coauthor (with Harvey Washington Wiley and Willard Dell Bigelow) of the authoritative United States compendium of standard methods for chemical analysis of dairy products. Even a cursory examination of the 84-page Wiley, Van Slyke, and Bigelow compendium shows how dramatically analytical methods had changed (and improved) during the thirty years after Liebig's initial proximate analysis of milk.

L. L. Van Slyke was born in Centerville, Allegany County, New York. His family soon moved to Pike, a small town in adjoining Wyoming County. He attended local district schools, and then prepared for college (from 1872 to 1875) at Pike Seminary. Pike Seminary had been a Free Will Baptist school since 1859. After graduating, he spent the fall semester 1875 at Hillsdale College, Hillsdale, Michigan. Hillsdale College was said to be one of only two colleges in the nation affiliated with the Free Will Baptist denomination. In January 1876, he matriculated at the University of Michigan in Ann Arbor, seventy miles northeast of Hillsdale. He entered the College of Literature, Science and the Arts. He graduated in June 1879 with the A.B. degree, and spent the next year teaching Latin and Greek back home at Pike Seminary.

L. L. Van Slyke entered the chemistry graduate program at the University of Michigan in 1880. He received the A.M. degree in 1881, and the Ph.D. in 1882. He was Assistant in Chemistry at the University of Michigan from 1881 to 1885. He then took a position in Honolulu as Professor of Chemistry and Natural Science, and Government Chemist, in the Chemical Laboratory of Oahu College. Oahu College was founded in 1841 as Punahou School for children of missionaries serving throughout the Pacific. It was Oahu College from 1853 to 1934. Then it took back its original name. Punahou School now claims to be the largest coeducational, independent K–12 school on a single campus in the United States.

He was at Oahu College from 1885 to 1888. He was then appointed Lecturer on General Chemistry at the University of Michigan for the 1888–1889 academic year, replacing a faculty member on a one-year leave. Van Slyke was "fellow-by-courtesy" at The Johns Hopkins University during 1889–1890 year, looking for a more secure situation. He applied for a position at the Michigan Mining School (Houghton, Michigan). President Marshman Edward Wadsworth wrote: "Your name was very favorably considered, but amongst the candidates was found one who it was thought had a training more nearly in our special needs. No objection was raised against you." Van Slyke had been keeping University of Michigan President James Burrill Angell informed of his job search. In a letter to Angell, written in Pike on June 18, 1890, Van Slyke quoted President Wadsworth, and closed with: "So I am afloat again and ready to catch on to the first good thing that comes along." A "good thing" did come along, seventy-five miles west of Pike in Geneva. Stephen Moulton Babcock (1843–1931), who had been an agricultural chemist at the New York State Agricultural Experiment Station in Geneva since 1881, resigned to become Chair of the Agricultural Chemistry Department of the University of Wisconsin Agricultural Experiment Station. Van Slyke replaced Babcock, and became Chief Agricultural Chemist at the Geneva Station. Van Slyke moved to Geneva and joined the First Presbyterian Church, where he was an Elder for 36 years.

Bosworth and Van Slyke published many joint papers, reporting on their research into the chemistry of milk. While on the staff of the New York Agricultural Experiment Station, Alfred Bosworth enrolled in a graduate program at Harvard University in Cambridge, Massachusetts, working with the clinical biochemist Otto Knut Olof Folin (1867–1934). Harvard awarded Bosworth the A.M. degree in 1913. As early as 1913, Bosworth was collaborating in Boston with Henry I. Bowditch, M.D., on methods of chemical analysis of milk. After Alfred Bosworth left Geneva, he and H. I. Bowditch worked closely together in the Chemical Laboratories of The Boston Floating Hospital. A series of at least fourteen research papers—"Studies of Infant Feeding"—resulted from this collaboration.

The Boston Floating Hospital began in 1894 as a rented excursion boat towed around Boston Harbor, giving mothers and their sick babies medical care, fresh air, and relief from summer heat. It was also a pediatric affiliation site for nursing students enrolled at Boston Training School for Nurses (founded in 1873) and for nurses in training at other schools throughout New England. The Floating Hospital continues. The Floating Hospital is now on land (on Washington Street in Boston) as the Floating Hospital for Children at Tufts Medical Center. It is an infant and childcare hospital, and a pediatric teaching and research center.

Bosworth and Bowditch took the opportunity for summer cruises on the Floating Hospital to tend sick infants, to perfect their infant formula in the Floating Hospital laboratory, and to observe how well infants tolerated various versions of their "recon-structed milk for infants." On July 1, 1918, Bosworth applied for a U. S. Patent for a process for making reconstructed milk "which will be almost perfectly digestible and assimilable, particularly for infants." He assigned the patent to The Boston Floating Hospital, Inc. Henry I. Bowditch was Physician-in-Charge at the Boston Floating Hospital until a severe illness necessitated his retirement in 1925. He died in 1927.

The methodology of Bosworth and Bowditch in conducting their nutritional research differed in an important way from the methods of their early predecessors. Whereas Justus von Liebig invoked what he believed to be the "simple laws of nutri-tion" to guide his attempts to produce a chemical equivalent of mother's milk, Bos-worth and Bowditch added their own clinical observations of infants on the Boston Floating Hospital to their chemical studies of various formulations of reconstructed milk. They recognized explicitly that a formulation was satisfactory for a particular infant only when the infant thrived on that diet. Their studies were not clinical trials with twenty-first-century protocols, but they were studies that focused on the well-being of the babies themselves.

The work of Bosworth and Bowditch came to the attention of Columbus, Ohio, dairymen Harry Clinton Moores (April 16, 1881–February 28, 1965) and Stanley Melvin Ross (1882–March 22, 1946). Moores and Ross had been classmates at the Edminston and Johnson Business College in Columbus. Moores became a book-keeper in Columbus in 1901. Ross continued his education at the Y.M.C.A. School of Commerce in Columbus, graduating in 1903.

Stanley Ross was one of the first graduates of the Y.M.C.A. School of Com-merce, established in 1889. From 1902 to 1965, the seal of the school gave the name as "Franklin University—Columbus YMCA." From its inception, the School of Commerce stressed practical education and low cost. It was modeled on the concepts of The Public Academy of Philadelphia, founded in 1749 by Benjamin Franklin. The Public Academy of Philadelphia evolved into the University of Pennsylvania. The School of Commerce *officially* became Franklin University in 1933. It today describes itself as "a student-centered, nonprofit, independent institution."

The Ross family was active in the affairs of the Y.M.C.A. School of Commerce and then Franklin University. Richard M. Ross and Elizabeth M. Ross, son and daughter-in-law of Stanley Melvin Ross, were major benefactors of the University.

"Libby" Ross gave two million dollars in 2001 to establish the Stanley M. and Richard M. Ross School of Management and Leadership at Franklin University.

Mrs. Paul Frank of Dallas, Texas, made a substantial contribution "to breathe new life and energy" into the Campus Center of Capital University in the Columbus neighborhood of Bexley. The renovated and "reimagined" student center opened in 2013 as the Harry C. Moores Student Union at Capital University. Capital was founded in 1830 as the Theological Seminary of the Evangelical Lutheran Synod of Ohio. Today, Capital describes itself as "a comprehensive, independent university grounded in the Lutheran tradition." Harry Moores and his wife Lydia formed the Harry C. Moores Foundation, which has given money to Capital University and to charitable organizations in Franklin County area.

How did Mr. Moores and Mr. Ross earn the wherewithal to become benefactors of two independent universities in Columbus?

In June 1903, Harry Clinton Moores and Stanley Melvin Ross formed a dairy products partnership—the Moores & Ross Milk Company. Their enterprise was very successful. For a quarter century, the company focused on daily home delivery of fresh bottled milk in the greater Columbus area. Moores & Ross also produced ice cream, butter, cream, and cottage cheese. Then, in 1925, the two men negotiated an agreement under which they would produce and market the Bosworth and Bowditch infant formula. They hailed their product as "the first commercial milk-based infant formula."

Moores & Ross initially sold the infant formula under the name "Franklin Infant Food." In related moves, Moores & Ross sold their traditional dairy business to Borden (in 1928), changed the name of Franklin Infant Food to "Similac" (1930), and formed the M & R Dietetic Laboratories to produce and market Similac and to engage in pediatric research. Moores & Ross used profits from the dairy business to establish the research laboratories, which in turn reaped handsome profits. M & R Dietetic Laboratories became Ross Laboratories in 1956, and in 1964 merged with Abbott Laboratories. The Similac brand name survives in 2014 for an extended line of pediatric products, marketed by Abbott Laboratories.

Coinciding with the agreement allowing Moores & Ross to market the infant formula was a professional move by Alfred Bosworth from Massachusetts to Ohio. For four years, from 1930 to 1934, he was an honorary Graduate Fellow in Physiological Chemistry at The Ohio State University in Columbus. In 1934 and 1936,

Alfred was Instructor of Physical Chemistry at Ohio State. In 1939 and 1940, he was Assistant Professor in "Medicine/Biochemical Research" at Ohio State. He taught classes that Ohio State listed in their course catalog. However, he received no salary from The Ohio State University during this decade. Bosworth summarized his very productive research career for The Ohio State University News Bureau with two short phrases: "About 90 scientific papers. Several patents."

The move to Ohio also had personal consequences. On Monday, September 18, 1933, Martha Dorothy Riegle and Alfred Willson Bosworth were married.

S. M. A.

In Cleveland, Henry John Gerstenberger (1881–1954) was the lead member of a research program to produce "an artificial milk similar in all its important characteristics to the best food for the human infant, namely, breast milk." Born in Cleveland, Gerstenberger received the M.D. degree from Western Reserve University Medical School in 1903. He then studied pediatrics in Berlin and Vienna. Together with Edward Fitch Cushing (1862–1911), he was an incorporator in 1904 of Babies' Dispensary and Hospital in Cleveland. Edward Cushing had studied at Cornell University (B.Ph. 1883) and Harvard University (M.D. 1888), and was Professor of Diseases of Children at Western Reserve from 1894 until his death. Gerstenberger became Medical Director of Babies' Dispensary and Hospital when the facility opened in 1911. At the same time, he was Head of the Department of Pediatrics at Cleveland's Metropolitan General Hospital, as well as Director of the Tuberculosis Contact Clinic, the first such clinic in the Western Hemisphere. Western Reserve appointed him Professor of Pediatrics at the University Medical School in 1913.

As early as December 1908, Henry Gerstenberger and Howard Davis Haskins (1871–1933) were collaborating in metabolic studies involving dietary milk products. Haskins was Instructor in Organic and Physiological Chemistry in the Western Reserve University Medical School. The two men reviewed progress of other researchers who were interested in producing artificial milk for infants, and (in December 1913) planned their own research strategy. Gerstenberger recalled: "It was immediately realized that the only hope lay in the use of an homogenizer, in which I had become interested a few years previously in an attempt at the Walter-Gordon Laboratory to make a very fine curd for casein milk. It was then learned that the Belle Vernon-Mapes Dairy Company was planning to put an homogenizer in the new plant which they were building …"

Walter-Gordon laboratories were located in many cities in the United States. The Cleveland Walter-Gordon Laboratory had been established in 1897, "a scientific laboratory for the modification of cow's milk, according to their own ideas of infant-feeding."

Belle Vernon-Mapes Dairy Company was created in 1903 by the merger of the Mapes Milk Company and the Belle Vernon Farms Dairy Company. Then (on January 29, 1915), Vernon-Mapes merged with Telling Bros. Ice Cream Company to become Telling-Belle Vernon Company, with general offices at 3821–3835 Cedar Avenue in Cleveland, the same address as Walter-Gordon Laboratory. Telling Bros. had begun in 1891 as a one-man milk route operated by William E. Telling (1868–1938). In partnership with his brother, John C. Telling, William organized the Telling Bros. Ice Cream Company in 1895. The firm incorporated in 1905. By 1913, Telling Bros. had yearly sales of 4.2 million quarts of ice cream. After the merger with Mapes, the business became the largest dairy operation in the Cleveland area. Always an innovator, William Telling started the Laboratory Products Company as an infant-formula venture, selling its products under the Formulac brand. Telling used profits from the dairy business to establish research laboratories.

National Dairy Products Corporation purchased Telling-Belle Vernon Company in 1928. National Dairy Products introduced the Sealtest brand name for Telling-Belle's products. Telling's Laboratory Products Company became the Sealtest Laboratories, and then the S.M.A. Corporation. American Home Products Corporation purchased S.M.A in 1938. The Formulac baby food brand name survived in the marketplace for at least another decade.

Henry John Gerstenberger had multiple simultaneous professional associations. So did many of the other persons involved in this narrative. In addition, the laboratories and companies themselves were involved in complex mergers and acquisitions. An especially confusing name to follow is "Wyeth." Convoluted as the Wyeth story may be, it brings together two of the men chosen by Albert Germann for his next research group.

John Wyeth (1841–1907) was a son of a druggist. John studied at the Philadelphia College of Pharmacy (founded in 1821, the first college of pharmacy in North America), now a part of the University of the Sciences in Philadelphia. John opened a retail drug business in 1860 with his brother Frank. Their drugstore expanded into a manufacturing facility (a mass-production compounding pharmacy) with a substantial pharmaceutical laboratory. John Wyeth & Brother incorporated in 1899. When John died, his son Stuart (1862–1929) became President of the corporation. Stuart Wyeth bequeathed the corporation to Harvard University. Harvard (in 1931) sold Wyeth to American Home Products. In 1938, American Home Products acquired the S.M.A. Corporation. The enlarged American Home Products Corporation reverted to the Wyeth name in 2002.

The significance of Wyeth in our narrative is that Wyeth produced infant formula until 1996 in Mason, Michigan. In 1954, the Research and Development Department, Nutritional Division, Wyeth Laboratories, Mason, Michigan, contributed a research paper on milk nutrition. Mason was a small city (population 2,575 in 1930), the county seat of Ingham County. Both Vernon Jersey and Otto Ungnade were living in Mason in the early 1930s. It is intriguing to speculate that Wyeth Laboratories attracted Jersey and Ungnade to Mason. Both Jersey and Ungnade were associated with S.M.A. at the same time. Both were to become founding members (together with other S.M.A. associates Albert Germann, Robert Cross, and Harold Barnett) of Quintrex in 1934.

H. J. Gerstenberger, H. D. Haskins, H. H. McGregor, and H. O. Ruh at Telling's Laboratory Products Company were developing artificial milk for infants in 1915. They called their artificial milk "G–R milk," shorthand for Gerstenberger–Ruh modified milk. They numbered successive formulations, as for example "G–R milk No. 2." Gerstenberger realized that incorporating the results of future discoveries in chemistry, physics, bacteriology, and biology into G–R milk meant that no specific formulation would represent a finished product. Gerstenberger and Ruh wrote in 1919: "The anticipation of such a development was the main reason why the personal name of 'G–R' was first given this new fat adapted preparation, in place of the special one that logically might have been used, 'fat adapted milk.' Since then it has been realized that the general, broad comprehension of the problem could be retained without attaching the personal element to it, and so that designation 'G–R' was replaced by 'S. M. A.' (Synthetic Milk Adapted)."

Gerstenberger and Ruh coined the S. M. A. abbreviation for "Synthetic Milk Adapted." The initials persisted for decades, but not every person who used the initials credited the 1919 publication. Not all persons agreed what words the initials signified. The spaces and the periods were vulnerable to deletion.

Carotene

Albert Germann returned to Cleveland in 1925 as Research Director at William Telling's Laboratory Products Company. Telling began selling his infant formula under the Formulac brand name. Telling was also preparing to market artificial milk by underwriting research by Gerstenberger, Haskins, McGregor, and Ruh. Albert Germann had been involved with the Gerstenberger–Ruh research before he went to Stanford. Albert and a Western Reserve chemistry colleague received the following acknowledgement in 1919: "We wish to take this opportunity to express our great indebtedness to the chemical department of Adelbert College for cooperation and advice; especially are we appreciative of the help given by Professors [Hippolyte] Gruener and Germann."

Although in different departments, Albert Germann and Howard Davis Haskins were colleagues at Western Reserve. Haskins taught Organic and Physiological Chemistry in the Western Reserve University Medical School, courses often elected by chemistry students enrolled in Adelbert College. Haskins and John James Rickard Macleod (1876–1935) had written the textbook *Organic Chemistry: Including Certain Portions of Physical Chemistry for Medical, Pharmaceutical, and Biological Students* (New York: John Wiley & Sons, 1st ed., 1907). Haskins later became Professor of Biochemistry at the University of Oregon. J. J. R. Macleod and Frederick Banting would share the 1923 Nobel Prize in Physiology or Medicine "for the discovery of insulin."

Two Frohring brothers were closely involved with William Telling's enterprises. William Otto Frohring (July 1, 1893–September 13, 1959) and Paul R. Frohring (August 2, 1903–January 14, 1998) were born in Cleveland, sons of Martha L. Bliss and William E. Frohring. William O. Frohring was awarded the B.S. degree by The Ohio State University in 1915. He was a member of the Division of Contagious

Diseases of the Cleveland City Hospital. He was closely associated with the Department of Pediatrics of Western Reserve University Medical School, where H. J. Gerstenberger had been Professor of Pediatrics since 1913. William O. Frohring later (from 1941 to 1943) enrolled in graduate-level research courses in the Western Reserve University Department of Biochemistry. Paul Frohring graduated from Cleveland's East Technical High School in 1922, and received a bachelor's degree in chemical engineering from the Case School of Applied Science in 1926.

William Otto Frohring had been Director of Laboratories at Telling Belle Vernon Company in Cleveland from 1916 to 1925. When Albert Germann became Research Director at Laboratory Products Company, William O. Frohring became Vice-President and General Manager.

William Telling began to promote S.M.A. as "the first artificial baby formula." Telling had made his fortune in home delivery of fresh milk. Telling purchased a milk wagon, and began a milk route at age 23. He and his brother John expanded the milk route into the Telling Brothers Company. They added product lines such as ice cream. They bought out competitors. Telling's dairy company was the first in the Cleveland area to deliver milk in reusable glass bottles. A series of similar marketing innovations kept them on top of competition.

A consumer revolution was in the wings. The kitchen icebox was about to be replaced. General Electric introduced its Monitor-Top refrigerator in 1927. The Kelvinator Four refrigerator followed in 1929. The future market for daily home delivery of fresh bottled milk was problematic. And there was vigorous competition in the increasingly crowded baby-formula market.

There was also increasingly crowded research activity related to milk products and to milk for infants. The work of Justus von Liebig, Gustav Mellin, James Horlick, Henri Nestlé, Gail Borden, George Ham Page, John Baptist Meÿenberg, Louis F. Latzer, Elbridge Amos Stuart, Lucius Lincoln Van Slyke, Alfred Willson Bosworth, Henry I. Bowditch, Henry John Gerstenberger, and their associates over six decades had revealed that the chemistry, physics, and biology of milk is much more complicated than earlier dairy scientists had imagined. Chemical and clinical research was documenting that dietary needs and tolerances sometimes varied greatly from infant to infant. A single modified formula that was best for all infants seemed an unattainable goal. It was suspected that there were undiscovered components in raw milk and in processed milk that sometimes produced significant dietary effects.

Research results that would revolutionize nutritional science were being published in the first decades of the 20th century. Vitamins were discovered and chemically studied; their nutritional significance was being explored clinically. Milk sugars were chemically characterized, and their enzyme-catalyzed reactions were beginning to be studied. Physical chemical methods were being applied to complex systems such as milk, and to chemical substances such as milk proteins. Fresh milk is an unstable colloidal dispersion of micelles, macromolecular assemblies that keep water-insoluble fats in suspension by surrounding the fats with water-soluble molecules. Almost everything that is done to fresh milk affects the micelles and also the proteins. Although milk may appear to be a simple liquid, milk is actually a very complicated natural product in which the terms solvent, solute, and solution fail to have simple meanings. Scientists were beginning to appreciate the nutritional and biochemical complexities of fats, proteins, and sugars. They recognized that proximate analysis of milk, such as used by Liebig, overlooked vital chemical details. For example, Liebig's inclusive mineral category—"ash"—was yielding in the laboratory to quantitative chemical analysis for specific individual elements.

The Frohring brothers began to separate themselves from the S.M.A. origins, while keeping the name. Public distinctions vanished among the names Laboratory Products Company, Sealtest Laboratories, and S.M.A. Corporation. The SMACO brand was introduced. William O. Frohring remained Vice-President and General Manager of S.M.A. until 1938, when American Home Products Corporation purchased S.M.A.

William Frohring and Paul Frohring were to seek their fortunes, not by expanding and extending the Telling milk enterprises, but by vigorous engagement in the emerging field of specialty biochemicals. The name "Laboratory Products Company" best described their new commercial direction.

The specialty biochemical carotene was foremost in Albert Germann's plans for his own professional future. It would soon become the focus of his commercial aspirations. Carotene's biochemical importance for humans and other animals arises because it is a "pro-vitamin A," a compound that many animals can convert into their essential nutrient Vitamin A. Carotene is a red-orange pigment found in many plants. It has a color similar to other food coloring substances such as annatto, paprika, and lycopene.

Carotene was being investigated a hundred years earlier, long before the nutritional significance of vitamins was appreciated. Heinrich Wilhelm Ferdinand Wackenroder (1798–1854), as a graduate student at the University of Göttingen, was looking for a plant source of anthelmintics, substances capable of eliminating human intestinal parasites. His doctoral dissertation in 1826 was on this subject. Wackenroder investigated carrots as a source of anthelmintics. He published experimental preparation methods in 1831, describing how he pressed carrots to obtain juice. Ether was used to extract carotene (to which he gave the name "carotin") from the juice. Then a ruby-red pigment was crystallized from the ethereal solution. Wackenroder found that the crystals dissolved in butter to impart a beautiful yellow color.

Wackenroder and his successors had difficulty separating carotene from similar substances. Because they could not obtain a pure product, their chemical analyses failed to yield consistent molecular formulas. Richard Martin Willstätter (1872–1942; Nobel laureate in Chemistry 1915) and Walter Mieg (born 1878) definitively determined the molecular formula of carotene ($C_{40}H_{56}$) in experiments published in 1907. Extensive further research established the molecular structure of beta-carotene (the most common vegetable carotene) as a polyunsaturated hydrocarbon with eleven "conjugated double bonds" (alternating single and double chemical bonds joining carbon atoms). This system of conjugated double bonds allows each molecule to absorb specific frequencies of visible light and is the molecular reason that carotene has its characteristic color. The unsaturation means that carotene is an antioxidant. That property is a nutritional plus. The unsaturation also means that carotene is unstable in light, and that it is readily degraded by free radicals and other oxidants. In many animals, an intestinal enzyme cleaves each forty-carbon carotene molecule into two twenty-carbon Vitamin A fragments. The resulting Vitamin A is then ready to be absorbed into the blood stream.

Germann Assembles a Research Group

Albert Germann assembled his own research group from members of S.M.A. to investigate the isolation, purification, and commercial production of carotene. His agricultural source would be carrots. His cohorts were Vernon Jersey, Robert Cross, Harold Barnett, and Otto Ungnade.

Vernon Jersey (September 1, 1898–September 6, 1984) had been a member of Albert Germann's first research group at Western Reserve University. At that time, Jersey and Germann were studying phosgene solutions. Jersey earned the A.B. degree in chemistry from Adelbert College of Western Reserve University in 1920. As a graduate student, Jersey was Assistant in Chemistry at Adelbert College and at the College for Women during the 1920–1921 year. He received the A.M. degree from Western Reserve in 1921.

Several of Albert Germann's later graduate students at Stanford University continued the phosgene experiments begun by Vernon Jersey. However, Jersey's chemical interests evolved away from the poisonous phosgene and toward biochemistry. He began research collaboration with biochemists J. Lucien Morris, Howard Horace Beard, and Charles T. Way in the Laboratory of Biochemistry at the Western Reserve University School of Medicine. He was Demonstrator in Biochemistry at the Western Reserve School of Medicine during the 1921–1922 and the 1922–1923 academic years, and was promoted to Instructor in Biochemistry for 1923–1924.

Then there was a one-year excursion to Ann Arbor, Michigan. Physiological chemist Victor Clarence Vaughan (1851–1929) had retired from the University of Michigan (Ann Arbor) in 1921 after thirty years as Dean of the Medical School. Vaughan's retirement coincided with planning of a new building that would house modern facilities for physiological chemistry. Vaughan's retirement also created an opportunity for the Medical School to reshape its physiological chemistry curriculum and redirect its research focus. A move to adopt the name "biochemistry" failed. Howard Bishop Lewis (1887–1954) was hired in May 1922 as Professor of Physiological Chemistry. Robert Gesell (1886–1954) was hired in May 1923 as Professor of Physiological Chemistry. Both men began to assemble research groups composed of graduate students, and Vernon Jersey decided to investigate this research activity. Jersey obtained an appointment as Instructor in Physiological Chemistry at the University of Michigan Medical School for the 1924–1925 academic year. After a year in Ann Arbor, he returned to the familiar territory of Cleveland. He resumed his position as Instructor in Biochemistry at Western Reserve School of Medicine for the 1925–1926 year.

Vernon Jersey was a research chemist for the Cleveland Varnish Company from 1927 to 1929. This was an era when Waterlox Chemical and Coatings Corporation;

Sherwin, Williams and Company; Glidden Varnish Company; and Harshaw Chemical Company were the largest of the many Cleveland manufacturers who were developing new products from plant and insect sources. Chemicals that traditionally had been used to make lacquers and varnishes were found also to be useful starting materials for synthesis of drugs and other medicinal substances. Vernon Jersey had not left biochemistry when he hired on at Cleveland Varnish Company. He was getting practical experience as an industrial biochemist.

He published three research papers from the Laboratory of Biochemistry: J. Lucien Morris and Vernon Jersey, "Chemical Constituents of Saliva as Indices of Glandular Activity," *Journal of Biochemistry*, vol. 56 (May 1, 1923), pp. 31–42; J. Lucien Morris, Vernon Jersey, and Charles T. Way, "Diuresis in the Sheep: Concentration of Uric Acid and Urea by the Excretory Mechanism of Sheep and Rabbit Compared," *American Journal of Physiology*, vol. 70, no. 1 (September 1, 1924), pp. 122–129; and Howard H. Beard and Vernon Jersey, "The Specific Rotatory Power of Glucose–Insulin Solutions in Contact with Muscle Tissue *in vitro*," *Journal of Biochemistry*, vol. 70, no. 1 (September 1, 1926), pp. 167–171.

Jersey continued his association with the Laboratory of Biochemistry, and pursued a Western Reserve doctorate. He earned the Ph.D. in Biochemistry in 1935 with the thesis "The Hydrolysis of Starch in High Concentrations by Malt Amylase." He must have kept professional contact with Marion Cleaveland, another member of Albert Germann's first research group. After teaching chemistry from 1921 to 1926 at the Western Reserve University College for Women, Marion Cleaveland entered a Columbia University doctoral program in New York City. Her 1929 Ph.D. thesis was "A Quantitative Study of the Influence of Certain Neutral Salts upon the Activity of Malt Amylase." Cleaveland and Jersey were both studying the chemical kinetics of the same enzyme: malt amylase. They were attempting to gain insight into the molecular mechanisms by which the enzyme catalyzes the conversion of long-chain starch molecules into sugars. With her Ph.D. in hand, Cleaveland returned to the Western Reserve chemistry faculty. She remained on the Western Reserve faculty until 1946.

As he was progressing towards a Ph.D., Jersey began an association with S.M.A. He submitted two patent applications in 1933: Vernon Jersey, "Preparation of Maltose and Dextrins," United States Patent 2,096,549; application June 14, 1933, patent granted October 19, 1937; and Vernon Jersey, "Method of Refining Fats and Oils,"

United States Patent 2,029,722; application June 7, 1933, patent granted February 4, 1936. In each case, he assigned the patent to the S.M.A. Corporation. He was in charge of dairy research at S.M.A. Corporation from 1929 to 1935.

Robert John Cross (November 7, 1884–April 23, 1955) was a graduate student at Stanford when Albert Germann was on the chemistry faculty there. Cross was born in Fresno, California. He attended Stanford University, receiving the A.B. degree in 1911. He was a chemist and an engineer at California Products Company from 1913 to 1917, and he worked with Henry R. Kohman and Robert Roy Irvin at the Mellon Institute of Industrial Research in Pittsburgh from 1917 to 1919. Multi-millionaire brothers Andrew William Mellon (1855–1937) and Richard Beatty Mellon (1858–1933) had founded the Mellon Institute in 1913. Cross may have held a Ward Baking Company Fellowship at the Institute. Kohman, Irvin, and Cross filed for two patents early in 1919: "Process for the Manufacture of Yeast" (assigned to the Fleischmann Company) and "Manufacture of Leavened Bread" (assigned to the Ward Baking Company).

Before the patent applications were filed, Robert Cross was back at Stanford University. He held a Sperry Flour Company Graduate Fellowship at Stanford for the 1918–1919 academic year, conducting research under the direction of Professor Robert Eckles Swain, senior member of the Chemistry Department. Cross received an A.M. degree from Stanford in 1920; his thesis was "A Study of the Amino-Acids of the Protein of Wheat Flours." Cross and Swain published this research in 1924 as "The Amino Acid Distribution in Proteins of Wheat Flours—With a Note on an Improved Method for the Preparation of Aldehyde-Free Alcohol."

Cross was a research chemist at the California Almond Growers' Exchange from 1923 to 1924. Decades later, Cross recalled that he continued graduate research at Stanford and "worked on his doctor's degree in science." In 1924, he worked for the United Verde Extension Mining Company in Jerome, Arizona. From 1925 to 1928, he was in Salt Lake City, Utah, at the Department of Agricultural Research Laboratories of the American Smelting and Refining Company.

Robert Cross became a research chemist and chemical engineer at S.M.A. in 1928. He filed a patent application on June 28, 1932, for an "Electroosmotic Process and Apparatus," and assigned the patent to the S.M.A. Corporation. He also filed a patent application on April 7, 1934, for a "Method of Recovering Carotene from Soaps," assigned to S.M.A. He gave his address for each patent application as Mason, Michigan.

Harold Montgomery Barnett (September 7, 1903–February 20, 1956) was born in Pawnee City, county seat of Pawnee County, Nebraska. He attended Nebraska Wesleyan University in Lincoln, where he was awarded the B.A. degree in 1925. He then entered the graduate program of the Division of Agricultural Biochemistry of the University of Minnesota, Minneapolis, where Dr. Ross Aiken Gortner (1885–1942), Chief of the Division, directed his research. During summers 1925 and 1926, he held student internships at the United States Department of Agriculture, Division of Plant Industry, field stations in Utah and Arizona. Barnett received the M.S. degree from Minnesota in 1927. His M.S. thesis title was "A Study of Acid and Base Binding by Proteins."

During the academic year 1927–1928, he was Instructor in Chemistry at Valparaiso University, Valparaiso, Indiana. At the time of Harold Barnett's faculty appointment (Saturday, May 14, 1927), Albert Germann was Acting President of Valparaiso University. Germann had recruited Barnett to join the Valparaiso faculty. Harold Barnett taught courses in organic chemistry and biochemistry at Valparaiso.

Harold Barnett continued in the Agricultural Biochemistry graduate program in Minneapolis. At the same time, he collaborated with Harry Goldblatt (1891–1977) at Western Reserve University School of Medicine in the Institute of Pathology. Barnett joined S.M.A. in Cleveland in 1929. Goldblatt was later to achieve international recognition for his research in human hypertension and for his inventions of related medical instruments. Barnett assigned a patent (application dated January 16, 1930) to S.M.A. Corporation.

In December 1931, Barnett completed the first draft of his doctoral thesis: "Studies on Leucine and Dileucine Hydrochloride and the Development of a New Method for the Isolation of Leucine from Proteins." The thesis was typewritten, probably with two carbon copies. He submitted the draft to Prof. Gortner. Neither the original nor a copy was deposited in the University of Minnesota library. Barnett took one copy with him to Cleveland where he consolidated his research results for publication. William Otto Frohring and Albert Germann gave him chemical and editorial guidance. Barnett submitted "Studies on Leucine and Dileucine Hydrochloride and a New Method for the Isolation of Leucine" to the *Journal of Biological Chemistry* on

November 28, 1932. The paper was published April 1, 1933. The copy of his Ph.D. thesis that the University library eventually accessed is a bound seven-page offprint of the *Journal of Biological Chemistry* paper. Harold Barnett received the Ph.D. degree (with a major in Agricultural Biochemistry and a minor in Plant Physiology) from the University of Minnesota in 1931.

Harold Barnett was associated with S.M.A. until 1935. In addition to his patent application dated January 16, 1930, he submitted further patent applications as the sole applicant, each patent assigned to S.M.A. Barnett, Frohring, and Germann submitted a joint patent application on November 11, 1932.

Otto Ungnade (abt 1883–March 30, 1963) was an expert in the processing of dairy products. He had published three books in German, in Germany. Their translated titles are *The Whey Protein (Ziger): Its Appearance, Its Essence, Its Nutritional Value, and Its Use in the Dairy* (1921); *Lactose: Its Production, Investigation, and Use* (1926); and *The Roller Dryer in the Dairy Industry: Progress in Milk Drying* (1929). A 1927 book review of *Lactose: Its Production, Investigation, and Use* identified the author as Chemiker Otto Ungnade, Hannover-Laatzen. Hannover-Laatzen is in the Hanover region of Lower Saxony, Germany.

In the early 1930s, Otto Ungnade submitted U. S. patent applications ["Manufacture of Citrates and Citric Acid" (1930), "Method of Preparing Meat Sauce" (1933), and "Method of Recovering Pigments" (1934)]. In each case, he assigned the patent to the S.M.A. Corporation. In each case, he gave his address as Mason, Michigan, the same small town where Robert Cross was living at the time.

The Valparaiso Interlude

With his new research group just beginning to function, Albert Germann did the unexpected in fall 1926. He responded to an emergency call from fellow Lutherans who needed a dependable, credentialed, and well-connected academic scientist in northwestern Indiana. Albert resigned his position with the Laboratory Products Company, and immediately began to play a central role in the rescue of Valparaiso University. The extended story of the rescue is related in Chapter 4. The continuing saga of the five-man research group is resumed in Chapter 5.

Sources and References for Chapter III

Page 166, *Two-pan analytical balance* ... Professor Morley's two-pan, equal-arm analytical balance did not survive into the 21st century. This photograph is of a similar balance, purchased in Göttingen in 1877 by John Tappan Stoddard (1852–1919) when he was completing his doctoral studies there. Stoddard became the first Professor of Chemistry at Smith College, Northampton, Massachusetts. Stoddard's balance is now on display in Ford Hall on the Smith College campus.

Page 167, *College for Women of Western Reserve University* ... The College for Women was founded in 1888. "The removal of Western Reserve University [from Hudson, Ohio, to Cleveland, in 1882] came at just the time when increasing numbers of women were seeking higher education. So many applied for admission that the university, faced with opposition by men students, established a separate college for women during the presidency of Dr. Hiram C. Haydn," *Cleveland Plain Dealer*, February 22, 1931.

Page 168, *Friedrich Wilhelm Ostwald* ... John Thomas Stock, *Ostwald's American Students: Apparatus, Techniques and Careers* (Concord, New Hampshire: Plaidswede Publishing, 2003).

Page 168, *His dissertation was* ... Olin Freeman Tower, *Studien über Superoxyd- Elektroden*, Inaugural-Dissertation (Leipzig: Wilhelm Engelmann, 1895), 38 pages. Reprinted from *Zeitschrift für physikalische Chemie*, vol. 18, no. 1 (1895). Ostwald was an editor of *Zeitschrift für physikalische Chemie*.

Page 168, *He took part in a classic calorimetric experiment* ... Olin Freeman Tower, "The First Five-Day Experiment with a Respiration Calorimeter," *Scientific American*, vol. 74, no. 25 (June 20, 1896), p. 387.

Page 169, *Frank Austen Gooch (1852–1929)* ... Professor of Chemistry at Yale from 1885 to 1918. Gooch graduated from Harvard College in 1872, with the degree of A. B. *cum laude, summos in Phys-icis et Chemia honores*. He stayed at Harvard, working closely with Professor Josiah Cooke. After several years of study with eminent scientists in Europe [detailed charmingly by Ralph G. Van Name, "Biographical Memoir of Frank Austin Gooch, 1852-1929," *Biographical Memoirs of the National Academy of Sciences* (Washington: National Academy of Sciences, 1931)], he was awarded the Ph.D. degree by Harvard. He was hired in 1885 by Yale to establish a modern curriculum in chemistry and to take the lead role in designing the Kent Chemical Laboratory (1888–1931). Kent lab was built on the corner of High and Library streets, now the location of the main entrance to Yale's Jonathan Edwards College. Sloane Physical Laboratory (1882–1931) had recently been built nearby on Library Street. Both labs were designed by architect Richard Raht. Both were demolished during construction of Jonathan Edwards College.

Page 169, *was published in "Silliman's Journal"* ... F. A. Gooch and H. W. Gruener, "A Method for the Determination of Antimony and its Condition of Oxidation," *American Journal of Science*, Series 3, vol. 42, no. 249 (September 1891), pp. 213–220. "Silliman's Journal" was founded at Yale in 1818 by Benjamin Silliman, and the editorship remained in the family until 1926. It is the oldest continuously published American scientific journal. In 1891, it was edited by Silliman's son-in-law, James Dwight Dana, and the title was *American Journal of Science*.

Page 169, *Flora Stone Mather College* ... The College for Women of Western Reserve University was renamed "Flora Stone Mather College" by the Western University Board of Trustees on February 21, 1931. Flora Stone Mather was the daughter of Amasa Stone, the man who moved Western Reserve from Hudson, Ohio, to Cleveland in 1882. She was a sister of Adelbert Stone, the man for whom Adelbert College was named.

Page 169, *a chemistry textbook* ... Hippolyte Washington Gruener, *Chemistry: The Science of Matter and Its Changes* (New York: P. F. Collier; New York and London: Harper & Brothers, 1922).

Page 169, *The popular chemistry book* ... Hippolyte Washington Gruener, *The Story of Chemistry: The Nature and Structure of Matter—How Chemistry is Utilized in Our Present Day Economic and Industrial Development* (New York: P. F. Collier, Popular Science Library, 1922, 1930, 1933, 1939, 1941, 1943, 1948).

Page 169, *an organic chemistry textbook* ... Hippolyte Washington Gruener and Herman Peter Lankelma, *Introduction to Organic Chemistry* (New York and Cincinnati: American Book Company, 1939). Hippolyte Washington Gruener, Herman Peter Lankelma (1896–1976), and Oliver Grummitt (1910–1989), *Laboratory Experiments in Organic Chemistry*. The hundred-page lab manual was printed in an 8.5 inch × 11 inch format by the Department of Chemistry, with annual revisions. The seventh edition was in 1946.

Page 170, *specialized apparatus for handling gases* ... Albert F. O. Germann, "A Modified Precision Barometer," *Journal of the American Chemical Society*, vol. 36, no. 12 (December 1914), pp. 2456–2462. Received October 17, 1914. O. F. Tower and A. F. O. Germann, "Vapor Pressures of Certain Alcoholic Solutions," *Journal of the American Chemical Society*, vol. 36, no. 12 (December 1914), pp. 2449–2456.

Page 170, *especially the density of oxygen from a variety* ... Albert F. O. Germann, "The Density of Oxygen," *Journal of Physical Chemistry*, vol. 19, no. 6 (1915), pp. 437–477.

Page 170, *existence of a mass-18 isotope of oxygen* ... See W. F. Giauque and H. L. Johnston, "An Isotope of Oxygen, Mass 18. Interpretation of the Atmospheric Absorption Bands," *Journal of the American Chemical Society*, vol. 51, no. 5 (May 1929), pp. 1436–1441.

Page 170, *Experiments revealing the dependence* ... Malcolm Dole, "The Relative Atomic Weight of Oxygen in Water and in Air," Communications to the Editor, *Journal of the American Chemical Society*, vol. 57, no. 12, p. 2731 (Submitted November 1, 1935; published December 1935).

Page 170, *could be more precise and more reliable* ... In the 1960s, single-beam, single-pan balances, with remote-controlled devices for placing working masses on the beam, and with numerical dial readout, were in general use in analytical chemistry laboratories, dramatically reducing the time required for a single weighing. In the following decades, electronic balances supplanted mechanical balances, not only in chemistry laboratories but also in grocery supermarkets. Direct digital display, and digital connectivity to computers, became standard features. Special vibration-controlled balance tables, as well as separate environmentally controlled balance rooms, disappeared from architectural standards for chemistry laboratory design. The concepts of buoyancy corrections and multiple calibrations throughout the range of a balance vanished from chemistry laboratory manuals. Weighing became more efficient, while the fundamental principles of mass comparison became farther removed from direct experience and from the consciousness of experimental chemists.

Page 171, *Germann found (and reported in two scientific publications)* ... Albert F. O. Germann, "The Devitrification of Glass. A Surface Phenomenon. The Repair of Crystallized Glass Apparatus," *The Chemical News and Journal of Industrial Science* [London], vol. 122 (March 18, 1921), pp. 124–125; *Journal of the American Chemical Society*, vol. 43, no. 1 (January 1921), pp. 11–14.

Page 172, *colligative property* ... This term was introduced by Friedrich Wilhelm Ostwald. See Wilhelm Ostwald, *Outlines of General Chemistry*, translated with the author's sanction by James Walker (London: Macmillan and Company, 1890), p. 58. Ostwald credits Wilhelm Maximilian Wundt (1832–1920) with suggesting the word "colligative." Reference given in William B. Jensen, "Logic, History, and the Chemistry Textbook," *Journal of Chemical Education*, vol. 75, no. 6 (June 1998), pp. 679–687.

Page 173, *The talks were listed ... Journal of Industrial and Engineering Chemistry*, vol. 12, no. 10 (1920), p. 1025.

Page 173, *A fifth presentation* ... A. F. O. Germann and Marion Cleaveland, "The Cryoscopy of Boron Trifluoride Solutions. V. Systems with Methyl Ether and with Methyl Chloride," *Science* (New Series), vol. 53, no. 1382 (1921), p. 582.

Page 173, *Some chemistry departments had equipment* ... As early as 1875, the *Cornell University Register* reported: "In the Chemical Laboratory building a room has been fitted up with apparatus and conveniences for ... the making of photographic transparencies, or lantern slides, for scientific illustration." Elaine Engst and Blaine Friedlander, "Cornell Rewind: Lantern Slides Illuminated Lectures," *Cornell Chronicle*, October 21, 2015, https://www.news.cornell.edu/stories/2015/10/cornell-rewind-lantern-slides-illuminated-lectures, accessed February 3, 2016.

Page 174, *the density of air in Cleveland* ... Albert F. O. Germann and Harold Simmons Booth, "The Density of Air in Cleveland," *The Bulletin of Western Reserve University*, vol. 19, no. 8, pp. 45–54 (1916). "From a thesis presented to the Faculty of the Graduate School of Western Reserve University by Harold Simmons Booth, in partial fulfillment of the requirements of the degree of Master of Arts."

Page 174, *Hurlbut Professor of Chemistry* ... Frank Hovorka (August 5, 1897–April 9, 1984) followed Harold Booth as Hurlbut Professor of Chemistry, occupying the Chair from 1954 to 1968; Hovorka then became Hurlbut Professor of Chemistry Emeritus until his death. The Frank Hovorka Chair in Chemistry was established in 1973 with an endowment of over a million dollars. The gift from Hinman Hurlbut in 1865 was $11,000. The present Hurlbut Professor of Chemistry is Malcolm E. Kenney. Information was supplied by Helen Conger, Case Western Reserve University Archivist, via email on December 18, 2015. *See also* "Hovorka, Frank," *The Encyclopedia of Cleveland History*, http://ech.case.edu/cgi/article.pl?id=HF6, accessed

December 29, 2015; and *Find A Grave Memorials* #131430438 (Frank Hovorka) and #131430417 (Sophie Nickel Hovorka), Dale Cemetery, Connersville, Fayette County, Indiana, http://www.findagrave.com/cgi-bin/fg.cgi?page=gr&GRid=131430438, accessed December 29, 2015.

Page 174, *His graduate research, with Albert Germann* ... A. F. O. Germann and Vernon Jersey, "The Vapor Density of Technical Phosgene," *Science* (New Series), vol. 53, no. 1382, p. 582 (1921); and A. F. O. Germann and V. Jersey, "The Cryoscopy of Phosgene Solutions: I. System with Chloride," *Science* (New Series), vol. 53, no. 1382, p. 582 (1921).

Page 175, *cryoscopy of aqueous salt solutions* ... Ralph E. Hall and William D. Harkins, "The Free Energy of Dilution and the Freezing-Point Lowerings in Solutions of Some Salts of Various Types of Ionization, and of Salt Mixtures." *Journal of the American Chemical Society*, vol. 38, no. 12 (1916), pp. 2658–2676.

Page 175, *chlorine octaphosgenate* ... A. F. O. Germann and V. Jersey, "The Cryoscopy of Phosgene Solutions: I. System with Chloride," op. cit.

Page 175, *Chlorine octahydrate* ... Humphry Davy first reported this substance in 1811; H. Davy, "On a Combination of Oxymuriatic Gas and Oxygene Gas," *Philosophical Transactions of the Royal Society* [London], vol. 101 (1811), pp. 155–162; read February 21, 1811. A quantitative chemical analysis, yielding the formula $10H_2O \cdot Cl_2$, was reported by Michael Faraday in 1823; M. Faraday, "On Hydrate of Chlorine," *Quarterly Journal of Science, Literature and the Arts*, vol. 15, art. 10 (1823), pp. 71–74. Other investigators also studied the chlorine hydrate. By the close of the nineteenth century, the consensus was that eight water molecules are bound to each chlorine molecule in the hydrate. X-ray crystallographic studies in mid-twentieth century revealed a complex structure, essentially compatible with the empirical formula $8H_2O \cdot Cl_2$; Linus Pauling and Richard E. Marsh, "The Structure of Chlorine Hydrate," *Proceedings of the National Academy of Sciences of the United States of America*, vol. 38, no.

2 (February 15, 1952), pp. 112–118.

Page 175, *John Davy* ... John Davy, Esq., "On a Gaseous Compound of Carbonic Oxide and Chlorine," *Philosophical Transactions of the Royal Society* [London], vol. 102 (January 1, 1812), pp. 144–151. Read February 6, 1812. Communicated by Sir Humphry Davy, Knt. LL.D. Sec. R.S.

Page 176, *Constantin Fahlberg (1850–1910) gave this account* ... "The Inventor of Saccharine," *Scientific American* (New Series), vol. 55, no. 3 (July 17, 1886), p. 36.

Page 176, *Johann Lewinski reported* ... Johann Lewinski, "Über die Grenzen der Hippursäurebildung beim Menschen," *Archiv für experimentelle Pathologie und Pharmakologie*, vol. 58, no. 5 (April 28, 1908), pp. 397–398.

Page 177, *H. D. Dakin confirmed* ... H. D. Dakin, "The Fate of Sodium Benzoate in the Human Organism," *The Journal of Biological Chemistry*, vol. 7 (1909–1910), pp. 103–108.

Page 177, *organic chemistry laboratory exercise* ... Recalled by Prof. Harold Gomes Cassidy in an organic chemistry lecture, Yale College, 1954–1955.

Page 177, *Purdue University gave ten-year-old* ... H. O. Deay and G. G. Lehker, *Insects: How to Collect, Preserve, and Identify Them* (West Lafayette, Indiana: Purdue University Agricultural Extension Service, 1948; Purdue University Extension Bulletin no. 352). The ingredients were sodium cyanide (NaCN) and plaster of Paris ($CaSO_4 \cdot \frac{1}{2}H_2O$), both white powders.

Page 177, *If they were among the persons able to smell ... Princeton University Laboratory Safety Manual* contains the information: "The warning properties of HCN are very poor; 40–60% of the population is unable to smell the characteristic odor of bitter almonds and there is a wide variation in the minimum odor threshold." http://web.princeton.edu/sites/ehs/labsafetymanual/cheminfo/hcn.htm, accessed July 8, 2014.

Page 177, *isolation of each from rotting flesh* ... Ludwig Brieger, *Weitere Untersuchungen über Ptomaine* (Berlin: August Hirschwald, 1885), pp. 39, 43.

Page 177, *Chemists routinely purified contaminated mercury* ... A simple purification apparatus was described (with a detailed drawing) by German chemist Julius Lothar Meyer (1830–1895), "Bequeme Vorrichtung zur Reinigung des Quecksilbers," *Fresenius' Zeitschrift für Analytische Chemie*, vol. 2 (1863), pp. 241–242. For some typical methods used in the late nineteenth century, *see* Geo. M. Hulett, "The Purification of Mercury," *School Science*, vol. 1, no. 8 (January 1902), pp. 426–430; and Joel H. Hildebrand, "Purification of Mercury," *Journal of the American Chemical Society*, vol. 31, no. 8 (1909), pp. 933–935.

Page 177, *Gooch crucible* ... The Gooch crucible was invented by Frank Austen Gooch (1852–1929), Professor of Chemistry at Yale from 1885 to 1918. The crucible was made of porcelain, with perforations in its flat base. Acid-washed, long-fiber asbestos was placed inside to cover the holes, the crucible was inserted into a hard-rubber Gooch crucible holder atop a vacuum filter flask, and a solution (the mother liquor) containing a solid precipitate was transferred into the previously weighed crucible. The precipitate could then be collected, washed, and dried. The crucible with precipitate would be weighed, and the weight of the precipitate calculated by difference. The asbestos did not react chemically with either the precipitate or the wash solutions, and its weight did not change during drying. A problem arose in the late twentieth century when new regulations prohibited discard of the used asbestos filter pad. The classic porcelain Gooch crucibles were replaced with glass crucibles that had sintered-glass, porous collection bases. The sintered-glass could be cleaned and the crucible reused.

Page 178, *pigments and binders* ... Michael D. T. Clark, "Paints and Pigments." http://www.nzic.org.nz/ChemProcesses/polymers/10D.pdf, accessed May 30, 2014.

Page 178, *Both phosgene and chlorine did become*

deadly weapons ... Leo P. Brophy, Wyndham D. Miles, and Rexmond C. Cochrane, *The Chemical Warfare Service: From Laboratory to Field* (Washington: Center of Military History, 1959).

Page 178, *The first poison gas used* ... A detailed and authoritative account of poison gases in warfare is Amos A. Fries and Clarence J. West, *Chemical Warfare* (New York: McGraw Hill Book Company, 1921). *See also* Sarah Everts, "When Chemicals Became Weapons of War, *Chemical & Engineering News*, vol. 93, no. 8 (February 23, 2015), cover and pp. 6–21.

Page 179, *Technical grade* ... "Technical grade" and "practical grade" chemicals are of a purity suitable for many commercial or industrial applications. "Reagent grade" and "chemically pure (C.P.)" chemicals are high-purity chemicals suitable for many laboratory applications. U.S.P., N.F., and F.C.C. chemicals conform respectively to the requirements of the United States Pharmacopeia, the National Formulary, and the Food Chemicals Codex. These chemicals are regulated by the Food and Drug Administration of the United States Department of Agriculture. A.C.S. reagents meet specifications of the American Chemical Society Committee on Analytical Reagents.

Page 179, *phosgene for Germann's later experiments* ... A. F. O. Germann "visited Edgewood on September 16, 1924 to discuss phosgene." Personal communication from James A. Baker, Associate Director, Edgewood Chemical Biological Center, Aberdeen Proving Ground, MD 21010-5424, April 17, 2012.

Page 179, *cooperation with the chemical warfare service* ... A. F. O. Germann and Leland R. Smith, "The Limiting Density of Phosgene," *Science* (New Series), vol. 62, no. 1480 (May 11, 1923), p. 564.

Page 179, *for the generous supply of phosgene* ... Albert F. O. Germann and Glenn H. McIntyre, "The Properties of Phosgene Solutions: Vapor Tension Curves of Aluminum Chloride Solution at 0° and at 25°," *Journal of Physical Chemistry*, vol. 29 (January 1925), pp. 102–105.

Page 179, *From another paper* ... Albert F. O. Germann, "The Conductivity of Phosgene Solutions of Aluminum Chloride at 25°, 0°, and −45°," *Journal of Physical Chemistry*, vol. 29, no. 9 (1925), pp. 1148–1154.

Page 179, *enumerating peacetime achievements* ... Amos A. Fries, "By-products of Chemical Warfare," *Industrial and Engineering Chemistry*, vol. 20, no. 10 (October 1928), pp. 1079–1084.

Page 180, *but half of the commercial products* ... American Chemistry Council, "Economic Impact of Chlorine Chemistry," http://chlorine.americanchemistry.com/Chlorine-Benefits/Economic-Benefits, accessed April 20, 2015.

Page 180, *produced and consumed within the same industrial plant* ... When phosgene is produced and consumed within the same industrial plant, this production is termed "captive use." The largest American "merchant manufacturer" (producer for market sales) of phosgene in 2014 was VanDeMark Chemical. *See* "The Phosgene Family," *Inside Industry Magazine* (June 2014), http://www.vdmchemical.com/vdm/images/vdm/pdfs/INSIDE%20INDUSTRY%20MAGAZINE.pdf, accessed August 16, 2014. *See also* "Fine Chemicals," *Chemical & Engineering News*, vol. 92, no. 32 (August 11, 2014), p. 7.

Page 180, *Scientists at the Bureau of Mines* ... Van. H. Manning, "War Gas Investigations," *Bulletin 178-A* (Washington: Department of the Interior, Bureau of Mines, 1919). Advance chapter from Bulletin 178, *War Work of the Bureau of Mines*.

Page 181, *Captain Ralph E. Hall C.W.S.* ... Wilbur H. Siebert, "Wartime on the Campus," Part I of *The University in the Great War*, vol. IV of *History of The Ohio State University* (Columbus: The Ohio State University Press, 1934), pp. 205–207.

Page 181, *Mr. Schaufelberger was on the instructional staff* ... "Twenty-ninth Annual Register, 1919–20," *Stanford University Bulletin*, p. 127.

Page 181, *Schaufelberger submitted his thesis* ... The thesis was twelve typewritten pages, plus a plate with drawings of apparatus, and four graphs drawn on cross-section paper. Scanned copy was kindly provided by Daniel Hartwig, Stanford University Archivist. Kevin Gribble, Stanford University Transcript Administrator, supplied additional biographical information.

Page 182, *Marion Cleaveland (March 31, 1898–December 23, 1975)* ... "Mrs. Lange Dies at 77," newspaper obituary, December 24, 1975. John Przybys, "The Langes Gave a Lasting Gift to Erie County," *Sandusky* (Ohio) *Register*, November 25, 1982, p. B-5. Virginia Steinemann and Helen Hansen, "Langes Gave Before, After Death," *Follet House Scrapbook* (Follet House Museum, Sandusky), October 22, 1989. "Dietitian's Unique Job: She Fattens Bacteria," newspaper article profiling Marion Cleaveland, October 6, 1942. June E. Deeter, "Marion Cleaveland Lange," two-page typewritten tribute. Materials from the Norbert Lange Biographical File, Sandusky Library; copies supplied by Ron Davidson, Archives Librarian, April 23, 2012.

Page 183, *founded "by Western Reserve University and Case School of Applied Science* ... "Cleveland College," Case Western Reserve University Archives, http://www.case.edu/its/archives/downtown/clevelandcollege.htm, accessed October 4, 2015.

Page 183, *Marion Cleaveland kept her professional name* ... There are many examples of prominent women scientists who were not permitted to serve co-equally with their husbands in the same university department. Notable was Dr. Gerty Theresa Radnitz Cori (1896–1957; Nobel laureate jointly with her husband Carl Cori in 1947). From 1922 to 1931, Carl Cori held a senior position at the New York State Institute for the Study of Malignant Diseases, and Gerty Cori was hired only as an assistant pathologist. From 1931 to the year before they received the Nobel Prize, Carl Cori was Chair of the Department of Pharmacology at the Washington University School of Medicine in St. Louis, while Gerty Cori was just a research associate. Finally, as she was being nomi-

nated for a Nobel Prize, she was given a professorial appointment. ["Dr. Gerty Theresa Radnitz Cori: Biography." http://www.nlm.nih.gov/changingthefaceofmedicine/physicians/biography_69.html, accessed August 8, 2014.] Another example is Dr. Margaret McLean Bender (1907–2008), wife of University of Wisconsin chemistry professor Paul Bender (1917–2004). Margaret Bender taught nursing chemistry as a Lecturer in the University of Wisconsin Extension Division (in a campus building distant from the Department of Chemistry building where her husband taught) from 1951 to 1970. She was Director of the University of Wisconsin Radiocarbon Laboratory from 1963 until her retirement in 1981. Most of her thirty-one research papers at Wisconsin involved radiocarbon dating. She retired as Emeritus Senior Scientist in the Institute for Environmental Studies (at the University of Wisconsin Center for Climate Research), never having held a professorial appointment. ["Margaret McLean Bender Died," https://www.chem.wisc.edu/content/some-sad-news-margaret-mclean-bender-died, accessed August 8, 2014.]

Page 184, *A large chemistry building* ... "Post-Destruction Decisions 2: Old Chemistry Building," http://quake06.stanford.edu/centennial/tour/stop2.html, accessed February 26, 2014.

Page 185, *the Stanford chemistry faculty was aging* ... Information about the composition of the Stanford Chemistry Department, and about the courses taught by individual chemistry faculty members, was obtained from issues of the *Stanford University Bulletin*, "Announcement of Courses" and "Annual Register," for years from 1917 to 1926.

Page 185, *major treatise on thermodynamics* ... J. W. Gibbs, "On the Equilibrium of Heterogeneous Substances," *Transactions of the Connecticut Academy of Arts and Sciences*, vol. 3, pp. 108–248, 343–524 (1874–1878). A 323-page paper in any scholarly scientific journal was highly unusual, and unprecedented in the *Transactions*. Because the *Transactions* was not a journal widely available, Gibbs personally sent bound offprints of his paper to the major physical chemists of the western world with the hope that his work would be read. Wilhelm Ostwald translated his copy into German and published it as J. Willard Gibbs, *Thermodynamische studien: Unter Mitwirkung des Verfassers aus dem Englischen übersetzt von W. Ostwald* (Leipzig: Wilhelm Engelmann, 1892), 409 pages.

Page 185, *principles that would guide physical chemists … See, for example, the following standard textbooks and the many references therein*: Pierre Maurice Marie Duhem, *Thermodynamics and Chemistry: A Non-Mathematical Treatise for Chemists and Students of Chemistry* (New York: John Wiley & Sons, 1903); Olin Freeman Tower, *The Conductivity of Liquids: Methods, Results, Chemical Applications and Theoretical Considerations* (Easton, Pennsylvania: Chemical Publishing Company, 1905); Walther Nernst, *Experimental and Theoretical Applications of Thermodynamics to Chemistry* (New York: C. Scribner's Sons, 1907); Fritz Haber and Arthur Becket Lamb, *Thermodynamics of Technical Gas-Reactions* (London: Longmans, Green, 1908); Otto Sackur, *A Text Book of Thermo-Chemistry and Thermodynamics* (London: Macmillan, 1917); Gilbert Newton Lewis and Merle Randall, *Thermodynamics and the Free Energy of Chemical Substances* (New York: McGraw-Hill, 1923); Edward Armand Guggenheim, *Modern Thermodynamics by the Methods of Willard Gibbs* (London: Methuen & Company, 1933); Herbert Spencer Harned and Benton Brooks Owen, *The Physical Chemistry of Electrolytic Solutions* (New York: Reinhold Publishing Corporation, 1943); Robert Harold Stokes and Robert Anthony Robinson, *Electrolyte Solutions: The Measurement and Interpretation of Conductance, Chemical Potential and Diffusion in Solutions of Simple Electrolytes* (London: Butterworths Scientific Publications, 1955); Ronald Percy Bell, *The Proton in Chemistry* (Ithaca, New York: Cornell University Press, 1959); Edward Armand Guggenheim and Robert Harold Stokes, *Equilibrium Properties of Aqueous Solutions of Single Strong Electrolytes* (New York: Pergamon Press, 1969).

Page 186, *molar concentration* … "Molar concentration" has the units of moles/liter. A mole of H^+ is the number of H^+ cations that would be produced by the complete dissociation of a mole of H_2O into hydrogen ions and hydroxyl ions. A mole of ordinary H_2O has a mass of about 18 grams.

Page 187, *immersing a platinum electrode* … In practice, the platinum metal is "platinized," coated with a deposit of "platinum black." *For details on depositing the platinum black, see* Friedrich Kohlrausch, "Ueber platinirte Electroden und Widerstandsbestimmung," *Annalen der Physik und Chemie* (Leipzig), vol. 60 (1897), pp. 316–332. Friedrich Wilhelm Georg Kohlrausch (1840–1910) was one of the important early electrochemists. *For a later survey of recommended platinizing procedures, see* A. M. Feltham and M. Spiro, "Platinized Platinum Electrodes," *Chemical Reviews*, vol. 71, no. 2 (1971), pp. 178–193.

Page 187, *A very different indicating electrode* … Fritz Haber and Zygmunt Klemensiewicz, "Über elektrische Phasengrenzkräfte," *Zeitschrift für physikalische Chemie, Stöichiometrie und Verwandtschaftslehre*, vol. 67 (1909), pp. 385-431. Their invention was described at a meeting of the Karlsruher chemischen Gesellschaft on January 28, 1909. *See also* Barbara Marczewska and Krzysztof Marczewski, "First Glass Electrode and its Creators F. Haber and Z. Klemensiewicz—On 100th Anniversary," *Zeitschrift für Physikalische Chemie International*, vol. 224, no. 5 (June 2010), pp. 795–799. Haber had been developing other electrodes, especially an electrode that involved the reversible hydrogenation of quinone to yield quinol (Gleichgewicht von Chinon und Hydrochinon) [Fritz Haber and Rudolph Russ, "Über die elektrolytische Reduktion," *Zeitschrift für physikalische Chemie, Stöichiometrie und Verwandtschaftslehre*, vol. 47 (1904), pp. 257-335; *see especially* "Reversible Depolarisatoren," pp. 294–297]. By 1920, this electrode had been improved in Copenhagen to the extent that it could be used to measure pH in dilute acidic aqueous solutions; *see* Einar Biilmann, "Sur l'hydrogénation des Quinhydrones," *Annales de Chimie,*" series 9, vol. 15 (1921), pp. 109–157; and Einar Biilmann, "Oxidation and Reduction Potentials of Organic Compounds," *Transactions of the Faraday Society*, vol. 19 (1923), pp. 676–690.

Page 187, *Fritz Jacobus Haber* ... Fritz Haber received the Nobel Prize for developing a practical method (the Haber Process) of synthesizing ammonia from hydrogen and atmospheric nitrogen. He also has been called the father of chemical warfare for his work in developing poisonous gases during World War I, and for his political efforts in Germany to have the gases deployed. He married Clara Immerwahr, a chemist and the first woman to earn a Ph.D. at the University of Breslau. Dr. Immerwahr was totally opposed to Haber's work in chemical warfare. Haber personally oversaw the first successful military use of chlorine, with the release of 167 tons of chlorine gas at the Second Battle of Ypres on April 22, 1915. After an argument with Haber over the subject, she committed suicide on May 2, 1915, shooting herself in the heart with his service revolver. *See* Sarah Everts, "Who was Fritz Haber," *Chemical & Engineering News*, vol. 93, no. 8 (February 23, 2015), pp. 18–19. *See also* Jane Essex and Laura Howes, "Experiments in Integrity—Fritz Haber and the Ethics of Chemistry," *Science in School*, issue 29 (Summer 2014), pp. 5–8, http://www.scienceinschool.org/repository/docs/issue29_ethical_chemistry.pdf, accessed July 15, 2014. The Fritz Haber Institute of the Max Planck Society and the Max Planck Institute for the History of Science held an international commemorative symposium, "100 Years of Chemical Warfare: Research, Deployment, Consequences," in Berlin on April 21 and 22, 2015.

Page 188, *Fifteen years later, Walter S. Hughes* ... Walter S. Hughes, "The Potential Difference between Glass and Electrolytes in Contact with the Glass," *Journal of the American Chemical Society*, vol. 44, no. 12 (December 1922), pp. 2860–2867. Submitted September 14, 1922.

Page 188, *Kelvin quadrant electrometer* ... K. L. Aplin and R. G. Harrison, "Lord Kelvin's Atmospheric Electricity Measurements," arXiv preprint, http://arxiv.org/ftp/arxiv/papers/1305/1305.5347.pdf, accessed February 21, 2014.

Page 188, *Kenneth H. Goode* ... Kenneth H. Goode, "A Continuous-Reading Electrotitration Apparatus," *Journal of the American Chemical Society*, vol. 44, no. 1 (January 1922), pp. 26–29. Submitted August 22, 1921.

Page 188, *Arnold Orville Beckman (1900–2004)* ... Arnold O. Beckman, Zeta '21, "Instruments and Progress in Chemistry," *The Hexagon of Alpha Chi Sigma*, (Fall 1987), pp. 47–51, 70. *See also* "The Development of the Beckman pH Meter: A National Historic Chemical Landmark," (Pasadena: California Institute of Technology, March 24, 2004: American Chemical Society, Division of the History of Chemistry, and the A.C.S. Office of Public Outreach); Carl E. Moore and Bruno Jaselskis, "The pH Meter, a Product of Technological Crossovers," *Bulletin of the History of Chemistry*, vol. 21 (1998), pp. 32–38.

Page 189, *the ubiquitous solvent for living systems* ... Pure water is seldom encountered in living systems. The liquid contents of living cells are often so concentrated as to resemble gels. Indeed, many important biochemical substances do not dissolve in water. However, chemical interactions at interfaces between an aqueous (water-dominant) phase and a lipid (fat-like) phase are extraordinarily significant in maintaining the integrity and the functioning of each living cell, and water is a necessary partner in these interactions. Most twentieth century studies of individual enzymatic reactions were conducted in water solutions.

Page 189, *Gilbert Newton Lewis (1875–1946)* ... Lewis was to become a brilliant contributor to chemical bonding theory, chemical thermodynamics, and the discovery of heavy water. His proposals that chemical bonds are often electron pairs, and that acidity and basicity can be often be described in terms of donation of electron pairs, were central to the development of theoretical chemistry early in the twentieth century. The terms "Lewis acid" and "Lewis base" are still widely used. He was an influential leader in American physical chemistry. As Dean of the College of Chemistry at the University of California at Berkeley for many years, Lewis had an enormous effect in reshaping the chemistry curriculum throughout the United States. His biographers consistently fail to credit the influence of Franklin and the two years of undergraduate research at Kansas on development of the career of G. N. Lewis.

Page 189, *resemble water in its physical and chemical properties* ... Recollection quoted in Howard M. Elsey, "Edward Curtis Franklin, 1862–1937," *Biographical Memoirs of the National Academy of Sciences* (Washington: National Academy of Sciences, 1991), pp. 65–78.

Page 189, *The first ammonia experiments from Kansas* ... Hamilton P. Cady, "A New Explosive Compound Formed by the Action of Liquid Ammonia upon Iodin," *The Kansas University Quarterly*, Series A, vol. 6, no. 2 (April 1897), pp. 71–75; Hamilton P. Cady, "The Electrolysis and Electrolytic Conductivity of Certain Substances Dissolved in Liquid Ammonia," *Journal of Physical Chemistry*, vol. 1, no. 11 (1897), pp. 707–713.

Page 189, *then began research at Cornell University* ... Arthur W. Davidson, "American Contemporaries: Hamilton Perkins Cady," *Industrial and Engineering Chemistry, News Edition*, vol. 17, no. 20 (October 20, 1939), pp. 660–661.

Page 189, *Franklin and Kraus investigated the solubilities* ... E. C. Franklin and C. A. Kraus, "Liquid Ammonia as a Solvent," *American Chemical Journal*, vol. 20 (1898), pp. 820–836; E. C. Franklin and C. A. Kraus, "Determination of the Molecular Rise in the Boiling Point of Liquid Ammonia, *American Chemical Journal*, vol. 20 (1898), pp. 836–853; E. C. Franklin and C. A. Kraus, "Metathetic Reactions between Certain Salts in Solution in Liquid Ammonia," *American Chemical Journal*, vol. 21 (January 1899), pp. 1–8; E. C. Franklin and C. A. Kraus, "Some Properties of Liquid Ammonia," *American Chemical Journal*, vol. 21 (1899), pp. 8–14.

Page 190, *Olin Stafford's experimental research* ...

Edward C. Franklin and Olin F. Stafford, "Reactions Between Acid and Basic Amides in Liquid Ammonia," *American Chemical Journal*, vol. 27, no. 2 (August 1902), pp. 83–107.

Page 190, *and his books* ... Edward Curtis Franklin, *Reactions in Liquid Ammonia* (New York: Columbia University Press, 1927), 22 pages. Edward Curtis Franklin, *The Nitrogen System of Compounds* (New York: Reinhold Publishing Corporation, 1935), 339 pages; no. 68 in the American Chemical Society Monograph Series.

Page 192, *Read what reserved Professor Eric Hutchinson* ... Eric Hutchinson (1920–2005), *The Department of Chemistry Stanford University, 1891 to 1976: A Brief Account of the First Eighty-five Years* (Department of Chemistry, Stanford University, 1977), ix + 122 pp. Electronic version: http://www-sul.stanford.edu/depts/swain/history/index.html#file, accessed March 28, 2013. First quoted paragraph, p. viii; second paragraph, p. 10.

Page 194, *polarographic electrochemical technique* ... The polarographic method of chemical analysis was invented in 1922 by Jaroslav Heyrovský (1890–1967; Nobel laureate 1959).

Page 195, *study led by Ettore Cardoso* ... Ettore Cardoso, "Revision des constants critiques des gaz liquéfiables," *Archives des sciences physiques et naturelles*, cent dix-septiéme année [117th year], quatrième période [no. 4], tome trente-quatrième [vol. 34], pp. 20–31.

Page 195, *called the Rev. Paul H. D. Lang* ... Paul H. D. Lang graduated from Concordia Seminary in St. Louis in 1925, and was installed as the pastor of Trinity Lutheran Church in Palo Alto on December 6, 1925. "The Story of Trinity Evangelical Lutheran Church," http://trinitylutheranpaloalto.com/about/history, accessed July 10, 2014.

Page 196, *did groundbreaking laboratory work* ... "Frohring, Paul R.," *The Encyclopedia of Cleveland History* (internet site maintained by Case Western Reserve University: http://ech.case.edu/ech-cgi/article.pl?id=FPR, accessed May 9, 2013).

Page 196, *the controversial history of "infant formula"* ... Andrew J. Schuman, "A Concise History of Infant Formula (Twists and Turns Included)," *Contemporary Pediatrics,* vol. 20, no. 2 (February 2003), pp. 91–94, 97–98, 100, 103; Emily E. Stevens, Thelma E. Patrock, and Rita Picklet, "A History of Infant Feeding," *The Journal of Perinatal Education,* vol. 18, no. 2 (spring 2009), pp. 32–39; Samuel X. Radbill, "Infant Feeding through the Ages," *Clinical Pediatrics,* vol. 20, no. 10 (1981), pp. 613–621; Elsie M. Widdowson, "Preparations used for the Artificial Feeding of Infants," *Postgraduate Medical Journal,* vol. 54 (March 1978), pp. 176–179; Alex F. Robertson, "Reflections on Errors in Neoatology III. The 'Experienced' Years, 1970 to 2000," *Journal of Perinatology,* vol. 23 (2003), pp. 240–249; Silvia Diez Castillho and Antônio de Azevedo Barros Filho, "The History of Infant Nutrition," *Jornal de Pediatria,* vol. 86, no. 3 (2010), pp. 179–188; Jyllian Kemsley, "Deconstructing Breast Milk," *Chemical & Engineering News,* vol. 91, no. 27 (July 8, 2013), pp. 28–29. H. J. Gerstenberger, "Preventive Infant Feeding—Its Simplification," *The American Journal of Public Health* vol. 13, no. 3 (March 1923), pp. 185–195.

Page 197, *the father of organic chemistry* ... William H. Brock, *Justus von Liebig: The Chemical Gatekeeper* (Cambridge: The University Press, 1997).

Page 197, *Joseph Black (1728–1799)* ... Black was a pioneer in the development of the two-pan analytical balance and in establishing the experimental foundations of thermodynamics. He discovered the phenomenon of latent heat.

Page 197, *Joseph Priestley (1733–1804)* ... Priestley invented apparatus that allowed him to conduct experiments on "different kinds of air," discovering and characterizing the gases nitric oxide, nitrous oxide, anhydrous hydrochloric acid, ammonia, and oxygen.

Page 197, *Henry Cavendish (1731–1810)* ... Cavendish quantitatively studied the composition of air with high precision. His experimental data revealed that air contains an inert gas, although it was another hundred years before the significance of that observation was understood. His experiments established that hydrogen is an element.

Page 197, *Carl Wilhelm Scheele (1742–1786)* ... Scheele is credited with independent discovery of the elements nitrogen, chlorine, manganese, molybdenum, barium, tungsten, and oxygen. He was the first chemist to purify compounds such as benzoic, oxalic, citric, tartaric, lactic, and uric acids.

Page 197, *Claude Louis Berthollet (1748–1822)* ... Berthollet was the first to propose the concept of reverse reactions that lead to a state of chemical equilibrium. He used this idea to challenge the proposal of constant composition of compounds.

Page 197, *Joseph Louis Proust (1754–1826)* ... Proust proposed the laws of constant composition and of definite proportions. Disputes between Berthollet and Proust helped clarify the concept of "chemical compound."

Page 197, *Antoine François, comte de Fourcroy (1755–1809)* ... He was a major popularizer of Lavoisier's "new chemistry."

Page 197, *John Dalton (1766–1844)* ... Dalton's lectures on atomic theory of matter were the first to use molecular models to illustrate formation of molecules from elemental atoms.

Page 197, *Humphry Davy (1778–1829)* ... Davy discovered the elements sodium, potassium, calcium, magnesium, boron, and barium.

Page 197, *Antoine-Laurent Lavoisier (1743–1794)* ... Lavoisier is credited with dismantling the phlogiston theory. Phlogiston had been introduced into late alchemy by Johann Joachim Becher (1635–1682) to describe combustion and the chemical processes now known as oxidation. Phlogiston was named and popularized by Georg Ernst Stahl (1659–1734). Lavoisier supplanted the phlogiston theory with his own ideas about combustion, focusing on the central role of oxygen in combustion. He developed the fundamentals of the modern chemical nomenclature, expounded in his *Traité Élémentaire de Chimie* (1789), the first modern textbook of chemistry.

Page 197, *Marie-Anne Pierrette Paulze (1758–1836)* ... Antoine and Marie Lavoisier worked closely together in all aspects of their experimental and theoretical research. Marie prepared their publications, including all drawings. After the execution of Antoine in 1794, Marie was the effective publicist of their work.

Page 197, *Liebig observed in 1865* ... Justus v. Liebig, "Eine neue Suppe für Kinder," *Liebig's Annalen der Chemie und Pharmacie*, vol. 133 (March 1865), pp. 374–383. This article was reprinted in 1866 as a twenty-page octavo recipe booklet, "Suppe für Säuglinge," intended for wide distribution. An expanded second edition, a 35-page booklet "Suppe für Säuglinge: mit Nachträgen in Beziehung auf ihre Bereitung und Anwendung" [Soup for Infants: With Addenda Related to its Preparation and Application] was printed in 1867 by Friedrich Boewig & Sohn, Braunschweig. This second edition was translated by Baroness Elise von Lersner-Ebersburg as "Food for Infants: A Complete Substitute for That Provided by Nature" (London: James Walton). A third German edition was published in 1877.

Page 198, *Johan Gustav Christoffer Thorsager Kjeldahl (1849–1900)* ... Johan Kjeldahl, "Neue Methode zur Bestimmung des Stickstoffs in organischen Körpern," *Zeitschrift für Analytische Chemie*, vol. 22 (1883), pp. 366–382. *See also* Purificación Sáez-Plaza, Tadeusz Michałowski, María José Navas, Agustín García Asuero, and Sławomir Wybraniec, "An Overview of the Kjeldahl Method of Nitrogen Determination. Part I. Early History, Chemistry of the Procedure, and Titrimetric Finish," *Critical Reviews in Analytical Chemistry*, vol. 43, no. 4 (2013), pp. 178-223. There had been earlier quantitative methods. For example, a method for determining the analytical composition of indigo ($C_{16}H_{10}N_2O_2$) was published by Jean Baptiste André Dumas (1800–1884) in J. Dumas, "Recherches de Chimie organique," *Annales de chimie et de physique*, vol. 53 (1833), pp. 164–181.

His method of analyzing for nitrogen begins on page 171. Convenient use of Dumas' method awaited an automated instrumental adaptation, which has recently been developed.

Page 198, *Stephen Moulton Babcock (1843–1931)* ... S. M. Babcock, "A New Method for the Estimation of Fat in Milk, Especially Adapted to Creameries and Cheese Factories," *Bulletin No. 24* (Madison: University of Wisconsin Agricultural Experiment Station, July 1890), 18 pages.

Page 198, *relative amounts of individual amino acids* ... The major constituents of proteins are amino acids. The relative amounts of individual amino acids differ widely in different proteins. Because certain essential amino acids are not synthesized metabolically by humans, the nutritive value of particular proteins depends on their amino acid composition.

Page 198, *relative amounts of individual fats* ... Fats in foods are usually triglycerides or phospholipids, substances that contain long-chain carboxylic acids called fatty acids. Foods differ widely in relative amounts of various fatty acids. Because certain essential fatty acids cannot be synthesized in sufficient amounts by humans, the nutritive value of particular fats depends on their fatty acid composition.

Page 198, *Liebig's personal magazine of science* ... H. S. Van Klooster, "The Story of Liebig's Annalen der Chemie," *Journal of Chemical Education*, vol. 34, no. 1 (January 1957), p. 27.

Page 198, *replicated Liebig's published formula in 1866* ... Science Museum London, http://www.science-museum.org.uk/broughttolife/objects/display.aspx?id=92472, accessed April 9, 2015.

Page 198, *"Mellin's Food Method is a simple* ... *The Mellin's Food Method of Percentage Feeding* (Boston: Press of Mellin's Food Company, 1908; 183 pages), p. iv.

Page 199, *"Mellin's Food is a dry, soluble extract* ... ibid., p. 181.

Page 199, *Soda Fountain® Malted Milk* ... CTL-Foods, Colfax, Wisconsin: "the original home of

Soda Fountain Malted Milk Powder, an All-Natural, Kosher-Certified, Wisconsin-Made product. CTL has been blending and packaging Soda Fountain Malted Milk Powder since 1972." http://www.ctlfoods.com, accessed February 24, 2016.

Page 200, *The development of canned milk products ...* E. H. Parfitt, "The Development of the Evaporated Milk Industry in the United States," *Journal of Dairy Science,* 50th Anniversary Edition (1956), pp. 838–842. Otto Frederick Hunziker, *Condensed Milk and Milk Powder* (Lagrange, Illinois: 1st edition, 1914; 7th edition, 1949). Sue Ann Gardner, "Gail Borden" (1999), *Faculty Publications, University of Nebraska-Lincoln Libraries,* Paper 110; http://digitalcommons.unl.edu/libraryscience/110, accessed August 19, 2015.

Page 200, *Gail Borden (1801–1874) received patents ...* Gail Borden Jr., of Brooklyn, New York, "Improvement in Concentration of Milk," Letters Patent No. 15,553, dated August 19, 1856. "Improvement in Condensing Milk," U. S. Letters Patent 15,563, dated August 19, 1856. Reissued May 15, 1862; February 10, 1863; November 14, 1865.

Page 200, *After only limited financial success ...* His milk was condensed and canned at two plants in Litchfield County, Connecticut. One plant was in Wolcottville (now Torrington), beginning in 1856. The other was in Burrville, beginning in 1857.

Page 200, *Eagle Brand Sweetened Condensed Milk ...* J. M. Smucker Company, http://www.eaglebrand.com/history/Default.aspx, accessed June 6, 2013.

Page 201, *John Baptist Meÿenberg (1847–1914) ...* Obituary of John B. Meyenberg, *Kent* [Washington] *Journal,* October 29, 1914.

Page 201, *Louis F. Latzer ...* Biographical information, references, and copies of materials from the Archives of the University of Illinois at Urbana-Champaign were supplied by William J. Maher, University Archivist, and by Linda Stahnke Stepp, Archives Reference Specialist, in June 2013.

Page 201, *Meÿenberg had filed patent applications ...* John Meÿenberg, U. S. Letters Patent 308,421, "Apparatus for Preserving Milk," application February 16, 1884; U. S. Letters Patent 308,422, "Process of Preserving Milk," application July 9, 1884.

Page 202, *certain new and useful improvements ...* John Meÿenberg, U. S. Letters Patent 358,213, "Process of Preserving Milk," application June 12, 1886.

Page 202, *Louis Latzer took charge ...* "Louis F. and John A. Latzer Papers, ca. 1880–1924," courtesy of the University of Illinois Archives, record series 26/4/1.

Page 202, *A newspaper feature article ...* F. A. Behymer, "A Farmer Who Lived 75 Years on One Farm, and Made $5,000,000 on the Side," *St. Louis Post-Dispatch,* Sunday morning, April 13, 1924, p. 13, courtesy of the University of Illinois Archives, Alumni and Faculty Biographical (Morgue) File, record series 26/4/1, folder title: "Latzer, Louis F."

Page 202, *Elbridge Amos Stuart (1856–1944) ...* James Leslie Marshall, *Elbridge A. Stuart, Founder of Carnation Company* (Los Angeles: Carnation Company, 1949).

Page 202, *Meÿenberg continued his own research ...* John Meÿenberg of Kent Washington, U. S. Letters Patent 682,103, "Process of Making Substitutes for Mothers' Milk," application July 20, 1900; renewed February 14, 1901. He also filed an application (with his residence given as Buenapark, California), U. S. Letters Patent 677,159, "Process of Preparing Foods," application January 8, 1900; renewed November 10, 1900.

Page 203, *Harold Jackson discovered Meyenberg ...* Quotation from internet website of Meyenberg Goat Milk Products, Turlock, California: http://meyenberg.com, accessed June 11, 2013.

Page 203, *"the first commercial milk-based infant formula" ...* Quotation is from the Similac® internet website, http://similac.com/baby-formula/about-similac-infant-formula/timeline, accessed August 19, 2015.

Page 203, *His ancestors came to Hingham* … Alfred Willson Bosworth, "A Rhode Island Patriot," Lippitt Prize Essay, 1898, Rhode Island College. This undergraduate essay "chronicles the life and patriotism of Bristol, Rhode Island native Benjamin Bosworth, including his ancestry." http://digitalcommons.uri.edu/cgi/viewcontent.cgi?article=1033&context=lippitt_prize, accessed July 8, 2013. Reference courtesy of Marlene L. Lopes, Special Collections Librarian, Rhode Island College. Bosworth's papers were deposited in the Division of Rare and Manuscript Collections, Cornell University Library, where they are catalogued as "Alfred Bosworth papers, 1899–1956," Collection Number 22-2-3998. The finding guide to the papers: http://rmc.library.cornell.edu/EAD/htmldocs/RMA03998.html, accessed August 19, 2015.

Page 203, *the oldest public high school in the United States* … This quotation is from the Boston Public Schools internet website, http://www.bostonpublicschools.org/school/english-high-school, accessed July 6, 2013. This claim is disputed. For example, Boston Latin School claims to be "the oldest public school in America with a continuous existence. It was founded April 23, 1635 by the Town of Boston." http://web.archive.org/web/20070502223937/http://www.bls.org/cfml/l3tmpl_history.cfm, accessed July 6, 2013. Hopkins Academy, the public high school in Hadley, Massachusetts, uses different words to stake its claim: "The school was founded in 1664 with an endowment from a wealthy Connecticut merchant, Edward Hopkins. Hopkins died in 1657 and in his will he set up a trust naming John Davenport, Theophilus Eaton, John Cullick, and William Goodwin as trustees. Goodwin, who helped to settle Hadley, used part of Hopkins' trust to set up a fund for the then Hopkins Donation School. The Hadley townspeople donated land to help build up the trust to pay for educational costs. The Hopkins Trust is the oldest charitable fund to be in continuous use in the United States." http://www.ask.com/wiki/Hopkins_Academy?o=2801&qsrc=999, accessed July 6, 2013.

Page 203, *Van Slyke published a major book* … Lucius Lincoln Van Slyke, *Modern Methods of Testing Milk and Milk Products: A Handbook Prepared for the Use of Dairy Students, Butter Makers, Cheese Makers, Producers of Milk, Operators in Condenseries, Managers of Milk-Shipping Stations, Milk Inspectors, Physicians, Etc.* (New York: Orange Judd Company, 1st edition 1906).

Page 204, *textbooks for cheese making* … Lucius Lincoln Van Slyke, *Course in Cheese Making for Movable Schools of Agriculture*, United States Office of Experiment Stations, *Bulletin*, no. 166 (Washington: Government Printing Office, 1906). Lucius Lincoln Van Slyke and Charles Albert Publow, *The Science and Practice of Cheese-Making: A Treatise on the Manufacture of American Cheddar Cheese and Other Varieties, Intended as a Text-Book for the Use of Dairy Teachers and Students in Classroom and Workroom* (New York: Orange Judd, 1909). Lucius Lincoln Van Slyke and Walter Van Price, *Cheese: A Treatise on the Manufacture of American Cheddar Cheese and Some Other Varieties* (New York: Orange Judd, 1927).

Page 204, *books on plant fertilizers* … Lucius Lincoln Van Slyke, *Plant Food, Its Nature, Composition and Most Profitable Use: Prepared to Aid Practical Farmers* (New York: German Kali Works, 1896). Lucius Lincoln Van Slyke, *Fertilizers and Crops: The Science and Practice of Plant-Feeding; A Presentation of Facts, Giving Practical Methods for Using Fertilizers in Crop Growing, With Special Emphasis on the Reasons Underlying Their Use, and on the Conditions of Their Greatest Efficiency* (New York: Orange Judd, 1912). Revised posthumously by his son, Donald Dexter Van Slyke (1883–1971): *Fertilizers and Crop Production* (New York: Orange Judd, 1932).

Page 204, *standard methods for chemical analysis* … Harvey Washington Wiley, Lucius Lincoln Van Slyke, and Willard Dell Bigelow, *Methods of Analysis Adopted by The Association of Official Agricultural Chemists, September 5, 6, and 7, 1895* (Washington: United States Department of Agriculture, Division of Chemistry, 1895), 84 pages.

Page 205, *In a letter to Angell, written in Pike* … Copy of letter supplied by Emma E. Hawker, Assistant Archivist, Bentley Historical Library, University of Michigan. She also supplied biographical information, as well as copies of material (including obituaries, other newspaper clippings, and forms completed by Van Slyke) from the Bentley Library Necrology File for L. L. Van Slyke.

Page 205, *many joint papers, reporting* … For example, Lucius Lincoln Van Slyke and Alfred Willson Bosworth, "Effect of Treating Milk with Carbon Dioxide Gas under Pressure," New York Agricultural Experiment Station, *Bulletin*, no. 292 (Geneva: August 1907), pp. 371–384. Alfred W. Bosworth and Lucius L. Van Slyke, "Preparation and Composition of Unsaturated or Acid Calcium Caseinate and Paracaseinate," *Journal of Biological Chemistry*, vol. 14, no. 3 (April 1913), pp. 211–225. Lucius L. Van Slyke and Alfred W. Bosworth, "Preparation and Composition of Basic Calcium Caseinate and Paracaseinate," *Journal of Biological Chemistry*, vol. 14, no. 3 (April 1913), pp. 207–209. Alfred W. Bosworth and Lucius L. Van Slyke, "The Phosphorus Content of Casein," *Journal of Biological Chemistry*, vol. 19, no. 1 (September 1914), pp. 67–71. Lucius L. Van Slyke and Alfred W. Bosworth, "The Cause of Acidity of Fresh Milk of Cows and a Method of Determination of Acidity," *Journal of Biological Chemistry*, vol. 19, no. 1 (September 1914), pp. 73–76. Lucius L. Van Slyke and Alfred W. Bosworth, "Condition of Casein and Salts in Milk," *Journal of Biological Chemistry*, vol. 20 (1914), pp. 135–152.

Page 205, *collaborating in Boston with Henry I. Bowditch* … For example, H. I. Bowditch, M.D., and A. W. Bosworth, Geneva, N. Y., "Rules for Calculating the Approximate Composition of Milk from the Specific Gravity and Percentage of Fat as Determined by the Babcock Method," *American Journal of Diseases of Children*, vol. 7, no. 3 (March 1914), pp. 244–245. The authors cite an earlier paper by them in the same journal, vol. 6 (1913), p. 394. Stephen Moulton Babcock (1843–1931) invented the Babcock test in 1890 at the University of Wisconsin. The test quickly became an official analytical chemical method in most dairy states. *See, for example,* "The Babcock Method of Determining Fat in Milk and Cream for the Use of Creameries," *Bulletin* no. 106, The Connecticut Agricultural Experiment Station (New Haven, Connecticut: March 1891).

Page 205, *A series of at least fourteen research papers* … *A sampling:* A. W. Bosworth and H. I. Bowditch, "Studies in Infant Feeding. The Chemical Changes Produced by the Addition of Lime Water to Milk," *Journal of Biological Chemistry*, vol. 28 (1917), pp. 491–435. A. W. Bosworth, and H. I. Bowditch, M.D., "Studies of Infant Feeding. VIII. The Mineral Constituents (Ash) of Milk," *Boston Medical and Surgical Journal*, vol. 177, no. 8 (August 23, 1917), pp. 248–251; read before the new England Pediatric Society on March 30, 1917.

Page 205, *The Boston Floating Hospital* … Paul Beaven, "A History of the Boston Floating Hospital," *Pediatrics*, vol. 19, no. 4 (April 1957), pp. 629–638.

Page 206, *process for making reconstructed milk* … Alfred W. Bosworth of Milton, Massachusetts, U. S. Patent 1,341,040, "Reconstructed Milk and Process of Making Same," application July 1, 1918, patented May 25, 1920, assigned to The Boston Floating Hospital, Boston, Massachusetts, a corporation of Massachusetts.

Page 206, *Y.M.C.A. School of Commerce* … Lori Wengerd, *Shaping the Future, Celebrating 100 Years: Thoughts and Photographs Celebrating the Students, Alumni, Friends, and Family of Franklin University* (Columbus, Ohio: Franklin University Press, 2002). "Franklin University's name bespeaks its connection to one of the greatest visionaries in history, Benjamin Franklin," p. 23.

Page 207, *Mrs. Paul Frank of Dallas* … Information was supplied by Dr. Larry T. Hunter, Director of Institutional Research, Capital University.

Page 207, *the Harry C. Moores Foundation* … Email February 1, 2016, from Mary Cummins, Harry C. Moores Foundation.

Page 207, *the first commercial milk-based infant formula* … Although Bosworth developed the product, the actual self-serving quotation is from Abbott: "1925. The Moores and Ross Milk Company (today known as Abbott Nutrition) produced the first commercial milk-based infant formula—a new concept at the time. 1927. The new milk-based infant formula was named Similac®, for simulated lactation." http://similac.com/baby-formula/about-similac-infant-formula/timeline, accessed July 3, 2013.

Page 207, *M & R Dietetic Laboratories* … "M & R Dietetic Laboratories," *Ohio History Central*, http://ohiohistorycentral.org/w/M_&_R_Dietetic_Laboratories?rec=923, accessed February 24, 2016.

Page 208, *Born in Cleveland, Gerstenberger* … "Gerstenberger, Henry John," *The Encyclopedia of Cleveland History*, http://ech.case.edu/cgi/article.pl?id=GHJ; "Healthcare History in Cleveland," *The Encyclopedia of Cleveland History*, http://www.teachingcleveland.org/index.php?option=com_k2&view=item&id=512:healthcare-history-in-cleveland, accessed June 12, 2013.

Page 208, *Edward Fitch Cushing (1862–1911)* … "The Pioneer Families of Cleveland," www.heritagepursuit.com/Cuyahoga/Cleveland502.htm, accessed June 12, 2013.

Page 208, *were collaborating in metabolic studies* … Howard D. Haskins and H. J. Gerstenberger (from the Laboratory of Physiology and Biochemistry, Western Reserve University, Cleveland), "Calcium Metabolism in a Case of Infantile Tetany," *Journal of Experimental Medicine*, vol. 13, no. 3 (March 1, 1911), pp. 314–318.

Page 208, *planned their own research strategy* … H. J. Gerstenberger, six-page "Introduction" to H. J. Gerstenberger, H. D. Haskins, H. H. McGregor, and H. O. Ruh [from Babies' Dispensary and Hospital, the Departments of Pediatrics, Chemistry and Biochemistry of Western Reserve University, and from the Walker-Gordon Laboratory, Cleveland, Ohio], "Studies in the Adaptation of an Artificial Food to Human Milk," *American Journal of Diseases of Children*, vol. 10, no. 4 (October 1915), pp. 249–265. Pre-

sented at the Annual Meeting of the American Pediatric Society, Lakewood, N. J., May 24, 1915. Submitted for publication July 15, 1915.

Page 208, *Gerstenberger recalled* … loc. cit., p. 252.

Page 209, *according to their own ideas of infant-feeding* … Editorial: "Modified Milk," *Cleveland Journal of Medicine*, vol. 3, no. 1 (January 1898), pp. 20–21.

Page 209, *a one-man milk route* … "Telling-Belle Vernon Co.," *The Encyclopedia of Cleveland History*, http://ech.case.edu/cgi/article.pl?id=TVC, accessed June 5, 2013. *See also* William Whitmoyer, "The Uncredentialed Professor" (Blog, posted Saturday, February 27, 2010), http://uncredentialed-professor.blogspot.com/2010/02/could-william-e-telling-dairy-king-of.html, accessed June 5, 2013.

Page 209, *The Formulac baby food brand name* … Formulac was a trademark of National Dairy Products Company, Inc., for "special dietary infant food derived from milk with mineral and vitamin supplements." The trademark's first commercial use was on February 12, 1944. It was registered with the United States Patent and Trademark Office (filing date March 28, 1944; registration date September 26, 1944). The trademark expired on January 10, 1986. http://www.trademarkia.com/formulac-71468760.html.

Page 210, *Gerstenberger and Ruh wrote in 1919:* … H. J. Gerstenberger and H. O. Ruh, in collaboration with M. J. Brickman, H. J. Leslie, and R. J. Ochsner [from Babies' Dispensary and Hospital, the Municipal Department of Child Hygiene, and the Department of Pediatrics, Western Reserve University, Cleveland], "Studies in the Adaptation of an Artificial Food to Human Milk. II. A Report of Three Years' Clinical Experience with the Feeding of S.M.A. (Synthetic Milk Adapted)" *American Journal of Diseases of Children*, vol. 17, no. 1 (January 1919), pp. 1–37. Presented before the Section on Diseases of Children at the Sixty-Ninth Annual Session of the American Medical Association, Chicago, June 1918. Submitted for publication

August 10, 1918. The quotation appears on page 9.

Page 211, *not every person who used the initials …* For example, "Simulated Milk Adapted," Andrew J. Schuman, "A Concise History of Infant Formula (Twists and Turns Included)," *Contemporary Pediatrics*, vol. 20, no. 2 (February 2003), p. 97; "Scientific Milk Adaptation," biographical sketch of Paul Frohring in the *Encyclopedia of Cleveland History*, http://ech.case.edu/ech-cgi/article.pl?id=FPR, accessed June 30, 2013; "Scientific Milk Adaptation," R. McL. Todd, "Infant feeding—A Comparison of Human, Evaporated, and Dried Milk," *The Practitioner*, vol. 184, no. 1101 (March 1960), pp. 352–354.

Page 211, *our great indebtedness …* H. J. Gerstenberger and H. O. Ruh, et al., "Studies in the Adaptation of an Artificial Food to Human Milk. II. A Report of Three Years' Clinical Experience with the Feeding of S.M.A. (Synthetic Milk Adapted)" *American Journal of Diseases of Children*, vol. 17, no. 1 (January 1919), footnote on page 22.

Page 213, *enzyme-catalyzed reactions were beginning to be studied …* Lactase was one of the first enzymes that hydrolyze milk sugars to be discovered. *See* Martinus Willem Beijerinck, "Die Lactase, ein neues Enzym," *Centralbl. Bakteriol. Parasitenkd.*, vol. 6 (1889), pp. 44–48, *cited in* R. J. Rouwenhorst, J. T. Pronk, and J. P. van Dijken, "Reflections on Biochemistry: The Discovery of beta-Galactosidase," *Trends in Biochemical Sciences*, vol. 14, no. 10 (October 1989), pp. 416–418.

Page 213, *The SMACO brand was introduced …* The brand persisted. In 1939, Carotene–SMACO (manufactured by the S. M. A. Corporation, Cleveland, Ohio) was listed as a "new and nonofficial remedy," together with SMACO Carotene in Oil, SMACO Carotene with Vitamin D Concentrate in Oil, and SMACO Carotene and Vitamin D Concentrate in Cod Liver Oil. *New and Nonofficial Remedies, 1939: Containing Descriptions of the Articles Which Stand Accepted by the Council on Pharmacy and Chemistry of the American Medical Association on January 1, 1939* (Chicago: American Medical Association, 1939), pp. 491–493.

Page 214, *plant source of anthelmintics …* The active search for anti-parasitic substances continued. For example, the Nobel Prize in Physiology or Medicine was awarded in October 2015 to Tu Youyou, Satoshi Omura, and William C. Campbell for therapies (involving anti-parasitic compounds found in herbs and soil) that "have revolutionized the treatment of some of the most devastating parasitic diseases."

Page 214, *He published experimental preparation methods in 1831 …* H. Wackenroder, "Über das Oleum radicis Dauci aetherum, das Carotin, den Carotenzucker und den officinellen succus Dauci; so wie auch über das Mannit, welches in dem Möhrensafte durch eine besondere Art der Gährung gebildet wird," *Geigers Magazin der Pharmazie*, vol. 33 (1831), pp. 144–172. Cited in Theodore L. Sourkes, "The Discovery and Early History of Carotene," *Bulletin of the History of Chemistry*, vol. 34, no. 1 (2009), pp. 32–38. For a biography of Wackenroder, *see* Herta Hellmuth, "Heinrich Wilhelm Ferdinand Wackenroder: 8. März 1798–14. September 1854," *Pharmazie*, vol. 35, no. 5/6 (1980), pp. 321–323.

Page 214, *definitively determined the molecular formula of carotene …* Richard Willstätter and Walter Mieg, "Untersuchungen über Chlorophyll. IV. Über die gelben Begleiter des Chlorophylls," *Justus Liebig's Annalen der Chemie*, vol. 355 (1907), pp. 1–28.

Page 214, *readily degraded by free radicals …* The oxidative decomposition of carotene into a variety of carboxylic acids was described by P. Karrer, A. Helfenstein, H. Wehrli, and A. Wettstein, "Pflanzenfarbstoffe XXV. Über die Konstitution des Lycopins und Carotins," *Helvetica Chimica Acta*, vol. 13, no. 5 (1930), pp. 1084–1099.

Page 215, *He began research collaboration with biochemists …* J. Lucien Morris and Vernon Jersey, preliminary presentation, "Proceedings of the American Society of Biological Chemists: Seventeenth Annual Meeting," *Journal of Biological Chemistry*, vol. 55, no. 2 (February 1923), p. xviii; J.

Lucien Morris and Vernon Jersey, "Chemical Constituents of Saliva as Indices of Glandular Activity," *Journal of Biological Chemistry*, vol. 56, no. 1 (May 1923), pp. 31–42; J. Lucien Morris, Vernon Jersey, and Charles T. Way, "Diuresis in the Sheep. Concentration of Uric Acid and Urea by the Excretory Mechanism of Sheep and Rabbit Compared," *American Journal of Physiology*, vol. 70, no. 1 (September 1924), pp. 122–129; Howard H. Beard and Vernon Jersey, "The Specific Rotatory Power of Glucose–Insulin Solutions in Contact with Muscle Tissue *in vitro*," *Journal of Biological Chemistry*, vol. 70, no. 1 (September 1926), pp. 167–171.

Page 215, *University of Michigan (Ann Arbor)* ... Horace W. Davenport, *Not Just Any Medical School: The Science, Practice, and Teaching of Medicine at the University of Michigan, 1850–1941* (Ann Arbor: The University of Michigan Press, 1999). *See especially* chap. 6, "Physiological Chemistry, 1921–41," and chap. 7, "Physiology."

Page 216, *Malt Amylase* ... Amylase (diastase) catalyzes the hydrolysis of carbohydrates into sugars. It was the first biochemical catalyst to be described in the scientific literature. Erhard Friedrich Leuchs (1800–1837) described the effect of saliva on starch: "Wirkung des Speichels auf Stärke," *Poggendorff's Annalen der Physik und Chemie*, vol. 98, no. 8 (1831), p. 623; Erhard Friedrich Leuchs, "Über die Verzuckerung des Stärkmehls durch Speichel," *Archiv für die Gesammte Naturlehre*, vol. 21, (1831), pp. 105–107. The enzyme was isolated by Anselme Payen (1795–1878) and Jean-François Persoz (1805–1868): A. Payen and J.-F. Persoz, "Mémoire sur la Diastase, les principaux Produits de ses Réactions et leurs applications aux arts industriels," *Annales de chimie et de physique*, Series 2, vol. 53 (1833), pp. 73–92.

Page 217, *Mellon Institute of Industrial Research* ... "Mellon Institute of Industrial Research," National Historic Chemical Landmarks booklet (Washington: American Chemical Society, Office of Public Outreach, March 28, 2013).

Page 217, *Ward Baking Company Fellowship ... The Story of Our Research Products* (New York: Ward Baking Company, 1921), 71 pages.

Page 217, *Kohman, Irvin, and Cross filed...* Henry A. Kohman, Roy Irvin, and Robert J. Cross, U. S. Patent 1,325,327, "Manufacture of Leavened Bread," application February 11, 1919, assigned to the Ward Baking Company; Henry A. Kohman, Roy Irvin, and Robert J. Cross, U. S. Patent 1,475,494, "Process for the Manufacture of Yeast," application January 20, 1919, assigned to the Fleischmann Company,

Page 217, *Cross and Swain published this research* ... Robert J. Cross and Robert E. Swain, *Industrial and Engineering Chemistry*, vol. 16, no. 1 (1924), pp. 49–52.

Page 217, *Decades later, Cross recalled ... See* Obituary, *South Whitley* [Indiana] *Tribune*, April 28, 1955.

Page 217, *He filed a patent application on June 28, 1932* ... Robert J. Cross, U. S. Patent 1,986,920, "Electroosmotic Process and Apparatus," application June 28, 1932, assigned to S.M.A. Corporation; Robert J. Cross, U. S. Patent 2,032,006, "Method of Recovering Carotene from Soaps," assigned to S.M.A. Corporation.

Page 218, *Dr. Ross Aiken Gortner* ... "Register of Ph.D. Degrees," *The Bulletin of the University of Minnesota*, vol. 42, no. 31 (May 22, 1939), p. 130. *For a biography of Dr. Gortner, see* Samuel Colville Lind, "Biographical Memoir of Ross Aiken Gortner, 1885–1942," *Biographical Memoirs of the National Academy of Sciences* (Washington: National Academy of Sciences, vol. 23, sixth memoir, 1943), pp. 148–180.

Page 218, *collaborated with Harry Goldblatt ... See* Harry Goldblatt and Katharine Marjorie Soames, "The Supplementary Value of Light Rays to a Diet Graded in its Content of Fat-Soluble Organic Factor," *Biochemical Journal*, vol. 17 (1923), pp. 622–629. Goldblatt and Soames showed some dietary benefit from foods that had been irradiated. This interest was pursued, with a better understanding of vitamins D and A, as reported in Harry Goldblatt and Harold M. Barnett, "Carotene and Vitamin A," article 6425 in *Proceedings of the Society for Experimental Biology and Medicine,* vol. 30, no. 2 (November 1932), pp. 201–204. Barnett then continued with research at S.M.A.; *see* Harold M. Barnett, "The Determination of Carotene in Butter Fat," *Journal of Biological Chemistry,* vol. 105, no. 2 (May 1, 1934), pp. 259–267.

Page 218, *Barnett submitted "Studies …* Harold M. Barnett, "Studies on Leucine and Dileucine Hydrochloride and a New Method for the Isolation of Leucine," *Journal of Biological Chemistry,* vol. 100 (April 1, 1933), pp. 543–550. Leucine is an essential amino acid for humans; it is needed for human metabolism, but must be obtained from the diet. Dileucine is the dipeptide in which two leucine molecules are joined via a peptide bond.

Page 219, *application dated January 16, 1930 …* Harold M. Barnett, U. S. Patent 1,990,769, "Amino Acids," application January 16, 1930, assigned to S.M.A. Corporation.

Page 219, *as the sole applicant …* Harold M. Barnett, U. S. Patent 1,978,981, "Method of Preparing Carotene Pigment Material," application April 12, 1932, assigned to the S.M.A. Corporation, Cleveland, Ohio; Harold M. Barnett, U. S. Patent 2,009,868, "Method of Preparing Leucine," application May 1, 1933, assigned to the S.M.A. Corporation, Cleveland, Ohio; Harold M. Barnett, U. S. Patent 1,988,031, "Method of Recovering Caro-

tene," application September 30, 1933, assigned to the S.M.A. Corporation, Cleveland, Ohio.

Page 219, *Barnett, Frohring, and Germann submitted a joint …* Harold M. Barnett, William O. Frohring, and Albert F. O. Germann, U. S. Patent 2,032,165, "Method of Extracting Carotene," application November 11, 1932, assigned to the S.M.A. Corporation, Cleveland, Ohio.

Page 219, *The Whey Protein …* Otto Ungnade, *Das Molkeneiweiss (Ziger): seine Darstellung, sein Wesen, sein Nährwert und seine Verwendung in der Käserei* (Berlin: Druck von A. Parrhysius, 1921), 30 pages. Published in German.

Page 219, *Lactose: Its Production …* Otto Ungnade, *Milchzucker: seine fabrikation, untersuchung und verwendung* (Hidesheim: Verlag der Molkerei-Zeitung, 1926), 71 pages. Published in German.

Page 219, *The Roller Dryer …* Otto Ungnade, *Der Walzentrockner in der Milchindustrie. Fortschritte in der Milchtrocknung* (Kempten im Allgäu, Mühlstr. K 15 Süddeutsche Molkerei-Zeitung, 1929), 19 pages. Published in German.

Page 219, *A 1927 book review …* Review by O. Spengler. "Neue Bücher: *Milchzucker, seine Fabrikation, Untersuchung und Verwendung.* Von Chemiker Otto Ungnade, Hannover-Laatzen. Verlag der Molkerei-Zeitung, Hildesheim. 1926," *Angewandte Chemie,* vol. 20, no. 17 (April 28, 1927), p. 499.

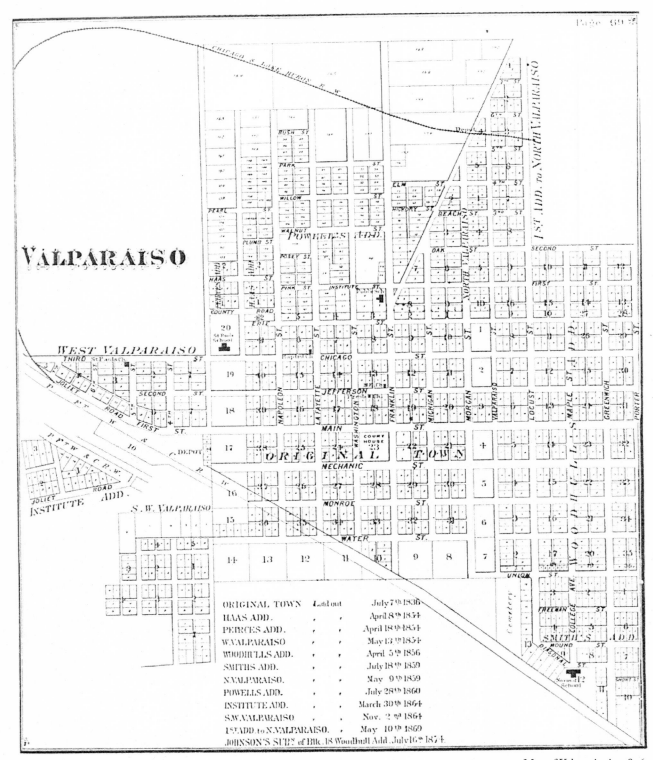

Map of Valparaiso in 1876

IV.
Valparaiso

ON FRIDAY, October 22, 1926, *Science* (the national journal of the American Association for the Advancement of Science) reported: "Dr. A. F. O. Germann has resigned his position with the Laboratory Products Company, where he was in charge of development and research, in order to organize work in chemistry at Valparaiso University, Indiana."

Albert Fredrick Ottomar Germann had been communicating with members of the Lutheran University Association and the separate Valparaiso University Association, both incorporated in July 1925. Those prominent Lutheran leaders persuaded Dr. Germann to take an active role in strengthening and "Lutheranizing" a faltering Valparaiso University. Dr. Germann was on campus as Professor of Chemistry and Head of the Department of Chemistry when classes opened in fall 1926. He was a senior member of the faculty on Sunday, October 3, 1926, when the Board of Directors of the Valparaiso University Association inaugurated William Herman Theodore Dau as the first Lutheran President of the University.

Albert Germann did much more during less than a year at Valparaiso University than "organize work in chemistry." He found and hired three strong chemists and a strong physicist for a reconstructed science faculty. He investigated "the insufficiency" of the Dean of Pharmacy. He served as Acting President of the University. He became Acting Dean of the School of Pharmacy. He secured institutional membership of the School of Pharmacy in the American Association of Colleges of Pharmacy.

The short news item in *Science* signaled a new and very different phase of the professional career of Albert Germann. To view that news with informed perspective, it is helpful to know some facts about Valparaiso—about the place, about its history, and about the times. It is helpful to know a bit about some political and cultural matters that were swirling around northern Indiana in the 1920s, including activities of the Ku Klux Klan, and controversies about biological evolution and historical geology. It is also helpful to know about the Lutheran clerical and lay leadership in Northern Indiana in the first quarter of the 20th century, and about ways that Albert Germann was connected to these leaders.

A Focused History of Education in Valparaiso

The present City of Valparaiso is the county seat of Porter County, Indiana. Porter County, in extreme northwestern Indiana, is bounded on the north by Lake Michigan, and on the west by Lake County (adjacent to Cook County, Illinois). European settlers arrived in the early 1830s. The Indiana General Assembly created Porter County in 1836. At that time, the county extended all the way west to the Illinois border. The General Assembly incorporated the Town of Valparaiso in 1850. It was another fifteen years before Valparaiso became a city.

Protestant denominations sent missionaries in 1831 to this frontier community of about three hundred folk. Presbyterians sent the Rev. Dr. J. C. Brown. Methodists sent the Rev. W. J. Forbes. Presbyterian and Methodist congregations were both holding regular church services by 1840. The Presbyterians built a wooden sanctuary in 1842. The Presbyterians moved that building at least once from its original location. It was still in use as late as 1876.

As was customary in other rural areas of Indiana at the time, district one-teacher common schools were established (usually by the township trustee, sometimes by a group of parents). A neighborhood school typically served families living within walking distance of the school building. Educational funding was local and often erratic. Families commonly supplemented township contributions, sometimes with money, often with "in-kind" donations such as firewood for winter heat in the one-room school building. In 1854, the Town of Valparaiso built a public high school, quickly nicknamed "The Old Seminary." Old Seminary was short-lived. The building burned to the ground in fall 1857. The town did not rebuild it.

Although the Town of Valparaiso took more than a decade to replace the functions of Old Seminary, the Methodists and the Presbyterians moved more quickly.

Methodists in 1859 opened the Valparaiso Male and Female College with a mission to be pioneers in coeducation. Its first class had an enrollment of seventy-five students, some having completed just a district-school course of study, others with even less formal education. A temporary wooden building was ready for students on Wednesday morning, September 21, 1859. The Methodists soon built a permanent brick school building, quickly christened "Old College." They laid the cornerstone in 1860. They added a tall tower and a wing to the east of Old College in 1867; the new wing was a dormitory for female students from out of town. The campus was at the southern end of College Avenue, in Woodhull's 1856 Addition to the original town.

A series of well-qualified Methodist men led Valparaiso Male and Female College. The first Presidents were educated at Indiana Asbury University. The University was named in honor of Bishop Francis Asbury (1745–1816), the first American bishop of the Methodist Episcopal Church. The Indiana General Assembly chartered the University on January 10, 1837. Sponsored as a seminary of learning by the Indiana Conference of the Methodist Episcopal Church, Indiana Asbury University was located in the frontier town of Greencastle, at the center of Putnam County. Washington Charles DePauw (1822–1887), then perhaps the wealthiest man in Indiana, gave substantial funds to endow the University. In 1884, the institution changed its name to DePauw University.

The first President of Valparaiso Male and Female College was the Rev. Charles N Sims (1835–1908), an 1859 graduate of Indiana Asbury University. Sims received an honorary A.M. degree from Ohio Wesleyan University in 1860. Not to be outdone, Indiana Asbury University reciprocated with an A.M. in 1861. Before coming to Valparaiso, Rev. Sims had been Principal of the Methodist Thorntown Academy, a co-educational school in Sugar Creek Township, Boone County, Indiana. Because Sims wanted to complete his contractual year at Thorntown, the Rev. Francis D. Carley was Acting President when students first arrived at Valparaiso. Rev. Carley was Professor of Mathematics and Natural Sciences, and one of the six original faculty members of the College.

Charles Sims was President of Valparaiso Male and Female College for two years. These were tumultuous years in America. During his presidency was the November 6, 1860, election of Abraham Lincoln as President of the United States, the formation of the Confederate States of America, and the April 12, 1861, Confederate attack on Fort Sumter. It had been more than a decade since a schism within Methodism over the issue of slavery resulted in the creation of the Methodist Episcopal Church South.

Sims resigned from Valparaiso Male and Female College to become a minister in the Methodist Episcopal Church. Honors from Indiana Asbury University kept coming to Charles Sims—the Doctor of Divinity degree in 1870, and the Doctor of Laws degree in 1883. On June 28, 1881, he was inaugurated as Chancellor of Syracuse University, Syracuse, New York. Sims retired from Syracuse University in 1893 after a distinguished career there.

The Methodist Church (the Valparaiso congregation, with encouragement from many other local citizens and from the Northwest Indiana Conference of the Methodist Episcopal Church) was generous in supplying construction and current operating funds, but the College contracted debt, never had an endowment, and apparently did not seek endowment funds to cushion lean years in its future. President Sims learned a great deal about the need for long-term financial stability during his two years at endowment-less Valparaiso Male and Female College. When he moved to Syracuse University, he became Chancellor of an institution in financial crisis. Much of his time and energy at Syracuse had to be devoted to fund-raising, not only to deal with on-going costs but also to add several hundred thousand dollars to the endowment. Valparaiso Male and Female College and its successors were to learn, in the hardest way, that a non-public educational institution should not hope to survive through turbulent financial and political times without the buffer of an adequate and secure endowment.

The Rev. Erastus Herman Staley (born February 6, 1830) was selected in 1862 to succeed Charles Sims as President of Valparaiso Male and Female College. Staley, like Sims, was a graduate of Indiana Asbury University. He received both the A.B. and A.M. degrees in 1861. It had become a custom at several Indiana colleges and universities to award a master's degree simultaneously with an earned baccalaureate; there was a charge for the additional sheepskin diploma. Staley had been the first President of the Tippecanoe Battle Ground Collegiate Institute. The Northwest Indiana Conference of the Methodist Episcopal Church had formed the Institute, which opened in the town of Battle Ground (Tippecanoe Township, Tippecanoe County, Indiana) on December 16, 1857. Staley then became the founding head of the first high school in Frankfort, Clinton County, Indiana. Faced with the consequences of losing Valparaiso students who had joined Union forces in the Civil War, Staley expanded the Board of Trustees of Valparaiso Male and Female College from five to eighteen members, hoping to broaden support for the school. Staley resigned after less than a year to become President of Indiana Northern College in South Bend.

The Rev. Benjamin Wilson Smith (1830–1921) was also a graduate of Indiana Asbury University (A.B., A.M. 1858). He was Professor of Classics at Valparaiso Male and Female College when promoted to President in 1864. Smith worked hard to find new sources of students. He gave scholarships to Civil War orphans and veterans. Smith resigned in 1867 to pursue careers as a Methodist minister in Terre Haute, as Postmaster in Lafayette, and as a three-term member of the Indiana General Assembly.

The Rev. Thomas Bond Wood (1844–1922) followed Smith in the presidency. Wood graduated from Indiana Asbury University (A.B. 1863, A.M. 1866). After earning his baccalaureate degree at Indiana Asbury, he attended Wesleyan University, Middletown, Connecticut, where in 1864 he received the A.B. degree and his license to preach, and in 1867 the M.A. degree. Wesleyan University was chartered in May 1831 as a Methodist college—but significantly, it was an independent institution under the auspices (but not under the control) of the Methodist conference. While he was a student at Wesleyan University, Thomas Wood taught German, natural science courses, and astronomy at Wesleyan Academy in Wilbraham, Massachusetts. Wesleyan Academy, founded in 1817 in New Market, New Hampshire, claims to be the first coeducational boarding school in the United States. Wesleyan Academy moved to Wilbraham in 1825. It merged with Monson Academy (founded 1804) in 1971 to become the present Wilbraham & Monson Academy.

President Wood led a fund-raising campaign in 1867 to assist in construction of the new wing to Old College. In spite of his efforts to raise money, the construction project increased the College's debt. There seems to have been no attempt to create an endowment. Confronted by the institution's severe financial problems, Wood resigned. He went on to a notable career as a missionary and a developer of school systems in South American countries.

The last President of the Valparaiso Male and Female College, serving from 1869 to 1871, was the Rev. Aaron Gurney (March 21, 1832–September 20, 1891). He had been minister of the Stockwell Methodist Episcopal Church in 1859 and the Valparaiso Methodist Episcopal Church in 1860. From 1863 to 1874, including the years of his college presidency, Gurney was an editor in various incarnations of the *Porter County Vidette* newspaper. Indiana Asbury University awarded him the honorary degree *artium magister* (A.M.) in 1870, guaranteeing that Indiana Asbury had provided (or at least recognized) presidential leadership for the entire life of the College. Gurney recognized that the College's business model was seriously flawed. He attempted to raise money locally. There appeared no way to keep enrollment from declining. In 1871, the Board of Trustees closed the College. Methodists maintained ownership. The Board of Trustees formed a committee to locate a group who would use the property for educational purposes. It would be two years before such a group was located. That "group" was a single man.

At the same time that Valparaiso Male and Female College was founded, the Presbyterians opened the Valparaiso Collegiate Institute in the heart of the town. The site was a plot of land bounded by Washington and Franklin streets, and by a street that would soon be named Institute Street. The church had purchased the land in 1860 from Nancy Borst. The church constructed a two-story brick school building, with four classrooms and a small office. Valparaiso booster (and Valparaiso historian) Hubert M. Skinner described the building as a "beautiful airy structure."

The Institute opened on April 16, 1861. Head of Valparaiso Collegiate Institute from 1864 to 1870 was Benjamin Wilcox (1816–1875), an 1841 graduate of Williams College. Williams College, established in 1793 in Williamstown, Massachusetts, is the second oldest college in Massachusetts. Also on the faculty of the Institute were writer and Presbyterian minister Ambrose Yoemans Moore (1822–1904), Miss Sophie Loring, and the missionary Miss Tyler.

The Presbyterian Church and many local citizens were generous in supplying construction and operating funds for the Institute, but (just as with the College) the Institute never had an endowment and apparently did not seek endowment funds.

Valparaiso Male and Female College continued in operation for about fourteen years. Valparaiso Collegiate Institute lasted only about a decade. Even as the Methodist school and the Presbyterian school declined, there were beginnings of a Catholic school and a Lutheran school in Valparaiso.

The Rev. Edward Sorin and six companions, all members of the recently established Congregation of Holy Cross, in 1842 took possession of 524 acres that the Catholic Bishop of Vincennes had given them for missionary work in northwestern Indiana. With a total enrollment of just two pre-college students, they immediately declared establishment of l'Université de Notre Dame du Lac. Priests from Notre Dame served the few Catholics in and around Valparaiso as early as 1845, celebrating Mass in the Porter County Courthouse, in the David Barry Blacksmith Shop on Indiana Avenue, and in the open air at the P. T. Clifford farm. When the Right Reverend John H. Luers became Bishop of the Catholic Diocese of Fort Wayne in 1857, he quickly placed a resident priest in Valparaiso. The Rev. Paul Gillen (1808–1882), of the Congregation of Holy Cross, in 1858 began construction of Valparaiso's first Catholic sanctuary. It was a wood frame building, 100 ft × 50 ft. The Rev. Michael O'Reilly, pastor from January 1863 to August 1887, set in motion the creation of Saint Paul's School. He began to teach youngsters, starting in 1863. The two-story brick schoolhouse, 90 ft × 50 ft, was built in 1867. Saint Paul's School officially opened with three teachers in September 1872. In 1893, there were 113 pupils in eight grades. Every pupil lived within a mile of the school. Saint Paul Catholic School continues today as a K–8 school, with an enrollment of 331 students in 2015.

Forty-five German families formed a Lutheran congregation in Valparaiso in 1862. The Rev. H. Meyer was the first pastor of Immanuel German Lutheran Church. He arrived in November 1864. Pastor Meyer established the German–English Lutheran Parochial School. He was the only teacher for the one-room school during its first three years. C. Peters, one of the first graduates of Concordia Lutheran Teachers Seminary (1864–1913, in Addison, Illinois; after 1913, in River Forest, Illinois; since 2006, Concordia University Chicago in River Forest), took charge of the school in 1867. The school, enlarged several times during the next decades, was located on the corner of Pink and Chestnut streets (by 1893, the same site was "the corner of Academy and Chestnut streets"). In 1891, the Immanuel congregation constructed a brick Victorian Gothic church on the southeast corner of Washington and Institute streets. In recognition of its significance, this building was placed on the National Register of Historic Places in 1982. German–English Lutheran Parochial School closed in 1913 due to falling enrollment.

In 1869, the City of Valparaiso bought the Collegiate Institute building for $10,000. Valparaiso City Public Graded School opened its doors in the Institute building in 1870. This was thirteen years after Old Seminary had burned.

The city constructed a second building in 1871. The new building was on the former Institute land, just north of the original structure. The old and new buildings were physically connected. Their architectural style was the same. This building complex was home to Valparaiso High School, which (as a thriving institution) continues today. In its first year, there were four hundred students and ten teachers. Three years later, in 1874, Valparaiso High School conducted its first commencement ceremony.

Funding, administration, control, and mission of the educational enterprise in Valparaiso evolved during the three decades from the 1840s to 1870s. The striking feature of that evolution is that there was *continuity* of educational services available to young people of the community. In spite of a disastrous fire and in spite of precarious funding, with changing leadership and evolving sponsorship, there were always opportunities for graduates of the one-room district schools (and successors of those schools) to take their next steps on educational ladders. By 1873, local students had a choice: they could participate in, or they could insulate themselves from, the next phase of the Valparaiso educational evolution—Henry Baker Brown's Revival.

Brown's Revival

Henry Baker Brown (1847–1917) revived the Valparaiso Male and Female College in 1873. Brown reopened the institution as the Northern Indiana Normal School and Business Institute. When the first semester began in 1873, there were thirty-five students. The faculty included President Henry Baker Brown, Martin Eugene Bogarte (1855–1911), Ida Hutchison, Pearly Sherman, and Samantha Elizabeth "Mantie" Baldwin (1848–1933). W. A. Yohn, M.D. (1850–1892), was Director of the Preparatory Department; he would be Professor of the Natural Sciences until 1886. Benjamin Franklin Perrine (1848–1930) was a faculty member, as well as a bookseller and printer. His commercial establishment was located between College Avenue and Locust Street.

Samantha Baldwin and 18-year-old Martin Bogarte had been classmates of H. B. Brown at National Normal University in Lebanon, Ohio. Samantha Baldwin taught literature, rhetoric, history, and geography in Brown's new school, and played a skillful role in writing the advertising copy that enticed the first students to campus. She would be Professor of Rhetoric and Composition from 1875 to 1914. Martin Bogarte taught mathematics, surveying, elocution, and commercial subjects. B. F. Perrine taught Latin and physics.

Brown's revival marked a sharp change in the mission of the school. From 1859 to 1871, Methodist ministers had led the College. The influence of Indiana Asbury University had always been evident, both in the successive administrations and in the faculty of the College. The student body of the College included a great many children from local district schools. Brown was not a Methodist. He sought to appeal to a more diverse demographic group—especially students (including adults) who needed basic academic skills required by their new employers. He actively recruited students who lived outside of Valparaiso. Valparaiso City Public Graded School (opened in 1870), Valparaiso High School (opened in 1871), the Saint Paul Catholic School, and the German–English Lutheran Parochial School were now providing education for children and youth who lived in the city.

Henry Baker Brown was born on a farm near Mount Vernon, Ohio. Mount Vernon, county seat of Knox County, had a population of 3,711 in 1850. With only a district-school education, he began teaching as a teenager. He was younger than some of his students. He enrolled at Southwestern State Normal College, a teachers' college in Lebanon, Ohio. Southwestern State Normal College had opened in 1855. The College raised its nominal status in 1870 by taking the name National Normal University. Alfred Holbrook (February 17, 1816–April 16, 1909) was the first President of Southwestern State Normal College. Holbrook was the guiding force of the school for most of its existence.

Henry Baker Brown graduated from National Normal University with a Bachelor of Science degree in 1871. In a nineteenth-century version of a work-study program, Brown then taught at Northwestern Ohio Normal School in Ada, Ohio, where he concurrently earned a Bachelor of Arts degree in Classics.

The idea of a "normal school" was not new in the nation. The mission of a typical normal school was to transmit the norms of educational practice to prospective teachers. These norms included accepted standards for evaluating student performance. They also included practical techniques for leading and managing a classroom. In many respects, a normal school was a teacher training school. It also provided opportunities for graduates of district schools to continue their formal education in the academic subjects included in curricula of the new seminaries, high schools, and pre-collegiate institutes being created across the country. Whereas many earlier schoolteachers had been self-taught, normal schools aspired to develop standard paths to schoolroom leadership. The first normal school in the United States was probably the Columbian School, founded in 1823 in Concord, Vermont, by the Reverend Samuel Read Hall (1795–1877). The normal school movement rapidly spread westward.

Northwestern Ohio Normal School (where Henry Baker Brown was both a student and a faculty member) was founded by Henry Solomon Lehr (1838–1923), a recently discharged Union veteran from the Civil War. Henry Lehr came to Ada in search of a site for establishing a collegiate institution. The small village of Ada, laid out in 1853 along the Indiana and Ohio Railway, was surrounded by farmland. Lehr was hired as the local teacher in 1866. By 1870, he had established personal relationships in Ada that gave him confidence to ask the citizens of the community to provide funds to purchase land for a campus and additional funds to build an academic building. In August 1871, Northwestern Ohio Normal School (after 1885, Ohio Normal University; since 1903, Ohio Northern University) opened its doors in Ada.

Henry Baker Brown may have viewed Alfred Holbrook and Henry Lehr as exemplars. Brown followed similar career pathways. Twenty-six-year-old Brown visited Valparaiso in 1873 to assess the possibility of acquiring the campus of Valparaiso Male and Female College from the Methodists for his own school. Business leaders in Valparaiso were feeling the economic effects of losing the business of out-of-town students who formerly attended the College. They were receptive to Henry Brown's ideas of attracting students to a practical, no-frills school, with courses designed to prepare students for the jobs being advertised in the newspapers. Local businesses needed the new school, and Brown needed their support.

Henry Brown realized that the Chicago and Lake Huron Railroad and the Pittsburgh, Fort Wayne & Chicago Railroad, both with passenger depots in Valparaiso, provided easy access to his projected school for members of a youthful immigrant population who, with aggressive marketing, could be enticed to enroll. Chicago, the western terminus of each railroad, had seen dramatic population increases: from 4,470 in 1840, 29,963 in 1850, 112,172 in 1860, and 298,977 in 1870. The Great Chicago Fire in October 1871 decimated more than two thousand acres within the city; rebuilding began immediately, requiring additional workers in large numbers. Many of the new workers had only a minimal command of English, and most needed to improve their reading, writing, and fundamental arithmetic skills. They needed (and they knew that they needed) basic instruction for these job-entrance and job-advancement requirements, as well as familiarity with the new technology being introduced into factories and offices. There was a pool of potential applicants for affordable courses, courses designed (and adaptable) for whatever previous preparation those students offered. Entrance level, remedial, specialized, and advanced courses would all be available.

Brown was effective in raising local money from county and city governments, and from local businesses. The marketing pitch for support from the Valparaiso business community was direct. Students from Chicago needed rooms to rent, food to eat, and new clothes to wear. Brown argued that a thriving, populist, low-cost, no-frills institution would bring new cash to town from Chicago. Brown raised enough local money to purchase the brick building that the Methodists had built and called "Old College." Methodists laid its cornerstone in 1860. A tower and a dormitory wing completed the Methodist's building in 1867. Brown called this building "Old Main." Old Main would outlast Henry Baker Brown.

In its second year of operation, enrollment climbed to three hundred. The school originally had three departments: preparatory, teaching, and business. By the late 1870s, Brown had added additional programs. In 1875, enrollment was nine hundred students, making Northern Indiana Normal School the largest school of its kind in the nation. To provide a numerical context, Indiana University in Bloomington had only 28 graduates (in all academic areas) in 1881 and 164 graduates in 1901.

In an advertisement in the 1893 *Valparaiso City Directory* (Chicago: Kraft & Radcliffe), Northern Indiana Normal School and Business Institute boasted that it was "the largest and best equipped normal school in the United States." The ad listed the following departments: "Preparatory, Teachers (including Kindergarten Work, Teachers Training Class and Pedagogy), Collegiate (including Scientific, Classic and Select Courses), Special Science, Civil Engineering, Pharmacy, Commercial, Music,

Fine Art, Phonography [Pitman shorthand stenography, developed by Isaac Pitman (1813–1897)], and Typewriting, Telegraphic and Review." "School the entire year. Students may enter at any time and select their own studies."

"The Commercial Department in connection with the school is everywhere acknowledged to be the most complete Commercial College in the land. It is supplied with the most extensive line of offices ever attempted by any Business School." The "extensive line of offices" (which were practical business laboratory rooms) was a successful innovation. The Business Institute building contained model offices, equipped with telephones, graphophones, typewriters, autographs, adding machines, filing cabinets—the full range of new office technology that a secretary might encounter on the job.

By the late 1870s, intercity telephone service was beginning to rival telegraph communication for businesses. Alexander Graham Bell (1847–1922) formed the Volta Graphophone Company, and in the 1880s was marketing what would be called the Dictaphone in 1907. The Smith-Premier typewriter appeared in 1887. Thomas Alva Edison (1847–1931) invented his Autographic Stencil Printing system, with patents in 1870 and 1880. Albert Blake Dick (1856–1934) would later market Edison's invention as the Mimeograph. William Seward Burroughs (1857–1898) invented a mechanical adding machine in the 1880s, and in 1886 founded the American Arithmometer Company (later in 1905, the Burroughs Adding Machine Company). Edwin Grenville Seibels (1866–1954) in 1898 invented the vertical file, manufactured by the Globe-Wernicke Company to replace pigeonhole files that required documents to be folded and inserted into envelopes. It was a time of rapid change in the office workplace. Henry Baker Brown was leading the way, providing hands-on instruction to help workers meet the challenges of a changing employment market.

Henry Brown opened a law school in 1880. Another advertisement in the 1893 *Valparaiso City Directory* described the Northern Indiana Law School, with H. B. Brown, President. Faculty listed were lawyer A. Lyte Jones, lawyer H. A. Gillett, and postmaster/attorney Mark L. DeMotte. This school "in its first decade has fully demonstrated the fact that a thorough legal education can be secured at one-half the expense usually incurred in attending professional schools."

With "school the entire year," Northern Indiana Normal School and Business

Institute was a pioneer of the collegiate summer school. With student entry "at any time," the School and Institute avoided the calendric inflexibility of quarters or semesters. With the ability of students to "select their own studies," there was no pretense of an institution-wide curriculum. Except for private music lessons, all classes were included in one tuition fee. There were no entrance requirements. The Institute issued certificates and diplomas, but there were no pretentious graduation ceremonies.

As the school became more and more successful, administration of the increasingly complex proprietary enterprise became burdensome for Henry Brown. In 1878, Brown submitted articles of incorporation to the State of Indiana, and received a broadly inclusive charter. President Brown then made an offer to a college classmate, Oliver Perry Kinsey (1849–1931). Kinsey was born on a farm near the village of Freeport, Harrison County, Ohio. Freeport had a population of 288 in 1850. In 1866, he entered Harlem Spring Seminary (Carroll County, Ohio), and then taught school for a few terms. He moved to Lebanon, Ohio, in 1868 to enter Southwestern State Normal College. He remained there for a dozen years, first as a student, then as an instructor. During those years, Southwestern State Normal College became National Normal University. Kinsey majored in literature, completed the Commercial Course, earned A.B. and A.M. degrees, and taught English. On Thursday, August 24, 1876, O. P. Kinsey married Sarah Porter (1841–1922), also a National Normal University graduate and faculty member.

Brown's partnership offer was especially attractive. Kinsey was to employ his managerial skills and business acumen to keep the school profitable, while maintaining charges to students as low as possible. In return, Kinsey would become half owner of the school. Kinsey accepted in 1880, becoming co-owner and Vice-President. Sarah and Oliver Kinsey moved to Valparaiso in 1881.

Brown was becoming well connected in Valparaiso society. He became an elder in the Christian Church (Disciples of Christ). In 1886, he married Geneva Axe, daughter of Phebe White and Elias Axe, a prominent Valparaiso couple. Geneva Axe Brown (1858–1940) was a member of the Daughters of the American Revolution and a charter member of the Harriet Beecher Stowe Women's Club. She was to have a dominant role in the future of the school.

The Kinsey's also became involved with Valparaiso campus and civic affairs. They were active in the Methodist church. Sarah Porter Kinsey taught geography and grammar at Northern Indiana Normal School, and was the matron of East Hall, the school's first dormitory for women. Oliver Kinsey served on the city and county councils, and he helped establish the city waterworks. The Valparaiso Public Library was organized in 1904 and opened in 1905. Oliver P. Kinsey was on the first library board.

Northern Indiana Normal School rechristened itself in 1900; it took the name Valparaiso *College*. Its enrollment had climbed to 2,500 students. In 1905, with a law school in Valparaiso and with medical and dental school programs in Chicago, it declared itself Valparaiso *University*. Central to fashioning relationships between Valparaiso and the Chicago medical and dental programs was Jasper Newton Roe (1864–1921). His intriguing career spiraled around teaching and administration, around Valparaiso and Chicago, around pharmacy and metallurgy. In 1903–1904, Roe was Dean of Students and Professor of Chemistry, Pharmacy, and Toxicology at Valparaiso. From 1905 to 1913, his home address was in Chicago, and he was no longer Dean of Students at Valparaiso. In 1909–1910, he was Dean of the Department of Pharmacology at Valparaiso, and Professor of Chemistry and Metallurgy at the Chicago College of Dental Surgery. He was listed as a senior student in the 1914–1915 catalog of the Chicago College of Medicine and Surgery, and his title in the faculty listing had become Jasper Newton Roe, A.M., Sc.D., M.D. By 1918, the medical and dental programs had become part of the Loyola Medical School, and Dr. Roe was no longer listed as a faculty member.

By 1910, Valparaiso University was one of the largest American educational enterprises, claimed by its administration to be second in enrollment only to Harvard University and much larger than the undergraduate Harvard College. Enrollment at Valparaiso University continued to increase, peaking at 4,977 in 1914–1915.

Comparison with Harvard made for good student-recruitment publicity. Harvard in 1904 was overwhelmingly the largest American research university, but Harvard's enrollment was growing only insignificantly and Valparaiso's enrollment was soaring. In 1914–1915, Harvard University had 4,534 students. By then, Columbia (5,248), Cornell (5,078), Pennsylvania (5,736), California (5,848), Illinois (5,137), Michigan (5,522), and Wisconsin (4,874) had overtaken Harvard.

Henry Baker Brown was proud to have Valparaiso University called "The Poor Man's Harvard." Whether Valparaiso had ever been a university is debatable. It certainly was not among the institutions that were laying the foundations for becoming research universities. The Morrill Act, signed into law by President Abraham Lincoln on July 2, 1862, gave initial impetus for research as an integral component of higher education in the United States. The Morrill Agricultural College Act of 1890 supplied additional incentive. In earlier chapters, we have seen the beginnings of American research universities: Cornell University in 1865, University of Wisconsin (in 1866 as a land-grant university), Colorado School of Mines and the University of Colorado in 1876, Western Reserve University in 1882, Clark University in 1887, Stanford University in 1891, Indiana University (in 1904 when the Graduate School was established). In each of these cases, governmental funding and/or private philanthropy provided the stability necessary for an institution to weather economic cycles and to outlast any flight of students during wartime.

Brown suffered a debilitating stroke in 1912. Although he retained the title of President of the University, governance and leadership duties passed to Oliver Perry Kinsey. Henry Baker Brown died on September 16, 1917. Even after Brown's death, Kinsey refused the title of "President." Oliver Perry Kinsey retired to Florida in May 1919.

Henry Baker Brown and Oliver Perry Kinsey had been co-proprietors of Valparaiso University, with full prerogatives for dealing with all aspects of the institution. The school was financed from year to year by its students, by its alumni, and by the booster citizens of Valparaiso. The school proudly had no endowment. It had no governing Board of Trustees. The no-frills school had no elaborate graduation ceremonies. Forward-looking colleges and universities were discovering that commencement week, when students, parents, and alumni gather for memorable festivities, is an excellent opportunity for fund raising to increase endowment and provide future financial security. Valparaiso University gave scant evidence of planning for its long-range future.

Although Henry Brown's stroke was unexpected in 1912, the actuarial expectation had to be that an eventual transition of leadership and administration would occur. The two men did not make public their preferences for how a transition should take place. Geneva Axe Brown would control the transition.

When Geneva Brown realized the seriousness of her husband's stroke, she arranged for her 22-year-old son, Henry Kinsey (H. K.) Brown (1890–1941), to become Treasurer of Valparaiso University. Although Valparaiso University pre-

sented outward signs of stability, in retrospect it is clear that the institution had serious structural problems. The University had added new academic programs, in part
to keep pace with a burgeoning enrollment. The University built a Domestic Science
building, and financed its construction with a substantial loan. This may have been
the first borrowing by the school.

Although the consequences for Valparaiso University were not immediately
apparent, Archduke Franz Ferdinand was assassinated on June 28, 1914, in Sarajevo.
Registration for World War military conscription in the United States began in
1917. The University faced a major exodus of students during the 1917–1918 year.
By 1919, enrollment was 1,900, just 38 per cent of the 1914 figure. Because student
fees and tuition comprised most of the funding for on-going operations and for
campus fixed costs, day-to-day finances became problematic.

The United States War Department established the Students' Army Training
Corps (S.A.T.C.), an emergency program that used campuses and faculty of 524 colleges and universities across the country to train men for what might have been
lengthy American involvement in the European war. The War Department paid for
the food, housing, and instruction of these student soldiers. From May 1918 through
November 1918, eight thousand soldiers came to the Valparaiso campus. Federal
funding financed construction of eight temporary barracks, a canteen, and a YMCA
building near the gym. Federal financing vanished after the Armistice was signed on
November 11, 1918. The S.A.T.C. disbanded. The soldiers departed. The barracks
were taken down. Only the YMCA remained.

Emergency wartime measures, such as the S.A.T.C., delayed the day of reckon-
ing, but survival of Valparaiso University required fundamental changes.

In June 1916, some members of the Brown and Kinsey families had proposed a
reorganization plan for the University. Under this plan, ownership and control of the
University would be in the hands of an independent, self-perpetuating Board of
Trustees. The Board of Trustees would be empowered to raise funds, not only for current operations but also for an endowment. The Board would hire personnel, including the President. Implementation of the reorganization plan required that the
owners—Henry Baker Brown (and his family) and Oliver Perry Kinsey (and his
family)—transfer title to the new Board. Geneva Axe Brown would not consent to
the transfer. She had blocked the reorganization plan.

When Oliver Perry Kinsey retired in May 1919, Geneva Brown orchestrated the promotion of 29-year old Henry Kinsey Brown from Treasurer of Valparaiso University to President. A year later, H. K. Brown resigned from the presidency, although not from the administration. H. K. made public the details of the 1916 reorganization plan, but the plan was not implemented until 1920.

The man found to replace H. K. Brown was Daniel Russell Hodgdon. Hodgdon served as President of Valparaiso University for less than a year, from July 1920 to April 23, 1921. His immediate previous position was a stint of less than a year as President of the homeopathic Hahnemann Hospital and Medical College of Chicago. At Hahnemann, he was an outspoken advocate for the Chicago Memorial Foundation "to make Chicago the medical center of the world." Daniel Hodgdon was flamboyant, was marginally competent as an administrator, and perhaps was a charlatan. He certainly had a knack for overstating his academic credentials. He was dismissed for cause (indeed, for a series of enumerated causes) by the newly established Board of Trustees. Valparaiso Professor of German John Edward Roessler followed him, from April 23, 1921, to May 25, 1922. President Roessler served with a fifteen-member Board of Trustees. Six trustees were from the City of Valparaiso, three from Chicago, three from New York, and one each from Hammond, Gary, and Pittsburgh.

President Roessler's one-year term was followed by an even shorter presidency, that of Milo Jesse Bowman (May 25, 1922 to January 1, 1923), Dean of the Valparaiso School of Law. John Roessler and Milo Bowman were respected and capable men, but the presidential legacies of H. K. Brown and Daniel Hodgdon were overwhelming burdens.

Dr. Horace Martin Evans (April 15, 1860–June 1936) was President from January 1, 1923, to January 3, 1926. During these crucial three years, tempestuous outside forces buffeted the Valparaiso University of Brown and Kinsey. Major change was inevitable. Death of the institution seemed possible. Yet Presbyterian President Evans and Lutheran Acting-President John Baur were able to work productively together as capable administrators and personable leaders to smooth the transition into a new Valparaiso era. Before describing the tempest and the first days of that new era, we shall give a short account of Horace Martin Evans, a truly remarkable man.

Horace Martin Evans was born in Harrison County in southern Indiana, near the Ohio River. He was the eldest child of Mary C. McRae and Prof. Isaac W. Evans. Horace attended public schools there, and then entered Northern Indiana Normal School and Business Institute in Valparaiso. On Tuesday, May 30, 1882, he married Anna Maud Skinner of Valparaiso. He completed the business course at Northern Indiana Normal, graduating with a B.S. degree in 1886. It was the heyday of the administration of Henry Baker Brown and Oliver Perry Kinsey.

Brown and Kinsey hired Horace Evans as Professor of Natural Science immediately after his graduation. Evans remained on the Northern Indiana Normal School faculty until 1896. For three winters, he took leaves of absence to attend the Chicago Medical College on the south side of Chicago. Chicago Medical College was affiliated with Northwestern University, and in 1891 changed its name to Northwestern University Medical School. The M.D. degree received by Horace Evans in 1892 was awarded by Northwestern University. He opened a medical practice in Valparaiso in 1892, and continued to teach chemistry laboratory courses at Northern Indiana Normal School.

Drawing inspiration from the career of his father and from the careers of Brown and Kinsey, Horace Evans in 1896 organized the Chattanooga Normal University in Hill City, Tennessee. Evans was the first President of Chattanooga Normal, and one of a very few founding faculty members. The first class of forty-three students who arrived in January 1897 included two of his children (De Forest William and Anna Ruth) and two others from Valparaiso (Herman Lightcap and Fannie Skinner; Fannie was probably related to Mrs. Evans). Some of the students were not yet teenagers. Among the early faculty members was Mary Lyon (A.B. Indiana University, 1895; graduate studies at Adrian College 1897–1898), Chair of Latin and Biology for the year 1898–1899. Chattanooga Normal had a curriculum that nominally culminated in the B.S. degree.

In 1902, Dr. Evans returned for ten years to Valparaiso and to his medical practice. He was the Health Officer of the City of Valparaiso for eight years. He was the local surgeon for the New York, Chicago and St. Louis Railroad (The Nickel Plate Road), and medical director of a life insurance company. He was also active in Valparaiso business affairs: President of Valparaiso First National Bank (now the 1st Source Bank), Vice-President and Director of the First Trust Company in Valparaiso, President of a knitting mill, and President of the Valparaiso Pure Dairy

Product Company. He owned and managed several Porter County farms.

Horace Evans was back in Chattanooga in 1912, associated with a family business—the G. H. Evans Lumber Company, an export enterprise specializing in southern hardwoods. He was the company Vice-President. His son, De Forest, was Secretary and Treasurer. Horace became Secretary of the Chattanooga Chamber of Commerce.

At the outbreak of the Great War, Horace Evans joined the military at age 58. He was appointed Captain in the United States Army on September 25, 1918, to serve in the Reconstruction Division of the Office of the Surgeon General. He was promoted to Major, then to Lieutenant Colonel, and finally to Senior Surgeon, a position that he held in the Public Health Service from February 1, 1920, to June 30, 1922. As Senior Surgeon, he organized and trained staff for 154 educational centers that employed five hundred teachers in hospitals and communities. He was a member of the Federal Board for Vocational Education.

When the Board of Trustees appointed Horace Martin Evans President of Valparaiso University, Dr. Evans brought an impressive set of credentials to the position. He was an alumnus of Northern Indiana Normal School and Business Institute, and had served for a decade on its faculty during the brightest period of the institution. He had been President of Chattanooga Normal University for six years. He had served three years, nine months, and six days in the United States military. He held an earned doctorate from a prestigious university, and had served fourteen years in general medical practice. He had deep roots in the Valparaiso community. He had extensive executive, managerial, and business experience.

The question was not the capability or the dedication of the energetic new President. The question was whether there could be a viable institution under the mantle of Valparaiso University.

Most institutions of higher education in the United States were under stress during mobilization for the Great War and for the short time that the United States was militarily engaged in Europe. Valparaiso was not unique in this regard. However, most colleges and universities recovered quickly, and then experienced substantial growth after the War. Enrollments across the nation doubled between 1919 and 1929. At Valparaiso, however, enrollment declined precipitously. Enrollment in 1915 was 4,977. In 1922, it was 1,200. In 1923, when Horace Evans became President, enrollment was 800.

John D. Rockefeller Sr. pledged fifty million dollars in 1919 to increase endowments of private colleges and universities, each award contingent on the institution raising several times the Rockefeller contribution. Most colleges and universities initiated fund-raising campaigns, partly to increase endowments but mostly to provide new capital for physical facilities. Many institutions raised twice as much in 1929 as they had raised in 1919. For physical plant expansion, the money raised nationally in 1929 was 7.5 times the 1919 figure. With great fanfare in 1920, Valparaiso President Daniel Russel Hodgdon announced a million-dollar campaign. Other schools at the same time were able take advantage of the prosperity of the 1920s to conduct successful campaigns. Hodgdon's Valparaiso campaign was a dismal failure.

And then, with a debt of $375,000, with the North Central Association of Colleges and Schools refusing to accredit the University, with student enrollment plummeting, with the most qualified faculty seeking other positions ... *then* came the symbolic end of Henry Baker Brown's Poor Man's Harvard. Old Main, the building whose cornerstone laying in 1860 symbolized the Methodists' dream of Valparaiso Male and Female College, burned to the ground on Thursday, February 15, 1923. There was neither money nor volunteer labor to remove the charred remains. Little was left to salvage of the 1860 dreams and subsequent accomplishments of the Methodists. Little of tangible value was left of the 1873 dreams and subsequent accomplishments of Henry Baker Brown.

President Horace Martin Evans seemed to have had no choice but to sell out. His problem was that there seemed to be no buyer.

The Ku Klux Klan Enters

Many citizens of Valparaiso believed that the Ku Klux Klan was ready, willing, and able to buy the University in 1923, and that the University was willing to enter into buy-sell negotiations. The Knights of the Ku Klux Klan proclaimed that they were "an Invisible Empire." While activities of the Klan were often publicly visible, the organization was far from transparent. Several scholars have searched fragmentary records of the Indiana Ku Klux Klan and the archives of Valparaiso University to document plausible re-creations of relevant events of summer 1923. Extant contemporary records are scanty. There were few impartial witnesses. There certainly were no impartial major participants. Participants often kept only secret diaries and later burned incriminating papers. Few ever gave interviews.

This account begins with quotations from the contemporary public version of events written by (or at least sanctioned by) Milton Elrod, editor-in-chief of *The Fiery Cross,* a weekly Indianapolis publication of the Indiana Ku Klux Klan. Printed copies of the newspaper still exist. The Friday, August 24, 1923, issue of *The Fiery Cross* attracted widespread attention with the front-page, seven-column banner headline UNIVERSITY TO BECOME NATIONAL INSTITUTION screaming over a two-column sub-head "College at Valparaiso to Become a Monument to American Ideals and Principles." The long article began:

> "True to the announcement appearing in the newspapers throughout the United States last week, the Ku Klux Klan is ready to 'take over' Valparaiso University! ...
>
> "Klan committees from a number of states made favorable reports in regard to the organization behind Valparaiso and all was ready to consummate the deal last week until it was found that, as is usual in many transactions of this magnitude, it was necessary to iron out certain legal tangles before the final consummation of the contracts. Contracts are now being drawn to handle what has heretofore been a tangled mess of technicalities. Milton Elrod, editor of The Fiery Cross, will return to Valparaiso on Wednesday or Thursday with the hope that the matter will be ready for consummation.
>
> "... whatever the Ku Klux Klan starts out to do, it always does. In this instance, the Klan has started to make Valparaiso a great national institution; to make it a monument to American ideals and principles. It has started out to make Valparaiso a self-supporting and self-sustaining institution, amply financed and amply endowed with a $1,000,000 minimum. The title is to be invested in the trustees of Valparaiso University ...
>
> "The Klan has started out to clear the university of all indebtedness and to start it once again, free of encumbrance, rigidly along the path of the original plans of Dr. Henry Baker Brown, who founded the university fifty years ago ..."

Each member of the Valparaiso community had an individual reaction to the unfolding events. Well documented is the reaction of Hugh Cornelius Muldoon (May 7, 1884–May 4, 1956), Dean of the Valparaiso University School of Pharmacy, when the Friday, August 24, 1923 edition of *The Fiery Cross* hit the streets. And "hit the streets" it did. The newspaper had a reputed circulation of half a million. Copies of each issue were available at every Valparaiso store that displayed a TWK (Trade with Klansmen) sign in the window. Copies were distributed as propaganda pieces at frequent mass rallies—"konklaves"—organized throughout Indiana during summer 1923. Klan hawkers were on the streets of Valparaiso with the August 24th edition of *The Fiery Cross* to sell at 5¢ per copy. Teenagers were paid 2¢ for each copy that they sold or delivered to subscribers.

Dean Muldoon had become convinced early that the anti-Catholic Ku Klux Klan would quickly remove him from the faculty in any take-over. He had expressed this concern to President Horace Martin Evans when rumors of Klan interest first surfaced. President Evans promised the Dean to write "as soon as there were any developments that were of importance." The day after the August 24th edition of *The Fiery Cross* hit the streets, President Evans wrote in detail to Dean Muldoon. The Dean was vacationing at his family homestead at the corner of Chemung Street and Sawyer Place in Waverly, Tioga County, New York. The President's letter began with the Klan proposal: "It will mean that we will have all the debts of the Institution paid within ninety days, and within the next ninety days $150,000.00 will be given to the Institution to help meet its expenses the coming year and for repairs and buildings. Then a campaign will be put on for a half-million dollars to endow the school, all of which they hope to have within the year."

Dean Muldoon had previously signified to the President his desire to retire if the Klan took control. The President appealed in his letter to the Dean's loyalty to the Institution. The President continued: "I feel that in justice to our students who are partly through the course that it would be only fair for you to remain at least another year … There will be no desire on my part to have you retire at all … If you find it impossible to remain it would be a very great favor to me if you would suggest someone … to carry on."

Hugh Cornelius Muldoon graduated from Waverly High School and then taught school. He was Principal of Union School in Lockwood, Tioga County, New York, in 1906–1907 and 1907–1908. He entered the Albany College of Pharmacy (now the School of Pharmacy and Pharmaceutical Sciences, Albany College of Pharmacy and Health Sciences, Union University, Albany, New York) on October 5, 1908. After a year of formal study, he left college for apprenticeships at the Abigail M. Littlefield Pharmacy in Troy, New York; pharmacy department of Wm. Sautter & Co. in Albany, New York; and the P. J. Noyes Co. in Mount Washington, New Hampshire. He returned to Albany College of Pharmacy, graduating in 1912 as valedictorian of his class. His valedictory address, "Commercialism in Pharmacy," was printed in the graduation program. The address was also published in *The Druggists Circular* (June 1912), pp. 360–361. His degree was Ph.G. (graduate in pharmacy).

In fall 1912, Hugh Muldoon joined the faculty of the Massachusetts College of Pharmacy (now the Massachusetts College of Pharmacy and Health Sciences) in Boston. His appointment was as Instructor in Analytical and Organic Chemistry. In his second year on the faculty, he initiated a course in "Pharmaceutical Latin," and began writing a textbook for his course. John Wiley & Sons (New York) published his book, *Lessons in Pharmaceutical Latin and Prescription Writing and Interpretation*, in 1916. John Wiley published revised editions in 1925, 1937, and 1946. HardPress published a facsimile reprint which was for sale in 2014.

Hugh Muldoon left Massachusetts College of Pharmacy in 1918 to become Professor of Chemistry at his *alma mater*, Albany College of Pharmacy. As the school year began, Dean William Mansfield took a year's leave of absence because of illness, and Hugh Muldoon became Acting Dean of the College. After Mansfield returned, Muldoon became Head of the Department of Chemistry.

Daniel Russel Hodgdon, during his brief tenure as President of Valparaiso University (July 1920 to April 1921), hired Hugh Cornelius Muldoon as Dean of the Valparaiso School of Pharmacy, effective with the fall semester, 1920–1921. As we have observed, Hugh Muldoon in 1923 began looking for a new position. An opportunity presented itself.

The Very Reverend Martin A. Hehir (1855–1935) became President of Pittsburgh Catholic College (Pittsburgh, Pennsylvania) in 1899. He was to preside over three decades of expansion of the College. The School of Law, the College's first professional school, opened in 1911, and the institution then changed its name to Duquesne University of the Holy Ghost. President Hehir had ambitious plans for adding additional professional schools of Business, Pharmacy, Music, Education, and Nursing.

Hugh Muldoon and President Hehir were in communication about founding a School of Pharmacy at Duquesne. Muldoon had experience in practical pharmaceutical chemistry, in teaching at all levels, in pedagogical innovation, and in academic administration. He had published a well-received textbook, and he had two more books at an advanced stage of preparation, probably under contract: *A Textbook of Organic Chemistry for Students of the Medical Sciences,* and the accompanying *A Laboratory Manual of Organic Chemistry for Students of the Medical Sciences.* These latter two books would be published by P. Blakiston's Son & Co. (Philadelphia) in 1927, eventually going through three editions.

President Hehir wanted to be sure that his projected School of Pharmacy would be quickly accredited, but accreditation could be a problem. Nationally it was being expected that the credentials of a senior faculty member include a doctorate. Muldoon's only academic degree was a two-year 1912 Ph.G. from Albany College of Pharmacy. Although there is no extant documentary evidence, it is likely that there was back-and-forth communication among President Horace Evans of Valparaiso, President Martin Hehir of Duquesne, and Hugh Muldoon about this concern. In any case, Hugh Muldoon signed a contract on Monday, April 20, 1925, as the founding Dean of the School of Pharmacy of Duquesne University of the Holy Ghost. On Friday, June 12, 1925, presumably upon the recommendation of President Horace Evans, the Trustees of Valparaiso University conferred the honorary degree of Doctor of Science on retiring Dean Hugh Cornelius Muldoon. It is customary for an honorary degree to be accompanied by an explanatory citation, but no citation was deposited in the Valparaiso University Archives. Awarding the doctorate to Hugh Muldoon was one of the last actions of *that* Board of Trustees, if indeed the degree was voted in a formal session of the Trustees.

Hugh Muldoon then had an illustrious thirty-year career at Duquesne. He served as Dean of the School of Pharmacy from 1925 until his retirement in 1955. He was elected President of the American Association of Colleges of Pharmacy in 1937. In 1953, he received the Joseph P. Remington Medal of the American Pharmaceutical Association.

The Valparaiso University academic year began in September 1923, with Hugh

Muldoon continuing as Dean of the School of Pharmacy. Muldoon's successor as Dean (surely at Muldoon's suggestion) was Professor George Charles Schicks Jr. (May 11, 1893–July 16, 1961), ranking faculty member of the Valparaiso School of Pharmacy. George Charles Schicks had received the degree of Ph.G. (graduate in pharmacy) from Massachusetts College of Pharmacy on May 27, 1919. Schicks as a student and Muldoon as a faculty member overlapped for at least a year at Massachusetts College of Pharmacy. Schicks had joined the Valparaiso faculty in 1920 as Professor of Materia Medica and Histology.

Valparaiso University awarded George Charles Schicks the Ph.C. degree after a year on the faculty. The contemporary Valparaiso catalog listed the curricula of study in the School of Pharmacy, including "A curriculum comprising two years of three semesters each (72 weeks), and leading to the degree of *Graduate in Pharmacy*, Ph.G.," and "A curriculum comprising two years of four semesters each (96 weeks), and leading to the degree of *Pharmaceutical Chemist*, Ph.C." Dean Muldoon may have been uncomfortable with Schicks teaching in the Pharmaceutical Chemistry curriculum with only the lesser Ph.G. degree. Although perhaps not strictly an honorary degree, Schicks' Ph.C. was not a degree "earned in course" in the conventional manner. Perhaps the appropriate designation would have been Ph.C. *ad eundem*, a degree based on experience, rather than a degree based on explicit qualification.

Schicks was Dean of the School of Pharmacy during the academic year 1925–1926. We shall return to the Schicks affair later in this chapter.

The Klan's public account of take-over negotiations continued in the next issue of *The Fiery Cross*. From the Friday, August 31, 1923, issue, under the somewhat subdued front-page headlines VALPARAISO PLANS MOVING FORWARD, "Trustees Meeting Is Delayed One Week on Account of Snarled Mess Found:"

> "Legal problems covering a period of several years require adjudication. Plans of the Klan to perpetuate Valparaiso university are moving forward as rapidly as possible according to an announcement here today.
>
> "The affairs of Valparaiso university over a period of the last few years have become a tangled, snarled mass of deals and counter-deals, and legal technicalities, requiring considerable time and some of the best minds of the legal fraternity to iron them out.

"While it had been hoped to complete the transactions in connection with the university this week, and while the Klan lawyers are searching for ways and means by which the program can legally be carried out, nevertheless an additional delay of one week was announced when the trustees' meeting called for Valparaiso university on Tuesday, was set forward to September 5, at which time it is hoped to have the entire affair in such shape that public announcement can be made of the entire transaction."

Public clarification of the Klan interpretation of "legal technicalities" came a week later in *The Fiery Cross*. From the Friday, September 7, 1923, issue, under the page-one headlines VALPO TRANSACTION NOW BEING HELD UP BY LEGAL TANGLE, "Clause in Original Charter May Balk Plans of Klan to Aid University, Doubtful That Matter Can Be Legally Consummated, Which Means Abandonment of Plans:"

"The Invisible Empire, Knights of the Ku Klux Klan, may not be legally able to take control of Valparaiso University. Plans were about completed for the transaction which would have made this famous old school an institution national in scope and influence, when a legal snag was struck. It may be eliminated and the plans carried to completion, but the prospect is a gloomy one at present, attorneys claim.

"A clause in the original charter of the university reads in effect that no fraternal, benevolent or eleemosynary order or any religious body shall take over the control of the university at any future date under any consideration.

"The Knights of the Ku Klux Klan are distinctly a benevolent and eleemosynary order, their constitution states. There is the difficulty. ...

"Just when it appeared that the Knights of the Ku Klux Klan would have a national college at which the truest ideals of American national life would be promulgated, this snag was struck.

"Attorneys for the Klan and for the trustees of the school are working together in an effort to find a way out of the difficulty. If it is possible in any legal way to get around the clause in the charter, the representatives of the Klan will do so. Otherwise, the school will have to pass to other hands."

It is unlikely that a "legal snag" involving an eleemosynary order [eleemosynary: of, relating to, or supported by charity] was the reason that the Knights of the Ku Klux Klan publicly abandoned their plans to take control of Valparaiso University. Richard Baepler wrote: "… the deal was off because there was simply no money in the Klan's treasury for the purchase of VU, at least nowhere near the amount needed." Adam Laatz wrote: "The powerful leader of the Indiana Klan, D. C. Stephenson, had completed the final negotiations to purchase Valparaiso University during the summer of 1923. The state's Klan newspaper, *The Fiery Cross,* trumpeted the Klan's goal of turning 'Valpo' into a 'poor man's Harvard.' At the last minute, however, the national leadership pulled out of the deal, and the Indiana Klan could not afford the purchase on its own." According to Neil Betten: "… the only barrier was monetary; and despite the later denials by the University, the Klan, not the school, was the unwilling partner. The national Klan organization in Atlanta, Georgia, vetoed the scheme." Lance Trusty summarized: "Ultimately, greed and corruption [by David Curtis Stephenson (1891–1966), Grand Dragon of the Indiana Ku Klux Klan], rather than a genuine lack of money, halted the Klan purchase of Valparaiso University." In any case, Editor Milton Elrod's prediction would soon become reality. The school would pass to other hands.

Fort Wayne Lutherans Seize an Opportunity

Rev. George F. Schutes (abt 1878–1938), the progressive pastor of Immanuel Lutheran Church in Valparaiso, may have been the first person to advocate effectively for a Lutheran purchase of the University. He was a neighbor of University President Horace Martin Evans. Early in 1925, the two men informally discussed the practicalities of such a business deal. Rev. Schutes contacted Rev. Otto Hermann Pannkoke (1887–1969) and Rev. John C. Baur (1885–1984) to explore the idea further. Pannkoke and Baur were experienced Lutheran leaders, widely known as independent men capable of decisive and aggressive action. They understood practical politics. They knew how to move effectively and quickly.

Within just a few months, before the summer of 1925, Otto Hermann Pannkoke and John C. Baur had assembled their leadership team. During that summer,

Valparaiso University became the first Lutheran University in the United States.

There were already Lutheran institutions of higher education in the United States in 1925, but probably none were yet universities. As we have seen throughout this book, the word "university" has many definitions. For example, Finlandia University was founded in 1896 by J. K. Nikander (1855–1919) in Hancock, Michigan, as Suomi College and Theological Seminary. Rev. Nikander was a mission pastor of the Finnish Evangelical Lutheran Church of America. Originally a two-year institution, Suomi became a four-year college in 1996. Suomi College changed its name to Finlandia University on July 1, 2000. Many present-day Lutheran institutions were seminaries when they adopted the title "university." Capital University was founded in Canton, Ohio, on June 3, 1830, as the Theological Seminary of the Evangelical Lutheran Synod of Ohio. It took the name Capital University on March 2, 1850, when the institution became a seminary for the new Evangelical Lutheran Joint Synod of Ohio and Other States.

To understand how the amazingly rapid series of events occurred in Valparaiso, we need to know more about Pannkoke and Baur, and the men they recruited for their leadership team.

Otto Hermann Pannkoke was born July 12, 1887, in North Dakota. He attended Concordia Seminary in Fort Wayne, graduating in 1908. He was Pastor of St. James Lutheran Church, Golden Valley, North Dakota, from 1909 to 1912. He then moved to New York City to study at Columbia University and at Union Theological Seminary. Such a move was not typical of contemporary graduates of Concordia Seminary.

Union Theological Seminary summarizes its history and mission as follows: "At its founding in 1836, Union was Presbyterian in orientation. But even in those days we welcomed students from all denominations. This was a daringly ecumenical stance in the 19th century.... But Union's commitment to the historical criticism of the Bible thrust the Seminary into the middle of controversy. After the 1892 heresy trial of Union Professor Charles A. Briggs by the Presbyterian Church in the U.S.A., the Seminary rescinded the prerogative of the General Assembly of the Presbyterian Church to veto faculty appointments. This was an irrevocable commitment to academic freedom, to higher academic and scholarly standards, and to independence from any denominational control. The 1910 move to Union's present campus on upper Broadway was another forward looking step that would bring the Seminary into closer association with major New York institutions: Columbia University,

Teachers College, Barnard College, The Riverside Church, The Jewish Theological Seminary of America, and churches and community organizations in Harlem."

Otto Pannkoke became Head of the Lutheran Bureau. Lutheran Bureau was a nonprofit organization, established in 1914 to be independent of official church control but linked by faith and confession to the Lutheran tradition. The Bureau continues today as the American Lutheran Publicity Bureau.

The Lutheran Lenoir College, Hickory, North Carolina, hired Pannkoke in 1919 to direct a $250,000 fund-raising campaign to increase its endowment. When Robert L. Fritz, President of Lenoir College, retired in 1920, the Board of Trustees elected Otto Pannkoke as Fritz's successor. Pannkoke declined the offer, but he did remain associated with the College to direct a $750,000 campaign that began in 1923. Lenoir College awarded Pannkoke the degree Doctor of Divinity *honoris causa* in 1920. The school became Lenoir–Rhyne College in 1923, honoring Daniel Efird Rhyne (1852–1931), a major contributor to the second campaign. Since 2008, it has been Lenoir–Rhyne University.

Lenoir College opened in 1891 with very close ties to the Tennessee Synod of the Evangelical Lutheran Church. Today it is affiliated with the North Carolina Synod of the Evangelical Lutheran Church in America (ELCA), and is associated with the ELCA Lutheran Theological Southern Seminary in Columbia, South Carolina.

In contrast to the history of Lenoir–Rhyne, some other Lutheran educational institutions in the United States have evolved along rather different paths, paths that led to independence from control by a single congregation or a single synod. Augsburg in Minneapolis is an example. The school opened in September 1869, the first seminary founded by Norwegian Lutherans in America. Augsburg College was accredited as a liberal arts college in 1954. A self-study in 1962 defined the College's mission as "serving the good of society first and the interests of the Lutheran Free Church second." Augustana College in Rock Island, Illinois, tells a similar story. The Scandinavian Evangelical Lutheran Augustana Synod founded it as Augustana College and Theological Seminary in 1860. Today: "The College honors its roots and its affiliation with the Evangelical Lutheran Church in America. At the same time, Augustana's rich liberal arts environment is enhanced by diversity."

The shared vision of George F. Schutes, Otto Hermann Pannkoke, and John C. Baur was for Valparaiso to become the first American Lutheran *university*. Their wide experience within Lutheran communities convinced them individually that the ideals of an American university were compatible with the full spectrum of Lutheran beliefs, confessions, and practices, but incompatible with control by a single congregation or a single synod.

John Baur and O. H. Pannkoke were classmates at Concordia Seminary. They had worked together after graduation. They remained close friends. Baur was born November 16, 1885, in Connecticut and raised in New York. His first pastoral work was as a city missionary in New York. He then accepted a call to serve Trinity Suburban Lutheran Church in Fort Wayne, where he was pastor from 1914 to 1919. His residence was in Fort Wayne from 1914 until 1938. Baur was Field Secretary of the American Luther League from 1919 to 1927, with his office in Fort Wayne. Members of the American Luther League were laymen and parochial school teachers; clergy had only advisory roles. Baur was editor of *The Lutheran Layman* during those eight years.

Richard Baepler wrote: "Baur possessed boundless energy and was completely unafraid of crossing the boundaries of traditional formal organizations, not a typical trait of the Missouri Synod's clergy ... Church leaders in Kansas, Oklahoma, and Oregon requested his help in ... antiparochial school battles in their states. The biggest battle in this nationwide contest took place in Michigan, where the Klan, leaders of the Scottish Rite Masons, and other groups formed the Wayne County Civic Association as their political vehicle in a public referendum. Baur and ... Pannkoke formed an alliance of Michigan Lutherans, Roman Catholics, Seventh-Day Adventists, and Christian Reformed. In the end, they succeeded in fashioning a state policy that permitted religiously sponsored education to survive with basic public standards ... Crossing denominational boundaries provoked controversy in the Missouri Synod, and Baur's open disregard for many Missouri cultural and intellectual restrictions was well known."

Baur invited Schutes to meet with faculty (they were largely clergymen) of Concordia College in Fort Wayne, and with members (they all were laymen) of the American Luther League, to present the idea of Lutheranizing Valparaiso. The men of the Concordia College faculty did not seem interested. The men of the American Luther League were enthusiastic, including the National President of the League, Herman Duemling, M.D., a member of St. Paul's Lutheran Church in Fort Wayne.

Herman A. Duemling (September 18, 1871–February 4, 1927) was born in

Addison, Illinois, a village settled by German Lutherans in the 1840s. His parents were Jennie Suelzer and Herman Duemling (1845–1913). In 1864, the Concordia Lutheran Teachers Seminary opened in Addison. (The Seminary moved to River Forest, Illinois, in 1913, and became Concordia University Chicago in 2006.) One of the first teachers in the Valparaiso German–English Lutheran Parochial School, C. Peters, graduated from the Seminary, probably in 1867. The senior Herman Duemling was on the faculty of the Seminary from 1870 to 1874. According to Richard Baepler, Herman Duemling Sr. was "a science professor with a doctorate from a German university." The family moved to Fort Wayne, where the senior Herman Duemling joined the faculty of Concordia College. There he taught science and mathematics from 1874 to 1899. He published a series of arithmetic textbooks, *Practical Arithmetic for the Common Schools of North America*, parts 1, 2, 3, and 4 (St. Louis: Concordia Publishing House, 1880s). He was also an inventor; he patented a process for filling fiber in paper pulp.

The younger Herman A. Duemling attended St. Paul's Lutheran School. He graduated from Concordia College in 1889. In 1892, he received one of the first M.D. degrees awarded by Washington University (St. Louis). He probably received most of his medical education at St. Louis Medical College. St. Louis Medical College affiliated with Washington University in 1891, establishing the Washington University School of Medicine. The Missouri General Assembly chartered Washington University in 1853 as a nonsectarian institution. When chartered, it had no endowment, no connection with a religious organization, no single wealthy patron, and no assured governmental financial support. It survived and prospered, but many similarly situated institutions did not.

Dr. Duemling established a medical practice in Fort Wayne immediately after graduating from medical school. He also became Professor of Anatomy at Fort Wayne College of Medicine, a co-educational medical school established in 1876. It became the Medical Department of Taylor University in 1905. Fort Wayne College of Medicine was one of several predecessors of Indiana University School of Medicine. "… in the year 1902 a number of delegates from the various Lutheran churches of Fort Wayne and vicinity met for the purpose of organizing a hospital association and named it 'The Evangelical Lutheran Hospital Association' of Fort Wayne and vicinity. This association was incorporated in the State of Indiana on the 11th day of November, 1903." Dr. Duemling was appointed Chief Surgeon on the hospital medical staff in 1903.

Among the 1903 Lutheran Hospital officers was the Rev. Paul Stoeppelwerth, Vice-President of the Board of Directors. Paul Stoeppelwerth served Trinity German Lutheran Church in Fort Wayne until November 1, 1914, when he became pastor of St. John's Evangelical Lutheran Church in Peru. Rev. Stoeppelwerth officiated on July 25, 1916, at the wedding in Peru of his niece-in-law, Martha Knechtel, and Frank Erhart Emmanuel Germann.

John Baur sought advice from O. H. Pannkoke, who made an inspection trip to Valparaiso. The principals moved quickly during the last weeks of June 1925. A Central States Division of the National Lutheran Education Association was organized for the immediate purpose of acquiring Valparaiso University for the Lutheran Church. Within a day, the Central District elected an Executive Committee: Herman A. Duemling, President; W. Charles Dickmeyer, Vice-President; Paul F. Miller, Secretary; and Charles J. Scheimann, Treasurer.

W. Charles Dickmeyer (July 1, 1883–November 17, 1968) was a life-long Fort Wayne business executive and a member of the Redeemer Lutheran Church. He attended Lutheran schools. At the time of his death, he was President and Chairman of the Board of Wayne Candies, Inc.

Paul F. Miller, son of the Rev. Jacob William Miller, D.D. (September 16, 1860–May 11, 1933), was a pastor at St. Paul's Lutheran Church in Fort Wayne. He had served as assistant to his father since 1910. Rev. Paul Miller became senior pastor when his father resigned on January 1, 1929, and served St. Paul's for two decades until his own retirement in 1950.

Charles J. Scheimann (October 24, 1862–March 24, 1926) was a Fort Wayne businessman, associated with several enterprises, including the Fort Wayne *Freie Presse* (an evening German-language newspaper), and the Packard Piano Company (where he was Treasurer from 1897 to the day of his death). He attended the parish school of St. Paul's Lutheran Church and then Concordia College (where he was a Trustee for twenty-five years).

In addition to the Executive Committee (Duemling, Dickmeyer, Miller, and Scheimann), the Central District created an Incorporating Committee that included John Baur of Fort Wayne, and George Schutes and Herman Sievers of Valparaiso.

Herman Sievers was a prominent businessman and civic leader in Valparaiso. This group asked Martin H. Luecke Jr. to serve as legal counsel.

Fort Wayne attorney Martin H. Luecke (May 23, 1883–November 2, 1948) was born in the village of Bethalto, Madison County, Illinois, just across the Mississippi River from St. Louis, Missouri. In 1880, Bethalto had a population of 628. His father, the Rev. Dr. Martin H. Luecke (June 22, 1859–April 13, 1926), was President of Concordia College in Fort Wayne from 1903 until his death. The younger Luecke was a 1902 graduate of the Illinois Wesleyan University Law School in Bloomington, Illinois.

The Incorporating Committee members had extensive experience with internal Lutheran politics, and individually they were wary of any arrangements under which a synod or a group of churches could control finances of the University or control operation of the University. They gave Martin Luecke instructions to draft articles of incorporation for two independent entities: the Lutheran University Association and the Valparaiso University Association. The name "Central States Division of the National Lutheran Education Association" was not to appear in either document. The term Lutheran was to be inclusive, allowing the University to operate without certain cultural and intellectual restrictions that some Missouri Synod leaders had urged in the past.

The concept of separating an educational institution from control by a single person, a single congregation, or a single synod was not a new idea. Members of the Incorporating Committee had enough experience with church politics to be confident that such a wall of separation was necessary. Herman A. Duemling Jr., Otto Hermann Pannkoke, John C. Baur, Martin H. Luecke Jr., and Paul Stoeppelwerth had personal experience with consequences of not making this separation. They also had observed successful situations where a wall of separation had been put in place, consciously and conspicuously. Later in this chapter, we shall describe issues in Conover, North Carolina, that resulted from institutional control by a single person, a single congregation, and a single synod. Enmeshed in that Conover story were Otto Hermann Pannkoke, John C. Baur, and William Herman Theodore Dau.

Brothers Paul and Henry Stoeppelwerth (recall Chapter 1) observed a direct comparison of administrative models with and without a wall of separation. Henry in 1893 was the founding faculty member of St. John's College in Winfield, Kansas, where he taught Latin and History for 41 years. He watched Winfield businessman John P. Baden purchase personal control of the institution, even though nominal control was in a corporation and in a Board of Trustees. Henry had observed an alternative model, 350 miles north in Fremont, Nebraska, where Lutheran congregations formed the "Lutheran Orphans' Home Society of Nebraska" in 1892 to build and operate an orphanage in Fremont. The Home Society was explicitly a Lutheran organization without allegiance to any congregation or to any synod.

Early in his pastorate at Trinity German Lutheran Church in Fort Wayne, Paul Stoeppelwerth was involved in the formation of "The Evangelical Lutheran Hospital Association" of Fort Wayne and vicinity. The Association was incorporated on November 11, 1903, to build, organize, and operate the Fort Wayne Lutheran Hospital. He was appointed to the first Board of Directors of the Lutheran Hospital, and served as Vice-President. Herman A. Duemling Jr. was Chief Surgeon. Both clergy and laity were involved in forming the Association and in supervising the operation of the hospital, but a distinct line was drawn between the Fort Wayne Lutheran Hospital and individual church congregations or synods. In 2014: "Lutheran Hospital is directly or indirectly owned by a partnership that proudly includes physician owners, including certain members of the hospital's medical staff." It is a member of the Lutheran Health Network, but not under the control of any congregation or synod.

Martin H. Luecke Jr. was a prominent Fort Wayne lawyer, instrumental in forming the Irene Byron Tuberculosis Sanatorium in Fort Wayne in 1919. He was the first President of its Board of Directors, continuing as President until his death in 1948. He was also Business Manager and Superintendent of the Sanatorium. The Irene Byron Sanatorium was associated with the Indiana Society for the Prevention of Tuberculosis (and its successors), and received some funding from sales of Christmas Seals. President Luecke made sure that there was state and county funding, and that there was local control of the sanatorium. The site is on the National Register of Historic Places, 12371–12407 Lima Road (State Road 3), north of Fort Wayne in Perry Township, Allen County.

Articles of Incorporation of the Lutheran University Association were filed with the Indiana Secretary of State and with the Porter County Recorder on Wednesday, July 15, 1925. The Association was formed to acquire, hold, own, and control real estate and personal property for universities and colleges, and for other religious, charitable, and educational purposes. The Articles of Incorporation gave the Association authority to raise, maintain, invest, and control an endowment fund. Separate articles of incorporation of the Valparaiso University Association were notarized in Fort Wayne and in Valparaiso on Monday, July 27, 1925. This second entity was formed to construct, establish, maintain, operate, and conduct schools, colleges, and universities for educational, literary, scientific, and charitable purposes.

The range of responsibilities and prerogatives listed were traditional for trustees of "educational, literary, scientific, and charitable" institutions. For example, Benjamin Franklin (1706–1790), in a pamphlet that led to the founding of the Public Academy of Philadelphia (now the University of Pennsylvania), proposed "that some persons of leisure and publick spirit, apply for a charter, by which they may be incorporated, with power to erect an academy for the education of youth, to govern the same, provide masters, make rules, receive donations, purchase lands, &c. and to add to their number, from time to time such other persons as they shall judge suitable." The distinctive aspect for the Lutheranizing of Valparaiso University was placing a wall between fund raising and operation. The experienced Lutheran incorporators were wary of potential donors who might seek to influence curriculum, admissions, or staffing.

Milton Elrod had written in his Friday, August 24, 1923, issue of *The Fiery Cross* that "affairs of Valparaiso university over a period of the last few years have become a tangled, snarled mass of deals and counter-deals, and legal technicalities, requiring considerable time and some of the best minds of the legal fraternity to iron them out." Impressive minds were hard at work in summer 1925, but the Lutherans did not require "considerable time." By Tuesday, August 11, 1925, members of the Lutheran University Association Board of Directors had sorted through the tangles and had successfully negotiated with representatives of the Brown family and with all others holding liens against University property and assets. The deed conveying Valparaiso University to the Lutheran University Association was filed with the Porter County Recorder on Saturday, September 12, 1925.

Horace Martin Evans, serving visibly and competently in the presidency, provided the public appearance of continuity and stability when faculty and students arrived for the beginning of the fall semester. Behind the scenes, there was intense activity. On August 24, 1925, O. H. Pannkoke became director of an $883,000 fund-raising campaign, with a goal of $500,000 committed to endowment. Pannkoke already had an enviable fund-raising record of accomplishment. He had recently been director of two campaigns designed to increase the Lenoir College endowment by a million dollars. Pannkoke, reporting on December 14, 1925, that $750,000 was in sight for Valparaiso, turned over the responsibility of completing the campaign to John Baur. Baur also had successful fund-raising experience; he had been head of a $5,000,000 campaign for the Missouri Synod in 1923–1924.

A great many responsibilities were being turned over to John Baur. Baur was in charge of the massive refurbishment of the campus. This involved removal of the remains—fallen bricks, charred timbers, and worse—of Old Main, the historic campus building that burned to the ground in fall 1923. Campus refurbishment involved cleanup of all buildings, interior painting of most buildings, and repairs to a few critical aspects of campus infrastructure. It also involved some real estate transactions: acquisition of buildings and land (and sale of other buildings and land) to consolidate the campus into contiguous parcels.

John Baur was taking steps that he expected would lead to a seamless administrative transition into the new Valparaiso era. Horace Martin Evans would remain President until the work of the fall semester 1925 was completed. Because the Board of Directors of Valparaiso University Association was still searching for a replacement, John Baur became Acting President in January 1926 at the beginning of the spring semester. William Herman Theodore Dau accepted the call to the presidency on Friday, February 12, 1926. Dau would be President-Elect until his inauguration on October 3, 1926. For the next months, there was a *de facto* shared presidency, with roles and responsibilities of Baur and Dau often not clearly delineated.

Dr. A. F. O. Germann Receives a Call

Dean Hugh Cornelius Muldoon was not the only senior member of the faculty who sought and found positions at institutions where the future seemed brighter, or at least more nearly secure. Some of the remaining faculty were glaringly inadequate as teachers or scholars, and John Baur had to make dismissal decisions. Voluntary resignations and necessary dismissals were resulting in a very small continuing faculty.

Among John Baur's responsibilities was locating prospective new faculty. The task was especially challenging in the sciences. Deans at competing colleges and universities were also looking for young scientists with earned doctorates, offering each an attractive opportunity to pursue the experimental research that could launch a productive academic career. Valparaiso could not yet compete in terms of physical facilities. Valparaiso called itself a university, but it could not yet offer the enticement of graduate students and advanced undergraduates to be the working core of a research group. President Dau accepted the presidency because he saw the presidency as the capstone of his illustrious career. Maybe an outstanding scientist could be persuaded to come to Valparaiso with a capstone appointment. John Baur, who had many personal and professional connections in other academic areas, did not know any such scientist.

The enticements John Baur used to recruit faculty would not have tempted Dr. Albert Germann, at age 40 with a wife and three children in Cleveland, to leave Laboratory Products Company and come to Valparaiso for a permanent faculty appointment. John Baur needed Albert Germann for a very different role. Albert Germann had the experience and a network of personal connections for locating appropriate prospective science faculty. John Baur could appeal to Albert Germann's loyalty to education, loyalty to Indiana, and loyalty to the Lutheran Church, by asking him to take on the temporary assignment of salvaging the Chemistry Department and the School of Pharmacy.

How did John Baur identify Albert Germann as the man he needed? Albert Germann had been active in Hoosier Lutheran affairs, especially the Walther League. It was as a delegate from Peru to a Walther League convention in Detroit that Albert met his future wife, Ida Meinke. It would not be surprising (although it is not documented) if John Baur and Albert German had earlier met and even become friends. They were about the same age.

Paul Stoeppelwerth could have recommended Albert to John Baur. Rev. Stoeppelwerth knew the Germann family well. Mary and Gustave Germann (Albert's parents) were members of St. John's Evangelical Lutheran Church in Peru, where Paul Stoeppelwerth was pastor from 1914 until 1928. Mary and Gustave enjoyed praising the accomplishments of their two sons. Paul's niece-in-law, Martha Knechtel, married Frank Germann (Albert's brother) in Peru on July 25, 1916. The Rev. Paul Stoeppelwerth officiated at the wedding. *Herman A. Duemling knew Paul Stoeppelwerth.* Herman A. Duemling was President of the Executive Committee of the Central States Division of the National Lutheran Education Association. Dr. Duemling was Chief Surgeon at Fort Wayne Lutheran Hospital in 1903 when Paul Stoeppelwerth was Vice-President of the Board of Directors of Fort Wayne Lutheran Hospital. *John Baur and Paul Stoeppelwerth had slightly overlapping pastorates in Fort Wayne.* Baur was pastor of Trinity Suburban Lutheran Church in Fort Wayne from 1914 to 1919. Stoeppelwerth was pastor of the Trinity German Lutheran Church in Fort Wayne from 1902 to 1914; he then moved to Peru but remained active in regional Lutheran affairs.

The actual situation may have been quite simple. Strong and enduring friendships were created among Lutherans at colleges and universities. Informal networking relationships, such as those formed in the Indiana University Concordia Club, may explain why Baur reached out to Germann. As one example, see excerpts from a letter written on April 9, 1927, by Albert Germann to Ralph E. Richman, Chairman of the Board's Committee on Instruction:

> "Dear Friend Richman: I have just had a letter from brother Frank telling me about Dr. _____ one of the Lutheran boys at the university when he was there. I strongly suspect that you must have known _____ also. … Frank says he used to chum with him quite a bit; that he is quiet and reserved; but that he has not seen or heard of him since 1914. I do not want to write to _____ until I am sure of my ground. I want particularly to know whether he is still a good Lutheran before writing. Frank is not certain that he attended the meetings of the Concordia Club, but thinks he did. Therefore, there may be some mistake even about his being a Lutheran. Any dope you can give me on this will be very much appreciated."

This letter also reveals what may a significant piece of information. Albert Germann in the letter implies that Ralph Richman (Indiana University Class of 1913) knew Frank Germann (Indiana University Class of 1911) and perhaps Albert Germann (Indiana University undergraduate Class of 1909, A.M. 1910) from their student days. John Baur may have been told by the Chairman of the Committee on Instruction that his college acquaintance, Albert Germann, was the man Valparaiso University needed.

Beyond the speculation, here are the facts: Albert Fredrick Ottomar Germann, A.B., A.M., M.Sc., D.Sc., was Professor of Chemistry and Head of the Department of Chemistry at Valparaiso University when classes opened in fall 1926. He was a senior member of the faculty on Sunday, October 3, 1926, when William H. T. Dau was inaugurated as the first Lutheran President of the University. Albert Germann was later to be Acting Dean of the School of Pharmacy and also Acting President of the University.

Neither Albert Germann nor John Baur moved his family to Valparaiso. Germann's family—his wife Ida and their children Barbara, Edith, and Lucia—moved from Cleveland to Peru, Indiana, where they lived at 123 West 3rd Street with the children's paternal grandparents, Mary and Gustave Germann. The three girls attended the Lutheran St. John's Christian Day School in Peru during the 1926–1927 school year. Albert kept their permanent residence at 1532 East 86th Street, Cleveland, but he spent most of his time in Valparaiso. The home address of John C. Baur (1885–1984), his wife Helen (1882–1956), and their son John Baur Jr. remained 4105 South Calhoun Street in Fort Wayne from 1924 to 1930. The Baur family lived in Fort Wayne from 1914 to 1938.

One of the first candidates Germann brought to Baur's attention was chemist Harry Victor Fuller (October 23, 1880–January 8, 1948). Baur appointed Dr. Fuller Acting Professor of Chemistry for the 1927–1928 academic year.

Harry Fuller was born in Spring Valley, Fillmore County, Minnesota, "where the prairies meet the bluffs." He graduated from high school in Sioux Falls, county seat of Minnehaha County, South Dakota. Although Sioux Falls is now the largest city in South Dakota, it had only 2,164 inhabitants when Harry was born. He joined the 1st South Dakota Volunteer Infantry (as a Private in Company B) in the short Span-ish–American War. The War began with the sinking of the USS *Maine* in Havana Harbor on February 15, 1898; hostilities ended August 12, 1898. After the War, Fuller enrolled in the mechanical engineering course at the University of Minnesota from fall 1900 through spring 1903, receiving the Briggs Prize in Foundry Practice in 1902. He returned to the University in 1905–1906, but did not obtain a degree.

Instead, he travelled to Switzerland and entered the Polytechnic Institute of Zurich (the Eidgenössischen Polytechnikum in Zürich). There he was able to conduct research in analytical chemistry under Frederick Pearson Treadwell. The "Poly" had awarded its first doctorates in 1909. It had changed to its current name of Eidgenössische Technische Hochschule (ETH) before 1912, when Harry Fuller was awarded the Ph.D. with the dissertation "Beiträge zur Gasanalyse." With his doctorate, Fuller became a member of the chemistry faculty at Peiyang University, Tientsien, China. He was Professor of Chemistry at Peiyang until he joined the Valparaiso faculty. While in Tientsien, Fuller was also Head Chemist to the Mint of China and Head Chemist to the Port of Tientsien.

Albert Germann probably became aware of Harry Fuller when both Midwesterners were chemistry graduate students in Switzerland. Albert Germann was at the University of Geneva from the winter semester 1910–1911 through the winter semester 1911–1912. Fuller's mentor, Frederick Pearson Treadwell (born 1857 in Portsmouth, New Hampshire; died 1918 in Zurich) was already well known in the United States. He was author of the three-volume standard treatise *Analytical Chemistry* (first English edition published by John Wiley in New York in 1903). His earlier tabular outline of the methods of inorganic qualitative analysis, *Tabellen zur Qualitativen Analyse* (Berlin: 2nd edition, 1884), was popular among beginning chemistry students. Chemists in the United States were supposed to have a reading knowledge of German, but the "Treadwell Tables" were organized to be useful even for students with little German grammar competence.

The appointment was a capstone appointment for Dr. Fuller. The appointment brought needed prestige to the Valparaiso Department of Chemistry. However competent Dr. Fuller was as an analytical chemist and as an experienced chemistry teacher, he had no independent scholarly publication record as a research chemist and was unlikely to become the vigorous leader that the Department needed for its future. With Harry Fuller, Albert Germann had recommended a scientist with an earned doctorate, but probably not a practicing Lutheran. Fuller's obituary states that he was a member of Porter Lodge No. 137, Free and Accepted Masons, and that his Masonic lodge brothers were in charge of the final funeral rites.

For his research at Laboratory Products Company and at S.M.A., Albert Germann had been following the work of Leroy Sheldon Palmer (1887–1944) and Clarence Henry Eckles (1875–1933) in the Department of Dairy Husbandry of the University of Missouri (Columbia), especially their reports on the natural yellow pigments of milk fat and of plants. A graduate student (Walter E. Thrun) in the University of Missouri Dairy Chemistry Laboratory published a chemical paper in 1916 (with Leroy S. Palmer) that was of particular interest to Germann. The paper reported on methods of chemical analysis of carotene in oleomargarine and in butter. Germann thought that Walter Thrun might be a promising candidate for a faculty position at Valparaiso.

Walter Eugene Thrun (March 22, 1892–August 18, 1951) was born in Bloomfield, Walworth County, Wisconsin, near the Wisconsin–Illinois state line. After high school, he entered Northwestern College, Watertown, Wisconsin. Northwestern College had been established in 1865 by the Wisconsin Synod to train Lutheran pastors in Wisconsin. When the Wisconsin, Minnesota, and Michigan synods joined to form the Evangelical Lutheran Joint Synod of Wisconsin and Other States in 1892, Northwestern College became primarily a college for educating men to serve as pastors throughout that new synod. Perhaps because of a shift in career plans, Walter Thrun transferred to the University of Michigan in Ann Arbor. There he earned an A.B. degree in 1912 and an M.S. degree in 1914. He then received an assistantship in chemistry at the University of Missouri Agricultural Experiment Station in Columbia, and began graduate studies in the Department of Agricultural Chemistry of the University of Missouri. His research, on quantitative chemical analysis of proteins from beef, was under the direction of Perry Fox Trowbridge (April 25, 1866–May 15, 1937), and led to Thrun's Ph.D. degree in 1917.

Thrun's career over the next decade was punctuated by many starts and changes: Instructor in Physical Chemistry at the University of Illinois, World War service in the Army Division of Chemical Warfare and the Army Division of Nutritional Service, a fellowship in the School of Hygiene and Public Health at The Johns Hopkins University, Professor of Chemistry in the Baylor College Medical College, Associate Professor of Chemistry at the Mississippi Agricultural and Mechanical College, Instructor at Lehigh University, and Chemist at the Michigan State College Experiment Station. In reviewing this employment record, Germann must have thought that Walter Thrun could be enticed by a faculty position that held at least a hope of permanency. Germann contacted Thrun with an offer.

Walter Thrun accepted Germann's offer. Thrun was Assistant Professor of Chemistry at Valparaiso University in 1929. He became Associate Professor in 1931, Head of the Chemistry Department in 1932, and Professor in 1939. Perhaps his first research publication from Valparaiso was "A Study of the Soluble Lakes of Aurintricarboxylic Acid," *Journal of Physical Chemistry*, vol. 33, no. 7 (1929), pp. 977–983. This paper reported experimental results that were conducted (as was necessary at Valparaiso at the time) with minimal laboratory equipment. Further publications followed, most reporting research in the area of analytical chemistry.

Germann had a third recommendation for the Chemistry Department. Harold Montgomery Barnett (September 7, 1903–February 20, 1956) was born in Pawnee City, Nebraska. Pawnee City, county seat of Pawnee County, had a population of 1,610 in 1910. He attended Nebraska Wesleyan University in Lincoln, where he was awarded the B.A. degree in 1925. He then entered the graduate program of the Division of Agricultural Biochemistry of the University of Minnesota, Minneapolis, where Dr. Ross Aiken Gortner, Chief of the Division, directed Barnett's research. During summers 1925 and 1926, Barnett held student internships at United States Department of Agriculture Division of Plant Industry field stations in Utah and Arizona.

Ross Aiken Gortner (March 20, 1885–September 30, 1942) was a distinguished physical biochemist. He had a productive five-year research career at the Carnegie Institution's famed Cold Spring Harbor (Long Island, New York) Station for Experimental Evolution, beginning on September 1, 1909. He joined the faculty of the University of Minnesota on August 1, 1914. He was Chief of the Division of Agricultural Biochemistry at the University of Minnesota from August 1917 until his death. Among Gortner's many honors would be his election to the National Academy of Sciences in April 1935.

Albert Germann was looking for a promising young chemist for a Valparaiso University faculty appointment. He was also looking for a promising young chemist to join Laboratory Products Company back in Cleveland. It seems likely that Germann contacted Dr. Gortner late in 1926, asking whether Gortner had a student who might fill both positions, although not necessarily at the same time. Harold Barnett was far enough along in his graduate program to receive the M.S. degree in biochemistry and plant physiology in June 1927. His experimental studies on the amino acid leucine and the peptide dileucine were progressing, and Dr. Gortner felt confident that the work would be completed by the end of 1931. The University of Minnesota did award Barnett the Ph.D. degree in Agricultural Biochemistry and Plant Physiology in 1931.

On Germann's recommendation, the Committee on Instruction voted on Wednesday, May 11, 1927, to offer an instructorship in chemistry to Harold Barnett for the 1927–1928 year. Germann reported on Saturday, May 14, 1927, that Barnett had accepted the offer. Barnett joined S.M.A. in Cleveland in 1929.

Albert asked his brother Frank for recommendations. Frank was then a physical chemist and Professor of Chemistry at the University of Colorado. His earlier education and professional experience had been in physics. Frank Germann suggested Pleasant Ernest Roller as a candidate for a physics position. Frank Germann was familiar with Mr. Roller's credentials: very strong as a physical chemist, and also strong enough to be considered for a faculty appointment as a physicist. Roller had an M.A. in chemistry from the University of Colorado (1923) and an M.S. from the University of Nebraska (1925). He would receive the Ph.D. in chemistry from the University of Colorado at graduation in 1927.

On Albert Germann's recommendation, the Committee on Instruction voted on May 11, 1927, to "secure the services of P. E. Roller of the University of Colorado as the acting head and assistant professor of the Department of Physics." Roller accepted the offer, and joined the faculty for the 1927–1928 academic year. His wife was hired by Valparaiso University as Instructor in English.

Dr. Roller wanted to conduct his own electrochemical research experiments. Those experiments required apparatus that was unavailable in Science Hall at Valparaiso. He arranged to become a Visiting Scientist at the University of Chicago, and was given permission to make electrical measurements at the Sidney A. Kent Chemical Laboratory of the University of Chicago. In the well-equipped Kent Laboratory, he used a new Leeds and Northrup potentiometer with a sensitive wall-projection galvanometer to measure pH with a quinhydrone electrode. He used a precision water thermostat to keep the temperature of the electrode assembly and the sample controlled at 25 °C ± 0.02°.

Hiring P. E. Roller for the Valparaiso Physics Department also turned out to be successful recruiting for S.M.A. A 1931 paper by Roller was a "Contribution from the Research Division of The S.M.A. Corporation, Cleveland, Ohio." At the end of that paper: "It is a pleasure to acknowledge the valuable assistance rendered by Dr. A. F. O. Germann, Director of the Research Laboratory of The S.M.A. Corporation."

William Herman Theodore Dau

The inauguration of William Herman Theodore Dau (February 8, 1864–April 21, 1944) as the first Lutheran President of Valparaiso University was on campus, Sunday, October 3, 1926. The outside temperature was 75 °F, and it was raining heavily in Valparaiso. Then the rains ended. The Monday morning sunlight revealed the bright colors of glistening autumn leaves on the campus hardwood trees. It was the first week of a new Valparaiso University.

William Dau was born in the town of Lauenburg (now Lębork) on the western periphery of Pomerelia (now part of the Polish Pomeranian province). The Dau family came to America in 1881, and settled in Detroit, Michigan. His family joined many Lutherans who had emigrated from Pomerelia, reacting to forced mergers of Prussian Calvinist and Lutheran confessions ordered in 1817 by King Friedrich Wilhelm III. The first wave of about three thousand Lutherans arrived in America from 1839 to 1843. Tens of thousands followed during the next decades.

The Rev. Johannes Adam Heugli (1860-1902), pastor of Trinity Lutheran Church in downtown Detroit, noticed young William Dau reading Latin in his father's tailor shop. Heugli encouraged him to prepare for the Lutheran ministry. William Dau entered Concordia College in Fort Wayne in 1882. At that time, Concordia College served as a German Gymnasium, a Missouri Synod preparatory school for Concordia Seminary in St. Louis. Dau followed the conventional educational route directly from Gymnasium to Seminary, entering the Seminary in 1883. Founded in 1839, Concordia Seminary was the second oldest Lutheran seminary in the United States. Its primary mission was to educate Lutheran pastors, missionaries, and church leaders. Dau graduated from Concordia Seminary in 1886 at age 22.

His first pastorate was "The German Evangelical Lutheran Trinity Church of the Unaltered Augsburg Confession of the City of Memphis, State of Tennessee" (now Trinity Lutheran Church in Memphis), established thirty years earlier by a student missionary from Concordia Seminary. When W. H. T. Dau arrived in Memphis, he found an empty new church building that had been constructed between 1874 and 1878. The building was unfurnished and unused because of the devastating yellow fever epidemic of 1878. Sixty percent of the population of Memphis fled during the epidemic; few returned. Most people who remained in the city became ill; five thousand died. A major task of Dau's first two years was leading the congregation's recovery effort. Services finally were held in the new sanctuary in 1888. Dau also taught in Trinity's parochial school.

Sherrie Otte, Trinity Lutheran Church Historian, reports: "We are very fortunate in having the church council meeting minutes from that time translated and compiled from their original German into English. In reviewing these notes, it appears that Pastor Dau not only served Trinity well, but he was also very active in working with Lutheran families in the region. He traveled often to many areas in Tennessee; in the first few months of 1891, for example, he visited Milan, Jackson, Trenton, Nashville, Greenbriar, Ridgetop, and Mimmick (cities spread out over 5 counties in western and central Tennessee), offering communion and baptism to Lutheran families, while also researching the possibilities of establishing new congregations.

"Pastor Dau was apparently much loved and respected at Trinity. In April, 1891, in response to a call to Pastor Dau from Evangelical Lutheran Church in Lenox, Michigan, the elders at Trinity wrote a letter, which reads in part: 'We your dear brothers of the congregation in Memphis, Tennessee, have decided to write to you dear brothers in the Ev. Luth. congregation in Lenox to please leave our dear Pastor to us and not to covet him. We decided that we will not let him go. We hope you will be strong and get a pastor soon'."

Rev. Dau stayed with the Memphis parish until 1892, when the congregation of Concordia Lutheran Church (Conover, North Carolina) called him to be their pastor. Conover installed him on Sunday, May 29, 1892. The congregation also called George A. Romoser (1870–July 9, 1936), a spring 1892 graduate of Concordia Seminary. Romoser was ordained and installed on Sunday, July 31, 1892. The two men were called formally to serve a single church, but that church did not need two ministers. Dau and Romoser were called to help unravel an entrenched entanglement with an educational institution in Conover and another educational institution in nearby Hickory. There were also significant synodic disputes.

Concordia College in Conover began as Concordia High School in 1877, with

Robert Anderson Yoder (August 16, 1854–May 16, 1911) and his wife Rosa Eliza-beth Fisher (March 11, 1855–April 12, 1924) as its only teachers. The Concordia College Association of the Evangelical Lutheran Church was soon formed, and a school building was constructed. Mr. Yoder organized a group of Lutherans that met for worship in the College assembly hall, beginning Sunday, September 8, 1878. There appears to have been little desire to separate the Church and the College. Mr. Yoder served the Concordia Congregation as pastor and the Concordia College as head and teacher.

Ten miles away in Hickory, Watauga County lawyer Walter Waightstill Lenoir (1823–1890) had offered 17½ acres of land "to any Protestant church which would establish a college." Lenoir had served as a Captain of Company A of the 37th North Carolina Infantry Regiment in the Civil War. After Captain Lenoir died in July 1890, his executor made the offer more enticing by adding thirty-six adjoining acres to the bribe. At the same time, jurisdictional divisions surfaced between the Tennes-see Synod and the English Synod of Missouri. Mr. Yoder, many faculty members, and some students decided to leave Concordia College to form Highland College in Hickory. Highland College opened in September 1891, under the auspices of the Tennessee Synod. Four months later the College changed its name to Lenoir Col-lege, acknowledging its Hickory financial benefactor.

There may have been compelling theological or doctrinal reasons for the decision by some Conover folk to leave the English Synod of Missouri. Robert Anderson Yoder may have been a charismatic leader. A contigent of faculty and students fol-lowed Yoder ten miles to Hickory. Walter Waightstill Lenoir and his executor may have bought their allegiance. There may have been face-to-face confrontations. There certainly were heated confrontations in print. Yoder published a 48-page tract [Rob-ert Anderson Yoder, *The Situation in North Carolina* (Enterprise Job Office, 1894)] that provoked a prompt 46-page printed response [W. H. T. Dau, Geo. A. Romoser, J. M. Smith, L. Buchheimer, C. L. Coon and C. H. Bernheim (on the title page: "by a committee"), *Review of Prof. Yoder's "Situation in North Carolina"* (1894)].

Recall Otto Hermann Pannkoke, the man who (with John C. Baur) had a central role in making possible the Lutheranization of Valparaiso University. Lenior College would hire O. H. Pannkoke in 1919 to direct a $250,000 fund-raising campaign. Len-ior College offered Pannkoke its presidency in 1920, and awarded him the honorary

Doctor of Divinity degree in 1920. It seems unlikely that Pannkoke, working so closely with Lenoir College and its prospective benefactors, could have been unaware of the Concordia College–Highland College schism, and the role played by W. H. T. Dau in a fiery in-print exchange between Conover and Hickory partisans in 1894.

The Tennessee Synod severed all ties with Concordia College. In March 1892, the English Synod of Missouri accepted Concordia College as its own institution, appointing members to the Board of Trustees, supplementing faculty salaries, and executing a complete transfer of the College and its assets to the Synod. There had been no realistic separation of church and college in Conover, and it was the undisguised intention of the congregation for Rev. Dau to become President of Concordia College. Within a year of his installation, W. H. T. Dau resigned as *pastor* "to enable him to devote his time and strength to his other work"—the presidency of the College.

In practical terms, physical separation was required for the church to thrive. The church had been worshipping in the auditorium of the College administration building for sixteen years. The congregation needed its own sanctuary. It hired an architect, but decided to serve as its own contractor. Bricks for the construction were handmade by the members from Conover clay, baked in the sun to dry, and then fired in kilns built along the railroad tracks. The College buildings were renovated at the same time. The Church dedicated its new building on Reformation Day, October 31, 1897. Concordia College continued until a fire destroyed the main building in 1935. The successor Missouri Synod church is St. John's Lutheran Church, on Saint John's Church Road in Conover.

Rev. W. H. T. Dau served as President of Concordia College from 1892 to 1899, followed by George Romoser from 1899 to 1911. Dau was called in 1899 to be pastor of St. Paul's Evangelical Lutheran Church in Hammond, Indiana, almost on the Indiana–Illinois state line. Hammond and Valparaiso are 35 miles apart in the "Calumet Region" of extreme northwest Indiana. Dau came to Hammond just in time to participate in construction of a new building, a building that the congregation boasted "was the first Protestant church of its size in the Calumet Region." The church was dedicated in 1903. Dau remained in the Hammond pulpit until 1905.

The career of William Herman Theodore Dau moved into a different phase in 1905. What was also happening in 1905?

Theodore Roosevelt was President of the United States. Albert Germann was a student at Indiana University in Bloomington; he had matriculated on June 24, 1904. Ida Helene Johanna Meinke had just completed school in the Village of Royal Oak, Michigan. Frank Germann was a junior in Peru High School; he would graduate in 1906. Martha Minna Maria Knechtel was a freshman in Fremont (Nebraska) High School. Rev. Paul Stoeppelwerth was serving Trinity German Lutheran Church in Fort Wayne. Alumnus Horace Martin Evans had been on the faculty of Northern Indiana Normal School and Business Institute, and was practicing medicine in Valparaiso; he had received the M.D. degree from Northwestern University in 1892. John C. Baur and Otto Hermann Pannkoke were classmates at Concordia Seminary in Fort Wayne; they would graduate in 1908. In 1905, with a law school in Valparaiso and with medical and dental school programs in Chicago, Valparaiso College declared itself a university. By 1910, Valparaiso would claim to be the second largest university in the United States, "The Poor Man's Harvard." Henry Ford had been manufacturing automobiles since 1903; there would be nineteen models until he introduced his Model T on August 12, 1908. In Huntington, Indiana, Nick Freienstein (1876–1941) began selling breaded tenderloin sandwiches; the iconic pork tenderloin would still be at the top of the menu at Nick's Kitchen in 2014.

From 1905 until 1926, W. H. T. Dau was back in St. Louis at his Alma Mater, Concordia Seminary. One of his first duties at the Seminary was to replace the late Augustus Lawrence Gräbner (July 10, 1849–December 7, 1904; professor at Concordia Seminary, St. Louis, 1887–1904) as editor of the *Theological Quarterly*. Professor Gräbner had been one of Dau's teachers at Concordia Seminary before 1886. It appears that Dau's entire formal education in the United States was at Concordia College and Concordia Seminary. He had the title of Professor of Theology in 1905.

Among the first of his many publications during his tenure at Concordia Seminary was a ninety-page collection of seven Holy Week meditations—*He Loved Me, and Gave Himself for Me: For the Quiet Hour During Holy Week* (St. Louis, Missouri: Concordia Publishing House, 1910). He authored a three-volume series, *Leaves from the Story of Luther's Life:* "The Leipzig Debate in 1519" (St. Louis: Concordia, 1919; preface dated November 19, 1918); "The Great Renunciation" (St. Louis: Concordia, 1920); and "At the Tribunal of Caesar" (St. Louis: Concordia, 1921). Dau also collaborated with Gerhard Friedrich Bente (January 22, 1858–December 15, 1930) in editing and translating the *Concordia Triglotta: The Symbolical Books of the Evangelical*

Lutheran Church, German-Latin-English (St. Louis: Concordia, 1921), 1285 pages.

Professor Dau served as vacancy pastor at Trinity Lutheran Church in St. Louis from April 1914 until January 1915. Trinity Lutheran Church, established in 1839, was the first German Lutheran church in St. Louis, and is the oldest Lutheran congregation west of the Mississippi River. Trinity was the mother church of Holy Cross, Immanuel, and Zion Lutheran churches in St. Louis.

William Herman Theodore Dau accepted the appointment as President of Valparaiso University on February 12, 1926. At age 62, his reputation as a Lutheran theologian was secure. His appointment brought reassurance to many Lutherans that the University was in theologically safe hands. He had received the degree of Doctor of Divinity *honoris causa* from the Lutheran Immanuel Seminary in North Adelaide, Australia, in 1923. After two decades as a seminary teacher and respected scholar, Dau may have envisioned his new role as comparable to the gracious living enjoyed by Franz August Otto Pieper (June 27, 1852–June 3, 1931), then President of Concordia Seminary.

In many respects, however, his new role was as a rebuilder, reminiscent of the demanding physical tasks in his first pastorates. He had been restoration pastor of The German Evangelical Lutheran Trinity Church of the Unaltered Augsburg Confession of the City of Memphis. He had been a literal bricks-and-mortar builder when pastor of Concordia Lutheran Church in Conover. He had played a central role in completing physical construction as pastor of St. Paul's Evangelical Lutheran Church in Hammond. As he worked alongside John Baur, Dau's role at Valparaiso was reminiscent of his experiences in sharing leadership with George A. Romoser at Concordia Lutheran Church and Concordia College in Conover, where the delineation between Church and College, between pastor and president, was often unclear. As successor to President Horace Martin Evans at Valparaiso, Dau was replaying his 1890s role when he had replaced Robert Anderson Yoder during a dramatic institutional change in Conover.

Biological Evolution in the Curriculum

Richard Baepler wrote: "In the 1920s and 1930s, the most visible intellectual issue for many religiously traditional church colleges was evolution. The course on evolution disappeared from the [Valparaiso] catalog when the Lutherans remodeled the University, and President Dau checked the textbooks used on the campus for signs of this controversial theory. He reported that there was no 'objectionable' textbook in use except for one in geology. But he believed that the 'skill and piety' of the professor would adequately deal with whatever issues arose in this regard."

Biological evolution was certainly visible on campus and throughout the nation when William Herman Theodore Dau became President of Valparaiso University. The Scopes Trial was front-page news in summer 1925, as Clarence Seward Darrow (1857–1938) and William Jennings Bryan (1860–1925) argued the case *State of Tennessee v. John Thomas Scopes* in the Rhea County courthouse in Dayton, Tennessee. John Thomas Scopes (1900–1970) had been arrested for teaching evolution in a Tennessee public high school, in violation of a just-enacted 1925 state law. Clear-channel WGN in Chicago aired the first on-the-scene radio coverage of a criminal trial. Defense attorney Clarence Seward Darrow called biologist David Starr Jordan, former President of Indiana University and the first President of Stanford University, to testify in defense of Mr. Scopes and in defense of biological evolution. Presbyterian layman and three-time United States presidential candidate William Jennings Bryan argued for the prosecution, characterizing evolutionary ideas as the nemesis of Christian civilization. Prominent on the national stage, vehemently criticizing evolution and evolutionists, were such flamboyant Protestant evangelists as Billy Sunday (William Ashley Sunday, 1862–1935), then preaching from his tabernacle in Winona Lake, Indiana; and Aimee Semple McPherson (1890–1944), a vocal supporter of Bryan during the Scopes Trial. Bryan died just after the trial, on July 26, 1925, in Dayton, Tennessee.

Dau could not have avoided the influence of Augustus Lawrence Gräbner (July 10, 1849–December 7, 1904; Dau's predecessor as editor of the *Theological Quarterly*) and his son Theodore Conrad Graebner (November 23, 1876–November 14, 1950; professor at Concordia Seminary, St. Louis, 1913–1950). A. L. Gräbner was managing editor of the *Theological Quarterly* in 1902 when he published an article, "Science and the Church," in the *Quarterly*. In the article, he wrote:

"There is, however, one thing in which a Christian synod can be and should be a unit, and that is the doctrine of the inerrancy of the Bible, the whole Bible, from Genesis to Revelation. And as the word of God is truth, God's truth, and as two contradictory propositions cannot both be true, a Christian synod can and should unanimously reject whatever, be it in theology or elsewhere, it may find in open conflict with any statement of the word of God. The Bible is not a textbook of Zoology or Biology or Astronomy, claiming for itself the authority secured by the most careful and extended human investigations, observation and speculation. Its claims are infinitely higher. The authority of human scientists is never more than human; that of the Scriptures is everywhere divine. The omniscient Creator knows more about his handiwork than any created mind. Where the statements of many and great scientists are in conflict with those of the Bible, the latter must prevail, not although, but because, the Bible is not a scientific text-book, but more, the word and truth of God. A Christian may not, and a whole church, under present conditions, cannot, be familiar with the science of Biology, and no man is competent either to approve or to disapprove what he does not know. But when Darwinists assert that man is a product of ages of evolution from inferior organisms, while the Bible plainly teaches a different origin and descent of man, every Christian of average intelligence may consistently and promptly reject the said Darwinian error where or in whatever form it may confront him, and a synod might and should unhesitantly condemn it whenever it crossed its path, though no member of the synod had read the *Origins of Species* or the *Descent of Man.*"

Theodore Conrad Graebner was a prolific anti-evolution writer. He disagreed with his father's assertion that "two contradictory propositions cannot both be true." The Rev. John A. Leimer, pastor of the Hope Evangelical Lutheran Church in Chicago, in 1938 wrote T. C. Graebner: "A young man of my church, a graduate of

Northwestern university, a student of geology, is troubled with respect to his faith in the divine inspiration of Scripture." Graebner's immediate reply: "Your young man must keep his geology and his Genesis in two compartments with a water-tight bulkhead between. He must not deny evident facts which are disclosed by the earth's layers and he must not give up his faith in the Bible because he cannot harmonize historical geology with the record in Genesis. It may be said that such contradictions imply an either/or, but experience proves that we get along with others of the same nature right in the field of science and they don't trouble us. Nothing can be more contradictory than the theory which makes light composed of waves and the other theory which deals in quanta, or small particles. Light cannot be both yet IT IS."

Regardless of President Dau's views on Biblical inerrancy concerning creation, he knew that the University could not afford politically to become involved with the explosive evolution controversy. How could he recruit outstanding young scientists who would, in good conscience and without compromising their intellectual integrity, keep evolution out of their classrooms?

Among the first faculty recruited by Dau and Baur were young scientists Louis Frederick Heimlich (April 13, 1890–October 12, 1928) and Alfred Herman Ludwig Meyer (February 27, 1893–February 27, 1988). Heimlich, just completing his doctorate at the University of Wisconsin when offered a position at Valparaiso, was appointed Professor of Botany and Head of the Department of Botany. He was soon named Dean of the College of Liberal Arts. He was immediately given wide responsibility for "remodeling the science curricula." On March 18, 1927, the Committee on Instruction appointed Heimlich to additional positions: Acting Head of the Department of Geology and Acting Head of the Department of Zoology. Alfred Meyer had a 1921 B.A. in General Studies and a 1923 A.M. in Geology from the University of Illinois. Meyer's appointment was as Instructor in Geology at Valparaiso.

Louis Frederick Heimlich was born in the small town of Reynolds, Honey Creek Township, White County, Indiana. Reynolds had a population of 348 in 1890. He attended the public and Lutheran parochial schools of Monticello and Lafayette, Indiana. He entered Purdue University in 1910, and received the B.S. degree in 1914 and the M.S. degree in 1916, both in Botany. He taught at Purdue, beginning in 1914. He pursued graduate studies at the University of Wisconsin during summers, and then in

1924 for an entire year. Heimlich received the Ph.D. from the University of Wisconsin in June 1926 with the dissertation "The Development and Anatomy of the Staminate Flower of the Cucumber." He was an active member of the Lutheran Church.

If Louis Frederick Heimlich perceived a conflict between his religious beliefs and biological evolution, he found ways to direct his biological research to sidestep any such conflict. He focused on taxonomy and morphology of existing Indiana flora. He collected native Hoosier plants, systemizing his collections by constructing a detailed taxonomic key. He used his privately published key in classes at Purdue and at Valparaiso. Heimlich was revising this key at the time of his death. Seven publications of his botanical research from 1914 to 1927 appeared in the *Proceedings of the Indiana Academy of Sciences*. His last scholarly paper, "Microsporogenesis in the Cucumber," appeared in the prestigious *Proceedings of the National Academy of Sciences*.

Heimlich's untimely death from pneumonia at the beginning of the 1928–1929 school year initiated a faculty search for another young biologist who could carry forth a creditable research program that was independent of evolutionary theory. The man selected was zoologist Frank Roy Elliott (May 19, 1888–October 17, 1965).

Born in the unincorporated village of Spartansburg, Greensfork Township, Randolph County, Indiana, Frank Elliott was reared and educated as a Quaker. He graduated from Richmond (Indiana) High School, and studied at Earlham College in Richmond. He received the B.S. degree in 1911 and the A.M. degree in 1912, both from Earlham. Frank Elliott taught at the Quaker colleges Earlham and Wilmington (Wilmington, Ohio), and at The Ohio State University (Athens, Ohio), while pursuing doctoral studies at Ohio State. He spent summers 1913, 1915, and 1916 at the Lake Erie Biological Station of The Ohio State University (on Sandusky Bay at Cedar Point), working with Herbert Osborn, Director and Professor of Zoology and Entomology. Frank Elliott was awarded the Ph.D. degree in 1929 by Ohio State, with the thesis "An Ecological Study of the Spiders of the Beech–Maple Forest." The focus of his doctoral research was an eighty-acre beech and maple woodland, known as Lewis Woods, near Earlham College.

Elliott was appointed Associate Professor at Valparaiso for the 1929–1930 academic year. During his quarter-century career at Valparaiso, he became the preeminent spider specialist in Indiana and the recognized authority on classification of existing Indiana spiders. Frank Roy Elliott may have felt able in his zoological research to insulate his classification of spiders from evolutionary theory. He may have believed that he could avoid confrontation with evolutionary theory when teaching about diversity of spiders. Many present-day philosophers of biology believe that such insulation is, at best, naive.

The philosophy of the Department of Biology in 2015 with respect to evolution: "The biology faculty is dedicated to the highest standards of scientific ethics and intellectual integrity, and those values lead to the department's philosophical position on teaching evolution. The faculty uses evolutionary principles as a central, unifying framework for understanding the unity and the diversity of the living world, while remaining sensitive to the faith roots of its students and alumni."

The eighteenth- and nineteenth-century European scientific revolution in *chemistry* seems remarkably free of conflicts with religious orthodoxy, even though some eminent practitioners of chemistry were able get themselves into deep personal trouble with the establishments. The house of Joseph Priestley (1733–1804) was burned in the name of religion, and Antoine-Laurent Lavoisier (1743–1794) was guillotined. Neither action was in reaction to the man's science. There is no suggestion that either Albert Germann or Frank Germann (or any of the new faculty appointees at Valparaiso in physics, chemistry, or pharmacy) publicly expressed a conflict between theology and their professional work in the laboratory or in the classroom. However, a significant issue *did* arise at Valparaiso University in geology.

Dau discovered an "objectionable" geology textbook in use at Valparaiso, but expressed confidence in the "skill and piety" of the professor to deal with evolutionary issues. The professor was Alfred Herman Ludwig Meyer (February 27, 1893–February 27, 1988).

Alfred Meyer was born in Venedy, Washington County, Illinois, a rural village with a population of only 177 in 1900. Venedy was founded as Die Evangelishe Brockschmidt Hill about 1840 by Lutheran pastor Ottomar Fuerbringer and six families. At the center of the village is St. Salvator Lutheran Church. Rev. Fuerbringer helped found the "German Evangelical Lutheran Synod of Missouri, Ohio, and Other States" (now the Missouri Synod) in 1847. The St. Salvator congregation joined the new Synod in 1848.

Alfred was the youngest of the eight children of Marie (September 1, 1853–January 4, 1934) and William (December 26, 1842–August 5, 1932) Meyer. William was a pioneer flour miller in Venedy. Alfred attended the one-teacher St. Salvator

Lutheran School during the mornings and the Venedy public one-teacher school during the afternoons. With mastery of the common-school curriculum, and with evident motivation toward self-education, he was hired in 1910 at age seventeen to be the teacher in a one-room public school in Linneman, six miles south of Venedy.

Conforming to the local agricultural planting, cultivating, and harvesting calendar, his teaching duties were confined to the late fall, the winter, and the early spring. From 1911 to 1914, he was the teacher in the Venedy public one-room school. Summer was thus available for him to continue his formal education. Alfred enrolled at Southern Illinois State Normal University at Carbondale (now Southern Illinois University) on June 12, 1911. Southern Illinois advertised that its spring and summer terms were designed to accommodate the teaching schedules of local schoolteachers: "By entering first part of spring term and remaining throughout summer session one may get a full half-year of normal training." Southern Illinois offered a full range of high school "review courses," and served as the high school for many of its students.

Alfred attended Eastern Illinois State Normal School in Charleston (now Eastern Illinois University) in 1912–1913. He entered as a member of the "First Year of the Four-Year Course," meaning that he had about the educational attainment of someone with two years of high school. Some of that attainment may have been the result of self-education; part of it was certainly earned the previous year at Southern Illinois State Normal University. Alfred's name appears again in the Southern Illinois State enrollment register for the spring 1914 term. He may have attended Eastern in the summer of 1915.

He matriculated at McKendree College at Lebanon on September 16, 1916, attending classes during the fall and spring terms. Originally named Lebanon Seminary, McKendree is the oldest college in Illinois. The school became McKendree University in July 2007.

Alfred entered the University of Illinois at Urbana on September 20, 1917. He had already registered for the pre-World War military draft, and he may have joined the Students' Army Training Corps organized on campus a year later (on September 2, 1918). Among courses offered Students' Army Training Corps students who wished to become officers were "Surveying" and "Map-Making." Alfred served in the Special Officers Training Company at Camp Hancock near Augusta, Georgia.

In senior year at the University of Illinois, Alfred was a member of the Chemistry Club and the Lutheran Concordia Club. His major was Geology. He received an A.B. degree in General Studies on Wednesday, June 15, 1921. He then enrolled in the graduate program in Geology at the University of Illinois. He submitted a master's thesis, "Geological Survey of the Vermont, Illinois Quadrangle," and was awarded the A.M. degree in Geology in 1923. He also matriculated at the Graduate School of the University of Chicago on Wednesday, June 8, 1921 (a week before he received his A.B. from the University of Illinois), and took classes during the summer quarters of 1921, 1924, and 1926.

Ronald L. Numbers has written about experiences of Missouri Synod Lutheran Geologist Alfred Meyer: "… early in 1923, as he was completing the requirements for a master's degree in geology from Illinois, he plunged into a heartrending crisis of confidence. Having recently read antievolution books by [George McCready] Price and fellow Lutheran Theodore Graebner, he despaired of being able 'in good faith even [to] take up the practice as I had planned to do, that is, to seek employment as an oil geologist to do field, laboratory, or office work.' He greatly admired Price's 'high Christian ideal' and hoped that the crusader's forthcoming *New Geology* would 'reform science as Luther had reformed religion.' Sinking slowly into a quagmire of scrupulosity, he came to fear that even using the language of historical geology was sinful. After submitting a copy of his thesis to the university library, he began obsessing about a chapter that mentioned the phrase 'Biological Development.' So great was his 'spiritual anguish,' he considered petitioning to have his thesis withdrawn and destroyed."

Did Alfred Meyer take action to withdraw his thesis? The answer does not seem to be a matter of existing record. The University of Illinois maintains a card catalog of all theses submitted for graduate degrees, and in that catalog is a card for "Meyer, Alfred Herman. 'Geological Survey of the Vermont, Illinois quadrangle.' call number 1923 M57." However, there is no entry for the thesis in the most recent University online electronic library catalog. The Curator of the University Rare Book & Manuscript Library believes that the thesis is not in the main collection ("it has a particular kind of call number that doesn't match with anything else," so there would be no shelving location for it in the book stacks). The thesis is not in the Rare Book & Manuscript Library, and it is not in the University Archives. The Curator states:

"I'm uncertain where this thesis may have gone, as it appears the University did at one time hold a copy of this thesis."

Determined to avoid a career in geology, Meyer investigated possibilities in the kindred academic fields of geography and cartography where he might avoid confrontation with Scripture. He appears to have attended seminars and perhaps classes at Northwestern University during summers while teaching in Chicago area schools. He may have taught from 1925 to 1926 at Luther Institute, a secondary school in Englewood on Chicago's south side. As noted earlier, he attended the University of Chicago as a graduate student in the summer quarters of 1921, 1924, and 1926.

As a practicing Missouri Synod Lutheran living in the Chicago area, and a credentialed scientist in search of employment, Meyer must have been aware of the Lutheran activity in nearby Valparaiso. When the deed conveying Valparaiso University to the Lutheran University Association was filed with the Porter County Recorder on September 12, 1925 (with extensive newspaper coverage), the time would have been ripe for Meyer to apply for a teaching position at the "new" Valparaiso University. However the initial contact was made, we do know that Meyer joined the faculty for the 1926–1927 academic year as Instructor in Geology.

Although appointed to teach geology at Valparaiso University, Meyer sought to avoid the word *geology* (and, insofar as he was able, the subject matter of historical geology), both in his teaching and also in his research. He persuaded the University to create a Department of Geography and Geology, allowing him to focus on what he thought were the theologically safe fields of cartography and *geography*. He was able to shift the departmental emphasis further away from geology; by 1931, the department had become the Department of Geography and Meteorology, a name that continues to this day.

While continuing to teach at Valparaiso, Meyer entered a graduate program in geography at the University of Michigan, Ann Arbor, where he received the Ph.D. degree in June 1934. His dissertation was "The Kankakee 'Marsh' of Northern Indiana–Illinois." A paper copy and a microfilm edition are shelved in the University library. Two years later he published the dissertation in *Papers of the Michigan Academy of Sciences, Arts and Letters* [vol. 21 (1936), pp. 359–396]. The Kankakee Valley Historical Society scanned the original paper and posted it on its internet website.

Valparaiso University promoted Alfred Meyer to Associate Professor and Head of the Department of Geography and Meteorology in 1931. He became Professor in 1942. He remained Head of the Department until age 74, and retired from the faculty at the age of 80. He recruited like-minded John H. Strietelmeier for the geography faculty. Meyer and Strietelmeier collaborated in many ways, including co-authoring an influential geography textbook. Meyer's influence on curricular content continues to this day. Geology vanished from the Valparaiso University curriculum with Meyer's appointment, and geology never returned to the campus. In 2014, Valparaiso students could elect courses in Geology and Earth Sciences off campus in Gary at Indiana University Northwest, a regional campus of Indiana University, as part of a consortium called the Valparaiso–Indiana Geography and Geology Association.

The Germann Administration

Albert Germann was hired to teach chemistry. He was rewarded with the highest faculty salary in the University. It was always the expectation by John Baur that Germann would have institutional responsibilities well beyond the chemistry classroom. At first, those responsibilities involved identifying candidates for faculty positions. Then, probably unexpectedly, those responsibilities expanded dramatically.

Six months after W. H. T. Dau's inauguration as President of the University, there was evidence that Dau's physical condition was deteriorating. He was not keeping abreast of correspondence and he was neglecting some administrative obligations. Paperwork was piling up on the President's desk. At the urging of his family, Dau consulted the family physician, who reported subnormal blood pressure and signs of nervous exhaustion. Dau then went to Detroit, accompanied by Harry A. Eberline (1874–1952), President of the Lutheran University Association and a resident of Detroit, and by Oscar Carl Kreinheder, Chairman of the Committee on Instruction, for an independent physical examination by Henry L. Ulbrich, M.D. (1883–1962), a prominent Lutheran layman. Dr. Ulbrich reported on Wednesday, April 27, 1927, that the examination revealed very low blood pressure, heart pulsations on exertion, and some tax on the nervous system. He concluded that the President should be given an extended vacation of several months. "It is also my opinion that it is imperative that his vacation begin immediately."

The Executive Committee of the Lutheran University Association held a special meeting on Sunday, May 1, 1927, to consider the medical report from Dr. Ulbrich. The Executive Committee voted to grant W. H. T. Dau an immediate two-month leave of absence. At the same meeting, the Executive Committee voted "to ask Dr. Albert F. O. Germann, head of the Chemistry Department at Valparaiso, to be the Acting President during Dr. Dau's absence." Harry A. Eberline "agreed to present these resolutions to Dr. Dau in person." John Baur, who had earlier served as Acting President (and would later again be Acting President), was Secretary Pro Tem of the Committee for this crucial meeting.

Acting President Germann acted quickly to dispatch the accumulation of presidential paperwork, including unanswered letters of inquiry from interested faculty candidates. The Committee on Instruction, within ten days, approved eight faculty appointments submitted by Germann. The Committee instructed Germann to investigate five other specific candidates, and instructed Germann to "submit suitable candidates to head the Departments of Education, Economics, Music, and Mathematics." The Committee on Instruction was composed of Ralph Edward Richman (1891–1972) of Cincinnati, Fredrick Henry Wehrenberg (December 29, 1890–December 24, 1963) of Fort Wayne, and the Rev. Oscar Carl Kreinheder (November 10, 1877–March 26, 1946) of Detroit. The Committee had been appointed in January 1927 by Herman A. Duemling, President of the Board of Directors.

W. H. T. Dau resented (and appeared at times not to accept) the appointment of Germann as Acting President. Relations between Dau and Germann were curt. For example, see the full text of a letter from Dau, who was still on leave:

> Dr. A. F. O. Germann, Valparaiso, Indiana. Dear Doctor:
>
> Merely as a matter of record, I wish you to note that I am in Valparaiso, returned from my journey nearly two weeks. I have also proof that you have known of my presence and I am a little surprised that so far I have received no visit from you.
>
> I should desire, in particular, a report of the Convention of the Third Region of State Boards of Pharmacy and Colleges of Pharmacy in Indianapolis, for which I furnished you credentials.

Another matter that you have, no doubt, noted already, is I have reversed your decision not to hold any religious exercises during the Summer School, also the weekly Assembly meeting, which you likewise abolished, has been restored.

Very truly yours, W. H. T. DAU, D.D., PRESIDENT.

Dau referred to Albert Germann as "Dr. A. F. O. Germann" and "Dear Doctor," he signed the letter as "W. H. T. Dau, D.D." Dau seems to have been uncomfortable with Germann's academic credentials. No evidence has been found that Dau had an earned doctorate; he had received the honorary degree of Doctor of Divinity from the Lutheran Immanuel Seminary in North Adelaide, Australia. Using the letters D.D. postnominally for an honorary degree is conventional. Others, however, often referred to him as "Doctor Dau," as do many published references. Use of the prenominal "Dr." is stylistically questionable when the degree is honorary.

Committee on Instruction asked Albert Germann to become Acting Dean of the School of Pharmacy. W. H. T. Dau did not approve of this action. On Thursday, July 21, 1927, Dau wrote to Germann as follows:

> Referring to our conversation last Saturday, I want to confirm by this note the opinion I expressed to you, to wit:
>
> That I fear harm from making our formerly prosperous School of Pharmacy, even in appearance, a mere dependency of our Department of Chemistry. In the public opinion it will be that if you were to be the Acting Head of the School of Pharmacy.
>
> Moreover, you were instrumental in discovering the insufficiency of the former Dean of the School of Pharmacy and it is known the Dean harbored particular animosity against you personally. I think, therefore, it is utterly tactless that you should take his place. Need I explain why?
>
> Nothing in this letter is to be interpreted as a depreciation of your real worth in our Department of Chemistry. In what I say to you, I mean well with you.

Dau earlier condemned the pharmacy school as a mere trade school, but on July 21st he characterized the School as "our formerly prosperous School of Pharmacy" that should not even appear to be "a mere dependency of our Department of Chemistry." If a curriculum focused only on training students to be dispensing druggists, then "trade school" might have been appropriate. However, Albert Germann knew from his most recent professional experience that the pharmaceutical sciences were rapidly becoming closely associated with the biochemical sciences, interrelated with biology and chemistry in potentially transformational ways. He believed that the mission of the School of Pharmacy should be scientific education rather than commercial training.

In the meantime, Germann was active as Acting Dean of the School of Pharmacy. He wrote to Ralph Richman: "Your letter of May 24, received while I was in Detroit with the Pharmics. I had 56 students with me. The total expense to each student for transportation and for two nights' hotel accommodation was $7.00. I think that this is a record for economy. More than that—we had the best service that anyone would ask, both in the way of transportation and hotels."

The "Schicks Affair" illustrates an example of a problem, quite prevalent in the 19th century. Some American colleges and universities were making appointments at professorial ranks to persons whose academic credentials included only a few courses beyond high school. Frank Germann noted in 1919 that the Colorado School of Mines faculty then included many "who know little if anything beyond what they have to teach." If many faculty were incompetent even in "what they have to teach," if many had insufficient knowledge, training, or credentials, then there would be an institutional problem.

W. H. T. Dau reminded Albert Germann "you were instrumental in discovering the insufficiency of the former Dean of the School of Pharmacy [George Charles Schicks Jr.]." Extant records may not reveal the substance of that "insufficiency," but the problem was considered serious enough to result in the dismissal of Dean Schicks from the Valparaiso faculty during the 1926–1927 academic year.

After Valparaiso, George Schicks went to Rutgers University. He was appointed Professor of Pharmacy in the Rutgers University College of Pharmacy in 1928, and was named Assistant Dean a year later. He resigned in 1945 to become director of the Perth Amboy (New Jersey) General Hospital. In 1950, he became Executive Director of Saint Barnabas Hospital, the oldest and largest non-profit, non-sectarian hospital in the state. At the time of his death, he was directing expansion into the new $10,000,000 Saint Barnabas Medical Center in Livingston, New Jersey.

Others exaggerated Schick's academic credentials over the years. He had earned the degree of Ph.G. (graduate in pharmacy) from Massachusetts College of Pharmacy in 1919. After a year on the faculty, Valparaiso gave him the courtesy degree Ph.C. (pharmaceutical chemist), perhaps because it was embarrassing to have an instructor in the pharmaceutical chemistry program without at least the Ph.C. degree. Even though Schick's biographical entry (which he himself wrote) in *American Men of Science* (6th edition, 1938) clearly states that his degrees were Ph.G. and Ph.C., Saint Barnabas Hospital listed him as "George Schicks, Ph.D." His *New York Times* obituary includes the phrase: "Dr. Schicks, who received a Doctor of Philosophy degree from the Massachusetts College of Pharmacy in 1919, ..." No documentation of any doctorate has been found.

Schicks claimed (*American Men of Science*, 6th edition) that he had been Dean of the Valparaiso College of Pharmacy from 1925 to 1927, but Albert Germann wrote (July 27, 1927): "It has been my constant hope that it might be possible to find a man properly qualified to step into the position left vacant by the dismissal of Mr. Schicks last year ... Since the talk I had with Mr. Cox [Cyrus L. Cox, B.S., a member of the faculty of the Pharmacy School at Valparaiso University for several years, appointed Instructor in Pharmacy on June 7, 1927] I have been more worried than ever about the situation in the Department of Pharmacy."

From the minutes of the May 11, 1927, meeting of the Valparaiso Committee on Instruction: "It was moved ... that ... the acting president [A. F. O. Germann] be asked to negotiate with Mr. Uhl who has taken the place of Mr. Schicks in the Department of Pharmacy ..." In a June 7, 1927, letter to the Members of the Educational Committee of the Board of Directors of Valparaiso University Association, Germann wrote: "Mr. Arthur H. Uhl, formerly assistant instructor in the Department of Pharmacy at the University of Wisconsin, and since April 7 instructor in pharmacognosy at Valparaiso University, will accept an appointment as instructor in pharmacognosy ... for ... 1927–28."

Pharmacognosy is a branch of pharmacology that deals with the chemical composition and the therapeutic uses of drugs of biological origin, especially medicinal substances obtained from plants. Arthur Hoyt Uhl (1900–1980) was especially well qualified to teach this subject. He had just completed all requirements for the M.S.

degree from the University of Wisconsin, and would have his M.S. diploma before classes opened in fall 1927. His 1927 thesis had a two-part title: "A Century of the *United States Pharmacopoeia, 1820–1920: Podophyllum peltatum.*"The second part was prelude to his 1930 Wisconsin Ph.D. thesis: "A Study of *Podophyllum peltatum* Linne." *Podophyllum peltatum,* commonly called mayapple, is an herbaceous perennial, native to all of eastern North America. Uhl's thesis titles reflect the importance of the study of medicinal plants to the research programs of the Wisconsin School of Pharmacy and the Wisconsin Pharmaceutical Experiment Station, with its 2½-acre medicinal plant garden on the Madison campus.

After Valparaiso, Arthur Uhl returned to the University of Wisconsin to complete his doctoral studies. He then joined the University of Wisconsin pharmacy faculty. He became Dean of the School of Pharmacy, had an illustrious career at Wisconsin, and retired on July 31, 1968. He was proud to be one of the six founders of the American Institute of the History of Pharmacy (in Madison, January 22, 1941).

According to John Strietelmeier, Germann was Acting President from May to September, 1927. During that time, the School of Pharmacy had been accepted as a member of the American Association of Colleges of Pharmacy, and judged to be conforming to the Association's standards.

Two months after the first physical examination, Dr. Ulbrich and a Dr. Reye examined the President again in Detroit. President Dau reported to the Board of Directors of the Valparaiso University Association on Saturday, September 3, 1927: "The Detroit physicians have advised my immediate resignation. It is hard to convince myself that I should take this step. … my office is at the Directors' discretion, and I shall not stand in the way of any change which the Directors may decree in the interest of the school."The Board granted President Dau a year's leave. During Dau's leave of absence, John C. Baur served as Acting President of the University. Baur had been Business Manager of the University since his first stint as Acting President from January 1926 to February 12, 1926. The presidential transition from Germann to Baur occurred during the first week of September 1927.

Return to Cleveland

Albert Germann accepted his initial appointment at Valparaiso University as a temporary assignment. He had no desire in summer 1927 to remain in Valparaiso after completion of his immediate administrative duties. To avert any move to transform one of his "acting roles" into a permanent position, he submitted a *pro forma* letter of resignation from the faculty to the Committee on Instruction on June 13, 1927.

As the summer ended, Germann again expressed his desire to resign. Ralph Richman wrote Germann on August 9, 1927: "By unanimous vote the Committee on Instruction has refused to accept your resignation and each member strongly urges that you remain with Valparaiso University."

Germann had often spoken candidly with members of the Committee on Instruction about his roles at the University. During the first weeks of August, he met with Ralph Richman and Oscar Kreinheder of the Committee, and with John Baur, discussing again his resignation. Fred Wehrenberg, the other member of the Committee, was in Tacoma, Washington, at a meeting of lumber dealers, unavailable for in-person consultation. Wehrenberg was in Tacoma as President and General Manager of the Fort Wayne Standard Lumber and Supply Company. German also met in Cleveland with William O. Frohring, Vice-President and General Manager of Laboratory Products Company. And he spent a few days at home with his family in Cleveland.

Albert Germann, in his own judgment, had completed his work in Valparaiso. Albert did not believe that he was still needed in Valparaiso, and he must have felt that W. H. T. Dau did not want him there. Albert's family needed him. The family had returned to Cleveland from Peru. School in Cleveland was beginning for his three children, with the first classes just before Labor Day, Monday, September 5. Barbara was 11, Edith would be 10 on September 6, and Lucia was 7. There was also a very attractive professional inducement from William O. Frohring.

In a letter to Ralph Richman on August 6, 1927, Germann wrote: "I have delayed writing a refusal to the Laboratory Products Company of their offer to me, pending disposition of my resignation here. I have just received a letter from the Vice-President and General Manager of the Company, Mr. Frohring, asking that I delay decision until I can have a personal conference with him. I shall doubtless be in Cleveland some time next week and shall see him then. I must admit that his offer is very tempting, especially so since my family is still tied up in Cleveland and my acceptance there would solve that difficulty at one stroke." Baur reported to Richman "that the company still wants Germann to come back and offers to build a new research laboratory for him."

The Valparaiso phase of the professional career of Albert Germann closed at the end of August 1927. Richman wrote to Germann on Thursday, September 1, 1927: "President Eberline has written to me that you have finally decided to go back to your place in Cleveland. On behalf of the Committee on Instruction, which has been working with you for the selection of faculty, I express our regrets at this decision. We have found you faithful and conscientious to the last degree and learned to value highly the tremendous energy and zeal which you displayed in your work for us."

Sources and References for Chapter IV

Two standard references for the history of Valparaiso University, each written by a member of the Valparaiso faculty, are: John Strietelmeier, *Valparaiso's First Century: A Centennial History of Valparaiso University* (Valparaiso, Indiana: Valparaiso University, 1959); and Richard Baepler, *Flame of Faith, Lamp of Learning: A History of Valparaiso University* (St. Louis: Concordia Publishing House, 2001). For an account of the early years until the presidency of John E. Roessler, see George William Stimpson, *The Story of Valparaiso University: Including an Account of the Recent Period of Turbulence* (Published by the author. Chicago: W. B. Conkey Co., printer, 1921). *See also* Powell A. Moore, *The Calumet Region: Indiana's Last Frontier* (Indiana Historical Bureau, 1959; Indiana Historical Collections, vol. 39), chap. 23 "Education", pp. 453–471.

Page 238, *Map of Valparaiso* ... "Street and Plat Map of Valparaiso, Indiana," A. G. Hardesty, *Illustrated Historical Atlas of Porter County, Indiana* (Valparaiso: A. G. Hardesty, 1876), p. 69.

Page 239, *the national journal* ... The weekly publication *Science*, founded in 1880, has been the official journal of the American Association for the Advancement of Science since 1900.

Page 239, "*Dr. A. F. O. Germann has resigned his position ... Science* (New Series), vol. 64, no. 1660 (October 22, 1926), p. 404.

Page 239, *to know some facts about Valparaiso* ... A valuable contemporary account of the early days of Valparaiso village is Hubert M. Skinner, *History of Valparaiso from the Earliest Times to the Present*, by A Citizen [pseud.] (Valparaiso: Normal Publishing House, 1876).

Page 241, *Bishop Francis Asbury (1745–1816)* ...

John Wesley (1703–1791) appointed Francis Asbury and Thomas Coke in 1784 as his co-superintendents of the Methodist movement in America. This appointment created the first two Bishops of the Methodist Episcopal Church in America. John Wesley, often called the founder of Methodism, was joined by his brother Charles Wesley (1707–1788) and by George Whitefield (1714–1770) in establishing and spreading Methodism. Indiana Asbury University originally admitted only male students. Women were first admitted in 1867, eight years after Valparaiso Male and Female College opened as a coeducational institution.

Page 241, *The first President of Valparaiso Male and Female* ... "Chancellors Papers: Charles N. Sims," Syracuse University Archives; Rev. Charles N. Sims," Boone County Genealogy, http://www.ingenweb.org/inboone/biographies/biography-sims-charles.htm, accessed April 7, 2013. President Sims did not use a period following his middle initial.

Page 242, *creation of the Methodist Episcopal Church South* ... The Methodist Episcopal Church South was formed in 1844. The African Methodist Episcopal Church had separated from the Methodist Episcopal Church in 1816.

Page 242, *Rev. Erastus Herman Staley* ... Valparaiso University, "Past Presidents," http://www.valpo.edu/150/history-presidents/staley.php, accessed April 7, 2013. *See also* "*Frankfort High School Yearbook, 1907,*" *http://indianagenweb.com/inclinton/vitals/yearbooks/Frankfort_High_School_1907.html, accessed* February 26, 2016,

Page 242, *Staley, like Sims, was a graduate of Indiana Asbury University* ... *Alumnal Register of Officers, Faculties and Graduates, 1837-1900* (Greencastle, Indiana: DePauw University, 1901), p. 57.

Page 242, *Tippecanoe Battle Ground Collegiate Institute* ... George P. Salen, "The Battle Ground Collegiate Institute" (1952), from *The Battle Ground Story: Northwest Indiana Conference, Methodist Church* (circa 1965). http://www.battleground.in. gov/HBGDC/HistoryBG.doc, accessed January 26, 2014.

Page 243, *Benjamin Wilson Smith (1830–1921) was also* ... DePauw *Alumnal Register,* op. cit., p. 53.

Page 243, *Thomas Bond Wood (1844–1922) followed* ... DePauw *Alumnal Register,* op. cit., p. 67.

Page 244, *Gurney was an editor* ... He may have founded the newspaper. According to *Chronicling America,* United States Library of Congress (http://chroniclingamerica.loc.gov/lccn/sn86058328/, accessed June 7, 2015), successors have included *The Evening Messenger* (1891–1927), *Valparaiso Daily Vidette* (1911–1927), *The Vidette-Messenger* (1927–1989), and *Vidette-Messenger of Porter County* (1989–1995). A biographical sketch of Aaron Gurney (with two references) is embedded in Donna Potter Phillips, "Preachers and Printers in the Family," *Ancestry,* vol. 22, no. 2 (March–April 2004), p. 66. *See also* E. E. M'Kay, "Mrs. Janette Gurney" [widow of Dr. Aaron Gurney], Obituary, *Minutes of the Rock River Annual Conference of the Methodist Episcopal Church,* held in Austin Church, Chicago, Illinois; reprinted in *Northwestern Christian Advocate,* vol. 51 (April 8, 1903), p. 30; and "Aaron Gurney," *Portrait & Biographical Album of Sangamon County, Illinois* (Chicago: Chapman Brothers, 1891), http://sangamon.illinoisgenweb. org/1891/gurney.htm, accessed October 8, 2015.

Page 244, *Indiana Asbury University awarded him the honorary degree* ... DePauw *Alumnal Register,* op. cit., p. 320.

Page 244, *Presbyterian minister Ambrose Yoemans Moore* ... Among his publications were: A. Y. Moore, *The Life of Schuyler Colfax* (Philadelphia: T. B. Peterson & Bros., 1868); A. Y. Moore, *History of the Presbytery of Indianapolis* (Indianapolis: J. G. Doughty, printer, 1876); Ambrose Yoemans Moore, *Memorial Sermon, Sabbath, May 25, 1890, to the*

John Dunn Post, G.A.R. in the Presbyterian Church, Hanover, Ind. (Madison, Indiana: 1890); A. Y. Moore, *Sermon Preached at the Funeral of Rev. Levi Hughes, in Walnut St. Presbyterian Church, Bloomington, Indiana, Nov. 4, 1870* (Washington, D.C.: printed by Wm. H. Moore, 1871).

Page 245, *The Rev. Edward Sorin* ... Information about the establishment of the Catholic school in Valparaiso was obtained from "St. Paul's School, Valparaiso, Porter Co.," *Parochial Schools of the Diocese of Fort Wayne, Ind.* (vols. I–V, 1893); "Valparaiso. St. Paul's Church. 1858," Rt. Rev. H. J. Alerding, *The Diocese of Fort Wayne: A Book of Historical Reference* (Fort Wayne, 1907), pp. 268–270; and The Most Rev. John F. Noll, *The Diocese of Fort Wayne: Fragments of History* (Fort Wayne, 1941), vol. II, pp. 402–403. Copies of the relevant pages were supplied by Janice L. Cantrell, Archivist, Diocese of Fort Wayne–South Bend Archives, Fort Wayne. Also consulted was "Parish History: Saint Paul Catholic Church," http://saintpaulvalpo.org/about-us/, accessed April 26, 2015.

Page 245, *celebrating Mass in the Porter County Courthouse* ... The first Porter County Courthouse was of wood frame construction, built in 1837. It was replaced on the same site in 1853 by a brick building.

Page 245, *Congregation of Holy Cross* ... Congregation of Holy Cross (Congregatio a Sancta Cruce, C.S.C.) was founded in 1837 by Basil Anthony-Marie Moreau in Le Mans, France. Father Moreau envisioned C.S.C. as an apostolic missionary community. He sent missionaries to Algiers, to Eastern Bengal, and to northwestern Indiana.

Page 245, *Rev. Paul Gillen (1808–1882)* ... He was the first resident pastor at Michigan City. He also served pastorates in Chesterton, Walkerton, and Hobart, each in the extreme northwest corner of Indiana.

Page 245, *a Lutheran congregation* ... *Eightieth Anniversary* (Valparaiso: Immanuel Lutheran Church, September 17, 1944). Copy provided by Chris Martel, Genealogy Department, Valparaiso Public Library.

Page 245, *C. Peters, one of the first graduates* … It would be interesting to know more about C. Peters and the Seminary. However, "In 1913 when the college moved from Addison to River Forest, unfortunately a major fire in 1913 destroyed almost all records of the time in Addison." Email from William M. Ewald, Archivist, Concordia University Chicago, April 19, 2015.

Page 249, *Indiana University in Bloomington had only 28 graduates* … Indiana University advertisement in the 1902 *Narcissus*, yearbook of Peru (Indiana) High School. Copy in the Peru Public Library.

Page 251, *he married Geneva Axe*… "Geneva Axe Brown, Biography." http://www.inportercounty.org/Data/Biographies/Brown173.html, accessed May 19, 2013. Transcribed from Thomas H. Cannon, H. H. Loring, and Charles J. Robb, *History of the Lake and Calumet Region of Indiana Embracing the Counties of Lake, Porter and Laporte.* Vol. II (Indianapolis: Historians' Association, 1927). pp. 781–782.

Page 252, *he helped establish the city waterworks* … "In 1866, water works (so-called), were put up with some help from the county, supplying several cisterns and occasionally a fountain (so-called) in the public square. While it is ridiculous to call these water works, the people could hardly get along without them." Weston A. Goodspeed and Charles Blanchard, *Counties of Lake and Porter, Indiana: Historical and Biographical* (Chicago: F. A. Battey and Company, 1882), p. 128.

Page 252, *was on the first library board* … Information supplied by Larry Clark, Porter County Public Library System.

Page 252, *Jasper Newton Roe (1864–1921)* … "Jasper Newton Roe, Sc.D., M.D., Professor and Head of the Department of Chemistry, Secretary of the Board of Trustees of the Medical Department of the Valparaiso University. Dr. Roe was born at Markle, Indiana, July 17, 1864. His early education was received in the public schools of Indiana. Later he came to the Valparaiso University and obtained the Sc.D. and A.M. degrees; Ph.G., Northwestern

University. In 1893 he organized the Valparaiso University College of Pharmacy; 1902, the Chicago College of Medicine and Surgery; and in 1906, secured the Chicago College of Dental Surgery as part of the Valparaiso University. "Throughout his entire connections with the institution, Dr. Roe has been a faithful, energetic worker, ever keeping the vital interests of the college uppermost in mind." Dedication page of *The Medicos 1917*, published by the Senior Class of the Chicago College of Medicine and Surgery (Medical Department Valparaiso University). Information from the catalogs of the Chicago College of Medicine and Surgery (1903–1917) was supplied by Gloria Leischner, Administrative Assistant, Loyola University Stritch School of Medicine.

Page 252, *enrollment only to Harvard University* … Roger L. Geiger, *To Advance Knowledge: The Growth of American Research Universities, 1900–1940* (New York: Oxford University Press, 1986), Appendix A.

Page 255, *President of the homeopathic Hahnemann Hospital and Medical College of Chicago* … "Hodgdon Dinner" invitation, full-page portrait, and "A Welcome To Our New President," *The Bulletin of the Hahnemann Hospital and Medical College of Chicago*, vol. 6, no. 2 (September 1919), pp. 1–3. Copy supplied by Susan M. Sacharski, Archivist, Northwestern Memorial Hospital.

Page 255, *outspoken advocate for the Chicago Memorial Foundation* … "The Chicago Memorial Foundation," *The Clinique*, a monthly abstract of the clinics and of the proceedings of the Clinical Society of the Hahnemann Hospital of Chicago (Chicago: Illinois Homeopathic Association), vol. 41, no. 2 (March 1920), pp. 99–102. Copy supplied by Susan M. Sacharski, Archivist, Northwestern Memorial Hospital.

Page 255, *He certainly had a knack for overstating* … [Hodgdon was] "an ill-tempered autocrat with a genuine bachelor's degree from Bates College buried under a collection of phony diplomas (M.A., M.S., Sc.D., LL.D., Ph.D.)," Lance Trusty, "All Talk and No 'Kash': Valparaiso University and the

Ku Klux Klan," *Indiana Magazine of History*, vol. 82, no. 1 (March 1986), pp. 1–36; quotation from page 11. "[several students] determined that Hodgdon's Bachelor of Arts from Bates College was the only legitimate degree of the six he claimed to possess. His Master and Doctor of Science degrees were from 'Potomac University,' which turned out to be a correspondence school unrecognized by any state educational authority or university. Hodgdon's LL.D. was honorary, having been conferred by Henry Kinsey Brown. The M.D. he had received was from the Hahnemann Medical School, where he was the president. The Ph.D. that he claimed to have earned from Columbia University was entirely a fiction." Richard Baepler, op. cit., pp. 98–99.

According to an entry, probably written by Mr. Hodgdon himself, in *Genealogical and Family History of the State of Maine*, George Thomas Little, ed. (New York: Lewis Historical Publishing Company, 1909): Daniel Russell Hodgdon "was born in Winthrop, Maine, 1885. He became a pupil in the high school at Winthrop, and obtained a liberal education at Bates College, and at the University of Maine and the University of Chicago. He studied for the ministry and supplied the church at Pittston, Maine, during his collegiate course. He taught the schools of Freeport, Strong, Abbot and Wayne. He came to Corinna in 1907 and is the very efficient principal of the Union Academy in that town."

His entry in Marquis *Who Was Who in America* (vol. 7, 1977–1981), compiled posthumously from material supplied by Mr. Hodgdon, continues: Vice-Principal, Maine State Normal School, 1908–1910; Head of Science Department, Rutgers College Preparatory School, 1910–1911, Passaic High School, 1911–1913, New Jersey State Normal School, 1913–1918, State Summer School for Teachers, New Jersey, 1913–1918; Director of Newark Technical School, and founder and President of the College of Engineering, 1918–1920; President of Hahnemann Medical College and Hospital, Chicago, 1920–1922, Columbus School, New Rochelle, New York, "since 1922;" Lecturer, New York University Institute of Arts and Sci-

ences, 1917–1919, 1925–1926; … It is significant that he does not mention the presidency of Valparaiso University in his *Who's Who in America* resumé, and that he extends the dates of his employment at Newark and Hahnemann to cover his months at Valparaiso.

He published a book, *Elementary General Science* (New York: Hinds, Hayden & Eldredge, copyright 1918; 553 pages). The content appears to have been cut and pasted from a great many sources. On the title page: Daniel Russell Hodgdon, Sc.D., LL.D., President, Valparaiso University; formerly President of Hahnemann Medical College and Hospital of Chicago; Director Industrial Educational Bureau; President of College of Technology, Newark; Lecturer, Newark Institute of Arts and Science; Member of Faculty, New York University and New Jersey State Normal School. The copyright date must precede the printing date of the title page by a couple of years.

In 1919, Hodgdon presented an expansive view of his own credentials. He may have completed an authentic doctoral program a decade later. In 1931, Hodgdon submitted a two-volume typescript thesis, *Legal Aspects in the Administration and Control of Public School Property*, as partial fulfillment of the requirements for the Ph.D. of the School of Education, New York University.

Page 257, *Enrollments across the nation doubled between 1919 and 1929…* Roger L. Geiger, op. cit., p. 108.

Page 257, *Enrollment in 1915 was 4,977…* Richard Baepler, op. cit., p. 89.

Page 257, *In 1922, it was 1,200…* ibid., p. 101.

Page 258, *Many institutions raised twice…* Roger L. Geiger, op. cit., p. 125.

Page 258, *records of the Indiana Ku Klux Klan …* It is misleading to view the Ku Klux Klan as a monolithic, national organization with a coherent history. Myths abound. Unbiased sources of Ku Klux Klan history are rare, so it is undesirable to rely on just a few writers. A recent book with a lengthy bibliography is Kelly J. Baker, *Gospel According to the Klan: The KKK's Appeal to Protestant America, 1915–1930* (Lawrence: University Press of Kansas, 2011).

Page 259, *Friday, August 24, 1923, issue* ... *The Fiery Cross* (Indianapolis), vol. II, no. 43 (Friday, August 24, 1923), pp. 1, 7. This and other issues of *The Fiery Cross* were accessed in July 2013 from the Indiana University internet site http://www.libraries.iub.edu/index.php?pageId=4667, "Collection: Digital Archive: Fiery Cross."

Page 260, *frequent mass rallies—"konklaves"*... A konklave in Valparaiso on Saturday, May 19, 1923, brought 50,000 to the city for "a gigantic frolic," a parade of 6,000 Klan members (3,000 in robes), and an afternoon and evening carnival that included a barbecue, circus acts, and fireworks [*The Fiery Cross*, vol. II, no. 26, May 25, 1923, pp. 1, 2]. The zenith Indiana konklave may have been the gathering on Independence Day 1923 in Kokomo. Eight-year-old Robert Coughlan attended that Klan Konklave on July 4, 1923. Years later, Coughlan (by then an editor with Harcourt, Brace & Co., *Fortune*, and *Life)* wrote: "The Klan's official estimate, which probably was not far wrong in this case, was that two hundred thousand members were there. Kokomo then had a population of about thirty thousand, and naturally every facility of the town was swamped." ["Konklave in Kokomo," *The Aspirin Age* (New York: Simon & Schuster, 1949; edited by Isabel Leighton), chap. 1923, pp. 105–129.] *See also* Allen Safianow, "'Konklave in Kokomo' revisited," *Historian*, vol. 50, no. 3 (May 1988), pp. 329–347.

Page 260, *Teenagers were paid 2¢ for each copy* ... Garland Stickler, in 1986, recalled that this was the rate in Columbia City, Indiana, at the time. *See* Willadene Egner, "Whitley County Survives the Ku Klux Klan," *Bulletin of the Whitley County Historical Society*, vol. 24, no. 5 (October 1986), p. 15.

Page 260, *President Evans promised the Dean* ... Letter, dated August 25, 1923, from H. M. Evans, President, to Dean H. C. Muldoon, 418 Chemung Street, Waverly, New York. Copy courtesy of Judy Miller, Special Collections Librarian, Valparaiso University.

Page 260, *Hugh Cornelius Muldoon graduated* ... Much of the biographical information is from James A. Ingram and Louis D. Vottero, *Hugh Cornelius Muldoon: An* Appreciation (privately printed in 2001): "Supported in part by the Paul and Nancy Wherry Endowed Fund in the History of Pharmacy at The Ohio State University College of Pharmacy, and by Duquesne University School of Pharmacy." Further information was supplied by Gwen Weldy, Archivist, Albany College of Pharmacy and Health Sciences, and by Kathy Krathwohl, Library and Learning Resources, Massachusetts College of Pharmacy and Health Sciences. In addition, substantial information about Dean Muldoon's tenure at Duquesne is in a biography file at Duquesne; Thomas White, University Archivist and Curator of Special Collections, Duquesne University, supplied copies from that file.

Page 262, *Trustees of Valparaiso University conferred the honorary degree* ... Information supplied by Judy Miller, Special Collections Librarian, Valparaiso University.

Page 263, *Professor of Materia Medica and Histology* ... Pharmacology is a modern synonym of "materia medica." Histology is the identification and study of cells and tissues, ordinarily using the optical microscope.

Page 263, *negotiations continued in the next issue* ... *The Fiery Cross* (Indianapolis), vol. II, no. 44 (August 31, 1923), pp. 1, 8.

Page 264, *Public clarification of the Klan interpretation* ... *The Fiery Cross* (Indianapolis), vol. II, no. 45 (September 7, 1923), p. 1.

Page 265, *Richard Baepler wrote* ... Richard Baepler, *Flame of Faith, Lamp of Learning: A History of Valparaiso University* (St. Louis: Concordia Publishing House, 2001), p. 107.

Page 265, *Adam Laatz wrote* ... Adam Laatz, "Red Schoolhouse, Burning Cross: the Ku Klux Klan of the 1920s and Educational Reform," *History of Education Quarterly*, vol. 52, no. 3 (August 2012), pp. 323–350. Quotation from page 337.

Page 265, *According to Neil Betten:* ... Neil Betten, "Nativism and the Klan in Town and City: Valparaiso and Gary, Indiana," *Studies in History and Society,* vol. 4 (spring 1973), pp. 3–16. Quotation from page 12.

Page 265, *Lance Trusty summarized* ... Lance Trusty, "All Talk and No 'Kash'; Valparaiso University and the Ku Klux Klan," *Indiana Magazine of History,* vol. 82, no. 1 (March 1986), pp. 1–36. Quotation from page 32.

Page 265, *the first person to advocate effectively* ... The timeline of the events that culminated in the Lutheranization of Valparaiso University is reported in John Strietelmeier, *Valparaiso's First Century: A Centennial History of Valparaiso University* (Valparaiso, Indiana: Valparaiso University, 1959), pp. 82–92. This timeline is based in large part on retrospective interviews by John Strietelmeier with John C. Baur and with Walther M. Miller on February 4, 1950, and with W. C. Dickmeyer on February 19, 1957.

Page 266, *Finlandia University* ... http://www.finlandia.edu/finlandia-fast-facts.html, accessed January 12, 2016. *See also* "Finlandia University," Wikipedia, accessed January 12, 2016.

Page 266, *Many present-day Lutheran institutions* ... Forty-one Lutheran colleges and universities are listed by the Lutheran Educational Conference of North America, an inter-Lutheran organization formed in 1910. http://www.lutherancolleges.org, accessed January 15, 2016.

Page 266, *Capital University* ... http://www.capital.edu/About-Capital/Mission-and-Vision/, accessed January 12, 2016. *See also* "Capital University," Wikipedia, accessed January 12, 2016.

Page 267, *Union Theological Seminary summarizes* ... Union Theological Seminary internet website, http://www.utsnyc.edu/about/union-theological-seminary-history-mission, accessed July 20, 2014.

Page 267, *Lenoir College opened in 1891* ... "History of Lenoir-Rhyne University," website, http://www.lr.edu/visitors/history-of-lenoir-rhyne,

accessed February 13, 2014. With timeline.

Page 267, *Augsburg in Minneapolis* ... "A College of the Church," http://www.augsburg.edu/about/history/, accessed February 13, 2014.

Page 268, *Augustana College* ... "Mission and History," http://www.augustana.edu/general-information/mission-and-history, accessed February 13, 2014.

Page 268, *Baur was editor* ... Dr. Gerald Perschbacher, editor of *The Lutheran Layman*, the flagship printed newspaper of Lutheran Hour Ministries, has pointed out: "The Lutheran Layman is the current name of our publication. That name has been carried for most of the decades since formation in 1929 under the initial title of Lutheran Laymen's League Bulletin. The Lutheran Laymen's League was formed in 1917 during a convention of the Missouri Synod." [email July 16, 2013]. It thus appears that the American Luther League and the Lutheran Laymen's League are distinctly different organizations, and the two publications with the name *The Lutheran Layman* are also distinctly different. Dr. Perschbacher continued: "I recall no mention made of Baur in the 33 years I have been on staff and during which time I founded our archives and gathered its collections." For an examination of Baur's role in the American Luther League, and a comparison of the American Luther League and the Lutheran Laymen's League, see E. Fred Vonderlage, "The American Luther League, A One-Purpose Organization," *Concordia Historical Institute Quarterly,* vol. 36, no. 2 (July 1963), pp. 33–42.

Page 268, *Baur possessed boundless* ... Richard Baepler, *Flame of Faith, Lamp of Learning: A History of Valparaiso University* (St. Louis: Concordia Publishing House, 2001), p. 143.

Page 268, *Church leaders in Kansas, Oklahoma, and Oregon* ... Rev. R. G. Messerli, on behalf of the Oregon Lutheran Schools Committee, in 1922 wrote to John Baur for advice in combating a ballot initiative known as the Compulsory Education Bill. "The bill proposed to make it a misdemeanor for any parent or guardian of a child eight to sixteen years old to fail to send her or him to a public school. The bill was openly supported by the Klan, the Scottish Rite Masons, and by gubernatorial candidate Walter Pierce, who was elected to office that year. It was naturally opposed by many churches and religious organizations, including the Lutheran Schools Committee. Principal leaders of the Committee were Paul J. Hillman, principal of the Zion Lutheran School, Portland; and clergyman R. G. Messerli. The measure passed by a comfortable majority, however, but was later declared unconstitutional by the U. S. Supreme Court in 1925, on an appeal brought by the Hill Military Academy of Portland and the Sisters of the Holy Names of Jesus and Mary." Oregon Historical Society Research Library, "Guide to the Lutheran Schools Committee Records, 1921-1925," http://nwda.orbiscascade.org/ark:/80444/xv11984, accessed June 20, 2015.

Page 268, *was born in Addison, Illinois* ... Biography of Herman A. Duemling *in* Bert J. Griswold, *Builders of Greater Fort Wayne* (Fort Wayne: 1926), pp. 132 and 675. Obituary of Herman A. Duemling, Fort Wayne *News-Sentinel*, Saturday, February 5, 1927, p. 24. *See also* material relating to the elder Herman Duemling: "Biographical Note," *Herman Duemling Collection*, http://www.lutheranhistory.org/collections/fa/m-0105.htm, accessed July 20, 2013; "History of Our Seminary," *Addison Normal School Yearbook* (Addison, Illinois: 1912), pp. 11–13. http://users.tbc.net/~weilfamily/genealogy/ANS/ANS_12.html, accessed July 20, 2013; Herman Duemling of Fort Wayne, Indiana, "Improvement in Processes for Filling Fiber in Paper-Pulp," U. S. Letters Patent No. 157,198, application filed October 10, 1874. The quotation regarding a German doctorate is from Richard Baepler, *Flame of Faith, Lamp of Learning: A History of Valparaiso University* (St. Louis: Concordia Publishing House, 2001), p. 150.

Page 269, *in the year 1902* ... "Hospital History," *The Debris-ette*, The First Annual of the Lutheran Hospital Training School for Nurses, 1921, 60 + xiii pages.

Page 270, *W. Charles Dickmeyer (July 1, 1883– November 17, 1968)* ... Biography of W. Charles Dickmeyer *in* Bert J. Griswold, *Builders of Greater Fort Wayne* (Fort Wayne: 1926), pp. 132 and 675. Obituary, Fort Wayne *Journal Gazette*, Monday, November 18, 1968, p. 1, cols 4 and 5.

Page 270, *Paul F. Miller* ... Mildred L. Burger, *Short History of the Lutheran Church—Missouri Synod in Fort Wayne, Indiana* (Fort Wayne: Fort Wayne Public Library, 1967). *See also* Obituary of Rev. Jacob W. Miller, Fort Wayne *News-Sentinel*, Friday, May 12, 1933, p. 1, col. 3; p. 10, cols 2 and 3.

Page 270, *Charles J. Scheimann (October 24, 1862– March 24, 1926)* ... Biography of Charles J. Scheimann *in* Bert J. Griswold, *Builders of Greater Fort Wayne* (Fort Wayne: 1926), pp. 508 and 758.

Page 271, *businessman and civic leader in Valparaiso* ... Herman Sievers served on the May 1918 Porter County Red Cross War Committee, which also included Henry Kinsey Brown, Mr. and Mrs. O. P. Kinsey, and Mrs. H. B. Brown. *The Vidette-Messenger* centennial edition, vol. 10, section 2 (August 18, 1936), p. 21.

Page 271, *born in the village of Bethalto, Illinois* ... Biography of Martin H. Luecke, lawyer, *in* Bert J. Griswold, *Builders of Greater Fort Wayne* (Fort Wayne: 1926), pp. 346, 717, 718, 719. *See also* Obituary: "Martin Luecke, Sanatorium Head, Civic Leader," Fort Wayne *Journal Gazette*, Wednesday, November 3, 1948, p. 1, p. 8.

Page 272, *Lutheran Hospital is directly or indirectly owned* ... Lutheran Hospital internet website, http://www.lutheranhospital.com, accessed January 16, 2014.

Page 273, *pamphlet that led to the founding* ... Benjamin Franklin, *Proposals Relating to the Education of Youth in Pensilvania* (Philadelphia: Franklin and Hall, Printers, 1749), 32 pages.

Page 276, *a letter written on April 9, 1927...* Copy supplied by Judith Miller, Valparaiso University Archives.

Page 277, *Albert kept their permanent residence ...* In

the margin of letter from Albert Germann to Ralph E. Richman, dated August 6, 1927, Germann wrote: "During this week, I can be reached most quickly at 1532 East 86th St., Cleveland, Ohio." Copy of letter supplied by Judith Miller, Valparaiso University Archives.

Page 277, *4105 South Calhoun Street* … Annual Fort Wayne City Directories, 1920–1938; Mildred L. Burger, *Short History of the Lutheran Church–Missouri Synod in Fort Wayne, Indiana* (Fort Wayne: Fort Wayne Public Library, 1967), p. 14 lists John Baur as pastor of Trinity Lutheran Church from 1914 to 1919; email from Cindy Venderley, Secretary, Trinity Lutheran Church, Fort Wayne, February 8, 2013, confirming that Trinity Lutheran Church had a parsonage when John Baur was pastor.

Page 277, *Harry Victor Fuller (October 23, 1880– January 8, 1948)* … Obituary, Valparaiso *Vidette-Messenger* and *Vidette-Times*, Friday, January 9, 1948, p. 1.

Page 277, *where the prairies meet the bluffs* … http://www.springvalley.govoffice.com, accessed October 10, 2015.

Page 277, *but did not obtain a degree* … "Complete Directory of the Alumni of the University of Minnesota," *The Minnesota Alumni Weekly*, vol. 8, no. 12 (November 30, 1908), pp. 17–160. Retrieved January 1, 2016, from the University of Minnesota Digital Conservancy, http://purl.umn.edu/53305.

Page 278, *entered the Polytechnic Institute of Zurich* … In 2015: "[Admission to] Bachelor programmes is open to everybody. ETH Zurich may, however, require you to pass an entrance examination before admitting you." https://www.ethz.ch/en/studies/registration-application/bachelor/other-certificates.html, accessed January 2, 2016.

Page 278, *Harry Fuller was awarded the Ph.D.* … Harry Victor Fuller, *Beiträge zur Gasanalyse* (Zürich: Buchdruckerei E. Liechti, 1912), 69 pages. Thesis (doctoral), Universität Basel, 1912. This citation is from WorldCat, and contradicts the implication in the text that his Ph.D. degree was awarded by ETH.

Page 278, *Fuller's obituary states… Vidette-Messenger*, op. cit.

Page 278, *the work of Leroy Sheldon Palmer* … Leroy S. Palmer and C. H. Eckles, "Carotin—The Principal Natural Yellow Pigment of Milk Fat: Its Relations to Plant Carotin and the Carotin of the body fat, *corpus luteum* and Blood Serum: I. The Chemical and Physiological Relation of the Pigments of Milk Fat to the Carotin and Xanthophylls of Green Plants," *Journal of Biological Chemistry*, vol. 17 (March 1, 1914), pp. 191–210; Leroy S. Palmer and C. H. Eckles, "Carotin—The Principal Natural Yellow Pigment of Milk Fat: Its Relations to Plant Carotin and the Carotin of the Body Fat, *corpus luteum* and Blood Serum: II. The Pigments of the Body Fat, *corpus luteum* and Skin Secretions of the Cow," *Journal of Biological Chemistry*, vol. 17 (March 1, 1914), pp. 211–221; Leroy S. Palmer and C. H. Eckles, "Carotin—The Principal Natural Yellow Pigment of Milk Fat: Its Relations to Plant Carotin and the Carotin of the Body Fat, *corpus luteum*, and Blood Serum: III. The Yellow Lipochrome of Blood Serum," *Journal of Biological Chemistry*, vol. 17 (March 1, 1914), pp. 223–236; Leroy S. Palmer and C. H. Eckles, "Carotin—The Principal Natural Yellow Pigment of Milk Fat: Its Relations to Plant Carotin and the Carotin of the Blood Serum, Body Fat and *corpus luteum*: IV. The Fate of Carotin and Xanthophylls During Digestion," *Journal of Biological Chemistry*, vol. 17 (March 1, 1914), pp. 237–243; Leroy S. Palmer and C. H. Eckles, "Carotin—The Principal Natural Yellow Pigment of Milk Fat: Its Relations to Plant Carotin and the Carotin of the Blood Serum, Body Fat and *corpus luteum*: V. The Pigments of Human Milk Fat," *Journal of Biological Chemistry*, vol. 17 (March 1, 1914), pp. 245–249. Palmer had just published the first full review of the field of carotinoids: Leroy Sheldon Palmer, *Carotinoids and Related Pigments: The Chromolipoids* (New York: The Chemical Catalog Company, Inc., 1922), 316 pages.

Page 278, *Leroy Sheldon Palmer (1887–1944)* … "Leroy Sheldon Palmer (1887–1944) was the first

American who utilized chromatography in the investigation of carotenoids present in animals, specially in milk, butter and selected tissues, and in the food intake of the animals. His work represented most likely the first use of chromatography after Tswett's [Mikhail Semyonovich Tsvet (1872–1919)] basic publications in 1906," L. S. Ettre and R. L. Wixom, "Leroy Sheldon Palmer (1887–1944) and the Beginnings of Chromatography in the United States of America," *Chromatographia*, vol. 37, nos 11 and 12 (December 1993), pp. 659–668. For an extended biography of Palmer, see Egbert Jennes and Richard W. Luecke, "Leroy Sheldon Palmer (March 23, 1887–March 8, 1944)," *The Journal of Nutrition*, vol. 63, no. 1 (1957), pp. 1–18.

Page 279, *Clarence Henry Eckles (1875–1933)*… "On April 17, 1901, the Missouri Legislature approved the establishment of a department of dairy husbandry in the University of Missouri's College of Agriculture. Clarence Henry Eckles was chosen as the first department head. He was one of the 17 founding members of the ADSA [American Dairy Science Association] in 1906," F. Martz, J. R. Campbell, R. Ricketts, and J. N. Spain, "100 Years of Dairy Science at the University of Missouri—Columbia," http://www.adsa.org/archive/centennial/posters/17732_umc.pdf, accessed September 14, 2014. Adapted from F. Martz, *Missouri Agricultural Experiment Station Special Report 564* (2006).

Page 279, *A graduate student (Walter E. Thrun)* … Leroy S. Palmer and Walter E. Thrun, "The Detection of Natural and Artificial Pigments in Oleomargarine and Butter," *The Journal of Industrial and Engineering Chemistry*, vol. 8, no. 7 (July 1916), pp. 614–618. For an extended examination of controversies involving colorants in oleomargarine, see William Shurtleff and Akiko Aoyagi, "History of Soy Oil Margarine: History of Margarine in the United States," in *History of Soybeans and Soyfoods, 1100 B.C. to the 1980s,* (Lafayette, California: Soyfoods Center, unpublished manuscript, 2004), http://www.soyinfocenter.com/HSS/margarine2.php, accessed October 10, 2015.

Page 279, *Walter Eugene Thrun (March 22, 1892–August 18, 1951)* … Obituary, Will E. Edington, "Walter Eugene Thrun," *Proceedings of the Indiana Academy of Science*, vol. 61 (1951), pp. 27–28.

Page 279, *chemical analysis of proteins from beef* … Walter E. Thrun and P. F. Trowbridge, "Determination of Various Forms of Nitrogen in Bovine Flesh, Including the Products of Hydrolysis of Some of the Proteins." First paper: "The Hexone Bases of Some Flesh Proteins," *The Journal of Biological Chemistry*, vol. 34, no. 2 (1918), pp. 343–353. Second paper: "The Bromination of the Hydrolysates of Some Beef Flesh Proteins," *The Journal of Biological Chemistry*, vol. 34, no. 2 (1918), pp. 355–362.

Page 280, *Ross Aiken Gortner (March 20, 1885–September 30, 1942)* … Samuel Colville Lind, "Biographical Memoir of Ross Aiken Gortner, 1885-1942," *Biographical Memoirs of the National Academy of Sciences* (Washington: National Academy of Sciences, vol. 23, 6th memoir, 1943), pp. 147–180.

Page 281, *very strong as a physical chemist* … Pleasant Ernest Roller, "The Maximum Boiling Point and the Minimum Freezing Point of Alcohol, Glycerine, and Water," chemistry M.A. thesis, University of Colorado, 1923; "Reactions of Acetaldehyde as Studied from the Standpoint of Electromotive Force," chemistry M.S. thesis, University of Nebraska, 1925; "The Cannizzaro Reaction of Furfural," chemistry Ph.D. thesis, University of Colorado, 1927. *See also* Saul B. Arenson, Pleasant Ernest Roller, and D. J. Brown, "The Reactive Nature of Aldehydes from the Standpoint of the Apparent Electromotive Force," *Journal of Physical Chemistry*, vol. 30, no. 5 (January 1925), pp. 620–627.

Page 281, *Sidney A. Kent Chemical Laboratory* … Funds to build, furnish, and equip the Kent Chemical Laboratory were provided by Sidney Albert Kent (1834–1900), President of the Chicago Packing & Provision Company, Director of the Chicago Board of Trade, and President of the Corn Exchange Bank. The building was constructed in 1894. The results of

Roller's electrochemical measurements were reported in P. E. Roller, "The Application of the Quinhydrone Electrode to Solutions of Phenol and Cresols," *Journal of Physical Chemistry*, vol. 34, no. 2 (January 1929), pp. 367–372.

Page 281, *to be successful recruiting for S.M.A.* ... P. E. Roller, "The Effect of Wheat Germ Oil on the Keeping Qualities of Fats and Food Rations," *Journal of Physical Chemistry*, vol. 35, no. 11 (1931), pp. 3286–3292. This subject was to be of keen interest to Albert Germann for the rest of his life. *See also* P. E. Roller, Ph.D., Cleveland, Ohio, "A Study of Breast Milk," *The Journal of Pediatrics*," vol. 4, no. 2 (February 1934), pp. 238–241; "From the Research Laboratory of S. M. A. Corporation, Cleveland, Ohio;" "Acknowledgment is made to Dr. A. F. O. Germann, Research Director of the S.M.A. Corporation, Cleveland, Ohio, for valuable suggestions ..."; at the end of the article, Roller gives the address Barboursville, West Virginia. Barboursville is a village in Cabell County, near the city of Huntington. In 1930, Barboursville had a population of 1,508.

Page 282, *William Herman Theodore Dau* ... Concise biographical summary is given in Erwin L. Lueker, Luther Poellot, and Paul Jackson, eds., *Christian Cyclopedia*. Internet version produced by The Lutheran Church—Missouri Synod, 2000. http://cyclopedia.lcms.org/default.asp. Reference Librarian Shawn Barnett, Concordia Seminary Library, St. Louis, Missouri, supplied additional information by email December 12, 2013. *See also* "Our History," Historic Trinity Lutheran Church of Detroit, http://historictrinity.org/trinhist.html, accessed January 16, 2016.

Page 282, *His first pastorate was* ... "History of Trinity," http://trinitymemphis.org/?page_id=301, accessed July 27, 2013. *Also,* email from Martha Israel, Parish Assistant, Trinity Lutheran Church, Memphis, Tennessee, July 29, 2013.

Page 283, *Trinity Lutheran Church Historian* ... Email from Sherrie Otte, July 30, 2013.

Page 283, *when the congregation of Concordia Luth-*

eran Church ... Howard J. Patten, *Concordia: "Hope Is Remembering With Praise,"* (Conover, North Carolina: Concordia Lutheran Church, 1980), 138 pages, no pagination. This book was written from the perspective of Conover. A significant source used by Rev. Patten is W. H. T. Dau, Geo. A. Romoser, J. M. Smith, L. Buchheimer, C. L. Coon and C. H. Bernheim (on the title page: "by a committee"), *Review of Prof. Yoder's "Situation in North Carolina"* (n.p., 1894), 46 pages. The *Review* was written and published in response to Robert Anderson Yoder, *The Situation in North Carolina* (Enterprise Job Office, 1894), 48 pages. A sympathetic biography of Rev. Yoder was written by the Rev. Dr. John Hall, son-in-law of Robert Anderson Yoder, and republished in *Yoder Newsletter Online*, issue 14 (October 1989), http://www.yodernewsletter.org/YNL/vol14.html, accessed July 29, 2013. *See also,* "History of Concordia College," http://school.concordianc.org/uploads/files/History%20of%20Concordia%20College.pdf, accessed January 17, 2016.

Page 283, *George A. Romoser (1870–July 9, 1936)* ... George A. Romoser was born in Baltimore, Maryland. He graduated from Baltimore City College. In 2016: "Baltimore City College, founded in 1839, is the third oldest public high school in the United States. Committed to the pursuit of excellence, we are a citywide college preparatory institution with selective admissions and an emphasis on the liberal arts and sciences," http://www.baltimorecitycollege.us/apps/pages/index.jsp?uREC_ID=270306&type=d, accessed January 17, 2016. Romoser then attended The Johns Hopkins University in Baltimore, and Concordia Theological Seminary in St. Louis. He was awarded the degree Doctor of Divinity *honoris causa* by Concordia Seminary in 1930. He served as President of Concordia College in Conover until 1911, and then joined the faculty of Concordia Institute in the village of Bronxville, Westchester County, New York, as a teacher of Greek. The Institute was founded in 1881 in Manhattan as a part of the Lutheran Church of St. Matthew, and was a preparatory school for Concordia Seminary in St. Louis. Its

Bronxville campus opened on January 4, 1910, with a hundred students. After three years on the faculty, Romoser was elected President of Concordia Institute. He served as President for eighteen years, "raising the institution to be a fully accredited high school and one of the first fully accredited junior colleges in New York." W. H. Luecke, "In Memoriam: George A. Romoser," *Church History*, vol. 5, no. 4 (December 1936), p. 386.

Page 287, *Professor Dau served as vacancy pastor* ... Email October 7, 2014, from Dennis Rathert, Archivist of Trinity Lutheran Church, St. Louis.

Page 287, *Franz August Otto Pieper (June 27, 1852–June 3, 1931)* ... Pieper became Professor of Dogmatics and Pastoral Theology at Concordia Seminary in 1878, and in 1887 became President of Concordia Seminary, a position that he would hold until his death. He was President of the Missouri Synod from 1899 to 1911.

Page 288, *the most visible intellectual issue* ... Richard Baepler, *Flame of Faith, Lamp of Learning: A History of Valparaiso University* (St. Louis: Concordia Publishing House, 2001), p. 169.

Page 288, *Theodore Conrad Graebner (November 23, 1876–November 14, 1950...* Mark E. Braun, "Theodore Graebner: Bellwether of Changes in the Missouri Synod," *Wisconsin Lutheran Seminary Online* (1977), pp. 186–216, www.wlsessays.net/files/BraunTheodoreGraebner.pdf, accessed September 15, 2014.

Page 289, *"Science and the Church"* ... A. G. [A. L. Gräbner], "Science and the Church," *Theological Quarterly*, vol. 6 (1902), pp. 37–45. *Theological Quarterly* was a publication of the Evangelical Lutheran Synod of Missouri, Ohio, and Other States, 1897–1920 (St. Louis: Concordia Publishing House).

Page 289, *The Rev. John A. Leimer* ... John A. Leimer to Prof. Th. Graebner, November 28, 1938. T. G. to Rev. John A. Leimer, November 30, 1938. Copies of both letters (from Archives of the Concordia Historical Institute, box "Theo. Graebner, F–G", folder labeled "Geology—Correspondence, 1924–1949") were supplied by Mark J. Bliese,

Research Assistant, Concordia Historical Institute, 804 Seminary Place, St. Louis, Missouri.

Page 290, *appointed Heimlich to additional positions* ... Minutes of the meeting of the Committee on Instruction, March 18, 1927. Copy supplied by Judith Miller, Valparaiso University Archives.

Page 290, *Louis Frederick Heimlich was born* ... Fred Kaufmann, Valparaiso University; Edwin J. Kohl and C. L. Porter, Purdue University; Obituary, "Louis Frederick Heimlich," *Proceedings of the Indiana Academy of Science*, vol. 38 (1928), pp. 29–30.

Page 291, *"Microsporogenesis in the Cucumber"* ... L. F. Heimlich, "Microsporogenesis in the Cucumber," *Proceedings of the National Academy of Sciences of the United States of America*, vol. 13, no. 3 (March 1, 1927), pp. 113–115.

Page 291, *Frank Roy Elliott (May 19, 1888–October 17, 1965)* ... "Elliott, Dr. F(rank) R(oy)," *American Men of Science*, 6th edition (New York: The Science Press, 1938), p. 412. *See also* Fay Kenoyer Daily, Obituary, "Frank R(oy) Elliott: Spartansburg, Indiana, May 19, 1888; Angola, Indiana, October 17, 1965," *Proceedings of the Indiana Academy of Science*, vol. 76 (1966), pp. 45–46.

Page 291, *summers 1913, 1915, and 1916* ... Andrea M. Wilson, "Participants at the Lake Erie Biological Station of The Ohio State University, 1896 to 1982," CLEAR Technical Report no. 271 (Columbus: The Ohio State University Center for Lake Erie Area Research, December 1982), pp. 15–17.

Page 291, *with the thesis* ... The thesis was published in *The Ohio Journal of Science*, vol. 30, no. 1 (January 1930), pp. 1–22.

Page 292, *Many present-day philosophers of biology* ... *See, for example,* Thomas A. C. Reydon, "Classifying Life, Reconstructing History, and Teaching Diversity: Philosophical Issues in the Teaching of Biological Systematics and Biodiversity," *Science and Education. Contributions from History, Philosophy and Sociology of Science and Mathematics*, vol. 22, no. 2 (February 2013), pp. 189–220. Contains a useful six-page bibliography.

Page 292, *The philosophy of the Department of Biology in 2015* ... Valparaiso University Department of Biology internet webpage, http://www.valpo.edu/biology/about/, accessed November 20, 2015.

Page 292, *Alfred Herman Ludwig Meyer (February 27, 1893–February 27, 1988)...* Biographies of Alfred Meyer have appeared in scholarly journals, in a book of biographies, and on a Valparaiso University internet website. Chauncy D. Harris, Committee on Geographical Studies, University of Chicago, "In Memory: Alfred H. Meyer, 1893–1988, *Journal of Geography*, vol. 87, no. 6 (November 1, 1988) contains significant factual errors. A balanced memorial, Fay Kenoyer Daily, "Alfred H(erman) L(udwig) Meyer: Venedy, Illinois, February 27, 1893; Valparaiso, Indiana, February 27, 1988" appeared in *Proceedings of the Indiana Academy of Science*, vol. 98 (1988), pp. 49–50; it has at least two errors. A biography with portrait appears in Thomas Frank Barton and Pradyumna P. Karan, *Leaders in American Geography, Volume 1: Geographic Education* (Mesilla, New Mexico: New Mexico Geographical Society, 1992), pp. 148–151. Meyer's contribution as a geographer is the focus of Jon T. Kilpinen, "Alfred H. Meyer: The Life and Work of a Midwestern Geographer" (1996), internet website of the Department of Geography and Meteorology at Valparaiso University, http://www.valpo.edu/geomet/histphil/biograph/meyer/meyer.html, accessed September 13, 2013.

Page 293, *he was hired in 1910 at age seventeen* ... As we have seen in earlier chapters, it was not uncommon for a teacher to be hired with just a common-school education. *See, for an example,* this fictional account of rural schooling in southern Illinois: Arno Bratten (with an introduction by Eli Gilbert Lentz), *The Redemption of Arthur True: A Rural School Story* (Marion, Illinois: Stafford Publishing Co., 1909). Arno Bratten would later be Principal of the Marion Township High School, a member of the summer school faculty of Southern Illinois State Normal University, and President of the Southern Illinois Teachers' Association.

Page 293, *Alfred enrolled at Southern Illinois State Normal University* ... Email September 6, 2013, from Matt Gorzalski, University Archivist, Southern Illinois University, Carbondale, Illinois.

Page 293, *Alfred attended Eastern Illinois State Normal School* ... Email September 6, 2013, from Prof. Robert Hillman, University Archivist, Booth Library, Eastern Illinois University, Charleston, Illinois.

Page 293, *McKendree College at Lebanon* ... Letter dated October 11, 2013, from Deborah L. Larson, Assistant Dean and Registrar, McKendree University, Lebanon, Illinois.

Page 293, *University of Illinois at Urbana* ... Email August 29, 2013, from Ellen D. Swain, Archivist for Student Life/Culture, University of Illinois at Urbana–Champaign, and email September 4, 2013, from Helen Sullivan, Archives Research Center, University of Illinois at Urbana–Champaign.

Page 294, *also matriculated at the Graduate School* ... Email September 18, 2013, from Thomas Whittaker, Reference Assistant, Special Collections Research Center, The University of Chicago.

Page 294, *Ronald L. Numbers has written* ... Ronald L. Numbers, *The Creationists* (New York: Alfred A. Knopf, 1992), p. 274.

Page 294, *[George McCready] Price* ... George McCready Price (1870–1963) had already written several antievolution books, including *Outlines of Modern Christianity and Modern Science* (Oakland, California: Pacific Press, 1902); *Illogical Geology: The Weakest Point in the Evolution Theory* (Los Angeles: Modern Heretic, 1906); *God's Two Books; or, Plain Facts About Evolution, Geology, and the Bible* (Washington: Review and Herald Publishing Association, 1911); *The Fundamentals of Geology and Their Bearings on the Doctrine of a Literal Creation* (Portland, Oregon: Pacific Press Publishing Association, 1913); and *Q.E.D.; or, New Light on the Doctrine of Creation* (New York: Fleming H. Revell Company, 1917). The crusader's forthcoming book was *The New Geology: A Textbook for Colleges, Normal Schools, and Training Schools; and for the General Reader* (Mountain View, California:

Pacific Press Publishing Association, 1923), 726pp.

Page 294, *Did Alfred Meyer take action ...* Emails September 5 and 6, 2013, from Reference, Research, & Scholarly Services, University of Illinois Library, and from Marten N. Stromberg, Curator, Rare Book & Manuscript Library, University of Illinois.

Page 295, *His dissertation was "The Kankakee ...* Email September 5, 2013, from Bentley Historical Library, University of Michigan. *Also,* email August 30, 2013, from John P. Hodson Founder and President, Kankakee Valley Historical Society, Inc., 22 West 1050 South Street, Kouts, Indiana; http://www.kankakeevalleyhistoricalsociety.org.

Page 296, *co-authoring an influential geography textbook ...* Alfred H. Meyer and John H. Strietelmeier, *Geography in World Society: A Conceptual Approach* (Philadelphia: J. B. Lippincott Company, 1963), 846 pages.

Page 296, *Harry A. Eberline (1874–1952)...* Harry A. Eberline was born in Logansport, Indiana. When he was thirteen, his family moved to Fort Wayne, where he completed his education. He graduated from Concordia College. He started work in Fort Wayne as an office boy at Salamonie Mining and Gas. There he worked his way up to the position of Secretary as the business grew. Eberline moved on to become Secretary–Treasurer of William L. Carnahan and Company, a wholesale boot and shoe company. He invested in other businesses in the Fort Wayne area. In 1901 (or 1905), Eberline moved to Detroit, becoming a partner in the Crowley Brothers Wholesale Dry Goods Company. He married Adelaide Foellinger (1881–1977). They had two children. The family lived at 888 Chicago Boulevard in Detroit during the 1910s and 1920s. *History of the Boston–Edison Neighborhood* [Detroit], http://www.historicbostonedison.org/history/people_bus.shtml, accessed January 16, 2016. Obituary, Fort Wayne *Journal Gazette*, May 20, 1953, p. 18, col 1. Allen County Indiana Cemetery Project, Lindenwood Cemetery, Section G, http://www.rootsweb.ancestry.com/~inallcem/wayne/lindenwood/section-g-a-e.html, accessed January 16, 2016.

Page 296, *imperative that his vacation begin immediately* ... Minutes of the meeting of the Executive Council of the Valparaiso University Association held on May first, 1927. A written report from Dr. Ulbrich was included in the Minutes. Copy supplied by Judith Miller, Valparaiso University Archives.

Page 297, *approved eight faculty appointments* ... Minutes of the meeting of the Committee on Instruction, May 11, 1927. Copy supplied by Judith Miller, Valparaiso University Archives.

Page 297, *Ralph Edward Richman (1891–1972)* ... Ralph Edward Richman was born February 16, 1891, son of Margaret Waltz and Charles H. Richman. He graduated from Tipton High School, Tipton, Indiana, in 1908. While in high school, he was already selling fire insurance as Tipton agent for Fidelity Fire of New York. He graduated from Indiana University in 1913, with an A.B. degree in Economics. He was a member of Sigma Rho ("an interorganization composed of those interested in public speaking and oratory"), a member of the Debating Team for three years, and a member of the Lutheran Concordia Club. He was elected to Phi Beta Kappa, and served as an undergraduate Teaching Assistant in the Department of Public Speaking for three years. Active in campus politics, he was President of his Class in 1910 and 1911, President of Y.M.C.A. in 1911 and 1912, Chairman of Student Marshalls in 1912, and member of the Board of Directors of the Indiana Union in 1911, 1912, and 1913. He later was a graduate student at Harvard, focusing on insurance. Richman was Deputy Fire Marshal of Indiana (in Indianapolis) as early as 1915. He joined National Underwriter in Cincinnati in 1916. There he started and edited *Accident and Health* bulletins in 1924, and served as manager of the Cincinnati office from 1919 to 1933. He then went to Hartford, Connecticut, to develop New England business of National Underwriter, later moving his headquarters to Boston. In 1943, he became the editor of the *Casualty Insurer*. He also edited *Fire Protection*. Richman's first involvement with Valparaiso University was his election to the first permanent Board of Directors in April of 1926 to a one-year term. In January 1927, Dr. Herman A. Duemling, President of the Board, appointed Richman, Fredrick Henry Wehrenberg, and Oscar Carl Kreinheder to serve as the Committee on Instruction. The Committee first met in February 1927, and quickly became very active in curriculum and staff development. Richman later served as Vice-President and then President of the Board of Directors, before submitting his resignation in 1933. Sources: Ethan Stoppenhagen, Assistant in Archives, Valparaiso University Archives & Special Collections, email January 22, 2016. Tipton High School yearbook, the *Tiptonian*, vol. 10 (1908), http://www.tiptonpl.lib.in.us/yearbooks/1908tiptonian.pdf, accessed January 22, 2016. *The 1913 Arbutus*, yearbook of the Indiana University Class of 1913, https://ia902306.us.archive.org/22/items/arbutus_1913indi/arbutus_1913indi_bw.pdf, accessed January 22, 2016. Ralph E. Richman, "Fires Caused by Lightning—Best Method of Protecting Farm Property," prize winning essay, *Safety Engineering*, vol. 30, no. 4 (August 1915), pp. 154–155.

Page 297, *Fredrick Henry Wehrenberg (December 29, 1890–December 24, 1963)* ... Fredrick Henry Wehrenberg was born in Fort Wayne, son of Wilhelmina Albersmeyer and Henry Karl Wehrenberg. He attended the parish school of St. Paul's Lutheran Church and then International Business College in Fort Wayne. He served with Herman A. Duemling on the Board of Directors of the Lutheran Hospital Association, and with Martin H. Luecke Jr. on the Board of Directors of the Irene Byron Tuberculosis Sanatorium in Fort Wayne. At his death, Wehrenberg was President and General Manager of the Fort Wayne Standard Lumber and Supply Company, and also President and General Manager of the New Haven (Indiana) Lumber and Supply Company. The New Haven enterprise had been formed by his father and his uncle, Fred Albersmeyer, in 1906. Fredrick Wehrenberg became manager of the firm in 1915. Sources: Biography of Fredrick Wehrenberg *in* Bert J. Griswold, *Builders*

of Greater Fort Wayne (Fort Wayne: 1926), pp. 612 and 777. Obituary of Fred H. Wehrenberg, Fort Wayne *Journal Gazette*, p. 1, cols 5 and 6; p. 2A, col. 1, Thursday, December 26, 1963.

Page 297, *Rev. Oscar Carl Kreinheder (November 10, 1877–March 26, 1946)* ... Oscar Carl Kreinheder was born in Buffalo, New York. He prepared for seminary at Concordia Collegiate Institute in Bronxville, New York, graduating in 1920. One of his teachers was George A. Romoser. Kreinheder graduated from Concordia Seminary, St. Louis, Missouri, and was ordained by The English Evangelical Lutheran Synod of Missouri and Other States. He was pastor of a Lutheran church in East St. Louis, Illinois (1901–1903); of the English Evangelical of the Redeemer Lutheran Church, St. Paul, Minnesota (1903–1920); and of a Lutheran church in Detroit, Michigan (1920–1930). He was President of the English District of the Missouri Synod (1918–1927). He served as President of Valparaiso University from 1930 to 1939. Sources: *Christian Cyclopedia* (Erwin Lueker, ed.), electronic edition, http://cyclopedia.lcms.org/display.asp?t1=K&word=KREINHEDER.OSCARCARL, accessed January 16, 2016. "1910 St. Paul Churches–Lutheran," *St. Paul City Directory* (Chicago: R. L. Polk & Company, 1910), http://www.kinsource.com/ED1910Census/StPaulCLutheran.htm, accessed January 16, 2016.

Page 297, *full text of a letter from Dau* ... Letter from Dau to Germann, dated June 30th, 1927. Copy supplied by Judith Miller, Valparaiso University Archives.

Page 298, *as do many published references ... see, for example,* "Valparaiso University: Presidents," http://www.valpo.edu/150/history-presidents/dau.php; "Dau Church History Library," http://www.historictrinity.org/dau.html; "Valpo Tea," https://historictrinity.org/valpotea.html; "In Memory of William Herman Theodore Dau," *Concordia Theological Monthly*, vol. 15, no. 12 (December 1944), p. 793. Internet sites accessed October 21, 2015.

Page 298, *On July 21, 1927, Dau wrote to Germann* … Letter, beginning "My dear Doctor:" and signed "W. H. T. Dau, D. D., President." Copy supplied by Judith Miller, Valparaiso University Archives.

Page 298, *as a mere trade school* … Richard Baepler, *Flame of Faith, Lamp of Learning: A History of Valparaiso University* (St. Louis: Concordia Publishing House, 2001), p. 159.

Page 299, *I had 56 students with me* … Letter dated May 28, 1927. Copy supplied by Judith Miller, Valparaiso University Archives.

Page 299, *Professor of Pharmacy in the Rutgers University* … Roy A. Bowers and David L. Cowen, *The Rutgers University College of Pharmacy: A Centennial History* (New Brunswick: Rutgers University Press, 1991), p. 62. Thomas J. Frusciano, Rutgers University Archivist, provided sources of this biographical information.

Page 299, *he became Executive Director of Saint Barnabas* … "1950. New Faces Lead the Way. George Schicks, Ph.D., Becomes Hospital Administrator," *Saint Barnabas, Our History: 1900–1955*, http://www.barnabashealth.org/hospitals/saint_barnabas/aboutus/1900.html, accessed August 4, 2013.

Page 300, *includes the phrase* … Obituary, *The New York Times*, July 18, 1961, p. 29. In fact, he received the degree of Ph.G. (*graduate in pharmacy*) from Massachusetts College of Pharmacy on May 27, 1919.

Page 301, *Wisconsin Pharmaceutical Experiment Station* … "History of the Zeeh Pharmaceutical Experiment Station," internet website of the School of Pharmacy, University of Wisconsin, Madison: http://www.pharmacy.wisc.edu/zeeh-pharmaceutical-experiment-station/history-zeeh-pharmaceutical-experiment-station, accessed July 24, 2013.

Page 301, *one of the six founders* … "AIHP Celebrates 60 Years," *Apothecary's Cabinet*, vol. 1, no. 2 (spring 2001), p. 6.

Page 301, *According to John Strietelmeier* … John Strietelmeier, *Valparaiso's First Century: A Centennial History of Valparaiso University* (Valparaiso, Indiana: Valparaiso University, 1959), p. 101.

Page 301, *my office is at the Directors' discretion* … "my final report for the first year of my administration." To the Board of Directors of the Valparaiso University Association, dated September 3, 1927. Copy supplied by Judith Miller, Valparaiso University Archives. According to John Strietelmeier (*Valparaiso's First Century: A Centennial History of Valparaiso University*, op. cit., p. 101), Germann was "acting president, May to September, 1927." As indicated in this "final report" and in letters quoted in the text, Dau would not have agreed with Strietelmeier's assessment.

Page 302, *letter of resignation from the faculty* … Copy supplied by Judith Miller, Valparaiso University Archives.

Page 302, *Ralph Richman wrote Germann on August 9, 1927* … Richman to Germann (in Cleveland). Copy supplied by Judith Miller, Valparaiso University Archives.

Page 302, *In a letter to Ralph Richman* … Copy supplied by Judith Miller, Valparaiso University Archives.

Page 303, *Richman wrote to Germann on Thursday, September 1, 1927* … Letter from Ralph E. Richman, Secretary and Acting-Chairman, Committee on Instruction. Copy supplied by Judith Miller, Valparaiso University Archives.

Sanborn-Perris Map of South Whitley in 1900

V.
Nutritional Research
Associates

L UISE BARBARA GERMANN POOK recalled, in third person:
"Her childhood was spent in many locations and in many schools as her
father, a Chemistry professor at Western Reserve University in Cleveland,
took other positions. At age 5 her family moved to Palo Alto, Calif., when her father
became a professor at Stanford University. At age 9, her family moved back to Cleveland, Ohio, when her father took a Research Chemist position with Laboratory
Products Co. At age 10 she lived with her grandparents in Peru, while her father was
at Valparaiso University helping them get their Science departments' credentials in
order and get accredited, first as Head of the Chemistry Department, then acting
Dean of the Pharmacy School, then Acting President of the University. At age 11
her family moved back to Cleveland, when her father became Director at S.M.A.
Corporation. In 1934 her father and four others of his research team formed Quintrex Corporation which then was renamed Nutritional Research Associates, Inc.
Her grandfather G. Adolph Germann of Peru found a building available in South
Whitley, and Barbara went with her father from Peru to South Whitley when he
first saw and went through the building and then bought it. The family then gradually moved to South Whitley with Barbara interrupting her college studies to
help her father with running the office, and with whatever other help was needed.
She then also took a job as a proofreader with Stump Printing Co., which was the
publisher of the *South Whitley Tribune* and many other publications, so she could
finish her college degree.

"A graduate of Cleveland East High School in 1933, she attended Flora Stone Mather College of Western Reserve University from 1933–36. After moving to South Whitley and helping start her father's business, she completed her bachelors degree at Manchester College in 1940. She spent an additional year at Manchester College and several summers at Ball State University doing graduate work and getting additional teaching credentials.

"She always supported in any way possible and was part owner of her family's business founded by her father, Nutritional Research Associates, Inc., since its founding in 1934. Her interest and support only increased when Nutritional Research Associates, Inc. purchased her father-in-law Ervin Pook's Pook Feed & Coal Co. in 1956 at his retirement which was then renamed Whitley Feeds and also with her son Jonathan's interest and involvement in the business from high school until the present."

Most of this final chapter is set in the small town of South Whitley, Cleveland Township, Whitley County, Indiana. This is the town where Nutritional Research Associates, Inc., established its physical facilities in 1935. It is the town to which Ida and Albert Germann gradually moved their family, the town where they finally settled.

South Whitley was indeed a small town then, and it still is. Throughout the first half of the twentieth century, South Whitley's population was stable at just over a thousand persons: 1,113 in 1900, 1,176 in 1910, 1,074 in 1920, 1,102 in 1930, and 1,118 in 1940. Palo Alto in 1920 had a population of 5,900. Peru, the only other small town or city that Barbara had known, grew from 6,518 in 1920 to 8,736 in 1936. By contrast, Cleveland (where Barbara lived from age eleven until she completed her junior year in college) was the fifth largest city in the nation, with a population of about 900,000.

South Whitley sits on the banks of the Eel River in southwestern Whitley County, between Peru, Indiana (home of Barbara's Germann grandparents) and Van Wert County, Ohio (birthplace of her grandfather Germann). It is 45 miles from Peru to South Whitley, 26 miles from South Whitley to Fort Wayne, and another 40 miles to the city of Van Wert. Many members of the Germann extended family were living in the 1930s between Peru and Van Wert County, especially in Fort Wayne. South Whitley was in familiar territory for Gustave Adolph Germann.

Chapter 4 closed with Albert Germann's departure from Valparaiso University on Thursday, September 1, 1927. Labor Day was Monday, September 5; the first day of school for his daughters was the previous week. Barbara Germann entered Addison Junior High School in Cleveland on Friday, September 2, 1927; she would graduate from Cleveland East High School in June 1933. Her sisters Edith and Lucia entered Wade Park Elementary School. Edith would later attend Addison Junior High School and then graduate from Cleveland East High School in June 1935. Lucia attended Addison Junior High School and Cleveland East High School, leaving in September 1936 for South Whitley. Lucia received her diploma from South Whitley High School in 1938, one of twenty-five members of her graduating class.

The Germann family lived at 1532 East 86th Street in the Hough section of Cleveland. Hough extends from East 55th Street to East 106th Street, and includes the area between Superior Avenue on the north and Euclid Avenue on the south. Euclid Avenue was "Millionaire's Row" before the Great War, with "beautiful elm-lined sidewalks and ornate mansions situated amid lavish gardens." The post-war exodus of the extremely wealthy to suburbs transformed Hough into the middle-class neighborhood that was the Germann family's Cleveland home.

At the eastern edge of Hough is University Circle, since 1880 the home of Case School of Applied Science (predecessor of Case Institute of Technology) and since 1882 the home of Western Reserve University. Within the Hough neighborhood in 1927 were Wade Park Elementary School at 7600 Wade Park Boulevard, Addison Junior High School at 1725 East 79th Street and Hough Avenue, and Cleveland East High School at 1380 East 82nd Street and Decker Avenue. Cleveland built Wade Park Elementary School in 1898. The old Wade Park building was demolished and replaced with a new Wade Park Elementary School in 1975. Addison Junior High School was built in 1914. Cleveland East High School was built in 1900; it closed in 1975. At the northeast corner of Hough was St. Paul Lutheran Church–Missouri Synod, 5406 Spencer Avenue (just off East 55th Street).

Albert Germann resumed work as Research Director of Laboratory Products Company and S.M.A. in Cleveland. William Telling, who had made his fortune in the dairy business, promoted the principal product of S.M.A. as "the first artificial baby formula." The names Telling Laboratory, Laboratory Products Company, Sealtest Laboratories, and S.M.A. Corporation were used interchangeably in labeling, in publicity, and in advertising.

Telling's Director of Laboratories from 1916 to 1925 was William O. Frohring.

When Albert Germann became Research Director at Laboratory Products Company in 1925, William Frohring was elevated to Vice-President and General Manager, positions that he would hold until 1938. William and his brother Paul decided that their prospects for future financial success indicated a move from dairy products into the field of specialty biochemicals. They made that move. They were successful.

Quintrex

When Albert Germann returned to Cleveland, he began to assemble his own research group from members of S.M.A. The specialty biochemical carotene was prominent in his plans. His cohorts were Vernon Jersey, Robert Cross, Otto Ungnade, and Harold Barnett. In 1934, these five S.M.A. research scientists decided to form the Quintrex Corporation. They had been broadening their research and business perspectives beyond the increasingly crowded infant-formula business. They were about to capitalize on the vitamin revolution.

The scientific community was rapidly learning about vitamins. Just a few decades earlier, nutritionists had focused on carbohydrates, fats, and proteins as the important components of a good diet. Vitamins, with significant effects when present in only trace amounts, were becoming recognized as additional dietary components that needed to be understood. Because the molecular structures were still being investigated, systematic chemical names were unavailable for individual vitamins. Besides, a name such as "levo-hexuronic acid" for a nutrient was often deemed intimidating or worse. It sounds like the name of an unnatural product. The first letters of the alphabet were used to name successive new vitamins. This convention persists.

By 1913, Marguerite Davis (1887–1967) and Elmer Verner McCollum (1879–1967) at the University of Wisconsin, and Thomas Burr Osborne (1859–1929) and Lafayette Benedict Mendel (1872–1935) at Yale, had isolated a yellow, fat-soluble nutrient from butterfat and from cod liver oil. This yellow substance (carotene) was later to be identified with Vitamin A. As we observed in Chapter 3, Heinrich Wilhelm Ferdinand Wackenroder published experimental preparation methods in 1831, describing how he pressed carrots to obtain juice, and how he extracted carotene from the juice. Early in the twentieth century, Richard Martin Willstätter and Walter Mieg studied this yellow material as a chemical compound. Willstätter and Mieg determined the empirical formula of carotene to be $C_{40}H_{56}$; the results of their experiments were published in 1907.

Japanese agricultural chemist Umetaro Suzuki (1874–1943) and Polish biochemist Kazimierz (Casimir) Funk (1884–1967) independently isolated the anti-beriberi factor from rice bran in 1911. The water-soluble anti-beriberi factor was initially called Vitamin B. During the next decades, researchers found this nutrient to be a mixture of many chemical compounds, collectively called the "Vitamin B Complex." Individual members of the complex were numbered: B_1, B_2, and so forth.

In his 1914 book, Funk presented evidence for at least four vitamins: one that prevents beriberi, one that prevents scurvy, one that prevents pellagra, and one that prevents rickets. Beriberi, scurvy, pellagra, and rickets, once scourges of humankind, became preventable conditions merely by changes in diet.

This was just the beginning of the vitamin revolution. By 1932, the Hungarian Albert Szent-Györgyi de Nagyrápolt (1893–1986; Nobel laureate 1937) and the American Charles Glen King (1896–1988) had identified and chemically characterized the anti-scurvy factor (Vitamin C) as levo-hexuronic acid, later also named L-ascorbic acid. By 1923, Harry Steenbock (1886–1967) at the University of Wisconsin had shown that irradiation of milk with ultraviolet light increases the concentration of the anti-rickets factor (Vitamin D). Steenbock patented his invention. Proceeds from his patent (until 1945, a royalty payment from every quart of irradiated milk) led to the formation of the Wisconsin Alumni Research Foundation (WARF), the pioneer organization for university technology transfer.

Quintrex was incorporated in Fort Wayne on Monday, November 5, 1934. The *Quint*rex name implies five incorporators. Albert Germann and three other men moved to Indiana. The fifth, Harold Barnett, went west to Long Beach, California. These five men of Quintrex had individual expertise that they would collectively soon put to use commercially by extracting carotene (a metabolic precursor of Vitamin A) from carrots. Elsewhere in 1934, there were many systematic experimental investigations of the nutritional requirements of humans and also farm animals for vitamins. In chemical laboratories throughout the world, vitamins and their metabolic precursors were being identified, isolated, and purified. Their molecular structures were being determined. The stage was set for exploiting the beaker-and-flask results of desktop chemistry for efficient and profitable commercial production of vitamins.

Vernon Jersey had been a member of Albert Germann's first research group at Western Reserve University from 1920 to 1921. Mr. Jersey began his association with S.M.A. Corporation while he was a doctoral student at Western Reserve. He was in charge of dairy research at S.M.A. from 1929 to 1935. He received the Ph.D. in Biochemistry from Western Reserve in 1935. Dr. Jersey moved to South Whitley in 1937. He married Evelyn Bippus (1920–2009) on Sunday, March 24, 1940.

Robert Cross had been a graduate student in chemistry at Stanford University when Albert Germann was on the chemistry faculty there. He earned his A.B. (1911) and A.M. (1920) degrees from Stanford. In 1928, Robert Cross became a research chemist and chemical engineer at S.M.A. He lived in Mason, Michigan. He married Pearl Bingham on Wednesday, January 1, 1930. The family moved to South Whitley in 1941.

Otto Ungnade had published three books in Germany (in 1921, 1926, and 1929) on the chemistry of milk and on the technology of drying milk. By 1930, he was associated with S.M.A. He submitted U. S. Patent applications in 1930, 1933, and 1934, in each case assigning the patent to the S.M.A. Corporation, and in each case giving his address as Mason, Michigan. According to his obituary, he moved to Fort Wayne, Indiana (26 miles east of South Whitley) in 1929. Perhaps he maintained two residences for several years. Otto Ungnade characterized his occupation in Indiana as "a self-employed research chemist."

Albert Germann had recruited Harold Barnett (when Albert was Acting President of Valparaiso University) for the position of Instructor in Chemistry at Valparaiso University for the academic year 1927–1928. Barnett remained a candidate for the Ph.D. degree at the University of Minnesota while collaborating in Cleveland with Dr. Harry Goldblatt at the Institute of Pathology of the Western Reserve University School of Medicine, and also with William Otto Frohring and Albert Germann at S.M.A. The University of Minnesota awarded him the Ph.D. degree in Agricultural Biochemistry and Plant Physiology in 1931. Harold Barnett was associated with S.M.A. from 1929 to 1935. He then moved west, and in 1936 established Barnett Laboratories at 1120 East Artesia Boulevard, Long Beach, California. He was Director of Barnett Laboratories, Inc., for two decades, from 1936 until his death on February 20, 1956.

Barnett's move to California was prompted by his interest in extracting carotene from carrots. Barnett wanted to be close to his source. Carrots were becoming an important agricultural crop in California. Acreage devoted to carrot production in the state was increasing exponentially, doubling almost every year from 1925 to 1929. As Barnett anticipated, California continued through the next decades to be an excellent source of carrots harvested during winter, spring, and fall growing seasons, the months when carotene content is highest. United States Department of Agriculture ten-year average data (1938–1947) place California in first place among the states for winter harvests (with more than 50% of United States production), for spring harvests (with 70% of national production), and for fall harvests (with 42% of national production).

After Harold Barnett's departure, the four remaining scientists—Albert Germann, Vernon Jersey, Robert Cross, and Otto Ungnade—renamed their enterprise. The corporation became Nutritional Research Associates, Inc., on Thursday, March 28, 1935. Albert Germann became President, Vernon Jersey became Secretary-Treasurer, and Robert Cross became Chief Chemist and Chemical Engineer. The Quintrex brand name did not disappear. For example, Quintrex Aqua-Vite, a solution of water-soluble vitamins to be added to drinking water for fur-bearing mammals, pets, caged birds, and other animals, was still advertised by Nutritional Research Associates, Inc., in 2013.

Albert Germann consulted with his father G. Adolph Germann about a location for a research laboratory and a manufacturing facility. Albert wanted to begin processing tons of carrots right away, and (as Harold Barnett had found) the likely source of carotene-rich carrots was California. Access to long-haul freight-train service was therefore essential.

South Whitley

As a knowledgeable and experienced building contractor in Peru, Indiana, Gustave Adolph Germann was personally well connected with real estate agents in the greater Peru area. Gustave learned of a commercial building that was for sale in South Whitley, 45 miles east of Peru. It was an ideal site, just east of the grade crossing of the tracks of two railroad lines: the Vandalia Railroad and the Nickel Plate Road.

The Vandalia was a 93-mile line completed in 1874 as the Detroit, Eel River and Illinois Railroad. South Whitley was incorporated on the northwest bank of the Eel River. After 1879, the railroad's shop facilities were in Peru. The Vandalia name appeared when the Pennsylvania Railroad acquired the Detroit, Eel River and Illinois in 1901. The Vandalia crossed the New York to Chicago main line of the Pennsylvania Railroad at grade in Columbia City, ten miles northeast of South Whitley. Columbia City, the county seat, is located at the center of Whitley County. The Vandalia was locally called the Panhandle, a name inherited from the Pennsylvania Railroad's Panhandle Division, whose tracks passed through the Northern Panhandle of West Virginia.

The Nickel Plate Road opened in 1882 as the New York, Chicago and St. Louis Railroad. The Vandalia crossed the main line of the Nickel Plate in South Whitley at grade, a half-block west of State Street, the main business street of the town. South Whitley was the only Nickel Plate passenger stop in the 1940s between Fort Wayne and the Chicago commuter region.

When Barbara Germann traveled to South Whitley with her father in 1935 to visit the building that her grandfather had located, she saw the building as part of a cluster of structures that housed enterprises dependent on railway access via the Vandalia and the Nickel Plate. Several of these enterprises were also dependent on farm-to-market roadway access by trucks and wagons. The cluster included the Nickel Plate depot, the Vandalia depot, grain elevators and feed mills, and large buildings that until recently had housed a major printing plant and a manufacturing plant. The Pook Feed and Coal Company was located between the tracks of the two railroads on the east side of State Street. Farther to the east along the tracks was the Mayer Grain Elevator. West of State Street was the Farmers Elevator.

The site of Springfield Academy was on the east side of State Street, just south of the railroad tracks. Springfield Academy was South Whitley's first high school. The Academy opened on August 5, 1867. It was superseded in 1887 by the construction of a two-story brick town school (with a belfry) on the east side of Calhoun Street, between Columbia Street and Market Street. Calhoun Street was named for John Caldwell Calhoun (1782–1850). Before that time, only Wayne Street had been named for a person.

G. M. Naber was the first Superintendent of the Calhoun Street School. Naber probably taught all high school classes. Elementary students were taught on the first floor of the building. Only two students—Nettie Baker and Sadie Vaux—completed the high school requirements in the first three years. They graduated on Thursday, June 19, 1890. Columbia City lawyer Thomas Riley Marshall (1854–1925) delivered their commencement address. Marshall would later serve as Governor of Indiana (1909–1913) and two terms as Vice-President of the United States (1913–1921) in the administration of Woodrow Wilson.

After the Calhoun Street School opened, the two-story brick Academy building housed the Atoz [pronounced "A-to-Z"] printing plant (eventually operated by Robert E. Hicks), and the offices and machinery of the Grip Nut Company, manufacturer of threaded steel bolts and patented steel grip nuts. A large room on the second floor of the Academy building continued to function for a half century as an assembly hall and as an indoor basketball court for the town.

The building that G. Adolph Germann had located was adjacent to the Nickel Plate tracks, on Broad Street, at the corner of Broad Street and a stub of Randolph Street. Randolph Street, running north and south, was two streets east of Calhoun Street. The building was a remnant of the estate of Robert E. Hicks. The late Robert Hicks was a flamboyant and charismatic personality, well known throughout the area. F. A. Schack, administrator of the Hicks estate, offered the property for sale. Albert Germann purchased the building on Saturday, September 7, 1935, in the name of "Nutritional Research Associates, Inc., an Indiana Corporation." He paid $500.

The career of Albert Fredrick Ottomar Germann moved into a new phase in 1935. What was also happening at that time?

Franklin Delano Roosevelt was President of the United States. *The Reader's Digest* was in its 14th year of publication. The American Chemical Society cited Frank Germann's method of producing dry ice as among the "High Points in Chemistry" for 1933. Arnold Beckman demonstrated his Model G pH Meter at the 1935 national meeting of the American Chemical Society. On February 28, 1935, Gerard J. Berchet and Wallace Carothers, working at duPont, synthesized Nylon. The Social Security Act was signed into law on August 14, 1935. The Rural Electric Administration was created in 1935 to bring electricity to rural areas. Adolph Hitler introduced military conscription in Germany, undoing the Treaty of Versailles. Notorious Indiana bank robber

John Dillinger died in an FBI gun battle on July 22, 1934, in Chicago. Ross Lockridge Jr. was writing his novel about a fictional Hoosier community "which had no boundaries in time and space," the antithesis of South Whitley in 1935. In 1935, Shirley Temple was starring in "The Little Colonel," "Our Little Girl," "Curly Top," and "The Littlest Rebel." In May 1934, soil conservation pioneer Hugh Bennett (1881–1960) was testifying before Congress when the Great Dust Bowl Storm deposited top soil from the Great Plains onto the Capitol Building in Washington; he used the unprecedented meteorological event to argue effectively for the Soil Conservation Act of 1935.

Albert Germann was investing in the future, even while the world was economically still in the depths of the Great Depression. Small-town South Whitley, surrounded by family farms that produced milk, butter, eggs, chickens, steers, hogs, and grain, survived the Depression with less individual suffering than occurred in many urban areas and in the drought-stricken Great Plains. Many folks in town had their own backyard gardens. Some farmers rented out small plots as "truck patches" where other families could grow vegetables. Most canned any excess produce, using glass jars made by the Ball Glass Works, seventy miles south in Muncie.

Today the farmland around South Whitley is planted largely to corn and soybeans. There was much more agricultural diversity in 1935. Oats, wheat, and alfalfa were also grown as part of systematic crop-rotation schemes. Tomatoes were a popular cash crop. Picked by hand by teenagers, field-ripened tomatoes were hauled to Pierceton (twelve miles north, eight miles west) to the Reid-Murdock plant. There they were processed into catsup, chili sauce, and canned tomatoes, then sold under the Monarch Brand. Cucumbers, also harvested by hand before the school year began, were hauled to the Reid-Murdock pickle factory in Columbia City.

South Whitley grocer Eugene Weybright (1907–1990) recalled: "If you had a job at the time, that was the main thing. Overtime pay was not heard of. You were paid so much a week; in our case (Kroger) we worked 80 to 90 hours a week, without complaining. Friday and Saturday the store was opened at 6:30 a.m. and remained open until about 11 or 12 p.m. I recall some of the prices at that time: butter solid prints (quarters were not in use then) about 19 cents a pound, potatoes were featured regularly at 69¢ for 100 pounds, hamburger at 3 pounds for 25¢, picnic hams at 7½¢ a pound; sugar was always featured in canning season at about $5.29 for a hundred-pound bag."

Depression recollections from two school teachers: "Some of the high school boys came to school barefoot until Thanksgiving. I sponsored a Senior High School class bus trip to Washington, D.C. for one week [1934]. It cost each student $14, all expenses except food. In 1932, $1 would provide a steak dinner, a ticket for the movie, a hair cut, and have money left for gasoline for the car. On $100 a month, I got married and raised four children." "I was fortunate in the Depression, always on teacher's salary, from September 1929. My salary began at $1,200, then $1,350, then cut to $1,150. No hardship. I bought a fine Plymouth new coupe in 1932 for $643 and kept it 18 years."

Depression recollections from a farm wife: "During 1927–1933 we paid $600 cash rent on a 200-acre farm in Union Township [in Whitley County, northeast of South Whitley], milked 8–12 cows by hand, churned our own butter, hatched our own baby chicks. One winter we got 10 cents per dozen eggs—one week we got 7 cents. We canned 400–450 quarts of fruits, vegetables and meat—had plenty of good food and plenty of meat. We raised our own potatoes—one year we had 40 bushel which we couldn't even give away. Each week we would trade potatoes for fish from the 'fish man' from Columbia City.... I belonged to the Union Township Home Division Club. Nothing better than a print dress was permitted to be worn to the club meetings. We used Purdue University study lessons and exchanged helpful hints of all kinds, discussed feed-sack dresses, best methods to bleach and to make sheets, pillow cases, etc., how to make home-made soap—you name it."

Depression recollections from a Democratic Township Trustee: "Then we had the P.W.A. [Public Works Administration] and it was cursed and damned by the Republicans but it was a God-send. They condemned it, but roads were built and Court Houses, too, and many others....with the advent of cotton pickers, corn pickers, tomato pickers and all the automatic machinery we had men out of employment."

An attractive residential property, on the other side of town from the newly purchased Nutritional Research Associates building, had also been part of the Robert E. Hicks estate. Two houses were located on an 11.54-acre parcel of land in Cleveland Township, outside the incorporated town of South Whitley but adjacent to the west corporation boundary of the town. Mae and Elmer Hicks (Elmer was a son of Robert E. Hicks) had owned this property, but they had just sold it to Elmore and Hiram Augsburger. Albert Germann decided to keep a watchful eye on the property. Two months later, the Augsburgers sold the place to Clara and Fern Orr. Less than a year later, the Orrs sold the houses and land (on Thursday, August 27, 1936) to Ida Helene Germann for $6,000. Then the Germann family gradually moved to South Whitley and settled in.

The Germann houses were within easy walking distance of the new two-story brick South Whitley–Cleveland Township High School building, dedicated Wednesday, February 17, 1932. Harry Guyer Leslie, Governor of Indiana, was the main speaker at the dedication ceremony. Fred Fox introduced the Governor. We shall have more to say about Harry Guyer Leslie and about Fred Fox.

The new consolidated school building housed classes from junior high school (grades seven and eight) through the four years of high school. There was a spacious library, a chemistry/physics laboratory room (with individual student work stations and a fume hood) for hands-on science, an attached greenhouse and aquarium for experimental biology, a wood, metal, and automotive classroom-shop, a home economics classroom with sewing machines and kitchen work stations, an office-style commercial-studies classroom, and a sound-insulated band and chorus room. The concept of a school cafeteria apparently had not yet dawned on school architects. There was an elevated stage at the end of what the architects called the "multi-purpose gymnasium and auditorium." The stage provided facilities for school dramatic productions, with theater-style curtains hung from overhead tracks. However, it was apparent to all that the primary purpose for the room was Hoosier high school basketball. The room had enough permanent bleacher seating for most of the townspeople. The gym was quite a contrast to the second-floor, low-ceiling basketball court in the old Springfield Academy building.

Elementary school classes continued in the pre-consolidation 1887 brick Calhoun Street School, also within walking distance of the Germann houses. School buses brought farm students to both schools from throughout Cleveland Township. Farm kids arrived with lunch pails, and spent the whole day in town. Town kids often walked home for lunch; the lunch "hour" was 90 minutes long. The bells in the belfries of the schools signaled the beginning of afternoon classes.

The 1932 building was a highly visible symbol of the end of an era in the evolution of the local public schools. In 1891–1892, there were thirteen one-room, one-teacher district schools in rural Cleveland Township. No student needed to walk more than two miles to a district school; when weather permitted, almost all the students did walk. Half the district schools had disappeared by 1919–1920, and a few four-room replacement buildings were built. Only one district school remained in Cleveland Township in 1931–1932, the year of the final consolidation into South Whitley.

The new consolidated school system, with a common calendar for all grades throughout the township, formalized the demise of the district-school year that in earlier decades had been synchronized with the farm planting, cultivating, and harvesting seasons. Consolidation also permitted implementation in Cleveland Township of curricular ideas of Hoosier educator Charles Allen Prosser (1871–1952). Prosser had championed the concept of including vocational education as a separate part of the curriculum of a comprehensive high school. The school population was large enough to justify individual teachers for agriculture, homemaking, and commercial subjects, and to create separate academic and vocational tracks.

The school had a vocational agriculture and shop teacher, a home economics teacher, and a commercial teacher, each with a dedicated classroom. The home economics and vocational agriculture teachers were paid extra to organize summertime 4-H (Head, Heart, Hands, and Health) student homemaking and agriculture clubs for girls and boys, each in conjunction with the Purdue University Cooperative Extension Service. Substantial external funding for these three teachers was provided under the umbrella of the 1917 Smith–Hughes Act, Federal legislation based on recommendations of Charles Allen Prosser.

It was the expressed intent of the Smith–Hughes Act to isolate vocational education from academic education in the nation's public schools. The South Whitley–Cleveland Township High School student body was large enough to permit separate vocational classes and teachers, but too small to permit effective separation of students in most of the curriculum, certainly not isolation.

The first graduation ceremonies at the new building were in the third week of April 1932. Folding chairs were set up on the hardwood floor of the basketball court for more than five hundred graduates, families, and townsfolk who attended three end-of-year school events that week. Ministers of the Methodist Episcopal Church, the Church of the United Brethren in Christ, and the Church of God conducted a Baccalaureate Service for the Class of 1932 on Sunday evening, April 17. The *South*

Whitley Tribune reported that all the churches co-operated by dispensing with evening services to give their members the opportunity to attend Baccalaureate at the new school. Class Night was Wednesday, April 20, when Senior Class President Lewis David Reiff (1914–2002) "passed the emblem to a representative of the Junior Class." Janice Peabody was valedictorian and Dora Byers was salutatorian. Students from all classes who had been attending the new school that semester had parts in the program. The entire building was open in afternoon and evening, with exhibits and displays in all departments.

Principal Lee LeVere Eve (1903–1992) presented diplomas and Bibles to thirty-one high school graduates at Commencement on Friday, April 22. Garbed in black caps and gowns, the students processed while pianist Isabelle Harrop, school music instructor, played a march. The Rev. Dr. James H. Lightbourne of Troy, Ohio, addressed the graduates. The high school orchestra provided music.

Lee Eve

Lee LeVere Eve was still Principal of South Whitley High School in 1936 when Ida Helene Germann bought the Hicks property and began to move the family to South Whitley. He was Principal during the years when Lucia Germann was a high school student at South Whitley. He was Principal when Barbara Germann completed her undergraduate studies at Manchester College, Lee Eve's alma mater.

Lee LeVere Eve was born February 17, 1903, near South Whitley. He grew up in a farming family. His parents Charlotte R. Cummins (1882–1932) and John Jacob Eve (1878–1948), and his paternal grandparents Anna M. (1846–1925) and John Jacob Eve (1850–1915), lived on adjacent farms in Richland Township, just north of Cleveland Township.

He attended elementary school and high school in the small Richland Township town of Larwill, seven miles north of South Whitley. The population of Larwill was 264 in 1920. He graduated in a class of nineteen in 1919. His future wife, Mary Irene Noble (1901–1975), graduated from Larwill High School in a class of thirteen in 1920. They were married on August 17, 1924.

Lee attended Manchester College in North Manchester (twenty miles southwest of

Larwill, eleven miles west of South Whitley), graduating in 1924 with an A.B. degree.

Albert Germann and Lee Eve were a little less than a generation apart. Albert graduated from Peru High School the year after Lee was born. Their early experiences as Hoosier school teachers were similar. Albert began teaching at Bunker Hill High School just after graduating from high school, and he worked his way through Indiana University by teaching near his home in Miami County. Lee pursued a similar course, teaching junior high school classes at Larwill while taking courses at Manchester College. He taught at Larwill from 1921 to 1926.

Lee began graduate studies at Indiana University in summer 1926, and received the Master of Arts degree in Education from Indiana University on October 25, 1928. He was a graduate student at Teachers College, Columbia University, New York City, from May 1930 to August 1948. He graduated from Teachers College on December 22, 1937, receiving the diploma "Superintendent of Schools," and then continued in a doctoral program at Teachers College, the nation's premier graduate school of education.

Mr. Eve's entire teaching career was in Indiana. It began in Whitley County, first as a junior high school teacher in Larwill, next as Principal of Coesse High School (in Union Township, fourteen miles east of Larwill) from 1926 to 1929, and then as Principal of South Whitley High School from 1929 to 1941. At South Whitley, he was actively involved with planning the new high school building and implementing an expanded comprehensive curriculum consistent with Smith–Hughes legislation. He was also active in the Indiana High School Athletic Association. In December 1933, he was elected by his fellow high school principals to a four-year term on the twenty-five member state Athletic Council, the legislative body of the Indiana High School Athletic Association.

With augmented academic credentials from Teachers College, Lee Eve left South Whitley in 1941 to become Principal of Westchester High School in Chesterton. In 1943, he became Superintendent of the Delphi–Deer Creek Township schools near Lafayette. Four years later, on August 11, 1945, he was chosen from a field of twenty-one candidates to be Superintendent of Schools at Crown Point. He resigned on July 6, 1950, to become Superintendent of Schools at Crawfordsville, seat of Wabash College, where he remained for nine years. When leaving Crown Point, he wrote to the Board of School Trustees: "You have been as nearly a 'perfect

Board' as a school city can have." An opportunity for professional advancement prompted his move. After Crawfordsville, he was Superintendent of Schools at Goshen from 1959 to 1966.

In 1967, Lee Eve joined the very small faculty in the Department of Education at Huntington College, Huntington, Indiana, where he was Chairman of the Division of Professional Studies and Assistant Professor of Education until 1972. After formal retirement, he continued at the College as Consultant in Education. Huntington College in 1969 awarded him the honorary degree L.H.D., Doctor of Humane Letters. In 1970, the Huntington College students voted him "Distinctive Teacher of the Year." He was back in South Whitley on October 11, 1970, as speaker for dedicating the new community library. Larwill historian Dorothy Minnick calculated that Lee Eve taught in Indiana for 52 years.

Lee LeVere Eve died March 6, 1992. He was buried in the South Whitley Cemetery with his wife, his parents, and his paternal grandparents.

Robert Hicks

Robert E. Hicks built two houses on his 11.54 acres at the west end of Columbia Street. According to his nephew [James Harold Doran (May 13, 1902–October 27, 1989)], the taller house is older than the big, one-story house. "I came [to South Whitley] in 1923. They were just finishing up the big house when I came. ... that house is solid. The whole thing is solid masonry. A full basement under it, three bedrooms on this end of the house plus a bathroom, their big bedroom and bath and a large living room and a study. There was a dining room and a breakfast room and then the kitchen and two bedrooms back of that. A full basement which they eventually put more bedrooms down there. One of the rooms which was about the size of the Town Hall here. It's a big darn thing. ... When I came the painters were finishing the inside ... beams and ceilings, all the doors, everything had three coats, three coats sanded off, just like a piano all over the house."

Ida and Albert christened the big house "Ger Manner." Ger Manner remained in the Germann family into the twenty-first century. A linoleum-block print of Ger Manner adorned the Germann's annual Christmas letter for many years. The graphic artist, who probably was a Germann, did not cut identifying initials into the face of the linoleum printing block, so the artist remains publicly anonymous. The letterpress printing of each Christmas letter was by Stump Printing Company in South Whitley. Stumps used a different color of ink for the linoleum-block print each year.

Entrance to Ger Manner was via a long curving driveway that visually was an extension of Columbia Street, 2½ blocks west of State Street. Eventually, when South Whitley extended its corporation limits to include the Ger Manner entrance, the address became 307 West Columbia Street. On the south side of Columbia Street, closer to State Street, was the imposing brick Hicks Tavern.

Who was Robert Hicks?

"In March of this year (1921) Robert E. Hicks, the Chicago editor and publisher, purchased a complete printing outfit and building at South Whitley, Indiana, worth $110,000 for $36,250. This transaction marks a climax in one of the most unusual struggles of self-mastery and success the world has ever known.

> Twenty years ago Hicks was a mail order swindler,
> He almost froze to death during a drunken spree.
> He had done time in a penitentiary.
> He was pardoned by President Wilson.
> He became a noted religious worker, in New York.
> He has come clean in confessing his wrong-doing."

Thus wrote Orison Swett Marden (1848–1924), author of many popular publications, including the immensely influential self-help book, *Pushing to the Front; or, Success Under Difficulties; A Book of Inspiration and Encouragement to All Who Are Struggling for Self-Elevation Along the Paths of Knowledge and of Duty* (New York: Thomas Y. Crowell Company, 1894; Boston: Houghton, Mifflin, 1894).

Robert Emmet Hicks (February 25, 1858–March 17, 1932) was born in Liberty Township, near Edina, the county seat of Knox County, Missouri. He claimed that he was born in a log farmhouse. He was the son of Sarah Selsor and Elisha Hicks.

Robert attended the local district school. He wrote that his formal education extended only to fourth grade. His nephew said that Robert's older sister (who became a schoolteacher in Sioux City, Iowa) "practically raised him." Robert seems to have been "home schooled." By the time Robert was twelve years old, Edina had a population of 807.

To support himself as a teenager, he worked on local farms. At the age of fourteen, Bob "loaded his pockets with tubes of cement for mending dishes and sallied forth to sell them to his neighbors in the little town of Kirksville." Kirksville, with a population of about 1,500, was county seat of adjoining Adair County to the west. It was the nearest "big city" where he could practice door-to-door selling in relative anonymity. He tried peddling other products, especially patent medicines, and was prudent in moving his huckster operations systematically from neighborhood to neighborhood, from town to town, in an effort to maintain his anonymity.

Bob learned the fundamentals of newspapering as an apprenticed printer's devil at the weekly *Sentinel* in Edina. He then moved east to Monticello, the county seat of adjacent Lewis County. There he put to work his recently acquired practical knowledge of printing and his self-taught knowledge of journalism. He founded a weekly newspaper, the *Monticello Journal*, in 1877. The paper became the *Lewis County Journal*. Its present-day descendant is the *Lewis County Press–News Journal* in Canton, Missouri.

Monticello was (and remains) a very small place. On a surveyor's map, the Town of Monticello in 1878 had platted residential building lots, but it may have had no residences. Twenty houses were located on larger parcels surrounding the town proper. Two decades later, after houses had been built on some of the small, in-town platted lots, the population was estimated to be 350. The 2010 United States Census counted ninety-eight residents in the town. No county seat in the State of Missouri (perhaps anywhere in the nation) has a smaller population.

Robert Hicks, editor and publisher (and bookkeeper, typesetter, pressman, and janitor) of the *Monticello Journal*, enthusiastic booster of the town, must have been the source of the often paraphrased description of the business district in 1878: The Monticello Savings Bank and the United States Post Office faced the Lewis County Courthouse across Lafayette Street. The Lindell Hotel sat northeast of Courthouse Square, at the intersection of Lafayette and Perry streets. South of the courthouse was the Southern Hotel on Jefferson Street, and west of the square on Washington

Street was the Monticello House. Also in town were the Monticello Public School, the Christian Church, the Baptist Church, the Methodist Episcopal Church South, the Methodist Monticello Seminary, and a weekly newspaper, the *Monticello Journal.*

The central fact was that the courthouse had been built (and was staffed and maintained) with county money. The bank, the post office, and the hotels existed to serve the courthouse functions. Folks living in the surrounding township came into town for church, for school, and for work. Robert Hicks demonstrated his journalistic ability to imply a bustling and thriving commercial center (in a town with a population close to zero) while staying close to verifiable facts. This ability impressed officers of the Atchison, Topeka and Santa Fe Railway. They already had formulated an ambitious fundraising scheme. They needed a willing, energetic, and qualified publicist.

Congress had granted land in Kansas to the Atchison, Topeka and Santa Fe to subsidize a portion of the projected transcontinental rail system. The railroad laid tracks across the flat lands of southwestern Kansas in the early 1880s. Kansas topography presented few construction obstacles. However, financial viability of the railroad seemed in jeopardy. Revenue from long-haul freight awaited completion of connecting lines farther west. Absence of substantial economic activity along the sparsely populated Kansas prairie rights-of-way had a severe impact on day-to-day cash flow.

To encourage settlement on land granted by Congress, and to attract investment funds from New York speculators, the railroad manipulated local Kansas politics to site new towns, preferably designated as county seats, next to the tracks. It established a real estate office in each town. The railroad's offer to Robert E. Hicks was for him to found a weekly newspaper in each new town. Without hesitation, Hicks accepted the offer.

A. T. & S. F. provided him minimal equipment to set up a print shop in each town. Hicks cultivated personal relationships within each emergent community. He collected and manufactured columns of newspaper copy—church news, legal news, society news, and lots of local business ads—to suggest, describe, and document on newsprint a thriving community. As each edition of the weekly newspaper was printed, bundles of copies were shipped by rail to New York to convince would-be settlers and investors that the Kansas frontier was inviting, safe, and booming.

With two years of experience at the helm of the *Monticello Journal,* Robert Emmet Hicks was employed by A. T. & S. F. for the decade 1878–1888 as a peripatetic newspaperman. He moved from county seat to new county seat, establishing newspapers.

Some readers may find the story of these dozen years implausible, or at least exaggerated. The documented journalistic beginnings of Robert Hicks turn out to be far from unique, and his recollections are consistent with (and parallel to) autobiographies of some contemporary Midwestern printers and newspapermen.

Edgar Watkins Howe (May 3, 1853–October 3, 1937) wrote a novel, *The Story of a Country Town*, that tells a similar story. Much of the book is thinly disguised autobiography. Howe writes that he began to learn the printing trade in Bethany, Harrison County, Missouri, at the age of ten. He then worked as an itinerate printer in towns throughout Missouri, Iowa, Nebraska, and beyond. He owned and published the weekly *Globe* in Golden, Colorado, from 1875 to 1877. The Colorado School of Mines had opened in Golden in 1873 under the auspices of the Episcopal Church, and the School of Mines became a public institution with an influx of funds from the Colorado Territorial Legislature on March 14, 1876. This should have been an excellent time for the *Globe* to prosper, but the youthful Howe ran the newspaper into bankruptcy. Eventually, in Atchison, Kansas, his reincarnation of the *Globe* was a financial success. The Santa Fe Railway was chartered in Atchison in February 1859; the railway was the Atchison, Topeka and Santa Fe Railway when Howe began publishing the *Atchison Globe*. He wrote an undisguised autobiography, *Plain People*, late in his life. Howe opened *Plain People* by retelling the years of his youth as a tramp printer.

Dudley Reid was born February 21, 1872, on a farm in Daviess County, Missouri, 3½ miles northwest of Winston. Winston was on a thirty-two-mile branch line of the Chicago, Rock Island and Pacific Railroad. Building of the branch line began at Jamesport in 1870. The branch line was completed to Cameron in 1871. The Reid farm was near the village of Alta Vista (population thirty-six in 1880). Reid's entrance into journalism was as a teenager, writing as the Alta Vista neighborhood correspondent for the *Gallatin Democrat*. Gallatin, also on the C. R. I. & P. R., was the county seat. It had a population of two thousand, and had two newspapers. Later, he was employed as a staff writer on the *Gallatin Democrat*. In spring 1902, he bought the *Sentinel* newspaper in Winston. That adventure lasted about two years. Then he travelled twenty miles and bought the *Gilman City Guide*. Gilman City was a town of four hundred inhabitants. The *Gilman City Guide* was a handset weekly, printed on a Washington hand press. In succession, Dudley Reid owned the *Nodaway Forum* in Maryville and the *Democrat* in Bethany. Then, in August 1912, he was back in Gilman City, again owner of the *Guide*.

Loren Dudley Reid (born 1905, son of Dudley Reid) wrote about the first sixteen years of his life in Gilman City, Harrison County, Missouri, in *Hurry Home Wednesday: Growing Up in a Small Missouri Town, 1905–1921.* "Gilman City came into being because of the construction of a thirty-four-mile stretch of railroad track," an extension of the Quincy, Omaha and Kansas City Railway. He tells of his introduction to the printing trade at about age seven from his parents as they wrote, set type, and printed the weekly *Gilman City Guide.* Robert Hicks, Edgar Howe, Dudley Reid, and Loren Reid had very different subsequent lives, but their beginnings had the similar smells and smudges of printer's ink, the pervasive influence of railroads, and their shared perception of the centrality of journalism in their own small Midwestern communities.

Hicks did not brag about surmounting his difficulties in setting up print shops on the Kansas frontier. He may not have encountered significant problems. Twenty-five years earlier, establishing a newspaper in Kansas might have been an heroic act. William H. Adams began printing the *Kansas Weekly Herald* in Leavenworth on September 15, 1854, even before the town had been laid out and before there was a building for his newsprint, type, and press. He "set type for his first issue in the open air, under an elm tree." There were many hazards for other pioneer newspaper publishers in Kansas in the late 1850s. The fiery politics leading to the Civil War often resulted in destruction of print shops soon after the first issues of offending newspapers appeared.

The biggest logistic challenge in establishing a newspaper was transportation of heavy printing equipment to proto-towns in unfriendly territory. Hicks had an advantage. His printing press could be carried by rail by his patron and employer, A. T. & S. F. It would not be surprising to learn that A. T. & S. F. provided a newspaper office, printing facilities, and living quarters in a railroad car, temporarily consigned to a siding. If this were the arrangement, then the whole operation could be moved quickly to the next location, by and at the convenience of A. T. & S. F.

The years when Robert Hicks was learning and plying his trade were years of vigorous newspaper creation in the small towns of the Midwest. In 1875, when he apprenticed at the weekly *Sentinel* in Edina, there were 6,144 weekly newspapers in the United

States. By 1890, two years after Hicks had completed his stint with A. T. & S. F., the nation had 13,795 weeklies. The newspapers that he founded, some probably with very short lives, were among more than five hundred weeklies added each year to the count of the living. The number of survivors peaked at 16,899 in 1910. There were still 12,390 commercial weekly newspapers in the nation in 1935, one in South Whitley, Indiana. Probably all were letterpress papers. Some were still handset in 1935.

Robert Hicks, while working as printer and journalist for A. T. & S. F., was also busy initiating dodgy financial endeavors. Hicks wrote that he began experimenting with questionable mail-order schemes when he had his own printing press at the *Monticello Journal.* "My first mail-order venture was to print fifty cards for 10 cents. Then I sold school supplies by mail, such as reward-of-merit cards and other helps for school teachers."

After he left Monticello, Hicks began to drink heavily. "Ever since I was twenty years old I had used intoxicants excessively—I was what is known as a 'periodical'." He continued with moneymaking schemes, increasingly shady. "I started with such schemes as selling outfits for collecting names and addresses, starting beginners in the mail order business, circular distributing schemes, medical schemes of all kinds by which money could be secured through the medium of the United States mails.... So far as making money was concerned, I was a success. It was in 1898 that I went to New York and started various mail order schemes, among which was the Geneva Chemical Company, a medical scheme which, like many other fraudulent schemes I had conducted, was a financial success until in 1902 … I was arrested, gave bond, and in May, 1903, was tried … I was convicted and sentenced to ten months … I gave bond pending the appeal and immediately went to Europe. I remained there for some time, returning to this country in the Fall of 1903.... There is nothing of particular interest in my life from the time I returned to this country until I surrendered to the government on May 31, 1915."

Those dozen years *are* of particular interest in our story. In 1903, he assumed the name of Robert E. Gammon and went to Chicago, penniless. There he secured a commission from the owner of the Atoz printing plant in South Whitley. "Gammon's" task was to start a distribution business in connection with the printing of large editions of advertising booklets. James E. Remington (September 3, 1876–January 5, 1941), cashier at the Gandy State Bank, recalled the 1903 arrival of Hicks in

South Whitley. Mr. Hicks impressed Mr. Remington as a portly gentleman, bold and loud in speaking, and very convincing in his speech. In South Whitley, Hicks worked at the Atoz printing plant, doing his commissioned work for a salary of $15 a week, later raised to $50. However, his associates sensed the shady nature of his enterprise, and disapproved of his propensity for alcohol. They gave him a hundred dollars and asked him to leave town.

Atoz was a very large facility for printing commercial booklets. It had the capacity for daily production of a half-million 32-page printed pamphlets, saddle-stitched with covers. Atoz generated its own electricity for lighting and for operating an assemblage of five Miehle flatbed printing presses. The plant consumed a railroad carload of paper each week. Atoz shipped ten carloads of advertising matter from South Whitley in one day on October 5, 1905. Atoz boasted that this was one of the largest single shipments of printed matter ever made in the United States. At one time in 1907, Atoz had a hundred employees. The population of South Whitley was then just over a thousand men, women, and children.

Hicks recounted the years from 1902 to 1915 in his widely distributed booklet, *A Conscience Unburdened,* and in inspirational sermons during which, it was said, he held congregations spellbound. As he told his tale, he had been rescued in mid-winter from the backroom of a riverfront dive in New York's Bowery, and taken to the Helping Hand Mission. There he was saved and born again. He became a sought-after speaker and preacher. Reflecting on his injustice to his many victims, he confessed at a Mission meeting on Sunday, May 30, 1915. He surrendered to authorities, and entered the New York Penitentiary on Blackwell's Island in the East River. Hicks was in jail for forty days. Ministers and other friends persuaded President Woodrow Wilson to free him from prison; Mr. Wilson signed the commutation on Wednesday, July 14, 1915. President Calvin Coolidge granted him a "full and unconditional pardon, for the purpose of restoring his civil rights" on Monday, June 6, 1927.

After the commutation, it was back to South Whitley.

Many details of the story for the years between 1915 and 1921 rely on recollections of Robert Hicks that he himself wrote down, published, and personally distributed. Hicks enjoyed publicizing his "down-and-out" to "up-and-in" redemption melodrama. "He arrived in South Whitley in August [1915] with his family, $222.32 in money, credit for two printing presses, and that was all. He gained an agreement with Frank Edgar Miner [1871–1936], owner of the Atoz Printing Company, that he might work there in his effort to start his 'dream' magazine, at a small wage. For a place to live, he found two upstairs rooms in a house with kitchen privileges downstairs. Just feeding his family was a daily problem. His new experimental little magazine, which he named the *Canvassers Magazine,* nearly failed. Advertisers were solicited, but they replied slowly. A first issue did appear, in November 1915, advocating honesty in sales and solicitation." That issue lost money, and he had few local sources of deficit financing. Mr. Hicks was evicted from the printing plant, but he rented a small office downtown. For a time, he continued his efforts. Then he decided to try publishing his new magazine again in Chicago. He sold his cook stove to get money for his family's tickets to Chicago on the Nickel Plate.

The enterprise in Chicago proved highly successful. Advertising revenue flowed into the Robert E. Hicks Corporation. Hicks changed the name of the publication to *Specialty Salesman Magazine.* When he discovered that the Atoz Printing Company was in financial trouble, this time he had the financial means to negotiate its purchase.

It was back to South Whitley again.

Competition from large Chicago printing corporations had caused the decline and fall of Atoz. Hicks was able to buy the Atoz Printing Company in South Whitley at a bankruptcy price in spring 1921—its land, its buildings, and all of its printing equipment. The equipment included several Miehle flatbed cylinder sheet-fed presses, Intertype line-of-type composition and hot-metal casting machines, and a Monotype typesetting and typecasting system.

An Intertype machine produced each line of justified characters as a single "slug" of lead, tin, and antimony alloy, typically 84–85% lead, 3.5–4.0% tin, and 11.5–12.0% antimony. A Monotype system produced justified lines of individual pieces of type, one piece per character. A line of Monotype pieces mimicked a line of handset foundry type. There were four significant distinctions between Monotype and foundry type: composition by Monotype was faster; there was no way to run out of particular characters; the pieces of Monotype could be recycled by melting after use, instead of being distributed by hand, back into type cases; and the Monotype alloy was softer than foundry type metal, so that Monotype characters sometimes showed wear during a long printing run.

The Lanston Monotype Machine Company recommended 72% lead, 9% tin, and

19% antimony. Intertype and Monotype replaced handset foundry type for straight text in every commercial shop large enough to afford these complex and expensive machines. Foundry type is manufactured as individual characters to be reused many times. It is cast from an alloy with less lead, more tin, and more antimony. A typical composition is 54% lead, 18% tin, and 28% antimony. Sometimes as much as 2% copper is added to the mix. Foundry type melts at a substantially higher temperature than Intertype or Monotype metal. It is harder, more brittle, and more durable when subjected to repeated abrasion during the printing process.

Hicks bought 11.54 acres of farmland, bounded in part by the west corporation boundary of the town of South Whitley and by the Vandalia Railroad. Then he launched an ambitious program of building construction.

The first two buildings constructed were houses on the 11.54 acres. Although the land was outside the town corporation limits, the gated entrance was at the west end of Columbia Street. James Remington wrote: "The entrance to the grounds is between huge pillars hung with massive gates, suggesting the style of an English manor. A wide driveway circles the house, which is surrounded by ample yardage. To the front is a well kept lawn, while at the rear is a large garden of flowers, and shrubbery, forming a fitting setting for a graceful pergola, the whole being enclosed within a trellised fencing, between the posts of which are hung ponderous chains, the ensemble presenting a striking picture of symmetry and simple elegance. Flanking the drive is a pond of water lilies."

The next contemplated building was the Temple of the Square Deal, planned to be the administration building and permanent headquarters of the International Association of Specialty Salesmen (I.A.S.S.). The phrase "Square Deal" was already well known. Theodore Roosevelt (1858–1919; United States President 1901–1909) often used the phrase to characterize his progressive domestic political agenda. Hicks, with forty other men and one woman, had founded the I.A.S.S. in April 1920 in Chicago. Hicks was its first president.

I.A.S.S. planned to form local "assemblies" throughout the nation and beyond. South Whitley Assembly Number 13 organized on Saturday, September 30, 1922, with thirty-five charter members. The local officers elected were Robert E. Hicks, President; Orva A. Bollinger, Vice-President; Milton Earl Emerson, Secretary; Fred G. Eberhard, Treasurer; and William F. Norris, Louis Mayer, and Lloyd H. Warner, Directors. Orva A. Bollinger (September 8, 1878–December 14, 1968) was South Whitley manager of the Farmers Mutual Telephone Company. Milton Earl Emerson (December 2, 1884–October 17, 1962; South Whitley High School Class of 1903) was a banker and a real estate agent. Fred G. Eberhard (1889–1944) was a physician. William F. (Fred) Norris (1879–1960) was a druggist in South Whitley from 1901 to 1950. Louis Mayer (1875–1939) was a banker. Lloyd H. Warner (1891–1969) was a garage owner, dealer in Ford and Lincoln cars and Fordson tractors.

By that time, Hicks was President Emeritus of the I.A.S.S. and Albert Garrette Burns (1888–1951) was President. Burns would later (1931–1939) serve as President of the National Inventors Congress.

Hicks' plan was to build the Temple of the Square Deal with money that I.A.S.S. members would contribute by buying construction bricks for a dollar each. Members were to mail their money to Burns, who was also Chairman of the Building Fund. Hicks pledged land for the Temple, probably a portion of the 11.54 acres. Each issue of the *Specialty Salesman Magazine* chronicled progress in fund raising. The South Whitley High School Class of 1923 yearbook, *The Reflector*, had a half-page advertisement (on page 96) from The City Meat Market, operated by Firmer E. Snyder (1883–1959) and his sons Mark Snyder and Carrol Jennings Snyder. The ad proclaimed South Whitley as "Home of the Temple of the Square Deal." Similar words were emblazoned on a forty-foot signboard erected near the junction of railroads at the north State Street entrance to town.

Groundbreaking for the Temple of the Square Deal was on Tuesday, May 15, 1923. There was an impressive ceremony when the first shovels of soil were removed from the building site. Then a month later, on Sunday, June 17, 1923, the cornerstone was laid. The South Whitley band was on hand. Albert G. Burns was master of ceremonies. Robert Hicks, M. Cassium (Cash) Graham, Dr. Arthur J. Folsom (Pastor of the Plymouth Congregational Church of Fort Wayne and Chaplain of the I.A.S.S.), Robert B. Stout (Chicago, I.A.S.S. Vice-President), and Edgar Denson (Detroit, I.A.S.S. Corresponding Secretary) spoke.

Cash Graham (1869–1935), a South Whitley native, was well connected politically. He had been South Whitley Postmaster from December 20, 1902, to May 22, 1913. In 1923, he was serving in Indianapolis as Chief Deputy of the office of the Indiana State Fire Marshal.

In December 1923, with no explanation, *Specialty Salesman Magazine* stopped publishing articles about the Temple. In the February 1924 issue, Robert Hicks announced that money was missing from the building fund. He blamed Albert G. Burns for misuse of funds. In the next issue (March 1924) was the news that Albert G. Burns was suing Robert Hicks for $100,000. The lawsuit did not go anywhere, but neither did the Temple. The full extent of construction was just the ceremonial placing of the cornerstone. Perhaps the pond of water lilies marked the site.

Robert Hicks was a Baptist. The South Whitley Baptist Church building was then on Main Street at the west end of Market Street. Hicks' next building project was a new brick home for the South Whitley Baptists. In 1922, he began negotiations with other members of the congregation. The site chosen was two blocks south, at the northwest corner of Mulberry and Main streets. Hicks contributed about half of the projected cost, and loaned the congregation an equal additional amount. The building, with a large sanctuary and a total-immersion baptistery, was completed in 1926. Dedication was Sunday, January 9, 1927. Fund raising continued through the depths of the Great Depression. The congregation burned the mortgage in a church service on Sunday, May 2, 1937. The former Baptist Church building was later occupied by the Church of God congregation.

The Baptist project may have been an effort by Robert Hicks to compete with another local church. In April 1922, the South Whitley Church of the Brethren formulated plans to construct a church building just down Mulberry Street from the projected site of the new Baptist building. The original congregation began at a tent meeting in fall 1913 on the same lot where the Baptists in 1922 intended to build their church. On December 11, 1912, the Middle Indiana District Mission Board of the Church of the Brethren organized a mission church in South Whitley. Membership of the mission church came largely from nearby rural Church of the Brethren congregations: Tunker, Pleasant View, and Spring Creek. The Mission Board supplied some of the 1922 construction funds to complement local contributions. The church dedicated its new brick edifice in 1923.

The last Robert Hicks building project in town was an outstanding success. He built the brick Hicks Tavern on the south side of Columbia Street (in 2014 street numbering, 106 and 108 West Columbia Street), between Main Street and State Street. The Tavern grand opening was Wednesday, May 11, to Friday, May 13, 1927.

"The Tavern was luxurious. The dining room seated 100 under beautiful lights, while the banquet room below, with a fireplace, had room for 200. The stairway was walnut and the carpets were thick. There were two suites of four rooms each, 17 rooms up and three down. The draperies were lovely and there were telephones in all rooms."

The opening celebration was an exercise in pomp and circumstance. Businessman and inspirational speaker Arthur Nash came from Cincinnati to be master of ceremonies. Nash was widely known for his autobiography, *The Golden Rule in Business* (New York: Fleming H. Revell Company, 1923). Nash died a few months later, at age 59, on October 30, 1927. Arthur Raymond Robinson (1881–1961), United States Senator from Indiana, spoke. Hugo Fox, a South Whitley native who was also the Principal Bassoon of the Chicago Symphony Orchestra, provided music for the banquet.

Fred Fox, brother of bassoonist Hugo Fox, managed the Hicks Tavern for several years. The Hicks Tavern, as we shall see, underwent a metamorphosis after Mr. Hicks retired to Florida. The building became the Kaadt Diabetic Institute for a decade. Then, on December 19, 1946, Fred Fox opened the Palm Room, a place for fine dining under the chandeliers of the resurrected Hicks Tavern.

Throughout his life, Robert Hicks cultivated acquaintanceships with influential people. He acquired friends who could persuade President Woodrow Wilson to free him from prison in 1915. He found friends who could persuade President Calvin Coolidge to restore his civil rights. He became sufficiently acquainted with evangelists Billy Sunday (1862–1935) and Homer Rodeheaver (1880–1955) to be invited to their Gospel Tabernacle at Winona Lake, Indiana. There he addressed a great audience on July 15, 1924, speaking on "Tithes of Human Souls," telling the story of his life. There was also an intriguing friendship with the Governor of the State of Indiana.

At the beginning of his third South Whitley incarnation, Hicks in spring 1921 sought the friendship of Indiana Secretary of State Edward L. Jackson (1873–1954). The voters of Indiana elected Jackson Governor in 1924. According to a 1980 interview with James Harold Doran, "Mr. Hicks accompanied Governor Jackson in a private railroad car to the governors' conference in Colorado, and the governor spent week-ends with Mr. Hicks in South Whitley, well entertained, of course. On one occasion the governor bought a new car in South Whitley, a popular Whippet, and that called for a speech to the townspeople assembled. Before the first visit of the governor, Mr. Doran received a telegram from Mr. Hicks stating that the governor was coming to South Whitley but to say nothing to anyone. Mr. Doran correctly read the mind of Uncle Bob and relayed the message to Fred Fox and Lou Mayer, who proceeded to arrange a welcoming party for Ed Jackson and Uncle Bob. Therefore, there were music and well-chosen remarks and plenty of handshaking at their arrival. Uncle Bob was not at all disgruntled by the 'failure' to keep the secret."

Senator Arthur Raymond Robinson and Governor Edward L. Jackson were political figures with high-profile liabilities in some circles. Jackson was a member of the Indiana Ku Klux Klan, and he had solicited Klan support when he ran for Governor of Indiana. Klan members then held half the seats in the Indiana General Assembly. "Jackson saw the Klan as an immensely popular, bipartisan group that had packaged a message of morality, Americanism, Protestantism, and Prohibition lifted wholesale from the state's churches and patriotic organizations." David Curtiss Stephenson (1891–1966), Grand Dragon of the Indiana Klan, encouraged Jackson's candidacy. While still Secretary of State, Jackson granted the Klan an official state charter. Presumably on orders from the Grand Dragon, Jackson also tried to bribe millionaire Governor Warren Terry McCray (1865–1938) to appoint several Klan members to state offices. McCray refused, but he did not make public the attempted payoff. Soon after Jackson was elected Governor of Indiana, United States Senator Samuel Ralston died. It was the Governor's prerogative to appoint a replacement. Grand Dragon D. C. Stephenson urged the appointment of Indianapolis lawyer Arthur Raymond Robinson, and Jackson acquiesced. Arthur Robinson became United States Senator Robinson from Indiana. The next year, Jackson pardoned Edward Shumaker, an important Klan member who had been sentenced to serve time on the Indiana State Farm (the Putnamville Correctional Facility). Shumaker's pardon was overturned. Governor Jackson's troubles got worse and worse. On November 14, 1925, D. C. Stephenson was convicted of the rape and murder of Madge Augustine Oberholtzer (November 10, 1896–April 14, 1925), and sentenced to life in prison. When Jackson refused to pardon the Grand Dragon, Stephenson told the *Indianapolis Times* about the earlier bribe attempt. After ugly legal actions, Jackson finished his term but left office in disgrace.

Edward L. Jackson was Indiana Secretary of State from January 22, 1920 to November 27, 1924, and Governor from January 12, 1925 to January 14, 1929. He was Secretary of State, with strong connections to the Klan, when (on Friday, August

24, 1923) *The Fiery Cross* announced that "the Ku Klux Klan is ready to 'take over' Valparaiso University!" Jackson was Governor when (on Friday, October 22, 1926) the journal *Science* reported: "Dr. A. F. O. Germann has resigned his position with the Laboratory Products Company, where he was in charge of development and research, in order to organize work in chemistry at Valparaiso University, Indiana."

Harry Guyer Leslie (1878–1937) followed Jackson in the Governor's office. He was Governor from January 14, 1929 to January 9, 1933. Leslie had mixed relationships with the Klan throughout his political career.

The Klan made a public appearance in South Whitley after Christmas in 1922. Just after dark, a twenty-five-foot-high wooden cross was set up between the tracks of the Vandalia Railroad and the Nickel Plate Road at the north end of State Street. The cross was set afire about 8:30 p.m., and it burned for several hours. Many residents interpreted this fiery cross (preceded by a burning cross a week earlier in Columbia City) as evidence that the Ku Klux Klan had organized in Whitley County.

More than 850 persons attended a lecture by a Rev. Blair on Thursday, January 18, 1923, in Columbia City. Nine men in white robes, wearing white hoods and masks, accompanied the speaker. Rev. Blair asserted that twenty percent of the male population of Indiana belonged to the Klan, as did thirty or forty members of the Indiana General Assembly. He denied that the Klan was "anti-anybody." He asserted that the Klan was simply pro-American, pro-Protestant, pro-White, and pro-Native. This would be the theme of many speeches by Protestant ministers before large crowds throughout 1923, 1924, and 1925 in Whitley County. Indiana Grand Dragon David Curtiss Stephenson presented a charter in 1923 to Whitley County Klan No. 25.

On Saturday, June 23, 1923, the Klan orchestrated a parade down State Street in South Whitley. "A robed Klansman carrying an American flag led the parade. Behind him came six robed horses and riders and automobiles decorated with crosses and flowers, followed by robed Klansmen. Before the parade, a Klan speaker had delivered an address from a truck at the lumber yards." There would be more parades in South Whitley during the next two years, and a cross burning by the Junior Klan. On Friday, July 13, 1923, the Ku Klux Klan held a meeting in an open field a few miles east of South Whitley. "In addition to the large crowd, the fiery cross and the discharge of dynamite, this meeting was marked by the first overt anti-klan action in the county. One of the robed guards on the edge of the field was stoned."

"A picnic held in Fox Grove near South Whitley in September [1925] was well advertised. It was to be the closing outdoor meeting of the season. The day came and went with what had to be 'low-key' reporting of the event. A Whitley County minister conducted devotional services, and after the picnic dinner there was a forty-five minute concert by the Elk-Klan Band of 40 pieces. The speaker, sponsored by the Kamelia [the women's auxiliary of the Klan] then addressed the crowd for over an hour, making this plea, for 'a return to the Americanism as practiced by the founders of this nation.'… It was a large crowd and, according to what newspaper you read, it was estimated at 'three to four thousand with over eight hundred cars' or it was 'between 2500 and 3000 with 550 cars'."

In every community, there are "joiners." There were Hoosiers in the 1920s who joined the Klan to become members of just another civic organization or just another ritualistic secret society. Some joiners saw the active involvement of mainline Protestant ministers in Klan Konklaves to be an indication of Klan respectability. The Klan was effective in using slogans associated with religion, morality, and patriotism. For some local Klan members, it took a nearby traumatic experience to change the perception of respectability, and to trigger apprehension about the meaning of Klan membership. That experience was a double lynching in Marion, forty miles south of South Whitley, thirty miles southeast of Peru. Two African American teenagers—Thomas Shipp (1911–1930) and Abram Smith (abt 1910–1930)—were dragged from prison and then hanged on Thursday, August 7, 1930, hanged from a tree on the lawn of the Grant County Courthouse. A shouting and jeering mob witnessed the lynching. Members of the Ku Klux Klan, some in full Klan regalia, were publicly participating. Two accused mob leaders were tried, but a jury of twelve white men acquitted each.

The mob also wanted the life of sixteen-year-old James Cameron (1914–2006). He was tortured and imprisoned, but he lived to tell his story fifty years later in his book, *A Time of Terror: A Survivor's Story* (Baltimore: Black Classic Press, 1982). The story of the lynching was also told and interpreted by James H. Madison in his book, *A Lynching in the Heartland: Race and Memory in America* (New York: Palgrave for St. Martin's Press, 2001).

South Whitley and county seat Columbia City may have been Klan towns. They certainly were Chautauqua towns. In Columbia City, Chautauqua programs were held under large tents from 1913 to 1923, with a break only for the Great War. William Jennings Bryan spoke for 2½ hours in Columbia City to more than 1,200 persons at a Chautauqua event on July 24, 1922. "Near the end of his lecture, Mr. Bryan declaimed long and loud on the evils of the theory of evolution." In South Whitley, the Redpath Chautauqua tent was set up on the grounds of the Calhoun Street School on August 9–14, 1922, and again on July 16–20, 1923.

Robert Hicks was personally very interested in the Chautauqua movement. He probably hoped to become an inspirational speaker on the Chautauqua tent circuit. Chautauqua figured prominently in his retirement plans. In 1928, Hicks began to make plans for retiring to the Florida center of Chautauqua activity. About 1929, he sold *Specialty Salesman Magazine* to National Trade Journals, Inc., of Chicago and New York. Atoz continued to publish the magazine in South Whitley until 1932. Robert Hicks moved to DeFuniak Springs in the panhandle of Florida. His son and daughter-in-law, Elmer and Mae Hicks, remained in Cleveland Township, living in the "big house" at the west end of Columbia Street.

As he was making plans for retirement, Hicks became involved with Lombard College in Galesburg, Illinois. The *Lombard College Catalog* lists Robert Emmet Hicks as a member of the Board of Trustees in 1926–1927 and 1927–1928. Lombard College was founded in 1853 by the Universalist Church as the co-educational Illinois Liberal Institute. Benjamin Lombard became a major benefactor, and the Institute changed its name in 1855 to Lombard College. The Great Depression hit Lombard hard financially, and Hicks was a Trustee in the last years of the institution. The final class graduated in 1930. It seems likely that the relationship between Hicks and Lombard College was part of an effort to save the College. That effort failed. Hicks moved to Florida.

DeFuniak Springs was the hometown of Robert's third wife, Margaret May Davis Joy. The town had been established in Walton County during the 1880s as a final-destination resort. The development was a joint enterprise of the Louisville and Nashville Railroad and the Florida Chautauqua Association (1884–1927). The Florida Chautauqua Association held its first assembly in DeFuniak Springs in February 1885. The Association built the four-thousand-seat Chautauqua Hall of Brotherhood on Lake DeFuniak in the center of town in 1910. Hicks bought land near the boundary between Walton County and Bay County. This land is now included in Camp Helen State Park, bordered on three sides by the Gulf of Mexico, by Phillips

Inlet, and by shallow Lake Powell, one of the largest coastal dune lakes in Florida.

For Robert Emmet Hicks, DeFuniak Springs was his final destination. He died there on March 11, 1932. His death was attributed to heart disease. Robert's daughter, Margaret Hicks Savage, wrote: "My mother, Margaret Davis Hicks built the 'Lodge' [in Camp Helen State Park] in 1931/33 on the 185 acres bought by my father, Robert E. Hicks, in 1928. My mother sold the property in 1945 to the Avondale Mills people [Avondale Textile Mills of Sylacauga, Alabama] for a modest sum. I was married in that house, and my son was born there. Our family gathered there for holidays. The summers were magical."

Hubert A. Stump

When Barbara Germann and her father visited South Whitley in 1935, they probably stopped by the offices of the weekly *South Whitley Tribune* to pick up a copy of the latest issue. The *Tribune* always kept a stack of earlier issues for sale. A half dozen issues would reveal a great deal about the community. In each issue, the Germanns would have found the weekly editorial column, "Hube A's Says Sos," written by editor, publisher, and owner Hubert A. Stump (April 18, 1904–December 25, 1949). Hubert Stump was also the man who set type on the *Tribune's* Intertype hot-metal, line-casting machine. He bragged (and visitors to the print shop confirmed) that he wrote his editorials seated at the Intertype keyboard, without paper copy or even notes. Some "Hube A's Says Sos" were opinion pieces, but most were folksy comments on the week about town.

On Thursday afternoon, August 15, 1935, Hubert Stump wrote in Hube A's Says Sos: "South Whitley is about to have a new industry—for which we are thankful as a community." Maybe he was referring to the imminent return of the Grip Nut Company. Maybe he had heard rumors of a forthcoming purchase of the Hicks Tavern. More likely, a local real estate agent had dropped by the *Tribune* office to report that the Nutritional Research Associates Corporation was on the verge of purchasing Hicks property next to the railroad junction. Three weeks later, on Saturday, September 7, 1935, Nutritional Research Associates, Inc., consummated that purchase, and South Whitley had the beginnings of a new industry. The new industry would in time become known locally as "The Carrot Factory."

Hubert A. Stump was born in Washington Township, just east of South Whitley. He graduated from the Washington Center High School in 1922. Hubert established the Stump Printing Company in South Whitley four years later in 1926. At first, "Stumps" was a minimal letterpress shop, with handset type and a 12" × 18" Chandler & Price Gordon-type hand-fed platen press.

He bought the *South Whitley Tribune* on October 30, 1933, from Albert Clyde Yearick (1885–1966). Yearick, previously editor and publisher of the *Argos* [Indiana] *Reflector*, had owned the *Tribune* since May 1, 1931. An Intertype machine and a flatbed sheet-fed newspaper printing press came with this 1933 purchase.

In common with all other small letterpress newspapers across the nation, lead-tin-antimony type, brass rules, and cuts (type-high relief mirror-image illustrations) for each page were assembled (imposed) on a page-size imposing stone and then locked into a rectangular page-size steel chase. Each heavy form (type locked in a chase) was carried to the press and placed on a horizontal steel flat bed (hence the "flatbed" name, and the phrase "putting the newspaper to bed"). During the printing, composition rollers automatically inked the type, individual sheets of newsprint were hand fed into the press, and each sheet was pressed against the inked type by a large steel impression cylinder (its circumference equal to the length of the sheet of newsprint) that rolled over the type.

With the newly acquired equipment, Hubert Stump became proprietor of a now fully equipped "job printing shop," as well as editor and publisher of the town's weekly newspaper.

It was a two-day printing process to produce each week's eight-page *Tribune*. The first step was to print pages 2, 3, 6, and 7 on one side of a single sheet of newsprint, four times the size of a finished page. The next day, each of these large sheets was hand fed into the press to print the other side—pages 1, 4, 5, and 8. As each sheet was printed, an attached automated contraption folded and cut each sheet, folded again, and then delivered an individual copy. The configuration of the machinery mandated an eight-page issue, whether or not there was enough local news and advertising. To fill a scant column or an empty page, Western Newspaper Union boilerplate was used. If only four pages of new material was available, then Hubert Stump resorted to "preprint," full sheets with short stories and ads already printed on one side. The ads were for national mail-order items such as proprietary nostrums—untested and largely unregulated "patent medicines." The ratio of column inches of ads to "news" conformed to postal regulations that governed content of a newspaper if it were to be mailed at a low rate. Western Newspaper Union sold the preprint at a cost slightly below the cost of unprinted paper; the advertising on preprint produced the revenue and profit for WNU.

It was job printing with an innovative slant that permitted entrepreneur Hubert Stump to translate a dream into a successful business. He was quite familiar with school-sponsored social functions such as school receptions. He became aware of the work of commercial artist George Earl Buzza (1883–1957), who had begun to produce slim gift books for such events. At the South Whitley High School Senior-Junior Reception, held at the Hicks Tavern on Friday evening, May 10, 1929, a take-home copy of *The Meanin' o' Gladness* was put at each person's place. The Buzza Company of Minneapolis published that booklet, with text by Lawrence Hawthorne, for just such purposes. The content was minimal, but the booklet was a handsome keepsake; one copy was kept for more than eighty years. It was "printed on one side of double leaves folded once in Japanese style." Hawthorne and Buzza collaborated on several of these books. Possibly significant is "The Trail of Memories," text from the writings of Lawrence Hawthorne, copyright 1920 by Buzza of Minneapolis. Hubert Stump was headed along his own trail of Memories.

The dream of Hubert Stump was to produce "personalized" specialty items designed for (and targeted to) high school activities, items available at an affordable cost. He introduced a booklet keepsake, printed to order especially for a specific school and for a specific event, printed with the names of all the students, priced affordably. Senior-junior receptions, proms, and graduations were the targeted events. Pricing was crucial. Even as the Great Depression hit bottom, new orders from schools increased. Stump marketed the booklets in many designs, each with the word "Memories" printed on the cover.

South Whitley graphic artist Alta Marian Graf Gerard (September 3, 1910–August 7, 2001) designed and drew the first Memories cover. She drew dozens of Memories covers during the next decade. Mrs. Gerard was on the staff of the *South Whitley Tribune* for ten years and was the staff photographer for twelve years. She lived on Poplar Street, a block away from the Stump residence.

The Midwestern small-town world of the 1930s was a world of small high schools, a world that Hubert Stump understood well. He learned how to market to high school principals. His enterprise took off spectacularly. He focused increasingly on Memories booklets, and sold off the newspaper-publishing portion of his business on July 29, 1943, to Basil Adams of Indianapolis.

About 1946, Stump bought all the printing equipment of the Franklin Press in Franklin, Indiana. His purchase included Brandtjen & Kluge automatic-feed platen presses, another Intertype, and an 8" × 12" Chandler & Price hand-fed platen press. Stump added the Intertype and the Kluge presses to his rapidly expanding printing facility on South State Street near the Eel River Bridge.

His direct-mail catalog included a wide range of personalized items for banquets and receptions. Because setup was quick and simple with a Kluge press, personalizing invitations, Memories booklets, place cards, and napkins by letterpress was equally quick and simple—and decidedly profitable. With the inventive aid of South Whitley machinist Eldon Leroy Krieg (July 14, 1904–May 30, 1987), Stump constructed an attachment that collected each freshly printed Memories cover from a Kluge press, gave the wet ink a spray of metallic powder, and then applied heat, resulting in raised printing that simulated expensive engraving.

Hubert A. Stump died on Christmas Day 1949, wealthier than he could have imagined in 1935. His funeral was at the Evangelical United Brethren Church, across Main Street from his home. The ballad "Memories" was sung at the funeral. Very popular in 1949, "Memories" had been recorded by crooner Bing Crosby two years earlier.

Hubert Stump's company continued to grow. In business in 2014 in South Whitley both as Stumps and as Shindigz, the company is prospering as "an American-owned, family-operated store specializing in personalized party items and decorations." It is now largely an internet-based mail-order enterprise.

Peter and Charles Kaadt

Hube A's Says Sos, Thursday, November 14, 1935: "There has been somewhat of a movement started for the town to purchase the Hicks Tavern for a town hall, etc." A similar item appeared on December 5, 1935. On Thursday, December 19, 1935: "The

Hicks Tavern, recently leased by Martin Daly of Indianapolis whose lease expired a few weeks ago, has been leased to a Mr. McArthur of Huntington for a year's time." Then a regular news item in the *South Whitley Tribune*: "Authorized word has been received that the Hicks Tavern, taken over on Sept. 15th [1936] by B. N. Lovelace of Chicago, will henceforth be under the management of Dr. C. F. Kaadt, a specialist in diabetic cases, who expects to convert the hotel into a sanitarium for diabetes."

The hotel needed very little architectural alteration for conversion into a "sanitarium for diabetes." The hotel simply needed a change of management. Dr. C. F. Kaadt provided that change.

Thirteen years and thousands of patients later, Dr. C. F. Kaadt and his brother Peter would be fined and sentenced to prison for violations of the 1938 Federal Food, Drug, and Cosmetic Act. James Harvey Young would devote a chapter of his book, *The Medical Messiahs: A Social History of Health Quackery in Twentieth-Century America,* to these "two gentlemen from Indiana." Their activities, judged by a Federal Court to be fraudulent and criminal, were conducted openly in South Whitley at the Hicks Tavern.

Dr. C. F. Kaadt was Charles Frederick Kaadt (1872–1957). Charles, his brothers Christian Gottlieb Kaadt (1868–1905) and Peter Simon Kaadt (1871–1951), and his sister Marie (1867–1957) were born in Denmark. His brother Edward Kaadt (1879–1942) was born in Iowa.

Charles Kaadt received the M.D. degree on April 14, 1902, from the Keokuk Medical College, and his medical certificate from the Iowa State Board of Health a month later on May 15, 1902. Keokuk Medical College opened in Davenport, Iowa (or perhaps just across the Mississippi River in Rock Island, Illinois) in 1849 as the College of Physicians and Surgeons of the Upper Mississippi. The next year it moved downstream to Keokuk in Lee County, Iowa. The Iowa General Assembly recognized the transplanted Keokuk College of Physicians and Surgeons as the official Medical Department of the State University of Iowa. Keokuk continued as the state-sponsored medical college for another twenty years, and then as an independent institution for an additional four decades. In 1908, Keokuk College merged with the former Iowa College of Physicians (by then the Medical Department of Drake University) to become the Drake University School of Medicine in Des Moines.

The requirements for admission and for graduation at any of the three medical schools in Iowa, although similar to standards at other schools in the Midwest at the time, were at best imperfect. "The competition for students was such that no school up to that time had the courage to raise the standard of admission, or extend the course of medical instruction." Charles Kaadt must have taken some courses in residence at Keokuk, but he probably completed most of the requirements for his M.D. degree by "three years study with a reputable physician." In this case, the study may have been a medical apprenticeship with his older brother Peter Kaadt, physician and surgeon in Clinton County, Iowa. In 1901, Kaadt brothers lived with their widowed mother [Ellen Marie Clausen Kaadt (1839–1919)] in Clinton, county seat of Clinton County. Their father was Christian Kaadt (1829–1879). The family had immigrated in 1874.

Peter moved around a lot. We can document some places and dates in his medical career. Peter received his M.D. degree from the Rush Medical College in Chicago on May 22, 1895, and his medical certificate from the Iowa State Board of Health on November 8, 1895. The *Clinton Daily Age* newspaper (published in Clinton, Iowa, from 1894 to 1896) reported on Tuesday, April 21, 1896, that Dr. P. S. Kaadt, "a Clinton boy," had moved from Bryant, Iowa, to Peru, Indiana, to work in the Wabash Railroad Hospital there. Bryant, fifteen miles northwest of Clinton, was an unincorporated farming community in northeastern Clinton County. The Wabash Railway Employees Hospital was on the north edge of Peru. The hospital had been established in 1886; a new brick building was being built in 1896. Peter was admitted to the practice of medicine, surgery, and obstetrics in the State of Indiana in 1897. He then moved back to Clinton. He later moved to Portland, Oregon, where he was licensed in 1910. Peter practiced medicine in Portland until he joined Charles in South Whitley in 1938. Between 1910 and 1915, he was also a Demonstrator of Anatomy at North Pacific College in Portland.

Charles Kaadt set up a medical practice in Fort Wayne. For thirty years, he was on call by the Wabash Railroad as a surgeon. The Fort Wayne *Journal Gazette* and *News-Sentinel* daily newspapers often had short news articles about him attending victims of railroad-related accidents. He also advertised his specialty as "stomach and bowel medicine."

"Stomach and bowel medicine" would seem to be closely related to "digestive diseases." Fort Wayne was the home of the first scientific journal devoted exclusively to the medical subspecialty of digestive diseases. Fort Wayne physician Beaumont Sanfield Cornell (1892–1958) founded *The American Journal of Digestive Diseases* in March 1934. In August 1934, the *Journal* became the official periodical of the American Gastroenterological Association. Paralleling the career of his Fort Wayne compatriot Charles Kaadt, who was already peddling a fraudulent cure for diabetes, Dr. Cornell used the *Journal* enthusiastically to promote his treatment of cancer as "a deficiency state," earning the ire of many fellow gastroenterologists. Cornell called his nostrum "anomin." It was an herbal product, probably a mixture of material obtained from plants *Ocimum sanctum* (holy basil), *Eugenia jambolane* (Madagascar java plum), *Zingiber officinale* (ginger), *Curcuma longa* (turmeric), and *Archetto musica* (bow rasa).

Edward Kaadt was a member of the Brotherhood of Locomotive Engineers and an engineer on the Wabash Railroad. He resigned from the railroad in 1932 to join Charles in managing Charles' Fort Wayne medical practice. The practice had expanded greatly. Many patients were coming to his Fort Wayne office, seeking a diabetes cure. There were already complaints from local doctors about Dr. Kaadt's "cure." There were also formal inquiries by the American Medical Association and by the Federal Food and Drug Administration. According to his obituary, Edward was "associated with his brother in operation of the Kaadt Diabetic Institute at South Whitley." At the end of his life, Edward lived in Fort Wayne at 339 West Brackenridge Street, the address of the home and office of Charles Kaadt. Edward may have had no medical role in the South Whitley enterprise. He was never charged with improprieties. At the end of 1941, Edward became seriously ill. He died on July 21, 1942.

Mrs. Marie C. Kaadt Graham, a sister of Charles, Peter, and Edward, was living in South Whitley in 1940 and 1942, probably with Charles. Her husband, Alexander Graham, died between 1910 and 1920, probably in Portland, Oregon. Marie was never charged with improprieties related to the Kaadt Diabetic Institute.

There may be no way to know if either Kaadt physician kept abreast of the methodical nineteenth-century medical studies that led incrementally, step by step, to understanding the biology and chemistry of *diabetes mellitus*. Paul Langerhans (1847–1888) first described the pancreatic islets of Langerhans in his 1869 dissertation. Joseph Freiherr von Mering (1849–1908) and Oskar Minkowski (1858–1931) demonstrated the importance of the pancreas in carbohydrate metabolism in 1890.

Eugene Lindsay Opie (1873–1971) in 1901 described degeneration of the islets of Langerhans in cases of *diabetes mellitus.* Neither the Keokuk nor the Rush curriculum would have introduced medical students to this emerging science when the Kaadt brothers were in classes. The earliest research publications would not have been easily available to Midwestern teachers or students.

However, it is unlikely that any physician with a diabetic patient in the 1920s would have failed to notice the highly publicized results of Frederick Grant Banting (1891–1941), John James Rickard Macleod (1876–1935), Charles Herbert Best (1899–1978), and James Bertram Collip (1892–1965). At the May 3, 1922, meeting of the Association of American Physicians in Washington, D.C., the quartet announced to the medical world that they had discovered insulin, and that insulin is effective in treating *diabetes mellitus.* Eli Lilly and Company in Indianapolis quickly began to manufacture purified insulin. On August 19, 1922, Eli Lilly began shipping dosages of insulin. The 1923 Nobel Prize in Physiology or Medicine went to Banting and Macleod "for the discovery of insulin." For the first time in human history, *diabetes mellitus* could be treated successfully. Type I diabetes had previously been a fatal disease, with no known treatment; in 1922, its symptoms could be controlled, and juvenile patients could anticipate a productive and rewarding adult life.

The medical science and the clinical evidence of the significance of insulin were conclusive and were quickly accepted by most members of the medical profession. Publicity, in medical journals and in the popular press, was positive and overwhelming. Yet Peter and Charles Kaadt practiced medicine in South Whitley from 1936 to 1948 in a manner contrary to this medical evidence. Thousands of gullible patients flocked to the Kaadt Diabetic Institute in the former Hicks Tavern. The financial rewards to the brothers were substantial. The consequences for many patients were disastrous.

"For one year prior to October 6, 1946, he [Peter Simon Kaadt] maintained his office, designated at times as a diabetic institute, in South Whitley, Ind. During this period this office had at least 100 patients a day, and there were over sixty rooming houses in South Whitley taking care of these patients. In October 1945 the respondent and his brother practiced at that office. They made representations to patients that they could cure diabetes and on at least one occasion made such representations to an admitted patient who had been suffering for at least six years. They also told her that she could eat about anything and gave her a diet sheet, which stated that most anything that has been made with sugar that has been thoroughly cooked is beneficial to one suffering from this disease....

"Patients were advised to attend the institute for three days, for which there was a charge of $30.00 including board; on leaving they were given a three months' medical treatment to take home with them, for which there was a charge of $30.00. The medicine which was to be taken home consisted of 1 gallon of liquid in a glass container, the liquid consisting of vinegar to which had been added potassium nitrate, some pepsin and takadiastase. The wholesale cost of this liquid was 93 cents per gallon. In addition the patient was given a box of cathartic and digestive pills to take during his home treatment."

South Whitley's population was 1,118 in 1940. Excluding office and examining rooms used for the medical practice, Hicks Tavern had about twenty sleeping rooms for patients. The South Whitley Hotel on State Street, owned and operated by Prince Immanuel of Jerusalem, was located about halfway between the Nickel Plate passenger depot and the Hicks Tavern. The South Whitley Hotel building had twenty-two rooms, but not all were sleeping rooms available for Kaadt patients. The daily need to house the patients, even with sixty households accepting roomers, was certainly close to the town's limit.

The Kaadt brothers were conducting a classic case of medical fraud. On its face, their enterprise was a clear violation of the landmark Pure Food and Drug Act of 1906, signed into law by President Theodore Roosevelt in 1906 as part of his Square Deal progressive agenda. Pioneer Hoosier chemist Harvey Washington Wiley (1844–1930), as Chief Chemist of the Bureau of Chemistry in the United States Department of Agriculture, provided the crucial leadership for passage of the 1906 Act. As happens so often, the bill as drafted by Congress contained compromise language introduced to obtain key votes necessary for passage. Some ambiguous language undercut significant provisions of the legislation.

A legal dispute arose over the meaning of drug labeling provisions of the 1906 law. Amazingly, the United States Supreme Court ruled in *United States v. Johnson* in 1911 that the law did not prohibit false therapeutic claims. The product involved was labeled "Dr. Johnson's Cure for Cancer." According to the Supreme Court, the law's prohibition was only against false and misleading claims on the label regarding the *ingredients* or the identity of the drug. In 1912, Congress enacted the Sherley Amendment, an ineffective compromise that merely prohibited false therapeutic claims that were "intended to defraud" the consumer. It turned out to be difficult to prove in court that a proprietor knew his drug to be worthless.

Litigation involving the patent medicine Banbar must have been noticed by any Kaadt lawyer. The liquid Banbar was marketed as a cure for diabetes. The principal ingredients were derived from the plants *Equisetum hyemale* Linnaeus (scouring rush horsetail) and *Leptandra virginica* Linnaeus (Culver's physic). Banbar's solvent was a mixture of water and alcohol. Other ingredients included magnesium sulfate, potassium acetate, and strychnine. For diabetics who were rejecting insulin injections in favor of Banbar, the product was particularly dangerous. The United States Food and Drug Administration (FDA) seized the product in the mid-1930s, charging the proprietor with fraud under the Sherley Amendment. In his defense, the proprietor submitted testimonial letters written to him, thanking him for the product. Government lawyers selected a representative group of testimonial letters and matched them side-by-side with death certificates of the same individuals, indicating that each had died from diabetes. Although the public health threat seemed obvious to observers, the court ruled that the proprietor had not intended to defraud his customers. Banbar gave drug regulators their first direct experience interpreting drug data from historical records, from selective testimonials, and from uncontrolled trials instead of direct clinical trials. Banbar remained on the market until Congress enacted the Federal Food, Drug, and Cosmetic Act in 1938. The 1938 Act required that drugs be proven safe before marketing. The Act appeared to regulate labeling of drugs.

Charles Kaadt probably began to treat diabetic patients soon after moving to Fort Wayne. As an advertised specialist on stomach and bowel diseases, practicing medicine in the city where *The American Journal of Digestive Diseases* was founded, it may have seemed reasonable to Dr. Kaadt (before the insulin breakthroughs of Banting, Macleod, Best, Collip, and Eli Lilly) to treat diabetes as if the disease were the result of faulty digestion of sugars and carbohydrates.

Charles did not retreat. Even as evidence accumulated in the early 1920s that insulin therapy is effective, Charles began to expand his non-insulin diabetes practice at his home and office at 339 Brackenridge Street in Fort Wayne. He concocted a remedy that he called his "Diabetic Ferment Treatment." The noun *ferment* refers generally to enzymes, particularly to enzymes that catalyze reactions of sugars and carbohydrates. Such enzymatic reactions in the stomach liberate glucose. Glucose, quickly absorbed into the blood stream, exacerbates many symptoms of diabetes.

Many of Kaadt's Fort Wayne colleagues in the Allen County Medical Society were uncomfortable with his diabetic treatment methodology. The local doctors had reason to believe that the "treatment" was not just ineffective, but that it actually was dangerous. They were increasingly concerned when his claims spread beyond his office into regional and national advertising. He was sending both promotional material and the remedy itself in the mail. Responding to a complaint from the local medical society, the American Medical Association in 1930 initiated an inquiry into the composition of the remedy. Then in 1932, the Food and Drug Administration charged that the remedy was misbranded. Dr. Kaadt agreed to remove all claims regarding diabetes from his labels. The Food and Drug Administration did not pursue the matter further.

Notwithstanding removal of explicit claims from the label, Charles Kaadt's Fort Wayne diabetic practice continued to expand. Within four years, the patient activity increased far beyond the capacity of his Fort Wayne office. The Hicks Tavern was available in South Whitley, and the stage was set in 1936 for moving the Kaadt Diabetic Institute there. Peter Kaadt moved from Portland, Oregon, to collaborate with his brother in South Whitley. They hired Robert S. Benson to be the administrative superintendent of the Institute. Peter commuted between Portland and South Whitley for a few years, and then in 1944 closed his Portland practice and spent full time in South Whitley.

The United States Post Office Department decided to investigate. A postal inspector, posing as a patient, submitted by mail a sample of synthetic urine prepared by an FDA chemist. The pseudo urine contained no sugar. Charles Kaadt responded that, by chemical analysis, he found the urine sample to contain sugar, indicating treatment. Without examining the patient, he prescribed by mail. The inspector mailed money, and Kaadt mailed his medicine. The FDA chemist analyzed the medicine. Chemical analysis revealed that the liquid was essentially a vinegar solution of potassium nitrate. Small quantities of what may have been denatured digestive enzymes (pepsin and takadiastase) were also present in the medicine, giving the liquid a cloudy yellow-brown appearance but having no effect in combating diabetes.

The FDA investigation revealed several problems. The Kaadt medicine was over-

priced, costing thirty times the cost of its ingredients. The medicine had no therapeutic value for treating diabetes. The medicine would be dangerous if taken by a
person in good health, likely to irritate the gastrointestinal tract and the kidneys.
Because the medicine was to be taken by a diabetic in lieu of dietary restrictions and
in lieu of insulin therapy, this medical regime could result in premature death.

Charles Kaadt must have been aware of those problems. He must have known
their significance. As the Indiana Supreme Court (in considering an appeal of revocation of Dr. Kaadt's medical license) was to conclude fifteen years later, "the
respondent was a man of broad professional experience, sufficiently educated in his
profession. [One cannot attribute] the acts complained of to mistake[s] arising out
of inexperience or lack of knowledge."

The Post Office Department initiated a show-cause hearing, asking why the
practices of the Kaadt Diabetic Institute should not be declared fraudulent and
why the Institute should not be denied use of the mails. Drs. Charles and Peter
Kaadt went to Washington for the hearing. After three days of testimony, the
brothers stipulated (on June 20, 1938) that they would cease using the mails to further the interests of the Institute.

The Kaadt products were henceforth shipped to patients from South Whitley by
the Railway Express Agency to avoid using the Post Office. It was not so easy to
avoid use of the mails for communicating with actual or prospective patients, or for
receiving payments for orders of Diabetic Ferment Treatment and similar Kaadt
nostrums. The Post Office Department brought suit in Federal Court against Dr.
Charles Kaadt, charging him with six counts of violating the June 20, 1938 stipula-
tion. The jury found Charles guilty of only one count. The judge was skeptical even
of the single guilty verdict. He wrote: "It is hard to conceive that the defendant
devised a scheme to defraud and had the intent to defraud in the face of these witnesses who honestly believe in the efficacy of the treatment." The judge voided the
guilty verdict and granted a motion for a new trial. That trial was never held.

The Clinic had its defenders and supporters. Charismatic Peter and Charles
Kaadt personally projected credible medical authority. Many of their patients were
eager to testify that these physicians were effective healers. Prominent persons were
among the believers; a knowledgeable local resident claimed that Cordell Hull
(United States Secretary of State from 1933 to 1944) had secretly been treated at the

Clinic. Some of the allegiance may have been purchased. The Kaadt brothers contributed funds (perhaps all the funds) to build a new Veterans of Foreign Wars building at 234 South State Street in South Whitley. Rumors abounded that the Kaadts were heavy contributors to local churches; the Methodist minister announced that he would testify in court to the excellent character of each brother.

The town's economy certainly benefited greatly from the activity surrounding the Clinic. Sixty householders supplemented their weekly incomes by taking in roomers. Prince Immanuel was filling his rooms at the South Whitley Hotel. Several South Whitley residents worked at the Clinic. Milton Earl Emerson was raising Angus steers on his farm at the south edge of town to provide beef steaks for the Clinic dining room. Conway Geist (1905–1967) was operating a taxi service whose primary role was to meet each Nickel Plate passenger train, and to transport patients to and from the Clinic. He also met every bus from Fort Wayne at the bus stop (the W. F. Norris Rexall Drugstore). Snell Bus Lines had two round trips daily from Fort Wayne to North Manchester via South Whitley. Fred Norris, with his Rexall Drugstore next-door to the Clinic, benefited from sales (other than Kaadt products) to the many visiting seriously ill patients and their families. Also nearby on State Street was the pharmacy of D. C. Scott, "The Old Time Druggist." After Durant C. Scott's retirement in September 1936, the establishment became the Howard Keister Walgreen Drugstore.

William F. Norris was a dispensing pharmacist and also a compounding pharmacist. A prescription from a local physician would often be a recipe, giving the names and quantities of ingredients and the directions for preparing the drug. Mr. Norris had supplies of the required chemicals, as well as scales, graduates, mortars and pestles, a tablet press, and assortments of empty gelatin capsules, ready to be filled with medicine. He would also sell small quantities of almost any chemical to a trustworthy customer. For example, he would replenish chemicals supplied in the popular Chemcraft home chemistry sets that the Porter Chemical Company sold for decades after 1914. Fred Norris was the judge of the appropriateness of each such sale.

The pages of the *South Whitley Tribune* had few critical comments about the Kaadt enterprise that was bringing business to town. Stump Printing Company was producing informational pamphlets. With a moratorium imposed by the Post Office Department on moving funds by mail, both Western Union and the Mayer State

Bank must have been profiting from alternative modes of money transfer.

Counterbalancing its defenders and supporters, powerful organizations were arrayed against the Institute (by then the Kaadt Diabetic Clinic), including the Indianapolis Better Business Bureau, the Indiana Board of Medical Registration and Examination, the Federal Food and Drug Administration, the American Diabetes Association, and *The Indianapolis Star.* The United States Post Office Department was continuing its surveillance. *The Indianapolis Star* assigned an investigative reporter to probe the affairs of the Clinic.

The Better Business Bureau petitioned the Board of Medical Registration and Examination to revoke the medical licenses of both Charles and Peter Kaadt. Charles entered a plea of *nolo contendere* before judgment was passed. Charles agreed to accept cancellation of his Indiana medical license with prejudice, and he promised never again to practice medicine in the state. The Board continued proceedings against Peter, revoking his license. South Whitley is in Whitley County, and Peter appealed the revocation to the friendly Whitley County Circuit Court. The Circuit Court restored his license, but the Board immediately appealed to the Indiana Supreme Court.

"The board's evidence showed that the respondent prescribed for patients without any physical examination and that he prescribed and gave medicine for diabetes to persons who were free from that disease. In no case was the necessary blood test made for sugar before prescribing for patients. Insulin and diet are the only known and accepted methods of treatment for diabetes; there is no oral treatment recognized by the medical world; removing patients suffering from this disease from insulin is dangerous and may be fatal. The consumption of sugar by a diabetic person is injurious to him, and the fact that sugar has been cooked does not render it harmless. The treatment adopted by the respondent is not approved by any other person in the profession. There have been no clinical tests or experimental stage in the development of this medicine; the treatment and medicine prescribed by the respondent is of no benefit to diabetic persons. The giving of the same has at times injured the patients, and some have died from its effect."

The Indiana Supreme Court in March 1948 overruled the Whitley County Circuit Court, and reinstated the order of the Board of Medical Registration and Examination to revoke the medical license of Peter Kaadt.

The Federal Food and Drug Administration did not believe that revocation of medical licenses was sufficient penalty. Federal indictments were returned Saturday, January 31, 1948, in the Northern District of Indiana against Charles Kaadt, Peter Kaadt, and Clinic Superintendent Robert S. Benson on seven counts of misbranding the Kaadt Diabetic Treatment, in violation of the 1938 Federal Food, Drug and Cosmetic Act. The trial was held in Fort Wayne in April 1948. The jury returned verdicts of guilty against each of the three defendants on each of the counts. Judge Patrick T. Stone imposed fines of $7,000 and costs, and imprisonment for three years, on each of the Kaadt brothers. Defendant Benson was sentenced to pay a fine of $350 and to serve one year in prison; Benson's prison sentence was suspended. Charles Kaadt and Peter Kaadt appealed to the United States Court of Appeals for the Seventh Circuit [*United States v. Kaadt,* 171 F.2d 600 (7th Cir. 1948)]; the appeal was rejected and the judgment of the District Court was affirmed on Tuesday, December 7, 1948. A request for a rehearing was denied on Monday, January 3, 1949.

Peter was released from prison because of ill health; he died in 1951. Charles served his full prison term; he died in 1957.

Fred Fox, Hugo Fox, and Fred Graham

There were at least five grocery stores in South Whitley in 1935: the Kroger Store, Firmer Snyder's I.G.A. (Independent Grocers Alliance), Craw's Corner Store, Howard McGlennen's Quality Bakery, and the Bee Hive Grocery. Canned goods were on high shelves behind the counters in the food stores, and many products were behind glass in display cases on the counters. The transition to a semblance of a self-serve supermarket would occur in the late 1940s. Earl Bayman (August 23, 1891–December 27, 1958) and Fred Fox (May 10, 1883–May 8, 1969) were proprietors of the Bee Hive. Earl was the skilled meat cutter, and Fred was the amiable personality at the front counter. Everybody in South Whitley knew Fred Fox, and he could call just about everybody by name.

South Whitley was an incorporated town with a town council, not a city with a mayor. Fred filled the mayoralty vacuum. Fred Fox facilitated a full-fanfare reception for Governor Edward L. Jackson when he came to visit Robert E. Hicks in South

Whitley. Fred was the genial host and general manager of the Palm Room, the banquet room of the Hicks Tavern.

Fred Fox was born in the village of Sidney in Kosciusko County, Indiana, son of Elizabeth Miller and William B. Fox. Sidney village, one mile north and six miles west of South Whitley, was incorporated as a town in 1914. The population of Sidney in 1920 was 223. In 2010, it was down to 83. The Fox family moved to South Whitley about 1897. Fred graduated in a class of five from South Whitley High School in 1901, and then attended Purdue University.

By 1905, South Whitley High School had graduated 126 students. The time had come for a school reunion. Roy Norris, Class of 1896, was chosen President of the new S.W.H.S. Alumni Association; Bertha Fager, Class of 1898, was named Secretary; and Fred Fox became Treasurer. The Alumni Association decided to hold reunions every three years. The 1905 officers served again in 1908. When Roy Norris died unexpectedly from complications of scarlet fever on January 21, 1911, Fred Fox became his successor.

Fred Fox quickly became the personification of the Triennial Alumni Reunion. He was President of the Alumni Association in 1911 and for the next three reunions, Vice-President in 1923, and then President again in 1932 and 1935. Many of the reunions were held south of town in Fox's Grove at Cuppy's Corner (the southwest corner of what is now the junction of state roads 14, 5, and 105). After a World War II hiatus, the Triennial Alumni Reunion resumed in 1946, and Fred Fox was elected President Emeritus, a position he held until his death. Part of the triennial ritual was a parade through town, featuring the high school band, the town's fire trucks, and usually an open convertible with Grand Marshal Fred Fox waving to spectators lining the streets. Fred loved a parade.

Fred cultivated influential connections. It was often said that when South Whitley needed a favor from the State House in Indianapolis, Fred would personally call the Governor, whether Edward L. Jackson, Harry Guyer Leslie, or Columbia City's Ralph Fesler Gates.

Fred Fox was South Whitley's Fire Chief for a quarter century. Always smoking a cigar, he would show up for a surprise fire drill at a school building to ring the fire bell. The cigar fumes gave away any pretense of a surprise. As Fire Chief, Fred maintained connections with South Whitley native Cash Graham, who for thirteen years was Chief Deputy of the office of the Indiana State Fire Marshal in Indianapolis. Cash Graham had been South Whitley Postmaster from December 20, 1902 to May 22, 1913, followed as Postmaster by Fred's father.

On a sunny day, Fred was likely to be found chatting with folks on State Street. He enjoyed people, and he enjoyed being on stage. He was a greeter at the Methodist Episcopal Church, and often passed the collection plate at Sunday services. Rev. M. C. Morrow quipped: "With Fred in action, the Nickel Plate comes right down the center aisle."

Fred once was smuggled on stage at a concert of the Chicago Symphony Orchestra. Fred had become friends with many members of the orchestra when they were visiting his brother Hugo at Fox's Grove. Musicians surreptitiously seated Fred in the trumpet section, across the concert stage from unsuspecting bassoonist Hugo. Fred several times held a trumpet to his lips, but he didn't sound a note. Hugo was not amused.

Hugo Eugene Fox (February 3, 1897–December 27, 1969) was born in Sidney. He played alto saxophone in the South Whitley High School Band. Band music often arrived from a publisher with separate parts scored for bassoon. In the absence of a bassoonist, the director sometimes asked Hugo to play those parts on his saxophone. While still in high school, Hugo decided to try an actual bassoon. His first bassoon teacher was John L. Verweire in Fort Wayne. Born in Belgium, Verweire graduated from the Royal Conservatory of Brussels before immigrating to the United States. He came to Fort Wayne in 1896, where he conducted the Fort Wayne City Band. City Band morphed (under Verweire's direction) into the Packard Piano Company Band, the Elks Band (perhaps also the Elk-Klan Band), the General Electric Band, and eventually the Fort Wayne Symphony Orchestra. John Verweire was also director of Fort Wayne's Mizpah Shrine Band, the Concordia College Band, and the *News-Sentinel* Newsboys Band.

Hugo was a member of the Agony Band, a group of fifteen who organized in 1912 at the 1887 Calhoun Street School in South Whitley. Hugo played alto saxophone, and School Superintendent W. W. Wells played D-flat and C piccolos. The others were Ellis Miller, cornet; Gene Glassley, Vernon Gresso, and Lee Nichols, trombone; Ernest Jewell and Gerald Horner, E-flat horn; Carper Hathaway, E-flat mellophone; Herbert Harley, clarinet; Lloyd Holben, baritone; Robert Harley and

Boyd Sickafoose, E-flat tuba; Keith Glassley, snare drum; and Frank Dimmick, bass drum. Most members were students at South Whitley High School. The band had several successful seasons, but disbanded at the outbreak of the Great War.

There were other bands in South Whitley then, continuing a tradition that dated back to a bugle, fife, and drum corps formed in Civil War times, and to a town band organized in 1885. The Atoz Printing Company sponsored the ATOZ Band as early as 1906. The Norris Pharmacy Orchestra, organized in May 1908, gave Saturday night concerts at the W. F. Norris Pharmacy on State Street. The Knights of Pythias lodge financed the K. of P. Band, with each musician getting fifty cents for a rehearsal and twenty-five cents for each performance.

With encouragement from School Superintendent Alvin R. Fleck, the Agony Band reorganized on December 19, 1924. Phil Farren, who was already directing five other school bands, was hired to lead the new band. Robert E. Hicks provided substantial financial support. There were sixty-two band members, drawn from as far down into elementary school as ability would permit. Mr. Farren continued as high school band director until 1927. He was followed by Gene Glassley and then by R. E. Melton.

Hugo Fox was valedictorian of the South Whitley High School Class of 1914. After graduation, he traveled on the Nickel Plate Railroad to Chicago every two weeks to study bassoon with Adolph Weiss (1891–1971). Adolph Weiss was second bassoonist of the Chicago Symphony Orchestra from 1913 until 1916.

As the United States prepared to enter the Great War, draft registration (for men between the ages of 21 and 31) began on June 5, 1917. Hugo was 20, not yet of draft age. Not waiting for the draft, he enlisted in the Navy. He received his recruit training at the Great Lakes Naval Training Center north of Chicago, and became a member of the bassoon section of its band. Eventually, he was transferred to the Philadelphia Naval Shipyard, where he served until discharged in 1919. The Armistice had been signed on November 11, 1918.

After the Navy, Hugo played in various musical ensembles in Indiana and Ohio, including the B. F. Goodrich Band in Akron, Ohio. In 1921, he moved back to Chicago to study bassoon with Julius Walter Gütter (1895–1937). Gütter was a member of the Chicago Symphony Orchestra from 1915 to 1922, except for a year off for the Great War.

Walter Gütter departed for the Philadelphia Orchestra in 1922. Gütter recommended that Hugo Fox replace him as Principal Bassoon. Legendary Music Director and Conductor Friedrich August Stock (1872–1942) agreed, and appointed twenty-five-year-old Hugo Fox the Principal Bassoon of the Chicago Symphony Orchestra. Sitting in the second bassoon chair was Hjalmar Rabe; Rabe had been Principal Bassoon during the wartime season when Gütter was away. Stock was already a legend in Chicago. He was hired as a violinist in 1895, became assistant conductor in 1899, and then was music director and conductor from 1905 to 1942.

Hugo Fox was Principal Bassoon of the Chicago Symphony for twenty-seven seasons, retiring at the close of the 1948–1949 season. For fifteen of those years, Hugo Fox was Instructor of Bassoon in the Northwestern University School of Music. He also taught bassoon in the Civic Orchestra of Chicago, the only training orchestra affiliated with a major American orchestra. After his retirement as a teacher in Chicago, he published a student instruction booklet, *Let's Play Bassoon*.

Bassoonists have always known that their performance depends critically on the quality of the reed they use. Professionals made their own double reeds. Hugo Fox's study with Adolph Weiss and with Walter Gütter included training in the techniques of making bassoon reeds. During the late 1930s, Hugo Fox began to sell reeds that he had meticulously crafted by hand. As demand increased, he began to mechanize some routine steps of reed manufacture. South Whitley inventor Eldon Leroy Krieg constructed some experimental machines. Hugo enlisted his brother Fred to test and operate prototype machinery.

Hugo Fox had dreams far beyond manufacturing reeds. He had never been satisfied with commercially available bassoons. He discussed with many people the practicalities of designing and manufacturing better instruments. Hardened wood of the sugar maple tree has long been the traditional material for constructing the body of lower-register woodwinds. Hugo sought sources of sugar maple timber, and considered properties of wood from the two subspecies that are native to Indiana: *Acer saccharum saccharum* and *Acer saccharum schneckii*. He investigated methods of curing and hardening the maple wood. He also investigated other quite different materials for the bassoon body, including phenolic plastics, cellulose acetate butyrate, and polypropylene.

The sit-down soda fountain at the Rexall drugstore on State Street in South Whitley may seem an unlikely place for Hugo's technical consultations on bassoon design, but this was location of many such discussions between Hugo Fox and Frederick Milo Graham (January 29, 1872–February 6, 1959). The soda fountain was a community gathering place, and Hugo Fox and Fred Graham had specific shared interests.

Fred Graham was born in Nelson Center, Ohio, son of Anna Snook and David Graham. Nelson Center was the crossroads at the exact center of Nelson Township, Portage County, Ohio. Fred attended Hiram College in Hiram, Ohio. He began his professional career with a two-year stint (probably summers of 1893 and 1894) with the United States Coast and Geodetic Survey, the premiere earth-science agency of the country and today the oldest element of the National Oceanic and Atmospheric Administration. He served in the surveying field party of topological engineer Dr. Charles Harrod Boyd (1833–1919). In his published report for 1894, Dr. Boyd acknowledged "the very acceptable service rendered" by F. M. Graham, who was assigned to Boyd's party as a rodman. The field party was charged with completing the topographic resurvey of the Connecticut River, and the hydrographic resurvey of Boston Bay and Boston Harbor. One product of Graham's time with the Survey was a Boston Harbor map that he framed and proudly displayed in his home office in South Whitley.

Fred Graham received the Bachelor of Science degree in 1897 from the Case School of Applied Science in Cleveland. Case School originated in 1877 with a large endowment gift by Leonard Case Jr. It became the Case Institute of Technology in 1947, and merged with Western Reserve University in 1967. Fred wrote an undergraduate engineering thesis, "The Design of a System of Sewers for Ravenna, Ohio," during the 1896–1897 school year. Ravenna is the county seat of Portage County, Ohio, thirty-five miles southeast of Cleveland. Cleveland was just beginning to implement a professionally planned sewerage system. His thesis was especially timely.

Fred Graham was a research engineer for the Pennsylvania Railroad for forty-seven years, involved in both theoretical and experimental research. He held patents for as many as twenty inventions to improve connections and fastenings of rails. He was especially interested in using the physics of acoustics to monitor rail roadbed conditions. He devised practical methods of using sound beams focused downward toward the roadbed and a microphone that detected sound reflected from within the roadbed. One of his devices compared the generated and reflected signals to reveal voids in the ballast or in the underlying foundation materials.

In Fort Wayne, he met his future wife, Claudine Scott (August 20, 1881–September 3, 1960). She was the only child of Melissa Porter (October 9, 1860–September 27, 1921) and Durant Charles Scott (July 14, 1859–April 21, 1938). Durant Scott was proprietor of the D. C. Scott Drug Store in South Whitley for fifty years. In the 1930s, the Grahams lived in Hollidaysburg, Pennsylvania. Hollidaysburg is the county seat of Blair County, seven miles south of Altoona. Claudine and Fred Graham retired to South Whitley in 1942, moving into the house at 111 North State Street where Mrs. Graham had spent her childhood. They spent winters in Sebring, Florida.

In their wills, Claudine and Fred Graham provided for Ameila Leochner Campbell (1894–1968), their housekeeper and companion for thirty years. The residue of the estate after Ms. Campbell's death was bequeathed to the South Whitley Library for construction of a new building. That building, at the southeast corner of Front Street and Maple Street, was dedicated on Sunday, October 11, 1970. Former South Whitley High School Principal Lee LeVere Eve was speaker at the ceremony. The library building, with additions, still serves the South Whitley community.

Fred Graham loved mathematics. He enjoyed explaining to high school students how mathematics had been employed when the proposed route of Pennsylvania Railroad tracks was plotted through mountainous Pennsylvania terrain. Trains could not negotiate steep grades. It was necessary to cut away portions of mountains and to fill portions of adjacent valleys to provide foundations so that tracks would be almost level. He explained that integral calculus was used to calculate how much rock would have to be blasted from mountains to provide the required amount of fill.

Case today characterizes itself as "the best small private university for engineers 'plus'—those whose interests and abilities allow them to excel beyond engineering … go as far as their imaginations will take them." Fred Graham exemplified the ideal of excelling wherever imagination leads. When several of his colleagues feted him on his 85th birthday, they recalled: "Mr. Graham once came to the rescue of a bassoon manufacturer who was commissioned by a U. S. Government symphonic band to build an instrument capable of playing a note a full tone lower than any existing bassoon could sound. The Graham knowledge of music, mathematics, oscillation and pitch produced the diagrams by which that bassoon was constructed." There is no record of whether that bassoon manufacturer was Hugo Fox. However, there were eyewitnesses and eavesdroppers to many conversations between Hugo Fox and Fred Graham about similar matters at the Norris drugstore soda fountain.

Another topic of conversation was surely the design of an electronic frequency analyzer that would enable bassoonists other than Hugo to evaluate the individual characteristics of each Fox bassoon. Fred Graham had worked with many other engineers to design and construct acoustic instrumentation for the Pennsylvania Railroad. By about 1950, Hugo Fox had a one-of-a-kind frequency analyzer in operation at Fox Products. To the end of his life, Hugo remained fascinated with musical applications of acoustic spectrum analysis.

Back to Hugo Fox, double reeds, and the Fox bassoons.

Hugo Fox retired from the Chicago Symphony in 1949, and founded the Fox Products Corporation at Cuppy's Corner south of South Whitley. Mass production of bassoon and oboe reeds put Fox Products on the double-reed mail-order map. His first source of tube cane was Fréjus in the Provence–Alpes–Côte d'Azur region of southeastern France. He aged the cane for eight years before beginning the cutting, gouging, carving, and shaping operations required to fabricate individual reeds.

Each reed is made with two blades of reed (hence the name "double-reed") bound together and wrapped with many turns of silk thread. Bassoon, oboe, and English horn double reeds each have a coat of paint near and over the thread wrappings. In 1949, many commercial paints were poisonous. Hugo Fox commissioned development of a special paint that could be certified by the federal government as non-toxic, safe for use on reeds.

There were only three employees in summer 1951 at Fox Products: Hugo Fox, Fred Fox, and Mary Lou Bowers Smith. Every reed was tested before the reed received the Fox seal of approval. Hugo Fox tested the bassoon reeds. Mary Lou Smith tested the oboe and English horn reeds. Before leaving the shop, each reed was sterilized with a germicidal lamp and packed in an individual vial.

Hugo's heart, however, was in the manufacture of better bassoons. His first bassoon was completed in December 1951. "Hugo was quite pleased with the results, so much so, that he played his instrument 'all the way along the winding lane to the (nearby) Fox residence'."

Northeastern Indiana was already a manufacturing center of quality band instruments, with C. G. Conn, Selmer, and others located in Elkhart. Selmer was world-famous for clarinets and flutes, and the company was experimenting in the 1940s with making a commercial oboe. South Whitley High School Band Director Reba

M. Geist (1902–1994) convinced Selmer to use her band as a test site for their prototype oboe. She talked with Hugo Fox, who matched Selmer's offer with both his first bassoon and also with private lessons for the South Whitley student who would be subjected to his experimental instrument.

The first of the four joints of the bassoon went into production in spring 1951. Twelve complete bassoons were produced in 1952, and yearly production gradually increased over the decade. The company then expanded significantly. It was still in business at Cuppy's Corner in 2014, manufacturing oboes, English horns, bassoons, and contrabassoons.

Traditional maple continued to be the classical material for the body of bassoons. Hugo realized that wood is inherently temperamental. Variations in ambient temperature and humidity influence the timbre and the pitch of the wooden instrument. On April 1, 1961, he filed a patent application for a polypropylene bassoon. In the text of the application, he included test results that demonstrated markedly better pitch stability of his polypropylene bassoon relative to a traditional maple bassoon when each was subjected to a high-humidity atmosphere for a week. He began to market a polypropylene instrument, targeted to military bands, university music programs, individuals seeking a durable second instrument, and budget-conscious purchasers for a first instrument. Two models of polypropylene bassoons were listed in the 2014 Fox instrument catalog.

Because of failing health, Hugo retired from active involvement in the company in 1962. His son Alan became President.

Prince Immanuel of Jerusalem

A stroll in 1935 from the railroad junction toward the Hicks Tavern would have taken Barbara and Albert Germann past the Immanuel Clinic (at 215 North State Street, in 2014 numbering). The Clinic was in a three-story Victorian residence with twenty-two rooms. The house was built in the Second Empire style by Eleanor Combs (1825–1909) and Caleb W. Edwards (1820–1894) in 1869, just after the Civil War. Caleb Edwards was a pioneer South Whitley physician. Nina Briant and Prince Albert Edwards (son of Eleanor and Caleb Edwards) raised their children—

Helene, Briant, and Eugene—in that house. Helene married Ralph Fesler Gates (1893–1978), a Columbia City attorney who would become the 37th Governor of Indiana, serving from 1945 to 1949. The paternal grandfather of Gov. Gates, John T. Gates, did the ornate interior plastering of the Edwards house.

For twenty years, from about 1926 to about 1946, Prince Immanuel (1874–October 1, 1949) was proprietor of the Immanuel Clinic. Over those two decades, he gave the Clinic several different names—South Whitley Hotel, Immanuel Health Center, Abbey of Immanuel, the South Whitley Health Society, Immanuel Sanitarium, and perhaps others. During the winter months, the interior of the Clinic was bedecked with potted dwarf Citrus trees and a banana plant. When the weather had warmed reliably, the trees and the banana were moved outdoors to grace his spacious front lawn. The Clinic was an enigma. For many residents of South Whitley, so was Prince Immanuel.

Prince Immanuel was born in Newport, Wales, son of Augusta Zadeck and Robert Immanuel. Augusta was Prussian and Robert was probably Welsh. Newport is an ancient cathedral city in southeast Wales. It was the site of a populist armed insurrection, the Newport Chartists Rising of 1839. Newport was an important shipping port when Prince was a boy there. It was a time when English-only language policies prevailed in most classrooms in Wales. Prince probably grew up bilingual in Cymraeg and English. He became fascinated with linguistics.

About 1883, when Prince was nine years old, he and his family moved to Johannesburg, South Africa. That unlikely move may have been triggered by the discovery of gold in southern Africa at Pilgrim's Rest in September 1873, at Jamestown in 1881, and then in Concession Creek on June 20, 1883. The Concession Creek discovery set off a gold rush to the Johannesburg area. The Immanuel family was in Johannesburg when prospectors located vast deposits of gold on Langlaagte in the Transvaal in 1886. Within a decade, this became the richest gold mining area in the world. Fortunes were made.

Prince Immanuel said that he was educated at the Medical School of the University of Berlin. That institution must have been Humboldt University of Berlin, the only university in Berlin at the beginning of the twentieth century. Efforts to document his medical education have been unsuccessful, but he often used the title Doctor.

He also said that he was head of a school in the City of Jerusalem for nine years.

Neither the dates nor the nature of this school have been discovered. It was during this period that he adopted the name Prince Immanuel of Jerusalem. He published a book in Jerusalem in 1907 with the title *The Order of the Golden Rule of Jerusalem*. Linguist Arika Okrent credits Prince Immanuel with creation of Universal, an invented language that she classifies as an *a posteriori* language, a language that, like Esperanto, takes most of its material from existing natural languages. She refers to a book by Prince Immanuel, published in Cairo in 1914. Prince Immanuel claimed that he knew twenty languages.

Dr. Okrent found a postcard, printed in Cairo, "with a picture of 'Prince Immanuel of Jerusalem' on it—a slight, bearded, turn-of-the-century-optometrist-looking fellow in some sort of sash-and-medallions regalia." Prince Immanuel's self-description: "My physiognomy and physique are unusual and always attract attention. I am five feet two inches, have a thirty-nine chest, and weigh one hundred fifty pounds, so you can well imagine that I am too Napoleonic around the waist for any active abstainer of forty. My hands and feet are tiny and delicate like those of a lady, yet I can walk fifty miles a day, and wring the neck of a giant. But it is my tri-colored Vandyke beard and heavy upturned mustaches, black, brown and grey, that create the cynosure."

He came to the United States before the outbreak of the Great War. By 1921, he had written and published his 258-page book *Criminals of Chicago*. The book was a sensational fictional tour of Chicago dens of iniquity, intended to popularize the work and recommendations of William J. Hickson, Director of the Psychopathic Laboratory of the Municipal Court of Chicago. An indication of the direction of some of the activities of the Psychopathic Laboratory is its publication in 1922 of the book *Eugenical Sterilization in the United States*.

Prince Immanuel came to South Whitley to work at the Atoz Printing Company as a proofreader. He probably felt that an association with Atoz would open a practical way for him to publish his writings. One of his unpublished works is a five-act play "Lupus and Fidus." The Indiana University cataloguing information for the manuscript of this play identifies the author as "Dr. Prince Immanuel (1874–1949), a Whitley County (Indiana) author, and operator of the South Whitley Health Society (according to the Department of Investigation, American Medical Association: 'apparently a diploma mill run by Prince Immanuel')."

His 79-page book, *Gospel According to Im-anu-el: Extracts from the Gospels, Com-*

piled and Arranged, With Additions, by P. Immanuel, of South Whitley, Ind. was printed in South Whitley in 1936. The book named the publisher as "Abbey of Immanuel." Anne Shoemaker Metzger (April 18, 1886–February 5, 1972), librarian of the South Whitley Public Library, said that he donated a copy to the library, but the contents were inappropriate for the library collection.

The writings of Prince Immanuel did not appeal to his hometown librarian. Editor Basil Adams of the *South Whitley Tribune* reported in a front-page article on Thursday, October 12, 1944: "Dr. Prince Immanuel, local physician, is among the authors whose work appears in 'Of America We Sing.' … Dr. Immanuel has presented a copy of this new book 'Of America We Sing' to the local library." If the book were ever accessioned, it has since been discarded. No writing attributed to Prince Immanuel as author is listed in the library's current on-line catalog.

When Albert Germann purchased a building for Nutritional Research Associates, Inc., in 1935, Dr. Immanuel was publishing an occasional column, "Health Chats," in the *South Whitley Tribune.* At that time, he gave his South Whitley address as Immanuel Clinic. Stump Printing Company used the type composed for each Health Chats article to print a circular that Prince Immanuel would then mail to persons on his commercial address list.

In 1947, Prince Immanuel published *Chaos: Written for the Illiterati, not the Litertai.* The OCLC FirstSearch database (WorldCat) describes this forty-five-page, 8½" × 11" book, as an "American Drama." The *South Whitley Tribune* set the type and printed the book, although the publisher was identified as World Press, Columbia City, Indiana. A few years later, he published *Chaos II* in the same format. The *Tribune* again set the type. This time, the *Tribune* printed about a thousand copies, but the pages were not immediately collated and bound. When Prince Immanuel needed a few copies, he would call the *Tribune* office (United Telephone Company #15) and additional copies would be assembled, bound, and delivered to his combined home, office, and Health Center, then in Columbia City. As late as 2010, a substantial number of unsold copies were still in storage at the *Tribune* office.

When he disposed of his hotel and home in South Whitley (about 1946), he opened a less pretentious Health Center ten miles away in Columbia City. He donated the dwarf Citrus trees and the banana plant (probably a Dwarf Cavendish) to the South Whitley High School science room, which had a small attached greenhouse.

Valentine Hennig

In 1935, there were five churches with sanctuaries within the corporation limits of South Whitley: the Methodist Episcopal Church, the Church of the United Brethren in Christ, the Church of the Brethren, the Church of God, and the Baptist Church. Each was Protestant. Although the five denominations differed in forms of governance, the local congregations and their ministers did not have sufficient theological disagreements to prevent them from organizing joint vacation Bible school classes for children of the community. Nationally, the Church of the United Brethren in Christ denomination merged with the Evangelical Church in 1946 to form the Evangelical United Brethren Church, which in 1968 merged with the Methodist Episcopal Church to form the United Methodist Church. The overall effect in South Whitley of the 1968 merger was that two congregations (Methodist Episcopal and Evangelical United Brethren) joined their congregations, and disposed of their buildings and real estate in town. They constructed a new sanctuary south of town, at the southeast corner of the junction of state roads 14, 5, and 105, across the intersection from Cuppy's Corner and across from the present location of Fox Products.

The *South Whitley Tribune* ran weekly church announcements, which in 1935 included the rural Lutheran Parish, Rev. W. E. Weber pastor. Lutheran Parish was a consortium of Eberhard and St. Peters churches, both located near the border between Washington and Columbia townships in Whitley County. Eberhard and St. Peters were members of the American Evangelical Lutheran Synod. Eberhard is still an active congregation, now a member of the Evangelical Lutheran Church in America Synod, a successor (in turn) of the American Evangelical Lutheran Church Synod and then the Lutheran Church in America Synod. St. Peters did not survive. Nearby, although not recognized by the *Tribune* for inclusion on the church page in 1935, was St. John's Lutheran Church (Missouri Synod), six miles east of South Whitley. St. John's is still active. Its historic sanctuary is at 2465 West Keiser Road.

Valentine (Val) Hennig (December 19, 1889–September 11, 1961) had been pastor of St. John's Lutheran Church for more than a decade when the Germann family moved to Whitley County. Val Hennig's tenure at St. John's Lutheran Church was thirty-seven years. He retired in 1960.

Val was one of ten children of Catherine Mohr and Valentine Hennig. He attended First St. Paul's Lutheran Parochial School in Chicago, and then Milwaukee's Concordia College, a preparatory school for the St. Louis Concordia Lutheran Seminary. He graduated from Concordia College *cum laude* in 1908, and matriculated at St. Louis Concordia Seminary. He received his degree in theology from the Seminary in 1911, and was ordained into the Lutheran Church–Missouri Synod ministry at Moorehead, Nebraska, in the same year. There he served three congregations in a joint ministry at Moorehead, Curtis, and Wellfleet. In his two years at Moorehead, the young minister had a literal bricks-and-mortar leadership role, actively engaged in constructing a new church building. He married Laura Luebeck on Wednesday, August 27, 1913.

After Nebraska, Val was called to Zion Lutheran Church (Missouri Synod) outside of Gordonville, a small village in rural Cape Girardeau County, Missouri. He was pastor in Gordonville for seven years, beginning in late 1914. Three of the children of Laura and Val were born during that time, each baptized at Zion Lutheran Church. Val was a leader in constructing the present sanctuary at 176 County Road 226. He was interim pastor at Oak Park, Illinois, for a few months, and then served eighteen months at the Saint Peter Lutheran Church (Missouri Synod), a mile west of the outskirts of the unincorporated rural village of Waymansville, Jackson Township, Bartholomew County, in southern Indiana.

In fall 1922, the Hennig family settled in Whitley County. Val was installed as pastor of St. John's in December. He also became Head of the St. John's Parochial School. His years at St. John's were years of gradual change for him and for the congregation. At first, German was the language for almost all services at St. John's. Later, for seven years, bilingual services were held each Sunday. After 1940, all services were in English. St. John's Parochial School was discontinued after four years, but Val found other ways to foster Lutheran education. For many years, he was the only German-language teacher living near South Whitley. In 1922, men at St. John's sat on the left side of the nave, women on the right side, and children on benches in front. Integrated seating for worship began in the 1930s. In 1942, communion became integrated.

St. John's Lutheran church welcomed Ida and Albert Germann and their family into its fellowship. Val Hennig became their pastor.

St. John's and the Rev. Val Hennig were associated with several other folk who appeared earlier in this book. For example, Pastor Val Henning performed the marriage of Mary Magdalene Dreyer and Charles Marshall Bowerman on February 5, 1939 at St. John's Lutheran Church. Charles Bowerman is mentioned in the Preface as an editor and publisher of the *South Whitley Tribune*. Val Hennig married 109 other couples in his years at St. John's.

More central to the theme of this book are members of the Pook family. Carl Frederick Pook (February 25, 1848–September 28, 1932), born in Herckendorf, Germany, was a pioneer farmer near South Whitley in Washington Township, and a member of St. John's. A son, Ervin H. Pook (April 26, 1885–February 14, 1974), married Margaretha Magdalena Kunberger at St. John's on May 23, 1909. They set up housekeeping on the Pook farm. In spring 1929, they established the Pook Feed and Coal Company at the Vandalia Railroad and the Nickel Plate crossing in South Whitley. A son of Margaretha and Ervin, Clarence Henry Louis Pook (July 16, 1912–April 13, 1996), was valedictorian of the South Whitley High School Class of 1930. He attended DePauw University on a four-year scholarship (the Rector Scholarship, DePauw University's oldest and preeminent academic merit award), graduating in 1934. He worked at Pook Feed and Coal Company until November 1937, when he was named Acting Postmaster of South Whitley. On Wednesday, May 18, 1938, he brought thirty-eight airmail letters from the South Whitley Post Office to the first (and perhaps only) direct airmail service from Whitley County to anywhere. Pilot for the open-cockpit biplane flight to Fort Wayne was Harold Tschantz, then Intertype operator at the Columbia City *Post* and *Commercial-Mail* daily newspapers, and seven years later co-owner of the *South Whitley Tribune*. Clarence Pook became South Whitley Postmaster in August 1939, and held that position until July 1977. He was the senior member of the South Whitley Post Office staff throughout investigation of the Kaadt Diabetic Institute by postal authorities and during subsequent litigation.

Luise Barbara Germann married Clarence Henry Louis Pook on Sunday, June 4, 1944, at St. John's Lutheran Church.

Nutritional Research Associates

The Preface to this book promised that the small-town South Whitley venue of Nutritional Research Associates would be examined in this final chapter, using vignettes of Lee LeVere Eve, Robert Emmet Hicks, Hubert A. Stump, Peter and Charles Kaadt, Fred and Hugo Eugene Fox, Frederick Milo Graham, Prince Immanuel of Jerusalem, and Valentine Hennig to illuminate the locale of Nutritional Research Associates and of Ger Manner. This cast of lively South Whitley contemporaries of the 1920s, 1930s, and 1940s illuminates many aspects of pioneering productive science side by side with fraudulent pseudoscience, and risk-taking free enterprise sometimes combined with charismatic exploitation.

This was the community into which Ida and Albert Germann finally planted their family. In Barbara Germann's phrase, the family gradually moved to South Whitley. Although Albert wanted to proceed rapidly with production of carotene, it turned out that establishment of the operations of Nutritional Research Associates would also be a gradual process. Dr. Vernon Jersey moved to South Whitley in 1937. Albert Germann was President of the Nutritional Research Associates Corporation, and Jersey was Secretary-Treasurer. Robert Cross, who had been a research chemist and chemical engineer at S.M.A., moved to South Whitley with his family in 1941. Cross became the chief chemist and chemical engineer in the South Whitley plant.

The enterprise had several components. Biochemical and nutritional research continued when transferred to the South Whitley laboratory. Albert Germann monitored the increasing volume of publications from other research groups. He began to write, publish, and distribute the *Bulletin* of the Nutritional Research Associates, summarizing the latest findings by scientists, and promoting his slowly developing line of nutritional products. Major challenges in the South Whitley plant involved both chemical engineering and mechanical engineering.

The chemical engineering challenge required modifying reaction conditions in small steps from the chemistry lab bench up to an efficient and reliable commercial process for producing pure and stable carotene. It is expected that a chemical reaction investigated in a small test tube may require altered experimental conditions when scaled-up to larger volumes in a beaker or flask. For example, agitation of reactants in a test tube can often be accomplished merely by gently stroking the glass tube. More vigorous stirring may be required in a larger container. Temperature control becomes progressively more complex as volume increases. The ratio of surface area to volume of a liquid can affect the thermodynamics and the chemical kinetics of a process; this ratio can change significantly as a reaction moves from desktop manipulation to production scale operations. Different proportions of reactants may be required for optimum yields. Temperature and pressure may have to be changed. Thus it is often necessary to construct and operate medium-size "pilot-plant" equipment to discover adjustments needed before committing to full-scale production.

Any cook who has attempted to convert a one-person dish into a casserole for a many-person carry-in meal can appreciate the scale-up complications. Cooking time and temperature often need to be changed. Surprisingly, even relative proportions of ingredients may require alteration. Conversion of that casserole recipe to instructions for feeding a hundred persons at a banquet poses yet another set of adjustments.

The mechanical engineering challenge required modifying commercially available equipment or designing new specialized machinery. South Whitley in the 1930s had a wide range of expert mechanics. Some had worked at Atoz and at Grip Nut. These were days when many local persons were repairing and modifying automobiles, small airplanes, and even massive steam-powered farm equipment. Operations at the Pook Feed and Coal Company, at the Farmers Elevator, and at the Mayer Elevator involved equipment like the grain hammermills that would be used to process carrots. There were at least three men in South Whitley who held U. S. patents on mechanical devices. Tinsmith Gilbert C. Gerard (February 3, 1900–September 16, 1968) had designed a simple and effective ventilation system for the Federal Works Progress Administration rural outhouse project. His system met the WPA requirements. Working in the Gerard Tin Shop at the south end of State Street, he mass produced thousands of copies of his device in the 1930s. Albert Germann prided himself on his glass-working abilities, but there were others with such skills in South Whitley. Johnson Brothers Neon Sign Company had been in business in South Whitley since 1929, employing several glassblowers. Aden U. Benner (1876–1948) had been an electrician in South Whitley since before 1918; he had a collection of intricate glass Geissler tubes made in Germany, and was attempting to duplicate similar gas-discharge tubes in South Whitley. Machinist Eldon Leroy Krieg designed and built a two-person self-standing elevator on his front lawn to carry amateur astronomers up to his telescope, mounted above neighboring trees. That structure held the first television aerial in town to capture broadcast signals from Chicago and Fort Wayne. There were many persons locally with engineering expertise, specialized skills, and certainly lots of advice.

Vernon Jersey described the process of extracting carotene from carrots in a 1946 interview with Marjorie Barnhart, Regional Feature Writer for the *Fort Wayne News-Sentinel:*

"First you cook the carrots slightly, shred them, put them in a press, squeeze all the juice out of them, and throw it away. The pulp you shred again, put on trays and dry to the consistency of potato chips. This you put in a hammermill and grind into an orange-colored flour. Into it you add petroleum ether which dissolves the yellow color (Vitamin A) and carries it off into a tank.

"There you have captured the color, which you were seeking, but it is mixed with the petroleum product [petroleum ether] which would give the consumer a stomach ache. The petroleum is removed in the next step, leaving pure carrot oil and the color which is carotene. The carotene is crystallized out of the oil—and eureka—pure Vitamin A." Petroleum ether is "normal hexane," a volatile saturated hydrocarbon whose molecules are linear (not branched) chains of carbon atoms, and have the empirical formula C_6H_{14}. Other names for petroleum ether are naphtha and ligroin.

When Marjorie Barnhart interviewed Albert Germann, Albert mentioned that cow's milk also contains Vitamin A, but a ton of carrots contains more than fifty times as much Vitamin A as does a ton of milk. Peter or Charles Kaadt might have made analogous claims about their nostrums. But whereas the Drs. Kaadt expected their patients to trust only them, Dr. Germann characteristically pulled his copies of the standard vitamin manual and a United States Department of Agriculture compilation of vitamin content of foods from his bookshelf to show the journalist the source of the data for his calculation.

She asked why most of the carotene supplies go for animal consumption. Albert laughed: "Carotene is a better but more expensive source of Vitamin A than fish oils. Farmers spending the higher price for it know they will get their money back on the market. When humans buy food or medicine for themselves, however, they want to get the cheapest things, and are willing to pay a doctor if need be. They know that a sick animal is a loss and they don't take the chances with it that they do with themselves."

Vernon Jersey described a step in the processing of carrots by noting that dried pulp was ground into an orange-colored flour. Robert Cross had previously carried out experimental research on several aspects of flours, although these were not carrot flours. He held a Sperry Flour Company Graduate Fellowship at Stanford University, conducting research on the amino acids of proteins in wheat flours. He received joint patents for "Process for the Manufacture of Yeast" and "Manufacture of Leavened Bread." The professional staff of Nutritional Research Associates had a wide range of credentials applicable to the South Whitley operations. Cross was just the person to consult with operators of nearby grain mills for the best methods of grinding dried carrot pulp.

Just prior to World War II, Albert Germann and Vernon Jersey assumed full ownership of the Nutritional Research Associates Corporation. Germann handled sales, research, and development, while Jersey was in charge of production operations and accounting. At peak times, the number of employees might reach fifteen.

Albert Germann had long been concerned about the stability of carrot-oil products. The possibility that wheat germ oil might improve the stability of fats and oils had been investigated by Pleasant Ernest Roller, the man whom Germann had recruited for a faculty position in physics at Valparaiso University. Roller's results were suggestive but not conclusive. Roller conducted his wheat-germ research at S.M.A. in Cleveland where Albert Germann was Director. Albert continued to monitor related research. A decade later, Albert became particularly interested in the doctoral research of Erich Heftmann at the University of Rochester School of Medicine and Dentistry, Rochester, New York. Heftmann concluded that a class of organic compounds called tocopherols protect carotene from oxidation. He found that "the tocopherol content of carrot oil is considerable; it has been estimated at about 0.5 to 1%." Germann consulted with Heftmann during Heftmann's research. Germann also supplied a gift of carrot oil for Heftmann's experiments.

By the fifteenth anniversary of the formation of the corporation, the South Whitley plant was also extracting wheat germ oil as a source of Vitamin E (alpha-tocopherol). The principal activities of the plant were "the extraction of carotene and carrot oil from carrots, wheat germ oil from wheat germ, and the development of stable carrot oil products and of mixtures with other vitamins for use in fortifying animal feeds, human foods, and pharmaceuticals."

When Ervin H. Pook retired from his Pook Feed and Coal Company in 1956, Nutritional Research Associates purchased his adjacent business, buildings, and land. This landmark South Whitley enterprise was renamed "Whitley Feeds," and Whitley Feeds became a division of Nutritional Research Associates, Inc.

Albert wrote, in "The South Whitley Germann Family Letter for 1957" (December 1957): "Albert Senior probably shows his advanced age more than other members of the family. On May 3rd last he suddenly keeled over unconscious at the office—without any advance warning—and Dr. Jersey rushed him to the hospital in Columbia City, where he was revived by Dr. Ridlon [Albert Maurice Ridlon, M.D. (1918–1996)] and permitted to return home the next day. The doctor pronounced it Atherosclerosis—a circulatory ailment, caused by a deposit of cholesterol in the arteries of the brain, thus shutting off circulation. Albert returned to the office on May 15th. For several months he has been taking a newly developed mineral mixture, a product of Nutritional Research Associates, which should reduce the amount of cholesterol in the blood, if studies on rats reported from Harvard University apply to humans. Actually, he has been much stronger since beginning this routine." In the same family Christmas letter: "Albert and Ida are happy to announce that their son, Albert II, has practically completed his [Ph.D.] studies at Purdue University, and that he and Jean, with their first born, have removed to South Whitley … Albert II is working at the factory, where he is beginning to take over the responsibilities of his father …"

Also in the 1957 Christmas letter: "We are generally at home, especially on Sundays (we go to church at 10:00 a.m., but are home again by noon) and welcome any of our friends or relatives."

Over the years in South Whitley, Albert Sr. wrote, printed, and distributed health and nutrition bulletins, typically with many references to the scientific literature. Bulletin No. 66 (second edition, 1966) was prefaced with an atypical personal testimonial: "*A Scientist's Evaluation. The author, Dr. Albert F. O. Germann, who celebrated his 80th birthday on February 18, 1966, has been supplementing his diet with Carrot Oil, said to be rich in Vitamin E as well as in Carotene, the vegetable form of Vitamin A, since its first commercial development under his directorship in the early 1930's.*"

Until the close of his life, he maintained membership in civic and professional organizations, including the Board of Trustees of the South Whitley Community Public Library, Cleveland Museum of Art, Society of the Sigma Xi, Alpha Chi Sigma, Phi Beta Kappa, Indiana Academy of Science, American Chemical Society, American Pharmaceutical Association, American Association of University Professors, and Société Suisse de Chimie.

Ida Helene Johanna Meinke Germann died August 12, 1976, at the age of 92. Albert Fredrick Ottomar Germann died December 22, 1976, at the age of 90. Both were buried in the cemetery of the St. John's Lutheran Church near South Whitley. Three daughters, one son, and eleven grandchildren survived them.

Sources and References for Chapter V

Page 320, *Sanborn-Perris Map* ... Adapted from a copy of a fire-insurance map of South Whitley, Whitley County, Indiana (New York: Sanborn-Perris Map Company, Ltd, December 1900). The original was drawn with the scale of 50 feet to an inch, on four sheets, each sheet 21 inches by 25 inches. Copy supplied September 8, 2015, by Joyce Hite, Local History Librarian, South Whitley Public Library.

Page 321, *Luise Barbara Germann Pook recalled* ... Obituary, "Barbara Pook," *South Whitley* [Indiana] *Tribune-News*, February 8, 2012. Internal stylistic evidence suggests that Barbara wrote most of her own obituary. She died at home in South Whitley, just two weeks shy of her 96th birthday.

Page 322, *the town where they finally settled* ... This chapter describes South Whitley in the decades encompassing 1935. In most respects, the description extends forward only to the 1950s. To learn about the town in the 1960s, see Amy McVay Abbott, *Whitley County Kid* (copyright 2015; *see* www.amyabbottwrites.com). Her engaging book mentions the family of Jean and Al Germann (pp. 99 and 108). "Al and Jean were close friends of my parents and their three daughters were dear childhood friends," email to the author from Amy McVay Abbott, October 2, 2015. Al Germann is Albert Fredrick Ottomar Germann Jr.

Page 323, *beautiful elm-lined sidewalks* ... "Millionaire's Row," *Cleveland Historical*, http://clevelandhistorical.org/items/show/10, accessed August 20, 2014.

Page 323, *Within the Hough neighborhood in 1927* ... "Cuyahoga County Schools," http://www.oldohioschools.com/cuyahoga_county.htm, accessed August 22, 2014.

Page 325, *Umetaro Suzuki (1874–1943)* ... U. Suzuki and T. Shimamura, "Active Constituent of

Rice Grits Preventing Bird Polyneuritis," *Tokyo Kagaku Kaishi*, vol. 32, no. 1, pp. 1–4, 4–17, 17–23, 80–93, 93–111 (1911), https://www.jstage.jst.go.jp/browse/nikkashi1880/32/1/_contents

Page 325, *In his 1914 book, Funk* ... Casimir Funk, *Die Vitamine, ihre Bedeutung für die Physiologie und Pathologie, mit besonderer Berücksichtigung der Avitaminosen: (Beriberi, Skobut, Pellagra, Rachitis). Anhang: Die Wachstumstubstanz und das Krebsproblem* (Wiesbaden: J. F. Bergmann, 1914).

Page 325, *Wisconsin Alumni Research Foundation (WARF)* ... The initials became familiar to the public when the anticoagulant dicumarol [3,3´-methylene bis(4-hydroxycoumarin)] was patented in 1945 by University of Wisconsin biochemists Karl Paul Gerhard Link (1901–1978), Mark Arnold Stahmann (1914–2000), and Miyoshi "Mike" Ikawa (1919–2006), and by WARF. The anticoagulant was given the name warfarin.

Page 326, *a self-employed research chemist* ... Obituary, "Dr. Otto Ungnade," Fort Wayne *Journal Gazette*, Sunday, March 31, 1963, p. 8A, col. 2.

Page 327, *Acreage devoted to carrot production* ... Harvested acres: 1925, 650; 1926, 1,560; 1927, 4,340; 1928, 6,570; 1929, 12,580. Source: "California Carrots, 1925–2011," *California Historic Commodity Data*, California Field Office, National Agricultural Statistics Service, United States Department of Agriculture, revised February 2012, http://www.nass.usda.gov/Statistics_by_State/California/Historical_Data/Carrots-A.pdf, accessed November 3, 2013. *See also Commercial Truck Crops. Annual Summary. Commercial Truck Crops for Fresh Market* (Washington, D.C.: Bureau of Agricultural Economics, United States Department of Agriculture, 1949), mimeographed report no. 1213: "Carrots."

Page 327, *Quintrex Aqua-Vite* ... Ingredients: vitamin A palmitate, d-activated animal sterol, d-alpha tocopheryl acetate, menadione sodium bisulfite, ascorbic acid, thiamin hydrochloride, riboflavin, niacin, di-calcium pantothenate, pyridoxine hydrochloride, folic acid, vitamin B-12, and dextrose, https://www.bunnyrabbit.com/info/aquavite.htm, accessed June 25, 2013.

Page 327, *the grade crossing of the tracks of two rail lines* ... T. R. Kneller, "Railroads of Whitley County, Indiana," http://www.oocities.org/trkneller/railroads.html, mirrored from Geocities at the end of October 2009, accessed June 25, 2013. The tracks of the Vandalia have been removed in South Whitley, and a portion of the roadbed is now Pennsylvania Avenue. According to T. R. Kneller, traffic on the Vandalia "diminished over the years and abandonment came piece by piece beginning in 1954 and ending in 1977 with the last section. This last section ran to the southwest through South Whitley from Columbia City's connection with the Pennsylvania Railroad." In 2013, the Norfolk Southern Corporation operated the former Nickel Plate railroad through South Whitley.

Page 328, *South Whitley was incorporated on the northwest bank* ... The Eel River begins near Fort Wayne, and flows southwest to South Whitley and then to North Manchester. The Eel River joins the Wabash River from the north in Logansport, 16 miles west of Peru. Logansport is downstream from Peru on the Wabash. The Miami name for the Eel River is said to have been the Kenapocomoco. *See* Otho Winger, *The Ke na po co mo co: Eel River, the Home of Little Turtle* (North Manchester, Indiana: 1934). That Miami term was the inspiration for naming the KenapocoMocha coffee shop, which opened in 2008 in North Manchester.

Page 328, *The site of Springfield Academy* ... Springfield was the original name of South Whitley. The town was laid out with 42 lots by Joseph Parret, Jun. in May 1837. He named the principal north–south street Main Street. The parallel State Street, eventually the main business street, was close to the river and only one block long. With no railroads

north of town in 1840, and no bridge across the Eel River, State Street had little significance in Mr. Parret's plan for the town. "Plat of the Town of Springfield," filed February 14, 1840, by Joseph Parret Jr.; Deed Book A, p. 135, Office of the Whitley County Recorder, Suite 206, Government Center, 220 West Van Buren Street, Columbia City, Indiana.

Page 328, *John Caldwell Calhoun (1782–1850)* ... Wayne Street was certainly named to honor Anthony Wayne (1745–1796), Commander of The Legion of the United States in an expedition that resulted in the destruction of Kekionga in 1794 and the establishment of Fort Wayne. According to Angus McCoy [Angus Cameron McCoy, *The Streets of Fort Wayne* (Fort Wayne: Allen County–Fort Wayne Historical Society, 1945)], Calhoun, Harrison, Clinton, and Franklin Streets in Fort Wayne were named for national figures at the time of settlement in the early 1800s. It is not certain why Calhoun was honored by South Whitley many decades later. At least one institution is rethinking such an honor. Yale President Peter Salovey, addressing incoming members of the Class of 2019, said: "Our residential colleges at Yale, into which you are being inducted this weekend, constitute one of our most cherished means of fostering an unusually close sense of community among undergraduates. About one in twelve of you has been assigned to Calhoun College, named when the college system was instituted in the 1930s for John C. Calhoun, a graduate of the Yale College Class of 1804, who achieved extremely high prominence in the early 19th century as a notable political theorist, a vice president to two different U.S. presidents, a secretary of war and of state, and a congressman and senator representing South Carolina. Calhoun died a decade before the outbreak of the American Civil War, and so he did not take part directly in the politics of secession and the breakup of the original Union. However, historians have long recognized that the secessionists of the time rested much of their thinking on Calhoun's political theory of nullification. Moreover, and what is more relevant to the concerns of the moment, Calhoun mounted the most powerful and influential defense of his day for slavery. In fact, he believed that the highest forms of civilization depend on involuntary servitude. Not only that, but he also believed that the races he thought to be inferior, black people in particular, ought to be subjected to it for the sake of their own best interests. I am not exaggerating. In a famous speech on the floor of the United States Senate in 1837, Calhoun said, 'I hold that in the present state of civilization, where two races of different origin, and distinguished by color, and other physical differences, as well as intellectual, are brought together, the relation now existing in the slaveholding States between the two, is, instead of an evil, a good – a positive good.' A year later, in another Senate speech, he noted, 'Many in the South once believed that slavery was a moral and political evil. That folly and delusion are gone. We see it now in its true light, and regard it as the most safe and stable basis for free institutions in the world'." Peter Salovey, "Launching a Difficult Conversation," August 29, 2015, http://alecollege. yale.edu/open-conversation/launching-difficult-conversation, accessed September 1, 2015.

Page 329, *Sadie Vaux* … Sadie Vaux (1871–1940), daughter of George Henry Vaux and <private> McDonald, wife of <private> Bauer, is listed on a Geni website, http://www.geni.com/people/Sadie-Vaux/6000000000988747830, accessed January 29, 2016. She would have been about 19 when she graduated from South Whitley High School.

Page 329, *Thomas Riley Marshall (1854–1925)* … Marshall was born in North Manchester, attended the common schools, and graduated from Wabash College, Crawfordsville, in 1873. He practiced law in Columbia City with William F. McNagny. He was Governor of Indiana (1909–1913) and Vice-President of the United States (1913–1921).

Page 329, *Randolph Street, running north and south* … Randolph Street was named for John Randolph (1773–1833), a long-time Congressman and then Senator from Virginia. He was one of the organizers of the American Colonization Society, an organization that helped found the colony of Liberia as a place in Africa for free-born American

blacks. Between Calhoun Street and Randolph Street was Jefferson Street, named for President Thomas Jefferson (1743–1826), cousin of John Randolph.

Page 329, *Albert Germann purchased the building* … Deed executed September 7, 1935. Deed Book 80, p. 414, Whitley County Recorder. The building was located on lots 11 and 12 in Webster's Third Addition to the Town of South Whitley. The sale included both the building and the two lots.

Page 330, *Reid-Murdock plant* … The Pierceton plant operated on the west edge of Pierceton from 1900 to 1956. It was a branch of Reid-Murdock & Company, a Chicago-based pickle, sauerkraut, and catsup manufacturer. *See* Joan E. Hostetler and Dorothy Nicholson (Manuscript and Visual Collections Department, William Henry Smith Memorial Library, Indiana Historical Society, Indianapolis), Collection #P 0263, "Walter J. Long Negatives, ca. 1920," http://www.indianahistory. org/our-collections/collection-guides/walter-j-long-negatives-ca-1920.pdf, accessed March 5, 2016. The collection includes an historical sketch and an image (abt March 1920) that depicts the storage yard and stacked crates of tomatoes at Reid-Murdock & Co., Pierceton. *See also* "Pickle Factory Paid Farmers Over $10,000," *Columbia City Commercial-Mail* (Friday, September 29, 1905): "The factory put up 362 casks of dill pickles this year and used 160,000 lbs. of salt."

Page 330, *Eugene Weybright (1907–1990) recalled* … "Many Stories Arise from the Great Depression!" *Bulletin of the Whitley County Historical Society*, vol. 17, no. 2 (April 1979), pp. 9–13.

Page 331, *Some of the high school boys* … Ford Fleck, ibid.

Page 331, *I was fortunate* … Cleon Fleck, ibid.

Page 331, *recollections from a farm wife* … Blanche E. Lawrence, ibid.

Page 331, *Democratic Township Trustee* … J. Lee Emery, ibid.

Page 331, *sold it to Elmore and Hiram Augsburger* …

Deed executed August 2, 1935. Deed Book 80, p. 227, Whitley County Recorder.

Page 332, *Augsburgers sold the place* ... Deed executed October 10, 1935. Deed Book 80, page 358, Whitley County Recorder.

Page 332, *to Ida Helene Germann* ... Deed executed August 27, 1936. Deed Book 81, p. 463, Whitley County Recorder.

Page 332, *Hoosier high school basketball* ... There were other school sports, but basketball was central throughout the first half of the twentieth century in the small schools of Indiana. Set in 1951, the movie *Hoosiers* (filmed in 1986, written by Angelo Pizzo, directed by David Anspaugh) was considered by many who were closely associated with "Hoosier hysteria" in 1935 to be faithful to the basketball culture that they remembered with fondness.

Page 332, *second-floor, low-ceiling basketball court* ... Cleon Fleck, "Heroes! [Sectional] Champions! 1922 Great Year at South Whitley," *Bulletin of the Whitley County Historical Society* (December 1974), pp. 17–19. Another indoor basketball facility in town was recalled in 2014 by 102-year-old Vera Lehman Plattner, South Whitley High School Class of 1931: "[A] tie barn was located behind the Norris drugstore. Dad would take care of the horses that had been driven into town. The barn had special stalls that were used to quarantine sick horses. Lawson Keller shoed the horses and Shorty Nutter also worked in the barn. There was extra room in the barn as fewer horses were driven into town as autos became more popular so one end of the barn was turned into a gymnasium about a half of a block long. Carl [Vera's brother] and I could play at the gym with our friends whenever there were no school teams practicing or playing. The court was used until the new high school was built." *South Whitley High School Alumni Newsletter*, no. 7 (December 13, 2014), p. 1.

Page 332, *end of an era* ... Cleon Fleck, "Here Comes the County Superintendent," *Bulletin of the Whitley County Historical Society* (June 1975), pp. 5–6. Writing about his father, Alvin R. Fleck

(Whitley County Superintendent of Schools, 1908–1921, 1925–1937; South Whitley School Superintendent, 1922–1925): "Although he was instrumental in the movement to consolidate schools, Mr. Fleck was, I think, a bit sad to see the one-room schools disappear."

Page 333, *a home economics teacher* ... "Home economics" was a twentieth-century addition to the curriculum. The term "domestic science," a holdover from the nineteenth century, was still used in South Whitley High School as late as 1919. The home economics movement began with chemist Ellen Henrietta Swallow Richards (December 3, 1842–March 30, 1911), the first woman to attend Massachusetts Institute of Technology. She founded the American Home Economics Association in 1908. The organization changed its name in 1994 to the American Association of Family and Consumer Sciences.

Page 333, *4-H (Head, Heart, Hands, and Health)* ... Although there were antecedents of 4-H clubs in Wisconsin, Minnesota, and Ohio as early as 1902, the Federal Smith–Lever Act of 1914 provided for national organization of 4-H clubs within the Cooperative Extension Service of the United States Department of Agriculture. Senator Michael Hoke Smith (1855–1931) of Georgia and Representative Asbury Francis Lever (1875–1940) of South Carolina co-sponsored the Smith–Lever Act of 1914.

Page 333, *Smith–Hughes Act* ... Senator Michael Hoke Smith (1855–1931) and Representative Dudley Mays Hughes (1848–1927), both from Georgia, co-sponsored the Smith–Hughes National Education Act of 1917.

Page 333, *separate vocational classes and teachers* ... Vocational courses previously had been offered, but the physical facilities in the Calhoun Street School did not permit much hands-on instruction, and the same teacher might teach both a vocational course and an academic subject. *See, for example,* the 1918–1919 South Whitley High School instructional staff: Superintendent Joseph Strickler taught Latin, Rose Jack taught English, Ethel Schuman taught

Domestic Science and Science, William Gregg taught Manual Training, Arithmetic, and Geography, and Lois Winch was Supervisor of Music and Art [Horace Ellis, *Directory of Indiana School Officials, 1918–1919* (Indianapolis: Wm. B. Burford), p. 157]. There were eleven high school graduates in 1919. In 1923, there were twenty-nine high school graduates. The high school faculty for 1922–1923 were listed in the school yearbook as: Alvin R. Fleck, Superintendent; Leigh L. Hunt, Principal; Ruth Van Natta Hunt, Latin and English; Delmar Mitzner, Science; Olive B. Perkins, French and English; Forest E. Albert, Music; Dennis Wright, Manual Training; and Celia Carson, Home Economics [Senior Class of South Whitley High School, *The Reflector*, vol. 6, 1923 (printed by the Robert E. Hicks Corporation), pp. 10–11].

Page 333, *The first graduation ceremonies* ... "Commencement Program," *South Whitley Tribune*, April 21, 1932; "Many Attend Baccalaureate Service," *South Whitley Tribune*, April 21, 1932; "Class Night," *South Whitley Tribune*, April 28, 1932; "Many Attend Graduation Exercises," *South Whitley Tribune*, April 28, 1932. Joyce Hite, Local History Librarian at the South Whitley Community Public Library, supplied copies of news articles.

Page 334, *Lewis David Reiff* ... Lewis Reiff (January 3, 1914–November 10, 2002) spent his formative years on a farm southwest of South Whitley. He married his high school classmate K. Willodean Moore on August 18, 1934. He spent many years in the steel industry in Michigan as an engineer and then as an executive. Obituary, *The Herald-Palladium* (Twin Cities of Benton Harbor and St. Joseph, Michigan), Wednesday, November 13, 2002.

Page 334, *Principal Lee LeVere Eve (1903–1992)* ... Biographical information was obtained from the following sources: "Alumni," *Reminiscence—'39*, Larwill High School Yearbook, p. 85; a listing of Principals in the program booklet of the 36th Triennial South Whitley High School Alumni Reunion, August 11, 2012; a listing of diplomas granted, in *Catalogue Number for the Sessions of 1938–1939* (Morningside Heights: Columbia University in the City of New York), p. 259; "Goldsborough Resigns; Eve New Principal," *Chesterton* [Indiana] *Tribune*, August 7, 1941; "Lee L. Eve Named Head of Delphi–Deer Creek Schools," *Delphi* [Indiana] *Citizen*, June 10, 1943; "Lee L. Eve Assumes Office as Head of School Here," *Delphi Citizen*, July 8, 1943; "Lee L. Eve Resigns as Superintendent of Delphi Schools," *Delphi Citizen*, August 16, 1945; Obituary, Columbia City [Indiana] *Post & Mail*, Friday, March 6, 1992; Obituary, Fort Wayne *Journal Gazette*, Monday, March 9, 1992, p. 4A, col. 1; and from information supplied by Tanya Kay Hagerty, Office of the Registrar, Indiana University–Bloomington; Jose Marte, Assistant Registrar, Teachers College, Columbia University; Debora K. Sheets, Benefits Coordinator, Whitley County Consolidated Schools; Jeff Van Drie, Principal, Chesterton High School; Serena Sutliff, Curator, and Eva Hopkins, Researcher, Westchester Township History Museum, Chesterton; Ralph Walker, Superintendent, Delphi Community School Corporation; Gayla Martin, Assistant Treasurer, Delphi Community School Corporation; John S. Williams, Director of Personnel, Crown Point Community School Corporation; the Reference Librarian, Crawfordsville District Public Library; Lori Martin, Executive Assistant to the Superintendent, Goshen Community Schools; Diane Miller, Librarian, Indiana Room, Huntington (Indiana) City–Township Public Library; and Randy L. Neuman, Associate Director, RichLyn Library, Huntington University.

Page 334, *Rev. Dr. James H. Lightbourne* ... James H. Lightbourne was pastor of the First Christian Church in Troy, Ohio (since 1957, the First United Church of Christ) from 1927 to 1934. He was very involved with planning of the church's educational building whose cornerstone was laid July 14, 1929; the building was dedicated March 2, 1930. It is 133 miles from South Whitley to Troy. One can speculate that Lee Eve and James Lightbourne, both involved with planning and then constructing new educational facilities, might have known each other between 1929 and 1932. Information is from the

Rev. Lauren L. Allen, Pastor, First United Church of Christ, Troy, Ohio; email March 31, 2015.

Page 334, *lived on adjacent farms* ... In 1918, his parents lived on 62 acres in Sections 20 and 21. His grandparents lived on 40 acres in Section 19. Their mail address was Rural Free Delivery, Route 3, South Whitley. Frank M. Hollis and J. F. Binder, "Directory of Richland Township," *Hollis & Binder's Complete Directory of Whitley County* (Columbia City, Indiana: Hollis & Binder, 1918), p. 132.

Page 334, *He graduated in a class of nineteen in 1919* ... Dorothy Minnick and others, *Larwill Alumni Reflections*. Digital scans supplied by Debbie S. Lowrance, Local History Librarian, Peabody Public Library, Columbia City, Indiana.

Page 335, *received the Master of Arts degree in Education* ... His A.M. thesis was "The Prognostic Value of the Indiana Composite Achievement Test as a Measure of Ability to do High School Work."

Page 335, *he was elected by his fellow high school principals* ... "Four New Members and Five Old Ones Elected to I. H. S. A. A. Athletic Council," *The Kokomo* [Indiana] *Tribune,* December 13, 1933. *See also* "History of the IHSAA," *By-Laws & Articles of Incorporation* (Indianapolis: Indiana High School Athletic Association, Inc., 2014–2015), p. 128.

Page 335, *"You have been as nearly* ... Letter, dated July 6, 1950, recorded in Minutes of the Board of School Trustees, copy supplied by John S. Williams, Director of Personnel, Crown Point Community School Corporation.

Page 336, *According to his nephew* ... "Memories of Harold Doran," transcript of a 1986 tape-recorded interview with Harold Doran (1986), pp. 6–7. South Whitley Community Public Library, South Whitley, Indiana, http://www.swhitley.libguides.com/home, accessed October 6, 2013.

Page 337, *Who was Robert Hicks?* ... Biographical information was obtained from the following sources: "Memories of Harold Doran," op. cit.; Cleon Fleck, "A Fantastic Career: The Amazing Robert E. Hicks," *Bulletin of the Whitley County*

Historical Society, vol. 18, no. 4 (August 1980), pp. 3–11; Robert E. Hicks, *A Conscience Unburdened* (South Whitley: Robert E. Hicks Corporation, 1925); containing a reprint of Robert E. Hicks, "A Conscience Unburdened—Cowardly Attacks Refuted," *Canvassers Magazine,* October 1916; "Robert E. Hicks," *Prison Problem League Magazine,* vol. 1, numbers 1, 2, and 3 (1925); *Who's Who in America,* vol. 15, 1928–1929 (Chicago: A. N. Marquis, 1928), p. 1028; James E. Remington, "Building a Magazine, Paying the Price," *Specialty Salesman Magazine* (November 1925), pp. 49–55; 194–195. Joyce Hite, Local History Librarian at the South Whitley Community Public Library, provided copies of material from the *Prison Problem League Magazine* and *Specialty Salesman Magazine.*

Page 337, *Thus wrote Orison Swett Marden* ... This passage was quoted in a three-part interview with Hicks in volume 1 of the *Prison Problem League Magazine; Devoted to the Principles of Prison Problem League, and to the Constructive Discussions of Prison Problems* (numbers 1, 2, and 3; May, June, and July 1925). The magazine had a lifespan of no more than a year. It was the official publication of the also short-lived Prison Problem League, formed and incorporated in 1923 in Muncie, Indiana.

Page 338, *practically raised him* ... "Memories of Harold Doran," op. cit., p. 4.

Page 338, *At the age of fourteen* ... James E. Remington, op. cit., p. 49.

Page 338, *The Town of Monticello in 1878* ... Map of "Monticello, 1878," from *An Illustrated Historical Atlas of Lewis County, Missouri* (Philadelphia: Edwards Brothers, 1878), p. 17.

Page 338, *description of the business district* ... For three versions of the description, *see* "Monticello, Missouri," *Wikipedia,* accessed October 16, 2013; *An Illustrated Historical Atlas of Lewis County, Missouri,* op. cit.; and National Register of Historic Places Registration Form, Lewis County Courthouse, November 24, 2004, section 8, page 12.

Page 340, *Edgar Watkins Howe (May 3, 1853–*

October 3, 1937) wrote a novel … E. W. Howe, *The Story of a Country Town* (Atchison, Kansas: Howe & Co., 1883). The first edition of 1,500 copies was self-published. Howe himself hand set the seven-point type, and printed it (four pages at a time) with a Gordon job press. J. R. Osgood & Co., Boston, Mark Twain's publisher at the time, published a copyedited edition in 1884. A later edition, lightly edited by Claude M. Simpson (who also supplied a substantial Introduction), was published as a handsome volume in the John Harvard Library, Howard Mumford Jones, Editor-in-Chief (Cambridge: Harvard University Press, 1961).

Page 340, *He wrote an undisguised autobiography* … E. W. Howe, *Plain People* (New York: Dodd, Mead & Company, 1929), 317 pages.

Page 341, *wrote about the first sixteen years of his life* … Loren Dudley Reid, *Hurry Home Wednesday: Growing Up in a Small Missouri Town, 1905-1921* (Columbia: University of Missouri Press, 1978), 291 pages.

Page 341, *Robert Hicks, Edgar Howe, Dudley Reid, and Loren Reid* … In the next pages, we shall examine aspects of the subsequent colorful life of Robert Hicks. Howe had a successful career as a writer and journalist. *The Story of a Country Town* went through many printings, several publishers (including Houghton, Mifflin & Co., Albert and Charles Boni, and Dodd, Mead & Company), and two modest revisions. He retired as editor and publisher of the *Atchison Globe* in 1911, and then spent thirty-two years as publisher of *E. W. Howe's Monthly*. Excerpts from the *Monthly* were printed in several of his books, including *Ventures in Common Sense* (New York: Alfred A. Knopf, 1919) with a 23-page introduction by H. L. Mencken. He also wrote and published two volumes of lay sermons, and at least five novels. Dudley Reid continued as a newspaperman. In February 1921, he went to Osceola, Iowa, and bought the *Tribune*. After a decade, he sold the *Tribune*, and bought the *Booster-Express* in West Des Moines. He concluded his autobiography: "Someday, perhaps, if you look closely and notice carefully, you may observe somewhere in six point

type, on the inside pages of your local newspaper, the final chapter of this little story." [Dudley Reid, *Ups and Downs: The Story of a Short-Legged Man and His Journey Through Life* (Des Moines: The Monitor Press, 1936), p. 408.] Loren Reid went to Grinnell College, earning the B.A. in 1927, the M.A. in 1930, and the Ph.D. in 1933. He was on the faculty of the University of Missouri for thirty-five years, and was a visiting professor at several institutions. He wrote many books, and was a founding member of the Speech Association of America. Professor Reid celebrated his 109th birthday on August 25, 2014: Ashley Jost, "Former MU Professor Reflects on Life as He Turns 109," *Columbia* (Missouri) *Daily Tribune*, Sunday, August 24, 2014, http://www.columbiatribune.com/news/local/former-mu-professor-reflects-on-life-as-he-turns/article_79f78462-0a63-5a9a-9077-41c646443cd3.html, accessed October 10, 2014.

Page 341, *William H. Adams began printing…* Douglas C. McMurtrie, "Pioneer Printing in Kansas," *Kansas Historical Quarterly*, vol. 1 (November 1931), pp. 3–16. Quotation from page 8.

Page 341, *hazards for other pioneer newspaper publishers* … G. Raymond Gaeddert, "First Newspapers in Kansas Counties," *Kansas Historical Quarterly*, vol. 10: "1854–1864," February 1941, pp. 3–33; "1865–1871," May 1941, pp. 124–149; "1871–1879," August 1941, pp. 299–323; "1879–1886," November 1941, pp. 380–411.

Page 341, *If this were the arrangement* … Such an arrangement would not have been unique. A biographer of Thomas Alva Edison (1847–1931) wrote that in 1862 the young Edison had a diminutive printing plant, a chemical laboratory, and an electrical workshop in a compartment of a Grand Trunk Railroad baggage car that rolled daily between Detroit and Port Huron, Michigan. George S. Bryan, *Edison: The Man and His Work* (Garden City, New York: Alfred A. Knoff, 1926), chap. 2.

Page 341, *years of vigorous newspaper creation* … Data from the N. W. Ayer and G. P. Rowell & Co. directories, cited in Eugene C. Harter (Dorothy

Harter, editor; Ann Harter Tucker, illustrator), *Boilerplating America: The Hidden Newspaper* (Lanham, Maryland: University Press of America, 1991), p. 51.

Page 342, *"My first mail-order venture ... A Conscience Unburdened,* op. cit., p. 7.

Page 342, *"Ever since I was twenty ... A Conscience Unburdened,* op. cit., p. 9.

Page 342, *"I started with such schemes ...A Conscience Unburdened,* op. cit., p. 8.

Page 342, *Those dozen years ...* "Building a Magazine, Paying the Price," op. cit., pp. 49–51.

Page 342, *James E. Remington ...* James E. Remington Sr. was born in South Whitley and graduated from South Whitley High School in 1891. He attended Manchester College for two years, and transferred to Northwestern University where he graduated in 1899. He joined the staff of the Atoz Printing Company in 1911, and later became Associate Editor of the *Specialty Salesman Magazine.* A son, James Remington Jr., graduated from South Whitley High School in 1926.

Page 343, *Atoz generated its own electricity ...* Municipal electric power for the rest of town came to South Whitley in 1899. The original municipal generator was steam powered. It supplied direct current. Alternating current came in 1929; three diesels replaced the steam engines.

Page 343, *Hicks recounted the years ...* "A Fantastic Career," op. cit., p. 5.

Page 343, *"He arrived in South Whitley in August ...* "A Fantastic Career," ibid.

Page 344, *Frank Edgar Miner [1871–1936] ...* Frank Edgar Miner was born in Columbia City, county seat of Whitley County, Indiana. He was a printer's devil as an adolescent at the Columbia City *Commercial* (predecessor of the *Commercial-Mail*), and bought the South Whitley *News* (predecessor of the *South Whitley Tribune)* in 1896. Miner aggressively expanded the newspaper's job-printing operations. By 1897, he had established the Atoz Printing Com-

pany (in partnership with E. R. Hibbard of Chicago and J. W. Hibbard of New York). He was publisher in South Whitley (with Editor John B. Stoll of South Bend) of the national magazine, *The Editorial,* from May 6, 1915, to April 19, 1917. Miner also published the short-lived *Merchants' Syndicate News,* a seven-column weekly newspaper that first appeared on April 9, 1915. Atoz printed five thousand copies of the first issue. *See* "Frank E. Miner," in Samuel P. Kaler and Richard H. Maring, *History of Whitley County, Indiana* (Indianapolis: B. F. Bowen and Co., 1907), pp. 650–651.

Page 344, *lead, tin, and antimony alloy ...* Imperial Type Metal Company, *Type Metal Alloys* (Imperial Type Metal Company: New York, Philadelphia, and Chicago, 1927). For slug-casting alloys, *see* page 60. For monotype alloys, *see* page 42.

Page 345, *"The entrance to the grounds ...* James E. Remington, "Building a Magazine, Paying the Price," *Specialty Salesman Magazine* (November 1925), pp. 194–195.

Page 345, *Flanking the drive is a pond ...* A photograph of the lily pond appeared in *Specialty Salesman Magazine* (November 1925), with the caption: "Bob Hicks and little Margaret beside the magnificent lily pond on Bob's estate. The rare and beautiful colors of the lilies make this pond one of the finest in the country. The house and barn are seen in the distance." "Little Margaret" is the daughter of Robert and his third wife, Margaret May Davis Joy. Reference was provided by Joyce Hite, Local History Librarian of the South Whitley Community Library.

Page 345, *the Temple of the Square Deal ...* Joyce Hite, Local History Librarian of the South Whitley Community Library, provided a summary of articles from *Specialty Salesman Magazine,* and also copies of the following articles from that periodical: Robert S. Clary, "South Whitley Sets the Pace" (November 1922); Albert G. Burns, International President, "Suggestions for Organizing Local Assemblies" (November 1922); "The Temple of the Square Deal at South Whitley" (December 1922), p. 576; E. R. James, "Temple of the Square Deal:

Cornerstone Laid, Sunday, Jun 17th" (August 1923), pp. 231–232.

Page 346, *Mark Snyder and Carrol Jennings Snyder* ... Carroll Snyder graduated from South Whitley High School in 1922. Mark Snyder graduated in 1924.

Page 346, *He had been South Whitley Postmaster* ... Stephen A. Kochersperger, Senior Research Analyst, Postal History, United States Postal Service. Email December 4, 2013.

Page 347, *a new brick home for the South Whitley Baptists* ... In 1900, the Baptist Church was on Main Street at the west end of Market Street (Sanborn-Perris map of South Whitley, dated 1900). See page 320.

Page 347, *The congregation burned the mortgage* ... *South Whitley Tribune*, April 29, 1937. Reference supplied by the Rev. Roy L. Emery in a letter to the author, dated February 3, 1955.

Page 347, *South Whitley Church of the Brethren* ... George M. Fleck, "Brethren Church Founded in 1913 at Tent Meeting," *South Whitley Tribune*, September 10, 1953.

Page 348, *"The Tavern was luxurious* ... "A Fantastic Career," op. cit., p. 9.

Page 348, *Nash died a few months later* ... Obituary, *The Indianapolis News*, October 31, 1927, p. 20.

Page 348, *a popular Whippet* ... The small, low-priced Whippet cars were produced from 1926 through 1931 by the Willys-Overland Company of Toledo, Ohio.

Page 349, *Jackson saw the Klan* ... Biographical information and the quotation are from Jason S. Lantzer, "Edward L. Jackson," in Linda C. Gugin and James E. St. Clair, *The Governors of Indiana* (Indianapolis: Indiana Historical Society Press, 2006), pp. 274–279. *See also* Leonard J. Moore, *Citizen Klansmen: The Ku Klux Klan in Indiana, 1921–1928*, chap. 6, "Political Power;" and David M. Chalmers, *Hooded Americanism: The First Century of the Ku Klux Klan, 1865–1965*, chap. 23, "Klan Castles in Indiana."

Page 350, *The Klan made a public appearance* ... Willadene Egner, "Whitley County Survives the Ku Klux Klan," *Bulletin of the Whitley County Historical Society*, vol. 24, no. 5 (October 1986), pp. 3–17. "All references in this account of the Ku Klux Klan in Whitley County can be found in the Columbia City Commercial Mail, Columbia City Evening Post (both the daily and midweekly) or the South Whitley Tribune for the years 1922 through 1926. However, whereas the newspapers mentioned names of farm owners, we have chosen to only locate the various sites of Klan meetings by township where they took place." Willadene Egner (January 24, 1915–December 13, 2003) was a retired medical research scientist when she wrote this extensively documented article. In 1986, she and the editor of the *Bulletin* felt it was too soon (after six decades!) to publish names of local participants.

Page 350, *"A robed Klansman carrying an American flag* ... Willadene Egner, loc. cit., pp. 4–5.

Page 351, *"A picnic held in Fox Grove* ... Willadene Egner, loc. cit., pp. 11–12.

Page 351, *They certainly were Chautauqua towns* ... Diana Reinhart, "Folks Bring Chairs and Fill Chautauqua Tent," *Bulletin of the Whitley County Historical* Society (December 1975), pp. 4–6.

Page 352, *Hicks became involved with Lombard College* ... The archives of Lombard College were transferred to Knox College, also in Galesburg. Information about Robert Hicks as a Trustee was provided by Maryjo McAndrew, Senior Archive Assistant, Knox College.

Page 353, *Margaret Davis Hicks built the 'Lodge'* ... Margaret Hicks Savage, February 9, 2010. Comment responding to Ellie Cominos, "Get in Tune with Nature at Camp Helen State Park," http://www.pcbdaily.com/get-in-tune-with-nature-at-camp-helen-state-park, accessed October 26, 2013. One of the children of Mrs. Savage bore the full family name: Robert Emmett Hicks Savage (February 15, 1945–April 9, 2006). Obituary of Robert Emmett Hicks Savage, *Houston Chronicle*, April 13,

2006, http://www.legacy.com/obituaries/houston-chronicle/obituary.aspx?pid=17403382, accessed January 29, 2016.

Page 354, *graduated from the Washington Center High School* … "Alumni," *The Washingtonian* (Washington Center High School yearbook: 1928), p. 42. Copy supplied by Virginia Doenges, Local History Librarian, South Whitley Community Public Library.

Page 354, *brass rules* … A 6-point-wide type-high brass rule often separated adjacent columns of text. When the printing surface was about ½ point wide, the resulting vertical hairline was almost invisible to the reader. In the nineteenth century, rules were sometimes inverted for obituaries, creating a 6-point black border around the text.

Page 354, *and cuts* … Many advertising agencies supplied, without charge, thin reverse engravings of commercial products. These zinc plates could be mounted on wooden blocks to produce type-high cuts to insert in an ad. Agencies also supplied cardboard "mats" with artwork as indented impressions. A stereocaster, with steel type-high bearer bars, allowed molten type metal to be poured over a mat, creating a solid type-high cut, a mirror image of the mat. A metal saw and a router were used to trim the casting into a rectangular cut with no protruding shoulders. A relief halftone cut of a photograph could be produced overnight by the Fort Wayne Engraving Company. Fort Wayne Engraving advertised that they were "Designers, Engravers, Electrotypers, Makers of Half-tones and Zinc Etchings for all kinds of High Class Printing."

Page 354, *type-high* … In America in 1885, the height-to-paper of a piece of type was defined as 0.9186 inch: "Uniform Type Bodies," *Typographic Advertiser* (Philadelphia: MacKellar, Smiths & Jordan Company), vol. 31, 1885, p. 117; cited by Richard L. Hopkins, *Origin of the American Point System for Printers' Type Measurement* (Terra Alta, West Virginia: Hill & Dale Press, 1976), p. 60. In 1927, height-to-paper was actually 0.918 inch: Imperial Type Metal Company, *Type Metal Alloys* (New York, Philadelphia, and Chicago, 1927), p.

80. Frank Romano, President of the Museum of Printing, North Andover, Massachusetts, confirmed the 0.918 inch dimension in an email December 17, 2014.

Page 354, *Western Newspaper Union* … For an examination of the role of Western Newspaper Union in supplying boilerplate and preprint to thousands of newspapers, see Dennis N. Mihelich, "George Joslyn: Western America's First Media Mogul," *Nebraska History*, vol. 82 (2001), pp. 26–36. Veteran Hoosier newspaperman Leigh S. Plummer recalled that boilerplate "supplied by WNU looked like the lead used in linotypes but was of sufficiently different composition so that it could not be used in the local typesetting machines. Otherwise some hard-up publisher would steal his metal and WNU wouldn't like that," *Bulletin of the Whitley County Historical Society*, vol. 20, no. 5 (October 1982), pp. 7–8. WNU boilerplate was supplied in column-wide, column-length plates, about ¼ inch thick, with the relief printing surface on one side and an indentation on the reverse. The indentation snapped into a matching projection on an iron base, so that that the pair produced a type-high stereotype that might include both text and illustrations. An assortment of iron-base parts was kept in the print shop; the thin plates were returned for remelting to WNU after use. Boilerplate could be sawed into short pieces, and portions could be routed to eliminate material not desired by the printer. Because the base and the boilerplate were used together with handset foundry type and Intertype slugs on the same page and often in the same column, the boilerplate system led to standardized newspaper column widths throughout most of the country. The *South Whitley Tribune* had 13-pica column width in 1935. In earlier years, brass rules separated columns of handset body type. The rules continued to be used after column-wide slugs replaced handset type, in part because these sturdy type-high rules reduced the tendency of boilerplate to dislodge during the printing process. For more history of boilerplate, see "Auxiliary Newspaper or Syndicate Services," chapter 10 in George A.

Kubler, *A New History of Stereotyping* (New York: J. J. Little & Ives, 1941).

Western Newspaper Union targeted the content of both preprint and boilerplate to specific localities. A shrewd publicist might have been able to get a political message into the boilerplate. For such an attempt, see letter from John Baur (recall Chapter 4) to Rev. R. G. Messerli, Lutheran Schools Committee, Portland, Oregon (September 25, 1922): "I want to thank you sincerely for letting me have Mr. Wheelwright's open letter to Mr. Malcolm. It is a classic and deserves the widest possible circulation. I hope that you have sent it out to all the prominent people in the state and also to all the editors. The letter, or a part of it, ought to go into the 'boiler plate' material for the Western Newspaper Union." Copy supplied by Elerina Aldamar, Research Specialist, Oregon Historical Society.

Page 355, *a take-home copy* ... The copy of *The Meanin' o' Gladness* is from the collection of Deloris Fleck. Quotation and bibliographic information are from the detailed catalogue record in the OCLC *FirstSearch* database (WorldCat).

Page 355, *Alta Marian Graf Gerard (September 3, 1910–August 7, 2001)* ... She was valedictorian of the South Whitley High School Class of 1928, and was editor of the yearbook, *The Reflector*. She continued her journalistic work—researching, recording, and writing local history for the *South Whitley Tribune*, the South Whitley Community Library, the South Whitley United Methodist Church, and the Whitley County Historical Society. Wayne Gerard has a large collection of Memories covers created by his mother (conversation with Wayne Gerard on November 8, 2014).

Page 356, *Basil Adams of Indianapolis* ... Mr. Adams sold the newspaper in 1945 to Charles M. Bowerman and Harold F. Tschantz, who continued its publication as a letterpress paper. Although they modernized many aspects of the printing operations, they kept Hubert Stump's 12" × 18" Chandler & Price hand-fed press for an occasional short-run job. Bowerman and Tschantz sold the newspaper to Linda and J. David Tranter in 1974. The Tranters computerized newspaper production, and switched from letterpress to offset lithography. The last letterpress newspaper in the Indiana-Ohio-Michigan region was *The Montpelier Herald* in Montpelier, Indiana, edited and published by Thomas Laymon. The final issue was printed on Thursday, September 22, 2005 (conversation with Thomas Laymon on November 8, 2014).

Page 356, *printing equipment of the Franklin Press* ... Hubert Stump disposed of the 8" × 12" foot-treadle-powered Chandler & Price platen press by transferring it to George Fleck, then a neighbor boy, in exchange for many hours of this printer's devil time, time spent distributing type into California job cases. Stump had hired a moving company to transfer the entire contents of the Franklin Press to South Whitley. The machinery arrived in operating condition. The movers deposited piles of type and printing accessories on the floor of a storage room. In return for sorting thousands of pieces of type, rule, leads, cuts, and assorted miscellany, the twelve-year-old obtained an adequately equipped letterpress print shop that was installed on the closed-in back porch at his home on Poplar Street.

Page 356, *The ballad "Memories"* ... Music for "Memories" was written in 1915 by Egbert Van Alstyne, with lyrics by Gus Kahn. Crooner "Bing" Crosby—Harry Lillis Crosby Jr. (May 3, 1903–October 14, 1977)—was the best-selling recording artist of the twentieth century.

Page 356, *In business in 2014* ... The company operates in the old Grip Nut Company buildings (on the site of Springfield Academy) and also in a sprawling facility at 101 East Carroll Road.

Page 356, *Hube A's Says Sos, November 14, 1935* ... *South Whitley Tribune*, vol. 51, no. 15 (November 14, 1935), p. 2.

Page 357, *James Harvey Young would devote a chapter* ... James Harvey Young, *The Medical Messiahs: A Social History of Health Quackery in Twentieth-Century America* (Princeton: Princeton University Press, 1967); chap. 10, "Two Gentlemen from Indiana."

Page 357, *two gentlemen from Indiana* … This chapter title refers to the novel: Newton Booth Tarkington (1869–1946), *The Gentleman from Indiana* (New York: Doubleday & McClure Company, 1899). The novel was the basis for the 1915 Paramount Pictures silent movie by the same name, written by Julia Crawford Ivers, Frank Lloyd, and Booth Tarkington. *See also* James Still, *The Gentleman from Indiana* (Woodstock, Illinois: Dramatic Pub., 2007), stage adaptation for contemporary theater audiences.

Page 357, *Charles Frederick Kaadt (1872–1957)* … There is contradictory documentation of the birth date of Charles Kaadt. A grave marker in the Adams Township, Allen County, Indiana, Catholic Cemetery (3500 Lake Avenue, Fort Wayne), Section K, is inscribed "Charles F. Kaadt, M.D., 1884 • 1957," photograph in http://www.rootsweb.ancestry.com/~inallcem/adams/catholic/section-k/kaadt-charles.jpg, accessed September 8, 2014. This marker was photographed by a volunteer of Mary Penrose Wayne Chapter, National Society Daughters of the American Revolution, Allen County Indiana Cemetery Project. Pam Rees (Iowa Heritage Digital Collections Coordinator and Reference Librarian, Iowa Library Services and State Library) wrote on November 13, 2013: "According to the 1940 American Medical Directory on page 668, Dr. Kaadt was born in 1872. He received his medical degree in 1902 and was licensed on November 6, 1905."

Page 357, *were born in Denmark* … *Registry of Physicians: Clinton, Clinton County, Iowa* (on microfilm #1005208 at the Clinton Library), copy supplied by the Clinton Public Library. The entry of "Denmark" in the Nativity column is ambiguous. Does Denmark refer to a local community or to a European country? Birthplaces of other persons on the same page were, in order of entry: Illinois, New York, Ohio, Illinois, and France, Russia, Iowa, Kansas, Iowa, Michigan, and so forth. The Wikipedia internet page "Denmark, Iowa," accessed October 30, 2013, states: "Denmark is an unincorporated community in northeastern Lee County, Iowa, United States. It lies along Iowa Highway 16 north of the city of Fort Madison, the county seat of Lee County. Its elevation is 722 feet (220 m). Although Denmark is unincorporated, it has a post office, with the ZIP code of 52624, which opened on 1846-04-07. The community is part of the Fort Madison–Keokuk, IA–MO Metropolitan Statistical Area." Columbia City (Indiana) physician O. F. Lehmberg said that "they were natives of Denmark" [Dr. O. F. Lehmberg, "Speech Given to the Historical Society," *Bulletin of the Whitley County Historical Society,* vol. 30, no. 6 (December 1992), pp. 3–9]. Documentation for the birthplace and birthdate of Edward Kaadt is even less secure. Census records (1910, 1920, 1930, and 1940) seem clear that the *country* of Denmark was the birthplace of Christian, Charles, Peter, and Marie. Those census records give a birth year of "about 1870," "about 1868," "about 1872," and "about 1875" for Marie. Marie is consistently listed as four years older than Peter. An 1874 immigration record shows that six passengers aboard the ship *City of Paris* arrived in New York from the ports of Liverpool, England, and Queenstown, Ireland, on August 3, 1874; the passengers were Maria Kaadt (wife, age 33), Chr. Kaadt (male, age 34), Kirstine Kaadt (female, age 5), Chr. Gottlieb Kaadt (male, age 3), Peter Simon Kaadt (male, age 2), and Carl Kaadt (male, age 1). The 1880 census records for Clinton, Iowa, include: Chris Kaadt, brick maker, age 50, born in Schleswig; Ella M. Kaadt, age 39, born in Schleswig; Mary Kaadt, age 14, born in Schleswig; Christian Kaadt, age 11, born in Denmark; Peter Kaadt, age 8, born in Denmark; Etta Kaadt, age 2, born in Iowa. Iowa gravestones: Christian Kaadt (1829–1879) and (November 15, 1829–November 27, 1879), Ellen Maria Kaadt (1840–1920); C. G. Kaadt (1868–1905). Springdale Cemetery, Clinton, County, Iowa, http://iowagravestones.org/search.php?new_cid=23&cfield=last&ctype=1&ctxt=kaadt&cfield2=first&ctype2=1&ctxt2=, accessed January 30, 2016.

Page 357, *Charles Kaadt received the M.D.* … University of Iowa Libraries, *Special Collections,* "Records of the Keokuk Medical & Dental Schools

(RG 15.03); Box 3," in a folder labeled "Alumni Lists by Year, 1890-1899, 1900-1907/08." Information supplied by Denise K. Anderson, Special Collections Department.

Page 357, *his medical certificate from the Iowa State Board of Health a month later on May 15, 1902* ... *Registry of Physicians,* op. cit. *But see also* "He received his medical degree in 1902 and was licensed on November 6, 1905," Pam Rees, op. cit.

Page 358, *The competition for students* ... David Sturges Fairchild, *History of Medicine in Iowa,* (Des Moines: Iowa State Medical Society, 1927); chap. 5, "The Iowa College of Physicians and Surgeons of Des Moines and the Medical Department of Drake University," p. 95. *See also:* "The average student [in 1850, at the University of Michigan Medical School] had not graduated from a college or a university, and he had probably learned his letters ... in a village school. The most important requirement was that a student have an apprenticeship to a respectable physician for three years." Horace W. Davenport, *Not Just Any Medical School: The Science, Practice, and Teaching of Medicine at the University of Michigan, 1850–1941* (Ann Arbor: The University of Michigan Press, 1999), p.1.

Page 358, *Kaadt brothers lived with their widowed mother* ... *Clinton City Directory* (1901), http://files.usgwarchives.net/ia/clinton/history/dir/1901H.txt, accessed October 27, 2013.

Page 358, *Peter received his M.D. degree from the Rush Medical College* ... Rush Medical College was named for Benjamin Rush, a physician from Pennsylvania who was also a signer of the Declaration of Independence. The College was chartered in 1837. It opened on December 4, 1843, with twenty-two students enrolled in a sixteen-week course. The college was affiliated with the University of Chicago from 1898 until 1942.

Page 358, *The Clinton Daily Age newspaper* ... http://iagenweb.org/state/textdisplay.php?file=/clinton/records/newspapers/c_age/ca/J.txt.

Page 358, *Demonstrator of Anatomy* ... Information supplied by Maija Anderson, Reference Librarian,

Oregon Health & Science University, Portland.

Page 358, *home of the first scientific journal* ... John T. Farrar, "The American Journal of Digestive Diseases, 1934–1977," *Digestive Diseases and Sciences,* vol. 24, no. 1 (January 1979), pp. 1–3.

Page 359, *Beaumont Sanfield Cornell (1892–1958)* ... Obituary, "Dr. Cornell Dies After Heart Attack," Fort Wayne *Journal Gazette* (September 17, 1958), p. 1. The Beaumont S. Cornell Scholarship is awarded by Indiana University–Purdue University Fort Wayne to graduates of Indiana high schools in Adams, Allen, or Huntington counties who are college students planning to become medical doctors.

Page 359, *to promote his treatment of cancer* ... B. S. Cornell, "A Preliminary Report on the Treatment of Cancer by a New Principle Extracted from Nuclear Material and Called ANOMIN," supplement to the August 1937 issue of *The American Journal of Digestive Diseases,* vol. 4 (1937). Cited by John T. Farrar, op. cit.

Page 359, *Edward Kaadt was a member* ... Obituary, "Edward Kaadt is Dead at 62," Fort Wayne *Journal Gazette,* July 22, 1942, p. 2, col. 6. This obituary is also a source of information about Mrs. Marie Kaadt Graham.

Page 359, *There may be no way* ... An excellent exposition of the early research on *diabetes mellitus* and the discovery of insulin at the University of Toronto in 1921–1922 is Louis Rosenfeld, "Insulin: Discovery and Controversy," *Clinical Chemistry,* vol. 48, no. 12 (2002), pp. 2270–2288.

Page 359, *Paul Langerhans (1847–1888)* ... P. Langerhans, *Beitrage zur mikroskopischen Anatomie der Bauchspeicheldrusse,* doctoral dissertation (Berlin: Gustav Lange, 1869).

Page 359, *Joseph Freiherr von Mering (1849–1908)* ... F. von Mering and O. Minkowski, "Untersuchungen über den Diabetes Mellitus nach Extripation des Pankreas, *Archive für Pathologie und Pharmacologie,* vol. 26 (1890), pp. 371–387.

Page 360, *Eugene Lindsay Opie (1873–1971)* ... Eugene L. Opie, "The Relation of Diabetes Mellitus to Lesions of the Pancreas. Hyaline Degeneration of the Islands of Langerhans," *Journal of Experimental Medicine*, vol. 5, no. 5 (1901), pp. 527–541.

Page 360, *Yet Peter and Charles Kaadt practiced medicine* ... *Board of Medical Registration and Examination of Indiana v. Kaadt*, 76 N. E. (2nd) 669 (Ind., 1948), reprinted in "Bureau of Legal Medicine: Medicolegal Abstracts," *Journal of the American Medical Association*, vol. 136, no. 15 (April 10, 1948), p. 1002.

Page 360, *"For one year prior* ... Board of Medical Registration, loc. cit.

Page 361, *some pepsin and takadiastase* ... Pepsin is a digestive enzyme that catalyzes the hydrolysis of food proteins into short peptides or amino acids. Takadiastase is a digestive enzyme that catalyzes the hydrolysis of starches into sugars. In the Kaadt medicine, both enzymes probably were denatured and thus inactive as catalysts.

Page 361, *A legal dispute arose over the meaning* ... Suzanne White Junod, "FDA and Clinical Drug Trials: A Short History," posted on the FDA Internet site, http://www.fda.gov/AboutFDA/What-WeDo/History/Overviews/ucm304485.htm, accessed October 28, 2013.

Page 362, *the patent medicine Banbar* ... Arthur J. Cramp, "Some Diabetes 'Cures' and 'Treatments'," *Hygeia*, vol. 13, no. 10 (October 1935), pp. 916–920. "Banbar ... For the Diabetic, originated and distributed only by L. B. Bartlett ... Pittsburgh," advertising circular, https://www.flickr.com/photos/fdaphotos/6800850262.

Page 363, *Many of Kaadt's Fort Wayne...* Young, *The Medical Messiahs*, op. cit., chap. 10, "Two Gentlemen from Indiana."

Page 363, *A postal inspector, posing as a patient* ... ibid.

Page 364, *initiated a show-cause hearing* ... ibid.

Page 364, *Railway Express Agency* ... In 1938, Railway Express Agency (REA) was owned by all the nation's railroads. REA operated much as United Parcel Service and FedEx do today. REA resulted

from the World War I nationalization of the United States railroads at the end of 1917.

Page 364, *The judge was skeptical* ... Facts regarding the Federal trial, and the quotation, are from Young, *The Medical Messiahs*, op. cit.

Page 365, *new Veterans of Foreign Wars building* ... That building became the home of both VFW Post 2919 and also AmVets Post 2919. VFW Post 2919 closed in 2014.

Page 365, *Several South Whitley residents worked* ... For example, Miriam Herr, just after graduating as valedictorian from South Whitley High School in 1945, worked for three years at the Clinic. She then began work at the South Whitley Post Office, later transferring to the nearby Larwill Post Office where she eventually became Postmaster. Obituary, "Miriam J. Bishop," *South Whitley Tribune-News*, vol. 129, no. 46 (Wednesday, June 11, 2014), p. 3A.

Page 365, *Chemcraft home chemistry sets* ... For a discussion of "portable cabinets of chemistry," see Kristie Macrakis, "The Hidden Past of Invisible Ink," *American Scientist*, vol. 102, no. 3 (May–June 2014), pp. 198–205.

Page 365, *Mayer State Bank* ... Theodore Mayer of Ligonier, his sons Louis Mayer and Moses Mayer, and Oscar Gandy established the Gandy State Bank in South Whitley in 1893. The bank was incorporated in 1923 as the Mayer State Bank.

Page 366, *"The board's evidence showed* ... Board of Medical Registration, loc. cit.

Page 367, *Federal indictments were returned* ... For an extended description of the investigations leading up to the trial, and of the trial itself, see James Harvey Young, op. cit.

Page 367, *Judge Patrick T. Stone imposed* ... Each doctor was sentenced to pay a fine of $1,000 and costs, and to serve one year in prison, on each of the seven counts, with the sentences on the first three counts to run consecutively. The sentences on the remaining counts were suspended. Each doctor was to be placed on probation when released from prison. Seizure dates: February 13, 1945, and

March 29, 1946. United States National Library of Medicine, History of Medicine internet website, http://archive.nlm.nih.gov/fdanj/items-by-subject ?subject=Kaadt+Diabetic+Treatment, accessed March 30, 2015.

Page 367, *because of ill health* … In December 1948, Peter was reported as "gravely ill in a Portland [Oregon] hospital, after a long illness." The context of that report was a sensational news story in the Roseburg, Oregon, *News-Review* on Tuesday, December 28, 1948: "Flagstaff, Ariz., Dec. 27 (IP). A woman who died in an auto court cabin with a man companion was identified by Coroner Vance G. White today as Mrs. Sayra S. Kaadt, Portland, Ore., club woman and former president of the Portland Parent-Teachers Association. She and a man identified as Harry E. Mathews, Chicago photo engraver, were found dead Friday where they had registered as 'Mr. and Mrs. H. Mathews.' A coroner's jury blamed the deaths on suffocation. Mrs. Kaadt's husband, Dr. Peter S. Kaadt, is gravely ill in a Portland hospital, after a long illness. Mrs. Kaadt, who was prominent in Portland clubwork, was named to the advisory board of the Oregon School for Delinquent Girls at Hillcrest, Ore., in 1943. She was a former school teacher in Portland." The *Long Beach Press-Telegram*, Long Beach, California, on December 25, 1948, wrote: "The couple was driving a Cadillac registered to Sayra S. Kaadt." Her obituary in the *Arizona Champion/Coconino Sun* (Flagstaff, Arizona) on Friday, December 31, 1948, contained clarifications; the woman was Mrs. Fayra Kaadt (January 1, 1898–December 24, 1948) who "Died of carbon monoxide poisoning from a gas heater." Other sources give her name as Fayra Myrl Kaadt (born Bagley), born 1891, christened 1895.

Page 368, *village of Sidney in Kosciusko County* … Since June 1963, Sidney and South Whitley have both been part of the consolidated Metropolitan School District of Whitko School Corporation. Whitko School Corporation serves areas of southwest Whitley and southeast Kosciusko counties, including the towns of South Whitley, Larwill, Pierceton, and Sidney, and rural areas of Washing-

ton, Monroe, Jackson, Richland, and Cleveland townships. In the 2015–2016 school year, 1,493 students were enrolled in two elementary schools, one middle school, and one high school.

Page 368, *Roy Norris, Class of 1896* … Roy Norris was born in 1879 and died in 1911, according to "South Whitley Cemetery," http://www.whitley-countyin.org/cem09.htm, accessed January 30, 2016. He died on January 21, 1911, at age 22 [should be age 32] years, 4 months, and 13 days, according to "South Whitley Funeral Home Records," http://whitleycountyin.org/funeral/1911. pdf, accessed January 30, 2016. Obituary, *Fort Wayne Sentinel*, Monday, January 23, 1911, p. 3, col. 5, gives date of death January 21, 1911: "O. R. Norris, a well known young drug clerk at the W. F. Norris drug store in South Whitley, better known as Roy Norris, died Saturday from a sudden attack of heart trouble, following an illness of one week's duration from scarlet fever."

Page 368, *Bertha Fager, Class of 1898* … Bertha Fager was born in 1880. She married Robert Jellison, South Whitley High School Class of 1897. She died April 17, 1981, at age 100. *See* "South Whitley Cemetery," http://www.whitleycountyin. org/cem09.htm, accessed January 30, 2016. *See also* Obituary, Fort Wayne *Journal Gazette*, Sunday, April 19, 1981, p. 9A, col. 2.

Page 369, *the Methodist Episcopal Church* … The brick Methodist Episcopal Church was on the northwest corner of Market Street and Maple Street. The parsonage was next door on Maple Street.

Page 369, *Hugo Eugene Fox (February 3, 1897– December 27, 1969)* … Biographical material was compiled from the author's recollections, and from the following sources: Obituary, *South Whitley* [Indiana] *Tribune* (December 30, 1969); "Listing of Principal Musicians of the Chicago Symphony Orchestra with Biographical Remarks," http:// www.stokowski.org/Principal_Musicians_Chi- cago_Symphony.htm; Information supplied by Frank Villella, Archivist, Rosenthal Archives of the

Chicago Symphony Orchestra; Internet web site of Fox Products, Inc., http://www.foxproducts.com, accessed December 5, 2013; Kathryn S. Camplese, "Fox Products Corporation—A Musical Miracle in Indiana's Farmland" (Muncie: Ball State University Honors Thesis, November 1984, http://liblink.bsu.edu/uhtbin/catkey/1249294).

Page 369, *His first bassoon teacher* … Biography of John L. Verweire *in* Bert J. Griswold, *Builders of Greater Fort Wayne* (Fort Wayne: 1926), pp. 592 and 773.

Page 370, *Most members were students* … The following are listed in the program booklet, 37th Triennial Alumni Reunion, South Whitley High School, August 1, 2015, as graduates of South Whitley High School: Hugo Fox, Class of 1914; Ellis Miller, 1913; Gene Glassley, 1917; Vernon Gresso, 1916; Lee Nichols, 1915; Ernest Jewell, 1914; Carper Hathaway, 1914; Herbert Harley, 1916; Lloyd Holben, 1913; Boyd Sickafoose, 1914; Keith Glassley, 1914; and Frank Dimmick, 1915. A photograph of the original Agony Band, with members identified, appeared in "Town Band Drew Crowds for Wednesday Night Concerts," *Bulletin of the Whitley County Historical Society* (April 1977), pp. 6–9.

Page 370, Phil Farren … Phil Farren was born in Italy on May 10, 1874. He immigrated as Phillippe Lorenzo Cianfarani in the early 1880s. In addition to his work as a musician, he was also a tailor in Columbia City.

Page 371, *student instruction booklet* … Hugo Fox, *Let's Play Bassoon* (South Whitley: Fox Bassoon Company, 1949), 22 pages, 15 × 23 cm, illustrated, with detailed fingering charts.

Page 372, *"the very acceptable service rendered"* … *Report of the Superintendent of the U. S. Coast and Geodetic Survey, Showing the Progress of the Work* (Washington: Government Printing Office, June 1894), part I, p. 21. Reference supplied by Simon Monroe and Mary Lou Cumberpatch, NOAA Central Library reference librarians.

Page 372, *Boston Harbor map* … One original is at

the National Archives. Digital Image: 246-06-1896; Type: Nautical Chart; Year: 1896; Scale: 1:20000; Publisher: US Coast & Geodetic Survey; Size: 45.434 × 36.891. http://historicalcharts.noaa.gov/historicals/preview/image/LC00246_06_1896, accessed December 19, 2013. Reference supplied by Mary Lou Cumberpatch, NOAA Central Library reference librarian.

Page 372, *undergraduate engineering thesis* … Information about the thesis was supplied by Jill Tatem, University Archivist, Case Western Reserve University.

Page 372, *Cleveland was just beginning to implement* … Funding for the first professionally engineered sewerage plan for Cleveland was approved in 1896. There was no plan for sewage treatment; raw sewage was emptied into the Cuyahoga River and Lake Erie. Treatment of sewage in Cleveland did not begin until 1922. *The Encyclopedia of Cleveland History;* "Sanitation," http://ech.case.edu/cgi/article.pl?id=S1; "Northeast Ohio Regional Sewer District," http://ech.case.edu/cgi/article.pl?id=NORSD; both internet sites accessed July 19, 2015.

Page 372, *He held patents* … Among his patents were: Frederick M. Graham, "Rail Joint Lubricating Device," U. S. Patent 1,889,313, application filed March 31, 1930; Frederick M. Graham and James B. McWilliams, "Rail Lubricating Device," U. S. Patent 1,890,605, application filed March 31, 1930; Frederick M. Graham, "Apparatus for Heat Treating Rails," U. S. Patent 1,882,417, application filed November 30, 1931; Frederick M. Graham, "Apparatus for Hardening the Ends of Track Rails," U. S. Patent 2,182,120, application filed March 12, 1938; Frederick M. Graham and Edgar E. Martin, "Elastic Tie Plate Anchor Spike," U. S. Patent 2,365,545, application filed June 17, 1943.

Page 373, *Dr. Lee LeVere Eve was speaker* … *South Whitley Tribune-News*, Thursday, October 8, 1970.

Page 373, *explaining to high school students* … The author's recollection of three tutorial sessions in summer 1952 in preparation for college calculus that fall.

Page 373, *his colleagues feted him* … Tribute quoted

in Obituary, *South Whitley Tribune*, May 21, 1959.

Page 374, *His first source of tube cane* ... Interview of Hugo Fox by the author for newspaper article: George M. Fleck, "From French Cane to Double-Reeds by Fox Products," *South Whitley Tribune* (vol. 65, no. 48, May 31, 1951), pp. 1, 4.

Page 374, *Mary Lou Bowers Smith* ... After high school, Mary Lou Bowers joined the Civic Orchestra of Chicago, the training orchestra affiliated with the Chicago Symphony Orchestra. She played oboe and English horn in the Fort Wayne Civic Orchestra and the Fort Wayne Philharmonic Orchestra. She was a graduate of Huntington College and Ball State Teachers College, and owned a music business in Huntington for many years. Biographical information submitted by Mary Lou Smith for the entry of her father, Harry Martin Bowers, *in* Huntington County Historical Society, *Huntington County, Indiana: History & Families, 1834–1993* (Paducah, Kentucky: Turner Publishing Company, 1993), p. 214.

Page 374, *"Hugo was quite pleased* ... Quotation from the Fort Wayne *Journal Gazette*, September 18, 1966. Cited by Kathryn S. Camplese, op. cit., p. 2.

Page 374, *Band Director Reba M. Geist* ... The South Whitley High School band acquired the Selmer oboe about 1950. The initial oboist was George Fleck, who switched to oboe from saxophone. Hugo Fox gave lessons on his first bassoon to Monica Fleck (December 14, 1937–May 12, 1994), who was in junior high school at South Whitley.

Page 375, *filed a patent application* ... Hugo E. Fox, "Bassoon," U. S. Patent 3,127,806.

Page 375, *three-story Victorian residence* ... Cleon Fleck, "A Homemaker and Our First Lady: That's Helene Gates," *Bulletin of the Whitley County Historical Society*, vol. 20, no. 6 (December 1982), pp. 3–7.

Page 376, *Efforts to document his medical education* ... I. A. S. Eitel, Humboldt University Archivist, reported that the name of Prince Immanuel does not appear in the Humboldt student directories

from 1890 to 1900. The archivist could not confirm a doctorate. Email January 9, 2014.

Page 377, *creation of Universal* ... Arika Okrent, *In the Land of Invented Languages: Esperanto Rock Stars, Klingon Poets, Loglan Lovers, and the Mad Dreamers Who Tried to Build a Perfect Language* (New York: Spiegel & Grau, 2009), p. 305. She amplified (email, December 22, 2013): "The reference to Universal came from a Russian bibliography of artificial languages, Alexander Dulichenko's *Mezhdunarodnye vspomogatel'nye jazyki* ('International Auxiliary Languages,' 1990. Talinn: Valgus). I think the reference was just 'Cairo, 1914'."

Page 377, *he knew twenty languages* ... Prince Immanuel of Jerusalem, *Criminals of Chicago* (Boston: Roxburgh Publishing Company, 1921), p. 31.

Page 377, *Prince Immanuel's self-description* ... *Criminals of Chicago*, op. cit., p. 30.

Page 377, *his 258-page book* ... *Criminals of Chicago* (op. cit.) was published by Roxburgh, a prestigious longtime Boston publisher. Thirteen libraries list the book in the OCLC FirstSearch database (WorldCat). The University of Illinois copy has been digitized by Hathi Trust and is freely available on the internet at http://hdl.handle.net/2027/uiuo. ark:/13960/t2k64c89p. The Forward suggests that the book was written in 1919. The Forward refers to methods "which I advocated thirty years ago in 'The Modern Bible';" the only publication with that title listed in FirstSearch is a 1901 sixteen-page reprint from *The Christian Register* by Charles Fletcher Dole.

Page 377, *Psychopathic Laboratory* ... *Report of the Psychopathic Laboratory of the Municipal Court of Chicago for the years May 1, 1914 to April 30, 1917* (Chicago: Fred Klein Co., Printers, 1917), https://archive.org/details/reportofpsychopaoochic. *See also* Harry Olson, "Psychopathic Laboratory Idea," *Journal of Criminal Law and Criminology* (vol. 6, no. 1, article 5, 1915), pp. 59–64.

Page 377, *publication in 1922 of the book...* Harry Hamilton Laughlin, D.Sc., *Eugenical Sterilization in the United States* (Chicago: Psychopathic Laboratory of the Municipal Court of Chicago, December 1922). The title page describes Dr. Laughlin as "Assistant Director of the Eugenics Record Office, Carnegie Institution of Washington, Cold Spring Harbor, Long Island, New York, and Eugenics Associate of the Psychopathic Laboratory of the Municipal Court of Chicago."

Page 377, *"Lupus and Fidus"*... Thirty-one-page carbon copy of a typescript manuscript, Sinclair Manuscripts ("Writings by Others," Box 39), Lilly Library Manuscript Collections, Indiana University, Bloomington, Indiana; copy supplied by archivist David F. Frasier. The subtitle, "The Mills of the Gods," was stricken out with red pencil. The Sinclair Manuscripts, 1890–1968, consist of correspondence, writings, and papers of the politically influential and prolific writer Upton Beall Sinclair (1878–1968).

Page 378, *Anne Shoemaker Metzger (April 18, 1886–February 5, 1972)* ... Anne Metzger told the author about the donation when the author was in high school. He may have misinterpreted her reasoning. She was a faithful Methodist, and he thought that she was offended by the additions to the *Gospels*. She was also the daughter and the widow of physicians, and she may have felt that Prince Immanuel's unorthodox medical pronouncements did not belong in the library's small medical reference collection. Her husband, Dr. Owen E. Metzger (1882–1917), practiced medicine in South Whitley.

Page 378, *among the authors ... Of America We Sing: A Contemporary Anthology of Patriotic Verse* (New York: Exposition Press, 1944), 503 pages.

Page 378, *United Telephone Company* ... The United Telephone Company (first called the Whitley County Telephone Company) had been formed in 1928 by consolidation of two competing local telephone companies: Whitley County (Home) Telephone Company and the Farmers Mutual Telephone Company. Before consolidation, most South Whitley businesses had a Home telephone number and a Farmers telephone number. Otherwise, a person with only a Home telephone

would need to place the call from a neighbor's telephone, or call the Farmers switchboard to place a Farmers call. Telephone service was free within most of Whitley County, but each subscriber was obliged to rent a telephone set from the company, at a monthly fee.

Page 379, *Valentine (Val) Hennig (December 19, 1889–September 11, 1961)* ... Fern (Labar) Tripcony, "Reverend Valentine Hennig," *Bulletin of the Whitley County Historical Society*, vol. 32, no. 4 (December 1994), pp. 13–15. *See also* Obituaries: "Rev. Val Hennig Dies at Hospital," *Fort Wayne News-Sentinel*, Tuesday, September 12, 1961, p. 16, col. 2; "Pastor's Widow Dies Suddenly," Fort Wayne *Journal Gazette*, Saturday, December 30, 1961, p. 13, col. 1.

Page 380, *Zion Lutheran Church* ... Information supplied by the Rev. Gary R. Hoffstetter, pastor of Christ Lutheran Church, Gordonville (email April 16, 2014), and the Rev. Wayne W. Schwiesow, pastor of Zion Lutheran Church.

Page 381, *Carl Frederick Pook (February 25, 1848–September 28, 1932)*... Obituary, "Death Claims Early Whitley Co. Resident," *Columbia City Post*, September 28, 1932.

Page 381, *he brought thirty-eight airmail letters* ... Franklin M. Bridge, "The Day We Flew the Mail from Orton Schoenauer's Pasture," *Bulletin of the Whitley County Historical Society*, vol. 21, no. 1 (February 1983), pp. 25–27.

Page 383, *Works Progress Administration rural outhouse project* ... Conversation with Gilbert Gerard's son Wayne on November 8, 2014. For more about the WPA project, see Ronald S. Barlow, *The Vanishing American Outhouse: A History of Country Plumbing* (El Cajon, California: Windmill Publishing Company, 1989), "The Outhouse Boom of 1933–1945," pp. 21–24.

Page 383, *Gerard Tin Shop* ... The firm was established about 1887 by Mr. Gerard's father, Marcellus Gerard. It was later known as Gerard Plumbing & Heating.

Page 384, *Vernon Jersey described the process* ... Marjorie Barnhart, "Carrots Get 'Squeezed' in Factory Making Vitamin A at South Whitley," *Fort Wayne News-Sentinel*, September 7, 1946. Copy of reprint supplied by Joyce Hite, Local History Librarian, South Whitley Community Library.

Page 384, *Albert mentioned that cow's milk* ... Marjorie Barnhart, loc. cit.

Page 384, *standard vitamin manual* ... Walter Hollis Eddy and Gilbert Dalldorf, *The Avitaminoses: The Chemical, Clinical and Pathological Aspects of the Vitamin Deficiency Diseases* (Baltimore: Williams & Wilkins, 1937), 338 pages. Williams & Wilkins was a premier publisher of medical manuals.

Page 384, *United States Department of Agriculture compilation* ... Lela E. Booher, Eva R. Hartzler, and Elizabeth M. Hewston, *A Compilation of the Vitamin Values of Foods in Relation to Processing and Other Variants: A Summary of the Vitamin A, Thiamin, Ascorbic Acid, Vitamin D, and Riboflavin Values of Foods in Terms of International Units or Absolute Weights of These Vitamins, As Recorded in the Literature Through December 1940* (Washington: United States Department of Agriculture, Circular No. 638, May 1942), 244 pages.

Page 385, *Just prior to World War II* ... "Nutritional Research Celebrates 50th Anniversary This Year," *South Whitley Tribune–Pierceton News*, vol. 100, Wednesday, February 22, 1984.

Page 385, *investigated by Pleasant Ernest Roller* ... P. E. Roller, "The Effect of Wheat Germ Oil on the Keeping Qualities of Fats and Food Rations," *Journal of Physical Chemistry*, vol. 35, no. 11 (January 1931), pp. 3286–3292. Contribution from the Research Division of The S. M. A. Corporation, Cleveland, Ohio.

Page 385, *doctoral research of Erich Heftmann* ... Erich Heftmann, "Antioxidant Properties of Carrot Oil," *Journal of the American Oil Chemists' Society*, vol. 24, no. 12 (December 1947), pp. 404–409.

Page 385, *The principal activities* ... Nutritional Research Associates, *15th Anniversary Historical Statement*, 1951.

Page 386, *an atypical personal testimonial* ... "Vitamin E and Your Health. A Frank Discussion of the Results of Research on the Importance of This Vitamin to the Health of the Nation" (South Whitley: Nutritional Research Associates, Inc., 1966), 8 pages.

Page 387, *Until the close of his life* ... Obituary, "Albert Germann," *Columbia City* [Indiana] *Post and Commercial Mail*, Wednesday, December 22, 1976.

REACTIONS IN PHOSGENE SOLUTION. II. FORMATION OF CHLORALUMINATES.*

BY ALBERT F. O. GERMANN AND KENNETH GAGOS

In a recent communication[1] one of us reported that potassium is attacked by phosgene containing dissolved aluminium chloride. The reaction in the ~~~sium is too slow for convenient study. The present investigation ~~~rvey of the behavior of other metals towards ~~~ to find, if possible, examples of ~~~ progress of the

THE PROPERTIES OF PHOSGENE SOLUTIONS: VAPOR TENSION CURVES OF ALUMINUM CHLORIDE SOLUTION AT 0° AND AT 25°

BY ALBERT F. O. GERMANN AND GLENN H. McINTYRE

The unusual chemical properti~ liquid phosgene recent~ which a l~

~lution of a~

CHEMICAL LABORATORY OF STANFORD UNIVERSITY]

NSTANTS AND VAPOR TENSION
PHOSGENE[1]

O. GERMANN AND QUIMBY W. TAYLOR

BER 12, 1925   PUBLISHED MAY 5, 1926

observation of the critical temperature o~
s is due to Hackspill and Mathieu,[2] who
direct observation. Paternò and Mazzuc
bexisting phases of phosgene, and by c~
th Young's curve for pentane deduce~
d the value 0.5135 for the critical d~
the critical pressure of phosgene ar
li,[3] using the modified van der W
)$_c$, deduced the value 51.5 atmos~
apor tension of phosgene has beer
ions. Atkinson, Heycock and P~
age of temperatures, from the boi
of water. Paternò and Mazzu
m —19° to +21°; each of tw~
ies of measurements througho
essive series of measurement~
e used in the preceding serie
n this way any more volatil
l any less volatile impuritie
of distillation on the vapor
ne (prepared from carbon
Germann and Birosel;[5] t~
ncluded in this article is fror
ent of Chemistry of Stanfor~
degree of Engineer in Chen~
eu, Bull. soc. chim., [4] 25,
chelli, Gazz. chim. ital., 50
nd Pope, J. Chem. Soc., ~

45

WESTERN RESERVE UNIVERSITY

ON THE DENSITY OF AIR IN CLEVELAND*

By ALBERT F. O. GERMANN and HAROLD SIMMONS BOOTH.

The fact that air had weight was first proven by Galileo in the
the seventeenth century, when he weighed a copper ball
~ssed air; but the actual determination of its
such difficulties that it was not until 1650,
~ump, that Otto von Guericke, of
first actual measurement of
~ses, the weight
~nd pres-
~ric

THE ORIGIN OF UNDERGROUND CARBON DIOXIDE[1]

FRANK E. E. GERMANN AND HERBERT W. AYRES
Department of Chemistry, University of Colorado, Boulder, Colorado

Received August 18, 1941

I. INTRODUCTION

Many theories of the origin of subterranean carbon dioxide have been advanced (4), and it is a reasonable assumption that there is truth in a number
of them. It is the purpose of the present paper to study only one of these,
i.e., thermal dissociation, and to show that actual underground conditions may
lead to quite different results from those obtained under idealized conditions
realized in a modern laboratory.
The first careful study of the equilibrium established between calcium carbonate, calcium oxide, and carbon dioxide was reported by Debray (2), whose
results are incorrect principally because of incorrect values assigned to the
temperatures of boiling cadmium and zinc. Since that time numerous studies
of the thermal dissociation of pure calcium carbonate have been reported and
the dissociation pressures over a wide range of temperatures are accurately
known.
Carbon dioxide has been encountered in various deep oil
States and Mexico. Volumes estimated as high
day have been reported from wells the r~

[1] Presented at the Eighteen~
Ithaca, New York, I~

Appendix A.

Graduate Students of
Frank Erhart Emmanuel Germann

This list of graduate students at the University of Colorado, with titles of their theses and references to joint research publications with Prof. Frank Germann, was compiled from "Publications of Frank E. E. Germann, Professor Emeritus of Chemistry, University of Colorado; Physical Chemist, National Bureau of Standards, Boulder, Colorado" (copy supplied by the Archives, University of Colorado at Boulder Libraries); and from Master's and Doctoral theses identified using the Chinook Plus Advanced Search electronic catalog of the University of Colorado Libraries, accessed via the internet February 2013. Most of the references to research publications were verified by inspection of the print journal itself, or by inspection of an electronic copy of the paper downloaded via the internet. The list is in approximate chronological order.

Ralph Newton Traxler, "The Adsorption of Iodine by Silver Iodide," M.A. thesis, 1922; Frank E. E. Germann and Ralph N. Traxler, "Adsorption of Iodine by Silver Iodide," *Journal of the American Chemical Society*, vol. 44, no. 3 (1922), pp. 460–464; Ralph N. Traxler and Frank E. E. Germann, "The Action of Red Phosphorus on Iodine in Organic Solvents," *Journal of the American Pharmaceutical Association*, vol. 14, no. 6 (June 1925), pp. 476–477; Ralph N. Traxler and Frank E. E. Germann, "The Decolorization of Carbon Disulphide Solutions of Iodine by Red Phosphorus," *Journal of Physical Chemistry*, vol. 29, no. 9 (1925), pp. 1119–1124; Frank E. E. Germann and Ralph N. Traxler, "Preparation and Melting Points of Pure Di- and Tri-Iodide of Phosphorus," *Journal of the American Chemical Society*, vol. 49, no. 2 (February 1927), pp. 307–312.

Malcolm Cleveland Hylan, "Adsorption in Photography," Ph.D. thesis, 1923; Frank E. E. Germann and Malcolm C. Hylan, "Dispersity of Silver Halides in Relation to Their Photographic Behavior," *Science*, (New Series), vol. 58, no. 1504 (October 26,

1923), pp. 332–333; Frank E. E. Germann and Malcolm C. Hylan, "The Photographic Sensitiveness of Silver Iodide," *Journal of the American Chemical Society,* vol. 45, no. 11 (November 1923), pp. 2486–2493; Frank E. E. Germann and Malcolm C. Hylan, "Dispersity of Silver Halides in Relation to Their Photographic Behavior," *Journal of Physical Chemistry,* vol. 28, no. 5 (1924), pp. 449–456.

Derk Vivian Tieszen (October 19, 1894–January 22, 1960), "Sodium Platinocyanide," M.A. thesis, 1928.

Oscar Brauer Muench (1891–1953), "Lithium Platinocyanide and a Micro Method for the Quantitative Determination of its Hydrates," Ph.D. thesis, 1928; Frank E. E. Germann and O. B. Muench, "Studies on the Physical and Chemical Properties of the Platinocyanides. I. The Hydrates of Lithium Platinocyanide," *Journal of Physical Chemistry,* vol. 33, no. 3 (1933), pp. 415–423.

Dzu-Kun Shen, "Photographic Sensitivity and the Latent Image," Ph.D. thesis, 1928; Frank E. E. Germann and Dzu-Kun Shen, "Studies in Photography. I. The Nature of Sensitivity and the Latent Image," *Journal of Physical Chemistry,* vol. 33, no. 6 (1929), pp. 864–872; Frank E. E. Germann and Dzu-Kun Shen, "Studies in Photography. II. The Rôle of Sensitizers in Photography and the Latent Image," *Journal of Physical Chemistry,* vol. 33, no. 10 (1929), pp. 1583–1592; Frank E. E. Germann and D. K. Shen, "The Relation Between Photographic Reversal and the Sensitivity of the Silver Halide Grain," *Journal of Physical Chemistry,* vol. 35 (1931), pp. 93–99; Frank E. E. Germann and Dzu-Kun Shen, "Sensitization and Desensitization of Silver Iodide," *The Journal of the Colorado-Wyoming Academy of Science,* vol. 1 (1929), p. 25.

Paul Reheard Frey (1902–1978), "Determination of the Hydrates of Uranyl Nitrate and the Description of Some of Their Properties," M.S. thesis, 1930; Frank E. E. Germann and Paul Reheard Frey, "The Hydrates of Uranyl Nitrate, Their Respective Vapor Pressures and Relative Stability of the Lower Hydrate," *The Journal of the Colorado-Wyoming Academy of Science,* vol. 1 (1929), p. 54.

Norman Jackson Harrar (1902–1941), "A Study of the Iron Compounds of Certain Organic Acids," Ph.D. thesis, 1930; Norman J. Harrar and Frank E. E. Germann, "A

Study of Organic Acid Iron Solutions. I. Concentrations and Colors," *Journal of Physical Chemistry*, vol. 35, no. 6 (1931), pp. 1666–1673; Norman J. Harrar and Frank E. E. Germann, "A Study of Organic-Acid Iron Solutions. II. Colloidal Properties," *Journal of Physical Chemistry*, vol. 35, no. 8 (1931), pp. 2210–2218; Norman J. Harrar and Frank E. E. Germann, "A Study of Organic-Acid Iron Solutions. III. Complex-Colloid Equilibrium," *Journal of Physical Chemistry*, vol. 36, no. 2 (1932), pp. 688–695. *See also* Frank E. E. Germann, "Norman Jackson Harrar: January 7, 1902–October 16, 1941," *Science* (New Series), vol. 94, no. 2448 (November 28, 1941), pp. 507–508.

Henry Carl Staehle (1896–1966), "Part 1: The Solubility of Carbon Dioxide in Oil Bearing Sands. Part 2: An Apparatus for the Determination of Melting Points," M.S. thesis, 1931; "Magnetic Birefringence," Ph.D. thesis, 1933.

Walter Edwin Rule, "The Determination of Vapor Pressures by the Smith and Menzie's Isoteniscope," M.S. thesis, 1933.

Aaron Gustaf Oberg, "The Dielectric Constants of Ortho-, Meta-, and Para-Fluoro-toluene," M.S. thesis, 1933; "A Study of the Absorption Spectra of Inorganic Salt Solutions," Ph.D. thesis, 1935; Aaron Oberg and F. E. E. Germann, "Application of the Study of Electric Capacities to the Study of Chemical Reactions," presented at the meeting of the Colorado-Wyoming Academy of Science, November 27, 1931.

Odon Stahlhut Knight, "A New Method of Preparation of Pure Triethanolamine," M.S. thesis (Chemistry), 1932; "Vapor Pressure–Temperature Data Accurately Represented by Line Co-ordinate Charts in the Pressure Range from Five Hundred to Nine Hundred Millimeters of Mercury," Ph.D. thesis (Chemistry), 1933; "A Chemical Engineering Laboratory for the University of Colorado: Including the Plan of a Course of Instruction and Specifications for the Laboratory Equipment," Ch.E. thesis (Chemical Engineering), 1935; Frank E. E. Germann and Odon S. Knight, "Vapor Pressure–Temperature Data Represented by Line Co-ordinate Charts," *The Journal of the Colorado-Wyoming Academy of Science*, vol. 1, no. 6 (1934), p. 14; Frank E. E. Germann and Odon S. Knight, "Line Coordinate Charts for Vapor Pressure–Temperature Data," *Industrial and Engineering Chemistry*, vol. 26, no. 4 (April 1934), pp.

467–470; and F. E. E. Germann and Odon S. Knight, *Boiling Points of Ring and Chain Compounds* (Boulder: Department of Chemistry, University of Colorado, 1934), including larger versions of the two charts from the *Industrial and Engineering Chemistry* paper; Frank E. E. Germann and Odon S. Knight, "The Preparation of Pure Triethanolamine (β, β', β"-Trihydroxytriethylamine)," *Journal of the American Chemical Society*, vol. 55, no. 10 (October 1933), p. 4150.

Anthony Rose Ronzio, "A Study of the Reaction between Nitrogen Trioxide and Sulphur Dioxide," M.S. thesis, 1932; "The Action of Aromatic Aldehydes upon the Addition Products Obtained from Aromatic Amidines and Glyoxal," Ph.D. thesis, 1935; Anthony Rose Ronzio, Joseph Johnston Coleman, and Frank E. E. Germann, "A Microcalorimeter," *The Journal of the Colorado-Wyoming Academy of Science*, vol. 2, no. 3 (1937), p. 59. He also collaborated at Colorado with Kenneth Gagos (a former Stanford graduate student of Albert Germann): A. R. Ronzio and K. A. Gagos, "An Improvement in the Victor-Meyer Method," *Journal of Chemical Education*, vol. 9, no. 10 (October 1932), pp. 1827–1828; and "A Study of the Reaction Between Nitrogen Trioxide and Sulfur Dioxide," presented by Ronzio and Gagos at the meeting of the Colorado-Wyoming Academy of Science, November 27, 1931.

Thomas Howard James (1912–2000), "The Influence of Salts upon Intermittent Photographic Exposures," M.A. thesis, 1935; "The Nature of the Latent Photographic Image from a Theoretical and Experimental Point of View," Ph.D. thesis, 1935; T. Howard James, F. E. E. Germann, and Julian M. Blair, "The Influence of Salts on Intermittent Photographic Exposures," *The Journal of the Colorado-Wyoming Academy of Science*, vol. 1, no. 6 (1934), p. 17; T. Howard James, F. E. E. Germann, and Julian M. Blair, "The Action of Water on the Latent Photographic Image," *Journal of Physical Chemistry*, vol. 38, no. 9 (December 1934), pp. 1211–1216; T. Howard James, F. E. E. Germann, and Julian M. Blair, "Action of Water on the Latent Photographic Image," *The Journal of the Colorado-Wyoming Academy of Science*, vol. 1, no. 6 (1934), p. 20.

Clarence Albert Neilson, "An Improved Apparatus for the Quantitative Estimation of Helium in Gases," M.S. thesis, 1933; "Magnetic Double Refraction in Organic Liquid Mixtures," Ph.D. thesis, 1935; Frank E. E. Germann, K. A. Gagos, and C. A. Neilson, "Improved Apparatus for Quantitative Estimation of Helium in Gases," *In-*

dustrial and Engineering Chemistry, Analytical Edition, vol. 6, no. 3 (May 15, 1934), pp. 215–217; Clarence Albert Neilson and Frank E. E. Germann, "The Cotton-Mouton Constants of Ternary Organic Liquid Systems," *The Journal of the Colorado-Wyoming Academy of Science,* vol. 2, no. 2 (1937), p. 23.

Joseph Johnston Coleman, "The Heat of Formation of Binary Liquid Solutions from Their Liquid Components," M.A. thesis, 1934; "Non-electrolytic Solutions," Ph.D. thesis, 1936; J. J. Coleman and Frank E. E. Germann, "The Heat of Formation of Binary Liquid Solutions from Their Liquid Components," *Journal of Chemical Physics,* vol. 1, no. 12 (1933), pp. 847–851; J. J. Coleman and Frank E. E. Germann, "The Heat of Formation of Binary Liquid Solutions from their Liquid Components," *The Journal of the Colorado-Wyoming Academy of Science,* vol. 1, no. 6 (1934), p. 15.

Charles Franklin Metz (September 23, 1904–February 10, 1974), "The Phase Diagram of the System Silver Iodide–Lead Iodide," M.S. thesis 1928; Frank E. E. Germann and Charles F. Metz, "The Phase Diagram of the System Silver Iodide–Lead Iodide," *Journal of Physical Chemistry,* vol. 35, no. 7 (January 1930), pp. 1944–1952; Charles Franklin Metz, "The Effect of Concentration on the Magnetic Double Refraction of Some Organic Salts," Ph.D. thesis, 1936; Charles Franklin Metz and Frank E. E. Germann, "The Effect of Concentration on the Magnetic Double Refraction of Some Organic Salts," *The Journal of the Colorado-Wyoming Academy of Science,* vol. 2, no. 3 (1937), p. 60; Frank E. E. German and Charles F. Metz ("Formerly Assistant in Chemistry and Research Fellow, University of Colorado; now Assistant Professor of Chemistry, Colorado State College of Agriculture and Mechanic Arts"), "Magnetic Double Refraction," *University of Colorado Studies.* Series D. Physical and Biological Sciences, vol. 1, no. 2 (October 1940), pp. 71–103.

Herbert Wilmot Ayres (1914–1989), "The Hydrolytic Dissociation of Oolitic Limestone," M.A. thesis, 1939; Frank E. E. Germann and Herbert W. Ayres, "The Origin of Underground Carbon Dioxide," *Journal of Physical Chemistry,* vol. 46, no. 1 (1942), pp. 61–68.

James William Hensley (March 5, 1915–June 24, 1975), "A Method of Capillary-Fluorescence Analysis," M.S. thesis, 1939; Frank E. E. Germann and James W.

Hensley, "Quantitative Capillary Luminescence Analysis, *Journal of Physical Chemistry*," vol. 44, no. 9 (September 1940), pp. 1071–1081; Frank E. E. Germann and J. W. Hensley, "A Direct Vision Fluorometer," *University of Colorado Studies.* Series D. Physical and Biological Sciences, vol. 1, no. 1 (March 1940), pp. 37–41.

Charles LeRoy Gibson (1911–December 8, 1944), "The Mechanism of the Dark Reaction Following the Photolysis of Malachite Green Leuco-Cyanide," M.S. thesis, 1936; "The Hydrolysis of Copper Sulfate," Ph.D. thesis, 1941; Frank E. E. Germann and Charles LeRoy Gibson, "Studies on the Reactions of the Leucocyanides of the Triphenylmethane Dyes. I. The Mechanism of the Dark Reaction Following the Photolysis of Malachite Green Leucocyanide," *Journal of the American Chemical Society*, vol. 62, no. 1 (1940), pp. 110–112.

Lester Everette Kuentzel, "A Study on the Photochemical Reactions of Leuco-Compounds of Malachite Green," Ph.D. thesis, 1941; Frank E. E. Germann and Lester E. Kuentzel, "A Study of the Photochemical Reactions of Leuco-Compounds of Malachite Green," *The Journal of the Colorado-Wyoming Academy of Science*, vol. 3, no. 2 (1942), p. 23.

Ray Alan Woodriff (January 22, 1909–March 1, 1983), "Investigation by an Improved Method of the Wavelengths of Fluorescence of Lead Tungstate–Calcium Tungstate Mixtures Excited by Various Wave Lengths of Ultraviolet Light," Ph.D. thesis 1942; Frank E. E. Germann and Ray Alan Woodriff, "Energy Distribution in Fluorescence," *The Journal of the Colorado-Wyoming Academy of Science*, vol. 3 (1946), p. 17; Frank E. E. Germann and Ray Woodriff, "Cross-Prism Investigation of Fluorescence," *The Review of Scientific Instruments*, vol. 15, no. 6 (June 1944), pp. 145–149.

Elmer Russell Alexander (February 19, 1902–August 26, 1987), "Ethylene Borate and Similar Borate Glasses as Media for Investigating Phosphorescence of Organic Compounds," Ph.D. thesis, 1949.

Robert George Rekers, "An Investigation of the Fluorescence of Certain Organic Compounds in Dilute Solution," Ph.D. thesis, 1951.

Appendix B.

Graduate Students of
Albert Fredrick Ottomar Germann

This list of graduate students, with titles of their theses, was compiled from "Publications of Albert Fredrick Ottomar Germann, Assistant Professor of Chemistry, Stanford University" (copy supplied by the Archives, Stanford University); and from research publications and patents accessed with Google Scholar, the WorldCat database, and other internet resources. Most of the references to research publications were verified by inspection of the print journal itself or by inspection of an electronic copy of the paper downloaded via the internet. The list is in approximate chronological order.

Western Reserve University

Harold Simmons Booth (1891–1953), "The Atomic Weight of Nitrogen," Ph.D. thesis, 1919. Albert F. O. Germann and Harold Simmons Booth, "On the Density of Air in Cleveland," *Western Reserve University Bulletin,* vol. 19, no. 8 (1916), pp. 45–54 [From a thesis submitted to the Faculty of the Graduate School of Western Reserve University in partial fulfillment of the requirements for the degree of Master of Arts]. Albert F. O. Germann and Harold S. Booth, "The Density of Silicon Tetrafluoride," *Journal of Physical Chemistry,* vol. 21 (1917), pp. 81–100. Albert F. O. Germann and Harold Simmons Booth, "Thermal Analysis of the System Boron Trifluoride–Hydrogen Sulphide," *Journal of Physical Chemistry,* vol. 30, no. 3 (January 1926), pp. 369–377; "The experimental work described here was performed in 1920 at the Morley Chemical Laboratory of Western Reserve University." [Submitted from Laboratory Products Company, Cleveland, Ohio, and Western Reserve University, Cleveland, Ohio.]

Vernon Jersey (1898–1984), "The Hydrolysis of Starch in High Concentrations by

Malt Amylase," Ph.D. thesis, 1935, Biochemistry, Western Reserve. A. F. O. Germann and V. Jersey, "The Cryoscopy of Phosgene Solutions: I. System with Chlorine," *Science* (New Series), vol. 53, no. 1382 (1921), p. 582. *See also* J. Lucien Morris and Vernon Jersey, "Chemical Constituents of Saliva as Indices of Glandular Activity," *Journal of Biochemistry*, vol. 56 (May 1, 1923), pp. 31–42; J. Lucien Morris, Vernon Jersey, and Charles T. Way, "Diuresis in the Sheep: Concentration of Uric Acid and Urea by the Excretory Mechanism of Sheep and Rabbit Compared," *American Journal of Physiology*, vol. 70, no. 1 (September 1, 1924), pp. 122–129; and Howard H. Beard and Vernon Jersey, "The Specific Rotatory Power of Glucose–Insulin Solutions in Contact with Muscle Tissue *in vitro*," *Journal of Biochemistry*, vol. 70 (September 1, 1926), pp. 167–171. [The *Journal of Biochemistry* and *American Journal of Physiology* papers are from the Laboratory of Biochemistry, School of Medicine, Western Reserve University.] *See further* Vernon Jersey, "Preparation of Maltose and Dextrins," United States Patent 2,096,549; application June 14, 1933, patent granted October 19, 1937; patent assigned to S.M.A. Corporation, Cleveland, Ohio. From obituary in *South Whitley Tribune:* born September 1, 1898; spent formative years in Cleveland, Ohio; died September 6, 1984. Moved to South Whitley, Indiana in 1937, and lived at Rural Route 1, South Whitley. He was "the chemist" for Nutritional Research Associates. After retiring, he operated the South Whitley Laundry, selling it shortly before his death.

Leland Stanford Junior University

Charles Russel Timpany, "Calcium Phosgeno-Aluminate: A Physico-Chemical Study," M.A. dissertation, Stanford University, 1925, 46 pages. Albert F. O. Germann and Charles Russel Timpany, "Calcium Phosgeno-Aluminate: A Physico-Chemical Study," *Journal of Physical Chemistry*, vol. 29, no. 11 (January 1925), pp. 1423–1431. After receiving the M.A. degree, Charles Timpany was a special-education teacher, then Assistant Superintendent of the Schools of Santa Clara County, California, from 1947 to 1957. He was also a graduate student in the School of Education at Stanford University, and earned the Ed. D. degree from Stanford in September 1950 with the dissertation "A Proposed Curriculum Reorganization in the Secondary Schools of Santa Clara County." He served as Superintendent of the Schools of Santa Clara County from 1957 to 1967. In 1979, the Santa Clara County Board of Education dedicated the Timpany Center of Santa Clara County "to Dr. Charles Russel Timpany, a pioneer in the field of special education."

Quimby W. Taylor, "The Critical Pressure and Temperature of Phosgene," M.A. thesis, 1923. Albert F. O. Germann and Quimby W. Taylor, "The Critical Temperature and Pressure of Phosgene," *Science* (New Series), vol. 58, no. 1503 (October 19, 1923), p. 310. Albert F. O. Germann and Quimby W. Taylor, "The Critical Constants and Vapor Tension of Phosgene," *Journal of the American Chemical Society*, vol. 48 (May 1926), pp. 1154–1159 [Part of the material is from a thesis submitted to the Department of Chemistry of Stanford University in partial fulfillment of the requirements for the degree of Engineer in Chemistry, 1923].

Kenneth A. Gagos (1896–1995), "The Formation of Chloraluminates in Phosgene Solution: The Phosgenates of Aluminum Chloride," A.M. thesis, 1924. Albert F. O. Germann and Kenneth A. Gagos, "Reactions in Phosgene Solution. II. The Reaction of Calcium with Phosgene," *Science* (New Series), vol. 58, no. 1503 (October 19, 1923), pp. 309–310. Albert F. O. Germann and Kenneth Gagos, "Reactions in Phosgene Solution. II. Formation of Chloraluminates," *Journal of Physical Chemistry*, vol. 28, no. 9 (1924), pp. 965–972. We note in Chapter 2 that Kenneth Gagos joined the faculty of the Department of Chemistry at the University of Colorado, where he was instructor in the "Physical Chemistry Laboratory" course and where he collaborated on several projects with Frank E. E. Germann.

Dionisio Martinez Birosel, "Reactions in Phosgene Solution: Phosgeno Salts," Stanford thesis for the degree of Chemical Engineer, 1925. Albert F. O. Germann and D. M. Birosel, "The Phosgene-Aluminates of Sodium, Strontium, and Barium," *Journal of Physical Chemistry*, vol. 29, no. 11 (January 1925), pp. 1469–1476. Albert F. O. Germann and D. M. Birosel, "An Ebullition Device for Low Temperature and Vacuum Distillation," *Journal of Physical Chemistry*, vol. 29, no. 12 (January 1925), pp. 1528–1532. Dionisio Birosel grew up in Santa, Philippine Islands, earned the A.B. degree from the College of the Pacific (San Jose, California) in 1922, the M.S. degree from the University of Southern California (Los Angeles) in 1923, and the M.A. degree from Columbia University (New York City) in 1925, the same year in which he received the Ch. E. degree from Stanford. He then entered the chemistry graduate program at the University of Iowa to work with Lemuel Charles Raiford (1872–1944), earning the Ph.D. degree on July 23, 1926, with the two-part dissertation: "I. The Behavior of Certain Mixed Ethers toward Bromine and Hydrogen Bromide. II. Compounds of Alkali Metals and Mixed Ethers Containing Isoalkyl Radicals." *The Daily Iowan* (vol. 26, no. 50, July 24, 1926, p. 1) reported that Birosel "received a tremendous outburst of applause when the diploma and insignia were given him." Biographical information was supplied by Denise Anderson, Archives Assistant, Special Collections Department, University of Iowa Libraries, email November 16, 2015.

Glenn Hazel McIntyre (October 10, 1902–November 29, 1998), A.B. in Chemistry, Stanford University, 1924. Albert F. O. Germann and Glenn H. McIntyre, "The Properties of Phosgene Solutions: Vapor-Tension Curves of Aluminum Chloride Solution at 0° and 25°," *Journal of Physical Chemistry,* vol. 29 (January 1925), pp. 102–105. Perhaps Albert Germann influenced Mr. McIntyre to consider Western Reserve University for further research. In any case, Glenn Hazel McIntyre became a graduate student in chemistry at Western Reserve University, about the same time as Germann returned to Cleveland. He received the M.A. degree in 1927 with the dissertation "Gases from Fused Silicates," was elected to the Western Reserve Chapter of Sigma Xi in 1933, and received the Ph.D. degree in 1939 with the dissertation "Fundamental Reactions Involved in the Formation of Porcelain Enamels." On May 9, 1939, Glenn McIntyre and Eugene E. Bryant filed a patent application for "Porcelain Enamel Ground Coat." United States Patent 2,321,763 was granted June 15, 1943, assigned to Ferro Enamel Corporation of Cleveland.

Index

This index does not include citations for articles in periodicals. It does not include material in the Sources and References.

A. & M. College of Texas, 106
Abbe, Ernst (1840–1905), 38
Academia Lutherana Philosophiæ, 138
Adams, William H., 341
Adamson, George P., 41
Addison Junior High School, 323
Addison, Illinois, 269
Agassiz, Louis (1807–1873), 98
Agony Band, 369
Albany College of Pharmacy, 261
Albert Ludwig University of Freiburg, 96
Albright College, 130
Alderson, Victor Clifton, 91, 99, 143
Alexander, Elmer Russell (1902–1987), 122, 414
Alpha Chi Sigma, 20, 102, 138
    The Hexagon of Alpha Chi Sigma, 138
Altman, Sidney, 139
American Association for the Advancement of Science, 116, 128, 143, 239
American Association of Colleges of Pharmacy, 239, 262, 301
American Association of University Professors, 92, 143
American Chemical Journal, 180
American Gastroenterological Association, 359
American Home Products Corporation, 210
American Journal of Digestive Diseases, 359
American Journal of Science, 97, 133
American Luther League, 268
American Lutheran Publicity Bureau, 267
American Medical Association, 363, 377
American Smelting and Refining Company, 217
Anglo-Swiss Condensed Milk Company, 201
Annalen der Pharmacie, 133, 198
Anomin, 359
Archer, Frederick Scott (1813–1857), 107

Argonne National Laboratory, 141
Argonne–West, 121
Armistice, 46, 90, 370
Armour Institute of Technology, 91
Arrhenius, Svante (1859–1927), 30
Arsenic in human cadaver, 100
Asbestos, 177
Asbury, Francis (1745–1816), 12, 241
Atchison, Topeka and Santa Fe Railway, 116, 341
ATOZ Band, 370
Atoz Printing Company, 329, 342, 344, 352, 370, 377, 383
Atwater, Wilbur Olin (1844–1907), 168
Augsburg College, 267
Augsburger, Elmore and Hiram, 331
Augustana College, 267
Augustana Synod of the Scandinavian Lutheran Church, 267
Aumann, Charles William, 59, 61
Axe, Geneva (1858–1940), 251, 253-255
Ayres, Arthur, 129
Ayres, Bert Wilmot, 129
Ayres, Herbert Wilmot (1914–1989), 129, 413
Babcock, Stephen Moulton (1843–1931), 198, 205
Babies' Dispensary and Hospital, 208
Baden, John P., 58, 272
Badger Chemist, 134
Bailar, John Christian (1904–1991), 102
Baker, George Fisher (1840–1931), 111
Baker, John Townsend (1860–1935), 40
Baker and Adamson, 41
Baker Laboratory, 112
Balance, equal-arm two-pan, 43, 166, 170
Ball Glass Works, 330
Baldwin, Samantha Elizabeth (1848–1933), 246
Ball State University, 13, 322
Banbar, 362
Bancroft, Wilder Dwight (1867–1953), 22, 55, 87, 105, 133, 189

Bands
    Agony Band, 369
    Akron, Ohio, 370
    Fort Wayne, 369
    Great Lakes Naval, 370
    Rochester Normal College, 17
    South Whitley, 332, 369, 374
Banting, Frederick Grant (1891–1941), 211, 360
Baptist Church (South Whitley), 347
Barium, 104
Barnard College, 53, 267
Barnett, Harold Montgomery (1903–1956), 280, 325, 326
Barnett Laboratories, Inc., 326
BASF, 39
BASF Wyandotte, 119
Bassoon, full tone lower, 373
Bassoon, polypropylene, 375
Baum, Eva M., 95
Baur, John, Jr., 277
Baur, John C. (1885–1984)
    Acting President (January 1926 to February 12, 1926), 274
    Acting President (September 1927), 301
    biographical summary, 268
    call to Albert Germann, 274
    de facto shared presidency, 287
    Incorporating Committee, 270
    meets with American Luther League members, 268
    meets with Schutes and Pannkoke, 265
    organizes Lutherans to acquire Valparaiso University, 268, 270
    retained Fort Wayne residence, 277
Baur, Helen (1882–1956), 277
Bayer, Friedrich (1825–1880), 40
Baylor College, 279
Bayman, Earl (1891–1958), 367
Beckman, Arnold Orville (1900–2004)
    Model DU spectrophotometer, 126
    Model G pH meter, 126, 188
Becquerel, Antoine Henri (1852–1908), 83
Beede, Joshua William, 28
Belen, New Mexico, 116
Bell, Alexander Graham (1847–1922), 250

Belle Vernon Farms Dairy Company, 209
Belle Vernon-Mapes Dairy Company, 209
Bellis, Arthur Emmons, 89
Bémont, Gustave (1857–1937), 83
Benedict, Francis Guano (1870–1957), 168
Benson, Robert S., 363, 367
Berthollet, Claude Louis (1748–1822), 35, 197
Best, Charles Herbert (1899–1978), 360
Bethel College, 113
Better Business Bureau (Indianapolis), 366
Bigelow, Willard Dell (1866–1939), 204
Bingham, Pearl, 326
Biological evolution. *See* Evolution
Bippus, Evelyn (1929–2009), 326
Birosel, Dionisio Martinez, 193, 417
Black, Joseph (1728–1799), 197
Board of Medical Registration (Indiana), 366
Bogarte, Martin Eugene (1855–1911), 246
Boilerplate, 354
Bollinger, Orva A. (1878–1968), 345
Booth, Harold Simmons (1891–1953), 173, 184, 415
Borden, Gail (1801–1874), 200
Borden-Milbank New York Condensed Milk Company, 200
Boron trifluoride, 172, 186, 191
Borosilicate glass, 38, 171
Boston Floating Hospital, 205
Bosworth, Alfred Willson (1879–1963), 203-208
Boulder Garden Club. 145
Bowditch, Henry I. (died 1927), 205
Bowerman, Charles Marshall, 381
Bowers, Florence A. (1891–1979), 115
Bowman, Milo Jesse, 255
Bowman, Robert L. (1916–1995), 123
Boyd, Charles Harrod (1833–1919), 372
Breed, Mary Bidwell (1870-1949), 21, 23-25, 30
Bridges, Harry (1901–1990), 141
Brown, Geneva Axe. *See* Axe, Geneva
Brown, Henry Baker (1847–1917), 246-253
Brown, Henry Kinsey, (1890–1941), 253-255
Brown, J. C., 240
Brown, Oliver (1873–1967), 5, 21, 22, 31
Brown University, 61
Brownie camera, 107

Brubacher, Abram Royer (1870–1939), 114

Brubacher, John Seiler (1898–1988), 114

Bryan, William Jennings (1860–1925), 288, 352

Bryan, William Lowe (1860–1955), 5, 24, 52, 92

Bryn Mawr College, 23

Bryn Mawr College Monographs, 24

Bunge, Paul (1839–1888), 38

Bunker Hill High School, 19, 45, 169

Bunsen, Robert Wilhelm Eberhard (1811–1899), 35

Bureau of Mines. *See* United States Department of the Interior

Bureau of Standards. *See* National Bureau of Standards

Burns, Albert Garrette (1888–1951), 346, 347

Burroughs, William Seward (1857–1898), 250

Butler, Ovid (1801–1881), 13

Butler Township, 19, 20, 45

Butler University, 12

Buzza, George Earl (1883–1957), 355

Byers, Dora, 334

Cadaverine, 177

Cady, Hamilton Perkins (1874–1943), 189

Calhoun, John Caldwell (1782–1850), 328

Calhoun Street School, 328, 332, 352, 369

California Institute of Technology, 128, 188

Cameron, James (1914–2006), 351

Campbell, Ameila Leochner (1894–1968), 373

Canvassers Magazine, 344

Carbon dioxide, 127

Carbon monoxide, 175, 194

Carley, Francis D., 241

Carlsberg Laboratory, 186, 189, 192

Carmichael, Emmett B., 94

Carnation® Infant Formula, 202

Carnegie, Andrew (1835–1919), 18, 86, 111

Carnegie Institute of Technology, 25

Carotene, 211, 279
  isolation from carrots, 214
  molecular formula, 214
  molecular structure, 214
  precursor of Vitamin A, 213

Carrots, 327

Cary, Howard H. (1908–1991), 125

Case School of Applied Science, 183, 212, 323, 372

Case Western Reserve University, 42, 183
  See also Western Reserve University

Cavendish, Henry (1731–1810), 197

Cech, Thomas R., 139

Central States Division, National Lutheran Education Association, 270, 271

Chatham College, 24

Chattanooga Normal University, 256

Chautauqua, 351

Chemcraft home chemistry set, 365

Chemical Abstracts, 30

Chemical Landmark, 42

Chemical Warfare Service.
  See United States Army

Chesterton, Indiana, 335

Chicago and Lake Huron Railroad, 248

Chicago Medical College, 256

Chicago, Milwaukee and St. Paul Railroad, 112

Chicago, Rock Island and Pacific Railroad, 340

Chicago Symphony Orchestra, 348, 369, 370, 374

Chili Technical College, 108

Chlorine, 175, 178, 180, 194

Chlorine octahydrate, 175

Chlorine octaphosgenate, 175

Church of the Brethren (South Whitley), 347

Ciamician, Giacomo Luigi (1857–1922), 35

Ciba-Geigy, 40

Circus Hall of Fame, 47

Clark University, 50, 253

Clavel-Oswald, Alexander, 40

Cleaveland, Marion (1898–1975), 173, 182, 183, 216

Cleveland College, 183

Cleveland East High School, 44, 322, 323

Cleveland Normal School, 45

Cleveland School of Education, 45

Cleveland School of Nurses, 45, 167

Cleveland Township, Whitley County, Indiana, 322

Coast and Geodetic Survey, 372

Coesse, Indiana, 335

Cold Spring Harbor Station for Experimental Evolution, 280

Coleman, Joseph Johnston, 413

Colgate University, 96, 100

Collip, James Bertran (1892–1965), 360

Colorado Agricultural College, 88, 120, 126, 130

Colorado School of Mines, 55, 87, 253, 299
    Alumni Association, 90
    The Colorado School of Mines Magazine, 90

Colorado State Normal School, 122

Colorado-Wyoming Academy of Science, 131

Colorimeter, 124

Columbia brand milk, 202

Columbia University, 123, 182, 216, 252, 266, 335

Columbian School, 248

Combs, Eleanor (1825–1909), 375

Common schools, 7, 9, 20, 47, 240, 332
    textbooks for, 8

Concordia Club, 20, 48, 276, 294

Concordia College (Conover), 283

Concordia College (Fort Wayne), 269, 270, 271, 282

Concordia College Association of the Evangelical Lutheran Church, 284

Concordia Lutheran Church (Conover), 283

Concordia Lutheran Teachers Seminary (Addison, Illinois), 245, 269

Concordia Seminary (Fort Wayne), 266

Concordia Seminary (St. Louis), 16, 57, 282, 283, 286–288

Conover (North Carolina), 283

Cooke, Josiah Parsons (1827–1894), 34

Coolidge, Calvin (1872–1933), 343, 348

Cornell, Beaumont Sanfield, 359

Cornell, Benjamin D., 94

Cornell University, 54, 252
    Baker Laboratory, 112
    Brown, Oliver, 22
    Foley, Arthur, 49
    Mathers, Frank, 25
    New York College of Agriculture, 203
    Physical Review, 50, 87
    Ramsey, Rolla, 50
    sabbatical leave, 111

Corning Glass Works, 171

Country Life Commission, 9

Country Life Movement, 136

County Unit Demonstration Projects, 10

Crawfordsville, Indiana, 12, 335

Crookes, William, 83

Cross, Robert John (1884–1955), 210, 214, 217, 324, 326, 382

Crowe, John Finley (1787–1860), 12

Crown Point, Indiana, 335

Cryoscopy, 172, 175

Cumings, Edgar Roscoe, 28

Cummings, Dwight A., 95

Cuppy's Corner, 368, 374, 375, 379

Curie, Pierre, and Marie Skłodowska-Curie, 83, 85, 104

Curtis, Harry Alfred (1884–1963), 93

Cushing, Edward Fitch (1862–1911), 208

Cyanide, 90, 177

Daguerre, Louis-Jacques-Mandé (1787–1851), 107

Dalton, John (1766–1844), 197

Daniels, Farrington (1889–1972), 32

Darrow, Clarence Seward (1857–1938), 288

Darwin, Charles (1809–1882), 98, 289

Dau, William Herman Theodore (1864–1944)
    born in Pomerelia, 282
    Concordia College (Fort Wayne), 282
    Concordia Seminary (St. Louis), 282, 286
    Conover, North Carolina, 283, 285
    German Evangelical Lutheran Trinity Church of the Unaltered Augsburg Confession of the City of Memphis, 282
    honorary Doctor of Divinity degree, 285, 298
    St. Paul's Evangelical Lutheran Church (Hammond), 285
    Valparaiso University
        biological evolution, 288
        health of President, 296, 301
        inauguration, 239, 282
        School of Pharmacy, 298

Davis, Marguerite (1887–1967), 324

Davy, Humphry (1778–1829), 84, 175

Davy, John (1790–1868), 175

Dayton, Tennessee, 288

de Forest, Lee (1873–1961), 188

Dean, Paul Marshall (born 1885), 94, 100

Dean of Women, 23-25

Deckert, Helena (1859–1948), 113

DeFuniak Springs, 352

Delphi, Indiana, 335
Delta Epsilon, 138
DeMotte, Mark. L., 250
Dennis, Louis Monroe (1863–1936), 25
Denson, Edgar, 346
DePauw University, 12, 241, 242, 243, 244, 381
DePauw, Washington Charles (1822–1887), 241
Derick, Clarence George (1883–1980), 101
Detroit, Eel River and Illinois Railroad, 328
Dewey, John (1859–1952), 92
Diabetes mellitus
    Banting, Frederick Grant (1891– 1941), 360
    Best, Charles Herbert (1899–1978), 360
    Collip, James Bertram (1892–1965), 360
    Diabetic Ferment Treatment, 362
    Langerhans, Paul (1847–1888), 359, 360
    Macleod, John James Rickard (1876–1935),
      360
    Mering, Joseph Freiherr von (1849–1908), 359
    Minkowski, Oskar (1858–1931), 359
    Opie, Eugene Lindsay (1873-1971), 360
Diabetic Institute, Kaadt, 348, 356-367
Dick, Albert Blake (1856–1934), 250
Dickmeyer, W. Charles (1883–1968), 270
Dimmick, Frank, 370
Diploma mill, 377
Distilled water, 33
District schools. *See* Common schools
Doran, James Harold (1902–1989), 336, 338, 348
Draft registration, 46, 370
Dreyer, Mary Magdalene, 381
Driver, Leotis Lincoln (1867–1960), 135
Druggists Circular, 261
Dry ice, 127
Duboscq, Louis Jules (1817–1886), 124
Duboscq colorimeter, 124
Duemling, Herman (1845–1913), 11, 269
Duemling, Herman A. (1871–1927), 268, 269, 270
du Pont, Eleuthère Irénée (1771–1834), 40
Duquesne University of the Holy Ghost, 261
Eagle Brand® condensed milk, 200
Earlham College, 12, 291
East Texas State Teachers College, 123
Eastern Illinois State Normal School, 293
Eastman, George (1854–1932), 107

Eastman Kodak Company, 107, 109
Eberhard, Fred G. (1889–1944), 345
Eberhard Lutheran Church, 379
Eberline, Harry A. (1874–1952), 296, 297, 303
Eckles, Clarence Henry (1875–1933), 279
Edgewood Arsenal, 119, 179, 181
Edina *Sentinel*, 338
Edinger, Albert (1865–1914), 96
Edison, Thomas Alva (1847–1931), 250
Edwards, Caleb W. (1820–1894), 375
Eel River, 328
Ehemant, Anna Clémentine Thérèse, 200
Eidgenössischen Polytechnikum (Zürich), 278
Ekeley, John Bernard (1869–1951), 96-101
Elliott, Frank Roy (1888–1965), 291
Elrod, Milton, 259, 265
Emerson, Milton Earl (1884–1962), 345, 365
Emmaus Evangelical Lutheran Church (Fort
    Wayne). *See* Emmaus Lutheran Church
Emmaus Lutheran Church (Fort Wayne), 17, 18,
    56
Engelhorn, Friedrich (1821–1902), 39
English Evangelical Lutheran Synod, 58
English Synod of Missouri, 284
Evangelical Lutheran Hospital Association (Fort
    Wayne), 269, 272
Evans, George Harlowe, 129
Evans, Horace Martin (1860–1936)
    Chattanooga Chamber of Commerce, 257
    Chattanooga Normal University, 256
    Chicago Medical College, 256
    G. H. Evans Lumber Company, 257
    married Anna Maud Skinner, 256
    Northern Indiana Normal School and Business
      Institute
      graduated, 256
      Professor of Natural Science, 256
    Northwestern University Medical School, 256
    Public Health Service, 257
    United States Army, 257
    Valparaiso and business enterprises, 256
    Valparaiso and medical practice, 256
    Valparaiso University
      Hugh Cornelius Muldoon, 260-263
      Ku Klux Klan, 258-265

Lutheran purchase, 265-273
Old Main burns, 258
President, 255-274
Evans, John (1814–1897), 140
Eve, Lee LeVere (1903–1992), 334, 373
Evelyn, Kenneth A., 125
Evelyn photoelectric colorimeter, 125
Evolution, 240, 288, 352
Evolution, Cold Spring Harbor Station for
    Experimental, 280
Fahlberg, Constantin (1850–1910), 176
Faraday, Michael (1791–1867), 84
Farine Lactée Henri Nestlé, 200
Farren, Phil, 370
Fasel, Anna Maria, 44
Fat adapted milk. *See* Gerstenberger–Ruh
    modified milk
Ferdinand, Archduke Franz, 45, 54, 254
Fiery Cross, The, 259, 263, 264
Fiery cross, 350
First German Evangelical Lutheran Church of
    Fort Wayne. *See* St. Paul's Lutheran Church
    (Fort Wayne)
Fisher, Rosa Elizabeth (1855–1924), 284
Fleck, Alvin R., 370
Floating Hospital, 205
Flora Stone Mather College, 169, 182, 322
Florida Chautauqua Association, 352
Flotation process, 90
Fluorescence experiments, 112
Foley, Arthur Lee (1867–1945), 5, 28, 49, 53, 83
Folin, Otto Knut Olof (1867–1934), 205
Folsom, Arthur J., 346
Food and Drug Administration,
    Ayres, Herbert Wilmot, 129
    investigation, 363
    Food, Drug and Cosmetic Act (1938), 362
    misbranding, 361, 367
    Pure Food and Drug Act (1906), 26, 361
    Sherley Amendment (1912), 362
    Wiley, Harvey Washington (1844–1930), 26,
        361
Forbes, W. J., 240
Ford, J. P., Company, 119
Ford, John Baptiste (1811–1903), 119

Ford Foundation, 142
Formulac baby food, 209
Fort Wayne College of Medicine, 269
Fort Wayne Female College, 13
Fort Wayne Lutheran Hospital, 270, 272
Fourcroy, Antoine François, comte de (1755–
    1809), 35, 197
Fowler, Louisa McEndree, 25
Fox, Fred (1883–1969), 348, 349, 367
Fox, Hugo Eugene (1897–1969), 348, 367
Fox Products Corporation, 374
Fox's Grove, 351, 368, 369
Frank, Mrs. Paul, 207
Franklin, Benjamin (1706–1790), 206, 273
Franklin, Edward Curtis (1862–1937)
    Advisory Board "on war problems," 180
    Albert Germann drawn to Stanford by, 192
    ammonia research, 190
    Edgewood Arsenal student research assistant
        ship, 181
    honors, 190
    personality, 192
    Stanford University, 190
    University of Kansas, 189
    Western Reserve University honorary degree,
        195
Franklin College, 12, 127
Franklin Infant Food, 207
Franklin University, 206
Freeman Academy, 113
Freezing-point depression, 172
Freie Presse (Fort Wayne), 270
Fremont, Nebraska, 56, 272
Fremont Normal School and Commercial
Institute, 61
Frey, Paul Reheard (1902–1978), 130-131, 410
Friedrich-Wilhelms-Universität, 169
Fries, Amos Alfred (1873–1963), 179
Fritz, Robert L., 267
Frohring, Paul R., (1903–1998), 196, 211-213, 324
Frohring, William Otto, (1893–1959), 196,
    211-213, 302, 323-324
Fuller, Harry Victor (1880–1948), 277-278
Funk, Kazimierz (Casimir) (1884–1967), 325
G–R milk. *See* Gerstenberger–Ruh modified milk

Gagos, Kenneth A. (1896–1995), 121, 135, 193, 412, 417

Gallatin Democrat, 340

Gammon, Robert E. (pseudonym), 342

Gandy State Bank, 342

Gates, Ralph Fesler (1893–1978), 368, 376

Geigy-Merian, Johann Rudolf, 40

Geist, Conway, 365

Geist, Reba M., 374

General Electric Fellowship, 51

Geneva Chemical Company, 342

Geologic time, 115

Geological history. *See* Evolution

George Washington Carver Junior High School, 62

Ger Manner, 332, 336, 382

Gerard, Alta Marian Graf (1910–2001), 355

Gerard, Gilbert, 383

German–English Lutheran Parochial School (Valparaiso), 245, 247, 269

German Evangelical Lutheran Synod of Missouri, Ohio, and Other States, 11, 292

German Evangelical Lutheran Trinity Church of the Unaltered Augsburg Confession of the City of Memphis, State of Tennessee, 282, 287

Germann, Albert Fredrik Ottomar (1886–1976)

  birth, 18

  children, 44, 111, 195, 277, 302, 321, 323, 334, 381, 386

  death, 387

  Carotene, 211

  Cleveland School of Nurses, 167

  Indiana University

    Alpha Chi Sigma, 20

    A.B. in Chemistry, 20

    A.M. in Chemistry, 30

    Concordia Club, 20

    Phi Beta Kappa, 48

  Laboratory Products Company, 196, 239, 323

  marriage, 44

  Peru High School, 18

  Quintrex, 324

  St. John's Christian Day School, 18

  teaching in Miami County

    Bunker Hill High School, 19

    Butler Township, 19

  University of Berlin, 38, 51

  University of Geneva

    doctorat ès sciences physiques et chimiques, 38

  University of Wisconsin

    M.Sc. in Chemistry, 31

  Western Reserve University, 41, 167

  Valparaiso University

    Acting Dean, School of Pharmacy, 298

    Acting President, 297

    call, 239, 274

    resignation, 302

Germann, Albert Fredrik Ottomar, Jr., 44, 386

Germann, Alfred W., 16

Germann, Barbara. *See* Germann, Luise Barbara

Germann, Carl (Charles) Adam, (1851–1932), 16

Germann, Edith (1917–1990), 44, 111, 302, 323

Germann, Edwin Jacob (1869–1942), 5, 17, 54

Germann, Frank Erhart Emmanuel (1887–1974)

  birth, 46

  children, 61, 62, 111, 127

  Colorado School of Mines, 55, 87

  Cornell University, 54

    Department of Physics, 86

    Carnegie Research Associate, 86

    Carnegie sabbatical research grant, 109

  death, 146

  Indiana University

    A.B. in Physics, 48

    Concordia Club, 48

    Department of Romance Languages, 53

    Phi Beta Kappa, 48, 116, 143

    Physics Club, 53, 85

  marriage, 55, 276

  memberships

    Alpha Chi Sigma, 138

    American Association for Advancement of Science, 143

    American Association of University Professors, 143

    American Chemical Society, 138

    Colorado–Wyoming Academy of Science, 131

    Delta Epsilon, 138

    Lutheran Academy for Scholarship, 138

Phi Beta Kappa, 48, 116, 143
Phi Lambda Upsilon, 138
Sigma Xi, 144
National Bureau of Standards–Boulder, 144
Peru High School, 46
St. John's Christian Day School, 46
teaching in Miami County
Pipe Creek Township, 47
Elmwood School in Peru, 47
University of Berlin, 51
University of Colorado
appointment, 93
graduate students, 409
Laboratory Manual of Physical Chemistry, 134
recommendation for Valparaiso hire, 281
sabbatical leave, 109
University of Geneva, 51
doctorat ès sciences physiques, 54
Germann, Gary E., 16
Germann, Georg Peter (1815–1901), 14
Germann, Gustave Adolph (1860–1940), 14, 275,
277, 321
Germann, Ida Helene Johanna Meinke. *See*
Meinke, Ida Helene Johanna
Germann, Jacob (1835–1918), 17
Germann, Jean, 386
Germann, Lois Marie (1921–2013), 62, 111, 127
Germann, Lucia May (1920–1998), 44, 111, 302,
323, 334
Germann, Luise Barbara (1916–2012), 44, 111,
302, 321, 323, 334, 381
Germann, Maria Elisabetha Hofmann, (1823–
1878). *See* Hofmann, Maria Elisabetha
Germann, Martha Minna Maria Knechtel.
See Knechtel, Martha Minna Maria
Germann, Mary Fredericke Mueller.
See Mueller, Mary Fredericke
Germann, Peter Friedrich (1849–1935), 17
Germann, Richard Paul (1918–2007), 61, 111, 127
Gerstenberger, Henry John (1881–1954), 208
Gerstenberger–Ruh modified milk, 210
Gesell, Robert (1886–1954), 215
Getman, Frederick Hutton (1877–1941), 32
Giaugue, William Francis (1895–1982), 38
Gibson, Charles LeRoy (1911–1944), 116-117, 414

Gilbert, Earl C., 130
Gillette, H. A., 250
Gillman City Guide, 341
Glass
Corning Glass Works, 171
Jenaer Glaswerk, 38, 171
Nonex borosilicate, 171
Pyrex® borosilicate, 172
repair of devitrified, 171
Glass blowing, 37, 135, 171, 383
Glass electrode, 188
Glassley, Gene, 369
Glassley, Keith, 370
Godfrey, Francois (1788–1840), 47
Golden, Colorado, 88, 101
Gooch, Frank Austen (1852–1929), 169
Gooch crucible, 28, 177
Goode, Kenneth H., 188
Gortner, Ross Aiken (1885–1942), 280
Goshen, Indiana, 114, 336
Goshen College, 114
Gräbe, Carl (1841–1927), 35
Gräbner, Augustus Lawrence (1849–1904), 288
Graebner, Theodore Conrad (1876–1950), 289,
294
Graham, Cassium (Cash) (1869–1935), 346, 369
Graham, Frederick Milo (1872–1959), 372
Graham, Marie Kaadt, 359
Gray, Asa (1810–1888), 98
Gray, Joseph William, 89
Grebner, Constantin, 11
Greeley (Colorado) High School, 122
Gresso, Vernon, 369
Grip Nut Company, 329, 353, 383
Gruener, Hippolyte Washington (1869–1961),
167, 169, 184, 211
Gurney, Aaron, 244
Gustavson, Reuben Gilbert, 139-143
Guye, Philippe-Auguste (1862–1922), 6, 35, 36,
38, 39, 41, 51, 52, 170
Haas, Rosa M., 114
Haber, Fritz (1868–1934), 187
Hagenbeck–Wallace Circus, 47
Hale, Horace Morrison, 99
Hall, Baynard Rush (1793–1863), 28

Hall, Ralph E., 175, 181
Hall, Samuel Read (1795–1877), 248
Hanna, Ulysses S., 28
Hanover College, 12, 26
Harlem Spring Seminary, 251
Harley, Herbert, 369
Harley, Lucia May Germann.
　　See Germann, Lucia May
Harley, Robert, 369
Harney, John Hopkins (1806–1868), 29
Harrar, Norman Jackson (1902–1941), 125, 126, 410
Harrop, Isabelle, 334
Harvard University, 6, 27, 29, 34, 97, 98, 174, 180, 205, 208, 210, 252, 258, 265, 286, 386
Haskins, Howard Davis (1871–1933), 208
Hathaway, Carper, 369
Hawthorne, Lawrence, 355
Hazard, William Jonathan, 89
Heath, Jane Rives, 25
Hehir, Martin A., (1855–1935), 261
Heimlich, Louis Frederick (1890–1928), 290
Helvetia Milk Condensing Company, 201
Hennig, Valentine (1890–1961), 379
Hensley, James William (1915–1975), 118, 413
Heugli, Johannes Adam (1860–1902), 282
Heyrovský, Jaroslav (1890–1967), 194
Hickory, North Carolina, 284
Hicks, Mae and Elmer, 331, 352
Hicks, Robert Emmet (1858–1932), 336-353
　　A Conscience Unburdened, 343
　　Atchison, Topeka and Santa Fe Railway, 339
　　Atoz Printing Company, 342, 344
　　Baptist Church building, 347
　　Billy Sunday (1862–1935) and Homer
　　　Rodeheaver (1880–1955), 348
　　Camp Helen State Park, 353
　　Lewis County Journal, 338
　　Monticello Journal, 338
　　Monticello, Missouri, 338
　　South Whitley I.A.S.S. Assembly, 345
　　Specialty Salesman Magazine, 344
　　Temple of the Square Deal, 345
Hicks Tavern, 347, 353, 356
Hickson, William J., 377
Higgins, Mary Etta, 129

Highland College (Hickory, North Carolina).
　　See Lenoir College
Hillsdale College, 204
Hippuric acid, 176
Hiram College, 372
Historical geology. *See* Evolution
Hodgdon, Daniel Russel, 255, 258, 261
Hofmann, Maria Elisabetha (1823–1878), 14
Holben, Lloyd, 369
Holbrook, Alfred (1816–1909), 247
Holleman, Arnold Frederick, 100
Holman, Omer, 127
Horlick, James, Sr. (1809–1879), 199
Horlick, James, Jr. (1844–1921), 199
Horlick, William (1846–1936), 199
Horlick's Malted Milk, 199
Horner, Gerald, 369
Horsford, Eben Norton (1818–1893), 98
Hoskins, William (1862–1934), 180
Hough section of Cleveland, 323
Hovey, Charles Edward (1827–1897), 97
Howe, Edgar Watkins (1853–1937), 340
Howe, William Warren, 94
"Hube A's Says Sos," 353, 356
Hughes, Walter S., 188
Huntington College, 22, 336
Huntzicher, Harry N., 106
Hurd, Albert (1823–1906), 98
Hutchinson, Eric, 192
Hutchison, Ida, 246
Hydrogen electrode, 187
Hydrogen sulfide, 177
Hylan, Malcolm Cleveland (1896–1944), 108, 409
Illinois Industrial University, 201
Illinois State Normal University, 97–98
Illinois Wesleyan University, 271
Immanuel, Prince, 361, 365, 375–378
　　Atoz Printing Company, 377
　　Chaos: Written for the Illiterati, not the Litertai,
　　　378
　　Chaos II, 378
　　Criminals of Chicago, 377
　　"diploma mill," 377
　　Gospel According to Im-anu-el, 377
　　"Health Chats," 378

Immanuel Clinic, South Whitley Hotel, Immanuel Health Center, Abbey of Immanuel, South Whitley Health Society, Immanuel Sanitarium, 376
Johannesburg, 376
"Lupus and Fidus," 377
Newport, Wales, 376
Order of the Golden Rule of Jerusalem, 377
Prince Immanuel of Jerusalem, 377
Universal language, 377
Immanuel Lutheran Church (Valparaiso), 265
Inerrancy, doctrine of Biblical, 290
Indiana Ashbury University.
See DePauw University
Indiana Constitution of 1851, 7
Indiana High School Athletic Association, 335
Indiana State Normal School, 13
Indiana Supreme Court, 366
Indiana University
advertisement in *Narcissus*, 19
Department of Chemistry, 21
Department of Physics, 49
Department of Romance Languages, 53
first Ph.D. in Chemistry, 29
founding, 13, 29
See also Brown, Oliver; Foley, Arthur Lee; Germann, Albert Fredrick Ottomar; Germann, Frank Erhart Emmanuel; Jordan, David Starr; Lockridge, Ross Franklin, Sr.; Mathers, Frank Curry; Ramsey, Rolla Ray
Indiana University Studies, 29, 132
Indianapolis Star, 366
Indianapolis Times, 349
Infant food
Bosworth and Bowditch reconstructed milk for infants, 206
Carnation® infant formula, 202
Carnation® sweetened condensed milk, 202
Eagle Brand® condensed milk, 200
Farine Lactée Henri Nestlé, 200
Fat adapted milk, 210
Formulac brand, 209
Franklin Infant Food, 207
Gerstenberger–Ruh modified milk (G–R milk), 210

Laboratory Products Company, 196, 239
Liebig's Soluble Food for Babies, 198
Lily brand cream, 202
Meÿenberg Columbia brand milk, 202
Meyenberg goat milk, 203
Meÿenberg Monroe brand milk, 202
Page's Anglo-Swiss sweetened condensed milk, 201
Pet Milk, 202
Reconstructed milk for infants, 206
Sealtest brand, 213, 209
Similac, 207
Synthetic Milk Adapted (S. M. A.), 211, 212
Wyeth Laboratories, 210
Insect killing jars, 177
Insulin, 360, 362
International Association of Specialty Salesmen, 345
International Critical Tables of Numerical Data, 195
Intertype, 344, 354, 356
Irene Byron Tuberculosis Sanatorium, 272
Isotopes of oxygen, 38, 170
Jackson, Edward L. (1873–1954), 348–350, 367, 368
James, Thomas Howard (1912–2000), 108, 109, 412
Jannach, P. E., 34
Jarvis Hall Collegiate School, 88
Jenaer Glaswerk, 38, 171
Jersey, Vernon (1898–1984)
Boron trifluoride, 173
education, 174–175, 215–217
extracting carotene from carrots, 384–385
Nutritional Research Associates, 382–385
Mason, Michigan, 210
Phosgene, 175, 178
Quintrex, 324–326
research and biographical summary, 415–416
S.M.A., 210
Jewell, Ernest, 369
Johannesburg, 376
John Wyeth & Brother, 210
Johns Hopkins University, 279
Johnston, Herrick Lee (1898–1965), 38
Jones, A. Lyte, 250

Jones, Frank, 62

Jones, Horace, 62, 146

Jones, Lois Marie Germann.
 See Germann, Lois Marie

Jones, Lorann, 62

Jordan, David Starr (1851–1931), 190, 288

Journal de Chimie Physique, 35

Journal of Physical Chemistry, 30, 32, 133, 189

Journal of the Colorado–Wyoming Academy of Science, 131

Justus Liebig's Annalen der Chemie und Pharmacie, 133, 198

Kaadt, Charles Frederick (1872–1957), 356–367
 death, 367
 Diabetic Ferment Treatment, 362
 Federal trial, 367
 imprisonment, 367
 Keokuk Medical College, 357
 Post Office suit in Federal Court, 364
 revocation of medical license, 366

Kaadt, Christian (1829–1879), 358

Kaadt, Christian Gottlieb (1868–1905), 357

Kaadt, Edward (1879–1942), 357, 359

Kaadt, Ellen Marie Clausen (1839–1919), 358

Kaadt, Marie (1867–1957), 357, 359

Kaadt, Peter Simon (1871–1951), 356–367
 death, 367
 Federal trial, 367
 imprisonment, 367
 North Pacific College of Dentistry, 358
 revocation of medical license, 366
 Rush Medical College, 358
 Wabash Railroad Hospital, 358

Kaadt Diabetic Institute
 Federal trial, 367
 Food and Drug Administration investigation, 363
 Post Office investigation, 363
 Show-cause hearing, 364

Kahlenberg, Louis Albrecht (1870–1941), 5, 31, 34, 48, 55, 106

Kansas University Quarterly, 132

Kansas Weekly Herald, 341

Kappa Mu Epsilon, 116

Keister Walgreen Drug Store, 365

Kellogg, Vernon Lyman (1867–1937), 190

Kelvin quadrant electrometer, 188

Kent Chemical Laboratory (Chicago), 281

Kent Chemical Laboratory (Yale), 169

Keppel, Frederick Paul (1875–1943), 86

Kern, Alfred (1850–1893), 40

Keyl, Agnes Magdalena, 16

Keyl, Caroline Emilie (1851–1924), 17

Keyl, Ernst Gerhard Wilhelm (1804–1872), 15–17

Keyl, Hermann Wilhelm, 17

Keyl, Martha Constantia, 15

Keyl, Sophie Amilie Vogel, 15–17

King, Charles Glen (1896–1988), 325

Kinsey, Oliver Perry (1849–1931), 251–255

Kinsey, Sarah Porter. *See* Porter, Sarah

Kjeldahl, Johan Gustav Christoffer Thorsager (1849–1900), 198

Klemensiewicz, Zygmunt Aleksander (1886–1963), 187

Knechtel, Alfred John (1881–1916), 56, 59, 61

Knechtel, Anna Olga Rosa (1884–1944), 56, 59, 61

Knechtel, Edwin Edward Lloyd (1877–1940), 56

Knechtel, Emma Friedericka Caroline (1871–1873), 56

Knechtel, Hilda Magdalena Margaret (1889–1890), 56

Knechtel, Ida Helena Christina (1879–1957), 56, 57, 59, 61

Knechtel, John (1843–1906), 56, 59

Knechtel, Martha Minna Maria (1892–1966)
 birth, 56
 children, 61, 62, 88, 111
 death, 145
 marriage, 55, 61, 276
 schooling, 59–61

Knechtel, Mary Ann Schneider.
 See Schneider, Mary Ann

Knight, Odon Stahlhut Knight, 411

Knights of Pythias, 370

Knox College, 98

Königlichen Friedrich-Wilhelms-Universität zu Berlin. *See* University of Berlin

Krafft, Friedrich (1852–1923), 22, 24

Kraus, Charles August (1875–1967), 189

Kreinheder, Oscar Carl (1877–1946), 296, 297, 302

Krieg, Eldon Leroy (1904–1987), 356, 371, 383

Ku Klux Klan, 12, 109–111, 258–265, 349–351

Kuentzel, Lester Everette, 414

Kunberger, Margaretha Magdalena, 381

Kurrentschrift, 11

Laboratory Products Company, 196, 210, 211, 213, 219, 239, 275, 278, 280, 302, 321, 323

Lafayette College, 40

Lake Erie Biological Station, 291

Land, Edwin Herbert (1909–1991), 109

Lane, Franklin Knight (1864–1921), 180

Lang, Paul H. D., 195

Lange, Marion. *See* Cleaveland, Marion

Lange, Norbert Adolph, 183

Langerhaus, Paul (1847–1888), 359

Larwill, Indiana, 334

Latent photographic image, 106–108

Latzer, Louis F. (1848–1924), 201

Lavoisier, Antoine-Laurent (1743–1794), 35, 197, 292

Lawrence, Abbott (1792–1855), 98

Lawrence Scientific School, 98

Lea, Matthew Carey (1823–1897), 105, 106

Lehigh University, 108, 279

Lehr, Henry Solomon (1838–1923), 248

Leimer, John A., 289

Leipzig University, 99, 133, 168, 192

Lenoir College, 267, 274, 284

Lenoir, Walter Waightstill (1823–1890), 284

Lenox, Lionel Reymond, 191

Leslie, Harry Guyer (1878–1937), 332, 350, 368

Lewis, Gilbert Newton Lewis (1875–1946), 189

Lewis, Howard Bishop (1887–1954), 215

Lewis County Journal, 338

Liebig, Justus von (1803–1873), 98, 133, 197–199, 206, 212

Liebig's Annalen, 133, 198

Lightbourne, James H., 334

Lilly, Eli, 360

Lily Brand cream, 202

Lincoln, Abraham, 241, 253

Little, Arlington P., 89

Locke, John Galen (1873–1935), 110

Lockridge, Ross Franklin, Jr., (1914–1948), 46

Lockridge, Ross Franklin, Sr., (1877–1952), 5, 46, 48

Log cabin, 12, 25

Log farm house, 26, 337

Log school building, 44

Lombard College, 352

Loring, Sophie, 244

Los Alamos National Laboratory, 137

Louisville and Nashville Railroad, 352

Lovejoy, Arthur Oncken (1873–1962), 92

Ludwig-Maximilians-Universität München, 169

Luecke, Martin H. (1859–1926), 271

Luecke, Martin H. (1883–1948), 271–272

Luers, John H., 245

Luminescence, 119

Luther Institute, 295

Lutheran Academy for Scholarship, 138

Lutheran Bureau, 267

Lutheran Hospital (Fort Wayne), 270, 272

Lutheran Immanuel Seminary (North Adelaide, Australia), 287

Lutheran Layman, 268

Lutheran Orphans' Home Society of Nebraska, 58, 272

Lutheran Parish (South Whitley), 379

Lutheran Schools (Fort Wayne) consortium, 11

Lutheran Teachers' Seminary, 245, 269

Lutheran University Association, 239, 271–273

McCollum, Elmer Verner (1879–1967), 324

McCray, Warren Terry (1865–1938), 349

McGuffey, William Holmes (1800–1873), 8–9

McIntyre, Glenn Hazel, 193, 418

McKendree College, 201, 293

McPherson, Aimee Semple (1890–1944), 288

Macalester College, 106

Macleod, John James Rickard (1876–1935), 211, 360

Mallinckrodt, Edward (1845–1928), 41

Mallinckrodt, Gustav (1840–1877), 41

Mallinckrodt, Otto (1847–1876), 41

Manchester College, 12, 322, 334

Manchester University. *See* Manchester College

Manhattan Project, 119, 137, 141, 142

Mapes Milk Company, 209

Marden, Orison Swett (1848–1924), 337

Margaret Morrison Carnegie College, 25

Marshall, Thomas Riley (1854–1925), 93, 329

Mason, Michigan, 210, 218

Massachusetts College of Pharmacy, 261

Mathers, Frank Curry (1881–1973), 5, 21, 25, 27, 29

Mathews, Joseph Howard (1881–1970), 5, 31, 32, 34, 138

Maxwell, Ruth Redfern (1885–1962), 53

Mayer, Louis (1875–1938), 345, 349

Mayer Grain Elevator, 328, 383

Mayer State Bank, 365

Medical College of Nashville, 27

Medical Schools

    Baylor College, 279

    Chicago College of Medicine, 252

    Chicago Medical College, 256

    Drake University, 357

    Fort Wayne College of Medicine, 269

    Indiana Medical College, 26

    Indiana University, 21, 269

    Keokuk Medical College, 357

    Loyola, 252

    Nashville, 27

    Northwestern University, 256

    Rochester, 385

    Rush, 358

    St. Louis Medical College, 269

    Taylor University, 269

    Tufts, 205

    University of Berlin, 376

    University of Colorado, 94

    University of Michigan, 215

    Valparaiso, 252

    Washington University, 269

    Western Reserve University, 170, 208, 211, 212, 215, 218

Meinike, Anna. *See* Fasel, Anna Maria

Meinike, Louis Henry, 44

Meinke, Ida Helene Johanna (1884–1976)

    birth, 44

    children, 44, 111, 195, 277, 302, 321, 323, 334, 381, 386

    death, 387

    Ger-Manner, 332, 336, 382

    marriage, 44

    schooling, 44

Mellin, Gustav, 198

Mellin's Food, 198

Mellon Institute, 126, 217

Memphis, Tennessee, 282

Mène, Charles, 124

Mendel, Lafayette Benedict (1872–1935), 324

Merck & Company, 39

Merck, Friedrich Jacob (1621–1678), 39

Merck, Heinrich Emmanuel (1794–1855), 39

Mercurous perchlorate voltmeter, 29

Mercury, 177, 194

Merritt, Ernest George (1865–1948), 50, 87, 132

Methodist Episcopal Church South, 242, 339

Metz, Charles Franklin (1904–1974), 135–138, 413

Mexican–American War (1846–1848), 27

Meÿenberg, John Baptist (1847–1914), 201–203

Meyenberg Goat Milk, 203

Meyer, Alfred Herman Ludwig (1893–1988), 292–296

Meyer, H., 245

Meyer, Viktor (1848–1897), 24, 34

Miami County, Indiana, 3, 14, 169

Miami Nation, 3, 14, 15, 47

Michelson Laboratory, 121

Michigan Academy of Sciences, Arts and Letters, Papers of the, 295

Michigan Alkali Company, 119

Michigan State College, 279

Midland College, 61

Mieg, Walter (born 1878), 214, 324

Miller, Ellis, 369

Miller, Jacob William (1860–1933), 270

Miller, Paul F., 270

Millikan, Glenn Austin (1906–1947), 125

Mills, Caleb (1806–1879), 7, 10

Miner, Frank Edgar (1871–1936), 344

Minkowski, Oskar (1858–1931), 359

Mint of China, 278

Mississippi Agricultural and Mechanical College, 279

Mitchell, John Pearce, 191, 192

Monotype, 344

Montana College of Agriculture and Mechanic Arts, 120, 121
Monticello, Missouri, 338
Monticello Journal, 338
Moore, Ambrose Yoemans (1822–1904), 244
Moore, John, 13
Moore, Richard B., 104
Moores, Harry Clinton (1881–1965), 206–207
Morley, Clarence Joseph (1869–1948), 110
Morley, Edward Williams (1838–1923), 36–37, 41–43, 168, 170, 171
Morrill Act (1862), 253
Morrill Agricultural College Act (1890), 253
Morse Hall, 55, 111
Mueller, Mary Fredericke (1864–1942), 4, 16, 18, 46, 277
Muench, Oscar Brauer (1891–1953), 114–116, 143, 410
Muldoon, Hugh Cornelius (1884–1956), 260–263
Mustard gas, 178
Narcissus, 18, 19, 46, 47
Nash, Arthur (1870–1927), 348
National Bureau of Standards, 144, 189
National Dairy Products Corporation, 209
National Institute of Standards and Technology, 144
National Institutes of Health, 123
National Lamp Works, 178
National Lutheran Education Association, Central States Division, 270, 271
National Normal University, 247
National Research Council, 195
National Technical Laboratories, 125, 189
Naughty-One, 18
Naval Research, United States Office of, 119
Nebraska Wesleyan University, 218, 280
Neilson, Clarence Alber, 412
Nela, 178
Nernst, Walther Hermann (1864–1941), 38
Nestle, Heinrich (1814–1890), 199
Nestlé Infant Food, 200
New Harmony, Indiana, 27, 46
New Mexico College of Agriculture and Mechanic Arts, 118
New Mexico Highlands University, 115
New York Agricultural Experiment Station, 205

New York, Chicago and St. Louis Railroad, 256, 328
New York State College for Teachers, 114
Nichols, Edward Leamington (1854–1937), 50, 87, 132
Nichols, Lee, 369
Nichols, William Henry (1852–1930), 180
Nickel Plate Road, 256, 328
Norlin, George (1871–1942), 111
Normal Schools
    Chattanooga Normal University, 256
    Cleveland Normal School, 45
    Colorado State Normal School, 122
    Columbian School, 248
    East Texas State Teachers College, 123
    Eastern Illinois State Normal School, 293
    Fremont Normal School and Commercial Institute, 61
    Illinois State Normal University, 97–98
    Indiana State Normal School, 13
    mission of, 247
    National Normal University, 247
    New York State College for Teachers in Albany, 114
    Northern Indiana Normal School and Business Institute, 246–258
    Northwestern Ohio Normal School, 247, 248
    Ohio Normal University, 5, 17, 248
    Rochester Normal College, 5, 17
    Southern Illinois State Normal University, 293
    Southwestern State Normal College, 247
    Teachers College, Columbia University, 123, 267, 335
    Wabash Teachers Seminary and Manual Labor College, 12
Norris Pharmacy Orchestra, 370
Norris, William F. (1879–1960), 345, 365
North Central Association of Colleges and Schools, 258
North Pacific College of Dentistry, 358
Northern Indiana Law School, 250
Northern Indiana Normal School and Business Institute, 246–258
Northwestern College (Watertown, Wisconsin), 279
Northwestern Ohio Normal School, 247–248

Northwestern University, 140, 256, 290, 295, 371

Norton, John Pitkin (1822–1852), 97

Nutritional Research Associates, Inc.
  incorporation, 327
  officers, 327, 382, 385
  purchase of building, 329
  purchase of Pook Feed and Coal Company, 386
  South Whitley, 382–386

Oahu College, 204

Oberg, Aaron Gustaf, 411

Ohio Normal University, 5, 17, 248

Ohio Northern University, 248

Ohio State University, 114, 207, 211, 291

Ohio Wesleyan University, 241

Oil shale, 91

Okrent, Arika, 377

Old College (Valparaiso), 241, 243, 249

Old Main (Valparaiso), 249, 258

Old Seminary (Valparaiso), 240, 246

Oolitic, Indiana, 129

Oolitic limestone, 33, 128, 129

Opie, Eugene Lindsey (1873–1971), 360

Oregon State Agricultural College, 120, 130

Orr, Clara and Fern, 332

Osborn, Edith Germann. *See* Germann, Edith

Osborn, Herbert, 291

Osborne, Thomas Burr (1859–1929), 324

Ostwald, Friedrich Wilhelm (1853–1932), 30, 34, 99, 133, 168, 192

Oswald, Margaret Ruby (1910–1999), 120

Owen, Richard Dale (1810–1890), 27

Oxygen, isotopes of, 170

Page, George Ham (1836–1899), 201

Palmer, Charles Skeele (1858–1939), 99

Palmer, Leroy Sheldon (1887–1944), 278

Palo Alto, California, 184, 195

Panhandle, 328

Pannkoke, Otto Hermann (1887–1969), 265–268, 270, 271, 274, 284

Parker, Anna, 34

Parker Fellowship, 34

Parsons, Charles Lathrop (1869–1954), 180

Paulze, Marie-Anne Pierrette (1758–1836), 197

Peabody, Janice, 334

Peiyang University, 278

Pennsylvania College for Women, 24

Pennsylvania Female College, 23

Pennsylvania Railroad, 328, 372

Pennsylvania State College, 127

Perkins, Frances (1880–1965), 141

Perrine, Benjamin Franklin (1848–1930), 246, 247

Perth Amboy (New Jersey) General Hospital, 299

Pet Milk Company, 202

Petroleum ether, 384

pH scale, 187

Phi Beta Kappa, 47, 48, 116, 143

Phi Kappa Phi, 116

Phi Lambda Upsilon, 138

Phillips, Wendell, 173, 174

Phosgene, 135, 173, 175–182, 191, 193–194

Phosphorescence, 122

Physical chemistry, first journals in
  Journal de Chimie Physique, 35
  Journal of Physical Chemistry, 30, 55, 133
  *Zeitschrift für physikalische Chemie, Stöichio
    metrie und Verwandtschaftslehre*, 30, 133

Physical Review, 50, 87, 133

Physics Club, 53

Pieper, Franz August Otto (1852–1931), 287

Pike Seminary, 204

Pipe Creek, 19, 47

Pitman, Isaac (1813–1897), 250

Pittsburgh Catholic College, 261

Pittsburgh, Fort Wayne & Chicago Railroad, 248

Planck, Max Karl Ernst Ludwig (1858–1947), 38

Plasterer, Eiffel G. (1899–1989), 84

Platinocyanides, 114, 115, 117

Plummer, John Thomas (1807–1864), 10

Plutonium, 119, 137

Poe, Charles Franklin (1888–1970), 94–95, 101–102, 111

Polytechnic Institute of Zurich, 278

Pook, Carl Frederick (1848–1932), 381

Pook, Clarence Henry Louis (1912–1996), 381

Pook, Ervin H., (1885–1974), 322, 381, 386

Pook, Jonathan, 322

Pook, Luise Barbara Germann. *See* Germann, Luise Barbara

Pook Feed and Coal Company, 322, 328, 381, 386

Poor, Edith, 18

Port of Tientsien, 278

Porter, Cole Albert (1891–1964), 47

Porter, Melissa (1860–1921), 373

Porter, Sarah, 251

Porter Chemical Company, 365

Porter County, Indiana, 240

Powell, John Wesley (1834–1902), 98

Preprint newsprint, 354

Price, George McCready, 294

Priestley, Joseph (1733–1804), 197, 292

Prosser, Charles Allen (1871–1952), 7, 333

Proust, Joseph Louis (1754–1826), 197

Proximate analysis, 197, 204, 213

Public Academy of Philadelphia, 206, 273

Public Works Administration, 331

Purdue University, 12, 27, 177, 290, 331, 333, 368, 386

Pure Food and Drug Act (1906), 27, 361
    Federal Food, Drug, and Cosmetic Act (1938), 362
    Sherley Amendment, 362

Putrescine, 177

Pyrex®, 172

Quincy, Omaha and Kansas City Railway, 341

Quintrex, 210, 324

Quintrex Aqua-Vite, 327

Radium, 37, 49, 83, 85, 90, 104, 105

Radium emanation, 104

Radon, 104

Rakestraw, Norris Watson, 192

Ramsey, Rolla Roy (1872–1955), 5, 50, 53

Randall, George Maxwell (1810–1873), 88

Ray, Joseph (1807–1855), 8

Reconstructed milk for infants, 206

Redeemer Lutheran Church (Fort Wayne), 270

Reid, Dudley (born 1872), 340

Reid, Loren Dudley (born 1905), 341

Reiff, Lewis David, 334

Reimann, Stanley P., 125

Rekers, Robert George, 121, 414

Remington, James E. (1876–1941), 342, 345

Remsen, Ira (1846–1927), 26, 99, 180

Reprints, 30

Reserve, Indiana, 19, 45

Resources for the Future, 142

Rhode Island College, 203

Rhyne, Daniel Efird (1852–1931), 267

Richards, Theodore William (1868–1928), 31, 34, 180

Richardson, George Mann (1863–1902), 190

Richman, Ralph E. (1891–1972), 276, 297, 302, 303

Ridlon, Albert Maurice (1918–1996), 386

Riffe, Inez Y., 95

Robinson, Arthur Raymond (1881–1961), 349

Rochester Institute of Technology, 109

Rochester Normal College, 5, 17

Rockefeller, John D., 10, 258

Rodeheaver, Homer Alvan (1880–1955), 348

Roe, Jasper Newton (1864–1921), 252

Roessler, John Edward, 255

Rogers, Emmet C., 95

Roller, Pleasant Ernest, 281, 385

Romance Languages, Department of, 53

Romoser, George A., 283, 285

Ronzio, Anthony Rose, 412

Roosevelt, Franklin Delano (1882–1945), 329

Roosevelt, Theodore (1858–1919)
    Commission on Country Life, 9
    Pure Food and Drug Act, 361
    Square Deal, 345

Rosa, Edward Bennett (1873–1921), 168

Ross, Stanley Melvin (1882–1946), 206–207

Royal Oak, Michigan, 44

Rule, Walter Edwin, 411

Rutgers University, 299

Rutherford, Ernest (1871–1937), 37

S. M. A.
    Albert Germann assembles research group
        Vernon Jersey, 215–216, 326–327
        Robert Cross, 217, 326–327
        Harold Barnett, 218–219, 326–327
        Otto Ungnade, 219, 326–327
    Henry Gerstenberger and Howard Davis Haskins, 208
    John Wyeth & Brother, 210
    Laboratory Products Company, 209, 323–326
    Quintrex, 324
    Research Director, 323–324
    Sealtest Laboratories, 209, 323
    Synthetic Milk Adapted, 211

"the first artificial baby formula," 212, 323
  Walter E. Thrun, 278–280
  William E. Telling and John C. Telling,
    209–212, 323–324
  William Otto Frohring and Paul R. Frohring,
    211–213, 323–324
Sabbatical leave, 109–112
Saccharin, 40, 176
Saint Barnabas Hospital, Livingston, New Jersey, 299
St. Clair (Nebraska) Post Office, 122
St. James Lutheran Church (Golden Valley, North
  Dakota), 266
St. Johannes Evangelical Lutheran Church (Peru),
  16, 18
  See also St. John's Lutheran Church (Peru)
St. John's Christian Day School (Peru), 11, 18, 45,
  46, 277
St. John's College (Winfield, Kansas), 58, 271
St. John's Lutheran Church (Conover, North
  Carolina), 285
St. John's Lutheran Church (Peru), 11, 16, 44, 61,
  270, 275
St. John's Lutheran Church (South Whitley), 379,
  380–381
St. Louis Medical College, 269
Saint Mary's College, 12
Saint Paul Catholic School (Valparaiso), 245, 247
St. Paul Lutheran Church (Amherst, Ohio), 57
St. Paul's Evangelical Lutheran Church (Fort
  Wayne).
  See St. Paul's Lutheran Church (Fort Wayne)
St. Paul's Evangelical Lutheran Church (Hammond),
  285, 287
St. Paul's Lutheran Church (Fort Wayne), 268,
  270
St. Paul's Lutheran School (Fort Wayne), 269, 270
St. Paul's School (Garden City, Long Island, New
  York), 96
Saint Paul's School (Valparaiso), 245, 247
St. Peters Lutheran Church (South Whitley), 379
St. Salvator Lutheran Church (Venedy, Illinois),
  292
Saint Servan, 53, 127
St. Timothy's School, 25
Sandoz, Edouard (1853–1928), 40

Sanford, Arthur H., 125
Sartorius, Florenz (1846–1925), 38
Scandinavian Evangelical Lutheran Augustana
  Synod, 267
Schaufelberger, William M., 175, 181–182
Scheele, Carl Wilhelm (1742–1786), 197
Scheimann, Charles J. (1862–1926), 270
Schicks, George Charles, Jr., (1893–1961), 263
  credentials exaggerated, 300
  dismissal, 299
  "insufficiency," 298
  Perth Amboy (New Jersey) General Hospital,
    299
  replacement by Arthur H. Uhl, 300
  Rutgers University, 299
  Saint Barnabas Hospital, 299
Schlesinger, Hermann Irving, 103
Schlundt, Herman, 104, 115
Schmidt, Werner, 201
Schneider, Mary Ann (1842–1935), 56, 59, 61
Schnetzler, Jean Balthasar (1823–1896), 200
Schott, Friedrich Otto (1851–1935), 38, 171
Schulze, Johann Heinrich (1687–1744), 106
Schutes, George F. (abt 1878–1938), 265, 267,
  268, 270
Science, 143, 239
Science News Letter, 128
Scopes, John Thomas (1900–1970), 288
Scopes Trial, 288
Scott, Claudine (1881–1960), 372
Scott, Durant Charles (1859–1938), 365, 373
Scott Drug Store, 365, 373
Scottish Rite Masons, 268
Sealtest Brand, 209
Sealtest Laboratories, 209, 323
Seibels, Edwin Grenville (1866–1954), 250
Sewall, Joseph Addison (1830–1917), 96–99
Sewerage systems, 4, 20, 372
Shafer, Winfield Scott (1852–1916), 17
Shakhashiri, Bassam Z. (born 1939), 84
Sheard, Charles, 125
Sheffield, Joseph Earl (1793–1882), 98
Sheffield Scientific School, 97
Shen, Dzu-Kun, 108, 410
Sherley Amendment, 362

Sherman, Pearly, 246

Shindigz, 356

Shinn, Frederick Lafayette, 22, 31

Shipp, Thomas (1911–1930), 351

Sickafoose, Boyd, 370

Sidney, Indiana, 368, 369

Sievers, Herman, 270

Sigma Xi, 144, 387

Sihler, Wilhelm (1801–1885), 12

Silliman, Benjamin, Jr. (1816–1885), 97

Silliman, Benjamin, Sr. (1779–1864), 97, 133

Silliman's Journal, 97, 133, 169

Similac, 207

Sims, Charles N (1835–1908), 241–242

Skinner, Anna Maud, 256

Skłodowska-Curie. *See* Curie

Sloan, William Henry, 192

Smart, James H., School, 61

Smith, Abram (abt 1911–1930), 351

Smith, Benjamin Wilson (1830–1921), 243

Smith, Leland R., 173, 174

Smith, Margaret V., 95

Smith, Mary Lou Bowers, 374

Smith–Hughes Act, 333, 335

Smucker Company, 200

Snell Bus Lines, 365

Snyder, Firmer E. (1883–1959), 346, 367

Sod house, 113

Soddy, Frederick (1877–1956), 37

Solvent systems, 184, 186, 193

    ammonia, 186, 189

    boron trifluoride, 172–173, 186

    general theory of, 194

    phosgene, 173, 175–182, 191, 193–194

    water, 186–189

Sørensen, Søren Peder Lauritz (1868–1939), 186–187, 189

South Whitley High School, 44–45

    building (1887), 329, 332, 352, 369

    building (1932), 332–334

    Triennial Alumni Reunion, 368

South Whitley Hotel, 361

South Whitley Postmaster, 346, 369, 381

South Whitley Tribune, 321, 353–356, 365, 378, 379, 381

Southern Illinois State Normal University, 293

Southwestern State Normal College, 247, 251

Spanish–American War (1898–1901), 277

Specialty Salesman Magazine, 344, 347, 352

Spectrophotofluorometer, 124

Spectrophotometer, 125

    Beckman Model DU, 126

Spectroscopy instruments, 112, 118, 124–126

Springfield Academy, 328–329, 332

Square Deal, 345–347

Staehle, Henry Carl (1896–1966), 411

Stafford, Orin Fletcher (1873–1941), 189

Staley, Erastus Herman (born 1830), 242

Stanford University, 184–185, 253, 321

    Chemistry Department, 184–185, 191–192

Stearns, Robert, 140–141

Steenbock, Harry (1886–1967), 325

Stephenson, David Curtis (1891–1966), 265, 349

Stewart, Alexander Turney (1803–1876), 96

Stillman. John Mason, 185

Stock, Friedrich August (1872–1942), 371

Stoeppelwerth, Henry John (1869–1934), 57, 58, 271

Stoeppelwerth, Ida Helena Christina Knechtel. *See* Knechtel, Ida Helena Christina

Stoeppelwerth, Paul Peter Christian (1872–1931)

    birth, 57

    death, 57

    Lutheran Hospital Association (Fort Wayne), 57, 271–272

    marriage, 57

    recommendation of Albert Germann to John Baur, 275–276

    St. John's Evangelical Lutheran Church (Peru), 57, 61, 275

    Trinity Geman Lutheran Church (Fort Wayne), 57, 276

    wedding of Martha and Frank, 61, 276

Stout, Robert B., 346

Strietelmeier, John H., 296, 301

Stromeyer, Friedrich (1776–1835), 35

Stuart, Elbridge Amos (1856–1944), 202

Students' Army Training Corps, 254, 293

Stump, Hubert A. (1904–1949)

    "Hube A's Says Sos," 353, 356

"Memories," 355
  South Whitley Tribune, 321, 353, 354
  Washington Center High School, 354
Stump Printing Company, 321, 337, 354
Sugar of lead, 177
Sunday, Billy. *See* Sunday, William Ashley
Sunday, William Ashley (1862–1935), 288, 348
Suzuki, Umetaro (1874–1943), 325
Swain, Robert Eckles (1875–1937), 191, 217
Swisher, Margaret, 95
Syracuse University, 242
Szent-Györgyi, Albert de Nagyrápolt (1893–1986), 325
Tait, Peter Guthrie (1831–1901), 84
Talbot, Henry Paul (1864–1927), 180
Talbot, William Henry Fox (1800–1877), 107
Tate, Magnolia (1887–1924), 122
Taylor, Quimby W., 193, 417
Taylor, William (1821–1902), 13
Taylor University, 12, 129, 269
Teacher colleges, *see* Normal Schools
Teachers College, Columbia University, 123, 267, 335
Telling, John C., 209
Telling, William E., (1868–1938), 209, 323
Telling-Belle Vernon Co., 209
Telling Bros. Ice Cream Co., 209
Telling Laboratory, 323
Temple of the Square Deal, 345–347
Tennessee Synod of the Evangelical Lutheran Church, 267, 284
Texas Christian University, 123
Texas Technological College, 122
Texas Transportation Institute, 106
Theobald, Jacob C., 5, 15
Theobald, Martha Constantia Keyl, 5, 15
Theological Quarterly, 288
Thomson, Joseph John (1856–1940), 37
Thorntown Academy, 241
Thrun, Walter Eugene (1892–1951), 279–280
Tientsien, China, 278
Tientsin, China, 108
Tieszen, Derk P. (1859–1946), 113
Tieszen, Derk Vivian (1894–1960), 112–114, 410
Timpany, Charles Russel, 193, 416

Tippecanoe Battle Ground Collegiate Institute, 242
Tocopherol, 385
Tower, Olin Freeman (1872–1945), 41, 43, 167–168
Township unit, 9
Traxler, Ralph Newton, 95, 105–106, 132, 409
Treadwell, Frederick Pearson (1857–1918), 278
Trevor, Joseph Ellis (1864–1941), 55, 87, 133, 189
Trinity German Lutheran Church (Fort Wayne), 57, 270, 272, 276, 286
Trinity German Lutheran School (Fremont), 56
Trinity Lutheran Church (Detroit), 282
Trinity Lutheran Church (Memphis), 282–293
Trinity Lutheran Church (St. Louis), 287
Trinity Suburban Lutheran Church (Fort Wayne), 268, 276
Trinity test, 137
Truman, Harry S., 119
Tschantz, Harold, 381
Tyndall, John (1820–1893), 84
Uhl, Arthur Hoyt (1900–1980), 300–301
Ulbrich, Henry L., (1883–1962), 296, 297, 301
Ungnade, Otto (c.a. 1883–1963), 210, 219, 326
Union Theological Seminary, 266
United States Army
  Air Force, 140
  Chemical Warfare Service, 119, 179, 181, 279
  Division of Nutritional Service, 279
  Edgewood Arsenal, 119, 179, 181
  Public Health Service, 257
  radio instruction, 50
  Signal Corps, 135
  Students' Army Training Corps, 254, 293
United States Coast and Geodetic Survey, 372
United States Department of Agriculture, 27, 168, 203
  Division of Plant Industry, 280
  Food and Drug Administration.
    See Food and Drug Administration
United States Department of the Interior
  Bureau of Mines, 145, 180, 181, 186
  Geological Survey, 98
  Public Works Administration, 331
  Works Progress Administration, 383

United States National Bureau of Standards, 144, 189
United States Post Office
    airmail from South Whitley, 381
    investigation, 363
    show-cause hearing, 364
    surveillance, 366
United States War Department, 254
United Verde Extension Mining Company, 217
Universal language, 377
University of Arizona, 142
University of Arkansas, 102
University of Berlin, 34, 38, 51, 376
University of California, 137
University of Chicago, 103, 113, 140, 141, 294
    Kent Chemical Laboratory, 281
    Metallurgical Laboratory, 141
University of Colorado, 61, 62, 93–145 sic passim, 253, 281
University of Colorado at Denver, 94
University of Colorado Journal of Engineering, 100
University of Colorado Laboratory Manual of Physical Chemistry, 134
University of Colorado Studies, 100, 132
University of Denver, 139
University of Evansville, 12
University of Geneva, 35, 51
University of Illinois, 101, 103, 188, 201, 279, 293–295
University of Kansas, 189, 190
University of Michigan, 204, 215, 279, 295
University of Minnesota, 218, 277, 280
University of Missouri, 25, 104, 115
University of Nebraska, 130, 142, 281
University of New Mexico, 116, 134, 137
University of Notre Dame du Lac, 12
University of Pennsylvania, 273
University of Rochester, 109, 121, 385
University of Wisconsin, 5, 22, 23, 29, 30–33, 48, 253, 290, 301
University of Wyoming, 132
Uranium, 85
Uranium nitrate, 86
Vail, Kenyon C., 95
Valparaiso City Public Graded School, 246

Valparaiso College, 252
Valparaiso Collegiate Institute, 244
Valparaiso High School, 246
Valparaiso–Indiana Geography and Geology Association, 296
Valparaiso Male and Female College, 241–244, 246–247
Valparaiso University, 12, 13, 29, 218, 239–303 sic passim, 321, 326
Valparaiso University Association, 239, 271, 273
van Nuys, Claude Cornelius, 89
Van Nüys, Thomas Charlton (1844–1898), 22
Van Slyke, Lucius Lincoln (1859–1931), 203–205
van 't Hoff, Jacobus Henricus (1852–1911), 30, 38
Van Valkenburgh, Horace B., 102–103
Van Wert, Ohio, 14, 17, 322
Vandalia Railroad, 328, 350
Vaughan, Victor Clarence (1851–1929), 215
Vauquelin, Louis Nicolas (1763–1829), 35
Venable, Francis Preston, (1856–1934), 180
Verweire, John L., 369
VFW Post 2919, 365
Vincennes University, 12
Vidette-Messenger, 244
Vitamin A, 213, 214, 324, 384, 386
Vitamin B, 325
Vitamin C, 325
Vitamin D, 325
Vitamin E, 385, 386
Vogel, Sophie Amilie, 15–17
von Mering, Joseph Freiherr (1849–1908), 359
Wabash and Erie Canal, 15, 17
Wabash College, 7, 12
Wackenroder, Heinrich Wilhelm Ferdinand (1798–1854), 214, 324
Wade Park Elementary School, 323
Wakeham, Glen, 95
Walker, William Hultz, (1869–1934), 181
Wallace, Benjamin E. (1847–1921), 47
Walter-Gordon Laboratory, 209
Walther League, 44, 275
Warner, Lloyd H. (1891–1969), 345
Washington, Missouri, 114
Washington and Lee University, 127
Washington University (St. Louis), 269

Waterworks, 4, 28, 33, 49, 252
Waverly High School, 260
Wayne County Civic Association, 268
Wehrenberg, Frederick H. (1890–1963), 297, 302
Weick, William H., 11
Wells, Herbert George (1866–1946), 84
Wells, W. W., 369
Weskott, Johann Friedrich (1821–1876), 40
Wesleyan Academy, 243
Wesleyan University, 167–168, 243
Westchester High School, 335
Western Military Institute, 27
Western Newspaper Union. 354
Western Reserve College, 36, 42
Western Reserve University, 41–45 *sic passim*, 61,
    167–175 *sic passim*
    Adelbert College, 43, 167
    Cleveland College, 183
    Cleveland Normal School, 45
    College for Women, 23, 43, 167, 182
    Department of Chemistry, 167–170
    Flora Stone Mather College, 169, 182, 322
    Phosgene, 175–182
    The Bulletin of Western Reserve University, 132
Western Union, 365
Westminster College, 50
Whitley County Circuit Court, 366
Whitley County, Indiana, 322
Whitley County Klan No. 25, 350
Whitley Feeds, 322, 386
Wilcox, Benjamin (1816–1875), 244
Wildi, John, 201–202
Wiley, Harvey Washington (1844–1930), 26, 204,
    361

Willard, John E. (1908–1996), 119
Williams, John Warren (1898–1988), 32
Williams College, 244
Willstätter, Richard Martin (1872–1942), 214, 324
Wilmington College, 291
Wilson, Merle (1894–1960), 114
Wilson, Woodrow (1856–1924), 179, 329, 343,
    348
Wittenberg College, 5, 17
Witter, Conrad, 10
Woland, Frances Elizabeth (1892–1967), 111
Wood, Thomas Bond (1844–1922), 243
Woodriff, Ray Alan (1909–1983), 119–121, 414
Worcester Academy, 47
Wyeth, John (1841–1907), 210
Wyeth, Stuart (1862–1929), 210
Wylie Hall, 20, 27
Wylie, Samuel Brown (1854–1890), 29
Xylyl bromide, 178
Y.M.C.A. School of Commerce, 206
Yale University, 47, 97, 133, 169, 185, 324
Yankton College, 113
Yearick, Albert Clyde (1885–1966), 354
Yerxa, Thomas E. (1851–1916), 202
Yoder, Robert Anderson (1854–1911), 284
Yohn, W. A., M.D. (1850–1892), 246
York College, 130
Young, Stewart Woodford, 182, 192
Zeiss, Carl Friedrich (1816–1888), 38
*Zeitschrift für physikalische Chemie, Stöichiometrie
    und Verwandtschaftslehre*, 30, 133

Designed by Hans Teensma and Nick Teensma
Text set in Adobe Caslon Pro

Printed on 60lb. Finch Cream White
by Bridgeport National Bindery

Published by Impress
Williamsburg, Massachusetts
www.impressinc.com